Coordinating Ombudsmen and the Judiciary

A comparative view on the relations between ombudsmen and the judiciary in the Netherlands, England and the European Union

Milan Remáč

Coordinating Ombudsmen and the Judiciary

A comparative view on the relations between ombudsmen and the judiciary in the Netherlands, England and the European Union

intersentia

METRO

Ius Commune Europaeum

Milan Remáč

Coordinating Ombudsmen and the Judiciary

A comparative view on the relations between ombudsmen and the judiciary in the Netherlands, England and the European Union

Intersentia Ltd
Trinity House | Cambridge Business Park | Cowley Road
Cambridge | CB4 0WZ | United Kingdom
Tel.: +44 1223 393 753 | Email: mail@intersentia.co.uk

ISBN 978-1-78068-218-1
D/2014/7849/68
NUR 828

Cambridge – Antwerp – Portland
www.intersentia.com | www.intersentia.co.uk

British Library Cataloguing in Publication Data. A catalogue record for this book is available from the British Library.

PREFACE

Voila! Here is the book I have been working on for the last four years! It is not as astonishing as the Holy Stone of Clonrichert, but I believe that it is the second-best thing. I hope that it will end up in a more suitable place than the Holy Stone, in your library, for example.

I would not have been able to write this book without the help of the following people.

First of all, I would like to thank my supervisors Philip Langbroek and Rob Widdershoven for their useful advice and (often) clear comments. Particularly, I wish to thank Philip for giving me considerable freedom in my research and enabling me to spread my 'academic wings' (and fly) and to Rob for dragging me back down to the substance of my research.

My special thanks go to Nick O'Brien and Brian Thompson who tried in an understandable way to introduce me to the most intriguing parts of the English legal system and the ombudsman system. Similarly, my special thanks go to Alex Brenninkmeijer, the former Dutch National Ombudsman, whose kind recommendation allowed me to start to work on a comparative part of my research. My thanks are also extended to all the ombudsmen and judges who, despite their full agendas, were willing to talk to me and to provide me with important information.

I would like to thank some of my colleagues who tried to be as collegial as possible (although I was usually not) namely Anoeska, Felix, Alberto, HK and Margot and also my friends Bara, Zdeněk and Jolien who entertained me during the dark times of my research.

Last, but not least, I would like to thank my parents (Ďakujem*! Bez Vašej podpory by to bolo ťažké. Táto kniha je pre Vás.*) and Marrit.

TABLE OF CONTENTS

ABBREVIATIONS

ABRvS	Administrative Law Division of the Council of State
ADR	alternative dispute resolution
AG	Advocate General
AJTC	Administrative Justice and Tribunal Council
Art.	Article
AWB	General Administrative Law Act
CBB	Trade and Industry Appeals Tribunal
CFI	Court of First Instance of the European Communities
CoJ	European Court of Justice
CPR	Civil Procedure Rules
CRvB	Central Appeals Tribunal
EUCST	European Union Civil Service Tribunal
EMA	European Medicines Agency
EN	England
EPSO	European Personnel Selection Office
EU	European Union
EUO	European Ombudsman
EUP	European Parliament
EURATOM	European Atomic Energy Community
FTT	First Tier Tribunal
GALA	General Administrative Law Act
EUGC	General Court of the European Union
GPPA	general principles of proper administration
HR	Supreme Court
HSO	Health Service Ombudsman
JOA	Judicial Organisation Act
LBIO	Landelijk Bureau Inning Onderhoudsbijdragen
LGO	Local Government Ombudsmen
MEP	Member of European Parliament
NO	National Ombudsman
NL	Netherlands

NZB	Nieuwe zaaksbehandeling
OLAF	European Anti-Fraud Office
PASC	Public Administration Select Committee
PAP	the Pre-Action Protocol for Judicial Review
PCA	Parliamentary Commissioner for Administration
PO	Parliamentary Ombudsman
Rb.	District Court (the Netherlands)
RMP	Royal Military Police
sec.	section
TCE Act	Tribunals, Courts and Enforcement Act
TEC	Treaty Establishing the European Community
TECSC	Treaty establishing the European Coal and Steel Community
TEU	Treaty on European Union
TFEU	Treaty on the Functioning of the European Union
TPR	Tribunal Procedural Rules
UK	United Kingdom
Vzngr.	provisional judge (the Netherlands)
WNo	the National Ombudsman Act

PART I

INTRODUCTION

Individuals in disputes with the state administration have several possibilities to protect their interests. Traditionally, they can resort to the *courts*. For a couple of decades and sometimes even longer, a part of the judiciary has been specialising in these disputes. This part of the judiciary is organised in the form of independent administrative courts, specialised tribunals or specialised chambers of ordinary courts. The courts are thus here in the position of a *traditional dispute resolution mechanism*. Apart from the courts and various administrative tribunals, an individual has several *alternative dispute resolution mechanisms* at his disposal that can deal with disputes in various, usually less formal ways. Depending on the legal system of the state, these mechanisms may include arbitration, mediation or the use of an *ombudsman* or some other institution. Within the sphere of public law, the ombudsman usually has a broader mandate and stronger powers than other ADR providers.[1] It is also one of the few bodies that has developed, in the last fifty years or so, from a *regional experiment* to a widespread institution.[2] In the last few decades ombudsmen have attracted a great deal of attention from the administration, individuals, society and possibly also from the judiciary.

This part of the book provides a general introduction to the research into the mutual relations between ombudsmen and the judiciary.[3] It delimits the main terms of the research, explains some choices and depicts the research design.

1 Gregory 2001, pp. 120-121.

2 In 2010/2011 the International Ombudsman Institute had 135 institutional ombudsman members (Annual Report of the Institute 2012). The number of *all* world ombudsmen is undoubtedly higher. For an explanation of the term 'regional experiment' see, section 1.1.

3 The term *ombudsman* as used in this book also covers women working in this position without discriminating against them. For the sake of consistency, the book does *not* use the terms *ombudswoman, ombudsperson*, *ombudsbody* or *ombuds*.

Chapter 1

GENERAL INTRODUCTION

1.1 Ombudsman – definition and functions

It is more than 200 years since the first ombudsman was introduced into the list of the Swedish constitutional authorities.[1] The role of this ombudsman was (and partially still is) to ensure compliance with the law by all state officials and judges.[2] This role was exercised on behalf of the *Riksdag* – the Swedish Parliament. Until the late 1960s, the ombudsman institution was a regional, *Nordic phenomenon;* however, the world soon discovered its advantages.[3] Nowadays, the ombudsman is present in almost all countries, although it does not necessarily always have the original Swedish name.[4]

The expansion of the ombudsman institution is connected with its flexibility. This has allowed the ombudsman to adapt to most political and societal circumstances. As noted by Abraham, one of the reasons for the international durability and popularity of the ombudsman institution is its ability to adapt to changing circumstances, to evolve, and to survive in a variety of political and legal habitats.[5] Over the course of time, the roles of the ombudsman have developed similar to the institution itself. The ombudsman has become a noticeable player in the field of *administrative justice* and in the latest decade also a valuable player in the field of the protection of *human rights*.[6] Nowadays, *ombudsmen come*

1 The Swedish *Justitieombudsman* dates back to the Swedish constitutional reform of 1809. However, the office had a predecessor in the office of the *Chancellor of Justice*, established in 1713 by the exiled Swedish King Charles XII. See, for example, Drewry 1997.

2 Cf. Stern 2008, p. 411 and <www.jo.se> (accessed on 31 July 2013).

3 The Scandinavian ombudsmen were established in 1920 in Finland, in 1955 in Denmark and in 1962 in Norway. The first non-Scandinavian ombudsman was established in 1962 in New Zealand.

4 For example, in Spain the title of the ombudsman is *Defensor del Pueblo*, in Portugal it is *Provedor de Justiça*, in Slovakia it is *Verejný ochránca práv*, in Poland it is *Rzecznik praw obywatelskich*.

5 Abraham 2008b, p. 672.

6 According to the *Paris Principles*, which the UN General Assembly annexed to its Resolution 48/134 and which define the minimum conditions that national human rights institutions must meet if they are to be considered as legitimate, also ombudsmen are considered as national *human rights* institutions. However, the European Court of Human Rights does not consider a complaint to an ombudsman to be an effective remedy for an individual. See, *Ananyev and others v Russia* (Application nos. 42525/07 and 60800/08) etc.

in all shapes and sizes[7] and *there is no 'one size fits all' model of the ombudsman institution.*[8] They are far from identical. It should be pointed out that apart from the *public service ombudsmen,* i.e. ombudsmen connected with the work of the state administration, there also is an increasing use of ombudsmen as alternatives to the courts in the private sector.[9]

Ombudsmen have not been placed in a normative vacuum, they rather adjust to the specifics of the systems in which they have been established. Because of that, from a contextual point of view one should define the term *ombudsman* so that it covers the institution stripped of all national specific features. As it is not the goal of this book to create a new definition of the institution, it uses the definition formulated in 1974 by the International Bar Association. The ombudsman is

> *an office provided by the constitution or by action of the legislature or parliament and headed by an independent high level public official who is responsible to the legislature or parliament, who receives complaints from aggrieved persons against government agencies, officials and employers or who acts on his own motion, and has the power to investigate, recommend corrective action and issue reports.*[10]

Apart from this definition one can also find a number of criteria for being admitted as an ombudsman to various regional or international ombudsman associations such as, for example, the *Ombudsman Association*[11] or the *International Ombudsman Institute.*[12] These criteria usually reflect the main points of the IBA definition while taking into account the specific purposes of the associations or their regional limitations.

On the basis of this definition one can identify several functions of the ombudsman which represent the core of his/her work. One can talk about the control function, the protection and dispute resolution function, the remedial function and the normative and potential educational function.

The control function of ombudsmen allows them to assess the conduct of institutions within their remit. This function is undoubtedly intrinsic to the vast majority of existing ombudsmen. Whether the ombudsmen deal with the concept of good administration, legality or human rights, the control function is present as a thin line that connects them all. The choices of particular institutions within the remit of the ombudsman depend on the legislator, and so does the normative concept of the ombudsman. The assessment of ombudsmen has characteristics that distinguish the institution from the control

7 Abraham 2008, p. 682.

8 Paunio 2009. For the ombudsman typology, see also, Kucsko-Stadlmayer 2008, Gregory 1999 or Remac 2013.

9 See, Reif 2004, p. 25ff or Seneviratne 2000.

10 The Ombudsman Committee, the International Bar Association Resolution, Vancouver: the International Bar Association, 1974. Despite its age, this definition is widely used by academics, scholars and ombudsmen. For example, Söderman described it as *one of the best attempts to define an Ombudsman's office* (in Söderman 1997). See also, for example, Ayeni 2000, p. 14, Reif 2004, p. 3, or Kucsko-Stadlmayer 2008, p. 4.

11 Ombudsman Association, Schedule 1 to the Rules, Criteria for the Recognition of Ombudsman Offices. <www.ombudsmanassociation.org/docs/OA-Rules.pdf> (accessed on 31 July 2013).

12 See Article 6, International Ombudsman Institute, By-laws, November 2012.

exercised by other bodies including the courts. Ombudsmen can assess the conduct of the administration. Generally they do not bind it other than morally, although they can opt for the route of a *publicity opinion*.[13] This inability to bind the administration provides the ombudsman with flexibility and it is often seen as one of the advantages of the institution.[14] For example, Buck et al. argue that if ombudsman's recommendations were legally binding on public authorities, it would override the legal discretionary authority of a public body to act.[15] Because of the legally non-binding character of the ombudsman's control, the acceptance of his/her recommendations to a large extent depends on the will of the controlled subject (the administration) to cooperate.[16] Thus, a huge role is played by the natural authority of the incumbent ombudsman and his/her power to persuade the administration to follow his/her recommendations and reports voluntarily. Ombudsmen do not have at their disposal any tools to enforce their findings. Their supervisory and control authority is not combined with the concept of coercive power.[17] The control exercised by the ombudsman does not depend on a relationship which entails being *subordinate to the administration*. Last but not least, this function can be exercised by means of a *complaint by an individual* or at *the ombudsman's own initiative.*

The protection and dispute resolution function is another general function of ombudsmen. It has two relatively independent sides. On the one side, there is the protection of an individual against the administration and, on the other, the resolution of disputes between these subjects. Ombudsmen are often perceived as a mechanism to protect individuals against abuses by the *machinery of the State*.[18] They are increasingly becoming an alternative to courts and tribunals.[19] However, ombudsmen as an alternative to the judiciary should be perceived in a broad sense, because, depending on the legal system, the alternative character of ombudsmen can range from a 'real' alternative to the proceedings of the judiciary to the subtle complementary nature of ombudsmen.[20]

The protection and dispute resolution function of ombudsmen is *an alternative* to the protection offered by the courts but also to other ADRs. The protection provided by ombudsmen depends on the powers that are attributed to them by the legislator. Critics of the institution tend to describe ombudsmen as *ombudsmice, toothless tigers, watchdogs that bark but don't bite* or *watchdogs in chains*.[21] They tend to point to the special character of the ombudsman's protection – *legally non-binding protection through persuasion.* Ombudsmen do not have the power to legally compel the administration to follow their recommendations, but they can refer to the need to follow common sense.[22] It is obvious

13 Harris 1999, p. 140.
14 Jacoby 1999, p. 21.
15 Buck et al. 2011, p. 40.
16 Seneviratne 2002, p.133
17 During their investigations ombudsmen *can* often exercise some coercive powers, i.e. in connection with requiring access to files, carrying out inspections or hearing witnesses. In Sweden, the ombudsman can even initiate disciplinary procedures against an official for misdemeanours.
18 Antoine 2008, p. 407.
19 James 1997, pp. 3-4.
20 See, Dragos & Neamtu 2014.
21 Gwyn 1973, p. 47.
22 See, for example, Report 2012/057 of 5 April 2012 of the Dutch National Ombudsman, Bevindingen, p. 5.

that ombudsmen's protection is different than the protection provided by the courts. Apart from that, their services are generally free.[23] They tend to be expeditious and deal with complaints within a short period of time.[24] They can also publicly highlight the problems of the administration as *publicity is their ultimate power*.[25] Ombudsmen can use naming, blaming and shaming methods. They often try to solve disputes in an informal way including telephoning, writing or emailing the administrative body concerned about the problem raised in the complainant. A fair amount of cases before ombudsmen end by using these informal mechanisms and only a small part of the admitted complaints lead to a written report.[26] Ombudsmen can also act as mediators standing between the individual and the administration,[27] or they can ask a special trained mediator to assist them in the conduct of an investigation.[28] Last but not least, ombudsmen can propose a friendly solution to both parties in the investigation that tries to bring these parties to a win-win situation.[29] However, in disputes they must always retain their *independence* and *impartiality*.

Ombudsmen also have *a remedial* or *redress function*. Pearce argues that one of the reasons for the establishment of the ombudsman was that traditional means of redress were not always satisfactory.[30] These traditional means can be hindered by high procedural fees, a high legal threshold or by their limited competences. However, the ombudsman can only *recommend a remedy*. He/she *cannot grant a remedy*. In the end it is the administration that has to decide whether a remedy, as recommended by the ombudsman, is in that particular case going to be granted or not. This function is directly connected with the need of the ombudsman to persuade the administration to act in accordance with his/her recommendations. The remedies that can be recommended by ombudsmen can be different from the remedies that are generally provided by other redress institutions. Very often, ombudsmen are not limited by the remedies included in statutes. Their recommendations can include apologies, explanations, ex gratia payments, reconsiderations of decisions or improvements to procedures etc.[31] The first remedy recommended by an ombudsman is usually the restitution of the individual to his original position. If that is not possible, the remedy should compensate him appropriately[32] while a financial remedy is not always

23 James 1997, p. 4.
24 See, for example, Dragos & Neamtu 2014.
25 Ramcharan 2002, p. xvi.
26 Informal techniques can be observed in the practice of various ombudsmen. For example, the intermediation (*tussenkomst*) of the Dutch National Ombudsman or the minor inquiry (*liten utredning*) of the Swedish Parliamentary Ombudsman.
27 See, for example, the French *Défenseur des Droits*. See, <http://defenseurdesdroits.fr/connaitre-son-action/la-mediation-avec-les-services-publics> (accessed on 31 July 2013).
28 As is the case of the Local Government Ombudsmen for England or the Parliamentary Ombudsman (UK).
29 See, the practice of the European Ombudsman.
30 Pearce 1999, p. 83.
31 See, for example, *The Ombudsman's Guide to the provision of redress* of the Irish Ombudsman, the Guidelines on Complaint Handling of the Ombudsman of Western Australia or the *Schadevergoedingswijzer* of the Dutch National Ombudsman.
32 See, for example, *Principles for remedies* of the Parliamentary and Health Services Ombudsman (UK).

sufficient.[33] Although ombudsmen exercise only *soft* powers, their redress function is directly connected with the task of *righting wrongs*.[34]

The *normative function* of ombudsmen is linked with the findings of ombudsmen and with their guidance. All ombudsmen evaluate the administrative conduct against some normative criterion or standard, be it maladministration, good administration or human rights. The normative standards and control criteria used by ombudsmen mostly depend on the will of the legislator who can formulate them differently.[35] They can range from legal rules to general normative concepts such as good administration. If the normative criteria are prescribed only as general normative concepts (good administration etc.) they often require a specification of their substance. This is often done by an active exercise of the normative powers of the ombudsman. Ombudsmen then develop these standards and often publish them in accessible collections or lists. Sometimes they only adopt the criteria developed by other ombudsmen or other institutions.[36] They can also decide that they will assess complaints on case-by-case basis without developing a list of normative standards. The normative standards of the ombudsman or the *ombudsnorms* are then the criteria against which the administrative conduct is evaluated.[37] They are developed by ombudsmen and their development is an ongoing process.[38] The ombudsnorms are not necessarily identical to legal norms.[39] They can be considered as parallel norms with a different character.[40] The lists of ombudsnorms that are often *published* by ombudsmen basically refer to the long-term experience of ombudsman offices in resolving disputes between individuals and the administration. Thus, the normative function of ombudsmen is reflected in the *development and 'codification' of normative standards* and in the *application of these normative standards* by ombudsmen in their investigative practice and by the administration in its actions.

The potential educational function of ombudsmen is a reflection of the work of ombudsmen on the administration and individuals. As Gregory and Giddings put it, ombudsmen exercise this function in connection with both public officials and the population.[41] Those who want to learn can approach various ombudsmen's publications usually online or in hard copy. These documents may have a potential double educative impact. On the one hand, administrative institutions have the possibility to learn how they can make their administrative processes more *user-friendly* and more *ombuds-proof*. On the other hand, the general public may learn what can be expected from the administration but also what can be expected from them in their dealings with the administration. As Maino

33 Guidance on proper redress (*Schadevergoedingswijzer)* of the Dutch National Ombudsman, Rule 2.
34 The term *righting wrongs* was used, for example, in Gregory & Giddings 2002, p. 15.
35 Kucsko-Stadlmayer 2008, p. 32.
36 This is for instance the case with the Public Services Ombudsman for Wales who adopted the Principles of Good Administration developed by the UK Parliamentary and Health Service Ombudsman.
37 Hubeau 2008, p. 370.
38 Langbroek & Rijpkema 2006, p. 95.
39 Langbroek & Rijpkema 2004, p. 20ff.
40 Langbroek & Remac 2011, p. 157.
41 Gregory & Giddings 2000, p. 14.

puts it, thanks to reports by and the results of the investigations of the ombudsman, the administration and individuals can refine their knowledge concerning the difference between right and wrong.[42] However, the position of ombudsmen as educative institutions is mainly passive. They provide guidance, but they cannot compel anybody to follow that guidance or to learn from it.

1.2 Administrative judiciary in the broadest sense

In general, it is not necessary to describe the functions and concepts of the judiciary in great detail as the judiciary is the traditional bearer of state powers and one of the essential pillars of democracy.[43] However, as this research tries to explain the relations between ombudsmen and the judiciary, one must also consider this subject. As the ombudsmen included in this research deal with disputes between individuals and the state administration it was necessary to look at that part of the judiciary that can also consider disputes between individuals and the state administration. Today, these disputes are often solved by the administrative judiciary. Generally, the administrative judiciary is connected with the *assessment of the lawfulness of actions by the administration or its decisions*. Depending on the national regulations the judiciary's assessment of compliance with the law can be connected with the actions of the administration, administrative decisions, factual acts etc.

Every administrative judiciary system reflects the national development and is connected with differences in each legal system. Because of that one can distinguish administrative courts, administrative tribunals or specialised administrative chambers of ordinary courts. Different structures of the administrative judiciary depend on the internal national organisation of the judiciary. However, one can discover several common features between these judicial bodies including resolving disputes between individuals and the state; legally binding and enforceable judgments; formal procedures and the development of legal principles. In general, administrative courts can be characterised as *specialised courts with jurisdiction limited to one or more classes of controversies between the Government and individuals, either at the original trial level or on appeal.*[44]

The *administrative judiciary* in this book is perceived in the *broadest sense* of the term as some of the courts (i.e. the European Union Courts, the High Court in the UK) are not administrative courts *stricto sensu* although they partially exercise the functions of administrative courts. Apart from that, also the civil courts sometimes deal with issues such as the non-contractual liability of the state. Thus, this book includes them within the *administrative judiciary* as well.

1.3 Relations between ombudsmen and the judiciary defined

An important term that is interwoven throughout the whole research is the term *relations between ombudsmen and the judiciary*. The book uses the term *relations* as it is defined

42 Maino 1999, p. 436.
43 Cf. Russell & O'Brien 2001.
44 Cadwell 1950, p. 14.

in the Oxford Online Dictionary, i.e. the way in which two or more people or things are connected.[45] Although ombudsmen and the judiciary can be related in several ways, this research approaches them as institutions that fulfil roles and functions connected with the exercise of state power (*state institutions*). Apart from institutional relations one can sometimes also see *interpersonal relations* between the incumbent ombudsmen and judges. It is possible that they know each other. However, as it is almost impossible to comprehensively assess this type of relation concerning the work of ombudsmen and the judiciary and from the methodological point of view it is difficult to engage in consistent research with regard to hundreds (or more) of national judges, these interpersonal relations are mentioned only randomly.

Hence, the term *relations between ombudsmen and the judiciary* as used in this research includes the *institutional relations between these institutions*. It refers to the way in which the judiciary and ombudsmen are *de lege* and *de facto* connected.

1.4 Choices and selection conditions of ombudsmen

Before going any further, it is important to explain the choices of ombudsmen included in the research. As there are hundreds of ombudsmen it was necessary to limit the research.

First of all, only *public service ombudsmen* are included in the research. They are *the ombudsmen that assess the conduct of bodies that exercise state powers*. Private ombudsman bodies such as banking ombudsmen, insurance ombudsmen or consumer protection ombudsmen that, in general, are not established on a statutory basis and are not directly connected with the exercise of state powers are *not* covered by this research.

Secondly, the ombudsman must assess the administrative conduct in question against a *general normative concept* that is acknowledged by the legislator. The research is connected with a general normative concept such as *good administration*, *proper administration* or *maladministration*. This excludes ombudsmen that *only* assess compliance with human rights or *only* compliance with the law. At the same time, the ombudsman should actively approach this general concept in order to explain its content and meaning.

These two necessary limitations were combined with *two practical issues*: my linguistic abilities and the interest in including ombudsmen from various legal cultures in the research. Because of that, the research includes ombudsmen from the continental legal system, from the common law system and from the supranational system:

45 <http://oxforddictionaries.com/definition/relation?q=elations > (accessed on 31 July 2013).

- *the National Ombudsman* (the Netherlands)
- *the Parliamentary Ombudsman* (UK) and *the Local Government Ombudsmen* (England),[46] and
- *the European Ombudsman* (the European Union).

All these four ombudsmen meet the previous conditions. They deal with a general normative concept (the Netherlands - proper behaviour, England - maladministration, the European Union - maladministration) and they all actively approach this concept. Undoubtedly, there are also other ombudsman systems that match these conditions.[47] However, because of the available *time* and *resources* it was not possible to include them all in the research. The results of this research and the potential design amendments of the systems can, however, also be applicable to other ombudsmen that meet the previous conditions.

46 The English Local Government Ombudsmen were included in the research for two main reasons that emerge during the research. According to the existing legislature in England, the Parliamentary Ombudsman cannot publish his/her investigation reports. Although in July 2013, parts of the reports (including special reports, digests of cases and annual reports) have been published, a huge part of his/her *ombudsprudence* is inaccessible. This fact was only discovered after several months of research into the topic of the PO. The second reason why the LGO was included in the research is the fact that when the senior English courts decide a case that involves the PO their findings are also *sometimes* applicable to the work of other ombudsmen including the LGO and vice versa.

47 For example, the Federal Ombudsmen in Belgium, the Commonwealth Ombudsmen (Australia), the Ombudsman of Malta or the Public Defender of Rights of the Czech Republic.

Chapter 2

RESEARCH DESIGN

This chapter identifies the design of the research. First of all, it discusses the goals of the research and explains its value. Furthermore, it points to theories, beliefs and prior research findings that guide or inform the research and thus create its conceptual framework. This is followed by highlighting issues that the research tries to explain. This is done by the delimitation of research questions. Methods that were used when looking for answers to these questions are discussed in this chapter as well. Last but not least, this section also tries to validate the research results and to limit, prevent or even eliminate the possible flaws in the results.[1]

2.1 Goals of the research

Despite the fact that the first ombudsman was established almost 200 years ago and despite a broad proliferation of ombudsmen in the final decades of the 20th century,[2] the ombudsman is, as regards to his/her relations with the judiciary, still an under-researched institution. The relations of ombudsmen with the executive are often extensively discussed by academics and by legal scholars.[3] The relations between the national parliaments and the ombudsmen are also often discussed in a comprehensive way as the ombudsman is often perceived to be a representative of parliament.[4] However, the existing research only marginally concentrates on the subject of the relations between ombudsmen and the judiciary. It occurs only in connection with a particular ombudsman,[5] or in connection with specific issues.[6] There are also some general comparative studies on ombudsmen but these relate to ombudsmen themselves rather than ombudsmen-judiciary relations.[7] A possible explanation for why ombudsmen-judiciary relations are still rather under-researched is the potential clarity of this relation without any specific or particular problems. Nonetheless, the lack of interest shown by research in these types of relations

1 This research design is loosely based on Maxwell 2005.
2 Cf. Reif 2004 or Gregory & Giddings 2000.
3 Cf. Harlow & Rawlings 2009.
4 See, for example, Gøtze 2009 or Abraham 2008, pp. 206-215 etc.
5 For example, Mendes 2009 or Montesh 2009 etc.
6 For example, Wakefield 2007 or Heede 2000 etc.
7 Cf. Kucsko-Stadlmayer 2008; or Mukoro 2008.

was observed, for instance, by Kirkham who points to *unanswered questions regarding the exact linkages between the work of the courts and that of the ombudsman.*[8] Although there are some attempts to describe these relations in individual national legal systems[9] a comparative study of these relations is still lacking. It is interesting that also some national institutions advocate the *strengthening and clarifying of the relationship between the ombudsmen and courts.*[10] Another reason for researching ombudsmen and their relations with the judiciary is the fact that most articles, commentaries and books on ombudsmen have been written by ombudsmen themselves or by members of their staff. A view from the *outside* is often missing. Despite some interest shown by academics, the *world of ombudsmen* is still partially unexplored. Thus, the research has four main goals: to *add to the existing collection of knowledge* about ombudsmen, *to pioneer and explore the area of ombudsman–judiciary relations* in a comparative way, *to broaden academic interest* in ombudsmen and *to highlight any possible amendments to the existing design of ombudsman-judiciary relations.*

2.2 Conceptual framework

A preliminary research into the topic confirms that ombudsmen and the judiciary can interact on different levels. This research concentrates on three main levels of this interaction: the institutional level, the case level and the normative level. The *institutional level* includes the general interplay between the ombudsman and the judiciary as state institutions. The *case level* includes the interplay between them as dispute resolution mechanisms. The *normative level* covers the interplay at the level of normative standards. The ideas behind these levels of interaction create the basis for a conceptual framework for the present research.

Although ombudsman–judiciary relations are somewhat overlooked by researchers, most books on administrative law, constitutional law and European Union law generally refer to ombudsmen. The judiciary as one of the main bearers of state power receives a great deal of attention and it often occupies centre stage in the attention of legal scholars. The position of ombudsmen and the judiciary within the constitutional system of state institutions is the general starting point of this research. Ombudsmen exercise their functions as state institutions, but so does the judiciary. Both institutions try to resolve disputes independently and impartially. They assess the complaints and applications of individuals and the actions of the administration and they protect the individuals in question. Nowadays, one cannot deny that ombudsmen exercise state powers. Nonetheless, the precise position which the ombudsman should occupy within the *trias politica* is not clear. When one looks at the characteristics of ombudsmen, one can see ties to all three traditional power bearers. An ombudsman can be seen as a kind of Parliamentary representative in connection with Parliament's control function but not with its legislative powers.[11] The ombudsman can control the actions of the government (the executive

8 Kirkham 2004, p. 301.
9 Dragoş et al. 2010, pp. 58-75.
10 The Law Commission Consultation Paper No. 187, para. 5.1.
11 Cf. Harlow & Rawlings 2009.

authority) although he/she stands outside it.[12] Similar to the judiciary, ombudsmen exercise some control function.[13] Naturally, these three premises are applicable only in a general manner. The individual national cases can be different. Also the theory often deals with the unclear position of the ombudsman in the state structure. For example, Addink notes that the ombudsman and other institutions, such as the court of audit or the council of state, create a so-called 'fourth power' of the state.[14]

Scheme 1 – **Ombudsmen and the *trias politica***

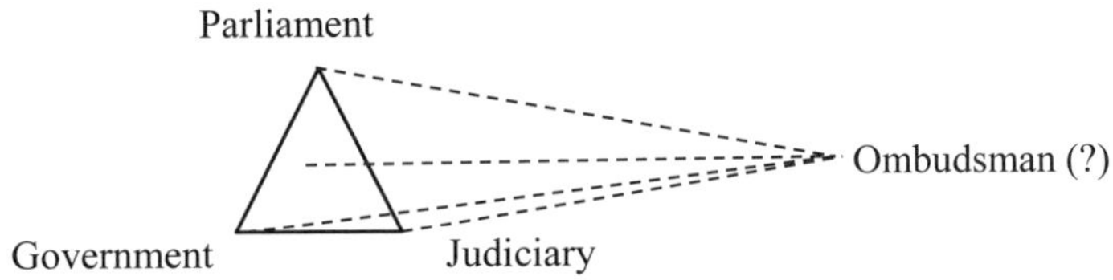

Ombudsmen exercise their powers and by doing so they undoubtedly contribute to *the checks and balances within the* democratic state.[15] In connection with the functions and the position of ombudsmen and the judiciary among the state institutions one can observe that their work is also directly connected with the *field of administrative law* or at least with *administrative justice*. Their work is connected with disputes between the state administration and individuals. An individual often has the possibility to protect his interests in a twofold way: through *an application to the courts* or *through a complaint to the ombudsman*. These institutions represent two different ways of dispute resolution and the protection of individual interests. The individual can usually decide which institution is more appropriate or suitable in his case. The consequences of following one route or the other usually vary and may have a different impact on their addressees.

Scheme 2 – **Ombudsman, court, administration and the individual**

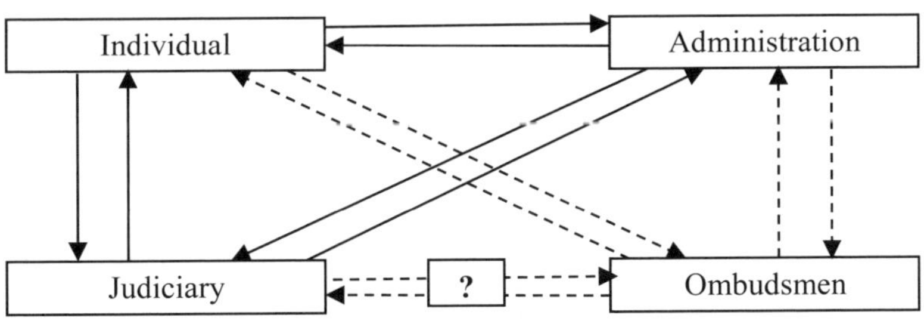

12 Cf. Heede 2000 or Gregory & Giddings 2002.
13 Cf. Reif 2004 or Buck et al. 2011.
14 See, Addink 2005b, p. 269-292.
15 Cf. Hubeau 2008, p. 388 or Brenninkmeijer 2012.

The inclusion of the ombudsman in the system of state bodies provides individuals with an additional possibility to have their interests, rights or feelings protected. It provides them with *an alternative* to the protection offered by the judiciary. From this perspective one can assume that there may be mutual *checks and balances between ombudsmen and the judiciary*. It would not be very effective to have two subjects doing the same things but with different results. Thus, there is a presumption that there is a certain coordination between the powers of these institutions and that cases where they can exercise their functions are somehow regulated. At the same time one must look at the fact that ombudsmen and the judiciary exist *alongside each other* and that they exercise their functions in disputes between the state administration and individuals. They both exercise *checks and balances against the administration* against another bearer of state power (the executive). In that respect they potentially impact and influence the work of the administration, whether in a particular case or generally. Because of that, one can presume that the powers of these institutions are used in a coordinated manner so that the individual's interests are fully protected.

Apart from the functional alternative, ombudsmen can be seen as a *moral alternative to the judiciary*. Their flexibility and the character of their normative concepts potentially allow them to cover categories of administrative actions beyond lawfulness. Jellinek once stated that *das Recht ist nichts anderes, als das ethische Minimum* – the law is an ethical minimum, and, in line with this statement, many ombudsmen consider legal principles to be a minimum standard for administrative conduct.[16] They often go beyond a legal assessment of the situation in question. It is however questionable how far ombudsmen can go when applying extra-legal standards. Legal theory does not cover these issues. Because of this one can approach the theories that discuss the relations between law and morality or law and ethics and try to apply them also to ombudsman-judiciary relations.[17] The judiciary usually covers only the legal side of administrative actions and the ombudsman can also be active in a sphere 'beyond' the law. While taking other theories into account one can approach this issue through the perception of Habermas who considers legal and moral rules as *different* but *mutually complementary* kinds of action norms.[18] He argues that a legal order can be legitimate only if it does not contradict basic moral principles. However, morality is not above the law, as though there is a hierarchy of norms. He rather argues that autonomous morality and statutory law stand in a *complementary relationship.*[19] He also alleges that the law and morality emerged simultaneously from the *encompassing societal ethos* in which traditional law and a conventional ethic were still intertwined with each other and only later were these norms differentiated.[20]

When applying this perception of law and morality to the positions of ombudsmen and the judiciary one can question whether ombudsnorms or the normative standards of ombudsmen are *only* moral norms. Surely, they can include moral norms but this

16 Widdershoven & Remac 2012, p. 405.

17 The issue of law and morality was tackled by Kant, Weber, Austin, Hart, Heidegger and many others.

18 Habermas 1996, p. 105.

19 Ibid., p. 106.

20 Ibid.

statement is not absolute. Because of that the approach that is included in this book is that *ombudsnorms* are *moral norms* and that they are *a priori different from legal norms*. This term includes *moral norms in a strict sense* (e.g. courtesy or politeness) and *broader moral norms* (e.g. procedural norms of administration or norms of an organisational character). This division is purely academic. Based on that, one can create a general scheme stemming from Habermas's perception that points to the fact that theoretically a value can be protected in double way: by ombudsmen or by the judiciary. These institutions, while protecting this value, apply certain normative standards that stem from encompassing societal ethos. It is however unclear whether there is a certain intermutation between these norms. That points to a complexity of ombudsnorms and legal norms as normative standards of these institutions.

Scheme 3 – **Ombudsnorms, legal norms and individual interests**

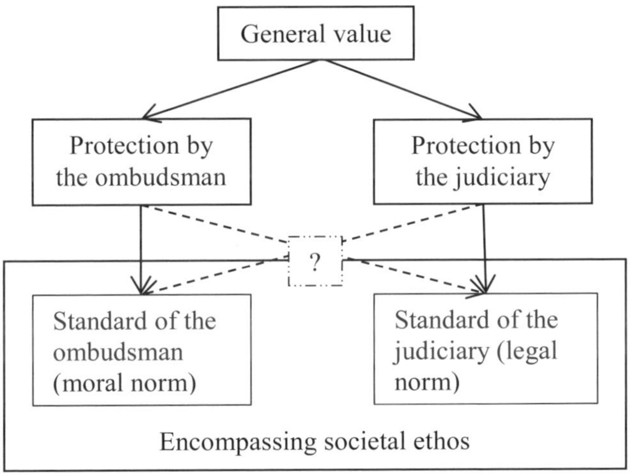

Although this scheme is rather theoretical, it shows that the ombudsman can be perceived as a *normative* and also a *moral alternative to the judiciary*. However, this institution can also be perceived as *a good administration alternative*. From the conceptual point of view, the matter of good administration or good governance and the application of principles of good administration receive a great deal of academic attention.[21] The debate on the principles of good administration can also be transformed into the interplay between the standards used by ombudsmen and those of the judiciary. This debate can only be connected with those ombudsmen that deal with a general concept such as good administration.

21 See, for example, Addink 2010 or Addink 2005.

Most of the second generation ombudsmen are directly connected with this concept.[22] These ombudsmen assess whether the administration exercises its functions in accordance with the requirements of general normative concepts such as good administration, proper administration or good governance. This leads to questioning the relation between the normative concepts such as good administration assessed by ombudsmen and the law, the domain of the judiciary.

A key term of this research is *coordination of ombudsman–judiciary relations*. This term, as used in this book, must be seen in a *neutral way*. It should *not* be perceived as a technique to attain *absolute coherence* between the ombudsman and the judiciary or something that should lead to *complete uniformity* in their decisions, norms or practices as it might decrease the inter-organisational independence of these institutions. Such coordination can lead to a destruction of the specific qualities of ombudsmen. Understanding this perception of coordination can be done with the help of organisation theory[23] and coordination theory.[24]

In connection with these two theories one can regard the *state* as an organisation that needs to be managed. State institutions are then formal structures of this organisation. Structures of an organisation need a certain level of *internal coordination* so that they are able to fulfil their roles and to attain their goals. As in any organisation, also in the State there is a functional division. The internal management of organisations can be included in various internal organisational rules. In the case of the State, these organisational rules are the law and other societal norms and applicable theories and doctrines such as the doctrine of the separation of powers or checks and balances. The state as a very complicated organisation covers many particular issues, thus these organisational rules require some generalisation and constant development. When looking at the state one can observe that its inner organisation must be coordinated so that its internal parts can exercise their roles properly. This includes coordination between ombudsmen and the judiciary.

One of the pioneers of organisation theory, Mintzberg, has built this theory on the presumption that every organised activity gives rise to two fundamental and opposing requirements: the *division of labour into various tasks* and the *co-ordination of these tasks to accomplish the activity*.[25] When one looks at ombudsmen and the judiciary one can see that they have their own tasks. Their primary division of labour can be exercised via constitutional, statutory or even sub-statutory legal acts and via the division of competences that are given to them by these acts. Coordination, according to Mintzberg, is based on several mechanisms that should be considered as the most basic elements of the

22 In general ombudsman theory one can distinguish three main ombudsman generations: ombudsmen reviewing legality, ombudsmen providing a review of general normative concepts such as good administration and ombudsmen reviewing human rights. Nonetheless, one can observe a hybridisation of these generations. See, for example, Reif 2004, p. 2f, Kucsko-Stadlmayer 2008, p. 61ff, Diamandouros 2007a, pp. 22-23 or Remac 2013.

23 *Organisation theory* is used to explain tendencies that drive effective organisations to structure themselves as they do. See, Mintzberg 1983, p. 3.

24 *Coordination theory* refers to different ways of coordination in diverse systems. Malone & Crowston 1994, p. 88.

25 Mintzberg 1979, p. 2.

structure, the glue that holds the organisation together. These mechanisms include mutual adjustment, direct supervision, the standardization of work processes, the standardization of output, the standardization of skills and the standardization of norms knowledge as mechanisms of coordination.[26] To put it simply, ombudsmen accomplish their own tasks while the judiciary also accomplishes its own. Because of that one can presume that there is a certain *institutional coordination* between ombudsmen and the judiciary. Coordination in this sense must be seen as a concept that may include different cooperative and competitive forms. As Malone and Crowston put it, good coordination is nearly invisible, and sometimes it is possible to notice it most clearly when it is lacking.[27] Coordination is thus *managing dependencies between activities*.[28] So if there is no dependence, there is nothing to coordinate.

When one looks at the ombudsman and the judiciary one cannot say that there is no dependence whatsoever. The fact that they exercise similar functions in a sphere of administrative justice and that they control the administration can create these dependences. Because of that one can think of the possible coordination of their tasks as dispute resolution mechanisms – *case coordination*. Last but not least, while ombudsmen and the judiciary are dealing with disputes between individuals and the state administration they apply normative standards. In this connection one can presume the existence of some form of *normative coordination* between these standards. The term coordination as it is used in this research has to be perceived as the *managing of cooperative, collaborating or competitive dependencies between ombudsmen and the judiciary in order to reach common goals (dispute resolution, the protection of the individual and the correct functioning of the administration)*.[29]

2.3 Research questions

The previous pages have generally outlined the goals of the research and its conceptual framework. While taking all this into account it was possible to create a set of questions that are central to the research. In this connection, I pose three main research questions.

The first research question:

How are the relations between ombudsmen and the judiciary as state institutions coordinated in the researched systems and what is the content of this coordination?

This research question covers the first issue of ombudsman-judiciary relations – *institutional coordination*. It tries to discover different institutional practices or different methods of organising the said relations in three different legal systems. The first research

26 Ibid., p. 3.
27 Malone & Crowston 1994, p. 90.
28 Ibid.
29 It is appropriate to distinguish here between the ombudsman's role as regards the *administrative behaviour* of courts themselves, where the coordination issue is not self-evident, and the *judicial role* of the courts where the coordination issue is the research object.

question is based on the following presumptions. In the majority of legal systems, ombudsmen and the judiciary exercise their functions within the sphere of administrative justice alongside each other. They render an independent and impartial assessment of administrative actions and disputes between individuals and the administration. The outcomes of their procedures are intended to offer an unbiased view of the dispute at hand and thus indirectly of the actions of the administration and the compliance of the administration with some normative standards. Thus, it is possible that these institutions will deal with similar cases, which may in the end lead to two different assessments of similar situations. Various legal systems may offer unique techniques and mechanisms for the institutional coordination of ombudsmen and the judiciary.

The second research question:

What is the mutual significance of the reports and the judgments and their content for the other researched institution and what are their interrelations?

This question is directly linked with *case coordination* – coordination connected with the results of the ombudsman investigation (reports)[30] and the proceedings before the judiciary (judgments). The reason for raising this question is the fact that the judgments and reports are one of the few visible manifestations of the actions of these institutions as they include and express their opinions and views on as well as their attitudes to certain conceptions (whether legal or factual). They represent the results of their constitutional functions. By assessing the case coordination one can discover whether the reports and judgments converge and whether there is some development in the acceptance of ombudsman reports by the judiciary and vice versa. Even individuals sometimes try to use the reports to support their statements or position in court proceedings. Similarly, parties to the ombudsman investigation sometimes try to support their arguments by a court judgment which they think is applicable in their case. It raises the question of coordination between the approaches of the judiciary and the ombudsmen but also the question of the mutual significance of judgments and reports in the procedures of the other institution.

The third research question:

What is the mutual significance of the normative standards of ombudsmen and the judiciary in the researched systems and what are the interrelations between these normative standards?

This research question is the narrowest of all three. It is a direct continuation of the previous two questions. Ombudsmen and the judiciary are state institutions exercising their state powers. Their work leads to certain findings. These findings assess administrative actions.

30 The report of the ombudsman is probably the best and most expressive term for the result of the ombudsman's investigation, although in some legal systems the name is different. Because of that, when dealing with a general description of the results of the ombudsman's investigation, the research uses the terms *report of the ombudsman* or *report*. However, when talking about a particular ombudsman, specific terms are used.

To do that, they use certain normative standards. These normative standards have a certain character, status and power. They *de facto* legitimise the ways of thinking and reasoning of ombudsmen and the judiciary while assessing administrative actions. These standards are usually directly or indirectly mentioned in judgments or reports. The applicability of similar assessment criteria in similar situations strengthens the uniformity of the case law of these institutions and the predictability of the results of their procedures. These standards can also have an impact on the administration. Its actions are assessed against them. They have the character of *assessment standards* but also of *standards of conduct*. Although ombudsmen and the judiciary exist within one system of administrative justice they may recognise different sets of normative standards. The judiciary is well known for a direct and active approach in the development and deducing of new legal standards, principles or unwritten rules – principles of law. Apart from the law there are also other societal standards such as ethical standards, moral standards, managerial norms or, lately, principles of good administration or of good governance. This is where the ombudsmen can step in. Their normative standards are connected with a normative concept such as the maladministration of proper administration. Their standards often represent a mixture of legal norms, principles of good administration, ethical or moral principles and standards of good administrative behaviour.[31] These normative standards can be substantively identical, but they do not have to be. That is why there is a presumption that there is some *normative coordination* between ombudsmen and the judiciary. This question addresses the mutual significance of normative standards used by the institutions with different constitutional roles.

2.4 Methods

After a preliminary research some *methods for data collection* were chosen. These methods are *documentary analysis* including a literature research, an analysis of the law and an analysis of the case work of the researched institutions (jurisprudence and ombudsprudence) and *individual interviews*.

Preliminary research proved that it is not possible to answer the research questions while using only one method. For instance, an analysis of the law could only reveal what the black-letter law actually entails but not the actual practice. The analysis of the case work could reveal the practice of these bodies but not the personal opinions of ombudsmen and judges. Given the limits of individual methods of data collection, a combination of all these methods could provide a sufficient and valid answer to the questions posed. The role of a multi-method design is in this particular case connected with the fact that it is necessary to cross-check between the sources of data and also with the necessity to supplement one kind of data with another.[32]

31 Remac 2013.

32 Spratt et al. 2004, p. 7.

2.4.1 Documentary analysis

After the selection of the ombudsman systems, written academic sources and literature written by ombudsmen were checked in order to find general *overview* data. The **literature research** did not reveal any answers to the research questions. Nonetheless, it has provided an important overview of the theoretical background and general understanding of the differences between the chosen ombudsmen–judiciary systems.

The *analysis of legal statutes* and their provisions was the second step in the research. It has provided a necessary check on the information accumulated in the literature but it also provided answers on the formal side of the coordination of ombudsman-judiciary relations. Two main types of legal documents were researched: legal acts establishing ombudsman institutions and their competences and legal acts establishing the judicial bodies and their competences. Some sub-statutory acts were researched as well including rules of conduct, rules of procedure or internal ombudsman statutes. Several internet search engines were used. In the case of the Netherlands this was the search engine http://wetten.overheid.nl/. In the case of English statutory law it was www.legislation.gov.uk and when researching EU law the research used the search engine http://eur-lex.europa.eu/. This particular method of data collection was used in the case of all three research questions, although in the case of the second and the third research question its applicability was rather limited as these research questions are more *practice orientated.* As laws are always developing it was necessary to limit this part of the analysis. Because of this only developments in the law until *31 July 2013* are taken into account.

The practice of ombudsmen and the judiciary was researched mostly through the jurisprudence of the judiciary and the ombudsprudence of the ombudsmen. The judgments and reports are the visible manifestation of the exercise of state powers by the judiciary and the ombudsmen.

Several internet search engines were used here as well. In the case of the reports of *the National Ombudsman* (NL) it was at his official internet site www.nationaleombudsman.nl/rapporten where one can find his investigation reports. In the case of *the Parliamentary Ombudsman* (UK) it was the official internet site www.ombudsman.org.uk/improving-public-service/reports-and-consultations. The ombudsprudence of the *Local Government Ombudsmen* (ENG) can be found at the official internet site of this ombudsman www.lgo.org.uk/decisions/search. The ombudsprudence of the *European Ombudsman* is published at his/her internet site www.ombudsman.europa.eu/en/cases/home.faces. As these institutions adopt hundreds of reports on a yearly basis it was necessary to limit the ombudsprudence. Because of that only reports (and other decisions) published between 1 January 2005 and 31 July 2013 were taken into account. Only the ombudsprudence of the Parliamentary Ombudsman was not limited in this way as the PO does not publish all investigation reports.[33]

33 In July 2013 only approx. 85 of the reports of the PO were posted on the official internet site. These included special reports, other reports and a number of digests of cases.

Also for the research into the jurisprudence several internet search engines were used. In the case of the Netherlands the research the used search engine http://uitspraken.rechtspraak.nl/ and www.raadvanstate.nl/uitspraken.html. In England, it was the search engines www.bailii.org/ and www.supremecourt.gov.uk/decided-cases/index.html. Several research engines were used to access the case work of the English Tribunals.[34] For access to the case law of the Court of Justice of the European Union the search engine posted on its official internet site http://curia.europa.eu/jcms/jcms/j_6/ was used.[35] As in the previous case, also here a time limitation was imposed. Only judgments delivered between 1 January 2005 and 31 July 2013 were researched. However, as the courts react to the ombudsman usually in the first years of the ombudsman's 'life' by trying to explain the mutual borders it was also important to take into account the *landmark* court judgments from the period before 1/1/2005. The choices of these judgments were based on the literature analysis.

There was no special limitation as to the number of courts or to the status of the courts (first-instance, second-instance or supreme courts) included in the research. This was done because of the specific character of all three legal systems included in the research. The book tries to use the judgments of all instances of the administrative judiciary. This approach is important, since researching this subject without taking into account the specifics of all three legal systems could negate some important differences between them and subsequently diminish its value.

2.4.2 *Individual interviews*

Despite the fact that the research primarily views ombudsmen and the judiciary as state institutions, traditional methods of data collection cannot answer the research questions in their entirety. Because of that, interviews were used as a tool for collecting information. Interviews are important not only in order to gain an understanding of the research[36] but they also present a coordinated way of obtaining the desired information.[37] They were used in the research in a twofold way. First of all, they were used in order to *illustrate certain points* that were considered of importance and/or of interest. In this case the interviews enable one to look beyond the letter of the law and into the real everyday practice. The persons interviewed provided their opinions of *what is actually happening*. Secondly, the interviews were used as the *source of fundamental information*. Often they were the only source of information as the issues covered by interviews were not covered by the law or included in the law books. Thus, the interviews not only function as the opinions of the

34 In connection with the English tribunals a necessary limitation was adopted. This limitation is connected with the complicated character of the tribunal system in England. Five individual tribunals were chosen for the research: Employment tribunals and four tribunals that belong under the umbrella of the First-tier Tribunal – Mental Health, Local Government Standards in England, Charity, Social security and Children protection. Because of the character of the English tribunal system, various research engines were used in order to access their casework. These specific research engines are mentioned further in the text. See, Part 3, Chapter 4 and Chapter 3.

35 One can argue that these search engines are not official sources of the law or that they do not include 'all' decisions of the courts. However, they have been either created by the judiciary, or the state or are supported by them. Plus, they include the most important or the most interesting judgments.

36 Maxwell 2005, p. 93.

37 Gubrium Holstein 2001, p. 3.

interviewees but also as an important source of data. In order to prevent the pitfalls of building the book on untrustworthy interviews, only field specialists were interviewed.

First of all, the incumbent ombudsmen in the researched systems who held their office until 2012 were interviewed. Apart from the ombudsmen also several members of their offices were interviewed. Secondly, several administrative law court and tribunal judges were interviewed. Thirdly, two members of a specialised institution that existed in the UK in July 2013, *the Administrative Justice and Tribunals Council,* were interviewed. The list of interviewed persons is included in Annex 2.

The choice of the interviewed judges was based on their connection with administrative law cases. It was also limited by their interest in and their willingness to give an interview, their time schedules, the development of the research and contacts among the judges. The judges were picked randomly. With the exception of the European Courts, the number of chosen judges represents only a small number of all judges working in the judiciary of the particular researched law system. At the same time the information received from judges represents only their individual opinions on the topic and not the official opinions of the 'national judicial bodies'. It is obvious that in comparison to other systems more judges were interviewed in England. This was necessary to properly understand the English tribunal system as the tribunals are nowadays part of the judiciary and they can be *de facto* described as *specialised first-instance administrative courts.*[38] The interviewed members of the AJTC were chosen because of their academic or practical connection with the work of ombudsmen. Both of the interviewed members of the AJTC were legal scholars.[39]

The interviews include three interconnected issues: the institutional relations ombudsman – the judiciary, the relations in connection with the judgments and reports and the relations linked to their normative standards. Although the research includes three different legal systems it was possible to create a list of core questions which is included in Annex 1. All the interviews were conducted between 2009 and 2013. The interviews were conducted after a general research (i.e. a literature research, a law and casework research) of each ombudsman and court system. They took place in English and only occasionally in Dutch. They were semi-structured and included a combination of open-ended and closed questions. They were recorded and subsequently transcribed and corrected. All transcripts of the interviews were sent to the persons interviewed, who then had an opportunity to change or adapt their statements. All the persons interviewed agreed to the publication of the interviews or parts thereof in the thesis. The interviews were mostly oral. Only occasionally were they replaced by a written questionnaire. The questions used in the questionnaire were identical to the questions used during the oral interviews.

38 There is still the question of to what extent the tribunals can be compared with continental first-instance administrative courts. This, however, is a question for further research.

39 As legal scholars they were subjected to a different set of questions. These questions are included Annex 1.

2.5 Validity

The validity of a comparative research has its importance. As it was not my intention to write fantasy or an academic fiction it was necessary that the results and facts of the research were confirmed and checked. This validation had several levels. First of all, all the information found in books, articles or internet sites had to be compared with the information received from other sources. The data were also checked against the provisions of the national laws.

Since the research was carried out in the period 2009 – 2013, a check on the accuracy of the information was carried out on a yearly basis. The latest validity check and subsequent modifications were done on 31 July 2013. As there is a continual development in statutory law, jurisprudence and ombudsprudence, an annual check on the validity of legal statutes and the jurisprudence and ombudsprudence of these institutions was also carried out. As noted before, the statutory laws, jurisprudence and ombudsprudence as included in the book reflect the valid situation up until 31 July 2013. An important check on the information was also done by interviews. Interviewees usually confirmed or conversely contradicted my presumptions and led me to recheck my research data. A partial validation of the data was also done by publishing academic articles, their presentation at conferences and their subsequent validation. An important part of this check was also the monthly meetings with my supervisors, who often questioned my data and my text. Last but not least, the validity and accuracy of the text was also ensured by a substantive check of my texts by scholars with an in-depth knowledge of each legal/ombudsman system included in the research. Because of all this I can presume that the data included in the research are not very far from being the factual and legal truth.

2.6 Summary

The research has several characteristics. First of all, it is a combination of *legal desk research* and *qualitative research*. The research tries to describe and analyse the mutual correlation and interplay between ombudsmen and the judiciary by researching the written law and jurisprudence of the judiciary, the casework of the ombudsmen and the academic literature. At the same time it goes further than just observing the status of written or unwritten law as it also tries to observe the actual practice of these institutions. Secondly, it is also a combination of descriptive and explanatory research since it tries to give an answer to the question of what is going on in ombudsman–court relations but it also tries to look at the issues from the position of why and how things are happening.[40] The research uses the theory building (construction) approach.[41] On the basis of three case studies of different ombudsman–judiciary systems one can generalise the results according to the similar systems of the ombudsmen and the judiciary. Because of that it includes an inductive reasoning and moves from an empirical level to a conceptual

40 For a more sophisticated explanation of descriptive and explanatory research see, De Vaus 2001, p.1ff.

41 Theory building is a process by which researchers seek to make sense of the observable world by conceptualizing, categorizing and ordering relationships among observed elements. Andersen & Kragh 2010, p. 50.

(abstract) one. As three different legal systems are included in the book, the research has the character of a comparative legal research.[42]

In general, ombudsmen and the judiciary provide an independent assessment of administrative actions. They try to solve disputes between the state and individuals and their practice can have a considerable impact on the work of the administration. In general, they should have common goals such as a contribution to the development of administrative justice, the better functioning of the state administration and an independent and impartial dispute resolution. At the same time their working methods differ, the results of their proceedings have a different character and they may have different areas of control. Last but not least, they may use different criteria to support their findings. Generally ombudsmen and the courts are similar, yet very different. As Abraham once put it, *ombudsmen and courts are like chalk and cheese: superficially similar, but of very different texture and ingredients.*[43]

42 See, for example, Zweigert & Kötz 1998.
43 Foreword by A. Abraham to Kirkham 2007.

PART II

RELATIONS BETWEEN THE NATIONAL OMBUDSMAN AND THE COURTS IN THE NETHERLANDS

Part II of the book describes the relations between the ombudsman and the judiciary in the Netherlands. As explained in the previous part in connection with the Dutch ombudsman institutions it is the *National Ombudsman* (NO) that is researched here. The other ombudsman institutions in the Netherlands are not a part of this research. This part also describes the court system in the Netherlands. It devotes its attention to the *administrative judiciary*.

Chapter 1 describes the position of the NO within the Dutch state authorities and within the Dutch ombudsman system. It discusses his powers and connects them with the general ombudsman functions discussed in Part 1. Chapter 2 describes the position, powers, structure and decisions of the Dutch judiciary while focusing on the administrative courts. Chapter 3 discusses the *institutional coordination* of the relations between the NO and the judiciary. By doing so it tries to answer the first research question. Chapter 4 tries to answer the second research question and clarifies the *case coordination* between the NO. The third researched question is addressed in Chapter 5 which discusses the *normative coordination* between the researched subjects.

Chapter 1

THE NATIONAL OMBUDSMAN

The institution of the NO was established in 1981 by the *National Ombudsman Act 1981* (*Wet Nationale ombudsman* – WNo).Two years later, the NO was also included in the Dutch Constitution in Art. 78a. With that, the institution has become one of the High Offices of the State (*Hoge Colleges van Staat*).[1] The legal theory includes the NO and the whole Dutch ombudsmen system into the system of external and independent complaint mechanisms that stand outside the administrative authorities.[2] The NO is also included in *the General Administrative Law Act 1994* (*Algemene wet bestuursrecht* – GALA) as amended by legislative changes. While the WNo almost exclusively deals with the establishment of the office of the NO, the GALA (Chapter 9) deals with procedural issues and the competences of the NO. The GALA also lays down rules for the other ombudsman institutions and the right to file an administrative complaint (*klachtrecht*). Nowadays the NO is a stable part of the administrative justice system in the Netherlands and specialises in the handling of complaints.

Since April 2011, there is also a specialised ombudsman institution – the Children's Ombudsman (*Kinderombudsman*) that is part of the NO Office.[3] Although the Children's Ombudsman is *ex lege* a *substitute National Ombudsman*[4] it is an independent body that is not subordinated to the NO. The law also presumes the existence of a specialised Ombudsman for Veterans *(Ombudsman voor veteranen).* In July 2013 the legal provisions establishing this ombudsman were not yet in force.

1.1 Functions of the National Ombudsman

Part 1 generally discusses the theoretical functions that can be connected with the ombudsman institutions – the control function, the protection and dispute resolution function, the redress function, the normative function and the educational function. As these functions are interrelated, it is rather difficult to separate them completely. One can

1 See, Meulenbroek 2008, p. 23.
2 See, Hubeau 2008, p. 377.
3 The Children's Ombudsman has a role in assessing whether the central and local state administration, but also private law organisations respect the rights of children (Art. 11b WNo).
4 Art. 9 (1) WNo.

also observe a similar situation in the Netherlands. The functions can be implied from the legal provisions or from the accepted practice of the ombudsmen.

1.1.1 Control function and protection and dispute resolution function

The *control function* of the NO can be implied from Art. 78a (1) of the Dutch Constitution. The article enables the NO to investigate the *conduct* (*gedragingen*) of the central government administrative authorities and the other administrative authorities designated by or pursuant to Act of Parliament. The actual rules for the exercise of this function are laid down in the GALA.[5] Investigating the conduct of administrative authorities fulfils the essential role of the ombudsman.[6] This function of the NO is connected with the investigation of the administrative conduct of institutions and matters within his competence.[7]

The NO can start to exercise his control function either based on a complaint or on his own initiative.[8] By dealing with complaints and by conducting investigations of his own motion the NO also exercises his *protection and conflict resolution function*. The NO describes his mission as protecting citizens against improper administrative actions.[9] The NO can protect the interest of the individual but also a certain value that forms the substance of the dispute. The majority of complainants file their complaint with the NO if they have a certain problem with the administration, or they have a different opinion on a certain issue covered by the administration and thus they are in dispute therewith. The GALA directly presumes that the NO stands between individuals and the administration as a dispute resolution mechanism. In this connection the NO can use several different methods, ranging from a formal investigation to intermediation between individuals and the administration.[10]

1.1.1.1 Subjects and matters within the competence of the National Ombudsman

When describing the subjects that fall within the competence of the NO, one must take into account the special organisation of the Dutch ombudsman system. The GALA distinguishes between two types of ombudsmen: the National Ombudsman and the ombudsmen established by specialised statutes that can be characterised as *municipal* or *specialised ombudsmen*. The competences of these ombudsman institutions stem from the statutes which establish them.[11] Based on these statutes, municipalities, provinces, water boards and other authorities can create their own complaints committee (called an

5 Art. 9:18 (1) GALA.
6 Cf. Annual Report of the NO 2005, p. 14.
7 Compare, Mein et al.2010, p. 11.
8 See, section 1.1.1.2.
9 Annual Report of the NO, 2010, p. 38 (*De burgers te beschermen tegen onbehoorlijk overheidsoptreden*).
10 See, section 1.1.1.3.
11 For instance, the Municipality Act (*de Gemeentewet*), the Provinces Act (*de Provinciewet*), the Water Boards Act (*de Waterschapswet*), the Act on the public bodies of Bonaire, St. Eustatius and Saba (*Wet openbare lichamen Bonaire, SintEustasius en Saba*).

ombudsman or an *ombudscommittee*).[12] If these institutions do not create such a body or subsequently abolish it,[13] the NO *ex lege* receives the competence to deal with complaints against the administrative bodies of these institutions.[14] Thus, in some cases the NO also acts as a *municipal ombudsman*.[15]

The list of institutions that are within the NO's competence is laid down in *Art. 1a (1) WNo.* It includes the Dutch ministries, the administrative authorities of the provinces, municipalities, water boards and decentralised agencies that do not have their own ombudsman institution, and administrative authorities charged with duties relating to the police etc. The NO investigates the *conduct (gedragingen)* of the institutions that are included in this act. Nonetheless, neither the GALA nor the WNo define the term *conduct (gedragingen).* The NO explains this term as 'primarily the conduct (actions) of the government that does not take the form of a decision.'[16] An assessment of the administrative decisions of administrative authorities is generally excluded from his competence.[17] Furthermore, he assesses whether this conduct was *proper* (*behoorlijk*) or not.[18] The list does not include the Dutch Parliament *(de Staten-Generaal)*, the King or the judiciary so any complaints against these state institutions are *a priori* excluded from his remit. This list can be changed by statutory legislation.[19]

The power of the NO is to certain extent limited by the law. There are several situations in which he does not have any jurisdiction to initiate or continue an investigation of a complaint at all (Art. 9:22 GALA). These situations include, for example, cases where the complaint relates to matters belonging to general government policy or generally binding rules; conduct against which one can file a complaint (*beklag*)[20] or an appeal (*beroep*);[21] conduct against which there is a pending complaint or appellate procedure; and conduct that can be supervised by the judiciary, i.e. an action that belongs to the jurisdiction of the courts.[22]

In some cases the NO can decide whether he will investigate the complaint or not (Art. 9:23 GALA). These situations include *inter alia* cases of an evidently unfounded

12 For example, the *Ombudsman of Amsterdam* or the *Ombudsman of Rotterdam.*

13 For example, in 2012 the Municipality of Utrecht decided to abolish the Municipal Ombudsman of Utrecht. The powers to assess the administrative behaviour of the municipal institutions in Utrecht passed to the NO.

14 Art. 1a (1) b) WNo.

15 In January 2013, 73 % (297) of all (408) the Dutch municipalities fell within the remit of the NO. <www.nationaleombudsman-nieuws.nl/nieuws/2013/nieuw-aangesloten-gemeenten-2013> (accessed on 31 July 2013).

16 See, for example, Annual Report of the NO, 2007, p. 134 (*De ombudsman beoordeelt hoofdzakelijk overheidsgedragingen die niet de vorm hebben van beschikkingen).*

17 See, section 2.2.

18 See, sections 1.1.3 and 5.1.1.

19 Dutch statutes are adopted in cooperation of the Dutch Government and the Dutch Parliament (*statutory legislation*). There is also legislation that is adopted by the institutions with a delegated power to legislate in special cases (*secondary or delegated legislation*).

20 Specialised complaint procedures can exclude the ombudsmen from the assessment of complaints.

21 According to Art. 1:5 (3) GALA the term 'appeal' includes an *administrative appeal* and an *appeal to the court.*

22 In relation with the Dutch judiciary, the NO's obligatory limitations are discussed in detail in section 3.1.1.

complaint; cases where the content of the complaint relates to conduct against which one can file an objection, an administrative appeal or a complaint; or cases where a complainant is not a person who is or has been directly influenced by the administrative conduct.[23] The NO is not obliged to investigate any conduct already investigated by relevant committee of any Chamber of Parliament (Art. 12 WNo).

1.1.1.2 Complaints and own initiative investigations

The right to file a *complaint with the NO* is a constitutional right.[24] However, the GALA contains several conditions that have to be complied with when exercising this right. Thus not every petition to the NO is a complaint and not every petition leads to his investigation.

Generally, the complaint should be written.[25] Nowadays a complainant can also file a complaint online by means of a complaint form (*klachtformulier*).[26] In practice, an oral complaint can be made at the NO Office. It is then written down by the staff and signed by the petitioner.[27] One can submit a complaint also in a language other than Dutch. However, if a translation of this complaint is necessary for its proper handling, the complainant has to bear the costs of such translation.[28]

Before complaining to the NO, the complainant must make a preliminary complaint or an objection with the body concerned (Art. 9:20 (1), GALA). Thus, he has to submit his petition to the administrative authority concerned, unless it cannot be reasonable to expect him to do so. The NO sees himself as a *voorziening in de tweede lijn* (a secondary remedy).[29] If this condition is not met the NO sends the petition to the appropriate administrative authority and informs the complainant thereof. According to Art. 9:24 (1) GALA the complaint to the NO has to be submitted within *one year* after the administrative authority has given notification of the findings of the investigation or since the handling of the complaint by the administrative authority has ended in some other way. This condition is strictly controlled.[30] The complaint must contain, as a minimum, are the name and address of the complainant, the date, the signature of the complainant, a description of the action concerned, the facts of the case, and the grounds of the complaint.[31] Generally, the complainant does not need to have an individual concern. Art. 9:18 (1) of GALA presumes that the complainant can ask the NO to investigate the way in which the administrative authority has acted towards *another person*. Still, the NO is not obliged to commence or to continue an investigation of such a complaint.[32]

23 In relation with the Dutch judiciary, the NO's discretionary limitations are discussed in detail in section 3.1.1.
24 See, (Art. 78a (1) Constitution)
25 Art. 9:18 (1) GALA.
26 <www.nationaleombudsman.nl/klachtformulier> (accessed on 31 July 2013).
27 Based on an interview with officials from the NO Office.
28 Art. 9:28 (2) GALA.
29 <www.nationaleombudsman.nl/over-de-nationale-ombudsman-0> (accessed on 31 July 2013).
30 *U heeft bij de Nationale ombudsman een klacht ingediend. En dan?*, De Nationale Ombudsman 2013, p. 3.
31 Art. 9:28 (1) GALA.
32 Art. 9:23 (d) GALA.

Besides the complaint, the NO can start an investigation also *on his own initiative*.[33] He usually starts an investigation on his own initiative when he wants to investigate structural problems in the public administration in order to *expose these problems* and *to help the administration to improve its services*.[34] These investigations are not very frequent but they are very influential. Between 2005 and 2013 only in 61 cases did such an investigation lead to a written report.[35] The greatest problem faced by the broader applicability of these procedures is an insufficient budget.[36] Neither GALA nor the WNo lay down specific conditions as to when the NO can start this type of investigation. Nonetheless, the NO cannot start an investigation on his own initiative in cases in which he cannot investigate a complaint.[37]

1.1.1.3 Investigation procedure

Before the NO decides whether he will proceed with an investigation, he has to decide whether the petition he has received is in fact a complaint. After the petition is received and its reception is confirmed a first test has to be applied. It is checked whether it meets six prima facie requirements so that it can be perceived to be a complaint. A petition is a complaint if it concerns the public administration (*overheid*); if it does not concern the content of legal norms or provisions of law; if it does not deal with a decision of a judge; if a complainant does not have the possibility to file an administrative appeal or commence an objection procedure; and if the problem to which the petition refers has occurred within less than one year and a complainant has already complained to the administrative authority itself.[38]

If the petition does not meet one of these requirements the NO will not continue the investigation and he will inform the petitioner of the reasons why he has decided not to investigate the complaint. Conversely, if it meets this test, then he can proceed with the investigation. An investigation can be conducted as an *intermediation* (*tussenkomst*) or as a *thorough investigation* (*uitgebreid onderzoek*).

An *intermediation* can best be described as a speedy and very informal investigation. It can be exercised through *intervention* (*interventie*) or *mediation* (*bemiddeling*). These tools are aimed at restoring the trust of an individual in the administration in concrete situations.[39] An example of an *intermediation* is a case where a complainant is in financial need because his allowance or his benefit has not been paid on time or if he has to wait for an administrative decision for a long time. During the intermediation the NO contacts the administrative authority concerned usually by telephone or email and proposes a solution. An intermediation provides the body concerned with the possibility to react speedily to the situation and it often enables an expeditious solution to a problem or a dispute. If the NO is content with the (proposed) solution of an administrative authority he informs

33 Art. 9:26 GALA and Art. 78a (1) Constitution.
34 Annual Report of the NO 2008, p. 40.
35 <www.nationaleombudsman.nl/onderzoeken-uit-eigen-beweging> (accessed on 31 July 2013).
36 Annual Report of the NO 2005, p. 12.
37 Art. 9:26 GALA.
38 *Geen gehoor bij de overheid? De Nationale ombudsman helpt*, De Nationale Ombudsman 2010, p. 5.
39 Annual Report of the NO 2011, p. 6.

the complainant about the solution and winds down the investigation. Intermediation does not lead to written and published reports.[40] However, if the NO is not content with this solution, he will proceed with a *thorough investigation*. An intermediation is a popular way of dealing with a complaint. Most cases that are received by the NO are dealt with by this particular method. For example, in 2012 more than 84% (3,444 cases) of all complaints accepted by the NO were dealt with by *intermediation*.[41] On average, an intervention requires 47 days, mediation needs 175 days and an investigation leading to a report requires 10 months.[42]

Although only a minority of all cases are investigated thoroughly (5% in 2012) this type of investigation has probably the greatest potential educational impact as it leads to a formalised and published report by the NO. A *thorough investigation* usually begins after the complaint passes the preliminary test and it is not possible to deal with the complaint by intermediation or this does not lead to satisfactory results.[43] A thorough investigation is usually a mixture of written and oral procedures. The NO has broad investigative powers. Administrative authorities, their employees, witnesses and the complainant have an obligation to provide the NO with the information necessary for his investigation and they have to appear in person before him when requested.[44] The NO can ask for any documents in possession of the administrative authority connected with the investigated conduct. Moreover, he is entitled to entrust certain activities to experts and obtain the assistance of interpreters. He can conduct an on-site investigation and for that purpose he can access any site, other than a dwelling, without the consent of the possessor. These powers can be limited due to state security.[45] The administrative authority is always given an opportunity to react to a complaint and to express its view.[46] Before closing the investigation, the NO sends the findings to the relevant authority, to the person to whose action the investigation relates and to the complainant. They can comment thereon. Once the NO receives their comments he writes his report.[47]

1.1.2 Redress function

Neither GALA nor the WNo include a list of remedies which can be granted by the NO. In fact, they do not even mention the possibility for the NO to remedy grieved complainants' situation. Based on the results of his investigation, the NO can only make recommendations to the administrative authorities.[48] His recommendations take the form of legally non-binding advice to the administration on how to remedy a situation

40 Annual Report of the NO 2010, p. 118.

41 According to the Annual Report of the NO 2012, in 2012 an intervention was used in 83% of all investigated cases. A report was written in 5% of cases and a letter in 4% of cases. Mediation was used in only 1% of cases (p. 43).

42 Annual Report of the NO 2011, p. 42.

43 *U heeft bij de Nationale ombudsman een klacht ingediend. En dan?*, De Nationale Ombudsman 2013, p. 4.

44 Art. 9:31 (1) GALA.

45 All these investigative powers are included in GALA, Arts. 9:31 – 9:34.

46 Art. 9:30 GALA.

47 For the types of reports, see, Paragraph 1.1.3.2.

48 Art. 9:27 (3) GALA.

in a particular case (*individual recommendation*) and/or on how to adapt the working processes so that the problem that needs to be remedied in an individual situation does not arise again (*structural recommendation*).[49]

In practice, the *individual recommendations* can request the administration, for example, to take a new decision in a case;[50] to reconsider any decision taken;[51] to remedy damage that has occurred to a complainant by an administrative action;[52] to meet the complainant and to discuss the issue with him[53] or to take certain specific steps to remedy a complainant.[54]

Structural recommendations can request the administration, for instance, to change the formulation of an official application;[55] to be active in communicating with parties, to reply more speedily and to use telephone contact more often[56] or to create a system in which citizens against whom an arrest warrant has been delivered, and who are not represented by a lawyer, receive this arrest warrant on time.[57] The recommendations of the NO depend on the particular case and can include a whole range of measures. Because of this one can also find different examples of recommendations.

The acceptance of the NO's recommendations depends entirely on the body concerned. Nonetheless, compliance with the recommendations of the NO is high, on average 92%.[58] For instance, in 2012 the NO included a recommendation in 78 cases out of which 92% of these recommendations were followed.[59]

The redress function can also be connected with the NO's guidance document – *Guidance on proper administrative compensation (Schadevergoedingswijzer)*.[60] This document contains 16 normative standards that should be used by the administration when providing complainants with compensation for damage.[61]

1.1.3 Normative function and educational function

The normative function and the educational function are closely linked with the general normative concept of the NO – proper administration (*behoorlijkheid*).

The *normative function* can be deduced from the GALA. In accordance with Art. 9:27 (1) of GALA the NO determines whether the administrative authority has behaved *properly*

49 See, for example, Annual Report of the NO 2010, p. 29.
50 See, for example, Report 2009/041 or Report 2009/127.
51 See, for example, Report 2010/219.
52 See, for example, Report 2010/323 or Report 2006/287.
53 See, for example, Report 2010/178.
54 See, for example, Report 2009/190.
55 See, for example, Report 2010/293.
56 See, for example, Report 2010/007.
57 See, for example, Report 2011/032.
58 This percentage is based on information included in the annual reports of the NO published between 2008 and 2012. See, Annual Reports of the National Ombudsman 2008-2012.
59 Verslag van de Nationale ombudsman over 2012: Mijn onbegrijpelike overheid, p. 44.
60 <www.nationaleombudsman.nl/sites/default/files/schadevergoedingswijzer_2.pdf> (accessed on 31 July 2013). This guidance document was written as a consequence of the NO's investigations in the cases *'Behoorlijk omgaan met schadeclaims'* (Report 2009/135 of 24 June 2009) and *'Behoorlijk omgaan met schadeclaims door gemeenten'* (Report 2011/025 of 15 February 2011).
61 Guidance of the NO is extensively discussed in section 1.1.3.1.

or not.[62] Based on this legal provision the NO is connected with the assessment of a *proper administration* (*behoorlijkheid*) that is his normative concept.[63] *Proper administration* is a very specific and very important term in the Dutch ombudsman system.[64] Another article of the GALA (Art. 9:36 (2)) explicitly requires the NO to state *which requirement of proper administration was breached* if he finds that the administrative conduct has been improper. Thus he is obliged to use the requirements of proper administration as assessment standards. However, the law does not define *proper administration or requirements of proper administration.*

During the adoption of the WNo and before this, there were various attempts to define the standard of control of the Dutch ombudsmen. Firstly, the ombudsman was supposed to base his reports or decisions on written and unwritten law and on other criteria against which he should have evaluated the actions of the administration.[65] The subsequent proposals decreased such a broad standard of control. Then the ombudsman should only have dealt with issues of *decency*.[66] Finally, the concept of *proper administration* was introduced as a standard of the ombudsman's control in order to distinguish his work from the protection exercised by the courts.[67] As there was no substantive consensus on the content of the term, the legislator decided to leave this issue for the discretion of the ombudsman.[68] The office holders seized upon this opportunity, and basically every one of them has introduced some form of novelty in the perception of proper administration and its requirements.[69]

Nowadays, proper administration is not only an awareness of the legal norms that can be assessed by the judge, but it is also represented by the individual who argues that 'this is not fair'![70] Unlawful conduct is not necessarily improper conduct. The NO must only find the administrative conduct improper if it is in breach of a specific requirement of proper administration, which can be enshrined in the law but does not necessarily need to be.[71] Proper administration hence goes beyond sole compliance with legal provisions. It requires the administration to comply also with special standards or requirements of proper administration set by the NO. In general, administrative conduct that passes the ombudsman's check and meets the requirements included in the list is proper

62 *De ombudsman beoordeelt of het bestuursorgaan zich in de door hem onderzochte aangelegenheid al dan niet behoorlijk heeft gedragen.*

63 Also Dutch municipal ombudsmen use proper administration as their normative concept.

64 The translation of the term *behoorlijkheid* is tricky. It has a few meanings and can be translated into English as decency, properness, adequacy or even as fairness. However, the leading Dutch scholars in ombudsman issues (for example, Langbroek and Rijpkema) but also the incumbent NO translate *behoorlijkheid* into English as properness, propriety or proper conduct. In order to be consistent, this book uses the term *proper administration* as a translation of *behoorlijkheid.*

65 See, Van der Vlugt 2011, p. 62.

66 Ibid.

67 Kamerstukken II 1976/77, 14 178, no. 3 (Memorie van Toelichting), pp. 19-20.

68 Of course, there was a broader discussion than is offered by this section. For more on the history of this term see, for example, Meulenbroek 2008, pp. 7-8 or Daalder et al. 1998.

69 See, section 5.1.1.

70 Annual Report of the NO 2005, pp. 72-73.

71 Brenninkmeijer & Van Hoogstraten 2008, p. 4.

administrative conduct. One can perceive proper administration as a Dutch version of good administration.[72]

By developing his own normative standards that explain the term proper administration the NO gives *guidance on proper administration*. This guidance and the standards are an expression of his normative function. This function is also expressed in the *results of the NO's investigation (reports)* where the normative standards are applied in practice as assessment standards. The reports have been described as reservoirs of experience from which general rules can be deduced[73] and warehouses of normative experience.[74]

These documents can have a potential educative impact on the administration and individuals. Thus, one can talk about the *potential educative function* of the NO. By setting standards and by pointing to administrative errors the NO enables the administration to learn from its mistakes and to provide better services. At the same time, this guidance enables individuals to learn what kind of service they can expect from the administration. The fact that the reports and the guidance of the NO are published on his official internet site and are generally accessible makes the potential educative impact of the NO's work rather broad. However, this function is only passive, since the NO cannot compel anybody to learn anything from his guidance.

1.1.3.1 Guidance of the National Ombudsman

The normative standards of the NO are included in several guidance documents. The most important document is the so-called *Guidelines on Proper Conduct*. They codify the requirements of proper administration. They also unify the perception and content of the term *proper administration*. Its latest version was developed as a result of cooperation between the NO and the majority of the municipal ombudsmen.[75] The list has the character of a checklist and a breach of one of the requirements leads to improper administration.[76] Thus, with the implicit blessing of the Dutch legislator which has acknowledged the existence of proper administration but has not specified its content, the NO has developed his own normative standards against which he assesses the proper conduct of the administration.[77] Apart from these recommendations and a general list of requirements of proper administration the NO also develops specific principles that are applicable to specific situations such as, for example, telephone contact with individuals or the enforcement of administrative decisions. These specialised requirements broaden the requirements of proper administration included in the *Guidelines on Proper Conduct* to specific situations.

The guidance of the NO is divided into three groups.[78] In the first group the NO includes guidance documents addressed to *individuals*, for example, documents such

72 See, Langroek & Remac 2011.
73 See, Langbroek & Rijpkema 2006.
74 Langbroek & Remac, p. 158.
75 Based on an interview with Dr. Brenninkmeijer, the National Ombudsman.
76 Based on interview with Mr. Van Dooren, the Substitute National Ombudsman.
77 See, also section 5.1.1.
78 See, <www.nationaleombudsman.nl/informatiemateriaal> (accessed on 31 July 2013).

as *Wat mag een slachtoffer verwachten van de overheid?* (What can a victim expect from the administration?), *Stop discriminatie kaart* (The stop discrimination card) or *Stop homopesten kaart* (The stop bullying homosexuals card). Apart from an explanation of conduct that individuals can expect from the administration they also include norms of proper societal behaviour.

The second type of guidance documents includes proper administration standards developed specially for the *administration*. These include, for instance, the *Beslissingwijzer* (Guidance on proper decision making), the *Correspondentiewijzer* (Guidance on proper correspondence), the already mentioned *Schadevergoedingwijzer* (Guidance on proper compensation) or the *Telefoonwijzer* (Guidance on proper telephone contact). These documents are collections of specialised proper administrative rules. Breaches of these requirements also lead to a breach of the general requirements of proper administration.[79]

The last group of guidance documents is addressed to *both the administration and individuals*. It clarifies general rules for participation (*Participatiewijzer*); rules applicable to objection procedures (*Bezwaarwijzer*); general rules connected with public demonstrations (the *Demonstratiekaart*) and the already mentioned general Guidelines on Proper Conduct.

1.1.3.2 Reports and other documents of the National Ombudsman

During the course of an investigation and thereafter, the NO can adopt several decisions.[80] The reports are the results of thorough investigations. In connection with Art. 9:36 (1) of GALA in a(n) *(investigation) report* he describes his findings and gives his verdict on the proper or improper character of the conduct. The reports can include findings (*rapport met een oordeel*) and sometimes also findings and recommendations (*rapport met een aanbeveling*). If he decides to include a recommendation, the administrative authority concerned has to notify him within a reasonable period of time of any action it intends to take based on this recommendation. If the administration does not accept the recommendation, it has an obligation to notify the NO and to state its reasons.[81] As noted above, in case of a finding of improper administration he is obliged to specify which *requirement of proper administration* was breached. If necessary, the NO can also communicate his findings to the chambers of Parliament, representative bodies of the provinces, municipalities, public bodies or water boards etc.[82] These reports are posted on the NO's official internet page.[83]

The NO submits an *annual report* (*verslag van zijn werkzaamheden*) to both chambers of Parliament, to the ministries and to other subjects.[84] Annual reports include a detailed analysis of the NO's work during the past year. The NO often uses annual reports also to point to a particular topic that is a part of the relation between an individual and

79 See, for example, Report 2012/194.

80 The term 'decision' does not refer to 'administrative decision' but refers to a general term covering the results of any process leading to a choice after thinking about several possibilities.

81 Art. 9:36 (5) GALA.

82 Art. 16 (3) WNo.

83 <www.nationaleombudsman.nl/rapporten> (accessed on 31 July 2013).

84 Art. 16 (1) WNo.

the administration.[85] Annual reports are made public and posted on the NO's official webpage.[86]

An annual report and investigation reports are the only types of reports the NO makes. The NO can also *inform the individuals concerned*[87] or send them *written notifications.*[88]

Although the NO is not the only ombudsman institution in the Netherlands, he has a central role in dealing with complaints against the administration. He controls the administration. He can protect the interests of citizens. He acts as an independent dispute resolution mechanism and he develops normative standards applicable to the administration and society which can have a possible educative impact.

85 For example, the Annual Report of the NO 2009 covered the issue of the polarisation and de-escalation of possible conflicts between the administration and an individual.

86 Art. 16 (2) WNo.

87 See, Art. 9:19 (1) GALA or Art. 9:18 (2) GALA.

88 See, Art. 9:25 (1) GALA.

Chapter 2

SYSTEM OF THE DUTCH COURTS

In general, the Dutch court system recognises two types of courts: *ordinary courts* with civil, criminal and administrative jurisdiction and *specialised administrative* (mainly appellate) *courts*.[1] There is no special constitutional court in the Netherlands and courts do not have the power to assess the constitutionality of statutory legislation and treaties.[2] This power belongs only to the Dutch Parliament that is the only institution that can change or amend the Dutch Constitution or statutes. The courts, however, are competent to review secondary legislation. They can test rules of lower legal authority against rules with higher legal authority.

Because of the connection between Dutch law and international law, the Netherlands clearly has a monist legal system.[3] The courts are able to assess the compliance of all national rules with self-executing international treaties.[4] A specific role is played by the ECHR and the case law of the European Court of Human Rights.[5] Because of the character of EU law, the courts are also competent to test national rules against Union law.[6]

2.1 The judiciary and the administrative courts

The development of an administrative judiciary is closely connected with the development of administrative law which started in the Netherlands in the final decades of the 19th century.[7] An increase in state interference in everyday life led to the development of a system of appeals against administrative decisions and orders.[8] Until 1985 the Netherlands had a whole range of special administrative appeals that provided safeguards for individuals in

1 It is not a goal of this chapter to give a comprehensive description of the Dutch law of administrative procedure. It only provides an overview of the most outstanding issues that can be connected with the relations researched. For a comprehensive description of Dutch procedural administrative law see, Damen et al. 2013.

2 Art. 120, Dutch Constitution. Some court decisions interpret this article very extensively. See, for example, HR 14-04-1989, AB 1989, 207.

3 See, for example, Sweet & Keller 2008, p. 684.

4 Art. 94, the Constitution.

5 See, for example, Blokker et al. 2006.

6 Cf. Kortmann & Bovend'Eert 2000, p. 134.

7 See, for example, Langbroek et al. 2013, p. 97.

8 Langbroek 1997, p. 88.

administrative disputes in specific areas of the law. Until then, one could appeal against an administrative decision in different internal administrative procedures, or to various specialised administrative courts or to the Crown (acting with the government),[9] which became the last instance in administrative disputes.[10] Between the mid-1980s and the mid-1990s the Dutch protection system in administrative law underwent massive reforms.

Nowadays, first-instance administrative law cases are dealt with by *administrative law divisions of district courts.*[11] There are also two special chambers of district courts that deal only with a specific type of administrative law actions.[12] There are currently (in July 2013) 11 district courts (*rechtbanken*) in the Netherlands with civil, criminal and administrative jurisdiction.

Against the judgments of district courts in administrative law cases, one can appeal to several appellate courts (*hoger beroep*). First of all, in tax cases (that in the Netherlands fall under the administrative law procedures) one can appeal to the tax chambers of the *Courts of Appeal (gerechtshoven).*[13] In cases stemming from social security disputes and matters concerning the civil service the appellate court is the specialised *Central Appeals Tribunal (Centrale Raad van Beroep).*[14] Another specialised appellate court is the *Trade and Industry Appeals Tribunal (College van Beroep voor het Bedrijfsleven)* which hears appeals against decisions in the area of economic administrative law.[15] Last but not least, there is the *Administrative Law Division of the Council of State (Afdeling bestuursrechtspraak van de Raad van State)* that deals with appeals against the decisions of first-instance administrative courts that are not expressly assigned to other administrative courts.[16] Against decisions of the Courts of Appeal one can file an appeal on a point of law (an appeal in cassation) with the *Supreme Court* (*Hoge Raad der Nederlanden*).

Despite the existence of different administrative courts that can decide the case at last instance one should not be concerned about the consistency of their rules. GALA in Art. 8:10a (4) enables the highest administrative courts, if they find it necessary in the interest of the consistency of jurisprudence and the development of the law, to form a *grand chamber* consisting of members of the highest administrative courts where these issues will be discussed.[17]

9 Because of the necessity for the minister to countersign the 'official' decision of the King/Queen. In practice, it was the Government that exercised this power. However, before the decision was taken, the Council of State gave its non-binding advice on the case, which could have been but did not have to be followed by the Government. See, Damen et al.2006, p. 38ff.

10 Specialised courts were, for example, the Court for civil servants, the Council for taxation disputes or the Council for appeal against some decisions concerning social insurances against illness. See, Langbroek 1997, p. 89.

11 Art. 43 JOA and Art. 8:7 (1) GALA.

12 These are the District Court in The Hague (division for migrant cases) and the District Court in Rotterdam (chamber for economic competition).

13 Art. 60 JOA and Art. 12, Annex 2: Competence Arrangement in Administrative Law Cases, GALA.

14 Arts. 9 – 10, Annex 2: Competence Arrangement in Administrative Law Cases, GALA. See also, <www.rechtspraak.nl/Naar-de-rechter/Hoger-beroep/Pages/Hoger-beroep.aspx> (accessed on 31 July 2013).

15 Art. 11, Annex 2: Competence Arrangement in Administrative Law Cases, GALA. See also, <www.rechtspraak.nl/Naar-de-rechter/Hoger-beroep/Pages/In-beroep-bij-het-CBb.aspx> (accessed on 31 July 2013).

16 <www.rechtspraak.nl/Organisatie/Raad-van-State/Pages/default.aspx> (accessed of 31 July 2013).

17 See also, Art. 8:12a GALA.

The legal framework of the Dutch courts includes numerous legal statutes that describe the organisation, composition, powers, jurisdictions and status of the administrative judiciary in the Netherlands.[18] An important statute is GALA, as it *inter alia* codifies the procedures against the administrative decisions before the courts.

2.2 Review of administrative decisions

The courts are expressly competent to deal with administrative orders (*besluiten*). According to Art. 1:3 (1) GALA an administrative order is a written decision of an administrative authority that constitutes a public law act.[19]

However, before submitting his case to the administrative court, an individual who is not content with an order by an administrative body should first of all deal with his case by means of the so-called *administrative objection procedure* (*bezwaar*).[20] This procedure gives the administrative body another opportunity to deal with the case. It also allows it to learn from its own mistakes and, if possible, to rectify such mistakes and thus to limit the number of cases that reach the courts. In general, individuals (interested persons) have 6 weeks to file an objection against an administrative order. Not adhering to this time limit makes this decision final without a possibility to appeal.[21] The objection procedure is generally an obligatory pre-trial procedure.[22] In limited cases, an individual can also file an *administrative appeal* with usually a superior administrative body (*administratief beroep*). However, the administrative appeal procedure is in decline and it has been mostly replaced by the objection procedure.[23] If objection proceedings do not satisfy the individual he can appeal to the previously mentioned courts (*beroep bij de bestuursrechter*).

Proceedings before the Dutch administrative courts are regulated in GALA, especially in Chapters 6 and 8.[24] If an *interested person (belanghebbende)*[25] is not content with an order by an administrative body he/she can file an appeal against this decision with an administrative court.[26] But the interested person must exhaust all available remedies which include the previously mentioned objection proceedings.[27] Secondly, GALA lays down an obligation to appeal within a time limit of six weeks after the decision is published. If this

18 For example, Judicial Organisation Act 1827 (*Wet op de Rechterlijke Organisatie*), Judiciary (Organisation and Management) Act 2001 (*Wet organisatie en bestuur gerechten*), Appeals Act 1952 (*Beroepswet*), Administrative Organisations Administrative Jurisdiction Act 1954 (*Wet bestuursrechtspraak bedrijfsorganisatie*) or the Council of State Act 1975 (*Wet op de Raad van State*). All acts have been subject to numerous changes and amendments.

19 *Onder besluit wordt verstaan: een schriftelijke beslissing van een bestuursorgaan, inhoudende een publiekrechtelijke rechtshandeling.*

20 Chapter 6 (Arts. 6:1 – 6:24) GALA.

21 Art. 6:12 (1) GALA.

22 The GALA includes cases where the objection proceedings are not obligatory and where an individual has to file an administrative appeal, or the administrative order includes its approval or its denial etc.

23 See, for example, Langbroek et al. 2013, pp. 97-120.

24 Chapter 6 generally covers objection proceedings. Chapter 8 describes appellate proceedings against the decision of an administrative body before the administrative courts.

25 Art. 1:2 (1) GALA.

26 Art. 8:8 GALA.

27 Sometimes it is obligatory to file an administrative appeal. See, for example, Art. 77, *Vreemdelingenwet*.

time limit is not adhered to the court declares the appeal inadmissible.[28] The appellant has to pay the respective court fee (*griffierecht*). In July 2013 the court fee was between € 44 and € 318.[29] And of course, the appeal has to be reasoned and signed. It is only possible to appeal against an administrative order (*besluit*) within meaning of the GALA.[30] But, for example, one cannot appeal against an order that contains a generally binding regulation or policy rules.[31]

The GALA distinguishes between preliminary proceedings (*vooronderzoek*)[32] and a hearing before the court (*onderzoek ter zitting*).[33] In both phases the judges have a number of powers that help them to decide the case. They can hear witnesses, hear the statements of experts in different fields, conduct an on-site investigation and, last but not least, they evaluate the written evidence.[34]

In *preliminary proceedings* the judge requires the administrative authority concerned to submit all the documents that were used by this authority when deciding the case.[35] Thus, this authority is given the possibility to react to the appeal. An appellant can react to this submission. If an appellant has some new evidence that would support his appeal he is obliged to submit it to the court at the latest 10 days before the hearing before the court.[36] Usually, the parties to the proceedings cannot submit new evidence during the hearing. *Hearings* are oral and generally in public. During this phase the court hears witnesses and experts and it deals with other evidence submitted by the parties. Legal representation during the hearing is not mandatory, but it is advisable.[37] Throughout the whole process the judge actively conducts the proceedings. He is *dominus litis* as he determines the course of the proceedings and of the case itself.[38] The hearing before the court leads to a judgment (*uitspraak*) delivered after the hearing, usually immediately or within a maximum time limit of 12 weeks.[39]

The court can reach four possible decisions. It can decide that it lacks jurisdiction; that the appeal is inadmissible; that the appeal is unfounded; or that the appeal is well-founded.[40] If the court declares that an appeal is well-founded, it quashes the original administrative order as a whole or partially. Then it can return the case back to the original decision maker who has to decide again. It can also decide that the original decision maker does not need to take a new decision or it can substitute its judgment for the challenged and quashed decision.[41]

28 Arts. 6:7 – 6:9 GALA.
29 Art. 8:41 GALA.
30 Art. 1:3 (1) GALA.
31 Arts. 8:4 – 8:7 GALA
32 Arts. 8:42 – 8:51 GALA.
33 Arts. 8:56 – 8:65 GALA.
34 Section 8.1.6 GALA.
35 Art. 8:42 GALA.
36 Art. 8:58 GALA.
37 Art. 8:24 GALA, see also Michiels 2006, p. 187.
38 See, Damen et al. 2006, p. 198ff.
39 Art. 8:66 (2) GALA.
40 Art. 8:70 GALA, see also Damen et al. 2006, p. 244ff.
41 Art. 8:72 (3) and (4) GALA.

The parties to the case do not have to be represented by a legal representative or other representative. In connection with the dispute, the court is bound by the appeal. However, the judge by virtue of his office can conduct further inquiries into the facts and is obliged to supplement the legal grounds for the appeal.[42]

If a party to the proceedings is not content with a judgment of a first-instance court, it can appeal against the judgment to one of the appellate courts (a higher appeal). The time limit within which to file an appeal is also six weeks. This limit starts to run on the day after the judgment of the court has been publicly pronounced. The appellate court assesses all the aspects of the case in the same way as the first-instance court has done. It does not limit itself only to the lawfulness of the judgment.[43] As the cassation procedure is in Dutch administrative proceedings limited to only decisions by the Courts of Appeal, the decision of the court on the *higher appeal* is mostly final.

One must here note the latest development in the Netherlands – *nieuwe zaaksbehandeling* (*a new way of dealing with cases*). The NZB has reacted to the fact that the administrative courts must respect the separation of powers and usually, after quashing a decision, refer the case back to the administrative body. This, however, takes a considerable amount of time and it is a formal solution which is not satisfactory for the appellant. Thus, at the heart of the NZB is a solution-focused court, the finality of the dispute resolution, speeding up the proceedings and the use of ADR.[44] The aim of this policy is to identify and solve the real problem of the dispute and to deal with it in a final way. During the NZB the judge tries to discuss with the parties to the proceedings the best possible way to solve the case, thus the NZB works towards an acceptable solution for all parties. This can lead to the solution of the problem by the judge but also by using the mediation techniques outside the court. This means that the case can be solved formally as well as informally.[45] If it is not possible to deal with the case using the informal method then the judge strives for a rapid and final solution to the case. This striving for finality can lead to one of the following consecutive possibilities: the annulment of the administrative decision while leaving its consequences untouched (Art. 8:72 (3) a. GALA), replacing the administrative decision with the court judgment (Art. 8:72 (3) b. GALA), the application of the *administrative loop* which entails giving the administrative authority the possibility to rectify an administrative decision within a specific time limit (Art. 8:51a GALA) or referring the whole case back to the administration (Art. 8:72 (4) GALA).[46] Most of the first-instance administrative courts have started to apply this policy in the majority of their administrative law cases.

42 Art. 8:69 GALA, see also Langbroek et al. 2013, p.115 or Damen et al. 2006, p. 213ff.

43 GALA distinguishes also specific procedures. For instance, the expedited procedure (*versnelde behandeling*) or the simplified procedure (*vereenvoudige behandeling*). See, for example, Damen et al. 2013.

44 See, Van Ettekoven & Verburg 2011or Aalberts 2011.

45 Burkens et al. 2012, p. 177ff.

46 Ibid, pp.182-194.

2.3 Normative standards of the courts

Over the years, the Dutch courts have developed specific criteria or standards for assessing the lawfulness of administrative decisions. Their development is directly connected with the increase in the administration and with an interest in protecting individuals.[47] Dutch legal theory and Dutch administrative law recognise *general principles of proper administration* (*algemene beginselen van behoorlijk bestuur – GPPA*). These legal principles were developed and discovered in the course of the judicial review procedure by specialised administrative courts and by the civil courts.[48] The Dutch administrative judiciary can review the compliance of administrative orders with codified but also uncodified rules. In truth, in 1994 the GALA codified a large part of judicially discovered and developed legal principles. Despite the codification, certain principles still exist in unwritten form and can be further developed.[49] Still, some principles have remained outside of the codification. The GPPA have two roles. First of all, they act as a *minimal legal standard of behaviour for the administration* and secondly, *they are used by the courts while assessing administrative decisions such as assessment standards.*[50]

In general, Dutch scholars and legal theory distinguish two types of the GPPA, *formal* and *material.*[51] The formal principles are connected with a preparation and adoption of the decisions and the material principles are bound by the content of decisions and their implementation. This division of the GPPA reflects the different impact of breaches of these principles on the administrative decision.[52] If a court quashes an administrative decision because of a breach of a formal principle, an administrative body can reach the same decision (if it deals with all the formalities). But if the court quashes an administrative decision because of a breach of a material principle, an administrative body has to change its decision as there was a problem with the substance of the decision.[53] As some of the GPPA have both formal and material aspects this part will approach them together without pointing specially to formal or material GPPA. The GPPA, as discovered and developed by the courts, are legal standards.[54] One has to note that neither the GALA nor any other statutory document bars the application of uncodified principles by the courts or the administration. The GPPA still retain some flexibility and if there is a need to change or adjust the principles to new conditions the courts can do this.[55]

Here one has to point to a possible confusion between the GPPA and the requirements of proper administration developed by the NO. They both refer to *proper administration.* This closeness can lead to a certain confusion as to their actual meaning. It must however be noted that while the GPPA are legal norms and are thus legally binding, the norms of

47 Ibid.
48 Cf. Langbroek 1997, p. 91 or Widdershoven & Remac 2012, pp. 381-407.
49 See, De Haan et al. 2001, p. 112, Ten Berge & Widdershoven 2001, p. 118 or Michiels 2006, p. 104.
50 Cf. Langbroek 1997, p. 88ff; Ten Berge & Widdershoven 2001, p. 117ff or Addink et al. 2010, p. 32.
51 Some scholars even talk about *borderline principles*. Cf. Adriaansen 2004.
52 Cf. Pennarts 1999.
53 Cf., Goorden 1997, p. 71 or Schlössels et al. 2006, p. 191.
54 Widdershoven & Remac 2012, pp. 383-385.
55 Cf. Schlössels & Stroink 2006, p. 189.

the NO are non-binding. Because of that Addink has called for their rebranding.[56] These standards are more comprehensively described in Chapter 5.

2.4 Remedies

An individual who is not content with an administrative decision by an administrative body can usually appeal to the courts. The courts, however, while providing the necessary remedies, have to stay within their statutory possibilities. Court remedies are in general enumerated in Chapter 8 of GALA. Based on the GALA if the court declares an appeal well-grounded, it quashes the challenged decision completely or partially.[57] The legal consequences of the challenged decision are also partially or fully quashed. After the court quashes the challenged decision it has a number of opportunities that are linked to the courts striving for the finality and speeding up of the case.[58]

First of all, the court can quash the decision but will maintain its legal consequences. At the same time the court can decide that its own judgment will replace the quashed decision or a part thereof.[59] The court always replaces its own judgment for the quashed decision if the quashed administrative decision was a decision concerning an administrative fine. Only if this is not possible does the court then oblige the administrative authority to make a completely new decision or to perform another act in compliance with its judgment. This rule was included in order to speed up administrative proceedings and to make the procedure more effective.[60] It also sets the term within which the administrative body has to take the new decision. At the same time it can decide that the statutory rules for the preparation of the new decision are not applicable.[61]

56 Addink 2010, p. 13.
57 Art. 8:72 (1) GALA.
58 See, section 2.2.
59 Art. 8:72 (3) GALA.
60 Cf. Barkhuysen & Claessens 2012, p. 84.
61 Art. 8:72 (4) GALA.

Chapter 3

INSTITUTIONAL COORDINATION OF OMBUDSMAN-JUDICIARY RELATIONS IN THE NETHERLANDS

The previous chapters have given a brief but compact review of the competences and functions of the NO and the activities of the Dutch administrative courts. One can note that although these state institutions are different, they can partially overlap when exercising their roles and functions. There are some similarities in the functions they exercise, goals they try to achieve as well as in the power to independently evaluate actions of administrative bodies. While taking into account the differences and possible overlaps between these institutions this chapter tries to find an answer to the first research question – *how relations between the National Ombudsman and the Dutch judiciary are coordinated on the institutional level and what is the content of this coordination.* In order to answer this question this chapter discusses the *formal institutional coordination of this relationship* (3.1). This is followed by the *practice* of possible *informal* institutional coordination between the NO and the courts (3.2). The last section of this chapter, the summary, tries to answer this research question (3.3).

3.1 Formal institutional coordination in the Netherlands

The formal institutional coordination mechanisms can be found in various sources. The first source is *statutory law adopted by the Dutch legislator* and *sub-statutory (secondary) legislation.* As the powers of the state institutions are set in the law and the NO and the Dutch courts are state institutions, one must start to look here.

Although the Netherlands has a continental law system and its courts do not have broad law creating powers as in the common law system, one cannot exclude the impact of case law on the development of institutional coordination. Because of that *the case law of the courts* is researched as well. However, the NO does not have any formal powers to make decisions that can bind the judiciary. Because of that it is questionable whether he can add something new to a *formal* institutional coordination of this relation.

3.1.1 *Statutory law and secondary legislation*

The institutional coordination of the NO and the courts is mainly included in *statutory law* adopted in cooperation between the government and Parliament.[1] Secondary legislation, also in connection with institutional coordination, is very limited.[2] Statutory law describes the powers of the NO and at the same time it underlines and determines the remit for the Dutch judiciary. One can here review the Constitution, statutes and secondary legislation that directly or at least indirectly deal with the powers of these institutions.

a) The Constitution
Although the Constitution establishes in Art. 78a a framework for the functioning of the NO in the Netherlands, it does not create or establish any mechanism of institutional coordination between the NO and the judiciary, which is also included in the Constitution (Arts. 112 and 133). The Constitution only delimits a general framework of the work of the NO and the courts. Still its provisions are broad and they leave the particular issues to be determined by statutory law and possibly by practice.

b) WNO and GALA
The WNo and GALA are the two main legal statutes which describe the functions and powers of the NO. As their contents are interrelated (at least in connection with Chapter 9 of GALA) one can approach them together. Although these two statutes do not completely describe the researched issue, they are the most comprehensive source of the institutional coordination of ombudsman-judiciary relations that can be found in Dutch statutory law. They deal with the *implied statutory bar*, the *mandatory statutory bar*, the *optional statutory bar*, the *referring of cases* and the *obligation of the NO to take into account the grounds of the court decision*.

1. Implied statutory bar of the NO
The implied statutory bar on the powers of the NO is included in Art. 1a (1) of WNo. The article enumerates the subjects whose conduct can be investigated by the NO. The WNo enumerates the institutions within the competence of the NO which include central, local and specialised administrative bodies.[3] The list does not include the courts. This article, in combination with Art. 78a (1) of the Constitution, which expressly allows the NO to investigate only the conduct of *administrative authorities (bestuursorganen)*, can be seen as the implied statutory bar for the NO and investigations on his own motion or complaint-based investigations. The Dutch courts or judges are not (for now) a subject whose conduct can be investigated by the NO. However, the administration of the courts is not excluded from the powers of the NO.[4]

1 For a description of the legislative procedure in the Netherlands see, for example, De Meij & Van der Vlies 2000, p.110ff.
2 Secondary legislation is legislation adopted through the delegation or empowerment of Parliament. For example, Orders in Council, ministerial regulations or rules adopted by the municipal authorities.
3 See, section 1.1.1.1.
4 See, section 4.2.1.1.

2. Mandatory statutory bar on the NO

The NO cannot investigate complaints or start an investigation of his own motion against improper conduct by state institutions in all situations. Art. 9:22 of GALA *inter alia* formally regulates and coordinates the possible simultaneous competences of the NO and the judiciary. In connection with the mandatory bar, GALA differs between *administrative courts* and *other than administrative courts* (ordinary courts). As the provisions of GALA are not easy to translate into English, for the sake of clarity this mandatory bar is described in the following scheme.

Scheme 1 – **Mandatory statutory bar on investigations by the NO**[5]

The NO can investigate the complaint if *in connection with a complained conduct*	**An individual *can (still)* appeal to the court (Art. 9:22 c. GALA)**	**The court already *rendered* its judgment (Art. 9:22 d. GALA)**	**The *proceedings* are *pending* (Art. 9:22 c. and e. GALA)**	**The judiciary* has *supervision* (Art. 9:22 f. GALA)**
Administrative court	No	No	No	No
Ordinary court	N/A	Yes (discretion-based)	No	No

* *De rechterlijke macht* (translation by the author).

By this mandatory statutory bar, GALA outlines the situations where the NO is unable to start or to continue his investigation. It establishes a clear formal delimitation of the competences of the court and the NO. If a court is dealing with conduct that is also a subject of the NO's investigation, the NO often has to stand back and drop the case. If there is a connection with the complained conduct, *ex lege* he does not have another choice. As stated above, the GALA differentiates between the administrative courts and ordinary courts. While the possible involvement of administrative courts stops or bars the NO's investigation, the involvement of the ordinary courts has this impact only in connection with pending court proceedings.

In connection with Art. 9:22 c. GALA where the NO is barred from an investigation in cases where the individual has a possibility to file an appeal (*beroep kan worden ingesteld*) i.e. cases where the appeal has not yet been filed but *can* still be filed in good time (within the 6-week time limit for filing an appeal). The expiry of this time limit opens a possibility for the NO to investigate the case.

5 Based on Arts. 9:22 c. – f. GALA

It is clear that the law here formally coordinates the interrelationship between the NO and the courts as state institutions.[6] If there was no such bar, the assessment of the same conduct by the NO and the courts could lead to two conclusions, which could be as similar as they could be different since these bodies may approach the issue from different angles or give different evaluations of the evidence etc. One can argue that such a *double control of administration* by two different institutions could in the end undermine the perception of legal certainty. Still, the individual cases as dealt with by the courts might not cover all angles of the administrative conduct that can be covered by the NO. Thus, the court decision might be unsatisfactory for an individual. The individual's satisfaction is here sacrificed for legal certainty.

3. Statutory bar based on the NO's discretion
Sometimes, the NO *can* discontinue the investigation or not start it at all. This discretion is laid down in Art. 9:23 GALA that in connection with the courts states that the NO is not obliged (*niet verplicht*) to start or continue his investigation. Similar to the previous case, the GALA differentiates between administrative courts and courts other than administrative.

Scheme 2 – **Discretion-based bar on investigations by the NO**[7]

The NO can decide *not to* investigate the complaint if	an individual *could have appealed* to the court (Art. 9:23 f. GALA)	the court already rendered its judgment (Art. 9:23 g. GALA)	it is *closely* linked with a case that is pending before a judicial body (Art. 9:23 j. GALA)	the complaint is *linked* with a conduct closely related to the substance of the proceedings leading to a judgment (Art. 9:23 k. GALA)
Administrative court	Yes	No (Mandatory bar)	Yes	N/A
Ordinary court	Yes	Yes	Yes	Yes

This bar enables the NO to decide whether he wants to start or continue the investigation. The law here establishes *formal institutional mechanisms* where it leaves the NO with discretion to decide about the investigation of the complaint if it has involved the action of the courts. Art. 9:24 (2) GALA sets another bar based on the NO's discretion that can be connected with the judiciary. In general, the NO is *not obliged* to investigate complaints if they were submitted to him one year after the complainant learned about the findings

6 The GALA, however, does not state what would happen if the NO has investigated the same conduct as the court, for example if this was necessary for a complainant. Obviously, in this situation this conduct by the NO would be unlawful as it would be in breach of the prohibition of an abuse of powers and/or other legal principles.

7 Based on Art. 9:23 f. – l. GALA

of the administrative institution or after the administrative complaint proceedings.[8] Based on this article, in connection with judicial proceedings before an *ordinary court* this time limit ends one year after the adoption of the court's judgment against which *no further remedy is possible.*

4. Referring cases

The GALA partially influences the referring policy of the NO. Its Art. 9:19 (1) gives the NO the discretion to refer the case to another competent body, which can be a court. He can do this if he reaches the conclusion that the petition that reached him is not a complaint but an appeal or an objection or a complaint to another institution. In this case he is obliged to inform the petitioner thereof as soon as possible and to transfer the petition to the competent institution. In this transfer he has to note the day when he received the petition. This can lead to the possibility that the individual, instead of appealing against the administrative decision to the court, sends his appeal to the NO, who should then send this appeal to the competent court. If the appeal is sent to the NO within the 6-week time limit for a judicial appeal, this leads to a statutory presumption that it has been filed in good time, unless there is a case of an evidently unjustified misuse of this provision.[9]

5. Obligation of the NO to take into account the grounds of the court decision

The GALA includes one more mechanism for the institutional coordination of the NO and the courts. In accordance with Art. 9:27 (2) if conduct that is the subject of the NO's investigation relates to a decision of a judicial body *(rechtelijke instantie)* the NO is obliged to take into account the legal grounds *(rechtsgronden)* upon which the decision partially or completely stands. As the term *rechtelijke instantie* includes ordinary as well as administrative courts, theoretically the NO must take into account the grounds of the court decision.

c) The courts' statutes

Statutes that establish the ordinary courts and/or administrative courts do not refer to relations between the courts and the NO. These statutes mostly deal with the status of the individual courts, their competences and partially with their procedures. They do not explicitly or implicitly address relations between the courts and the NO's working methods, processes, or the results of their proceedings. Only rarely do they refer to the NO. These references are usually connected with the impossibility of working as a judge, a representative of a court or a member of the court's administration while working as the NO.[10]

8 See, section 1.1.1.2.

9 Art. 6:15 (3) GALA.

10 See, for example, Art. 15 (8) f. *Wet op de rechterlijke organisatie*, Art. 26 (1) h. *Rijkswet Gemeenschappelijk Hof van Justitie*.

d) Other statutory law

An investigation of the Dutch statutes published at www.wetten.nl does not include other statutes that would expressly and directly deal with, modify or amend the institutional relations between ombudsmen and the courts.[11]

e) Secondary legislation

The research shows that secondary legislation does not deal with the issue of institutional coordination between ombudsmen and the courts. Occasionally it addresses issues of the financial remuneration of members of the highest courts and the NO.[12] Apart from that, secondary legislation does not bring anything new to this coordination.

3.1.2 The case law of the Dutch courts

Although the Dutch courts are connected with solving disputes and interpreting the law connected with a particular case rather than setting binding rules, one can find some examples where the courts, by interpreting the law, have explained, in an individually binding manner, the existing mechanisms predetermined in the statutory law. Although these examples are not numerous they express the courts' perception of the NO and they add to the understanding of the mechanisms included in the statutory law.

Furthermore, if an individual is not content with the conduct of the NO or his report he has only limited possibilities. He can file a complaint about this conduct with the NO office. His complaint will be assessed by a different employee of the NO than the person who dealt with the complaint.[13] If the individual is not content with the report of the NO or his decision not to begin an investigation, he has even less possibilities. Reports of the ombudsmen do not have the status of *a decision of an administrative authority that constitutes a public law act (order)* as defined in Art. 1:3 (1) GALA. They are not legal acts. Thus the reports of the NO do not fall within the administrative courts' scope of control. Their lawfulness cannot be assessed in a judicial review procedure. A theoretical possibility is to raise the issue with the ordinary (civil) courts. As I did not find such a case in the case law of the Dutch courts it is not clear whether the courts would accept such a case and how they would decide it.[14]

While taking into account these points one can find the following judgments where the courts interpreted the law applicable to the case at hand that was connected with the NO. For example, in the *judgment of the ABRvS of 3 February 1983* this court dealt with an appeal

11 One can however find statutes that deal with the financial remuneration of judges and the NO such as, for instance, *Wet rechtspositie Raad van State, Algemene Rekenkamer en Nationale ombudsman* of November 2008 or *Wet openbaarheid van Bestuur* of October 1991 on public access to information that can also be applicable to the NO and the courts. These statutes, however, do not deal with the relations researched here.

12 For example, *Besluit rechtspositie Raad van State, Algemene Rekenkamer en Nationale ombudsman* of 26 January 2009 deals with issues of the financial remuneration of members of the Council of State, the National Ombudsman and the substitute ombudsman.

13 See, Art. 6 *Klachtregeling bureau Nationale ombudsman* of 30 December 2003.

14 Cf. Meulenbroek 2008, p. 79.

against the decision of the administrative institution that rejected access to the documents submitted to the NO for the purpose of his investigation. The court here quashed the decision of the administrative authority and stated that the ombudsman's investigation does not bar the administrative authority from access to the documents sent to the NO, as the ombudsman's investigation and its results do not have the character of documents drawn up for internal deliberations in accordance with the then applicable provisions of the General Information (Public Access) Act (*Wet openbaarheid van bestuur*).[15]

In the *judgment of the ABRvS of 16 February 1987* one can see that the ABRvS *inter alia* tried to explain its own impossibility of dealing with an appeal against the report of the NO. As this was the case, from the beginning of the 1990s the court referred to the predecessor of GALA - *Act on administrative jurisdiction in administrative decisions* that expressly excluded the NO from the assessment powers of the Council of State. The ABRvS also pointed to the fact that there is no legal provision that would allow an appeal against the NO's actions. In its view, the NO must be seen as an instance to which an individual can complain about administrative conduct.[16] The court here confirmed its inability to review the reports of the Dutch ombudsmen.

Also the CRvB occasionally reacts to the status of ombudsmen. In *judgment of 7 March 1995* this court, *inter alia* dealt with the character and binding power of the report of the municipal ombudsman. It this connection, it stated that based on the then applicable law, the defendant (a provincial administrative body) was not bound by the report of this ombudsman and neither was it obliged to include the contents of that report in its deliberations. The court confirmed the non-binding character of the reports of the Dutch ombudsmen.[17]

Sometimes, one can find general opinions of the courts on the status of the ombudsman also in judgments of first-instance courts such as, for instance, in the *judgment of the District Court The Hague of 22 June 1994*. In this judgment the court ruled that the ombudsman's assessment that certain conduct was improper did not bind the civil judge to award damages for the unlawful conduct. Simply said, the civil judge is not bound by a report of the NO. In the same judgment the court stated that a compensation claim for the cost for legal representation before the NO are not recoverable.[18] Similarly, in a judgment of the *District Court Zutphen* of 12 October 1995 the court noted that during the NO's investigation there is no need to be represented by a legal representative. Because of this one cannot apply for the costs of legal representation during the NO investigation to be reimbursed.[19]

15 ABRvS 03-02-1983, AB 1984, 283.
16 ABRvS 16-02-1987, NJ 1990, 464.
17 CRvB 07-03-1995, JABW 1995, 248.
18 Rb. Den Haag 22-06-1994, V-N 1994/2526, 36.
19 Rb. Zutphen 12-10-1995, NJK 1996, 35.

3.1.3 *The 'ombudsprudence' of the National Ombudsman*

Recommendations, reports or other decisions of the NO are not legally binding. This means that *de facto* and *de iure* the NO cannot create mechanisms that can formally coordinate his relations with the judiciary. Of course, in his reports and in the annual reports the NO can explain his attitude towards the judiciary but these explanations do not alter his formal position towards the judiciary. The NO officially remains within the framework that is predetermined for him by the legislator. He remains within the bounds of his competence. A clear confirmation of the line between the courts and the NO is provided in the Annual Report 2011. Here the NO stated that:

> 'The work of the NO is based on the constitutional/statutory role of dealing with complaints or investigations at his own initiative. Based on this role one can expect that the work of the NO is comprised of reports following the investigation of individual cases and after an investigation of his own motion. In this connection one can make a comparison with the duties of the courts which leads to judgments as a result of their statutory role. Yet there is one more remarkable difference between the NO and the courts. ... [the NO]has to take into account also the social dimension of the relation between an individual and the administration. The legal questions are not the only concern of his work'.[20]

One can find the opinions of the NO about the courts also in his individual decisions. These are, however, closely described in the following chapter.[21] To sum up, the NO does not create new mechanisms to coordinate his relations with the courts.

3.1.4 *A short summary*

The Dutch legislator sets general mechanisms to coordinate NO-court relations. The written law provides a general framework for the work of the NO and the Dutch courts. It divides their competences and roles. A review of lawfulness is the domain of the courts while the NO assesses proper administration. The Constitution includes only a general delimitation of this framework. Statutory law deals more closely with these relations. The WNo establishes the NO and the GALA codifies the rules of the objection procedure, the administrative appeal procedure, administrative proceedings before the courts and complaint proceedings before the NO. Although the WNo includes some provisions on complaint proceedings, in comparison with the GALA they do not include any formal mechanisms that would considerably regulate NO-court relations. The GALA connects different legal consequences for the investigation of the NO with the work of the administrative and ordinary courts. While a judgment by an administrative court leads to an obligatory halting of the NO's activities, a judgment by an ordinary court allows the NO to exercise his discretion as to whether to start to investigate the complaint or not.

20 *Verslag van de Nationale ombudsman over 2010: 'Wat vindt u ervan?'*, p. 11.
21 See, section 4.2.1.1.

The case law of the courts does not create any real formal coordination mechanisms concerning the relations researched. However, the courts' interpretation of the law can be an addition to the clarity of existing mechanisms. The ombudsprudence of the NO does not create new formal coordination mechanisms. It only confirms those mechanisms that were predetermined by the law.

3.2 Informal institutional coordination in the Netherlands

The formal delimitation of the roles and functions of the courts and the NO does not answer all possible questions that can stem from the NO-court relationship. Because of that one can ask whether there are also some *extra legal* or *informal mechanisms* that coordinate the researched relationship in an informal or practice-based way. This section tries to find out whether there is something more than the formal institutional coordination.

As I did not find any external sources that would cover this particular issue, this section almost exclusively relies on the individual interviews which I conducted with the NO, his investigators and judges. The interviews were *de facto* the only source of information. The data received during the interviews are *only personal opinions* and they *do not* represent the *official* position of the institution.

3.2.1 Informal interaction between the NO and the Dutch courts?

The NO and the administrative judiciary deal *inter alia* with disputes between the state and individuals. As such their work and their functions should lead to *one goal* – an impartial and independent assessment of dispute resolution in order to attain administrative justice and to solve the existing problem. As their formal interaction is limited by the statutory bars[22] the question remains how, and whether at all, these two different institutions have some *informal* interaction that enables them to approach this goal in a coordinated manner.

All of the interviewees confirmed that all relations, including informal ones, between the courts and the NO are *limited.* In most cases they pointed to some interaction that exists beyond the formal coordination. Despite underlining their differences, they did not completely exclude the existence of some form of mutual informal interaction. During the interview the incumbent NO, Dr Brenninkmeijer, noted that:

> 'Informally there are many connections. To start with, every three months I have a meeting with the Chair of the Council for the Judiciary.[23] We discuss what is coming up and what is relevant. Secondly, they invite me more than once a year for an introduction

22 See, section 3.1.1.

23 The Council for the Judiciary (*Raad voor de rechtspraak)* is part of the judicial system. It has taken over responsibility for a number of tasks from the Minister of Justice. These tasks are in nature operational and include the allocation of budgets, the supervision of financial management, personnel policy, ICT and housing. The *Raad* supports the courts in executing their tasks in these areas. Another of its tasks is to promote the quality of the judiciary system and to advise on new legislation which has implications for how justice is administered. See, *The judiciary system in the Netherlands*, The Council for the Judiciary, 2004, p. 2.

or a comment or when there is a need to explain our position. The last contact was with the Working Group on the Improvement of Complaint Handling by Courts and they asked me for advice on that subject. They have their own complaints handling mechanism dealing with complaints against judges. Originally, that was supposed to be also one part of my competences, dealing with complaints against judges, but somehow the whole project shifted in the direction of the Supreme Court.[24] ... I have also discussed with the courts whether they should refer cases to us if they concerns questions of proper administration; which they never do. They seem to have a problem with this. They say "well it's not the role of courts to refer cases to the ombudsman".'

Also Mr Van Dooren (the Substitute NO) confirmed that:

'There are regular informative meetings of the National Ombudsman and the Chair of the Raad voor de Rechtspraak. These meetings occur usually every three months. They are not formalised. In connection with the courts, the National Ombudsman gives only additional protection...The NO office has more contact with the office of the Public Prosecutor than with the courts. Also there are regular meetings with the Chair of the College van procureurs-generaal which are informal.'

Also the senior employees at the NO office, Ms De Bruijn and Mr Prins, noted that:

'A certain communication with the courts also existed in previous years, especially in the case of complaints against the IND (Immigration and Naturalisation Service). There was an active exchange of information between the NO and the judges dealing with migrant cases on particular issues of immigration and migrant law and the application of legal provisions by the IND. The informative meetings were attended by the NO, members of his office dealing with these issues, judges dealing with these issues and other experts in immigration law. These meetings were a place where the NO could influence and partially coordinate the work of individual judges in this specific issue. However, it is the judge who has to make a decision in the end and not all judges joined these meetings.'

Individual judges at the different Dutch courts also confirmed the existence of informal meetings between judges and the NO. For instance, Ms Mondt-Schouten, a judge of the ABRvS, stated that:

'Occasionally, there are informal meetings during which we can exchange our views. Also from time to time we ask the ombudsman to give a lecture at the Council of State. These lectures are for judges, but also for jurists. He can explain about his work, especially how he tries to stimulate the administrative authorities to deal with the complaints in a proper way, for example, by trying to connect them via phone

24 This raises the question of whether the NO *should* be able to assess the conduct of judges. On the one hand, it can bring independence into the assessment of complaints against the behavior of judges as these complaints are currently *ex lege* assessed by the judges themselves. On the other hand, such a competence can be perceived as a certain shift in the perception of the role of the NO. For a discussion on this particular issue see, for example, Advice of the Council of State (W03.05.0306/I) of 27 October 2005 or generally in Pauliat 2008.

> and asking them what is the real problem. He tries to point to the human side of the administration. So basically, there are no official relations but sometimes there are these unofficial meetings when we can exchange our views and opinions.'

Mr Van Zutphen, the president of the CBB, noted that the official relations are limited by the law, but unofficial interaction is possible especially due to the fact that the NO is a former administrative judge. He also noted that although the NO does not deal with complaints against judges, his complaint handling procedures may have an impact on the complaint handling procedures for complaints against judges, as the NO has specialisation in dealing with the complaints.[25] He noted that:

> 'There are no official relations between us and the Ombudsman's office. We have our own system of complaint handling as far as judges are concerned... furthermore, I know the Ombudsman very well, he is one of my former colleagues. These unofficial relations are more on a friendly and convivial level. I meet him rather often and his work is of importance for the way we are dealing with and handling complaints that come to our court. So there is a sort of a 'shadow of the ombudsman' in the way we try to handle our complaints. He can be a mirror for handling complaints that come to the court. He has created a number of instruments and I think that that can potentially help the judiciary. Not as an official instrument but as an unofficial direction that can give us an opinion on how we could deal with our complaints and how we could encounter complainants in a specific case. So even if we are not bound by these instruments we know that they are there somewhere.'

He also noted that the NO can be helpful to the courts in an indirect way:

> 'The Ombudsman is also very active when it comes, for instance, to more general issues such as court fees and an increase in court fees as proposed by the government in 2011. He very firmly opposed this and he was a great help in that field for the judiciary. So in a more general way this is a sort of relationship because he is taking up the fight for those who have to pay the court fees and at the same moment the way in which he is putting this before the media and the public as well as politics is for us very important. In this field he was a great help.'

Mr Jansen, a judge at the CRvB, stated that there is no formal interaction between this court and the NO. However, he did not exclude informal interaction:

> 'Since both institutions are part of the dispute resolution system in the Netherlands, representatives of the National Ombudsman and the CRvB can occasionally meet

25 Nowadays, complaints against the behaviour of judges are first dealt with internally, usually by the president of the court where the judge against whom the complaint was filed sits. The courts adopt their own complaint procedures that are usually published on the website of each court and often also in the *Staatscourant* (official journal), for example, *Klachtenregeling van het College van Beroep voor het bedrijfsleven* (SC, No. 16749, 5 November 2009). Externally, complaint procedures are before the Supreme Court which receives the complaint from the Procurator General who can already exercise preparatory procedures. See also, Arts. 13a. – 13g. *Wet op de Rechterlijke Organisatie*.

> together at receptions and conferences. One of the employees of the Court has previously worked with the National Ombudsman.'

Also the first-instance judges confirmed that, indeed, despite the lack of any formal interaction between the NO and the courts, there is some informal interaction between them. Mr Verburg, a District Court judge, noted that:

> 'The ombudsman himself has been an administrative law judge for a long time, so there is informal contact between the courts and him especially nowadays since Alex Brenninkmeijer is the National Ombudsman. ... Still we, the judges and the ombudsman, think that we have a different approach towards and a different perspective concerning the cases at hand.'

Different competences that almost exclude interrelations between the NO and the courts were noted by Mr Van Schagen, a District Court Judge:

> 'The reason for almost non-existent relations of any kind is the fact that our competences, the court's and the ombudsman's, are different. The Ombudsman and the court are two different avenues of protection which the individual can follow. The Ombudsman deals only with complaints and administrative conduct against which it is possible to file a complaint and deals with these issues if there are no other possible legal avenues of protection. If it is an administrative decision (besluit) then we are competent.'

The experiences of the NO and the employees of his office and those of the judges of different Dutch administrative courts confirm that although there is no official formally predetermined interaction between these institutions, they do in fact interact, at least informally. They do not exist in an information vacuum. The interaction can often be unintentional. Often due to the career path of the persons in question it might remain at a subconscious level. The interaction is often connected with explaining their respective roles, different functions and working methods. It is based on a mutual acceptance of the existence of these bodies, sometimes connected with a general issue. Cooperation concerning such an issue may exist but it is not always sought.

3.2.2 Informal cooperation and exchange of information?

Formally, the law does not foresee any special cooperation between these two institutions. As they both work as dispute resolution mechanisms and they work in the same legal system, their general goal should presumably be the same. Because of that it is possible to presume that a certain level of informal cooperation can exist.

The interviews confirm the existence of informal cooperation between the NO and the courts, although it is rather exceptional. If it exists then it is usually only connected with a necessity to solve some specific problem in a coordinated manner. Nevertheless, despite this endeavour, any informal cooperation is only occasional.

The incumbent NO, Dr Brenninkmeijer, believes that certain cooperation can be positive:

> 'The ombudsman could offer the courts information about how things work in reality. The courts are working in quite a formal framework and they must admit these days that the application of the GALA has become too formal. So they are now working in the direction of a more informal approach, for example the inclusion of mediation. I think that the ombudsman could support these developments.'

He also pointed to the possibility of cooperation with the courts also in individual cases.

> 'Recently, we have opened a case which is related to the use of police cells in court buildings. Someone was kept there for 1½ hours without any provision of food or water etc. However, we are not competent to deal with the complaint and neither was the board of the court. So we said we are going to deal with this complaint and we have asked the court to cooperate on a voluntary basis in complaint handling and they approved this. So they will answer our questions. So basically, in this particular case we try to fill the gaps in the legal protection of citizens, because it was most probably only a mistake on the part of our legislator in dealing with this issue more clearly.'

At the same time he argues that a formal regulation of NO-court cooperation is not necessary as *the informal ways of cooperation or talking to each other are much more effective than the formal ones.* Mr Van Dooren (the Substitute NO) stated that despite the fact that the NO and the courts are part of the dispute resolution system, coordination with the courts is limited. He noted that:

> 'There is not so much cooperation with the courts as it may look. Sometimes it is difficult to talk to judges outside the courtroom.'

Ms De Bruijn and Mr Prins (senior employees at the NO office) contended that cooperation with the courts is limited to particular issues and very rare. They argued that:

> 'Cooperation with the courts as such is only very limited. For instance, in 2010 the Council of State asked the NO office to provide some information on certain issues that were covered by the Large-Scale Investigation of 'Handhaving'[26]. However, no further or any special cooperation with the courts (higher or lower) has been reported.'

The position of the interviewed judges was somewhat different. They mostly underlined the different character of the institutions, which makes the possibility of any cooperation very difficult. Ms Mondt-Schouten, a judge at the ABRvS, argued that cooperation with the NO does not in fact exist:

> 'In individual cases there is no cooperation. You cannot speak of cooperation as such, but sometimes in certain cases there is also an investigation by the ombudsman and then the applicants quite often inform the court thereof. Then, of course, we ask for the report because it can be interesting for our case. So basically, it depends on the deciding

26 *Handhavingwijzer* is one of the special guidance documents of the NO (see, section 1.1.3.1). This guidance sets twelve specific rules for the proper execution of maintenance requests by the municipalities. This guidance was developed in connection with Report 2010/235 of 14 September 2010.

> judges and on the particular circumstances of the case, and is also done in order to get a broader view of the case. Nonetheless, it can be important for the case in connection with the facts.'

Still, broad cooperation with the NO does not seem to be really necessary. She stated that:

> 'The reason is simple. Our tasks differ. The Ombudsman's role is different from ours and especially if the proceedings before the court are pending then it is impossible for the Ombudsman to deal with the case. He is not allowed to interfere.'

Mr Jansen, a judge at the CRvB, argued in very similar terms that:

> 'Both the National Ombudsman and the CRvB have their own role and function, they coexist together or rather they exist next to each other. As such there is no need for the CRvB to achieve or initiate any cooperation.'

Mr Verburg, a District Court judge, conversely pointed to the relatively personalised character of a possible cooperation between judges and the NO as this often depends on the interest of the individual judges. He noted that:

> 'This might be different from judge to judge. For myself, I would say that there is cooperation as we have written a book together [with the National Ombudsman] and he was also an editor of one of my other books. For other judges that depends... I believe we all understand that we have the same kinds of problems and we deal with the same kinds of developments over time. Procedural justice is an element we all know about. But there is no real court-ombudsman cooperation.'

He also pointed to some general issues where he can imagine their cooperation:

> 'For the last few years the approach of the National Ombudsman has been tied to procedural justice. He is worried about the behaviour and conduct of the administrative authorities. He has training sessions with them, he disseminates a lot of information to influence the authorities to make a change in their relations with individuals so that more procedural justice can be found there. At the same time we, the administrative law courts have been working on the subject of procedural justice as well. So what we have seen in the last two to three years is that there is a need for cooperation. So in January 2012 we invited the National Ombudsman to come to our administrative law section to discuss his ideas with us. Also in November 2012 I went to his office to discuss some issues with his investigators. So there you can see that in the field of procedural justice there is some unofficial and in no way institutionalised cooperation. But we can see that we are in the same process of change towards procedural justice.'

The potential interaction between the NO and the courts can also be seen in the exchange of information between these institutions. The reports of the NO and the judgments of the courts are the results of their work.[27] Nonetheless, these documents can be of importance

27 See, Chapter 4.

or of interest for the other institution. As the exchange of information is not directly covered by the formal coordination mechanisms it was presumed that it can occur in an informal way. The interviewees, however, confirmed that such an exchange of information is almost non-existent.

The NO, Dr Brenninkmeijer, did not specify any special way of exchanging information. He nonetheless confirmed that the case law of the courts has importance for his office. The employees of the Office, however, should access the case law on their own or they can consult the library. Ms De Bruijn and Mr Prins (senior employees at the NO office) confirmed that the exchange of information is limited and connected with ad hoc cases. They stated that:

> 'An exchange of information with the courts is very rare. One memorable informal meeting with the Council of State took place in 2010 concerning the 'Handhaving' investigation.'

Ms Bannier, an investigator at the NO office, confirmed that it is the role of individual investigators at the NO office to find whether specific case law is applicable to their case. In this connection there is no special exchange of information. She stated that:

> 'It is the responsibility of the investigators to check whether the present complaint has some relation to the courts and their case law. Investigators themselves check whether there is a judgment that could be useful in each particular case. They carry out the research via accessible websites of the courts or via the court case law that is collected in the library. They themselves have to assess to what extent the particular court decision is applicable in the case of the individual complaint.'

All interviewed judges stated that an exchange of information between the courts and the NO office does not exist. Mr Verburg, a District Court judge, stated that:

> 'As far as I know there is no exchange of information. Of course, once a year the Ombudsman sends his annual report to Parliament. And we can Google it of course. Also we can access his individual reports. But we don't send the judgments to the ombudsman if we think that this is an interesting decision for him.'

Mr Van Zutphen, the president of the CBB, added that:

> 'What we do, we make our decisions public for everybody on our website www.rechtspraak.nl where you can find all our judgments in important cases. There are criteria for choosing cases and for their publication. So anybody can access them, whether they are individuals or the Ombudsman. I have never seen a written request to give some information or advice. So no, I don't think there is any exchange of information. When we need some report we do it in the same way, we go to their website.'

Also Ms Mondt-Schouten, a judge at the ABRvS, observed that:

> 'We do not receive individual reports. Certainly not. But we read his annual report. And also some reports he has if it comes up during the case. For instance, already some years ago he had a number of cases about the IND (the Immigration and Naturalisation Service) and we read them closely as at that time we also dealt with cases with migration law. Of course, we can look up the reports of the National Ombudsman by ourselves on the internet.'

From the interviews with the members of the NO's office and of the judiciary one can reach some conclusions. Firstly, the roles and functions of the NO and the courts are often perceived as being completely different and this is often seen as a reason for not even trying to cooperate. This is linked with the formal institutional coordination that often excludes simultaneous proceedings of these institutions. Also the strict division of their powers does not help in their cooperation. Their cooperation is thus *a priori* perceived as non-existent. However, in some cases one can come across 'voluntary informal cooperation'. At the same time, a certain level of coordination can be perceived as suitable when one can get beyond the strict formal division of their goals and functions. Even if there is no direct cooperation in connection with individual cases, then at least in connection with the general perception of procedural justice and protection of individuals, cooperation between these institutions can be achievable and suitable.

As confirmed by the interviews, the exchange of information between the NO and the courts is rather rare, almost non-existent in fact. If it happens, then it is in a very general way (annual reports). As the case work of the NO and most of the case law of the courts is publicly accessible and posted on the internet, both institutions can access it.

3.2.3 A short summary

Informal coordination between the NO and the Dutch courts is limited. Despite this, there is some informal interplay between the NO and the courts. This happens during the meetings, conferences or presentations of the NO and the judges, whether they be regular or ad hoc. The NO tries to approach the courts actively. Administrative judges are aware of the NO and his office and they also confirm the existence of the interplay that goes beyond the legal provisions. This is often connected with the fact that the incumbent NO is a former administrative law judge. The interplay between the NO and the courts is usually connected with more issues that are common to both institutions and is usually connected with the explanation and reiteration of their own goals, functions and roles. Despite these informal connections, both institutions in their relations follow the provisions of the law and try to remain within their own sphere. Mutual cooperation, as well as the exchange of information, is almost non-existent. They are not premeditated and only on an ad hoc basis. If necessary, both institutions know where to look for the case law of the other institution. Although the NO and the courts are parts of the dispute resolution system in the Netherlands their informal interplay is fairly limited.

3.3 Summary

This chapter tries to give an answer to the first research question: *how are the relations between the National Ombudsman and the Dutch judiciary coordinated on the institutional level and what is the content of this coordination?*

The formal coordination mechanisms for NO-court relations in the Netherlands can be found in the Dutch law and possibly also in the case law of the judiciary. The Dutch Constitution, as the 'basic act' of the Kingdom, only sets the main and general areas in which these institutions can exercise their functions. Statutory law is broader and clearer. The most important legal provisions on this coordination are included in the WNo and the GALA. Here one can find mechanisms of the following character:

- *Formal barring mechanisms* which bar the powers of the ombudsman in connection with the judgments or proceedings of the judiciary. These include mandatory statutory bars, optional statutory bars, personal bars and implied statutory bars. All these bars are connected with an obligation on the part of the NO to halt or discontinue the investigation of a complaint if the previous court proceedings or judgments cover the same subject-matter. It distinguishes between the consequences of the actions of the administrative courts and those of the ordinary courts for the NO's investigation.
- *Referring formal mechanisms* which require the NO, if the necessary conditions are met, to refer the case to the courts. Such a mechanism does not exist vice versa.

Secondary legislation does not formally coordinate these relations.

The courts in their case law do not create new formal mechanisms but they provide an interpretation of the law and, by that, they can impact the development of the existing coordination mechanisms. They do this only on an ad hoc basis. The courts do not assess the lawfulness of the NO's reports and they cannot influence the NO in this way. Last but not least, the NO, because of his position, does not influence institutional coordination.

Informal institutional coordination between the NO and the courts is limited. Nonetheless, in the practice of these institutions one can find an informal interaction that goes beyond the formal mechanisms. The NO and the courts interact informally either in connection with a general problem that is mutual for both institutions or in connection with an individual case (the Handhaving case). However, the latter is relatively rare and it usually stems from the proactive policy of the NO or a need on the part of the courts. Practice-based mechanisms are closely connected with the reiteration and explanation of mutual roles towards the other institution.

As the law formally prescribes relatively different roles for the NO and the courts, these institutions closely adhere to their statutory functions and roles. Because of that, informal cooperation often does not exist. A similar conclusion can be reached also in connection with an informal exchange of information. It basically does not exist.

Chapter 4

CASE COORDINATION OF OMBUDSMEN – JUDICIARY RELATIONS IN THE NETHERLANDS?

The second research question is connected with the formal results of the pondering processes of the NO and the Dutch courts – their judgments and reports. This chapter tries to answer the question *concerning the mutual significance of the reports of the NO and the judgments of the Dutch judiciary and their content and concerning their possible interrelations.* The question is approached in twofold way. First of all, this chapter addresses this question from the position of a possible *formal case coordination* – coordination in the law and in the case law (4.1). Secondly, it devotes attention to the *practical interplay* between these institutions in the ombudsprudence of the NO and the jurisprudence of the courts (4.2). The chapter is concluded by the summary (4.3).

4.1 Formal case coordination of ombudsman-judiciary relations?

When looking for a formal case coordination of the relations which are the subject of the research one has to look at its possible sources: written law adopted by the legislator, the case law of the courts and possibly also the ombudsprudence of the NO.

4.1.1 Formal case coordination in the written Dutch law?

As described in the previous chapter it is mainly the written statutory law that coordinates the researched institutions on the institutional level.[1] Also concerning case coordination, statutory law plays its role. Here, however, one can observe that statutory law does not provide any special new mechanisms for case coordination. Nonetheless, one can point to the following law-established formal mechanisms of case coordination.

1. Approach of the NO towards court judgments

The most expressive formal mechanism covering case coordination is included in Art. 9:27 (2) GALA. This provision requires the NO to take into account the *legal grounds* upon which the judgment partially or completely stands. The NO is required to do this if a

1 See, section 3.1.1.

particular conduct that is the subject of his investigation *relates to a judgment of a judicial body.* The NO must approach the body in question and assess how far the conduct covered by his investigation and court proceedings interrelate. If they do interrelate, he has to take into account those grounds that the court included in the judgment when assessing the case. He must do this even though the case included in the judgment was not primarily connected with proper administration.

2. Evidence and arguments of the parties

A close inspection of the statutory law does not show any existence of a special formal mechanism that would *directly* describe the use of an NO report in court proceedings and the use of a court judgment in the NO's investigation.

Indirectly, however, a complainant and the administration are obliged to supply the NO with the necessary information.[2] The arguments and information can naturally be supported by the judgments of the Dutch courts. No provision of statutory law forbids the NO from approaching the judgments of his own initiative. He can approach the case law of the courts in an inquisitorial manner. This is connected with the character of his investigation and with the flexibility of the concept of proper administration but also with the fact that the NO can start an investigation on his own initiative.[3] Similarly, in court proceedings, the parties to the proceedings are obliged to give the courts the necessary information and to submit the arguments that support their statements.[4] These parties can support their case by the report of the NO. If the party to the proceedings does not comply with the obligation to support it with the necessary information or evidence the court can draw any conclusions which it sees fit.[5] However, it does not avail itself of the report of the NO of its own motion. The character of the court system is rather accusatorial. Still, the reports of the NO are not *a priori* formally rejected.

After a close inspection of the statutory law I did not find any other formal mechanism that would *directly* deal with case coordination between the NO and the courts. Although there is no specific description of these issues it is necessary to keep in mind the already mentioned institutional coordination mechanism in the form of the statutory bars set for the NO.[6] In this connection, the said acts *indirectly* recognise that court judgments have an impact on the NO's investigation. These provisions confirm a possible indirect impact of the court judgments on the NO's investigation.

4.1.2 Formal case coordination in the courts' case law?

Although, as explained in Chapter 3, the Dutch courts do not establish 'new' formal coordination mechanisms it is possible to find judgments that explain the courts' perception of the application of NO reports in their proceedings. For instance, the *ABRvS*

2 Art. 9:31 (1), GALA.
3 Art. 9:26, GALA.
4 Art. 8:29 (1), GALA.
5 Art. 8:31, GALA.
6 See, section 3.1.1.

in its *judgment of 8 December 2010 de facto* set a rule as to whether the courts can consider NO reports in their judgments and in their reasoning.

> The court here dealt with an appeal of an administrative body arguing that the district court inter alia erroneously referred to the report of the NO, as such a report does not bind the administration or the judge.[7] The ABRvS however stated that 'the fact that the report of the National Ombudsman does not contain any legally binding opinion does not mean that the District Court, in its further justification, has wrongly referred to the considerations of the National Ombudsman'.[8]

Although the ABRvS here does not expressly react to the issues covered by the report of the NO it confirms two important points. First of all, it confirms the fact that the Dutch courts in their judgments can refer to the reports of the NO and take them into account. The legally non-binding character of the reports does not change this fact. Secondly, the court confirms the legally non-binding character of the NO's reports.

In another judgment the same court explained that the report or the practice of the NO cannot influence the binding power of the decisions taken by the administration. In a *judgment of 1 May 2002* the ABRvS dealt with an appeal arguing that the applicant did not know about the consequences of the administrative decision and pointed to a different practice of the NO in similar cases.[9]

> The ABRvS however argued that his argument cannot succeed as the challenged 'decision on legal fees is based on an order in council (algemene maatregel van bestuur), based on the Act on Legal Assistance and is announced in accordance with the Publication Act. The argument of the appellant that he was not aware of the requirement for prior consent should therefore fail. The fact that the National Ombudsman informs complainants personally cannot influence the validity of the decision.'[10]

Thus, the court concluded that the NO's practice cannot influence the validity of secondary legislation. The appellant's plea for the application of the practice adopted by the NO is thus irrelevant. The applicability of the NO's reports in court proceedings can be limited by the fact that the concepts of proper administration and lawfulness do not entirely overlap. This issue was noted inter alia in a *judgment of the District Court of The Hague of 11 February 2009.*

> The applicant used the report of the NO as one of the arguments underlining the unlawfulness of the administrative decision. The court stated that 'in the present case there is no question of the unlawful conduct of the Fiscal Information and Investigation Service. The finding of the National Ombudsman does not lead to a different decision in this dispute. Still the National Ombudsman has not rendered a finding on the

7 RvS 08-12-2010, AB 2011, 55, para. 2.4.
8 Ibid, para. 2.4.2.
9 RvS 01-05-2002, JB 2002, 167, para. 2.4.
10 Ibid., para. 2.5.

> lawfulness of the administrative conduct but on the properness of this action. Improper administrative conduct does not necessarily mean that it is also unlawful.'[11]

The court here emphasised the difference between the findings of the NO and its own. The report of the NO can be used as evidence but it does not always lead to the same conclusions as the judgment of the court. A very similar conclusion was reached in appellate proceedings before the Court of Appeal of The Hague in a judgment of 14 December 2010.

> The Court of Appeal stated that 'the fact that the National Ombudsman has concluded that the FIOD-ECD had acted improperly by not actively informing the appellants, precisely as the District Court stated, does not mean that the State had acted unlawfully... The Court of Appeal does not find in the context of the report of the National Ombudsman any reason to conclude that the State had acted unlawfully.'[12]

The Court of Appeal here firstly underlined the fact that the NO's finding of a breach of the requirements of proper administration does not immediately mean a breach of the law. However, it did not exclude the possibility that the report could lead to such a result. It also confirmed that the courts take the reports of the NO seriously. When the individual supports his statements by the reports, the courts acknowledge and consider their content.[13] One can also point to the fact that the report of the NO is usually not enough for the court to decide that there has been a breach of the law.

Last but not least, one can also point to the *judgment of the CRvB of 4 May 2006*. The court here reached the conclusion that a complaint to the NO and the appeal against the administrative decision did not have the same consequences and could not be considered as identical.

> The court reacted to the arguments of the appellant who claimed that instead of sending an appeal to the court he complained to the NO. The Court stated that 'the complaint to the NO cannot be perceived as an appeal against the administrative decision'. [14]

Despite the fact that in their judgments the Dutch courts react only to ad hoc applications, their explanation can provide some clarity to the character of the reports of the NO.

4.1.3 Formal case coordination in the 'ombudsprudence'?

As noted previously, the NO cannot create mechanisms that would formally coordinate his relations with the judiciary.[15] This conclusion is also applicable to the case coordination.

11 Rb. Den Haag 11-02-2009, LJN: BH9325, para. 4.5.

12 Hof Den Haag 14-12-2010, LJN: BO7396, para. 8.

13 See also, for example, CRvB 20-08-2004, LJN: AQ7407 or Vzngr. Rb. Den Haag 02-03-2009, JA 2009, 69 or, Rb. Den Haag 20-08-2012, LJN: BX5425.

14 CRvB 04-05-2006, LJN: AX3238.

15 See, section 3.1.3.

4.1.4 A short summary

The formal coordination mechanisms that explain the character of the mutual connection between the judgments and the reports are limited. Statutory law does not create many 'special' formal coordination mechanisms that would only react to the results of the NO's investigations and court proceedings. It does not go beyond formal institutional coordination.[16] One can also note the NO's obligation to take into account the legal grounds of the court decisions.

The judgments of the courts in this connection are rather cautious. They generally allow the courts to refer to the NO's reports, but at the same time they underline the fact that the NO's reports on proper administration do not bind the court to reach the same judgment on the lawfulness of an administrative decision. The NO does not create new formal case coordination mechanisms between him and the courts.

4.2 Interplay between the National Ombudsman and the Dutch courts in connection with their findings

The previous pages show that the formal case coordination of the NO and the courts is not very extensive. The formal sources of the coordination of this relation do not describe the issue to the greatest possible extent. In order to answer the second research question in a more comprehensive manner, one should also look at the practical interplay between the NO and the courts in connection with their 'decisions'. This section tries to point to the perception of this interplay by the NO as well as by the courts. It is based on a combination of the data received through the interviews and research into the case law of the institutions.

4.2.1 Practice of the National Ombudsman

The formal case coordination mechanisms included in GALA require the NO to take into account the legal grounds of the previously rendered judgment. In practice this is not the only case when the NO and/or his investigators refer to or take into account the judgments of the Dutch courts. The interviews with the NO and members of his office confirm that the judgments of the Dutch courts are not overlooked. However, the information in the judgments is not taken into account indiscriminately. It must have a connection with the assessed complaint. Dr Brenninkmeijer (the National Ombudsman) confirmed that the jurisprudence is taken into account when assessing the compliance of the administrative conduct. During the interview, he stated that:

> 'Indeed, we do refer to court judgments. I have a couple of examples. I can start with the report on compensation (*Schadevergoeding*); in this report we referred to the case law.[17]

16 See, section 3.1.1.

17 Report 2009/135 of 23 June 2009, *Behoorlijk omgaan met schadeclaims.*

> There is also the report on enforcement (*Handhaving*) that includes the case law.[18] For instance, in the report on the freedom to demonstrate we have made an analysis of the case law of the European Court of Human Rights.[19] So if necessary we refer to the case law of the courts. Also in cases concerning the police and prosecution we very often use references to legislation and case law but then we are mostly implicit.'

The senior investigators at the NO Office, Ms Vegter and Ms Govers, added that:

> 'The National Ombudsman has to accept the judgment of the court as a fact. Nonetheless, in some cases it is more practical not to follow the strict rule of the law because proper administration and lawful administration are not identical. Not every unlawful conduct must necessarily be also improper. Thus, sometimes the investigators look at the decisions of the courts and in other cases there is no reason to do so. Everything depends on the individual case.'

Ms Bannier, an investigator at the NO Office, also confirmed that the case law of the courts is sometimes used by the investigators while assessing the complaints. She stated that:

> 'Sometimes the investigators refer to the courts' decisions only according to their number or in a very general sense. They don't need to quote the particular parts of the judgment to which they refer. The reason for this is that the reports are written in a style which is also understandable for individuals without a legal education. However, in some cases the investigators include a whole judgment or a part thereof in the background document which usually includes references to legal norms, internal norms and also judgments to which the investigators refer in the 'body' of the report. They do this usually in order to provide a better explanation. The investigators may also refer to important parts of court decisions in the 'body' of the report. That happens only in very important situations, especially while referring to a ground that has already been covered by the court.'

The interviews with the NO and his investigators confirm that they are well aware of the case law of the Dutch courts. They show that the case law of the courts is taken seriously. This is mostly connected with the previously discussed institutional coordination. The reports of the NO are accessible to the general public.[20] They are published on the official internet site of the NO.[21] Yearly around 341 reports are adopted and published.[22] References to the courts or to their case law can be found in almost every part of the investigation reports.[23] The NO refers to the courts only in connection with a particular complaint. This

18 Report 2010/235 of 13 September 2010, *Helder handhaven: Hoe gemeenten behoorlijk omgaan met handhavingsverzoeken van burgers.*

19 Report 2007/290 of 13 December 2007, *Demonstreren staat vrij: Veelgestelde vragen van demonstranten.*

20 Art. 9:36 (5), GALA.

21 <www.nationaleombudsman.nl/rapporten> (accessed on 31 July 2013).

22 This number is the average of reports adopted by the NO between 2005 and 2012. In 2005 he published 417 reports, in 2006 – 400, in 2007 – 334, in 2008 – 322, in 2009 – 295, in 2010 – 377, in 2011 – 379 and in 2012 – 209.

23 Usually, the reports of the NO include the following parts: *complaint* (*klacht*) that describes the problem of the complainant; *assessment of the issue at hand* (*beoordeling*) describing the facts of the case in

practice is only different in the annual reports, where he often expresses general opinions on the development of individual protection in the administration and the courts.

Between the years 2005-2013 the NO referred to the courts in numerous cases. The following scheme shows the numbers of references by the NO to different Dutch courts. These numbers are not absolute as the reports of the NO can refer to several courts or judgments in one report.

Scheme 3 – **References in the NO reports to the courts and their judgments**

References to courts found in the NO reports (1/1/2005-31/7/2013)	Amount of individual reports
District court	632
Court of Appeal	241
Administrative Law Division of the Council of State	128
Trade and Industry Appeals Tribunal	4
Central Appeals Tribunal	49
The Supreme Court	135
Judge *(rechter)*	1048
Judicial authority *(rechterlijke instantie)*	95

4.2.1.1 A typology of the cross-references to the courts

One can discover several types of NO cross-references to the courts. The following typology however represents only *theoretical and research-based categories* that should help one to understand the possible interplay between the NO and the courts. The NO *does not expressly use* or *recognise* the following typology.

1. Competence cross-references

For investigating a complaint the NO has to have the competence to deal with it. He has to make sure that he has such competence. At the same time his competence can be challenged and he must deal with these challenges. This practice then leads to competence cross-references to the courts where he explains his authority to entertain the complaint.[24] For example, in *Report 2010/297 of 14 October 2010* the NO included such a reference.

> He dealt with a complaint against officers of the regional police corps who had arrested the complainant. After the complainant was released, he complained to the NO that *inter alia* the minutes of his arrest taken by police officers were incorrect. The

chronological order; *findings of the NO* (*bevindingen*); and *conclusions* (*conclusie*) which explicitly include information as to whether there has been a breach of the requirement of proper administration. Some reports include a *recommendation* (*aanbeveling*). Reports can include the *research* (*onderzoek*) broadly discussing the facts of the case. Very often one can also find the *background information* (*achtergrond*) which includes the applicable legal acts, court decisions, and service rules that the ombudsman deems necessary for the case.

24 These references can be characterised as a specialized type of Explanatory references (see, section 4.2.1.1 (4)). But for the sake of the logic of the text, they are included first.

> administration of the police corps challenged the competence of the NO to deal with the case. It stated that the district court had previously dealt with these allegations and thus the NO no longer had competence. The NO however stated that 'from the decision of the District Court of Middelburg it does not appear that it was aware of the content of these minutes. At the same time nothing in the judgment deals with the situation that is covered in Art. 9:27 (2) GALA. Therefore the National Ombudsman does not see any bar that would prevent him from dealing with the complaint.'[25]

The NO analysed the applicability of the formal mechanism included in the GALA to his ability to deal with the complaint. After an assessment of objections of the administration and the provisions of the GALA, he decided that he did indeed have competence to deal with the case. The report is an example of the subsidiary role of the NO towards court proceedings and his obligation to accept the institutional coordination designed by the law. Sometimes, the NO *ex lege* limits his own powers to act. This is included, for instance, in *Report 2009/175 of 24 August 2009* where the NO dealt with a complaint against the former chairman of the Utrecht division of the Royal Notarial Association.

> During the investigation, the NO has discovered that the complainant filed an appeal against this decision at the administrative section of the district court. The NO then stated that 'Art. 9:22 c. of the GALA states that the National Ombudsman does not have jurisdiction to investigate if the complaint relates to conduct against which appellate proceedings are pending. In the present case the appellate proceedings are still pending before the court and this particular complaint has also been presented to the court. The National Ombudsman cannot exercise the functions of the judge and decide here as he has no authority to assess the conduct complained of and it is for the court to decide in this matter.'[26]

The NO thus here concluded that he was not competent to deal with the complaint and thus in accordance with the GALA he halted his investigation in connection with the part of the complaint that overlapped with the appeal to the court. He limited his investigation only to the issues that were not covered by the court proceedings. By these references the NO acknowledged the existence of formal institutional coordination connected with the courts. Similar references can be found in other reports.[27]

2. Factual (descriptive) cross-references

In order to describe the facts that were connected with the complaint the NO often enumerates them in the report. Sometimes, these facts also include previous court proceedings or judgments which can have some link with the complaint. The NO then refers to these court proceedings or the judgments. By these cross-references the NO describes the facts of the case in a way so that the reader of the report can appreciate all the facts of the case as they occurred. An example can be found in *Report 2007/197*

25 See, Report 2010/297 of 14 October 2010, *Beoordeling*, para. 1.

26 Report 2009/175 of 25 August 2009, *Beoordeling*, para. 6.

27 See, for instance, Report 2007/029 of 9 February 2007, Report 2008/143 of 13 August 2008, Report 2007/251 of 9 November 2007, Report 2009/125 of 16 June 2009 or Report 2006/038 of 6 February 2006.

of 20 September 2007. Here the complainant alleged that the *Landelijk Bureau Inning Onderhoudsbijdragen* (the National Maintenance Collection Agency, an agency with the competence to collect maintenance payments from and for divorcees – LBIO) had incorrectly indexed the maintenance payments.

> The report *inter alia* as a matter of fact referred to the judgment that had a connection with the complaint but it was not directly connected with his assessment of the received complaint. The report stated that 'by the decision of 17 November 2003 the District Court in The Hague had determined that the complainant has to pay his ex-wife maintenance of € 600 monthly for his children M. and S. This decision was registered in the Civil Status Register in The Hague on 22 April 2004.'[28]

Although this report is used as an example also in a later part of this section, these particular cross-references only point to the fact that there were previous court proceedings. Another example of this cross-reference is in *Report 2007/180 of 26 August 2007.*

> The NO here dealt with a complaint against the Institute for Employee Benefit Schemes (*UWV*) which despite all the actions by the complainant did not change her address in its system. The NO in his report inter alia cross-referenced to the judgment as a previous fact in the complainant's case. It noted that 'the complainant appealed against the decision about the objection of the UWV on 27 October 2005. The judgment of the District Court of 21 March 2006 upheld the appeal. The UWV appealed against this judgment. Until the issuing of the report, the proceedings before the CRvB are still pending.'

Since the complaint dealt with the *conduct* of the UWV and not with the content of its administrative decision, the NO referred to the court proceedings only as a matter of fact.

By factual or descriptive cross-references the NO only describes the facts of the case. This means that there was some previous involvement of the court. These cross-references do not refer to the substance of these cases. Similar references can be found in other reports.[29]

3. *Supportive cross-references and cross-references connected with the application of the court's rules*

Sometimes, the cross-references to the court go further than simply describing the facts of the case. They can be connected with the substance of the court proceedings. The NO occasionally makes cross-references to the judgments in order to support his own findings. Sometimes, he even uses the rules found by the courts. An example of such a cross-reference is in *Report 2010/289 of 4 October 2010.*

> The complainants here alleged that the Mayor and aldermen of a municipality refused to take measures that were necessary to remove the problem connected with the discharge

28 Report 2007/197 of 20 September 2007, *Beoordeling, Algemeen*, para. 1.

29 See, for example, Report 2006/002 of 11 January 2006, Report 2007/102 of 21 May 2007, Report 2009/172 of 18 August 2009 or Report 2010/096 of 25 April 2010.

> of rain water which led to the flooding of their estate. During the investigation, the NO discovered that the municipality, by breaching the requirement of legal certainty, had behaved improperly. He *inter alia* argued that the municipality had not reacted to any of the signals from the complainants about the problematic flooding situation and that it had not taken the necessary measures during the development of the residential area. In the background of this report the NO referred to a judgment that covered a similar situation but from the point of view of lawfulness. One can assume that this judgment was taken into account as one of the grounds to underline the obligations of the municipality in water management. The NO stated that 'in the judgment of 10 June 2009, the judge of the District Court of Middelburg had decided a dispute between one municipality in Zeeland and an individual that resulted from damage to the individual's apartment due to heavy rainfall. The judge inter alia considered that since 1 January 2008 municipalities have a wider obligation, in accordance with the Municipality Act, the Water Resources Act and the Environmental Management Act, to discharge rain and groundwater. The circumstances of this case suggest that the discharge of municipal sewage was insufficient due to heavy rainfall. Because of that fact the municipality did not meet its legal obligations (LJN BJ5625, Court Middelburg, Nr. 67489 / KG ZA 09-77).'[30]

From the wording of the report one can see that this judgment was not directly connected with the filed complaint. Still it was used as one of the supporting factors for the finding of improper administration. The NO here *inter alia* pointed to a breach of the municipalities' legal duty of care in relation to water management.[31] One can see that the NO sometimes gives considerable importance to judgments. This requires a substantive knowledge of the case law of the courts. Another example of this cross-referencing can be found in *Report 2007/197 of 20 September 2007.*

> In this case the complainant alleged that in 2004 the agency with the competence to collect maintenance payments (LBIO) had incorrectly indexed the maintenance payments in question. In the findings of the report the NO referred to court proceedings that determined the amount of maintenance as a matter of fact.[32] The complainant alleged that the LBIO should not apply any indexation as the judgment was registered in the Civil Status Register in April 2004. He argued that the indexation is done yearly by 1 January and by that date the judgment had not yet been registered. The director of the LBIO supported its case by a judgment of the Supreme Court.[33] The NO agreed with the director of the LBIO that the indexation for 2004 was correctly applied and noted that 'the Supreme Court had determined in its judgment of 23 October 1973(NJ 1975, 228) that the moment of pronouncing the divorce is decisive for the question of when the indexation can be applied. As the court in the present case pronounced the divorce on 17 November 2003, the LBIO could apply the indexation for 2004.'[34]

30 Report 2010/298 of 4 October 2010, *Achtergrond*, para. 3.
31 Ibid., *Beoordeling*, para. 11.
32 See, above the section on factual cross-references.
33 Report 2007/197 of 20 September 2007, *Bevindingen*, para. 2.
34 Ibid., *Beoordeling*, para. 9.

The NO here applied the rule that had previously been adopted by the Supreme Court. This shows an in-depth knowledge of the courts' case law. A similar example can be found in *Report 2010/219 of 16 August 2010*.

> Here the individual complained that the municipality refused to accept responsibility for the theft of an I-Phone from a well-functioning and properly adjusted locker at a municipality ice rink. In this case the NO used a definition of *deposit* as included in the Dutch Civil Code and the interpretation of this term included in the judgment of the District Court of Utrecht of 11 March 2009 where the court dealt with a case where a locker had been broken into. The judge decided that providing a locker to a user who has the sole key is not connected with confidentiality and therefore it is also not connected with a deposit.[35] The NO noted that individuals use these lockers at their own risk and it is only the court which can decide that this view is different in an individual case.[36] The NO decided that this complaint against the municipality was not well-founded.

Hence while investigating the complaint, the NO applied the legal definitions included in a statute and in the case law of the courts and thus *de facto* supported the credibility of his own findings. Again, considerable knowledge of the case law was shown. Still, one can argue that the NO could have decided the case without looking for support in the judgments. The last example of a supportive cross-reference is in *Report 2010/342 of 2 December 2010*.

> Here the NO used an explanation of a rule adopted in connection with criminal proceedings. The NO discovered that the police had confiscated the complainant's computer during a visit to the complainant's home because it was possible that he had defamed his ex-girlfriend, who was a family member of the police officer in question. Under Dutch law defamation is an offence which can only be prosecuted if an official complaint has been made by the aggrieved person. The NO made cross-references to two judgments of the Supreme Court (HR 03-05-1977, NJ 1978, 692 and HR 16-06-1998, NJ1998, 800) which explained the rule that a 'criminal prosecution for criminal defamation may only commence if there is an explicit request by the aggrieved person to the public prosecution to commence proceedings.'[37] This was not the case here. Two judgments were decisive in the present investigation. Also based on these judgments the NO concluded that the conduct of the police officer was in breach of the requirement of prohibition of the abuse of power.[38]

Here we can see an interesting application of the rule found by the court. The NO used the court's interpretation of the law in order to support his findings on a breach of proper administration. He used the persuasive power of the court's judgment to emphasise his own report. Similar references can be found in other reports by the NO.[39]

35 Report 2010/219 of 16 August 2010, *Bevindingen*, para. 5 a).
36 Ibid., *Beoordeling*, para. 13.
37 Report 2010/342 of 2 December 2010, *Beoordeling*, p. 6.
38 Ibid., *Beoordeling*, p. 6 and *Conclusie*, p. 8.
39 See, for example, Report 2006/288 of 17 August 2006, Report 2006/288 of 17 August 2006 or Report 2011/268 of 12 September 2011.

4. Explanatory cross-references
By these references to the courts or their judgments the NO tries to explain the applicability of the court judgment to the investigated case. These cross-references can be connected with the action of the NO or the actions of the parties to the proceedings. In the former case the NO applies a judgment in order to support his own findings and to explain the applicability of the judgment to the case.[40] In the latter case he deals with the judgments submitted to him by a party to the investigation who wants to support its arguments by referring to a judgment. An explanatory cross-reference can be found, for example, in in *Report 2009/151 of 22 July 2009* where the NO investigated a complaint concerning the decision of a water board which had rejected the complainant's request to compensate damage to a vessel.

> The water board stated that it is not responsible for the damage to the complainant's vessel as due to all the facts of the case it was not the manager of the said waterway. The NO discovered that the water board had sent a letter to the complainant in which it had *inter alia* stated that a judgment of the district court of The Hague, in an identical case, had confirmed the same view.[41] In the findings of the report the NO stated that 'the applicant held the water board responsible for the damage to his vessel in connection with the administration and management of the waterway. The water board refused to accept responsibility because its legal obligation concerns the good functioning of waterways and does not concern the maintenance of the waterway for shipping. This position has been supported by the judgment of 27 July 2005 of the Civil Department of the District Court of The Hague taken in a similar situation. Because of that the water board could have reasonably decided to reject the request to compensate the damage to the complainant. The conduct of the water board was in this connection proper.'[42]

Thus, the NO gave his own explanation and his own interpretation of the court's judgment. He assessed whether this judgment supported the arguments of the water board. He considered the circumstances of the case at hand and compared them to the circumstances of the case included in the judgment. One can see here an active approach by the NO towards the arguments of the parties to the investigation. Another example of this cross-referencing can be found in *Report 2011/216 of 28 July 2011*.

> Here the NO dealt with a complaint about the way in which an employee of the *Raad voor de Kinderbescherming* (Child Care and Protection Board) had prepared a meeting between the complainant's daughter and her ex-partner, the child's father. The complainant argued that the Board had ignored her objections against the meeting.[43] The Board stated, conversely, that it had received a request from the District Court of Maastricht to investigate meeting possibilities between complainant's daughter and her father. Also this investigation was opposed by the complainant.[44] The Board also recommended to the court the establishment of regular meetings between the daughter

40 From this perspective these references can overlap with the previous category of supportive references.
41 Report 2009/151, *Beoordeling*, para. 2.
42 Ibid., *Beoordeling*, para. 8.
43 Report 2011/216 of 28 July 2011, *Bevindingen*, para. 3.
44 Ibid., *Bevindingen*, para. 4.

> and her father as no serious objections were raised.[45] After the investigation the NO stated that the complainant's objections had not been ignored. He alleged that 'as the court had given the Board the assignment to investigate the possibility for parents to have access to their children, the Board's personnel have to follow this assignment despite the fact that the complainant was against it. The facts did not prove that the Board, while carrying out its assignment, had acted unprofessionally.'[46]

The NO here assessed the applicability of the arguments of the parties to the case. Based on the facts of the case he agreed that the administrative authority had acted properly as required by the court. Similar types of cross-references where the NO explains the applicability of the judgments to the investigated case at hand can be found throughout his ombudsprudence.[47]

5. Cross-references in complaints against the court administration

A special type of cross-referencing can be found in cases where the NO deals with complaints against the court administration. The administration of the court is undoubtedly connected with the actions of the courts but it is not connected with the resolution of disputes. Still it has an important role to play. In the ombudsprudence, one can find several examples where an individual who is discontent with the court administration complaints to the NO. Although the NO cannot deal with complaints against judges, he does deal with complaints against court administration.[48] Here he mostly decides on complaints against the registrar of the court (*griffier van de rechtbank)* or against the administration of the court (*bestuur van de rechtbank*). In these cases the NO deals only with the administrative work of the court *outside the courtroom*. For example, in Report 2010/351 of 9 December 2010 the NO dealt with a complaint against the administration of the District Court of Arnhem.

> The individual complained that the registrar of the court had lost the file with the evidence which she had delivered to the court and which was later not included in the court file, thus the judge could not take the necessary evidence into account when deciding the case. The NO indeed found that the documents had been lost by the court administration and this led to a breach of the requirement of administrative precision. He addressed a recommendation to the administration of the court to confirm the delivery of the documents, their number and character.[49]

A similar practice is included in other reports.[50]

45 Ibid., *Bevindingen*, para. 5.

46 Ibid., *Beoordeling*, para. 21.

47 See for example Report 2007/197 of 20 September 2007, Report 2011/172 of 9 June 2011, Report 2010/114 of 16 May 2010 or Report 2009/151 of 21 July 2009.

48 See, sections 3.1.1 and 3.2.1 and 1.1.1.1.

49 See, Report 2010/351 of 9 December 2010, Aanbeveling.

50 See, Report 2010/351of 9 December 2010, Report 2007/136 of 27 June 2007, Report 2008/191 of 22 September 2009, Report 2010/087 of 15 April 2010 or in Report 2007/240 of 6 November 2007.

6. Cross-references included in the NO's recommendations

Recommendations do not have to be included in every NO report.[51] Thus, cross-references to the courts in the NO's recommendations are rather unique. They do not have the character of factual references as they do not point to a specific fact, and neither are they used in order to support the findings of the NO. They express the NO's findings and report-making processes and the possibility for the administration to apply them in practice. An example of this practice can be found in *Report 2010/204 of 13 July 2010.*

> The complainant faced an action by the Child Abuse Counselling and Reporting Centre (*Advies- en Meldpunt Kindermishandeling Bureau Jeugdzorg Agglomeratie Amsterdam* (AKM)) which had received an anonymous complaint that the complainant had mistreated his son. During the investigation the AMK did not find any mistreatment. After the investigation the complainant asked the AMK to shred his file. However, his application was orally rejected without any justification being given. The NO concluded that when a body refuses an application to destroy a file it should inform the applicant of the grounds for this refusal and it should point to any possible legal remedies against this decision. This did not occur in this case.[52] The complainant received a reply one year after his application but the justification was unclear and it did not contain any reference to a possible legal remedy. The NO found a breach of the requirement of fair play. The NO made a general recommendation to the AKM in which he stated that 'the AKM should decide all future cases about destroying a file in writing and with motivated reasoned decision. In its decision it should also point to possible legal remedies against the decision such as, for instance, court proceedings.' [53]

Although this reference is a general one, the NO here underlined the position of the courts in administrative proceedings as one of the legal remedies and possible dispute resolution mechanisms. In some recommendations the NO makes cross-references to a particular judgment such as, for example, in *Report 2007/034 of 16 February 2007.*

> The NO here dealt with the way in which police officers had treated the complainant after his ex-wife had withheld custody of their children. Although the NO did not discover a breach of proper administration, he did discover that the police officers had taken the *Handbook on juvenile affairs* as a starting point when dealing with this case. The Handbook contended that if there is joint custody over children, the police can only mediate between the parents. It further claimed that a criminal law action (in accordance with Art. 279 of the Dutch Penal Code) is only acceptable if a parent without custody of a child refuses to return the child to a parent with custody and the police action can only take place after previous mediation. Conversely, the NO argued that the police should have taken as a starting point the *judgment of the Supreme Court of 15 February 2005* which stated that even in the case of joint custody, one of the parents may hinder the other from having custody of a child. In such cases the police can act in accordance with the Penal Code. The NO recommended 'that the administration of the regional police force should take as a starting point for police actions in problems

51 See, section1.1.2.

52 Report 2010/204 of 13 July 2010, *Beoordeling*, para. 15.

53 Ibid, *Aanbeveling 2.*

concerning the access of parents to their children the relevant case law of the Supreme Court (judgment of 15 February 2005, NJ 2005/218).'[54]

The NO thus recommended a change to the working methods of the police so that they can act in accordance with the jurisprudence. He here indirectly bolstered the protection of legal certainty. This practice is further confirmation that court judgements are not overlooked or ignored and that the NO is aware of the development in the case law. Similar references can also be found in other reports.[55]

4.2.1.2 A short summary

The previous examples prove that the NO in his reports occasionally makes cross-references to the courts or their case law. If there is a need to point to the facts of cases, to explain the application of the courts' case law or even to support his own findings with the court decision the NO can turn to the case law. It is also clear that the NO is aware of the jurisprudence. As confirmed by the interviews, the NO does not make cross-references to the jurisprudence indiscriminately. The cross-references depend on the circumstances of individual cases. Thus, he does not refer to the courts as a matter of principle but as a *matter of need*. And the cross-references as such do not always include quotations from particular court judgment. Here we can talk about three main (theoretical) roles involved in the practice of the NO making cross-references to the courts. Such cross-references:

- *inform* the readers as clearly as possible about the facts of the previous court proceedings, or the previous judgment directly or indirectly connected with the dispute;
- *explain* the choices of the NO whether in connection with competence challenges or in connection with the arguments of the parties to the investigation; and
- *underline the opinion* which the NO has reached based on the facts and the circumstances of the case. Sometimes the terms or notions that were already developed by the court are used. Thus the NO applies the court's interpretation of the law in his own working processes.

In general, one can state that in the practice of the NO the judgments of the Dutch courts, administrative or ordinary, higher or lower, play a visible role.

4.2.2 Practice of the Dutch courts

Formally, the Dutch courts are not bound by the reports of the NO. This is the first issue which differentiates the reports of the NO from the judgments of the Dutch courts. Nevertheless, one can find cases where the courts do take into account or even use the reports of the NO. This practice is not very extensive.

All interviewees confirmed that the courts sometimes use the reports of the NO or make cross-references to them. This practice has an *ad hoc* character and is connected only

54 Report 2007/034 of 16 February 2007, *Aanbeveling*.

55 See, for example, Report 2009/125 of 17 June 2009, Report 2008/179 of 10 September 2008, Report 2011/281 of 27 September 2011 or Report 2010/329 of 16 November 2010.

with individual cases. It is not premeditated. At the same time, they all confirmed that the NO's report as a piece of evidence does not have a special status. Although the report is a sophisticated opinion and not *just* an opinion, its persuasive authority in connection with unlawfulness is rather limited. As the courts can decide what to accept as evidence it is not excluded that they will accept the report but it should be presented as part of the file by one of the parties.

Ms Mondt-Schouten, a judge at the ABRvS, confirmed the possibility to take the NO's report into account but rejected any *special status* being given to the report in court proceedings. During the interview she noted that:

> 'We do not, a priori, exclude the reports of the Ombudsman from our decision-making process. But we must take into account that the report of the Ombudsman is not binding. Still, if some facts are proven in the report then we accept them, unless the parties can prove otherwise. But it is no different from other means of proving the facts, it does not have any special status. … the Ombudsman works very carefully and that gives us a certain trust in the facts that are included in the report. For example, quite often we get the reports of experts and then it is the same. You look carefully at the report and at the conclusions included therein to see whether they stem from the research carried out. But it is our responsibility to carefully assess all the issues and then to decide. So we have to check carefully if something is proven or if an expert's report is what it should be.'

Mr Van Zuthpen, the president of the CBB, noted that it is rather hypothetical to deal with the NO report in the procedure of this specialised administrative court. However, from a theoretical point of view he stated that the report of the NO can be used but not as *decisive proof*. Still, he expressed his doubts about the applicability of the report as evidence:

> 'I wonder whether I would really use it as evidence because, in essence, it is the opinion of a non-judicial officer. So it cannot be compared with a legal opinion. The Ombudsman's opinion is not 'just' an opinion but it is an opinion with a questionable legal quality … I can imagine that from the factual side of the case it can help. It can direct you towards a certain way of handling a case. It could pose new questions which you would like to have answered before you make your final decision. So in that way it can be of importance. However, if it was given a certain status, that it is proof that has to be accepted by the court, it could take away its effective social quality.'

Mr Jansen, a judge at the CRvB, mentioned that the NO's report can play a role in connection with the facts proven by the NO but from a legal point of view the report does not play such a role:

> 'During the determination of the facts in the case before the CRvB, the report of the National Ombudsman can play a certain role. However, during the interpretation and application of the legal provision upon which the Court has to decide, the report of the National Ombudsman will not be taken into consideration very quickly.'

Mr Verburg, a District Court judge, pointed to the character of the report:

> 'The report of the ombudsman is in itself authoritative but we are not willing to accept it as undeniable proof of the truth. Actually, a report from an accountant, a simple accountant, is stronger proof than the report of the ombudsman.'

He pondered on the actual possibility of the judge to accept the report as proof:

> 'Would I be free to do that? And if I did that, would I be free to make my judgment? Probably there are more different things than things in common, but I would compare it to this example. While reading a file, I find interesting information on Google. The question is: can I use it? For instance, somebody wants to get a permit for a gun. The permit was denied by the administration because of a criminal offence in the past. So I try to Google his name on the internet and I find that he has a blog on which he uses abusive language. Am I free to use that information? Am I free to Google his name in first place? And am I free to allow my judgment be influenced by that? It is similar to the ombudsman report. There are more differences than similarities between the ombudsman report and the internet, of course, but this one is the one that is in common. In itself the ombudsman report is public information, so there would be no reason not to read it apart from the question whether it can influence my sense of impartiality.'

Last but not least, Mr Van Schagen, a District Court judge, accepted that the report of the NO can be taken into consideration by judges:

> 'Everything that is included in the file is taken into consideration. However, the report of the ombudsman is not a decision of the court. It is a finding of a body that has assessed the complaint-worthy conduct. It does not confirm that the decision against which the applicant appealed is legally incorrect. A few weeks ago I received a file which included a report by the municipal ombudsman. I read it and took it into account when deciding. In the judgment I included a sentence saying that from the report of this ombudsman it does not result that the particular municipality in 2011 had behaved in a way that would lead to the quashing of the decision. This means that basically we accept that there was a complaint to the ombudsman. We state that it covered complaint-worthy conduct but that does not have an impact on the lawfulness of the challenged decision.'

Every year, the Dutch courts produce a vast number of judgements. In 2012, this number was around 1,712,590 cases.[56] Only around 6,6 % of these cases (113,800) came from the administrative courts.[57] These numbers should be increased by cases solved yearly by the Supreme Court. In 2012 this court dealt with 1,112 tax cases.[58] Although court cases have

56 See, Raad voor de Rechtspraak, Jaarverslag 2012, p. 73.

57 Based on the *Annual Report 2012 of the Council for the Judiciary,* the Dutch administrative courts dealt in 2012 with more than 113,800 cases. The majority of these cases were connected with general administrative law cases (*bestuurszaken*) – 45,700 cases. Other parts of decisions were connected with migration law (*vreemdelingenzaken*) – 40,390 cases and with tax cases (*belastingszaken*) – 27,670 cases. See, ibid.

58 See, Hoge Raad der Nederlanden Verslag over 2012, p. 96.

usually increased, in the last three years one can observe a minor decrease.[59] Even though the number of administrative law cases is relatively small it is not in the power of one human being to read through all of those decisions.

Because of that, the research only deals with the judgments included in the database posted on the official internet site of the Dutch judiciary (http://uitspraken.rechtspraak.nl/). The database includes judgments from different courts since 1999 and yearly more than 20,000 new judgments are added. The search criterion in this database was the term *'Nationale Ombudsman'*. Scheme 4 shows the application of this search criterion to the said database.

Scheme 4 – **References in court judgments to NO reports (1/1/1995-31/7/2013)**

Judicial institution	**Number of cross-references**
District court	160
Court of Appeal	55
Administrative Law Division of the Council of State	27
Trade and Industry Appeals Tribunal	4
Central Administrative Tribunal	80
Supreme Court (incl. the opinions of Advocates General)	72

The scheme shows that different Dutch courts indeed refer to the NO and/or his reports. Hence, the courts occasionally take into account the existence of the ombudsprudence. Before describing the way in which the courts approach the NO's reports it is necessary to reiterate that the NO's report is ***not*** an administrative decision *(besluit)* within the meaning of the GALA and it cannot be judicially reviewed.

4.2.2.1 A typology of court cross-references to the National Ombudsman

The typology of court cross-references to the NO includes only *theoretical categories*. The courts do not use them in their practice. They are only developed in order to explain the relations between the NO and the courts. By describing these categories one can discover how the Dutch courts react to issues that have already been covered by the NO. They can show how the courts deal with the reports that are submitted in the file by the parties to the proceedings. They can also clarify the courts' attitude towards the reports and also to the place of the NO in the sphere of administrative justice in the Netherlands.

1. Factual (descriptive) cross-references

Factual or descriptive references can be found in most of the judgments where the courts make cross-references to the NO. These references are included in those parts of judgments that do not express the court's opinion about a particular legal question but which describe the facts of the case. The courts often generally state that there has been

59 Ibid.

a previous NO investigation or that the NO has adopted a report. Very often this cross-reference to the NO is the only place in the whole judgment where the NO is mentioned. For instance, in the *judgment of the District Court of 's-Hertogenbosch of 30 December 2009* the court merely stated that:

> 'On 17 July 2009, the appellants filed a complaint with the Dutch Competition Authority (DCA) because they considered that the agreement is contrary to competition law. In consultation with the DCA, their complaint was withdrawn and it was submitted to another authority. As the appellants have not heard from the later authority they have filed a complaint with the National Ombudsman.'[60]

The following part of the judgment does not include any other reference to the NO. Thus, one cannot tell what the NO's report was about or what the findings were. Clearly the court here only described the facts of the case. Similarly, in a judgment of 2 August 2001, the CRvB only simply stated that:

> 'On behalf of a defendant a written defence was filed. Afterwards the appellants brought to the attention of the court a report of the National Ombudsman.'[61]

From this quotation from the judgment it is clear that the court was aware of the NO report. However, the report was not mentioned in the judgment thereafter. The reader of the judgment does not know what the content or conclusion of the report was. One can only presume that the court read the report and possibly took it into account without finding it necessary to mention it in the judgment. One can find similar factual references.[62]

2. Explanatory cross-references

The court can make cross-references to the NO with a different intention than just merely to state the fact that there was a previous NO investigation. Explanatory cross-references to the NO are connected with the substance of the report or with the powers of the NO. The courts can use them when it tries to explain the powers of the NO to the parties to the proceedings. For example, in the *judgment of the District Court of Haarlem of 31 March 2010* the court explained that *objections and complaints against decisions on remission could be raised in civil proceedings, or they could be submitted to the National Ombudsman.*[63] The court here only explained that there are also other possibilities to protect individual interests. These explanatory references do not go into the substance of the report.[64]

The court can however explain the content or findings of a report, and the applicability of the report for its proceedings. Such cross-references are connected with the *substance of reports*. The courts do this when parties to the proceedings support their

60 Vzngr. Rb. 's-Hertogenbosch 30-12-2009, JAR 2010, 34, para. 2.5.

61 CRvB 25-02-1999, TAR 1999, 70, *I. Ontstaan en loop van de gedingen.*

62 See, for example, CRvB 20-08-2004, LJN: AQ7407; ABRvS 30-03-2009, JB 2009, 128, para. 2.2; Rb. Dordrecht 04-06-1999, AB 1999, 330, para. 1; CBB 10-11-2010, LJN: BP0447, para. 1.

63 Rb. Haarlem 31-03-2010, NTFR 2010, 1150, para. 4.7.

64 See also, for instance, HR 11-07-2008, JOL 2008, 588, para. 3.4.4 or Rb. Den Haag 11-02-2009, LJN: BH9325, para. 4.5.

claims by means of the reports. Then they deal with a report and explain whether or not it is applicable to the case at hand. This type of reference can be found, for example, in a judgment of the *District Court of Assen of 19 February 2007.*

> The court here dealt with a claim for the compensation of immaterial damage connected with the disproportionate use of police force. The plaintiff first demanded this compensation from the police. After his claim was rejected by the police he appealed to the court. In the court proceedings he relied on the report of the NO who had previously declared his complaint against the disproportionate conduct of the police officers to be well-founded.[65] In this connection the court stated that 'the [plaintiff] based his claim on a disputed argument that a police officer had used disproportionate force against him and that, as a consequence, he suffered damage. He had to bear the burden of proof for his arguments. The plaintiff only provided general evidence which was not subsequently supported after the police submitted their detailed and reasoned objection. According to the judge this general character of his arguments stood in the way of his arguments being given binding authority. Instead of that, he repeatedly relied on the content of the report of the National Ombudsman and the content of three statements that inter alia led to the opinion of the Ombudsman… . It was *not shown* that the plaintiff suffered injury because of the damage or that there were any annoying or unpleasant consequences of the damage, or that he suffered financial loss as a result. A sound basis for the alleged damage was missing.'[66]

The court here underlined the fact that the report of the NO alone is not a 'sufficient argument' in this particular case.

> The court furthermore claims that 'the finding of the National Ombudsman that the complaint of the [plaintiff] – namely "after complainant's arrest on 10 February 2004 an official of the regional police corps of Drenthe used disproportionate force against the complainant, which caused him an injury"– is well founded, provides *serious indications of the unlawful character of the challenged conduct*, but in the case establishing the correctness of the basis of the claim of [plaintiff] it is *insufficient*, especially given the reasoned objection of the police. Therefore it may be required from the [plaintiff] to give concrete and more specific evidence. This is missing and the judge sees no reason – partly because it does not satisfy the burden of proof and partly as it lacks a proper basis for the justification of the (alleged) damage – to automatically trust his argument. The claim is rejected as being unfounded.'[67]

The court here did not disagree with the NO. It stated that the report *provides serious indications of the unlawful character of the challenged conduct.* But it is up to the plaintiff to support the indications with the necessary evidence. However, this evidence was not supplemented. Because of that the court concluded that the NO's report *alone* could not stand as evidence against the reasoned objection of the police which in this case apparently offered more proof than the report of the NO. Hence, based on the facts of

65 Rb. Assen 19-02-2007, LJN: AZ8836, para. 1.
66 Ibid., para. 3.
67 Ibid., para. 4.

the case, the NO's report was not enough to support the plaintiff's arguments without additional evidence.

Another explanatory cross-reference can be found in the *judgment of the District Court of The Hague of 19 May 2010.*

> The court here dealt with an appeal against the decision taken in accordance with provisions of the Immigration Act and the subsequent actions of the Ministry of Justice (the defendant). The plaintiff claimed that during his presentations to the Moroccan Authorities his rights had been breached because an interpreter was not present. The defendant alleged that an interpreter was not necessary because during the presentation to the Moroccan Authorities there was a representative of the plaintiff's alleged country of origin present. The plaintiff, however, required the application of the report of the NO of 27 February 2007: *Transparency of presentations: Presentations of asylum seekers who have exhausted all legal remedies to foreign representatives.*[68] The NO in this report *inter alia* recommended the administrative bodies dealing with asylum seekers to invite an interpreter to a presentation meeting if the employees of the Repatriation and Departure Service of the Ministry of Justice cannot converse in the language of the asylum seeker.[69] The Ministry of Justice argued that the report was not the law or a legally binding norm and that it did not have to be followed.

The court found that the NO's report was not applicable in this case. It noted two important conditions for its applicability. First of all, it found that the report was only applicable to *asylum seekers who have exhausted all legal remedies*[70] which was not the case here as the plaintiff was not an asylum seeker. Secondly, it found that according to the report an interpreter should assist *employees of the Repatriation and Departure Service* and not asylum seekers, as employees of the Service have to find out whether there are some issues that could endanger the person to be repatriated to his country of origin.[71] So based on the court's interpretation, the report was not intended to protect the procedural rights of an asylum seeker but to aid the employees of the Government. This case shows that the parties to the proceedings can support their statements with an NO report. Then the court can accept a report as evidence. The judge takes the report into account and assesses its relevance to the case. But if the report does not have a conclusive value for the case the court tries to explain this. Another explanatory reference can be found in the *judgment of the District Court of Alkmaar of 18 April 2006.*

> The court needed to decide whether the municipality's (the defendant's) written refusal to act and to take a decision and its delay can be legally excused and sustained by a report of the NO. Before the case was taken to court, the plaintiff had written several abusive letters after which the defendant, based on a report by the NO, decided to stop its communicating with the plaintiff. This conduct by the defendant subsequently led to a procedure before the court. The court here stated that 'with reference to the report

68 Report 2007/040 of 27 February 2007: *Transparantie in presentaties; Presentaties van uitgeprocedeerde asielzoekers aan buitenlandse vertegenwoordigers.*

69 Ibid., *Aanbeveling*, p. 26.

70 Rb. Den Haag 19-05-2010, LJN: BM9244, para. 4.

71 Ibid.

> of the National Ombudsman of 22 December 2002, AB 2003/55 the defendant argued that it was correct when it no longer responded to the plaintiff's letters because of the excessively insulting tone of his letter of 28 November 2002. The defendant pointed out that it had informed the plaintiff by letter of December 5, 2002 that he had violated the most basic standards that are decent in social communication. At this occasion the defendant also informed the plaintiff that it had decided to no longer communicate with him, in writing or orally, neither through its administrative service nor through its civil service.'[72]

In the following part of the judgment, court interpreted the content of the said report.

> 'In the aforementioned decision, the National Ombudsman alleged that an administrative body is, as a rule, always obliged to respond substantively to regular correspondence by citizens. According to the National Ombudsman, in certain circumstances there are exceptions to the requirement of proper administration for a timely and adequate response by administrative institutions. One of these exceptions occurs when there are offensive letters by citizens. These do not have to be substantively answered. But in those cases, according to the National Ombudsman, a written notification of why the letter is not going to be responded to is sufficient.'[73]

The court here substantively read, explained and interpreted the NO's report. The court did not quote the report literally but emphasized its most important conclusions. It applied the situation described in the report to the situation that was the subject of the case.

> It noticed 'that as the defendant in relation to previous correspondence with the plaintiff could have rightly taken the view, while relying on the report of the National Ombudsman, that some of the plaintiff's correspondence did not need to be answered, the defendant could not immediately and continuously maintain this position in connection with all petitions by the plaintiff. The court believed that every request by the plaintiff should have been assessed according to its merits. In connection with every correspondence it should be assessed whether there is a situation as described in paragraph 3.5.1.'[74]

The court here gave the report a legal interpretation. The court rejected the interpretation of the report as it was presented by the defendant and gave its own interpretation that should have been applicable in this case. The court did not reject the results included in the report but it rejected its interpretation by the defendant. One can only speculate what would be the judgment of the court if the facts of the case were the same as presumed by the report.[75] Similar cross-references, where courts refer substantively to the reports of the NO, can also be found in other judgments.[76]

72 Rb. Alkmaar 18-04-2006, LJN: AW8127, para. 3.4.
73 Ibid., para. 3.5.1.
74 Ibid., para. 3.5.6.
75 The court considered the appeal to be well-grounded mostly because of the breaches of the provisions of the GALA. See, ibid., para. 3.5.3.
76 See, for example, CRvB 20-08-2004, LJN: AQ7407; Rb. Den Haag 12-11-2007, JV 2008, 61; Hof Leeuwarden 02-12-2008, JA 2009, 34; Hof Den Haag 14-12-2010, LJN: BO9923; ABRvS 11-02-2009, AB

3. Distinguishing cross-references

Usually, the courts do not deal very profoundly with the NO's reports. However, occasionally there are also cases where the courts positively appreciate the NO's results and findings or conversely reject them. These cross-references to the NO are closely connected with the content and the substance of the reports. They represent an open attitude by the courts towards the results of the NO's investigation. They often directly or indirectly confirm or reject the results or findings of the NO. The first example of distinguishing references is in the *judgment of the District Court of 's-Hertogenbosch of 23 June 2004* dealing with a dispute between an individual and a regional police corps.

> The appellant was arrested by police officers on suspicion of assault after he voluntarily attended the police station. During his stay at the police station he emphasised that he had diabetes and that he needed to take his medication on time. During a body search medication was found on him. At the same time during his stay at the police station no doctor attended him although he required medical attention. He argued that the conduct of members of the police corps was unlawful. The district court found that in connection with the *conduct* of the police corps the complainant had complained to the NO who declared his complaint well-founded.[77] The court directly quoted the respective report where the NO found that 'the [plaintiff] had been detained in accordance with the definition of Art. 1 of the Office Instruction for the Police, the Royal Military Police and Special Police Personnel. Under Art. 32, a police officer should consult a doctor if the detained person requires this, if medication is found on him or if the detained person himself requests medical assistance. The Explanatory Memorandum states that also in the case where the detained person states that he needs to use his medication it is desirable to consult a doctor. It was undisputed that the [plaintiff] during his arrest (...) stated that he was diabetic and that he therefore needed to take his medication. It is also undisputed that during the [plaintiff's] body search (heart) medication in the form of a spray was seized, which was returned to the [plaintiff] when he requested it. (...) In any case, it was undisputed that the [plaintiff] asked the police to call his doctor, so that the police would be informed as to how to treat him if anything should happen during his stay at the police station. With regard to the Office Instruction and the Explanatory Memorandum, in the circumstances of the case the police had to consult a doctor.'[78]
>
> The court stated and concluded that 'it shared the same view as the National Ombudsman that the police, under these circumstances and with regard to Art. 32 of the Office Instruction, had to consult a doctor. Whether a doctor might have subsequently given information about the medical treatment of the [plaintiff] during his detention or about treatment in an emergency situation or consultation with the attending physician was not an issue that should be assessed by the police but by the consulted doctor.[79]From the above, it was apparent that the police had neglected their duty in this case and with that they had acted unlawfully against the plaintiff and they were therefore required to compensate the resulting damage.'[80]

2009, 102; Hof Leeuwarden 16-01-2004, BB 2004, 451 or CRvB 09-10-2007, USZ 2007.

77 Report 2002/135 of 1 May 2002.

78 Rb. Den Haag 23-06-2004, LJN: AP5823, para. 2.5.

79 Ibid., para. 2.6.

80 Ibid., para. 2.7.

The court thus accepted the report as an argument that would support the plaintiff's contention. Moreover, it agreed with the NO's assessment of this particular issue and shared the same view as the NO. The conduct of these police officers had resulted in improper administration as well as unlawfulness. The court also implicitly agreed with the facts found by the NO. Obviously, the court in this judgement went further than merely formally acknowledging the practice of the NO or stating as a matter of fact that there had been a previous NO investigation.

Another example can be found in the *judgment of the Court of Appeal of Arnhem of 13 July 2010* where the appellate court dealt with an appeal by the Inspector of the Tax Office against the judgment of the district court.

> The court of appeal here first of all as a matter of *fact* (factual reference) stated that 'the National Ombudsman had investigated a complaint about reducing a provisional tax assessment through an automatic reduction rather than carrying out an additional provisional tax assessment (No. 2008/314, December 22, 2008, VN 2009/9.6). The National Ombudsman found that the complaint was well-founded because of a breach of the requirement of proportionality. He recommended that the Minister of Finance should promote the system changes that would cover these situations also in the foreseeable future.'[81] In a further part of the judgment the Court expressly noted that 'the choice of the Inspector was not in accordance with the requirement of proportionality and it found support for this position in the opinion of the NO mentioned in paragraph 2.6.'[82]

The court here expressly acknowledged that the report of the NO that dealt with proper administration could also be used to consider the question of unlawfulness. For the finding of unlawfulness the court found support in the report of the NO. Another example that falls within this category can be found in the *judgment of the District Court of Arnhem of 24 September 2009* dealing with a dispute concerning a decrease in corporate tax.

> During the proceedings the court made cross-references to the NO's report.[83] It stated that it 'believed that the defendant had rightly taken the view that there was no legal basis to remedy the interest rates in the case where a (provisional) assessment had been automatically reduced on the basis of Art. 65 of the AWR (General Tax Act). At the same time there was no objection or appeal against a decrease in such an assessment. Inter alia as it resulted from the report of the National Ombudsman of 22 December 2008 (VN 2009/9.6) (2008/314), the defendant's policy was that, if the declaration so required, any possible automatic provisional assessment was firstly automatically decreased and then the (further provisional) assessment was imposed as a goal of budgetary considerations (in order to mitigate the amount of interest rates that should otherwise be compensated pursuant to Art. 30g of the AWR).'[84]

81 Hof Arnhem 13-07-2010, NTFR 2010, 2174, para. 2.6.
82 Ibid., para. 4.8 last sentence.
83 Report 2008/314 of 22 December 2008. The NO here found a breach of proportionality as one of the requirements of proper administration.
84 Rb. Arnhem 24-09-2009, LJN: BO9391, *4. Beoordeling van het geschil.*

The court therefore here considered the report to be a fact that confirmed the defendant's policy.

> The court dealt with this report and continued that 'the defendant had argued that a provisional refund could only be granted if the advance tax payments ... exceeded the amount of the tax that was likely to be owed. (...) In the opinion of the court these statements by the defendant had no basis in the law. This statement by the Ministry of Finance was not included in the aforementioned report of the National Ombudsman, where the Ombudsman reached the conclusions that "it is to be expected from the Ministry of Finance that it may have chosen the technique of imposing the further provisional tax assessment as well as a final tax assessment and not to automatically decrease such an assessment. The National Ombudsman further concluded that "because of this technique of choosing an automatic reduction (...) the Tax Office has acted improperly." The Court followed the National Ombudsman's opinion. The defendant had to meet these qualifications in its conduct while assessing the objection, where, as the court noted, the claimant had explicitly appealed against the violation of the general principles of proper administration.'[85]

As a result of the proceedings the court quashed the decisions of the Tax Office and ordered it to adopt a new decision that would follow its judgment and thus de facto also the report. The court here obviously took the report as one of the grounds for the judgment. The report played one additional role. It also implicitly confirmed that a breach of the normative standards of the NO and those of the court could lead to a similar result.[86] Other similar references can be found in other judgments.[87]

4.2.2.2 A short summary

From the previous examples of the cross-referring practice of the Dutch courts one can reach several conclusions. Firstly, the Dutch courts indeed sometimes refer to the NO. They do not make cross-references to the NO and his reports and decisions on a daily basis. They only do this if they are persuaded that such cross-referencing should be included in a judgment. If the report has a special interest for the outcome of the case, the court usually points thereto. References to the NO can be found in the judgments of all the courts. In general, one can talk about four main roles of the court's cross-references to the NO and to his reports. They:

- *inform the readers* of the judgments and as clearly as possible about the facts of the case, which might include previous NO investigations;
- *explain the applicability of the NO's reports* to the case at hand. As the reports are often submitted to support the contentions of the parties to the proceedings the courts have to deal with them. With that they can:
- *judicially interpret the content of the NO's report* and they give it a (binding) legal interpretation. Last but not least, the cross-references:

85 Ibid.

86 See, Chapter 5.

87 See for, example, Rb. Den Haag 12-03-2007, NJF 2007, 184; HR 28-09-2010, RvdW 2010, 1154 or Hof Arnhem 14-09-2010, NTFR 2010, 2334.

- *acknowledge the different role or position of the NO's investigation.* As the reports of the NO are not individually taken as a sufficient basis for the decision they confirm the additional character of the NO's investigation.

4.3 Summary

This chapter tries to give an answer to the question *about the significance of the reports of the NO and the judgments of the Dutch judiciary and their content for the other researched institutions and about their interrelations.*

The *formal case coordination* of NO-judiciary relations is rather limited. Statutory Dutch law does not provide a comprehensive answer to this question. Probably, the only formal mechanism of case coordination is the statutory requirement for the NO to take into account the legal grounds of court judgments if the issues covered by the court judgments relate to the issues covered by the investigation. *Indirectly,* a substantive part of this answer can be deduced from the institutional coordination between the NO and the judiciary discussed in the previous chapter.[88] The case law of the Dutch courts is not very extensive either, although it does clarify some issues. In this connection, the courts do not have a possibility to assess the lawfulness of the NO's reports as these reports are not public law acts according to the GALA. Thus the courts cannot officially prescribe the 'route' which the NO has to follow when assessing proper administration. The legally non-binding reports of the NO cannot add anything 'new' to formal case coordination.

In *practice*, the NO and the courts mutually acknowledge the existence of their findings. One can here find several similarities. Both institutions *occasionally cross-reference* the findings of the other institution and thus give some mutual importance to their findings. They do this in only *ad hoc situations* based on *necessity*. The cross-references are *not premeditated* and exist only in connection with *particular cases*. The cases where the NO and the courts mutually cross-reference each other represent only a fragment of all their practice.

The NO deals with the judgments *substantively* when the judgment in question is submitted to him as an argument to support the position of the parties to the investigation. He can also find and apply the judgment of the court or the rule included in the judgment of his own initiative. As confirmed by the interviews and the practice of the NO, judgments are used in the reports of the NO in order to *describe* the facts, to *explain* the applicability of the judgment to the investigated complaint and on certain occasions even to *support* the NO's findings. If there is a certain rule or some interpretation of the law by the court the NO can apply this rule as well. However, the NO does not indiscriminately adopt the judgments as applicable to the investigation. If the judgment is not applicable to the investigation the NO acknowledges its existence and explains the reasons for rejecting its applicability to the investigated case.

The courts deal in their practice with the reports of the NO only if the reports are submitted to them by the parties to the proceedings as one of the argument supporting their case. If the courts refer to the report of the NO they do this in order to *describe* the

88 See, section 3.1.1.

facts of the case, to *explain* the applicability of the report, to *interpret* its contents or to *explain* the powers of the NO. The reports of the NO do not have any special persuasive power in court proceedings. Although they are not 'just an opinion', they are not taken as indisputable confirmation of the unlawfulness of the administrative action. If the reports finding improper administrative conduct are not supported by additional arguments they are often not sufficient to prove the contention of the party to the proceedings and the unlawfulness of the administrative conduct. Interestingly enough, the courts occasionally legally interpret the reports in their judgments.

Chapter 5

NORMATIVE COORDINATION OF OMBUDSMAN-JUDICIARY RELATIONS IN THE NETHERLANDS?

As noted in chapters 1 and 2, the NO and the Dutch courts develop their own normative standards. The NO develops them when evaluating compliance with the concept of proper administration. The courts can do this while resolving legal disputes between individuals and the administration. The normative standards of these state institutions have attracted considerable interest in Dutch academic writing. Possibly every piece of Dutch academic literature on administrative law notes the existence of general principles of proper administration (GPPA).[1] Simultaneously, the NO's normative standards are a usual subject of academic literature, although due to their changes, this literature is often no longer *fresh* or innovative.[2] Only rarely are these normative standards discussed together.

The chapter tries to answer the question of *what is the mutual significance of the normative standards of the ombudsmen and the judiciary in the Netherlands and what are the interrelations between them.* In order to answer this question the chapter firstly discusses the normative standards *developed* by the NO and by the Dutch courts (5.1). It also tries to compare the normative concepts of proper administration and lawfulness. Furthermore, it questions the existence of normative coordination between the NO and the courts including their formal and substantive similarity (5.2). The next section provides a research-based description of the character of the normative standards as applied in the practice of the NO and the courts (5.3). The summary tries to answer the research question (5.4).

5.1 Development of normative standards by the National Ombudsman and by the Dutch judiciary

Despite the close nature of the proper administration and lawfulness concepts, they are not identical. According to the NO *proper administration* has an autonomous meaning.[3] Also some other writers note that it is not correct to equalize the concepts as they include

1 See, Pennarts 2008, Jansen 2006 or Burkens et al. 2006.
2 See, Ten Berge et al. 1992, Langbroek & Rijpkema 2004 or Meulenbroek 2008.
3 Brenninkmeijer & Van Hoogstraten 2008a, p. 34.

several differences.[4] However, their conceptual similarity must be underlined.[5] In general, nobody denies that there is an overlap between these normative concepts but it is not possible to conclude that they are the same.[6] Thus, proper administration and lawfulness should be considered as two distinctive, though partially overlapping and parallel concepts. Proper administration is also often considered to be broader than lawfulness.[7]

When one talks about *lawfulness*, one assesses the question whether a legal relation is in compliance with the law and legal norms. Conversely, *proper administration* gives content to the way in which the state administration and the individual interact.[8] It includes situations that exist outside of the domain of the law and can be covered by moral or ethical norms. The incumbent NO sees proper administration mainly as an *ethical category*.[9] And although ethical norms may be included or even codified in legal principles they cover also a huge part of behaviour or conduct that lies or exists *beyond lawfulness*. Clearly, the conduct of the administration has to be in *accordance with the law*, not only with written statutory law (the GALA or other legal statutes) but also with a number of uncodified legal principles (GPPA). *Proper administration* from the NO's perspective also includes lawful conduct; however, one must underline that the testing of legality has never been seen as a primary goal of the ombudsman's review.[10] The NO states that when it comes to questions of lawfulness the judge is the constitutional starting point. When it comes to questions of proper administration or good governance then a role is played by the NO.[11]

One can argue that every proper conduct is also a legal conduct and vice versa; however, that is not always the case. The NO, in his Annual Report of 2005, closely assesses the relationship between proper administration and lawfulness. He introduces and develops the so-called *ombudsmankwadrant,* that is a scheme describing the way in which one should perceive the relations between lawfulness and proper administration. Based on the following scheme one can find four possible types of administrative conduct.

Scheme 5 – **Ombudsman's quadrant on propriety and lawfulness**[12]

Administrative conduct	**Proper**	**Improper**
Lawful	Lawful and proper	Lawful but improper
Unlawful	Unlawful but proper	Unlawful and improper

4 See, Ten Berge et al. 1992.
5 See, Langbroek & Rijpkema 2004; Ten Berge et al. 1992 or Van der Heijden 2008.
6 See, Brenninkmeijer & van der Vlugt 2009, or Ten Berge 2007.
7 Michiels 2004, p. 259.
8 Annual Report of the NO 2005, p. 19.
9 Brenninkmeijer 2006.
10 See, for example, Brenninkmeijer & van Hoogstraten 2008.
11 Annual Report of the NO 2005, p. 14.
12 Ibid., p. 20.

The validity of this scheme has been discussed in several academic articles[13] and has sometimes even been questioned.[14] However, all four possibilities exist in the practice of the NO. *Lawful and proper administrative conduct* is found, for example, in Report 2006/165 of 24 April 2006.

> The report dealt with a complaint against police officers investigating a case of vandalism. During the investigation they were attacked by young men with snowballs. After they arrested one person for throwing a snowball they were verbally and later also physically harassed by friends of the handcuffed person. They had to use pepper spray and batons as a result. Eventually, these people were arrested and handcuffed as well. From the perspective of lawfulness the NO stated that given the situation the police officers did not breach the obligation to respect physical integrity. From the perspective of proper administration he stated that based on the circumstances of case the police officers had acted proportionally and also properly.

Unlawful and improper administrative conduct can be found in Report 2006/56 of April 2006.

> This report dealt with a complaint by a woman who allegedly did not have a valid train ticket. After the conductor did not accept her e-ticket she was handcuffed, dragged out of the train by two railway police officers and put into a police cell. From the position of the lawfulness of the conduct the NO stated that handcuffing and dragging the woman out of the train amounted to, in connection with her slim figure, an unlawful infringement of her bodily integrity. From the perspective of proper administration he stated that it is required from professionals that they exercise their roles proportionally and in order to de-escalate conflicts. This was not the case here.

Lawful but improper administrative conduct is included, for example, in Report 2006/322 of 18 September 2006.

> This report assessed the case where an 81-year old woman was suspected by the Social Insurance Bank (SVB) of pension fraud. In connection with the investigation the woman had been interrogated non-stop for 5 hours while the legally allowed time limit for such an interrogation was 6 hours. The NO here stated that this behaviour was lawful as the law enabled the SVB to subject suspects a 5-hour interrogation. However, the conduct of the SVB was not proper as the SVB did not take into account the age of the suspected person.

Unlawful but proper administrative conduct is the rarest of all the four cases. Still, one can find this concept in Report 2006/247 of 18 July 2006.

> Here, the NO assessed the case where a hostage-taking person was shot by a police officer who was using (at the time) a legally non-regulated type of ammunition (a bean-bag) that did not kill the attacker but only rendered him unconscious. The NO's investigation

13 Cf. Langbroek & Remac 2011, Van der Vlugt, 2010.
14 Cf. Damen 2008.

> was based on a complaint by the hostage taker. From the perspective of lawfulness this conduct was unlawful as the police officer did not use a type of ammunition which was allowed. From the perspective of properness the NO concluded that this case was proper because the police officer could have used permitted ammunition and killed the attacker. Based on the principle of proportionality this choice by the police officer was indeed proper.

From these examples one can see that the NO adopts a broad approach when assessing proper administration. This approach is not only 'black or white' but it definitely requires a further 'colouration'. If the administration does not act in accordance with the law then its conduct is unlawful. There is no other possibility. The law and its assessment have in this connection an absolute character. Conversely, an assessment of proper conduct has a gradual character with a whole spectrum of shades.[15] This also confirms the presumption that there is no equation between lawfulness and proper administration. However, it does not exclude a connection between them.[16]

5.1.1 Guidelines on Proper Conduct (Behoorlijkheidswijzer)

As noted before, the NO develops his own normative standards and publishes them.[17] Apart from the specialised guidance documents that cover specific types of the administrative conduct (e.g. telephone conversations, remedying damages or the decision-making process) the NO has also developed *general requirements of proper administration (vereisten van behoorlijkheid)*.These are nowadays 'codified' in the document *Guidelines on Proper Conduct.*[18] According to the NO the requirements form in a certain sense *a code of administrative conduct.*[19] Langbroek and Rijpkema argue that these requirements are developed as criteria for the democratic legitimacy of the administrative actions that from the perspective of the NO concretise the democratic basic rule of carefulness and respect for the actions of administration.[20] Meulenbroek notes that the NO has developed these requirements as a criterion for the assessment of administrative actions.[21] Last but not least, Gerrits-Jansens describes them as a quality standard for administrative services.[22]

The requirements of proper behaviour are not developed and applied only for the sake of a feeling of contentment as far as the ombudsman is concerned. As noted before,[23] the NO has an obligation to specify which requirement of proper administration has been

15 Annual Report of the NO 2006, p. 16.
16 See also, Schlössel 2013. In his article Schlössel discusses the relationship between legality and proper administration as developed by the NO. He concludes that proper administration should not be considered as legality.
17 See, section 1.1.3.1.
18 See, section 1.1.3.
19 Annual Report of the NO 2007, p. 160.
20 Langbroek & Rijpkema 2004, p. 20.
21 Meulenbroek 2008, p. 65.
22 *Een kwaliteitsnorm voor de dienstverlening van de overheid,* Gerrits-Jansens 2000, p. 134.
23 See, section 1.1.3.

breached if he finds that the administrative conduct was improper.[24] The GALA, however, does not specify what a 'requirement of proper administration' actually entails. It only *officially and legally acknowledges its existence*. As it is the NO who *ex lege* deals with *proper administration*, one must presume that he also develops or at least outlines the content of the requirements. And almost since the establishment of his office, the NO has been doing precisely that.

The first NO, Rang, argued that an important role to give content to proper administration is played by the *subjective ethical norms* described as *norms of decency* (*fatsoensnormen*). According to him, proper administration was interconnected with the ethics of administrative actions.[25] The second NO, Oosting, followed a more objective perspective. In 1987, he developed a list of requirements that were applicable to proper administration and which described its content. *Oosting's list* was the first attempt by the NO to give actual content to the term *proper administration* in the form of preventive norms of conduct. It became an important tool in the practice of the NO and even in the latest version of the list of requirements for proper administration one can feel its heritage.[26] However, it did not contain a *systematic* rendering of norms in context and it was not always applied in a similar fashion by subsequent officeholders.[27] An additional clarity concerning proper administration was brought by the third NO, Fernhout, who commissioned research into proper administration and into ombudsnorms. The research has led to a redeveloped list of *requirements of proper behaviour* by Langbroek and Rijpkema.[28] The list of requirements for proper administration was once again changed in 2011 when the incumbent NO, Brenninkmeijer, introduced its newest version.[29] He has tried to bring proper administration closer to the concept of fairness (*eerlijkheid*)[30] and to make the list simpler and without legal connotations. During an interview he noted that 'our new set of requirements for proper administration is less legal and it is closer to the idea of the Ombudskwadrant.[31] They are open to further development. The original norms in the Behoorlijkheidswijzer were reminiscent of the general principles of proper administration (GPPA).'

Nowadays, most Dutch ombudsmen use in their work the latest version of *Guidelines on Proper Conduct* as it was developed with the cooperation of the NO and the municipal ombudsmen.[32] The requirements are divided into four groups, each representing a specific type of conduct (Scheme 6). Their substance is included in Annex 3.

24 See, for example, Report 2009/199 of 22 September 2009, Report 2006/019 of 19 January 2006 or Report 2008/005 of 29 January 2008.
25 Annual Report of the NO 1985, p. 9.
26 Oosting's list can be found in, for example, Ten Berge et al. 1992.
27 Ten Berge & Langbroek 2005, p. 127.
28 See, Langbroek & Rijpkema 2004.
29 <www.nationaleombudsman.nl/sites/default/files/behoorlijkheidswijzer_nl_oktober_2012.pdf> (accessed on 31 July 2013).
30 Brenninkmeijer 2007.
31 See, Scheme 5, p. 69.
32 Based on the interview with Dr Brenninkmeijer.

Scheme 6 – **Requirements for proper administration (Guidelines on Proper Conduct – 2012)**

Open and clear	Respectful	Caring and solution focused	Fair and reliable
1. Transparent 2. Provide adequate information 3. Listen to citizens 4. Adequate reasons	5. Respect for fundamental rights 6. Promotion of active public participation 7. Courtesy 8. Fair play 9. Proportionality 10. Special care	11. Individualised approach 12. Cooperation 13. Leniency 14. Promptness 15. De-escalation	16. Integrity 17. Trustworthiness 18. Impartiality 19. Reasonableness 20. Careful preparation 21. Effective organisation 22. Professionalism

The requirements for proper administration as developed by the NO do not have the character of legal obligations for the administration. They are not legally binding or enforceable. According to the incumbent NO, the requirements for proper administration should not be legally codified as 'legal codification may hinder their development.'[33] Their advantage lies in the fact that they do not only cover legal norms but also norms that form the code of conduct of administrative bodies.[34] The relation between the general requirements of proper administration and the requirements included in the specialised lists (such as the Schadevergoedingwijzer)[35] was during the interview explained by the incumbent NO:

> 'The Guidelines on Proper Conduct present in general a set of requirements for proper administration with which the administration has to comply. The specialised 'wijzers' translate those norms into a certain subject. For instance, the Participatiewijzer and the Handhavingswijzer translate the requirements of proper administration into participation and into the issue of enforcement. So there is no difference between the general norms of proper administration and those 'wijzers' but they are more explicit and they are more dedicated to certain issues. What is more, we always prepare these specialised 'wijzers' and their norms in cooperation with the administration.'

5.1.2 General principles of proper administration (GPPA)

Although the Dutch courts do not have the same status as the common law courts, they have an undeniable normative function which can be found in their practice when assessing administrative actions and this function is connected with a potential *discovery of legal principles*. Already at the beginning of the 20th century a Dutch court, namely the Central Appeals Tribunal, had to assess conduct by an administrative body against standards other than written law. As Widdershoven and Remac state, this court, in order to decide the case, had to find an unwritten normative standard, in this case the general principle of legal certainty *that must be respected even in the absence of a provision of*

33 Based on the interview with Dr Brenninkmeijer.
34 Annual Report of the NO 2005, p. 12.
35 See, section 1.1.3.1.

written law.[36] The discovery of the first (unwritten) general principle of law paved the way for other courts, including the former post-war Tribunal for Food Affairs and the Supreme Court, to develop other general principles which should protect individuals against the all-powerful government.[37] Thus originally, the legal principles were developed in the course of the judicial review procedure by specialised administrative courts and by the civil courts.[38]

According to Dutch legal theory, one can find a basis for the judicial discovery of legal principles by the courts in the general legal consciousness *(het algemene rechtbewustzijn)* that can be derived from unwritten as well as written law. Hence, general principles of law do not reflect only the moral opinion of the individual judge or court but, in contrast, they can be presumed to be already present and hidden in the legal order, thereby having to be discovered by the courts.[39] On rare occasions the courts have even accepted the *contra legem* application of these principles. In these cases unwritten general legal principles prevail over written statutory law.[40] Originally, the GPPA were *judge-made* and *judge-applied* law. They were not codified in any statute or act, although since the late 1950s it was possible to find a general reference to general principles of proper administration in legal acts.[41] These principles were continuously used as a ground for judicial review (*toetsingsnorm*[42] or *toetsingsgrond*)[43] and they were later partially codified. As noted in section 2.3, since 1994, the GPPA have been partially codified in the GALA. A common explanation for only a *partial codification* is that some of the principles were not sufficiently ripe for codification[44] or that it was difficult to make a short, clear and comprehensive written legal provision that would include all specifics of a general and usually broadly unwritten principle.[45]

Nowadays, the GPPA generally[46] include:

1. The *prohibition of an abuse of power* (Verbod van détournement de pouvoir) is codified in Art. 3:3 GALA. The administration must use its power only for purposes given by the law.
2. The *prohibition of arbitrariness* (Willekeurverbod) is codified in Art. 3:4 (1) GALA. It requires the administration to weigh the interests directly involved in the case and not to take arbitrary decisions.
3. The *principle of proportionality* (Evenredigheidsbeginsel) is codified in Art. 3:4 (2) GALA. It requires that the adverse consequences of the administrative decision must not be disproportionate to the goals of that decision.

36 Widdershoven & Remac 2012, p. 382. See, CRvB 31-10-1935, ARB 1936, p. 168.
37 Widdershoven & Remac 2012, pp. 383-384.
38 Langbroek 1997, p. 93.
39 Widdershoven & Remac 2012, p. 385.
40 Ibid., p. 386 and HR 12-04-1978 (*Doorbraakarresten*), NJ 1979/533; HR 26-09-1979, AB 1980/210 or CRvB 18-02-1975, AB 1975/243.
41 See, for example, Nicolai 1990.
42 Michiels 2004, p. 272.
43 Michiels 2006, p. 102.
44 Goorden 1997, p. 69.
45 See, Ten Berge & Widdershoven 2001, p. 117 or Schlössels & Stroink 2006, p. 189.
46 One can also find a different typology of the GPPA. See, Seerden & Wenders 2012 or Pennarts 2008.

4. The *principle of specialisation* (Specialiteitsbeginsel) codified in Art. 3:4 (1) GALA requires that the administration, when exercising public law functions, may not cover public interests other than for which it was provided with powers.[47]
5. The *principle of carefulness* (Zorgvuldigheidsbeginsel) is codified in Art. 3:2 GALA. It requires the administration to carefully collect the information which must be taken into account, identify all the relevant facts and give the parties the opportunity to give the administration any additional information before the decision is taken.
6. The *principle of the justification for a decision (Motiveringsbeginsel)* requires the administration to provide reasons for its decision. It includes two rights for individuals, namely a right to knowable reasons for a decision (Art. 3:47 GALA) and the right to sound reasons (Art. 3:46 GALA).[48]
7. The unwritten, *fair play principle* (Fair play beginsel) requires the administration not to obstruct the procedural chances of an interested party. The codified principle (Art. 2:4 (2) GALA) gives the interested party the right to influence the decision-making processes.
8. The *prohibition of bias* (Verbod van vooringenomenheid) is codified in Art. 2:4 (1) GALA and requires the administration to act impartially, without any bias.
9. The principle of *equality* (Gelijkheidsbeginsel) codified in Art. 1 of the Constitution, requires the administration to treat equal cases in an equal way.
10. The unwritten *principle of formal legal certainty* (Formele Rechtszekerheidsbeginsel), requires the administration to formulate its decisions clearly so that individuals know their position in relation to administration. This principle is also connected with the predictability of the law.
11. The *principle of legitimate expectations* or *material legal certainty* (Vertrouwensbeginsel or materiële rechtszekerheid) is not codified and requires the administration to act as far as possible in accordance with the legitimate expectations that have been raised by legislation, individual decisions, policy rules, and precise assurances and promises.[49]

The role of the GPPA is to set a legal standard for administrative actions and to bring more clarity to the relations between the administration and individuals.[50] They are legal standards that limit the discretionary powers of administrative authorities.[51] The GPPA for the larger part are connected with the decision-making processes of the administration and they include the preparation of a decision (including the gathering of information), the weighing of interests, the decision itself and its communication. They represent *minimal standards for a legal or lawful administration.*[52]

According to Art. 8:77 (2) GALA if the judge decides to grant an appeal, he must include in the judgment those *written or unwritten rules or general principles of law that were breached or violated by the challenged and quashed decision*. Thus, even the law

47 Jans 2008, p. 36.
48 Widdershoven & Remac 2012, p. 395.
49 Ibid., p. 390.
50 Cf. De Haan et al. 2010, p. 103.
51 Romano 2002, p. 329.
52 Cf. Nicolai 1990 or Van Wijk et al. 2008.

presumes and requires the application of the GPPA. Thus, the Dutch courts can use written GPPA as codified in written statutes but also unwritten and uncodified GPPA. However, some authors argue that the further development of the unwritten part of the GPPA, after their codification, is dwindling. Especially in comparison with the use of the GPPA that are codified in the legal provisions of the GALA.[53] This point was also partially noted by Mr Verburg, a District Court judge, who during the interview noted that:

> 'The 1980s and the 1990s were the times of changes to the administrative law system in the Netherlands. It was also the time of discussions about the principles. I think it is true that in 1994, on the one hand, many people thought now we are ready, it is in the GALA and we are ready to apply it. On the other hand, it was also the 'zeitgeist'. We thought let's go with the flow. No more discussions about these principles.'

As argued by Ms Mondt-Schouten, a judge at the ABRvS, the development of the GPPA still exists:

> 'If you look, for example, at the principle of fair play. It is not written but if there is a case in which it is clear that there was no fair play then we will apply this principle. Of course, the GALA is important but that does not mean that it is the only source of principles.'

Thus, the development of legal principles by the courts is far from having reached its conclusion.

5.2 Formal normative coordination and the similarity of normative standards?

This section looks for the existence of *formal normative coordination* between the courts and the NO. It looks into the law and the jurisprudence of the courts. It also discusses the *formal* and *substantive similarity* between these normative standards.

5.2.1 Formal coordination between the normative standards of the Dutch courts and of the National Ombudsman?

When one looks at the statutory law, one can note that the law in Art. 9:36 (2) GALA expressly recognises and acknowledges the existence of the *requirements of proper administration*. It requires the NO to use these requirements of proper administration and to point to their breaches. The statutory law also partially codifies the GPPA. Apart from the partial codification of the general principles of proper administration in the GALA and the legal acknowledgement of the requirements for proper administration there is *no special statutory normative coordination* between the NO and the courts.

An investigation of the case law shows that the courts only very rarely deal with the normative standards of the NO. Apart from the cases noted previously,[54] one can point to

53 Cf. Addink 2011, p. 19.
54 See, section 4.2.2.

the *judgment of the District Court of The Hague of 27 July 2010.*[55] In this case, however, the court did not deal with the *general principles of proper administration* and the *requirements of the NO* but with the principles for civil courts to remedy damages.

> The court dealt with a dispute between a private company offering transport services and the Ministry of the Infrastructure and the Environment. The private company had been subjected to a fine which in its opinion was unlawful and improper and it requested damages before the civil court. The administrative conduct of the Ministry had been previously dealt with by the NO who found that its conduct was indeed improper and it breached the requirement of fair play.[56] Based on the report the private company argued that the state had not only acted in breach of proper administration but that it had also acted unlawfully.[57] The court assessed the content of the reports and the investigated administrative actions. In the end it concluded that 'although the NO had decided that the [administrative body] had acted improperly this did not mean that the [applicant] had a right to remedy the damages that allegedly existed as a consequence of these actions. For a claim to have one's damages paid *other rules are applicable*. The court did not reach the decision that the State had acted unlawfully by these [actions] so that its obligation to pay damages would not arise.'[58]

The court here did not directly deal with the clash between the GPPA and the requirements of proper administration. Nonetheless, it pointed to the lack of any connection between a breach of the normative standard of the NO (the requirement of proper administration) and the right for this to be remedied by the court. In this connection one has to take into account the case law where the courts have rejected statements that they are obliged to follow the findings of the NO.[59] When one translates this onto the level of normative standards, then this court does not follow the normative standards of the NO. The breach of the normative standards of the NO does not necessarily lead to a breach of the normative standards of the court.

5.2.2 *Similarity between the normative standards*

Despite the fact that there are only hints of a *formal normative coordination* between the NO and the courts, one can find, when looking at the normative standards of the NO and the courts, some similarities between these normative standards. When looking at the requirements for proper administration of the NO and at the GPPA one can notice a *formal* as well as *substantive* similarity between the normative standards.

Formal similarity between the normative standards of the NO and the Dutch courts exists in connection with the denomination of individual standards. Among the requirements for proper administration of the NO and the GPPA one can notice that there are standards that have the same or a similar name. This includes a formal similarity

55 The court referred directly to the NO's assessment criteria (*behoorlijkheidscriterium*) in judgment Rb. Rotterdam 20-03-2013, LJN: BZ5645, para. 4.7.1. Still, this judgment does not express an opinion thereon.

56 Rb. Den Haag 27-07-2011, LJN: BU1282, paras 2.09 and 2.10.

57 Ibid., para. 5.1.

58 Ibid., para. 5.20.

59 See, section 4.2.2.

between the requirement of proportionality and the principle of proportionality, the requirement of fair play and the principle of fair play as well as the requirement to provide adequate reasons and the principle of the justification of the decision. A certain formal similarity can also be found in the requirement of impartiality and the principle of the prohibition of any bias. However, the majority of these standards do not share this formal similarity. Furthermore, the *Guidance on Proper Conduct* does not resemble a statute. It is written in easy and understandable language. Every requirement also includes a short explanation. The English translation of the *Guidance on Proper Conduct* uses the term *should*. It has the character of general guidance and not a command. The Dutch equivalent is however a great deal more authoritative. It does not state that *the administration should behave* in a certain way but it requires that *the administration behaves* in a certain way (de overheid handelt, weegt, verzamelt, zorgt etc.). The diction of requirements that the administration *behaves* may possibly be reminiscent of a legal obligation.

Formal similarity between the normative standards of the NO and the courts is an indicator of a possible interrelation between these standards. It can theoretically lead to an erroneous conclusion that these normative standards are the same. However, as the normative standards with the same or similar names may have a different content, their substantive similarity and their application is more important.

Substantive similarity is connected with the *content* of the normative standards. When looking at the content of some of the requirements of proper administration and the GPPA, one can find that they both protect certain values. These values can be overlapping. As the requirements for proper administration are legally non-binding and the GPPA *are* the law, some values are protected by the courts during the assessment of compliance with the law or by the NO during the assessment of compliance with the general concept of proper administration. The protection of a certain value by both categories of normative standards can point to a substantive similarity between the researched normative standards. The following scheme identifies the protected values, the requirements of the NO and the GPPA and the law (as they are partially codified) protecting it as well as the identified substantial overlap.

Scheme 7 – **Substantive overlap between the requirements of proper administration and the general principles of proper administration or the written law**

	Requirement of proper administration of the NO	General principles of proper administration/written law	Value protected
	Examples*	Examples**	Overlap identified
1.	- Adequate reasons	- Principle of the justification of a decision - Arts. 3:46-3:47 GALA	Knowledge of the content of the administrative decisions and their conclusions.
	Report 2012/005, Report 2011/030 or Report 2011/141	ABRvS 15-02-2007, JV 2007, 168 or, Rb. Den Haag, 13-11-2007, LJN: BC1009.	Lack of reasons in the administrative decision may lead to a breach of the requirement of proper administration as well as the general principle of proper administration.
2.	- Respect for fundamental rights	- Principle of equality - Documents including human rights (ECHR, the Constitution etc.)	Fundamental (human) rights of individuals.
	Report 2011/224, Report 2011/076 or Report 2011/331	HR 23-04-2004, BNB 2004, 392 or Hof Leeuwarden 16-08-2012, BB 2012, 531 or Rb. Den Haag 11-07-2012, NJ 2012, 579.	Breach of fundamental rights may lead to unlawfulness but also to improper administration.
3.	- Fair play	- Principle of fair play - Art. 2:4 (2) GALA	Fairness of the administrative processes.
	Report 2001/207, Report 2011/319 or Report 2009/211	Rb. Den Haag 14-08-2008, JV 2008, 467 or HR 09-09-2011, NJ 2011, 553.	Obstruction of the procedural chances of the parties to the proceedings may lead to improper administration as well as to unlawfulness.
4.	- Proportionality	- Principle of proportionality - Art. 3:4 (2) GALA	Balance between aims and means of administrative actions.
	Report 2011/264, Report 2010/063 or Report 2009/246	HR 30-09-2011, BNB 2012, 69 or CBB 29-10-2010 LJN: BO2813.	Disproportionate administrative actions may lead to a breach of law as well as to improper administration.
5.	- Integrity	- Prohibition of an abuse of power - Art. 3:3 GALA	Proper use of administrative powers
	Report 2012/165, Report 2012/134 or Report 2012/027	Rb. Maastricht 08-02-2011, JWR 2011, 40 or HR 13-11-2007, JOL 2007, 754.	Using the powers of the administration for purposes other than those provided may lead to unlawfulness as well as to improper administration.

6.	**– Trustworthiness**	**– Principle of formal legal certainty – Principle of legitimate expectations – Prohibition of an abuse of power – Art. 3:3 GALA**	Legal certainty and the trust in the legal system.
	Report 2012/015, Report 2012/143 or Report 2012/111	HR 25-01-2011, JOW 2011, 31 or Rb. Den Haag 17-12-2007, LJN: BC5117.	Acting outside the framework of given powers and breaching legitimate expectations may lead to unlawfulness and to improper administration.
7.	**– Impartiality**	**– Prohibition of bias – Art. 2:4 (1) GALA**	Impartiality of the administration.
	Report 2012/182, Report 2011/128 or Report 2010/243	Rb. Amsterdam 07-02-2012, LJN: BW8475 or ABRvS 05-12-2007, AB 2008, 18.	Partial and biased actions of the administration may lead to a breach of proper administration and the law.
8.	**– Reasonableness**	**– Prohibition of arbitrariness – Art. 3:4 (1) GALA**	Reasonableness of the administrative decisions.
	Report 2012/015, Report 2012/004 or Report 2011/255	Rb. Den Haag 30-11-2010, BB 2011, 176 or HR 17-04-2009, BNB 2010, 114.	Not weighing all interests during the administrative decision-making process may lead to a breach of the law and to improper administration.
9.	**– Careful preparation**	**– Principle of carefulness – Art. 3:2 GALA**	Carefulness of the administrative proceedings.
	Report 2012/147, Report 2012/029 or Report 2012/130	HR 24-12-2010, BNB 2011, 82 or HR 16-12-1998, BB 2002, 634.	Insufficient identification and assembling of information or insufficient identifying of all relevant facts may lead to improper conduct but also to unlawfulness.

* These examples can include cases where the finding of improper administration is based on a combination of several acts of malpractice and not only on a breach of one particular requirement.

** Examples included here refer to cases where the said principle has been applied or developed by the court.

Based on the scheme and on a comparison of the NO's requirements and the GPPA one can distinguish two main groups: *overlapping normative standards* and *standards that do not overlap*.

In connection with the *overlapping normative standards* one can see that the majority of the discovered and applied normative standards have some similarity in their content. The similarity or overlap of the content does not mean that the standards are completely identical. This similarity is a sign of a similarity between the protected values. Thus, protecting similar values can bring the content of the overlapping normative standards also closer.

The scheme shows that in the *Guidance on Proper Conduct* one can identify at least nine cases where the requirements partially or even completely overlap with the GPPA that are primarily applied when assessing compliance with the law. This shows that the

Dutch courts and the NO use substantively similar standards when assessing compliance with two different normative concepts. The overlapping content of normative standards does not only bring the concepts of lawfulness and proper administration closer together but it can also bring the courts and the NO closer together. This overlap however does not make the requirements of the NO legally binding. It only underlines the fact that some social values simultaneously receive protection from the NO and the Dutch courts.

Sometimes, the requirements overlap with more than one legal principle. This is the case, for example, with the requirement of *Trustworthiness* that *inter alia* requires the administration to act within the framework of the law, to 'do what they say' and to comply with the judgments of the courts.[60] Although, as previously noted by the NO, the latest version of the *Guidelines* is less 'legal', in the case of substantively overlapping requirements it is possible to see an echo of the GPPA. Especially the second group (Respectful) and the fourth group of requirements (Open and clear) almost completely overlap with the legal principles.[61] Despite the substantive overlapping of these normative standards and despite the similarity between the protected general values, the character of the protection is different.

The *non-overlapping normative standards* include only the requirements of the NO. From Scheme 7 one can note that all the GPPA have their reflection in the requirements of the NO. Furthermore, the NO's standards can provide protection against administrative actions that are not covered by legal principles. This includes requirements such as listening to citizens, the promotion of active public participation, courtesy or the requirement of de-escalation. These requirements can be described as *exclusive ombudsman standards covering administrative conduct beyond the law*. In these cases, the general value is only protected by the NO as the legislator has not decided to also protect them by the courts.

5.3 Normative standards in practice

The previously discussed normative standards are actively applied in the practice of the NO and the courts. They have the character of *assessment standards* against which the NO and the courts assess the actions of the institutions within their competence. If this body does not follow these standards, its actions can be pronounced as unlawful and/or improper. One must here reiterate the fact that the Dutch courts assess the *legality of the administrative decision* while the NO assesses the *compliance of administrative conduct with requirements of proper administration.*[62]

As noted above, some of the general values are protected by the courts and by the NO. One can thus ponder whether the standards of the NO and the courts that protect the same general value are applied in a similar fashion and whether the fact that these institutions provide protection to the same general value leads to a mutual acknowledgement or probably even inspiration when developing these normative standards. The persons interviewed agreed that *in practice* one can see some overlapping between these standards while they underlined their different character. The incumbent NO, Dr Brenninkmeijer,

60 See, Annex 3.
61 See, Scheme 6 and Annex 3.
62 See, Chapters 1 and 2.

noted that the character of the requirements for proper administration is tied with the character of proper administration. Because of that the requirements must not be the same as legal principles. While being interviewed, he stated that:

> 'Our standards are different from the GPPA. Our norms go beyond what is the traditional perception of the law. I can give an example which is quite clear. It is connected with the freedom of expression. In general, this freedom implies that you can offend another person. So if I meet my neighbour in the morning the freedom of expression implies that I can tell him "Hey, asshole!" but he will be upset and my relationship with him will suffer. It is for the ombudsman to say "within the legal framework and freedoms you also have certain norms which you have to respect when you relate with others." And that's the difference which I would say is quite important. Our Ombudskwadrant points at it. It has two aspects; one is a substantive/legal aspect and the other is a relationship aspect so you combine this aspect with the law.'

He also provided another example as regards the right to be heard:

> 'Based on the GALA there are some situations in which the administration should hear the citizen. You can do that in quite a formal way. You organise the hearing and you hear the citizen. In the view of the ombudsman you can say that is only the beginning of the communication between the citizen and the administration because in the view of the ombudsman the right to be heard depends on whether you are really interested in the problems of the citizen, in what he is saying and that you take that into account. So you should be an interested listener.'

The substitute NO, Mr Van Dooren, confirmed an overlap between the requirements of proper administration and the GPPA:

> 'The GPPA used by the courts are strict legal principles. Principles included in the Guidance on Proper Conduct are not only legal principles although they are to a certain extent identical with the principles of constitutional, human rights and administrative law.'

All the interviewed judges agreed that the GPPA and the NO's requirements are different. Mr Van Zutphen, the president of the CBB, stated that:

> 'It is important to draw a line between the two sets of standards, because the GPPA are legal principles. They are legal concepts and should be seen within the legal context of handling cases in the courts. But I can imagine that the opinion of the NO that there has been improper administration can also lead the judges to a finding of unlawfulness or a breach of the GPPA. But that is a different type of identification of the behaviour within another framework. There must be differences although there may be a sort of overlap. In a way we are working from different positions but always towards a system in which democracy is protected. We follow the same goal from a basic position which is connected to the rule of law, equal treatment, respect for one's privacy etc. Those are common standards from where we start but we end with a different normative framework.'

Also Ms Mont-Schouten, a judge at the ABRvS, noted that in general:

> 'There might be a difference as the National Ombudsman goes a bit further beyond the law. For example, he assesses whether the government has acted properly, politely and correctly. I believe that that he goes further than us and I think it is his task to go further.'

Mr Verburg, a District Court judge, pointed to the fact that the standards of the NO are acknowledged by the courts but they are not very interesting for them:

> 'I cannot say that the Dutch courts in their practice extensively ignore the NO. But there is no power play. My colleagues are probably aware that the ombudsman is compiling a report on the conduct of some organisation if they have a similar case. In general, we perceive ourselves as institutions that are doing their own thing and the ombudsman does likewise. There is an overlap between our fields of work, but it is a small one. In the Netherlands you do not see very often that the judge takes the report of the ombudsman or the norms of the ombudsman and uses it or them. That is not our kind of work. We distinguish between lawfulness and proper administration.'

When looking at the Dutch courts one can see that they apply the law. Whether codified or not, the law is the domain of the courts. It is all they know. Conversely, when looking at the NO's normative standards one can see that they are not so clear. They are connected with a flexible concept of proper administration whose requirements *stem from the fundamental notions of decency that are included in fundamental rights, from GPPA and from legislation such as the GALA.*[63] The following subsections try to look at the application of statutory law (including human rights), GPPA and extra-legal principles such as the normative standards applied in the practice of the NO.

5.3.1 Statutory law as a normative standard of the National Ombudsman

The Dutch courts use the law as their main normative standard. That is what the courts do; they assess the lawfulness of administrative decisions and the compliance of those administrative decisions with the law. If, in the decision-making process, the administrative body breaches the legal requirements or the administrative decision does not include all the legally prescribed issues the courts can find such a breach.

On the other hand, the role of the NO is *not primarily connected* with the assessment of compliance with the law. It is not his role. Nonetheless, proper administration can overlap with lawfulness. One can here point to two requirements of proper administration: Integrity and Trustworthiness. The requirement of *integrity* requires *the administration to use its powers only for the purposes for which they were conferred*[64] and the requirement of *trustworthiness* requires *it to act within the framework of the law and to comply with the judgments of the courts.*[65] These two requirements for proper administration clearly

63 Annual Report of the NO 2007, p. 16.

64 Requirement 16, Integrity, *Guidelines on proper conduct*, October 2012.

65 Requirement 17, Trustworthiness, *Guidelines on proper conduct*, October 2012.

necessitate that the administration takes the law and legal provisions into account and acts within its legally given powers. In order to be able to assess compliance with these requirements for proper administration the NO *must know the law* which is applicable at the time of the assessment of the complaint and he *must be able to assess compliance with the law*. Thus, if the NO finds, during the assessment of a complaint, that the administration has acted unlawfully, he can reach a decision that there has been a breach of proper administration. He does not *formally* have the power to say that there has been a breach of the law. Still, he can express his opinion that the law has in fact been breached. But this finding does not have legal consequences as in the case of such a finding by the court. Thus, *de facto* he is giving a legally non-binding interpretation of the law.

Some academics highlight the importance of statutory law for the NO's assessment. For instance, Addink argues that the NO, while assessing proper administration, is led by the principles and the fundamental values that are codified in several places including the law.[66] Brenninkmeijer and Van der Vlugt underline that the requirements for proper administration display a close relationship with juridical legal norms and with the general principles of proper administration.[67] The connection of the NO with the law and the legal principles as normative standards has also been observed by Langbroek and Rijpkema who stated that in the years before 2002 the NO increasingly equated proper administrative conduct with lawful conduct while this equation was inconsistent with the proper function of the institution of the ombudsman.[68] In practice one can note several reports where the NO has actually assessed compliance with written law. This is, for example, the case in *Report 2013/006 of 16 January 2013*.

> The complainant argued that he had been wrongly arrested by the police for not being able to identify himself after he was considered to be a witness in a missing person case. He argued that the conduct of the police officer in question was not in accordance with their competences. The NO assessed his complaint and found that according to the law and the circumstances of the case the complainant could have been considered to be a witness and that the police officers were entitled to ask for his ID. According to the law a refusal to cooperate could lead to the person being detained.[69] However, the NO discovered that the complainant had actually initially identified himself. Despite this he was arrested in order to put pressure on him as a witness. Because of that the NO found that the conduct of the police officer in question was improper as he had *abused his competence* and breached the requirement of proper administration of integrity.

In this case the NO assessed (and de facto interpreted) the compliance of the actions of the police officer with the Police Act, the Compulsory Identification Act and the Criminal Code. These acts were used as a background for his report.[70] A similar example can be found in *Report 2010/267 of 24 September 2010*.

66 Addink 2008, pp. 3-26.
67 Brenninkmeijer & Van der Vlugt 2009, p. 47.
68 Langbroek, Rijpkema 2006, p. 90.
69 Report 2013/006 of 16 January 2013, *Beoordeling door de Nationale ombudsman*.
70 Ibid., Achtergrond.

> Here the NO dealt with a complaint against the conduct of the Royal Military Police (RMP) that according to the complainant had forced him to provide his fingerprints. He also complained about the use of handcuffs. The NO found that, based on the law, foreigners are obliged to cooperate with the RMP when asked for identification. Identification in the form of providing fingerprints exists only in reasonable cases, however.[71] As the complainant had previously applied for asylum in the Netherlands his fingerprints had already been taken. The NO found that the RMP wanted to take the complainant's fingerprints because of a query by the Repatriation and Departure Service. The RMP, however, did not ask the Repatriation Service about the reasons of this request. The NO argued that since the fingerprints of the complainant had been taken on a different occasion there was no reasonable reason to do this again. In his opinion this was an *abuse of the power* of the RMP and it resulted in improper conduct.[72] He also found that the RMP had acted improperly when they handcuffed the complainant as in the circumstances of the case the RMP did not have the competence to use handcuffs.[73]

The NO in this case clearly assessed the compliance of the RMP's conduct with the law: namely the Dutch Constitution, the Immigration Act and the Police Act. These two examples of assessing compliance with legal provisions were not out of the ordinary as one can discover more reports in which the NO has assessed compliance with statutory law.[74]

In the Netherlands, human rights are included in numerous international agreements and in the Constitution.[75] In general, compliance with human rights is assessed by the courts as human rights requirements are part of the legal requirements.[76] Human rights as a normative category are a legislative standard of control for many ombudsmen. In the case of some ombudsmen, especially those established in the last two decades, one can see a shift from general standards like good administration to human rights.[77] As human rights are a generally required standard in modern society they also find their way into the toolkits of the older ombudsmen. The Netherlands is not an exception in this regard.[78] Nowadays, human rights are part of written law. Still, the NO is not *ex lege* entrusted with the assessment of compliance with human rights. Neither the GALA nor the WNo expressly give the NO powers to assess compliance with human rights. However, due to the flexibility of proper administration, human rights *are* part of the NO's toolkit. Already in the1980s Oosting's list of compliance with human rights became a part of proper administration. Compliance with human rights is nowadays included in the *Guidelines on Proper Administration* in the requirement *respect for fundamental rights.* This requirement requires *public authorities to respect the fundamental rights of citizens including those that*

71 Report 2010/267 of 24 September 2010, *Beoordeling* I. a) para. 2.
72 Ibid., *Beoordeeling* I. a) para. 6.
73 Ibid., *Beoordeling* I. b) para. 7.
74 See for example, Report 2010/073 of 8 April 2010, Report 2012/052 of 9 March 2012, Report 2012/169 of 17 October 2012 or Report 2010/182 of 2 July 2010.
75 For a description of the human rights protection before the courts in the Netherlands see, for example, Akkermans et al. 2005.
76 After meeting all the requirements the case can continue before some international institutions such as, for instance, the European Court of Human Rights.
77 Cf. O'Reilly 2007or Remac 2013.
78 See, for example, Oosting 1995, pp. 115-136.

guarantee protection against government action or fundamental rights guaranteeing that public administration will take a certain action.[79] This shows that the concept of proper administration has grown.

An application of human rights by the NO as normative standards does not change the legal binding power of his reports or of the requirements of proper administration in general. However, the involvement of the NO in human rights protection can be a signal for the state administration. One can note a number of reports where the NO actually assessed the compliance of the administration with fundamental rights. This is, for instance, the situation described in Report 2011/224 of 2 August 2011.

> The complainant here *inter alia* argued that police officers, by using pepper spray against him, had not respected his right to privacy, his right to physical integrity and his right to personal liberty. When assessing these allegations the NO took into account a judgment of the Supreme Court, a decision by the European Court of Human Rights, the Constitution and the Police Act.[80] After assessing all the circumstances of the case the NO decided that the conduct of the police officers had not respected the fundamental rights of the complainant and because of that their conduct was improper.

The compliance of administrative conduct with fundamental rights was also assessed in *Report 2012/195 of 4 December 2012.*

> The complainant here argued that municipality had contacted a social assistance institution without her consent and had forwarded her letter to that institution. She argued that by doing this the municipality had breached her right to respect for private life as included in Art. 10 Constitution and Art. 8 ECHR. The NO found that the municipality had reacted to the complainant's cry for help. The municipality considered this to be necessary. The NO appreciated the proactive approach of the municipality but he stated that the letter was sent specifically to the mayor of the municipality and that forwarding it without the consent of the complainant showed insufficient respect for her privacy. He did not see any particular reasons that would substantiate the action of the municipality without the consent of the complainant.[81]

Thus the NO found that the conduct of the municipality was in breach of the requirement of proper administration – respect for fundamental rights (the right to respect for one's private and family life). Although the NO does not do this on a large scale, the assessment of compliance with human rights or rather the assessment of *respect for fundamental rights* is a stable component of his work. Similar cases can be found in other reports of the NO.[82]

79 Requirement 5, Respect for fundamental rights, *Guidelines on proper conduct*, October 2012.
80 Report 2011/224 of 2 August 2011, paras. 12-27.
81 Report 2012/195 of 4 December 2012, *Beoordeling*.
82 See, for example, Report 2012/103 of 14 June 2012, Report 2011/076 of 3 March 2011, Report 2011/331 of 8 November 2011 or Report 2012/207 of 27 December 2012.

5.3.2 General principles of law as a normative standard of the National Ombudsman

Apart from the statutory law and human rights that are used as normative standards one can see that the normative standards of the NO partially and substantively overlap with several GPPA (whether codified or not).[83] This can give rise to the question of to what extent are these substantively overlapping normative standards identical, i.e. whether they offer the same amount of protection. In order to provide a partial answer to this question this section points to the application of two substantively overlapping standards. The first example is the application of the GPPA *of providing justification for a decision* and the NO's *requirement of providing adequate reasons*. The second one is an overlapping normative standard of the *proportionality principle/requirement*.

The principle of justifying the administrative decision is a traditional legal requirement of Dutch administrative law. The principle as codified in the GALA (Arts. 3:46 and 3:47) entails a *right to knowable reasons for a decision* and *the right to sound reasons sufficiently justifying the content of the decision*. The NO's requirement of providing adequate reasons requires public authorities to supply clear statements of the reasons for their actions and decisions. These statements should explain the statutory bases for the action or decision, the facts taken into consideration and the way in which citizens' interests have been taken into account. Moreover, citizens should be able to understand the statements.[84]

In the jurisprudence of the Dutch courts breaches of this principle include *inter alia* cases where no reasons at all were given or the reasons provided were unsatisfactory or incorrect;[85] cases where the interests were not weighed or collected;[86] cases where the administration did not indicate the applicable legal rules or it indicated them incorrectly;[87] cases where the reasons given were inconsistent;[88] situations in which the arguments of the parties were not examined satisfactorily or not examined at all;[89] or cases where the reasons of the administration were not in compliance with the applicable law.[90] As indicated in the case law, the Dutch courts connect this requirement with their ability to understand the administrative decision and ascertain whether the reasons justify the content of the decision.[91] The courts here do not go into the content of the administrative decision, they only assess whether the reasons provided can confirm the decision which was reached or whether there are any reasons for the decision. Even if they quash the administrative decision because of a breach of this particular legal principle, the result of the administrative processes' newly adopted administrative decision might be the same.

As the NO does not need to stick closely to the courts' perception of *providing adequate reasons*, one can presume that the application of his standard is less stringent.

83 See, Scheme 7.
84 Requirement 4 – *Adequate reasons*, Guidelines on proper conduct.
85 CRvB, 28-05-1999, AB 2000, 262 or CRvB, 24-02-1998, USZ 1998, 107.
86 ARRS, 20-05-1988, AB, 423.
87 ABRS, 10-06-1999, JB 1999, 172.
88 ARRS, 10-03-1978, AB 1978, 486.
89 ABRS, 02-02-2005, AB 2005, 336.
90 Rb. Den Haag, 10-04-2003, TAR 2003, 124.
91 For more on this particular principle see, for example, Pennarts 2008, pp. 51-64.

In the following three examples one can observe the application of the requirement of providing adequate reasons in the practice of the NO. In *Report 2013/023 of 23 March 2013* the NO explained that there are four main aspects of this requirement: the legal provisions, the facts and interests, and the clear reasoning.

> The reasoning must be directed at the individual case and must be *understandable* for its recipient. The NO here dealt with a complaint about the refusal to remedy the whole sum of the damage caused by the police corps. The NO found that the police administrator, when assessing the application of the complainant to remedy the damage, did not take into account the assessment of an independent expert submitted by the complainant and that it based its decision solely on the assessment of its internal body. This, in the opinion of the NO, led to a breach of the requirement to provide adequate reasons and to improper conduct.[92]

In *Report 2012/208 of 28 December 2012* the NO again underlined that the reasons for the administrative decision must be *understandable* to individuals.

> This case dealt with a complaint against the action of the police corps which started an investigation against the complainant based on an anonymous tip. The complainant was a freelance journalist and the anonymous tip was about him being a child molester. The tip was investigated. The NO found that the police corps had made use of an investigation which included a visit to the complainant. The case was closed without any positive result. As the police suspected that the complainant had lied an additional investigation was carried out. The complainant was not however informed about its results. According to the NO it was unclear what kind of investigation was involved in the additional investigation. The NO found that during this investigation the police corps had acted in breach of the requirement of providing adequate reasons as they did not share the results of the additional investigation with the complainant. He reached the conclusion that the information was important as it underlined the decision of the police. The NO concluded that the police corps had breached this requirement in connection with the additional investigation.[93]

The third example is *Report 2011/141 of 14 May 2011*. The complainant here had bought a diesel campervan with a special filter installed in Germany.

> He wanted to register the vehicle in the Dutch register of vehicles. The RDW (the Centre for Vehicle Technology and Information) refused to register this van as it stated that it is the only body that can approve the instalment of such a special filter. It referred to the former secondary legislation on subsidies of the Ministry of Infrastructure and the Environment. The complainant did not agree and argued that the filter was installed in accordance with EU rules which must be accepted in the Netherlands. He complained that the RDW had approved the importation of the vehicle into the Netherlands but rejected its registration. As the intervention of the NO was not successful he started an investigation. During the investigation he found that the decision of the RDW referred only to secondary legislation concerning grants which in no way was applicable to the

92 See, Report 2013/023 of 23 March 2013, *Beoordeling*.
93 See, Report 2012/208 of 28 December 2012, *Bevindingen en beoordeling*, para. 6.1.

> present case. It was not clear which regulations were applicable to the present case and based on what regulation the RDW had rejected the registration. The NO found that the reasoning of the decision not to register the vehicle was not sufficient.

These examples of the NO's practice show that the application of his normative standards is *not that different* as regards the courts' application. One can see that the assessment of the principle depends on the individual circumstances of the case. In the previous cases one can observe that the NO found a breach of the requirement because of not taking into account the evidence submitted by the complainant (case 1), not sharing the results of the investigation that underlined the decision (case 2) and not being clear about the applicable rules (case 3). These three cases are very similar to the perception of the court's principle. One can argue that there is *not a big difference* in the application of the requirement to provide adequate reasons and the principle of justification. However, it is necessary to point to the fact that the NO in all three cases underlined the necessity for an *individual to understand the reasons for the administrative decision*. In this connection this requirement goes further than the GPPA. Neither the written nor the unwritten GPPA require that the reasons provided by the administration should be understandable for an individual. It is enough if the administration or the court in appellate proceedings can understand them.[94]

The principle of proportionality is another legal principle that is found in Dutch law. The principle is nowadays codified in the GALA. According to the GALA the adverse consequences of an *administrative decision* for the interested parties cannot be disproportionate to the aims that have to be attained by the decision. The NO's requirement of proportionality similarly requires the public authorities, in pursuing their aims, to avoid *measures* that have an unnecessary impact on citizens' lives or measures that are disproportionate to the aims concerned. As can be seen in Scheme 7 the normative standards discovered by the courts and developed by the NO protect the balance between the aims and means of administrative actions. The weighing of aims and means is important for both normative concepts and for both institutions.

After the codification in the GALA the principle of proportionality was also explained by an important 'landmark' *judgment of 9 May 1996 of the ABRvS*.[95] The ABRvS here stated that judges should not assess which adverse effects on an individual are disproportionate and which are not, or which outcome of the weighing of interests must be considered as the most balanced. The judge must exercise restraint in testing the weighing of interests as conducted by the administration.[96] Judges respect the discretion of the administration in its decision making and they only intervene in cases when the weighing of interests was *manifestly incorrect* and would amount to *arbitrariness*.[97] Thus, the courts should apply the so-called marginal test.

94 Among the published reports of the NO I did not find an example pointing to this part of the requirement.
95 ABRvS, 09-05-1996, JB 1996, 158 (Praxis en Maxis).
96 Ibid.
97 Seerden & Wenders 2012, p. 145.

The approach of the NO is described in the following three cases. It was included in *Report 2011/220 of 29 July 2011* where the NO dealt with a complaint against the way in which the complainant had been arrested.

> The complainant had been arrested by four police officers in the university library while sitting behind a computer. Here, without a single warning, he was grabbed by the neck from behind by a police officer while two other police officers grabbed him by the hands so that he could be handcuffed and brought to a police station. The NO found that the complainant often carried and used a pepper spray. In the past a pistol had been found on him and he allegedly possessed other weapons. The investigation, however, did not show that the complainant had resisted any previous arrest or that his actions were unpredictable because of drug misuse. In the opinion of the NO it was not necessary to arrest the complainant without warning with the use of force and to directly handcuff him. A less severe method of apprehension could have been used. Because of the disproportionality this action was thus improper.[98]

Another example can be found in *Report 2008/215 of 2 October 2008*. Here the NO assessed the conduct of the Employee Insurance Schemes Implementing Body (UWV) in connection with a disabled unemployed person.

> A specialist from the UWV originally found that the complainant could be reintegrated into the working process via special training. Later he changed his opinion about the complainant's abilities. The complainant inquired about the reasons for this change by means of several unpleasant, but not rude emails. Due to this he was prohibited from entering the UWV building and he was only allowed to communicate with the UWV in writing. In this connection the NO assessed the proportionality of this prohibition. The NO stated that the internal instruction of the UWV shows how to deal with aggressive or misbehaving clients. The NO found that the internal instruction allowed various measures to be used against misbehaving clients and refusing entry was one of the most severe. During the investigation the NO did not find that the communication of the complainant to the UWV was aggressive, abusive or that it expressed threats. He also did not find any physical violence on the part of the complainant towards UWV employees. Based on these facts the NO concluded that the action of the UWV had been disproportionate and thus improper.[99]

The third example can be found in *Report 2009/055 of 25 March 2009* that dealt with a complaint against a municipal forest ranger.

> The NO found that the complainant, while walking with his girlfriend and her dogs in a forest, had been stopped by a forest ranger who asked for their identity as their dogs were not on a leash as required by the law. The complainant's girlfriend, the owner of the dogs, gave a false name. After that they left by car. As soon as the forest ranger realised that a false identity had been given he wanted to stop their car. He did this by using his own car. He succeeded, and forced the complainant's car off the road and onto the kerb. Although providing a false identity and walking dogs without a leash in that particular

98 Report 2011/220 of 29 July 2011, *Beoordeling*.
99 Report 2008/215 of 2 October 2008, *Beoordeling*, para. 29.

> forest are punishable offences, the NO was not convinced that the force used by the forest ranger to stop the complainant was proportionate to the nature of the offences. According to the NO the investigating officer must in principle use the method that is the least burdensome for the suspect. He argued that the powers to arrest somebody even under criminal law must be moderate and proportionate. In this case he reached the conclusion that the use of force by the forest ranger was not proportionate and thus it breached the requirements of proper administration.[100]

Despite the fact that the value protected by the requirements and the principles is similar their application shows slight deviations. While the courts use this principle only in connection with the marginal test and find a breach only if there is a *manifestly incorrect* weighing of interests, the NO goes somewhat further. In all the cases described the conduct of the investigated institutions was consistent with the law. A person can be arrested (case 1), an entry can be prohibited (case 2) or a person can be fined (case 3).

The NO does not require *manifestly disproportionate conduct* in order to find a breach of the requirement of proper administration of proportionality. When one looks at the previous cases probably only in the last case can the weighing of interests be characterised as manifestly incorrect. In other cases the manifestly incorrect weighing of interests by the investigated institution is at least arguable. Thus technically, the NO can apply his normative standards in a more stringent fashion. He can do this because of/thanks to the greater flexibility of his standards. At the same time one can note that while the courts deal with the proportionality of the administrative *decision* and its adverse effects, the NO's requirement covers the proportionality of the administrative *measure* and/or its adverse effects.

5.3.3 Exclusively ombudsman principles as a normative standard

The Dutch courts are entrusted with the assessment of compliance with the law. They do not assess compliance with moral or extra-legal principles. Still, one can ponder how the courts 'discover' new principles of law. Can they find them within the sphere of morality or good governance? Can such a 'dormant' and possibly extra-legal principle become a legal principle? On the other hand, none of the requirements of proper administration that have been developed and 'codified' by the NO form the law. In Scheme 7 one can observe that there is a certain substantive overlap between the normative standards of the NO and the GPPA. However, not all of the normative standards overlap. Some of the requirements of proper administration do not have their reflection in the GPPA or the law, they are only extra-legal. The extra-legal character of some of the requirements does not mean that theoretically they cannot become binding legal rules. According to Addink, the requirements of proper administration can be seen as a *big group that includes legal norms in different stages of their development but also norms that are not nowadays considered to be legal norms.*[101] However, one must acknowledge that the NO cannot magically turn these extra-legal standards into legal ones, as only the legislator or a court can do that.

100 Report 2009/055 of 25 March 2009, *Beoordeling I*, para. 18.
101 Addink 2010, p. 13.

The normative standards of the NO that for now belong to the category of *exclusively ombudsman standards* can theoretically become legal principles. The same is applicable in the case of overlapping standards that provide broader or different protection. However, not all of the ombudsnorms probably have this potential. These standards can be found, for example, in cases where the NO assesses compliance with the requirements such as requirement 3 – *Listen to citizens*,[102] requirement 7 – *Courtesy*[103] or requirement 15 – *De-escalation*.[104] However, as the courts do not use these standards it is not possible to compare their application.

5.4 Summary

This chapter tries to answer the question of *what is the mutual significance of the normative standards of the ombudsmen and the judiciary in the Netherlands and what are the interrelations between these normative standards.*

One can observe that there is not that much *formal normative coordination* between the NO and the Dutch courts. The law expressly recognises the *requirements of proper administration* assessed by the NO and the GPPA. In the case of the latter category, the law even partially codifies most of the legal principles in one statutory document (GALA). However, it is silent about particular coordination between the standards. The case law of the courts is also rather silent although the courts can possibly discover more rules about the relation of the NO's requirements and the GPPA or the law in general.

Despite the limited formal normative coordination one can observe that the development of these normative standards is interconnected. Especially the requirements of proper administration are often an *extra-legal reflection of the legal principles*. Based on historical documents this reflection and a certain similarity as to the substance of the principles have existed since the first 'codification' of the NO's requirements in the 1980s. Similarity between the normative standards of the courts and of the NO has its *formal* and *substantive* part. While a formal part points to the denomination of the normative standards, a substantive part goes into the content (the substance) of the individual normative standards. This substantive similarity means that the NO and the courts can use their powers to provide protection against a certain type of administrative action and by that they protect a general value that encompasses both types of normative standards. This also means that some of the values are protected in a 'hard way' by the courts as well as in a 'soft way' by the NO. The NO potentially goes further as parts of his requirements do not reflect the legal principles and thus some general values are protected only in an extra-legal way by the standards of the NO. In general, he is not bound by the normative standards used by the courts in similar cases or the application of these standards by the courts. The NO does not specifically deal with administrative *decisions* but with

102 For the meaning of the requirement *Listen to citizens* see Annex 3 a). See, also Report 2012/024 of 21 February 2012, Report 2012/064 of 17 April 2012 or Report 2012/127 of 21 August 2012.

103 For the meaning of the requirement *Courtesy* see Annex 3 a). See, also Report 2013/060 of 29 May 2013, Report 2013/080 of 2 July 2013, or Report 2012/046 of 22 March 2012.

104 For the meaning of the requirement *De-escalation* see Annex 3 a). See, also Report 2012/111 of 21 June 2012, Report 2012/124 of 6 August 2012 or Report 2013/005 of 14 January 2013.

administrative conduct. He can go beyond the *marginal lawfulness test* that is applied by the courts to their decisions. As his recommendations are not binding he can go somewhat further as his powers are not glued to the law as the only applicable normative standard. Precisely this flexibility of proper administration makes the NO a *par excellence* protection for citizens which is additional to the protection provided by the courts.

PART III

RELATIONS BETWEEN OMBUDSMEN AND THE JUDICIARY IN ENGLAND

Part III of the book describes the relations between ombudsmen and the judiciary in England. The UK is one of the countries where the ombudsman is a stable part of the constitutional system.[1] It represents the oldest ombudsman system that is included in this book. It is also the system with a broad diversity of individual ombudsman institutions.[2] In July 2013, there are more than 20 bodies that meet the criteria of the Ombudsman Association and are recognized as ombudsmen and exercise their functions in the UK.[3] This part, however, deals only with two particular ombudsmen; the Parliamentary Commissioner for Administration (or the Parliamentary Ombudsman – PO) and the Commission for Local Administration in England (or the Local Government Ombudsmen – LGO). While in general, the PO has competence to control the UK government (the state administration) the LGO can only control local bodies in England (the local administration). However, this book *only* focuses on the situation in England. The UK in general, Scotland, Wales and Northern Ireland were excluded from this research. This part also describes the position of the judiciary in England including the courts and the tribunal system.

The competences, functions and decisions of the PO and the LGO are described in Chapter 1. Chapter 2 describes the court system and the system of tribunals in England. The formal and informal *institutional coordination* between ombudsmen and the judiciary is discussed in Chapter 3. Chapter 4 analyses the *case coordination* between these institutions. Chapter 5 examines their *normative coordination*.

1 Cf. Abraham 2008, p. 206 or Gay 2008, p. 2ff.

2 One can argue that with regard to population size, it is Belgium that has the highest concentration of ombudsman institutions. Cf. Longley & James 1999, p. 47 or Kucsko-Stadlmayer 2008.

3 <www.ombudsmanassociation.org/association-members.php> (accessed on 31 July 2013).

Chapter 1

THE PARLIAMENTARY OMBUDSMAN AND THE LOCAL GOVERNMENT OMBUDSMEN

1.1 The Parliamentary Ombudsman

The PO was the first ombudsman established in the UK. After long debates on the issue of the necessity and applicability of the ombudsman scheme in the British constitutional system, in 1967 the British Parliament enacted *the Parliamentary Commissioner Act 1967* (the 1967 Act).[1] The 1967 Act has been amended on multiple occasions and it is the main source of the PO's functions and competences.[2]

The PO was created as the *Parliamentary Commissioner for Administration* (PCA). This formal title is nowadays used only rarely, however. One of the reasons for this is the fact that the same person who is the PCA is also the *Health Service Commissioner for England.*[3] Because of this, these two institutions work together under the name of the *Parliamentary and Health Service Ombudsman* (PHSO). This book, however, deals only with *the parliamentary branch* of the PHSO office – the *Parliamentary Ombudsman* (PO).

1.1.1 Functions of the Parliamentary Ombudsman

This section delimits and describes the PO's functions according to the general model designed in Part 1.[4]

1.1.1.1 Control function and protection and dispute resolution function

The basis of the *control function* of the PO is the 1967 Act. According to sec. (1) of the 1967 Act the purpose of the PO *is conducting investigations.* Also the Statement of Responsibilities between the PHSO and the Cabinet Office, HM Treasury, Department of

1 Gregory & Giddings 2002, p. 12ff.

2 For the legal framework of the PO, see, <www.ombudsman.org.uk/about-us/who-we-are/history-and-legislation/legislation-for-the-po> (accessed on 31 July 2013).

3 Kirkham 2007, p. 21, note 1.

4 The *Law Commission* in its *Consultation Paper No. 186* distinguishes between three different functions: to address individual complaints, to address systematic failures and to disseminate knowledge across governance networks.

Health and the Ministry of Justice confirms that the role of the PO is *to provide a service to the public by undertaking independent investigations into complaints that government departments, the National Health Service in England and a range of other public bodies in the UK have not acted properly or fairly, or have provided a poor service.*[5] Investigations are an expression of the control function but also of the protection and dispute resolution function of the PO.

The protection and dispute resolution function is directly connected with individual complainants. It can be exercised through the complaints system.[6] The aim and vision of the PO's office is to provide an independent, high quality complaint handling service that rights individual wrongs, drives improvements in public services and informs public policy.[7] Sometimes the PO is described as a *citizen's defender.*[8] Undoubtedly, the PO protects individual complainants but it should be made clear that the PO cannot take sides as he/she must remain impartial and must take into account all of the circumstances of the case whether or not they favour the complainant. This function is also clearly present in the practice of the PO in seeking to conduct rapid, low-cost and informal dispute resolution.[9] This function is partially limited by the MP filter and the inability of the PO to conduct investigations of his/her own initiative.[10]

1.1.1.1.1 Subjects and matters within the competence of the Parliamentary Ombudsman

According to sec. 5(1) of the 1967 Act, the PO can investigate *any action taken by or on behalf of a government department* or *other authority,* to which the 1967 Act applies, and which has been *taken in the exercise of the administrative functions of that department or authority.* These actions have to *lead to injustice in consequence of maladministration.* The PO can also investigate failures to perform a relevant duty owed to members of the public (sec. 5 (1A) 1967 Act).[11]

The PO's competence is limited to those bodies that are expressly included in Schedule 2 of the 1967 Act (*Departments Etc Subject to Investigation*). The Schedule can be altered by an Order in Council.[12] In July 2013, the list of public authorities within the competence of the PO ranges from governmental departments (i.e. Department for Work and Pensions, Ministry of Defence) to non-departmental bodies (i.e. Standards Board for England, Tate Gallery) and agencies (i.e. Environment Agency, Food Standards Agency).[13]

5 Para. 5 of the Statement of Responsibilities.
6 See, section 1.1.1.1.2.
7 Annual Report 2011/12 (*Moving forward*), p. 4.
8 Purdue 2009, p. 882.
9 Cf. Parliament's Ombudsman: Information for the staff of MPs, PHSO-0112 August 2010, p. 5.
10 See, section 1.1.1.1.2.
11 These duties stem from codes of practice issued under Sec. 32 of the Domestic Violence, Crime and Victims Act 2004 (Code of practice for victims).
12 An *order in Council* is delegated legislation that contains a set of regulations relating to matters covered by the enabling power. It is issued by the Monarch on the advice of the Privy Council. See, Carroll 2003, p. 133ff.
13 See also <www.ombudsman.org.uk/make-a-complaint/how-to-complain/government-departments-and-other-public-bodies-which-the-ombudsman-can-investigate> (accessed on 31 July 2013).

According to Purdue, the 1967 Act (sec. 5(1)) also enables the PO to assess public services that have been contracted out to the private sector.[14]

According to sec. 5 (2) of the 1967 Act the PO cannot conduct an investigation with regard to any action in respect of which the person aggrieved has or had a right of appeal, or a reference or review to or before a tribunal constituted by or under any enactment or by virtue of Her Majesty's prerogative and with regard to any action in respect of which the person aggrieved has or had a remedy by way of proceedings in any court of law. This legal bar can only be overcome if the PO is satisfied that in the particular circumstances it is not reasonable to expect an individual to resort or to have resorted to these remedies.[15] Apart from matters that shall not be investigated there are also administrative actions that stand *ex lege* outside the PO's remit. Schedule 3 of the 1967 Act includes *matters that are excluded from the Parliamentary Ombudsman's jurisdiction*. According to the schedule the PO cannot expressly investigate, for example

- any exercise of the prerogative of mercy or of the power of a Secretary of State to make a reference in respect of any person to the High Court of Justice or the Court Martial Appeal Court;
- actions taken by any member of the administrative staff of a relevant tribunal, so far as that action is taken at the direction, or on the authority (whether express or implied), or any person acting in his capacity as a member of the tribunal or
- action taken by any person appointed by the Lord Chancellor as a member of the administrative staff of any court or tribunal, so far as that action is taken at the direction, or on the authority whether express or implied, of any person acting in a judicial capacity or in his capacity as a member of the tribunal.[16]

1.1.1.1.2 Complaints and own initiative investigations

If the PO wants to exercise his/her functions there has to be a *complaint*. This is a necessary prerequisite for each and every investigation. Complaints are connected with several requirements. According to sec. 5 of the 1967 Act, a complaint to the PO must be *duly made*. This includes a written complaint by the aggrieved person to a Member of Parliament within twelve months after the administration had a chance to deal with the complaint.

The PO cannot investigate complaints coming directly from individual complainants – only a *Member of Parliament* or, more precisely, a *Member of the House of Commons* can refer a complaint to the PO and ask him to investigate it. In practice, if the complaint is submitted directly to the PO it is forwarded to a constituency MP or some other MP who may submit the complaint back so that the precondition of the 1967 Act can be satisfied.[17] This *MP filter* is generally perceived as being outdated[18] and an obstacle to

14 Purdue 2009, p. 887.

15 This issue is discussed in depth in section 3.1.1 in connection with the judiciary.

16 Sec. 7, sec. 6B (1) and sec. 6A (1) Schedule 3.

17 Purdue 2009, p. 892.

18 Kirkham 2007, p.12 or *Report on the consultation on direct access to the Parliamentary Ombudsman*, Parliamentary and Health Service Ombudsman (2011) etc.

direct communication between complainants and the PO.[19] It is true that the PO, together with the *Assembly Ombudsman for Northern Ireland* (a part of the Northern Ireland Ombudsman), are probably the only European ombudsmen who cannot be directly accessed by complainants.[20] The *MP filter* represents the *first limitation* on the functions of the PO.

Sec. 5 (1) (a) of the 1967 Act expressly requires *a written complaint* to an MP. Oral complaints, complaints by telephone or complaints via email to the PO are considered as *an enquiry*. The complaint has to be made no later than *twelve months* from the day on which the person aggrieved first had notice of the matters alleged in the complaint. In special circumstances the PO may conduct an investigation even if the complaint was made after this time limit.[21]

The PO will only entertain a complaint *after* the complainant has tried to resolve his dispute with the administration, and received a response therefrom. The incumbent PO, Dame Mellor, argues that the body concerned should be given a chance to respond and, where appropriate, to try to put things right before the PO becomes involved.[22] Also, the former PO, Ms Abraham, was of the opinion that 'if [the public bodies] have not had an opportunity to handle the complaint, we consider such a complaint to have come to us prematurely, and we will generally decline to investigate it at that point and ask people to make full use of the local complaints process.'[23] If the body concerned has established a second-tier complaints handling body, it is normally expected that the complainant seeks to resolve the complaint by contacting that body before complaining to the PO.[24]

In accordance with sec. 5 (1) a) and 5A (1) a) of the 1967 Act, the complaint has to be made by 'a member of the public who claims to have sustained injustice in consequence of maladministration in connection with the action so taken or a member of the public who claims that a person has failed to perform a relevant duty owed by him to the member of the public.' Thus, the complaint must be submitted by a *directly aggrieved person*. Of course, if the person that has been directly aggrieved has died or is for any reason unable to act for himself or herself a complaint can be made by a personal representative or by a member of his or her family or by another individual who is suitable to represent the aggrieved person.[25] The 1967 Act gives the PO discretion in determining whether to initiate, continue or discontinue an investigation.

The *second limitation* on the PO's protection and dispute resolution function is connected with the absence of the PO's authority to conduct own-initiative investigations. For now,

19 Purdue 2009, p. 892 or Buck et al. 2011, p. 99 etc.

20 The Assembly Ombudsman for Northern Ireland has a similar filter. In this case, the complaint has to be taken to the Members of the Northern Ireland Assembly. Until the legislative changes in 2011, also the former French *Médiateur de la République* was only accessible through a Member of the French Parliament.

21 Sec. 6 (3) the 1967 Act.

22 *Bringing a complaint to the Parliamentary Ombudsman*, PHSO-0042 March 2012.

23 Annual Report 2008/09 *(Every complaint matters)*, p. 8.

24 <www.ombudsman.org.uk/make-a-complaint/information-for-mps/action-which-the-ombudsman-can-investigate> (accessed on 31 July 2013).

25 Sec. 6 (2) the 1967 Act.

the PO does not have formal competence to start such investigations. This is closely connected with the fact that the investigation of the PO can only be started following a complaint sent to an MP.

1.1.1.1.3 Investigation procedure

Apart from certain provisions, the law (including the 1967 Act) does not prescribe any general procedure as regards the PO's investigation or complaint handling. The PO has discretion in this connection. Thus, theoretically, each new PO can change or bring something new to the procedure. In the wording of the 1967 Act, 'the procedure for conducting an investigation shall be such as the Parliamentary Ombudsman considers appropriate in the circumstances of the case.'[26] In general, all investigations are conducted in private.[27]

The *complaints procedure* before the PO includes several stages. After the complaint is received (the '*Access*' stage), the PO checks whether the complaint falls within his/her competences (the '*Triage*' stage). After this the PO checks whether the complaint can be resolved quickly without the need for an investigation.[28] If this is not possible the PO, during the '*Investigation*' stage, informs the organisation concerned about the investigation. Based on the evidence the ombudsman comes to a *judgment* and informs both parties accordingly.[29] In general, the PO can use a number of investigative tools. It is possible to require an administrative body and/or other persons to provide information and to produce documents which are relevant to the investigation[30] or to hear witnesses.[31] Another stage, the '*Action*' stage, is connected with the action of the PO. If the PO upholds the complaint, he/she asks the body to take steps to resolve it (to provide an individual or future-oriented remedy). Generally, the investigation can lead to three possible results: there has been maladministration leading to injustice; there has maladministration which has not led to injustice; and there has been no maladministration. If the PO finds a case of maladministration he/she compiles an investigation report. If the investigation has not disclosed any maladministration the PO usually rejects the complaint without a report and he/she sends the MP and the complainant the *statement of reasons for not investigating the complaint*. At another stage, the '*Insight*' stage, the PO uses the experience from his/her investigations to help the public services to improve, to tell Parliament why things have gone wrong and to improve the complaints system. In the last potential stage, the '*Review*' stage, the PO considers complaints about his/her decisions or his/her service.[32]

In the practice of the PO one can also discover mechanisms of *informal dispute resolution*. The Annual Report 2009/10 addresses the so-called *intervention short of*

26 Sec. 7 (2) the 1967 Act.
27 Ibid.
28 Annual Report 2012/13 (*Aiming for impact*), p. 20.
29 A 'judgment' is the term used by the PO in the Annual Report 2012/13. See, ibid.
30 Sec. 8 (1) the 1967 Act.
31 Sec. 8 (2) the 1967 Act.
32 The new complaints procedure was introduced in April 2013 in order to decrease the *preliminary work* so that more *full investigations* can be carried out and more complaints can lead to *formal and final findings*. See, Annual Report 2012/13 (*Aiming for impact*), p. 20.

investigation when the PO informally intervenes with the administrative body to put things right quickly. Resolution through intervention can be attempted at any stage of the assessment process.[33] The body complained of is asked to provide a remedy which can resolve the complaint without the need for an investigation. The PO uses this approach where appropriate. An *intervention short of investigation* can lead, for example, to an apology and/or an explanation, but also to a request for financial compensation.[34] Intervention is a stable part of the PO's practice.[35] Although the latest Annual Report 2012/13 does not expressly discuss the practice of intervention, it implicitly confirms this practice. This annual report argues that in cases where the PO finds that an organisation has not acted correctly, the PO will ask it to take action to put things right. This can include apologies, compensation payments, wider remedies or other actions.[36] The changes introduced by the 1967 Act expressly allowed the PO to engage in *mediation*. In accordance with sec. 3 (1A) of the 1967 Act the PO may appoint and pay a mediator or other appropriate person to *assist him* in the conduct of an investigation under this Act. As is apparent from the PO's annual reports, mediation is not frequently used.

1.1.1.2 Redress function

The 1967 Act does not enumerate remedies that can be granted by the PO. In truth, it does not even give the PO any formal authority to *award* or *grant* remedies. The PO can only *recommend* a remedy by way of appropriate action that the body within his/her competence should take. The recommendations aim to remedy the injustice or hardship suffered and, where possible, to return the complainant to the position he or she would have been in if things had not gone wrong.[37] If the recommendations are not complied with, the PO cannot do much more. His/her reports, including recommendations to provide a remedy to an individual, are not legally enforceable. This lack of legal enforceability means that a complainant can be *de facto* left without a remedy.[38] The PO can however point to this fact in one of his/her reports and try to exert political pressure via Parliament.[39] But that is as far as the PO can go. The legally-binding character of the PO's recommendations or the enforcement of his/her decisions is sometimes considered to be counterproductive as it

33 Annual Report 2009/10 (*Making an impact*), p. 11.

34 Ibid., p. 14.

35 In 2000-01, 659 complaints (37% of the total) were the subject of an *intervention* with a positive outcome for the complainant (Annual Report 2000/01, p. 5). In 2010-11 intervention helped in only 107 parliamentary cases (Annual Report 2010/11, p. 10). In 2011-12, 491 cases were resolved this way (Annual Report 2011/12, p. 13). In 2010-11 intervention helped in only 107 parliamentary cases (Annual Report 2010/11, p. 10). According to *Responsive and Accountable? Statistical report on complaint handling by government departments and public organisations 2011-12* (December 2012) between 2011 and 2012 there were 100 cases of intervention.

36 Annual Report 2012/13 (*Aiming for impact*), p. 19.

37 <www.ombudsman.org.uk/make-a-complaint/information-for-mps/what-the-ombudsman-can-achieve-for-complainants> (accessed on 31 July 2013).

38 Seneviratne 2002, p. 132.

39 See, section 1.1.1.3.2. See also, Buck et al. 2011, p. 211ff and Appendix 7.

would 'alter the essential aspect of the ombudsman office, which is co-operation with the administration.'[40]

The major objective of the PO while remedying the injustice or hardship suffered is to 'return the complainant to the position he or she would have been in before this injustice caused by maladministration.'[41] This principle is connected with the complainant but also 'with others who have suffered injustice or hardship as a result of the same maladministration or poor service as the complainant.'[42] If the *restitution of the complainant to his position before maladministration* is not possible then the PO can recommend to the authority concerned that it apologizes, explains and/or acknowledges its responsibility;[43] that it reviews or changes a decision on the service given to the complainant, revises published material, revises procedures or policies to prevent the same thing from happening again, or trains or supervises staff[44] or provides a complainant with financial redress for direct or indirect financial loss, a loss of opportunity, inconvenience or distress.[45]

Although the acceptance of the PO's recommendations depends entirely on the body concerned, the recommendations are usually accepted. According to the Annual Report 2011/12, in 2011-12 the PO sought 1,730 remedies, *all of which* were accepted by the organisation complained about or were under consideration.[46] The latest Annual Report 2012/13 claims that in over 99% of cases organisations complied with her recommendations and resolved the complaint as she had asked them to do.[47]

1.1.1.3 Normative function and educational function

The *normative function* of the PO is generally accepted. In practice, the PO can try to counsel or advise the administrative bodies within his/her remit. One of his/her objectives is 'to work with others to use what she learns from complaints to help them make public services better and to lead the way in making the complaints system better.'[48] By sharing the lessons learnt from the complaints the PO tries to help to improve the way public services are provided.[49] Generally, the PO can try to influence and to improve the public services of administrative bodies through *recommendations, general guidelines* and practice-based *normative standards.*

The *potential educational function* is reflected in the effect of the normative function on the public bodies in question. The PO's educational function is partially limited. This limitation is connected with the fact that the PO does not and cannot publish all investigative reports. The 1967 Act accentuates the necessity of the private character of the

40 Seneviratne 2002, p. 132ff.
41 Getting it right, p. 6, *Principles for Remedy*, PHSO, 2009.
42 Acting fairly and proportionately, p. 9, *Principles for Remedy*, PHSO, 2009.
43 See, Report PA-3002/0058 (formerly C.1102/03) by the Parliamentary Commissioner for Administration (the Ombudsman). <www.pcaw.org.uk/files/ombud_report_pcaw.pdf > accessed on 31 July 2013.
44 Putting things right, p. 10, *Principles for Remedy.*
45 See, the PO's Special Report *A Debt of Honour*, para. 218.
46 Annual Report 2011/12 (*Moving forward*), p. 14.
47 Annual Report 2012/13 (Aiming for impact), p. 16.
48 <www.ombudsman.org.uk/improving-public-service> (accessed on 31 July 2013).
49 *Ombudsman's Principles publication*, Introduction, February 2010.

investigation which does not enable the publication of the PO individual reports.[50] Given the conditions, the administration and individuals can only learn from the *digest of cases*, *special* and *annual reports* and other guidelines or explanatory publications. Nonetheless, the potential educational function of the *investigation reports* is marginal.

1.1.1.3.1 Guidance of the Parliamentary Ombudsman

The PO has the ability to go beyond the individual case, to spot patterns of deficiency and to make recommendations for systemic changes that go much further than redressing the failings of a single individual's adverse encounter with an organ of the state.[51] The guidance practices of the PO are connected only with the recommendations of the reports, but the most outstanding example of the normative function of the PO are three sets of *Principles of Good Administration*. They are the PO's attempt to develop the role of the ombudsman from concentrating on individual complaints to diagnosing systemic failures through patterns of maladministration disclosed by a sequence of complaints.[52] The reason for presenting these principles was to be open and clear, with both complainants and public bodies within the PO's jurisdiction, about what is expected from the public bodies when they deliver certain services.[53] Apart from these principles,[54] the PO publishes the findings of his/her investigation such as the *NHS Governance of Complaints Handling research* or *customer satisfaction research*. One can also find guidance for individuals in several brochures such as *Your complaint and us: how we can help* or *Can we help you with your complaint?* etc.[55]

1.1.1.3.2 Reports of the Parliamentary Ombudsman

As noted by Woolf et al. the PO has *no power to make mandatory orders, but merely recommendations*.[56] The power of the PO's reports and recommendations, as is the case with the majority of the ombudsmen, depends on his/her ability to persuade the public bodies in question that it is better to comply with his/her reports and recommendations than to disagree with them. The 1967 Act (and also practice) recognizes several types of reports.

The investigation of the PO usually leads to a *report of the results of the investigation (investigation report)*.[57] An investigation report usually includes a description of the facts of the case, the criteria used, a description of the maladministration, a description of the injustice, statements by parties and possible recommendations by the PO.[58] If

50 The 1967 Act does not include an obligation or a right of the PO to publish investigation reports.
51 Abraham 2011, p. 11.
52 Gay 2008, p. 9.
53 Ombudsman's introduction to the Principles, p. 1.
54 They are discussed in greater detail in Chapter 5.
55 See, <www.ombudsman.org.uk/home> (accessed on 31 July 2013).
56 Woolf et al. 2007, p. 45.
57 Sec. 10 (1) the 1967 Act.
58 As investigation reports are not published and it is difficult to know their precise contents. These contents are created *per analogiam* with published *special* and *other* reports.

the investigation and its report do not lead to any results the PO can compile a *special report*. This is the strongest weapon in the PO's arsenal. The PO can lay this report before each House of Parliament in accordance with sec. 10 (3) of the 1967 Act if after an investigation it appears that injustice has been caused to a complainant in consequence of maladministration and this injustice has not been, or will not be, remedied. So far, the PO has only done this in 6 cases.[59] Special reports are always connected with substantive individual complaints. Thus his/her reports can be backed up by political influence and pressure from Parliament or Parliament's *Public Administration Select Committee.*

According to sec. 10 (4) of the 1967 Act the PO has an obligation to lay annually before each House of Parliament *a general report on the performance of his (her) functions* (*annual report*). These reports include general data on the complaints admitted, rejected and investigated. They usually also include examples of the most interesting individual reports. They describe the data and analyses of the complaints received during the year. They can also introduce new methods of or changes in investigation procedures.[60] Sec.10 (4) of the 1967 Act also enables the PO to submit from time to time before Parliament 'such other reports with regard to those functions as he thinks fit.' These *other* reports can include collections of cases against a particular departmental body or dealing with similar complaints. Specific types of 'other' reports are reports written together with other ombudsmen, for instance with the LGO.[61]

If the PO decides not to conduct an investigation, he/she has to send to the MP in question and to the body concerned *a statement of reasons for not conducting an investigation.*[62] The 1967 Act does not include an obligation for the PO to send the individual report or statement of reasons to the individual complainant; however, in practice these documents are also sent to this person. Apart from the reports, the PO can also express his/her opinions in *public consultations.*[63]

Despite the specific aspects of the English legal system, the previously discussed general ombudsman functions can also be identified in the practice of the PO. Generally, they overlap with the opinion of Harlow who notes that the *role of the Parliamentary Ombudsman should be that of an independent and unattached investigator, with a mandate to identify maladministration, recommend improved procedures and negotiate their implementation.*[64]

59 The first special report was submitted to Parliament in 1978, the case of *Rochester Way, Bexley*. It was followed by *Channel Tunnel Rail Link* (1995), *A Debt of Honour* (2005), *Trusting pension promises* (2006), *Injustice unremedied: the Government's response on Equitable Life* (2008) and *Cold Comfort (2009).*

60 See, Annual Report 2006/07 (*Putting principles into practice*) introducing the Principles of Good Administration or the Annual Report 2012/13 (*Aiming for impact*) introducing a new complaint procedure.

61 See, report *Environmentally Unfriendly* of 10 January 2010 or Report by the PO and the LGO to Ms A MP on *the results of an investigation into a complaint made by Mr and Mrs C and T* of 16 July 2013. These reports were jointly investigated by the PO and the LGO.

62 In one specific case the PO replaced this statement with a report to Parliament. The report explained the reasons for *not conducting* a particular investigation. See, *Report the Ombudsman's assessment of the loss of personal data by a Home Office contractor* of 22 March 2010.

63 <www.ombudsman.org.uk/improving-public-service/reports-and-consultations/consultations> (accessed on 31 July 2013).

64 See, Harlow 1978.

1.2 The Local Government Ombudsmen

In comparison with the PO, the NO or the EUO, there are *two* Local Government Ombudsmen. The Local Government Ombudsmen are members of the *Commission for Local Administration in England*, an independent body that supports their activities. Its role is to provide an independent means of redress to individuals for injustice caused by unfair treatment or service failure by local authorities, schools and care providers and to use its learning to promote good public service administration and service improvement.[65] The Commission has three members: two Local Government Ombudsmen (the LGO)[66] and the PO who is an *ex lege* member of the Commission.[67] The competence of the Commission and the LGO covers only the territory of England.[68] They were established by the *Local Government Act 1974* (the 1974 Act) as amended by other legislative changes.[69] Other statutory documents include, for example the Regulatory Reform (Collaboration etc. between Ombudsmen) Order 2007, the Health Act 2009 and other acts.[70]

1.2.1 Functions of the Local Government Ombudsmen

Despite their interconnected, overlapping and merging character, also in the case of the LGO one can distinguish the five ombudsman functions that were discussed in Part 1.

1.2.1.1 Control function and protection and dispute resolution function

The *control function* of the LGO is based on sec. 23 (1) of the 1974 Act, according to which the LGO were created for the purpose *of conducting investigations*. The Commissioners are independent complaint investigators. Seneviratne notes that 'they are at the apex of a complaints system which consists of internal and external review and they are the 'ultimate rung' on the complaints ladder, providing a final, independent mechanism for citizens' grievances.'[71]

Their *protection and dispute resolution function* is directly connected with the individual complainants. In accordance with the 1974 Act the LGO protect individuals if they approach them with a complaint against the conduct of a local authority. An individual complaint, however, is not the only possibility based on which the LGO can start their investigation and subsequent protection. The latest changes introduced by the 1974 Act enabled the LGO to go somewhat further. According to sec. 26D of the 1974 Act, the LGO can theoretically investigate *matters coming to their attention* without an express

65 < www.lgo.org.uk/working-for-us/the-commission-and-its-role/ > (accessed on 31 July 2013).
66 The following text uses the abbreviation *LGO* in the plural (Local Government Ombuds*men)*.
67 Sec. 23 (2) the 1974 Act.
68 For a particular division of the territory of England see <www.lgo.org.uk/about-us/who-we-are/> (accessed on 31 July 2013).
69 The 1974 Act created two *Commissions for Local Administration* in England and in Wales. The situation in Wales is dealt with by the *Public Services Ombudsman for Wales*.
70 <www.lgo.org.uk/about-us/legal-framework/> (accessed on 31 July 2013).
71 Seneviratne 2002, p. 222.

complaint.[72] However, the complaint remains the most important method of attracting the attention of the LGO.[73] In disputes the LGO stand between the local authorities and individuals. In their own words, they are not 'consumer champions'.[74]

1.2.1.1.1 Subjects and matters within the competence of the LGO

Sec. 25 (1) of the 1974 Act enumerates the bodies that are covered by the competences of the LGO. These bodies include all English *local authorities* and their members, officers, several committees or sub-committees.[75] In July 2013, these authorities included, apart from local authorities, for example the National Park Authorities, the fire and rescue authorities in England, and the police authorities established under the Police Act 1996. The list of bodies subject to an LGO investigation can be changed or extended by an HM Order in Council.[76] The LGO investigate matters which relate to *actions* taken *by* or *on behalf* of these bodies. Within the meaning of the 1974 Act *actions* also cover *failures to act*. In these actions the LGO look for *alleged or apparent maladministration* and *alleged or apparent service failure*.[77]

Sec. 26 (6) of the 1974 Act limits the LGO in their investigations. They cannot investigate 'actions in respect of which the person affected has or had a right of appeal, reference or review to or before a tribunal constituted by or under any enactment; actions in respect of which the person affected has or had a right of appeal to a Minister of the Crown and actions in respect of which the person affected has or had a remedy by way of proceedings in any court of law.' However, if in the particular circumstances it is not reasonable to expect the person affected to resort or to have resorted to such a remedy the LGO have discretion to investigate the matter.[78]

In connection with the LGO's investigative powers sec. 34 (3) of the 1974 Act notes that 'nothing authorizes or requires the LGO to question the merits of the decision taken without maladministration by an authority in the exercise of a discretion vested in that authority.'[79] The LGO are thus explicitly prevented from investigating the merits of the administrative *decision* in the absence of any administrative failure. This may sometimes be a challenge as in some cases it could be difficult to separate the finding of maladministration from a shortcoming in the merits.[80] Furthermore, schedule 5 of the 1974 Act explicitly enumerates the matters that are not subject to LGO investigations, for example, the commencement or conduct of civil or criminal proceedings before any

72 See, section 1.2.1.1.1.
73 Annual reports and the internet site of the LGO do not say much about dealing with *matters coming to the LGO's attention*.
74 <www.lgo.org.uk/about-us/> (accessed on 31 July 2013).
75 See also Annual Report 2011/12, p. 43 or <www.lgo.org.uk/making-a-complaint/who-you-can-complain-about/> (accessed on 31 July 2013).
76 Sec. 25 (2) the 1974 Act.
77 Sec. 26 (1) the 1974 Act.
78 In relation to the judiciary these limitations are discussed in detail in section 3.1.1.
79 There is not complete agreement on what this article actually means as several explanations can be found. See, for example, Crawford 2002, p. 122ff.
80 Endicott 2011, p. 220.

court of law or actions taken by any police authority in connection with the investigation or prevention of crime.

1.2.1.1.2 Complaints and own initiative investigations

The LGO may commence their investigation if they receive *a complaint*. In general, the complaint has to be *written,* though nowadays one can complain by email, phone or fax and online.[81] If the complaint is referred to the LGO by a local authority such reference must be made in writing.[82] The complaint can be made by a *member of the public who claims to have sustained injustice*[83] as a consequence of the matter or by a person authorised in writing by such a member of the public to act on his behalf.[84]

The removal of the *local councillor filter* in 1988 allowed direct access to the LGO. Nowadays, the LGO can be approached either *directly by a complainant* or *via the member of a local authority*. In the latter case the consent of the complainant to refer the case to the LGO is required.[85] The complaint has to be submitted within 12 months since the day on which the person affected first had notice of the matter. The LGO can accept complaints submitted after this time limit, however.[86]

In accordance with sec. 26 (5) and sec. 24A (3) b) of the 1974 Act, before the LGO starts to investigate the complaint, the local authority has to be informed about the complaint. The local authority should have the possibility to deal with the complaint before the LGO start their investigation. It must be given a reasonable opportunity to investigate the matter and to respond to it. A breach of this provision means that the complaint is rejected by the LGO as premature. A fair time for the council to investigate and reply to the complaint is up to 12 weeks.[87]

The LGO do not have the explicit formal competence to conduct own-motion investigations. The exercise of their functions can start almost solely by means of a complaint. However, the LGO can *investigate matters coming into their attention*.[88] These investigations virtually lead to the LGO conducting investigations of their own motion. This power gives 'extra 'teeth' to the LGO so that they can make enquiries and, if necessary, recommendations in respect of people other than the complainant.'[89] An example of this practice that is posted on the website of the LGO is the case where a complaint that discloses maladministration in a housing allocation case reveals that a third party, rather than the complainant, has suffered injustice because s/he should have been allocated a property.[90] Thus, the matter

81 Annual Report 2007/08, p. 6.
82 Sec. 26C (2) the 1974 Act.
83 Members of the public are individuals or a body of persons other than local or other public authorities (sec. 27 (1) the 1974 Act).
84 Sec. 26A (1) the 1974 Act.
85 Sec. 26C (2) the 1974 Act.
86 Sec. 26B (2) the 1974 Act.
87 <www.lgo.org.uk/making-a-complaint/submitting-a-complaint/> (accessed on 31 July 2013).
88 Sec. 24A (5) a) the 1974 Act.
89 <www.lgo.org.uk/guidance-on-jurisdiction/apparent-maladministration/> (accessed on 31 July 2013).
90 Ibid.

must come to the LGO's attention during the investigation of some other complaint and it must appear to them that a member of the public other than the complainant has, or may have, suffered injustice as a consequence of the matter.[91]

Because of the limited practice and interpretation of this legal provision by the LGO it is uncertain whether this power can actually lead to a *broad own-initiative investigation* as in the case of ombudsmen who have this authority *expresis verbis*. Buck et al. argue that this power is a *sensible solution* that provides the LGO with additional flexibility.[92] Still, it is more than what the PO can offer, but it is only a 'half-built house' compared to the ombudsmen who have this particular authority.

1.2.1.1.3 Investigation procedure

As the 1974 Act does not describe the LGO's investigation in any great detail, the Commissioners have a wide discretion as to how to conduct the investigation. Because of this the LGO have developed their own investigation procedure as regards complaints. There are two main stages of this procedure.

The first stage is the so-called *initial assessment*. During this stage the LGO assess whether they can accept the complaint for investigation, based on the facts submitted to them by the complainant. Here they follow their *Assessment Code*.[93] This code is applied to all complaints and it includes two sub-stages. In the *jurisdictional stage* the LGO check whether there are any legal restrictions on the investigation (including a premature complaint or a lack of competence etc.).[94] In the *discretionary stage* they deal with the choices that they can make in connection with the discretion to investigate given to them by the law. This second sub-stage includes the application of several tests. The injustice test assesses the level of personal injustice suffered by the complainant. The fault test assesses the scale and nature of the fault. The remedy test assesses how likely it is that a meaningful outcome to the complaint will be achieved and the public interest test assesses the level of the wider public interest arising from the individual case.[95] According to the Annual Report 2011/12 complaints are not investigated if the LGO do not have the power to investigate or there is no reason to use the exceptional power to investigate or an investigation is not justified.[96]

If the complaint passes these tests the LGO can commence an *investigation in a strict sense*. The LGO have a range of options that they can use in their investigations. These include informal contacts with the administration, visits to the authorities concerned, on-site investigations or the examination of files and the hearing of witnesses.[97] Both the local authority and the complainant are given an opportunity to comment on the draft results of the investigation or to provide further information. The final decision is also sent to both

91 Sec. 26D (1) c) the 1974 Act.
92 Buck et al. 2011, p. 126.
93 <www.lgo.org.uk/making-a-complaint/how-we-will-deal-with-your-complaint/assessment-code/> (accessed on 31 July 2013).
94 Sec. 26 (5) the 1974 Act.
95 All these tests are described in detail in the LGO's *Assessment Code* published on the LGO internet site.
96 Annual Report 2011/12 (*Delivering Public Value*), p. 41.
97 Sec. 29 (2) the 1974 Act.

parties. The investigations are conducted in private.[98] But conducting an investigation does not affect any action taken by the authority concerned, or any power or duty of that authority to take further action with respect to any matters that are the subject of the investigation.[99] At any stage of the investigation the LGO may consider conducting the investigation of a complaint jointly with other ombudsmen.[100]

The LGO can use various *informal dispute resolution mechanisms*. If the LGO find that the local authority has done something wrong they can *suggest that the body puts things right*. If the local authority accepts these suggestions they can discontinue their investigation.[101] Before April 2011 this practice of the LGO was called *local settlement*. A local settlement could occur at various stages of the investigation. In this connection the LGO stated that *councils sometimes volunteer settlements in response to our first enquiries about a complaint.*[102] After the views of both sides have been considered the LGO could either approve the settlement and discontinue enquiries or continue with the investigation. A fair number of cases were settled in this way. In 2009/10 around 28% of all complaints were settled in this way[103] and in 2010/11 this was around 26.8%.[104] The Annual Report 2011/12 replaced the term *local settlements* with the term *injustice remedied during enquiries.*[105] Around 21% of cases were solved in this way.[106] The Annual Report 2012/13 uses the term *an agreement to put things right*. This report however does not specify the number of cases solved in this way.[107] Sec. 29 (6A) of the 1974 Act enables the LGO to appoint and pay a mediator or another appropriate person to assist them in the conduct of an investigation. The last four annual reports of the LGO do not include comprehensive information on the use of a mediator. Nonetheless, some documents posted on the LGO internet site indirectly refer to this particular practice.[108]

1.2.1.2 Redress function

One of the aims of the LGO is to obtain redress for people who have suffered injustice as a result of something the council has done wrong (maladministration).[109] In general, there is no legal power for the LGO to *award damages* to a complainant. They can only *recommend* remedies that should put things, that went wrong, right. Generally, the LGO

98 Sec. 28 (2) the 1974 Act.
99 Sec. 28 (4) the 1974 Act.
100 Sec. 33ZA the 1974 Act.
101 Sec. 24 (7) b) the 1974 Act.
102 Annual Report 2007/08, p. 15.
103 Annual Report 2009/10, p. 12.
104 Annual Report 2010/11 (*Delivering Public Value*), p. 23.
105 Ibid., p. 41.
106 Ibid., p. 18.
107 See, Annual Report 2012/13 (*Raising the standards*), p. 9.
108 The LGO Annual Review: Southampton City Council for the year ended 31 March 2009, p. 5 or Local authority report – Cambridgeshire CC for the period ending – 31/03/2011, p. 3 etc.
109 Annual Report 2008/09, p. 21.

ask the organisation responsible for *the fault*[110] to take action to right the wrong in cases where this is still possible.[111] The local bodies *should* follow these recommendations.[112] If the LGO find maladministration, they can make recommendations to the local authority to remedy any injustice sustained by the person affected in consequence of the maladministration or the failure.[113] The 1974 Act does not specify the types of remedies that can be recommended by the LGO. The key focus of the LGO is on *restorative justice*.[114] This includes the following types of remedies: to apologise;[115] to take action (e.g. to carry out repairs to the complainant's council home)[116] and to review or reconsider the policies and procedures,[117] including taking a decision that should have been taken previously[118] or to reconsider a decision which has already been taken.[119] Only if such redress cannot be achieved should the local authority consider compensatory payments for the injustice caused.[120]

There is a very high rate of compliance with the recommendations of the LGO. It is around 99 per cent. This justifies the view that it is not necessary for the LGO to have powers to enforce their recommendations.[121] In 2011/12, *all LGO recommendations were accepted* in cases that were closed without a report and only two councils did not implement the recommendations made in the reports.[122] In the past, this was not always that the case and the LGO had many problems in persuading the local administration about the truth of their findings.[123]

110 The term *maladministration* is disappearing from the annual reports of the LGO. See, the last two annual reports.

111 Annual Report 2011/12 (*Delivering Public Value*), p. 26.

112 As will be noted later (in Chapters 3 and 4) the finding of maladministration by the LGO is *binding unless challenged in the judicial review procedure*.

113 Sec. 30 (1A), 31(2B) a) 31(2BA) a) the 1974 Act.

114 Annual Report 2011/12 (*Delivering Public Value*), p. 13.

115 See, Report on an investigation into complaint no. 08 014 087 against Brighton and Hove Council where the LGO recommended to apologize to the complainant for the failure in the procedure.

116 See, Report on an investigation into complaint no. 07/B/15371 against the London Borough of Lambeth where the LGO recommended the borough to agree to complete any works that were still required within three months from the date of the independent surveyor's report.

117 See, Report on an investigation into complaint no. 09 006 783 against Blaby District Council where the LGO recommended the council to review the procedures to ensure that officers were aware that flexibility is needed when policies are applied.

118 See, Report on an investigation into complaint no. 05/C/03367 against Redcar & Cleveland Borough Council where the LGO recommended the council to consider and reach a decision on the complainant's request and to establish internal arrangements as to how such requests will be considered and decided in the future.

119 See, Report on an investigation into complaint nos. 07B15825 & 08 007 844 against Havant Borough Council where the LGO recommended the council to reconsider the decisions regarding concessionary travel.

120 Annual Report 2011/12 (*Delivering Public Value*), p. 13. See, Report on an investigation into complaint no. 09 005 422 against Harlow District Council where the LGO recommended the council to pay compensation to the complainant.

121 Annual Report 2011/12 (*Delivering Public Value*), p. 13.

122 Annual Report 2011/12 (*Delivering Public Value*), p. 27. The Annual Report 2012/13 (*Raising the standards*) did not include any information on this issue.

123 Bailey et al. 2005, p. 195.

1.2.1.3 Normative function and educational function

The LGO are also active in creating guidelines and norms with a potential educational effect. Both functions are connected with the normative standards developed and applied in their practice. The normative and educational functions of the LGO are not expressly mentioned in the 1974 Act, although they can be implied therein. The normative function is directly connected with the *Commission for Local Administration in England*. The 1974 Act allows the Commission (and not the LGO), after consultation with the authorities concerned, *to provide to the authorities such advice and guidance about good administrative practice* as appears to be *appropriate*. The Commission may arrange for it to be *published for the information of the public.*[124]

1.2.1.3.1 Advice and guidance of the Local Government Ombudsmen

The *Commission for Local Administration in England* is the statutory body which provides the resources to support the activities of the LGO. It has powers to publish advice and guidance on good practice.[125] Such advice and guidance may be provided after appropriate consultation with the representative persons and authorities concerned. The 1974 Act enables the LGO to make recommendations that would *prevent injustice* being caused in the future in consequence of similar maladministration or in consequence of a similar failure in connection with the exercise of the authority's administrative functions.[126]

The guidance of the Commission and the LGO includes focus reports, joint publications, guidance notes and special reports. The *focus reports* are a new style of themed publications published by the LGO on particular subjects of complaints which draw on lessons learnt from complaints and include recommendations on good practice.[127] Collaboration between the LGO and other bodies may lead to the production of *joint publications.*[128] *Guidance notes* are written to provide guidance to bodies within the LGO's jurisdiction. They reflect the normative function of the LGO. In July 2013, they included four sets of documents, namely *Running a complaints system*, *Guidance on financial remedies*, *Guidance note on managing unreasonable complainant behaviour* and *Good administrative practice.*[129] The last guidance document is analysed in more detail in Chapter 5.

In the practice of the LGO/Commission one can find *special reports* that highlight the experience of the LGO in handling complaints, in particular subject areas with

124 Sec. 23 (12A) the 1974 Act.

125 Annual Report 2011/12 (*Delivering Public Value*), p. 4.

126 Sec. 31 (2B) b) and 31 (2BA) b) of the 1974 Act.

127 In July 2013, the LGO published six focus reports with the latest from November 2012, *Taking possession: councils' use of bailiffs for local debt collection*. See, <www.lgo.org.uk/publications/advice-and-guidance#focus> (accessed on 31 July 2013).

128 In July 2013, the LGO published only one joint publication from July 2011, *Aiming for the best: Using lessons from complaint to improve public services*. See, <www.lgo.org.uk/publications/advice-and-guidance#joint> (accessed on 31 July 2013).

129 <www.lgo.org.uk/publications/advice-and-guidance#guidance> (accessed on 31 July 2013).

recommendations on good practice.[130] These reports *highlight lessons learned from similar complaints across our three offices, and give general good practice advice from the Ombudsmen.[131]* These special reports have a different character to those of the PO as they are *not submitted* to Parliament in order to support the findings of the LGO. They are only documents containing general guidance.[132]

1.2.1.3.2 Reports of the Local Government Ombudsmen

According to sec. 30 (1) of the 1974 Act if the LGO complete an investigation into a matter, they have to prepare a *report of the results of the investigation* and send a copy to each of the parties concerned. The LGO *always* issue their reports *if a local authority does not accept their findings or recommendations*. They also do this if the case raises public interest issues or it elaborates the lessons learned for other bodies in similar circumstances.[133] The LGO can publish their individual reports. These reports are then posted on the official webpage of the LGO. Still, they reflect only a small fraction of their investigative practice.[134] A *statement of the reasons for the decision* can be sent instead if the LGO are satisfied with the action which the administrative authority concerned has taken or proposes to take, and it would not be appropriate to prepare and send a copy of a report to all the persons concerned.[135] The local authority has a duty to consider the investigation report and its recommendations. Within a period of three months, it should notify the LGO of the action which it has taken or which it proposes to take in connection with this report. If the LGO do not receive such a notification within this three-month period, and if they are not satisfied with the actions taken or proposed or if they do not receive within this period confirmation that the local authority has taken the proposed action to their satisfaction then they issue *further reports* setting out those facts and making further recommendations.[136] This report must be considered in full council. After the reports are adopted they are sent to the local body. This body then has the obligation, for a period of three weeks, to make copies of the report available for inspection by the public without charge during reasonable hours at its offices. Persons are also entitled to take copies of that report or extracts therefrom[137] and the local body has to supply a copy of the report to any person upon request.[138] It has to give public notice, by means of an advertisement in

130 The latest special report is *Local partnerships and citizen redress* (July 2007). See, <www.lgo.org.uk/publications/advice-and-guidance#special> (accessed on 31 July 2013).

131 Annual Report 2007/08, p. 21.

132 See, section 1.1.1.3.2.

133 Annual Report 2011/12 (*Delivering Public Value*), p. 27.

134 According to the Annual Report 2011/12 only 0.7% of all enquiries ended with a written report (p. 18). This number had slightly increased in the Annual Report 2012/13. This report refers to around 1% of all cases (p. 14).

135 Sec. 30 (1B) the 1974 Act.

136 Sec. 31 (2A) the 1974 Act.

137 Sec. 30 (4) the 1974 Act.

138 Sec. 30 (4A) of the 1974 Act.

(usually local) newspapers, that copies of the report will be available for a period of three weeks.[139] This is the so-called *sanction of publicity,* a sanction that the PO does not have.[140]

If a local authority's response to a further report is inadequate, the LGO may, by means of a *notice*, require the local authority to arrange for a *statement* to be published in accordance with the 1974 Act. The statement should consist of the details of any action recommended by the LGO in the further report which the local body has not taken. It may also consist of supporting material and the reasons why the local body has taken no action following the report. The statement has to be published in any two editions of a local newspaper within a fortnight. If it does not publish this statement then the LGO will arrange for such a statement to be published, and to be paid for by the local authority concerned.

Based on Article 23A of the 1974 Act the Commission lays a copy of the general report on the discharge of their functions (*annual report*) before Parliament and other authorities.

1.3 Maladministration in the English sense and injustice in consequence of maladministration

Maladministration is a very important concept for the majority of the public sector ombudsman systems in the UK.[141] The majority of publications or academic articles on the ombudsmen in England and most of the court judgments adopted in connection with the ombudsman touch upon this normative concept.

Maladministration is a *normative concept* of the PO and the LGO. This concept has been determined and acknowledged by the English legislator, and the PO and the LGO assess whether or not there is a case of maladministration in the actions of public bodies. The content of maladministration is not defined in Parliamentary statutes. As the ombudsmen deal with maladministration they should explain what the term means. While doing this, they exercise their normative function. However, they are not alone in this 'quest' for maladministration. They have several guidelines. In the history of the UK ombudsmen one can find some examples of the meaning of maladministration, especially in the statements of politicians, judgments of the courts and in the general reports of ombudsmen. A well-known definition of maladministration is the general definition given by Crossman who described maladministration as 'bias, neglect, inattention, delay, incompetence, inaptitude, perversity, turpitude, arbitrariness and so on.'[142] This definition is referred to as *the Crossman catalogue.*[143] It is clearly not exhaustive and especially the *and so on* part of the definition leaves the backdoor open and allows one to contemplate

139 Sec. 30 (5) of the 1974 Act.

140 Alder 2005, p. 294.

141 Maladministration is also used by the Public Services Ombudsman for Wales, the Scottish Public Services Ombudsman, the Ombudsman of Northern Ireland and many other ombudsmen.

142 R. Crossman was a Cabinet Minister in Wilson's 1964 Labour Government. He was responsible for introducing the ombudsman into the UK constitutional system. He gave this definition of maladministration as the Government spokesman during debates on the 1967 Act. See, Harlow & Rawlings 2009, p. 534ff.

143 Turpin & Tomkins 2007, p. 625 or Harlow & Rawlings 2009, p. 534 etc.

on the extent of maladministration. This definition has been partially confirmed by several judgments, for instance, Justice Sedley noted that 'it is accordingly accepted that maladministration includes bias, neglect, inattention, delay, incompetence, inaptitude, perversity, turpitude and arbitrariness in reaching a decision or exercising a discretion, but that it has nothing to do with the intrinsic merits of the decision itself.'[144] Sometimes judges define it differently. For example, Lord Justice Eveleigh uses the definition of maladministration given by the *Shorter Oxford English Dictionary.* He explains that maladministration means 'faulty administration or inefficient or improper management of affairs, especially public affairs.'[145]

In 1993, the PO (Sir William Reid) provided a list of examples that go beyond the original Crossman catalogue. In the Annual Report 1993 he added further examples of maladministration, which, according to Harlow and Rawlings, are of a *notably more bureaucratic flavour.*[146] Reid added to Crossman's definition, *for instance,* rudeness, an unwillingness to treat the complainant as a person with rights, a refusal to answer reasonable questions, neglecting to inform a complainant on request of his or her rights or entitlement, knowingly giving advice which is misleading or inadequate etc.[147] Maladministration in the perception of the LGO is rather similar. It includes delay, incorrect action or a failure to take any action, a failure to follow procedures or the law, a failure to provide information, inadequate record keeping, a failure to investigate, a failure to reply, making misleading or inaccurate statements, inadequate liaison, inadequate consultation and broken promises.[148] The Annual Report 2012/13 (*Raising the standards*) of the LGO characterises maladministration as cases where the council has not acted properly in carrying out its functions.[149] Maladministration is thus something negative, something not done correctly, properly or fairly by a public body.

Since the beginning of the 1990s one can however observe a shift in considering maladministration. The ombudsmen do not explain maladministration, but they explain its opposite – good administration. They have even created applicable lists of principles of good administration. In 1993 the LGO developed their *Guidance on Good Practice* that includes 42 Axioms of good administration.[150] At the beginning of the 2000s the PO developed and published three lists of what she considered to be good administration. Ms Abraham (the Parliamentary Ombudsman 2002-2012) in this connection commented:

> 'If I hadn't devised them [principles of good administration] somebody else would have had to, because people were constantly asking the ombudsman for a definition of maladministration. And from the minute I arrived to do this job, Parliamentary Committees and other people asked me to define maladministration. I decided I

144 *R v Parliamentary Commissioner for Administration (on the application of Balchin & Anor)* [1996] EWHC Admin 152, judgment of 25 October 1996, para. 13.

145 *R v Local Commissioner for Administration for the North and East Area of England, ex parte Bradford Metropolitan City Council* [1979] 2 All ER, at 314.

146 Harlow & Rawlings 2009, p. 534ff.

147 See, Annual Report of the Parliamentary Commissioner for Administration, 1993.

148 <www.lgo.org.uk/guide-for-advisers/maladministration-service-failure/> (accessed on 31 July 2013).

149 Annual Report 2012/13 (*Raising the standards*), p. 6.

150 See <www.lgo.org.uk/publications/advice-and-guidance#guidance> (accessed on 31 July 2013).

wouldn't do that. I would define good administration. That would be a more appropriate thing to do.'[151]

In the last few years one can observe at least one other terminological shift. Although the PO and the LGO work, according to their statutes, with maladministration, the term *maladministration* is slowly disappearing from their vocabulary. For example, the PO's Annual Report 2011/12 (*Moving forward*) does not use the term '*maladministration*' at all. It however uses terms such as 'good administration' and 'poor administration' as its opposite. In accordance with this annual report the PO describes her role as considering complaints that government departments, a range of other public bodies in the UK, and the NHS in England, have *not acted properly or fairly* or *have provided a poor service.*[152] The Annual Report 2012/13 (Aiming for impact) again uses this term and describes the PO's principal activities as 'the investigation of complaints from members of the public, referred to the PO by Members of Parliament, about maladministration in government departments, their agencies and some other public organisations in the UK.'[153]A shift can be also found in the practice of the LGO. In their Annual Report 2010/11 the LGO describe their mission as providing an independent means of redress to individuals for injustice caused by *unfair treatment* or service failure by local authorities, schools and care providers and use their learning to promote good public administration and service improvement.[154] A similar practice is highlighted in the Annual Report 2012/13 of the LGO. One can connect this practice with the endeavour of the PO and the LGO to make their documents simpler and more accessible.

The second key concept of the English ombudsman system is *injustice in consequence of maladministration*. The 1967 Act uses the phrase 'injustice sustained in consequence of maladministration in connection with the action so taken by or on behalf of a government department or other authority' and the 1974 Act speaks of 'injustice sustained in consequence of maladministration or service failure.'[155] These acts do not however say what constitutes injustice.

Again Crossman noted in this connection that 'we [the Government] have not tried to define injustice by using such terms as "loss or damage". These may have legal overtones which could be held to exclude one thing which I am particularly anxious shall remain – the sense of outrage aroused by unfair or incompetent administration, even where the complainant has suffered no actual loss.'[156] Thus, the concept of injustice in consequence of maladministration includes not only the injury that leads to certain material loss and can be traditionally raised before a court of law but also injustice in the sense of bad feeling, outrage aroused by unfair or incompetent administration, i.e. cases where the complainant has not suffered actual loss. Injustice in consequence of maladministration

151 Information provided by Ms Abraham during the interview.
152 Annual Report 2011/12 (*Moving forward*), p. 4.
153 Annual Report 2012/13 (*Aiming for impact*), p. 55.
154 Annual Report 2010/11, p. 4.
155 Sec. 5 (1) of the 1967 Act as amended and Sec. 26A (1) of the 1974 Act as amended.
156 The Rt Hon. Richard Crossman, Hansard: 18 October 1966 (col. 51).

'receives a wide interpretation which goes beyond some tangible loss or damage which may be suffered.'[157]

In both cases there must be an injustice *in consequence of* maladministration. This connection is important because maladministration may occur even without injustice or injustice can be caused by the complainant himself. Seneviratne notes that there may be poor procedures and maladministration revealed in the course of proceedings, but without injustice there is no requirement for the authority to do anything.[158] The LGO include among injustice also hurt feelings, distress, worry or inconvenience, the loss of a right or amenity, financial loss or an unnecessary expense of time.[159]

The absence of legal definitions of maladministration and injustice give these terms the necessary flexibility. The Law Commission argues that these terms were deliberately left undefined so that the ombudsmen would define them on the basis of their own case law.[160]

157 Hawke & Parpworth 1998, p. 267.
158 Seneviratne 2002, p. 214.
159 <www.lgo.org.uk/guide-for-advisers/injustice/ > (accessed on 31 July 2013).
160 The Law Commission Consultation Paper No. 196, p. 26.

Chapter 2

JUDICIAL AUTHORITIES IN ENGLAND

Similar to the other chapters of this book dealing with the position of the judiciary, this chapter does not cover the English judiciary in its entirety. It focuses only on those judicial bodies dealing with claims for review, with complaints and with appeals against the decisions of public bodies; matters that in continental law systems are usually covered by *administrative courts*. Until the impact of the European Courts, whether it is the Court of the European Union or the European Court of Human Rights, the development of the administrative judiciary in England was relatively independent and without many external influences. The development of the judiciary was going its own independent way. The system of administrative courts or rather the system of judicial institutions solving disputes between individuals and the state is not completely separated from the judicial bodies solving civil cases. The following pages give a brief overview of the main judicial bodies that solve disputes between individuals and the state administration, the courts and tribunals.[1]

2.1 Administrative courts in England?

As stated by Bailey et al. the courts of law are the most visible feature of the English legal system.[2] For laymen and also most probably for continental lawyers, the system of English courts may be unclear, even confusing. The courts are not the only part of the judiciary. Over time, England has developed a considerable number of tribunals.[3] The confusion can be amplified by the fact that the rules of law in the English legal system come from Parliamentary statutes and from common law.[4] The courts provide an authoritative explanation of the law and, when necessary, they create norms of behaviour. They can also exercise a limited *legislative function*. Cownie et al. noted that if the 'judges make the law, they do so only cautiously. They often attempt to explain that their law-making is either not law-making at all, or insofar as it is law-making, it is inevitable and fits closely with the established system.'[5] Because of this, relations between the courts and the law

1 For more on the English judicial system see, for example, Slapper & Kelly 2011 or Langbroek et al. 2013.
2 Bailey et al. 2002, p. 40.
3 Cownie et al. 2007, p. 23.
4 Ibid., p. 29.
5 Ibid.

are somewhat different from such relations in continental legal systems where the courts usually do not have the power to create or abolish the law as they only apply and interpret legal provisions.

The system of English courts is changing and developing. The development of the law during the last few decades has changed traditional views on the position of administrative decisions and the role of the courts in the sphere of administrative justice.[6] Administrative law, at least in the continental legal sense, has for a long time been considered to be outside the interest of the UK. At the beginning of the 20th century, Dicey argued that 'in England we know nothing of administrative law; and we wish to know nothing.'[7] However, much has changed since the 1920s. The growth of the power of the state went hand in hand with the growth of its administration and with the growth of expectations about its quality and responsibility[8] and also the English judiciary had to react to this development. As Leyland & Anthony note, the judicial oversight function has emerged as a response, and a potential counterbalance, to the vesting of powers in the modern state.[9] The courts had to deal with an increasing number of cases that called for a review of decisions by public bodies. As noted in 1963 by Lord Reid 'we do not have a developed system of administrative law – perhaps because until fairly recently we did not need it. So it is not surprising that in dealing with new types of cases the courts have had to grope for solutions, and have found that old powers, rules and procedures are largely inapplicable to cases which they were never designed or intended to deal with.'[10] Changes in society gradually led to the development of a body of law that can be described as administrative law.[11] Nowadays, administrative law has its place in the English legal system and is reflected in legal textbooks.[12]

For a considerable period of time there was no specialised court or courts that would *exclusively* deal with a review of the decisions of English public bodies. Until the late 1970s the judicial remedies in public law were extremely complex. In 1977, a new *Rule of the Supreme Court (Order 53)* was adopted. It created a procedure for an *application for judicial review*.[13] The purpose of the 1977 reform was to introduce a procedure whereby the prerogative remedies, and declarations and injunctions and, in appropriate circumstances, damages could be claimed in one claim.[14] These reforms introduced the reorganisation of the High Court and created within this court a specialised judicial body known as the *Crown Office* (and *the Crown Office List*) that covered judicial review, statutory appeals and similar matters.[15] The House of Lords confirmed these reforms in the 1982 judgment in *O'Reilly v Mackman* stating that 'the procedure of application for judicial review is a

6 See, for example, Harlow & Rawlings 2009, p. 4ff.
7 Leyland & Anthony 2008, p. 1.
8 Longley & James 1999, p. 29.
9 Leyland & Anthony, 2008, p. 14.
10 Lord Reid in *Ridge v Baldwin* [1964] AC 40, [1963] UKHL 2, p. 6.
11 Bradley & Ewing 2006, p. 657ff.
12 Wade & Forsyth 2009, or Bradley& Ewing 2006 or Leyland & Anthony 2008 etc.
13 Bradley & Ewing 2006, p. 765.
14 Lewis 2008, p. 4
15 Bradley & Ewing 2006, p. 765.

remedy specially connected with public law.'[16] The judicial review procedure can be briefly described as a means by which the courts control the exercise of governmental power.[17] As noted by Justice Brown 'judicial review is the exercise of the court's inherent power at common law to determine whether action is lawful or not; in a word to uphold the rule of law.'[18] After the reforms of the 1970s, the judicial review procedure was again reformed at the beginning of the 2000s. A part of the reforms that covered changes in civil procedure was themed along the lines of Lord Woolf's report *Access to Justice* in 1996.[19] These reforms *inter alia* recommended a consolidation of the rules applicable to civil proceedings and resulted in the *Civil Procedure Act 1997* (c. 12). Nowadays, the judicial review procedure is regulated by *the Civil Procedure Rules (Part 54)* and applicants have to take into account and follow the *Pre-Action Protocol.*[20]

At the beginning of the 2000s the *Bowman Committee Report on the Crown Office List* recommended changes to the procedure of the Crown Office List.[21] Following this report, the Crown Office List was replaced by (and rebranded as) *the Administrative Court* (October, 2000). The Bowman Report concluded that 'there is a continuing need for a specialist court as part of the High Court to deal with public and administrative law cases.'[22] Thus, the Administrative Court is not a brand new court. It is part of the *Queen's Bench Division of the High Court* and has functions which are not always covered by the judicial review procedure.

The Administrative Court deals with cases involving a judicial review of decisions by inferior courts and tribunals, public bodies and persons exercising a public function; statutory appeals and applications; applications for a writ of habeas corpus etc.[23] Although the Crown Office List and the Administrative Court were not the first English courts to deal with disputes between individuals and the state, they have been the *first judicial bodies that specialised in these issues.*[24] Against *some* of the decisions of the Administrative Court rendered in the judicial review procedure one can appeal to *the Court of Appeal* and sometimes even to *the Supreme Court*. These courts decide appeals after the refusal of permission for judicial review or appeals after substantive hearings were decided at first instance by the Administrative Court.[25]

16 Lord Diplock in *O'Reilly v Mackman [1983]* UKHL 1 (25 November 1983).

17 Barnett 2011, p. 722.

18 Justice Brown in *R v HM the Queen in Council, ex parte* Vijayatunga [1988] QB 322.

19 *Access to Justice Final Report*, The Right Honourable the Lord Woolf, Master of the Rolls, July 1996, <http://webarchive.nationalarchives.gov.uk/+/http:/www.dca.gov.uk/civil/final/index.htm> (accessed on 31 July 2013).

20 See, section 3.1.1.

21 *Bowman: Letter to the Lord Chancellor*, Judicial Review, Vol. 5, Issues 1-4, 2000, pp. 67-79.

22 Ibid., p. 68.

23 For the types of cases dealt with by the Administrative Court see, <www.justice.gov.uk/courts/rcj-rolls-building/administrative-court/types-of-cases> (accessed on 31 July 2013).

24 See, Morgan 2009.

25 The Court of Appeal deals with substantive appeals and with appeals after a refusal or permission in civil cases. The Supreme Court decides only on appeals after substantive hearings in criminal matters as there is no remedy in the domestic courts after a refusal of permission by the Administrative Court. See, sec. 19.4, Administrative Court Guidance (Notes for guidance on applying for judicial review).

The courts deciding on the judicial review procedure derive their core jurisdiction and procedures from various norms, for example, the Supreme Court Act 1981,[26] the Civil Procedure Rules – Part 54 (the CPR),[27] Practice Direction 54A – Judicial review,[28] Practice Direction (Administrative Court: Establishment) [2000] 4 All ER 1071, Pre-Action Protocol for Judicial Review (PAP)[29] or Administrative Court Guidance (Notes for guidance on applying for judicial review).[30]

2.1.1 The judicial review procedure[31]

The judicial review procedure is connected with a claim to review the lawfulness of an enactment or a *decision*, *action* or *failure to act* in relation to the exercise of a public function.[32] As the courts do not review administrative decisions *ex officio* there must be a written application. This must be filed promptly and in any event not later than 3 months after the grounds to make the claim first arose.[33] This rule does not imply that the claimant has 3 months to file a claim for a judicial review, because the claimant has to act *promptly*. Acting *promptly* is more important and it is connected with the date of the relevant decision and not with the applicant's subjective knowledge.[34] In this procedure the claimant can apply for a *mandatory order*,[35] a *prohibiting order*,[36] a *quashing order*,[37] an *injunction*,[38] a *declaration*[39] or damages, restitution or the recovery of a sum due. Claimants can apply for damages, restitution and the recovery of a sum due only in connection with any of the previously mentioned orders.[40]

While applying for a judicial review the applicants should follow the PAP. The judicial review procedure can be used only where there is no right of appeal or where all

26 Renamed the Senior Courts Act 1981 by the Constitutional Reform Act 2005, Schedule 1, para. 1.

27 Part 54 of the CPR describes Judicial Review and Statutory Review. The CPR are the rules of civil procedure before the senior English courts. They are created by the CPR Committee and adopted in the form of a statutory instrument. <www.justice.gov.uk/courts/procedure-rules/civil/rules> (assessed on 31 July 2013).

28 <www.justice.gov.uk/courts/procedure-rules/civil/rules/part54/pd_part54a> (accessed on 31 July 2013).

29 <www.justice.gov.uk/courts/procedure-rules/civil/protocol/prot_jrv> (accessed on 31 July 2013).

30 Guidance notes are created for individuals who wish to apply for the judicial review procedure. <www.justice.gov.uk/downloads/courts/administrative-court/judicial-review.pdf/ > (accessed on 31 July 2013).

31 This description of the judicial review procedure is only a general one and it does not discuss all its specific aspects.

32 Rule 54.1 (2) the CPR.

33 Rule 54.5 the CPR.

34 *R v Cotswold District Council, ex p Barrington Parish Council* (1997) 75 P & C.R 515.

35 A mandatory order is a direction to a public body to carry out some particular act specified in the order which under public law it has a duty to carry out. Supperstone & Knapman 2008, p. 103.

36 A prohibiting order is a direction to a public body forbidding that body from acting in excess of its statutory or other public law powers, or from abusing those powers. Ibid.

37 A quashing order is an order by which a decision of a public body is quashed. Ibid.

38 An injunction is an order to do something or to refrain from doing something. Longley & James 1999, p. 113.

39 A declaration is a judgment which clarifies the respective rights and obligations of the parties to the proceedings, without actually making any order as such. *Remedies in judicial review*, p. 2.

40 Rule 54.3 (2), the CPR.

avenues of appeal have been exhausted.[41] In accordance with the case law, a judicial review is a *remedy of last resort*.[42]

There are two stages in the judicial review procedure; the *permission stage* and the *hearing stage*. In the *permission stage*, the claimant has to apply for permission for a judicial review. Only if permission is granted can the second stage commence.[43] Before an individual can apply *for permission for judicial review, he should consult the PAP*.[44] According to the PAP the parties *should consider* possible alternative dispute resolution. They should exchange the *letter before claim*[45] and the *letter of response*. This stage has the function of filtering out those claims that have no prospect of success and to ease the pressure on the Administrative Court.[46] Applications for permission to proceed with the claim for judicial review are considered by a single judge on the papers.[47] All the information has to be provided in the application as the Administrative Court does not normally make use of an oral examination and it decides mainly upon written evidence. If permission is refused then the claimant may request that the *matter is reconsidered at a hearing*.[48]

If permission is granted the *hearing stage* can commence. During the hearing the parties present their case before the judge. They can refer to witness statements and to the case law of the court. Evidence is mostly written and oral evidence is heard only very rarely. The court considers the rival arguments and delivers a decision, either immediately or after taking time for consideration.[49] If the judicial review procedure is successful, it has a direct impact on the administrative action or administrative decisions challenged. The result of the proceedings is a legally binding and enforceable judgment. If the administrative decision is quashed, the court can remit the matter to the decision-maker and direct it to reconsider the matter and reach a decision in accordance with the judgment.[50] The court can also substitute its own judgment for the quashed decision although this power is limited to the decisions that were made by a *lower court* or *a tribunal*.[51]

Traditionally, only the decisions of inferior courts and tribunals were reviewed. Nowadays, however, the *state administration* is also susceptible to judicial review. As argued by Lord Diplock 'for a decision to be susceptible to judicial review the decision maker must be empowered by public law to make decisions that, if validly made, will lead to administrative action or abstention from action by an authority endowed by law

41 Sec. 2, the PAP.

42 *R v Sandwell Metropolitan Borough Council, ex p Wilkinson* (1998) 31 HLR 22 or *R v Law Society ex parte Kingsley* [1996] COD 59 etc. see also Jones & Thompson 2007, p. 228.

43 Rule 54.4, the CPR.

44 See, section 3.1.1.

45 The letter should identify the issues in dispute and establish whether litigation can be avoided. Sec. 8, PAP.

46 Judicial Review: A short guide to claims in the Administrative Court, Research Paper 06/44, p. 32.

47 Sec. 10.1, Administrative Court Guidance (Notes for guidance on applying for judicial review).

48 Rule 54.12 (3), the CPR.

49 Judicial Review: A short guide to claims in the Administrative Court, Research Paper 06/44, p. 24.

50 Rule 54.19 (2) a), the CPR.

51 Sec. 31 (5A) Senior Courts Act 1981.

with executive powers. In general, the body is amendable to judicial review if it derives its powers from written or unwritten law or if it discharges public functions or duties.'[52]

2.1.2 *Grounds for judicial review*

With a certain level of generalization one can create a list of grounds for judicial review used by the courts while assessing the legality of administrative actions. They are arguments which could be put forward before the court as to why it should hold a public authority's decision unlawful.[53] In theory and in the case law there are three main grounds for judicial review: *illegality*, *irrationality* and *procedural impropriety*. These grounds are noted in the landmark judgment in *Council of Civil Service Unions v Minister for the Civil Service* [1983] UKHL 6 (22 November 1983), 410. Naturally, there are also other grounds for judicial review.[54] Lord Diplock's formulation was a distillation of a great many legal principles developed on a case-by-case basis over a good many years.[55] These three grounds for judicial review are very broad and include other specialised (and earlier) grounds. The existence of other grounds (principles) was confirmed by Lord Diplock in the very same decision.[56]*Illegality* as a general principle includes, among other things, the ultra vires doctrine, fettering discretion, unlawful delegation or irrelevant consideration. Under *irrationality,* one can subsume unreasonableness and to a certain extent also proportionality[57] and *procedural impropriety* including a breach of principles of natural justice, a violation of statutory procedures, a failure to give reasons or the doctrine of legitimate expectations.[58]

Most of these principles were created by the practice of the senior English courts and have been applied for a longer period of time. The grounds are in a *state of constant development* and can be modified if the need arises.[59] These standards can stem from different sources, for example, from *procedural justice* but also from Union law. They are applicable to the whole system of English law not only to administrative matters. Some

52 *Council of Civil Service Unions v Minister for the Civil Service* [1983] UKHL 6 (22 November 1983). See also, Lord Justice Lloyd in *R v Panel on Takeovers and Mergers, ex p Datafin* [1987] QB 815.

53 Le Sueur et al. 1999, p. 226.

54 One can also find other grounds or their different division. Woolf et al. talk about the ground of legality and the ground of procedural propriety. Woolf et al. 2007, p. 479.

55 Jones & Thompson 2007, p. 239.

56 He noted that 'judicial review has developed to a stage when one can conveniently classify under three heads the grounds upon which administrative action is subject to control by judicial review. That is not to say that further development on a case by case basis may not in the course of time add further grounds. I have in mind particularly the possible adoption in the future of the principle of "proportionality" which is recognised in the administrative law of several of our fellow members of the European Economic Community.'

57 Proportionality as a ground for judicial review gives rise to discussion. See, Lord Slynn in *R v Secretary of State for Environment, Transport and Regions ex p Holding and Barnes* [2001] 2 All ER 929 at 975. Nonetheless, it is used when acting within the scope of Union law and in applying the Human Rights Acts Act, which allows the courts to deal with those provisions of the ECHR which have been incorporated into national law (Sec. 2(1)). See, also *R v Secretary of State for the Home Department, ex parte Daly [2001] UKHL 21.*

58 See, SH Bailey 2009.

59 Anthony 2002, p. 26ff.

authors narrow down the meaning of *principles of administrative* law to *grounds for judicial review,* i.e. a review of administrative decisions by the courts.[60] These grounds are discussed in more detail in Chapter 5.

2.1.3 Remedies

The fact that a public body has acted in a way that is unlawful in the public law sense does not in itself give rise to liability in the form of damages in English law.[61] Every remedy is fully discretionary and depends on the decision of the deciding judges.[62] The main remedies available in the *judicial review procedure* are, as already mentioned, the *prerogative remedies* (quashing order, mandatory order and prohibiting order), the *injunction* and the *declaratory order.*[63]

Sometimes in the judicial review procedure the courts can *award damages, order restitution* or the *recovery of a due sum.* Nonetheless, a claim for judicial review may not seek these remedies alone.[64] The claim for awarding damages, ordering restitution or the recovery of a due sum must be connected with one of the previously mentioned remedies. A claimant *can* be awarded damages in the judicial review procedure only if he joins his *application for judicial review* with a *claim for damages arising from any matter to which the application relates.* In order to be granted damages, the court must be satisfied that, if the claim had been made in an action begun by the applicant at the time of making his application, he would have been awarded damages.[65] Damages are usually awarded where the claimant can show a *tort* or a *breach of contract,* a *breach of European Union Law* or of *the Human Rights Act* 1998 (HRA 1998). Nevertheless, the award of damages by the Administrative Court is rather rare.[66]

2.2 Administrative tribunals in England?

It is true that tribunals were created as *ad hoc* bodies[67] but they are nevertheless an indispensable part of the English judiciary and they are often referred to as court substitutes.[68] For decades, they have been performing various judicial functions often connected with deciding statutory appeals against administrative decisions. This brings them very close to the perception of the continental administrative courts. However, without tribunals, the court system would simply break down and machinery for alternative dispute resolution

60 Cane 1996.
61 Supperstone & Knapman 2008, p. 116.
62 Stott & Felix, 1997, p. 27.
63 See, section 2.1.1.
64 Rule 54.3 (2), the Civil Procedure Rules.
65 Sec. 31 (4), the Supreme Court Act.
66 For the remedies in the judicial review procedure, see, Supperstone & Knapman 2008, p. 116ff.
67 Carroll 2003, p. 569 or Jones & Thompson 2007, p. 224.
68 Longley & James 1999, p. 95.

would need to be heavily augmented.[69] Last but not least, a description of the relations between the ombudsmen and the judiciary will not be complete without the tribunals.

As the English tribunal system is very broad and it is not possible to cover it completely in a couple of pages, this part is somewhat generalised. The generalisation starts with the description of the legal framework that is applicable to tribunals. It is rather complicated as the tribunals were created in an unsystematic and a rather spontaneous manner.[70] Nowadays the tribunal system is partially codified and unified by the *Tribunals, Courts and Enforcement Act 2007* (the TCE 2007 Act).[71] Apart from this act there are special statutes that establish individual tribunals and describe their competences.[72] There are also special statutes[73] and other statutory[74] or secondary legislation[75] which are taken into account by the tribunals while deciding cases.

2.2.1 The system of tribunals

Since the 1950s, the tribunal system has experienced an immense development. Traditionally, they have been considered as a faster, cheaper and less formal way of dealing with administrative disputes than the courts. But the tribunals were created as internal parts of the administrative bodies and that raised questions about their impartiality. Another problematic issue was the uncertainty about the body entitled to deal with appeals against their decisions. As the situation became rather complicated and unclear, in 2000 the Lord Chancellor, Lord Irvine of Lairg, decided to authorize Sir Andrew Leggatt to investigate tribunal reform. In 2001 Leggatt submitted the report *Tribunals for users - One system, One service* and advised on possible changes to the tribunal system.[76] The report also recommended the creation of one single, overarching structure of tribunals and the separation of the tribunals from the departments and other authorities whose policies and decisions are tested by these tribunals.[77] Most of Leggatt's recommendations were included in the later reform of the tribunal system. In 2007, Parliament passed the *TCE 2007Act* which created one *almost* entirely unified structure of tribunals. It established two new generic tribunals; *the First-tier Tribunal* (FTT) and *the Upper Tribunal.* It also transferred the existing jurisdictions of most of the existing tribunals to these two tribunals.[78]

69 Harlow & Rawlings 2009, p. 487.

70 Drewry 2009, p. 48ff.

71 For the TCE Act see, <www.legislation.gov.uk/ukpga/2007/15/contents> (accessed on 31 July 2013).

72 See, section 3.1.1.

73 For example, the FTT (Information Rights Tribunal) hears appeals from notices issued by the Information Commissioner under the Freedom of Information Act 2000, the Data Protection Act 1998, the Privacy and Electronic Communications Regulation 2003 and the Environmental Information Regulations 2004. See, <www.justice.gov.uk/tribunals/information-rights> (accessed on 31 July 2013).

74 For example, sec. 31A of the Supreme Court Act 1981describes a transfer of judicial review applications from the High Court to the Upper Tribunal.

75 For example, the Rules of Procedure of different tribunals, different orders of the Lord Chancellor, different Practice Statements made by the Senior President of Tribunals, etc.

76 See, <www.tribunals-review.org.uk/leggatthtm/leg-00.htm> (accessed on 31 July 2013).

77 Ibid., para. 2.23.

78 There are still some tribunals that exist outside this unified system. However, there is a gradual process of placing these tribunals under 'one roof'. For example, the former *Adjudication panel* became part of the First-tier Tribunal as the FTT (Local Government Standards in England) in January 2010.

Although there are still differences between the courts and tribunals, the tribunals, at least *at appellate level, stand in near proximity to the courts.*[79] Also the tribunals are considered to be *inferior to the normal courts.*[80] Another connection between the tribunals and the courts can be seen in an executive agency of the Ministry of Justice that is responsible for their administration – *the HM Courts & Tribunals Service.*[81] Although the role of this research is not to discuss the relations between the tribunals and the courts, it is appropriate to highlight the major characteristics of the tribunals in contrast to the courts.

The tribunals are forums in which disputes are settled by an impartial adjudicator.[82] They usually focus on a particular area of the law and they are specialists in certain legal (or factual) problems. The creation of a unified structure does not really endanger this specialization. The decision-making function of any tribunal depends on the legislation by which it was established.[83] In July 2013, the FTT had seven different chambers.[84] Each chamber deals with appeals against specific administrative decisions. The chambers include the tribunals with a similar jurisdiction or jurisdiction which brings together similar types of experts to hear appeals against the decisions of administrative bodies. The chambers operate under rules and procedures tailored to their specific needs.[85] The Upper Tribunal has four chambers.[86] It is an appellate body for the decisions of the FTT, although it can also have different functions.

In general, tribunals can be characterised as permanent bodies that are (still) less formal than the courts. They have a low cost and flexible practice. One can see a specialisation in a particular area of the law or in a specific type of dispute. They can adopt reasoned binding individual decisions that concern disputes within their jurisdiction. Their decisions are susceptible to judicial review. Apart from legal professionals (judges) they can also have lay members. Similar to the courts, the tribunals hold public hearings. Legal representation is permitted but only in a few cases does the state fund legal assistance. The tribunals were established by statutes that define their jurisdiction.[87] Since the FTT incorporates former tribunals that were originally different, there are *different shades of tribunals*. The tribunals were created in different times, by different statutes and they have different powers. Their actual connection with the law can differ, as some tribunals may decide on purely *legal entitlements* (social security) while others can be connected with *factual issues* (mental health). Their powers are definitely different from those of the Administrative Court. They are closely linked with the jurisdiction that is provided to them by the statutes in question.

79 Harlow & Rawlings 2009, p. 486.
80 Slapper & Kelly 2011, p. 565.
81 See, <www.justice.gov.uk/about/hmcts> (accessed on 31 July 2013).
82 Barnett 2011, p. 836.
83 Jones & Thompson in Seerden (ed.) 2007, p. 223.
84 Social Entitlement Chamber; Health, Education and Social Care Chamber; War Pensions and Armed Forces Compensation Chamber; the General Regulatory Chamber; Immigration and Asylum Chamber; the Property Chamber and Tax Chamber.
85 <www.justice.gov.uk/tribunals/rules> (accessed on 31 July 2013).
86 The Administrative Appeals Chamber, the Immigration and Asylum Chamber, the Lands Chamber and the Tax and Chancery Chamber.
87 See, section 3.1.1.

In general, tribunals deal with statutory appeals by individuals who are dissatisfied with the decision of the administrative body.[88] They do not only review the original decision, they decide thereon *de novo*. They can take every action available to the original decision maker and they subsequently substitute the original decision with their own. Until 2007, the tribunal system was supervised by the *Council on Tribunals*, an advisory non-departmental public body sponsored by the Ministry of Justice. In 2007, it was replaced by *the Administrative Justice and Tribunals Council* (AJTC) that has somewhat different functions.[89]

2.2.2 Discontent with tribunals

If an individual is not content with a decision by a tribunal he/she has several possibilities. First of all, the FTT and the Upper Tribunal can *self-review its own decisions*.[90] They can do this on their own initiative or upon an application by the person who has a right of appeal in respect of that particular decision. Secondly, an individual can *appeal with permission* against the decisions of the FTT to the Upper Tribunal.[91] Against the decisions of the Upper Tribunal one can *appeal on any points of law* to the Court of Appeal. In this case, however, permission to appeal is required.[92] The decisions of the tribunals or their actions that cannot be appealed are amenable to the *judicial review procedure* before the Upper Tribunal. This power closely links the tribunal system with the courts. In the judicial review procedure the Upper Tribunal is able to grant a mandatory order, a prohibition order, and a quashing order as well as declarations and injunctions.[93] The Upper Tribunal then applies the same principles as the High Court.

88 Cf. Slapper & Kelly 2011, p. 565ff.
89 See, section 3.1.1.
90 Sec. 9 (1) and 10 (1), the TCE Act.
91 Sec. 11 (1), the TCE Act.
92 Sec. 13 (1), the TCE Act.
93 Sec. 15 (1), the TCE Act.

Chapter 3

INSTITUTIONAL COORDINATION OF OMBUDSMAN–JUDICIARY RELATIONS IN ENGLAND?

With the help of the previous two descriptive chapters, this chapter seeks to answer the first research question: *how are the relations between the ombudsmen and judiciary as state institutions coordinated in England and what is the content of this coordination.* To find this answer the chapter addresses the institutional coordination of this relationship and the research question through discussing the *formal coordination of this relationship* (3.1). This is followed by the *practice* of possible *informal* coordination between the researched ombudsmen and the judiciary (3.2). A summary provides answers to the research question (3.3).

3.1 Formal institutional coordination in England

In the English situation it is necessary to look at two major sources that potentially include formal institutional coordination mechanisms for ombudsman–judiciary relations: the *primary legislation*[1] as adopted by Parliament and the *jurisprudence of the English courts* where the courts authoritatively interpret the law or even theoretically create a new rule of law. The tribunals can bind the other institutions only in a limited way and only in connection with an individual case. Neither PO nor the LGO can bind the judiciary. Because of that their ability to 'create' new rules of institutional coordination is considerably limited.

3.1.1 Primary legislation and other legal rules

Although English law is often wrongly perceived on the continent as unwritten law based exclusively on the case law of the courts, it is Acts of Parliament (primary legislation) that are the most important source of English law as they prevail over most of the other sources of law.[2] As noted by Jones & Thompson, thanks to the doctrine of the supremacy of Parliament, 'Parliament can by ordinary legislation do sorts of things which elsewhere

1 In England one can distinguish between *primary legislation,* i.e. laws enacted by Parliament, and *delegated or secondary legislation* where the powers are contained in primary legislation, but the detailed provisions have another procedure. See, Slapper & Kelly 2011, p. 79ff.

2 Elliot & Quinn 2008, p. 7.

might require a special procedure, or even amendment to the Constitution.'[3] This means that there are no legal limitations on the power of Parliament to legislate.[4] Based on the research of the statutes of Parliament, one can point to several statutes that include formal institutional coordination between ombudsmen and the judiciary.

a) The 1967 Act and the 1974 Act (statutes establishing the ombudsmen)

Although the PO and the LGO are two different ombudsman institutions, the provisions of the statutes that establish them are rather similar, at least in connection with their institutional relationship with the judiciary. In both cases, the extent of the coordination of this particular issue is marginal with one or two very important exceptions that actually create a *basis for their institutional relations.* The 1967 Act and the 1974 Act explicitly describe ombudsman-judiciary relations only in the following contexts: *subjects within the competence of the ombudsmen, statutory bars for ombudsmen, evidence* and *obstruction and contempt.*

1. Subjects within the competence of the ombudsmen

The first important formal institutional coordination between the researched ombudsmen and the English judiciary included in primary legislation is connected with the subjects and matters that fall within the competence of the researched ombudsmen. The statutes on the ombudsmen more or less expressly enumerate the bodies and authorities that are within the remit of ombudsmen investigations.[5] Neither the English courts, nor the tribunals are included in these lists. This is of importance because it confirms that these two ombudsmen cannot investigate actions of the judiciary or judges.[6] The PO can however investigate complaints against *the HM Courts and Tribunals Service* that provides administrative support to courts and tribunals. This body is not a court or a tribunal but an executive agency of the Ministry of Justice.[7]

2. Statutory bars for ombudsmen

Probably the most important provisions concerning the formal institutional relations between the two researched ombudsmen and the judiciary are included in sec. 5 (2) of the 1967 Act and in sec. 26 (6) of the 1974 Act. These provisions describe, in almost identical terms, the statutory bars on the ombudsmen and their discretion. They limit the ombudsmen in exercising their powers to start an investigation while leaving them with some discretion. In general, this bar was intended to prevent ombudsmen from trespassing on the jurisdiction of the courts and tribunals.[8] The following scheme shows these limitations.

3 Jones & Thompson 2007, p. 201.
4 Bradley & Ewing 2006, p. 55.
5 See, sections 1.1.1.1.1 and 1.2.1.1.1.
6 See, *Judicial Conduct and Appointments Ombudsman* dealing with judicial conduct and discipline.
7 It is included in Schedule 2 to the 1967 Act.
8 The Law Commission Consultation Paper No. 187, p. 109.

Scheme 1 – **Statutory bars for ombudsmen**

Ombudsmen shall not conduct an investigation in respect of any action in which the person aggrieved:	*has* a right of appeal, reference or review to or before a tribunal	*had* a right of appeal, reference or review to or before a tribunal	*has* a remedy by way of proceedings in any court of law	*had* a remedy by way of proceedings in any court of law
The PO	Yes	Yes	Yes	Yes
The LGO	Yes	Yes	Yes	Yes

In accordance with these two provisions ombudsmen cannot start their investigation if the claimant has commenced or already completed proceedings before a court or used his right to appeal to a tribunal, i.e. he/she has already exercised the legal remedy available (the *had* option). In these circumstances ombudsmen cannot act as they represent *a bar* to their investigations.[9] The obligation *not to investigate* is connected not only with the English courts or tribunals but with all courts and tribunals including the European ones. If an individual decides to go to court or to a tribunal the ombudsmen must remain passive. The same obligation is connected with a *theoretical* possibility where an individual only has a right to use this remedy, i.e. he/she has a possibility to use this remedy but has not yet made use of it (the *has* option).

These statutory bars are loosened by the existence of statutory discretion. Both the PO and the LGO can exercise their functions *if they are satisfied that in the particular circumstances it is not reasonable to expect the person aggrieved to resort or have resorted to it.*[10] Thus, this statutory bar does not have an absolute character. This *proviso* gives ombudsmen the power to investigate even if an individual can exercise or has already used a legal remedy and the ombudsman is not satisfied with the protection of the individual in that particular situation.[11] The ombudsmen only rarely exercise this discretion in favour of an individual, however.[12] Another problem is that if the complainant has *used* the legal remedy (i.e. he has appealed to a court or tribunal), it is difficult for the ombudsman to argue that it was not reasonable for an individual to do this.[13] According to the Law Commission these provisions acknowledge that there are overlapping jurisdictions between these ombudsmen and the courts and tribunals.[14] The Law Commission also points to the fact that the interpretation of the statutory bars can be different among ombudsmen and among the courts which makes the statutory bars *unsatisfactory and unclear.*[15] It even recommended a reform of these bars or their complete removal.[16]

9 See, The Law Commission Consultation Paper No. 187, pp. 108-109.
10 Sec. 5 (2) of the 1967 Act and sec. 26 (6) of the 1974.
11 Purdue 2009, p. 893.
12 The Law Commission Consultation Paper No. 187, p. 109.
13 Compare, ibid., pp. 109-110.
14 Law Commission (LAW COM No 329), June 2011, p. 21.
15 The Law Commission Consultation Paper No. 187, p. 111.
16 The Law Commission Consultation Paper No. 196, pp. 39-40.

3. Evidence, obstruction and contempt

When the ombudsmen collect evidence for an investigation the 1967 Act (sec. 8 (2), (5)) and the 1974 Act (sec. 29 (2), (7)) grant them powers similar to those of the High Court. In respect of the attendance and examination of witnesses and in respect of the production of documents they have the same powers as High Court judges. This power can be considered as one of the attributes of an ombudsman's independence; however, it does not really deal with the mutual relations between the ombudsmen and the judiciary and neither does it provide answers with regard to the judiciary's acceptance of evidence collected by the ombudsmen. The 1967 Act (sec. 9) and the 1974 Act (sec. 29) give ombudsmen the right to certify to the High Court if any person, without lawful excuse, obstructs them in the performance of their functions or if such a person is guilty of any act or omission in relation to an ombudsman investigation. This power is used rarely.[17] The ombudsmen can thus formally contact the High Court. However this power does not answer the question of the institutional relations between them.

b) Judiciary statutes

Neither the Supreme Court Act 1981 (the 1981 Act), nor the TCE 2007 Act *directly* discuss the institutional relations between the courts, tribunals and ombudsmen.[18] However, the TCE Act created one body that can potentially influence the work of the English administrative justice system: *the Administrative Justice and Tribunal Council* (AJTC).

Despite all the proposed changes in the system of state institutions in the UK, in July 2013 the AJTC still existed, although it was expected that on 19 August 2013 the AJTC would be abolished.[19] The AJTC was an advisory non-departmental public body that according to Schedule 7 of the TCE 2007 Act 'kept the administrative justice system under review; considered ways to make the system accessible, fair and efficient; advised on the development of the system'[20] and 'referred proposals for changes in the system or makes proposals for research into the system.'[21] In general, the AJTC reviewed the relationships between the various components of the administrative justice system (in particular ombudsmen, tribunals, the courts and the original decision-makers).[22] According to the AJTC administrative justice includes the procedures for making administrative decisions, the law that regulates decision-making, and the systems (such as the various tribunals and ombudsmen) that enable people to challenge these decisions.[23] In July 2013 it consisted of specialists in the field of administrative justice including academics, solicitors, former

17 See, *The Local Government Ombudsman's Annual Review: Corby Borough Council for the year ended 31 March 2009*, p. 5 or *The Local Government Ombudsman's Annual Review: The Royal Borough of Kingston upon Thames for the year ended 31 March 2009*, p. 5.

18 The 1981 Act, however, describes the judicial review procedure that is also applicable to the actions of the two researched ombudsmen. See, section 3.1.2.1.1.

19 <http://ajtc.justice.gov.uk/index.htm> (accessed on 31 July 2013).

20 The AJTC could also advise the *Senior President of Tribunals* (sec. 13 (2), d), Schedule 7, the TCE Act).

21 Sec. 13 (1), Schedule 7, the TCE 2007 Act.

22 Principles for Administrative Justice, November 2010, p. 10, See also, Department for Constitutional Affairs (2004): *Transforming Public Services: Complaints, Redress and Tribunals*, White Paper, p. 54.

23 <http://ajtc.justice.gov.uk/about/about-us.htm> (accessed on 31 July 2013) or The AJTC Information Leaflet Administrative Justice & Tribunals Council, p. 2.

members of tribunals or civil servants.[24] It was a forum which could bring together ombudsmen and tribunal judges and sometimes even court judges. The PO was an ex officio the member of the AJTC.

The AJTC could make recommendations and give advice. It also reviewed the relationships between the various components of the administrative justice system. It did not have the power to make binding decisions or to make the law or enforce it. It published various documents including a list of *Principles for Administrative Justice,* i.e. key values that go to the heart of effective and responsive frontline service delivery.[25] It held an annual conference for Presidents and Heads of tribunals, academics, the advice sector and others with an interest in administrative justice, and topical workshop events when the need arose.[26] The AJTC represented an official forum for a possible exchange of information between tribunals and ombudsmen. His Honour Judge Martin, President of the FTT (Chamber on Social Entitlements), noted that:

> 'There is no special formal way of exchanging information with the ombudsmen, only via the AJTC.'

Mr Laverick, a former senior officer of the LGO service (1975-1995) and a judge at the FTT (Local Government Standards in England), argued that:

> 'The AJTC is the place where I can go wearing a tribunal hat and would meet Anne [Seex] wearing an ombudsman hat. Courts are a bit thin on the ground there.'

Although the decision to abolish the AJTC was connected with the reform of the state administration and the economisation of the state, the interviewees expressed their doubts thereon. For instance, Ms Abraham (the Parliamentary Ombudsman 2002 - 2012) noted:

> 'I think that if the AJTC is abolished, it will make it much more difficult for the interfaces between the various aspects of the administrative justice to come together. The AJTC provides that umbrella. And it is populated with people who make the connections. All of us, whether we are ombudsmen, judges, tribunal judges, we do not proactively think about these connections by ourselves. So if there is nobody poking, prodding and making these connections, then it will get harder. And does it matter? Yes, it matters. It matters for the citizens trying to navigate their way around.'

Similarly, Judge O'Brien, FTT (Mental Health), agreed that:

> 'The abolition of the AJTC removes from the scene the only institution with any pretence to look across the administrative justice system as a whole and to include within its purview courts, tribunals and ombudsmen.'

24 <http://ajtc.justice.gov.uk/about/membership.htm> (accessed on 31July 2013).

25 Principles for Administrative Justice, November 2010, p. 15.

26 <http://ajtc.justice.gov.uk/about/how-we-work.htm> (accessed on 31 July 2013) and the AJTC Information Leaflet, Administrative Justice & Tribunals Council, p. 4.

Thus, the AJTC, as a specialised forum, could formally bring together representatives of a plethora of English tribunals, courts and ombudsmen.

c) Tribunal statutes

Apart from the general coordination of most of the tribunals under the TCE 2007 Act, the individual parts of the FTT have been established by special statutes that provide them with their powers. These parts of the FTT exercise their functions in close connection with these statutes. As noted in Part 1, because of the numerous tribunals in England only 5 former individual tribunals were included in this research, namely the *FTT (Mental Health Tribunal)*, the *FTT (Local Government Standards in England)*, the *FTT (Social Security and Child Support Tribunal)* and the *FTT (Charity Tribunal)*, together with the *Employment Tribunals* which remain outside the FTT. Thus, only five tribunal statutes (including the TCE 2007 Act) were studied.

The FTT (*Mental Health*) is a part of the Health, Education and Social Care Chamber. It hears applications under the *Mental Health Act 1983* (as amended). A close inspection of this Act did not reveal any specific references to two researched ombudsmen that would directly coordinate the formal institutional interplay between them and the tribunal.

The FTT (*Local Government Standards in England*), a part of the General Regulatory Chamber, was established by the *Local Government Act 2000* (as amended) as the *Adjudication Panel*. A close inspection of this Act did not reveal any specific references to two researched ombudsmen that would directly coordinate the formal institutional interplay between them and the tribunal.[27]

The FTT (*Charity*) is a part of the General Regulatory Chamber. It was established by the *Charity Act 2006* (as amended). A close inspection of this Act did not reveal any specific references to two researched ombudsmen that would directly coordinate the formal institutional interplay between them and the tribunal.

The FTT (*Social Security and Child Support*), now a part of the Social Entitlement Chamber, arranges independent hearings for appeals against decisions made by the Department for Work and Pensions. This tribunal was partially established by the *Social Security Act 1975* and the *Social Security Administration Act 1992* as the social security appeal tribunal and by the *Child Support Act 1991* as the Children Support Appeal Tribunal. A close inspection of these Acts (and other mainly statutory instruments and regulations) did not reveal any specific references to two researched ombudsmen that would directly coordinate the formal institutional interplay between them and the tribunal.

27 Nonetheless, this act refers to the ombudsmen. Its sec. 67 directly enables an ethical standards officer to consult the ombudsmen, namely the LGO and the Public Services Ombudsman for Wales. The ethical standards officers investigate cases that are referred to them by a body called *Standards for England* or other cases in which any such officer considers that a member or co-opted member of a relevant authority in England has failed, or may have failed, to comply with the *authority's code of conduct* and which has come to the attention of any such officer as a result of an investigation. See, sec. 59 (1) of the Local Government Act 2000. The ethical officers can consult the LGO if, at any stage in the course of conducting an investigation, he forms the opinion that the matters which are the subject of the investigation relate partly to a matter which could be the subject of an investigation by the LGO. These officers, however, are not members of this tribunal.

In July 2013, the *Employment Tribunals* remain outside the FTT. Originally, they were established by the *Industrial Training Act 1964* as Industrial Tribunals. Neither this act, nor other legal norms dealing with these tribunals directly regulate a possible formal institutional interplay between these tribunals and the two researched ombudsmen.

These five examples show that the special tribunal statutes do not formally coordinate the institutional relations between the PO and the LGO and the tribunals.

d) Other statutes

Other Parliamentary statutes published in the *UK Statute Law Database* that is made available online at <www.legislation.gov.uk/> do not (in July 2013) include any detailed or direct institutional coordination of the investigated relations.

e) Other norms

Other norms that can potentially institutionally coordinate relations between the ombudsmen and the judiciary can be found in the procedural rules of the courts and tribunals that do not have the character of Acts of Parliament. These include the CPR, the Tribunal Procedural Rules (TPR)[28] and the PAP.

The CPR, adopted as a *statutory instrument*, include general rules for the civil procedure before the High Court. The parts of the CPR that are applicable to the Administrative Court do not include a formal institutional coordination between this court and the ombudsmen. Their connection with the PO and the LGO is only indirect and is connected with a judicial review of their decisions and actions.[29]

The PAP is a *practice direction* for claimants when applying for permission for a judicial review. It includes procedural requirements that are prerequisites for court litigation with the aim being to enable the parties to avoid litigation by agreeing to a settlement, to exchange information about the claim and to support the efficient management of proceedings where litigation can be avoided.[30] It points potential applicants for judicial review towards other *alternative dispute resolution mechanisms*. The claimants should consider whether some form of alternative dispute resolution procedure would be more suitable than litigation. Although the PAP is legally non-binding claimants can be 'required by the Court to provide evidence that alternative means of resolving their dispute were considered. The Courts take the view that litigation should be a last resort, and that claims should not be issued prematurely when a settlement is still actively being explored.'[31] At the same time, parties should keep in mind that a claim for judicial review must be filed promptly and in any event not later than 3 months after the grounds to make the claim first arose. Sec. 3.2 of the PAP includes, as one of the options for resolving disputes without litigation, also *Ombudsmen,* namely the PHSO and the LGO who have discretion to deal with complaints relating to maladministration. Still, it warns them that the Ombudsmen are not able to look into a complaint once court action has been commenced.

28 The CPR and the TPR are secondary legislation.

29 See, sections 2.1.1 and 3.1.2.1.1.

30 Grainger et al. 2000, p. 141.

31 Sec. 3.1, the PAP.

The PAP thus directly recommends claimants to use other or alternative methods of dispute resolution including the ombudsmen before they actually file a claim for judicial review. Even though the PAP cannot compel the parties to use these procedures it recalls that they may be *asked* whether they have used them. Despite the use of the ADR the parties must file a claim for judicial review *promptly* and *in any event not later than 3 months (after the grounds to make the claim first arose)*. The expiry of this time limit leads to the expiration of the right to apply for judicial review. This means that if the parties decide to deal with their case by way of the ADR (including the ombudsmen), then it is possible that they will not have enough time to file an application for judicial review. If one takes into account 'the *has* option' included in Scheme 1 it is also questionable whether the ombudsmen can actually address the complaint where the complainant *has* a possible remedy in court proceedings, which the judicial review procedure clearly is. Still, although ADR (including the ombudsmen) is generally required by the PAP, its use may lead to the expiration of the right to have the case judicially reviewed. Moreover, compliance with the protocol alone is unlikely to be sufficient to persuade the court to allow a late claim.[32]

Also the TPR do not institutionally coordinate the relations between these tribunals and the ombudsmen. However, in all sets of procedural rules one can find references to ADR. All sets of the TPR include similar provisions asking the tribunals to bring to the attention of the parties the availability of any appropriate alternative procedure for the resolution of the dispute and if the parties wish and provided that it is compatible with the overriding objective, to facilitate the use of this procedure.[33] Thus, the tribunals can, if they find it appropriate, recommend the parties to use ADR. This can theoretically include also an investigation by the ombudsman although the TPR do not mention this explicitly.

3.1.2 Jurisprudence of the courts and the tribunals

One of the main specific aspects of the English legal system is the special role that is played by common law.[34] Because of that one can presume that some institutional coordination of ombudsman-judiciary relations is also included in the jurisprudence.

3.1.2.1 The case law of the courts

Generally, the English courts give an authoritative interpretation of the law and they also have a rule-creating function.[35] These two powers can definitely lead to an explanation for and the creation of institutional coordination between them and the ombudsmen. However, their special and rarely used power to *create the law* had not been exercised, by July 2013, in connection with the ombudsmen. Nonetheless, the courts by their rule-making and interpretative powers can explain and enforce the existing coordination mechanisms but also *push* the development of coordination. The impact of the power of

32 Footnote 1, the PAP.

33 See, The Tribunal Procedure (First-tier Tribunal) (General Regulatory Chamber) Rules 2009 S.I. 2009 No. 1976 (L. 20) or The Tribunal Procedure (Upper Tribunal) rules 2008 S.I. 2008 No. 2698 (L.15) etc.

34 Cf. Slapper & Kelly 2011 or De Cruz 2007, p. 99ff.

35 Cownie et al. 2007, p. 22ff.

the English courts on the ombudsman world is also considerably influenced by another important mechanism of institutional coordination – the courts' ability to judicially review the decisions of the two researched ombudsmen.

3.1.2.1.1 Judicial review of ombudsmen's actions

The power of the courts of judicial review requires a *reviewed* and a *reviewing subject.* This power is linked with the ability of the reviewing institution (a court) to quash the reviewed decision and to return the case to the reviewed institution (a public body). The two researched ombudsmen are not something special in this context. Their decisions[36] are amenable to judicial review. The statutes do not set different rules for the judicial review of ombudsmen's actions. Thus, the courts follow the CPR just like in any other case of judicial review.[37]

In connection with a decision or a report by the PO or the LGO no appeal is possible. If parties to the investigation are not content they can file a *complaint with the ombudsman* and ask him to review his/her decision.[38] An individual can also try to commence a judicial review procedure against this decision or action of the ombudsman. Applications for a judicial review of the decisions of the two researched ombudsmen are uncommon. Successful judicial review procedures are even rarer. Between 2006 and 2013 there were 78 applications for a judicial review of LGO decisions.[39] In 69 cases an application for permission was refused and in 4 cases the application for permission was withdrawn. The amount of applications for a judicial review of the PO's decisions is similar. Between 2006 and 2013 there were 55 applications for permission for judicial review out of which the court primarily refused the application in 41 cases.[40] Although 78/55 applications for a judicial review in 8 years may seem rather high, only a tiny fraction of these applications were accepted by the court for a hearing. Judges are not very eager to grant permission to review ombudsmen decisions. For instance, Prof. Seneviratne (a member of the AJTC) stated that:

> 'The courts are very reluctant to interfere with the recommendations of the ombudsmen or questions of their jurisdiction. Because the act about ombudsmen gives them such a wide discretion it is very difficult for courts to say that they have acted improperly in relation to that discretion. It has to be something very strange. Still they seem more

36 Buck et al. 2011, p. 174ff.

37 Very often a complainant is not content with a *decision of the ombudsman not to investigate* and not with a written report.

38 Complaints against an Ombudsman are dealt with by the Ombudsman himself or by one senior member of his/her staff. See, <www.lgo.org.uk/making-a-complaint/complaints-about-us/ > or <www.ombudsman.org.uk/make-a-complaint/unhappy-with-our-service> (both accessed on 31 July 2013).

39 In 2006/07 there were 14 applications for permission to apply for judicial review against the LGO. In 2007/08 – 8 applications; in 2008/09 – 9 applications; in 2009/10 – 13 applications; in 2010/11 – 7 applications; in 2011/12 – 8 applications; and in 2012/13 – 19 applications. See, the respective Annual reports of the LGO.

40 In 2006/07 there were 10 applications for permission to apply for judicial review; in 2007/08 there were 10 applications; in 2008/09 there were 7 applications; in 2009/10 there were 9 applications; in 2010/11 there were 9 applications; in 2011/12 there were 2 applications; and in 2012/13 there were 4 applications. See, the respective Annual reports of the PO.

> prepared to challenge the decisions of the Local Government Ombudsman than the Parliamentary Ombudsman.'

Dr Thompson (a member of the AJTC) also noted that:

> 'Where people take judicial review, it tends to be because the ombudsman has said that he is not going to accept the case. It happens in access, rather than in the report. But, by and large, it does not succeed. Quite often the applicants do not even get beyond the first stage of getting permission'.

The ombudsmen do not see the judicial review procedure as a negative aspect. Ms Seex (the Local Government Ombudsman) argued that:

> 'Judicial review is not a control of our decisions, it's a very proper exercise of overview. I feel very proud to be a part of the system where there is control over arbitrary and irrational decisions by the ombudsmen as well as by everybody else. That is entirely right. It is also extremely good for the citizen. It might help to change the citizen's view of the state and how the state operates its checks.'

Ms Abraham, the Parliamentary Ombudsman (2002-2012), in this connection added that:

> 'In practice, the courts have actually shied away from second-guessing the ombudsman in some judgments made and on a number of occasions the judicial review has either helped to clarify our jurisdiction, it has even reinforced our position, strengthened our position in some cases. Judicial review is time consuming, it's challenging and sometimes irritating but it is a useful safeguard and on a number of occasions it actually has been illuminating.'

Ms Knapman, the Deputy Master of the Administrative Court, added that it is quite difficult for an individual to succeed in these proceedings:

> 'The court really expects to have written evidence from the parties to set out what the ombudsman has found. If one of the parties disagrees with the facts of what the ombudsman found they would have quite a high hurdle to get over. But if you can clearly show that the facts that the ombudsman found were really wrong, then the court would not regard itself to be bound by the ombudsman's decision. But again we are talking about the facts that go to the merits of the decision so the court is unlikely to prove that witness A was correct and not witness B, unless you can show that witness B was clearly lying. If a claimant was trying to say that the ombudsmen have got a wrong fact, then that would be a high burden to discharge for a court to accept that they have got it wrong in fact.'

Although the practice of the courts to review ombudsmen decisions is not very extensive, it adds to the institutional coordination of ombudsmen and the courts. Judicial review can theoretically and practically lead to changes in ombudsmen practices. It is thus necessary to mention some of the 'landmark' judgments where the courts have institutionally influenced the ombudsmen. Before elaborating these judgments it is important to note that although the PO and the LGO are two *different and independent ombudsmen*, there is often a direct or implied application of the court judgments concerning the one ombudsman to the other. This is caused especially by the fact that the 1967 Act is perceived as a *model ombudsman statute*.[41] The statutes and also the roles of these ombudsmen are however *not identical* and the courts often highlight specific characteristics of particular ombudsmen.[42] The following examples point to some of the judgments where the courts institutionally *coordinated* the powers of the ombudsmen.

The case *R v Parliamentary Commissioner for Administration, ex p Dyer* is not the first case in which the parties to the PO investigation filed a claim to review the ombudsman's decision but it is the first substantive application for judicial review to have a PO's decision overturned in court.[43]

> Lord Justice Brown here argued that 'there is nothing about the Parliamentary Ombudsman's role or the statutory framework within which he operates so singular as to take him wholly outside the purview of judicial review.'[44] Nonetheless, he emphasized that the High Court will not be readily persuaded to interfere with the exercise of the PO's discretion and since this discretion involves a high degree of subjective judgment, it will always be difficult to mount an effective challenge against what may be called the conventional ground of Wednesbury unreasonableness. The Lord Justice of Appeal also stated that 'the discretion of the LGO is reviewable too, although only with inevitable difficulty.'[45]

In *R v Local Commissioner for Administration, ex p Bradford Metropolitan City Council* Lord Denning stated that if the LGO decides to investigate the complaint, the courts should not interfere with his decision 'except on one of the accepted grounds on which the courts can interfere with a discretionary power.'[46]

> He also noted that 'Parliament did not define maladministration. It deliberately left it to the ombudsman himself to interpret the word as best he could: and to do it by building up a body of case law on the subject.'[47] He highlighted that if there is no maladministration, the ombudsman may not question a decision taken by the authorities. He must *not go* into the merits of the decision and intimate any view as to whether it was right or wrong.[48] The court also clarified the fact that if the Commissioner carries out his investigation and in the course of it comes personally to the conclusion that a decision was wrongly taken, but is unable to point to any maladministration other than the

41 Cf. The Law Commission Consultation Paper No. 196, p. 27.
42 For example, in *R v Secretary of State for Work & Pensions & Ors (on the application of Bradley & Ors)*, [2008] EWCA Civ 36, the court underlined the difference between the PO and the LGO as on the local level there is no *real* separation of powers (legislative and executive), para. 58.
43 Gregory & Giddings 2002, p. 708.
44 R *v Parliamentary Commissioner for Administration, ex p. Dyer*, [1993] EWHC Admin 3, Lord Justice Brown.
45 Ibid.
46 R *v Local Commissioner for Administration, ex p Bradford Metropolitan City Council*, [1979] QB, 310.
47 Ibid., at 311.
48 Ibid., at 312.

> decision itself, he is prevented (by sec. 34 (3) of the 1974 Act) from questioning the decision.[49]

The court thus drew a hard line between an administrative decision and the manner in which the decision is taken, appearing to confine the ombudsman's remit to the latter, to matters of form and process rather than substance and content.[50]

In *R v Local Commissioner for Administration, ex p Eastleigh Borough Council* the Court of Appeal had to decide on appeal by the Eastleigh Borough Council and on a cross-appeal by the LGO against the judgment rejecting the application for judicial review.[51]

> The Court of Appeal held that a local council was entitled to a declaration that 'the LGO's conclusion was unauthorized by law and had no effect.'[52] Lord Donaldson in this connection reasoned that an LGO's report is neither a statute nor a judgment, thus it has to be written in everyday language and convey a message. He set out his view on the relationship between the local administration and the LGO stating that 'the parliamentary intention was that reports of the ombudsman should be loyally accepted by the local authority.'[53] As Parliament did not create a right of appeal against the findings in an LGO's report, this very fact, coupled with the public law character of the LGO's office and powers, is the foundation of the right to relief by way of judicial review.[54] He continued that 'in the absence of a successful application for judicial review and the giving of relief by the court, the local authorities should not dispute an ombudsman's report and should carry out their statutory duties in relation to it.'[55]

Based on this judgment one can summarise that the reports of the LGO should be followed by the administration unless challenged in a judicial review.[56]

The case of *R v Commissioner for Local Administration, ex p Croydon London Borough Council* gave some explanation in connection with a statutory bar on the LGO.

> The High Court here stated that 'the LGO is not concerned with considering whether in fact the proceedings would succeed. He merely has to be satisfied that the court of law is an appropriate forum for investigating the subject matter of the complaint.'[57] The LGO has an obligation to check during the *entire* proceedings whether the case cannot be better dealt with by another remedy. Lord Woolf ruled that if it becomes apparent during the course of an ombudsman's investigation that the issues being investigated are appropriate to be resolved in a court of law, the ombudsman is required to consider

49 Ibid., at 316.

50 Abraham & O'Brien 2006.

51 *R v Local Commissioner for Administration for the South, the West, the West Midlands, Leicestershire, Lincolnshire and Cambridgeshire, ex p Eastleigh Borough Council*, (1987) 86 LGR 145.

52 *R v Local Commissioner for Administration, ex p Eastleigh Borough Council*, [1988] QB, Lord Donaldson, at 866.

53 Ibid., at 855.

54 Ibid., at 868.

55 Ibid.

56 See also, Kirkham et al. who state *that the findings of the LGO are binding, provided they are made within the law* (Kirkham et al. 2008, p. 530).

57 *R v Commissioner for Local Administration, ex p Croydon London Borough Council*, [1989] 1 All ER at 1034 and 1035.

> whether it is appropriate to continue with the investigation. The extent to which the investigation has proceeded is a relevant consideration for the ombudsman to take into account in deciding whether or not to discontinue the investigation.[58] He also stated that the expertise of the LGO is not the same as that of a court of law. The issues whether the public body has properly understood the relevant law and the legal obligations are more appropriate for resolution by the High Court than by the LGO.[59]

The statutory bars for the ombudsman[60] were dealt with in case *R v Commissioner for Local Administration, ex parte H.*

> In this connection Justice Turner stated that 'it can hardly have been the intention of Parliament to have provided two remedies, one substantive by way of judicial review and one compensatory by way of the Local Commissioner.'[61] He furthermore explained that 'an essential feature of the legislation is the creation of a legal right to complain about a grievance, but in respect of which there had been no available form of redress whether through the common law or by means of judicial review. Where a party has ventilated a grievance by means of judicial review it was not contemplated that they should enjoy an alternative, let alone an additional right by way of a complaint to a Local Government Commissioner.'

This statement on the one hand interprets sec. 26 of the 1974 Act according to which the LGO cannot investigate if the individual has exercised his protection before the court or a tribunal. Somehow it overlooks *the proviso* included in sec. 26 (6) of the 1974 Act that enables the LGO to investigate even in the case of court proceedings. The LGO seem to follow this case law. They argue that if a complainant has exercised his right of appeal, reference, review or remedy by way of proceedings in any court of law, the proviso is irrelevant.[62] It is questionable whether the courts would apply this argumentation also in connection with the PO and what would be his/her position on this issue.

In the case *R (on application on Scholarstica Umo) v Commissioner for Local Administration in England* Justice Beatson ruled that *those advising individuals* regarding matters potentially giving rise to both local ombudsman investigations and to judicial review should first seek an investigation by a local ombudsman.[63] He also underlined that 'commencing proceedings by judicial review will, as a result of the statutory structure, deprive the ombudsman of jurisdiction thereafter to investigate.'[64]

The relation between maladministration and unlawfulness was covered in the case *R (on application of Liverpool City Council) v Local Commissioner for Local Government for North and North East England.*

58 Ibid., at 1045.

59 Ibid., at 1046.

60 See, section 3.1.1.

61 *R v Commissioner for Local Administration, ex p H*, [1999] COD 382,314.

62 <www.lgo.org.uk/guidance-on-jurisdiction/alternative-right-remedy/part-4/> (accessed on 31 July 2013).

63 *R (on the application of Scholarstica Umo) v Commissioner for Local Administration in England*, [2003] EWHC 3202 (Admin), para. 17.

64 Ibid.

> This judgment dealt with relations between maladministration and unlawful behaviour. Lord Justice Henry here highlighted, among other things, that 'maladministration comes in many guises, and while there is a substantial element of overlap between maladministration and unlawful conduct by councils or officers or councillors in local government, they are not synonymous.'[65] This view was supported by Lord Justice Chadwick who affirmed that the LGO investigate and report on maladministration and do not determine whether conduct has been unlawful. He also argued that 'the normative standards that are applied by the LGO must not be identical to those of the court.' He stated that 'there is no reason why, when exercising the power to investigate and report, the ombudsman should, necessarily, be constrained by the legal principles which would be applicable if he were carrying out the different task of determining whether conduct has been unlawful.'[66]

As highlighted by Lord Justice Chadwick, in principle there is no reason why the considerations which determine whether there has been maladministration should be the same as those which determine whether there has been unlawful conduct.[67]

Apart from these 'landmark' decisions of the judiciary one can point to cases where the courts have quashed the report of ombudsman. Although these cases are not very common they can occur. One of the few accessible examples was case *R v Parliamentary Commissioner for Administration (ex parte Balchin & Anor)* [1996] EWHC Admin 152 and the subsequent case *R v Parliamentary Commissioner for Administration (ex parte Balchin & Anor)* [1999] EWHC Admin 484. In these cases the High Court accepted the report of the PO for judicial review.

> The property of the complainants had been considerably negatively influenced and its price had been devalued by a road scheme proposed by the local council. The council submitted the scheme and the obligatory purchase orders to the Secretary of State for Transport. These obligatory purchase orders did not include the property of the complainants. They complained about the prepared road scheme and orders. The scheme and orders were confirmed by the Secretary of State while the Secretary of State called the local council for a 'sympathetic consideration by the council of the plight' of the complainants. The PO did not find maladministration in the actions of the Secretary of State for Transport which led the complainants to apply for a judicial review procedure against the PO's report.
>
> Mr Justice Sedley accepted the applicants' challenge that the PO's conclusion that there was no maladministration in the Secretary of State's failure to link his decision on confirmation to the county council's attitude to compensating the applicants was based upon a misapprehension of the Secretary of State's lawful power.[68] Based on the facts of the case, Mr Justice Sedley found that 'the PO had omitted a potentially decisive element from his consideration of whether the Department of Transport had caused injustice

65 *R (on application of Liverpool City Council) v Local Commissioner For Local Government for North and North East England*, [2000] EWCA Civ 54, para. 17.

66 Ibid.

67 Ibid.

68 *R v Parliamentary Commissioner for Administration (ex parte Balchin & Anor)* [1996] EWHC Admin 152 (25 October 1996), paras. 29-39.

> to the applicants by maladministration in its dealings with the county council,'[69] i.e. the PO did not consider all the necessary aspects of the case for his decision. Mr Justice Sedley concluded, however, that 'a certiorari order (now a quashing order) is necessary if the PO will undertake to reconsider his decision in the light of this judgment.'[70]
>
> The PO issued a further report on 14 July 1997, but it, too, became the subject of judicial review proceedings. Here Mr Justice Dyson for the second time quashed the PO's decision as there had been *a failure to give reasons for findings on a principal controversial issue.*[71] He noted that the PO did not considerably address the issue of injustice as it was one of *the principal controversial issues.* In this connection the PO was required to give reasons in relation thereto, which were sufficient to enable the parties to know what he had decided, and why.[72] In the opinion of Mr Justice Dyson 'the PO should have made it clear that he had considered it, and why he had decided that it did not involve injustice in this case.'[73]
>
> The PO reported again on 19 September 2000, but also that report became the subject of an application for judicial review and permission was granted in the High Court for a full hearing. For a third time, the Administrative Court quashed the PO's finding *that the maladministration had not caused injustice.* The Court concluded that 'the sense of outrage felt by the complainants had not been addressed.'[74] Because of that the Court found a serious flaw in the reasoning of the PO which went to the heart of the decision.[75]

The High Court in these three cases quashed the decision of the PO because the PO had not considered all the necessary aspects of the case or because he had failed to give reasons for his findings on the important issue in the case. The High Court thus applied *legal standards to the work of the PO.* This leads to the conclusion that the PO, when dealing with complaints and when assessing the facts, has to access matters *not only from the perception of maladministration*, but the PO has to be aware that there is a 'judge over his/her shoulder', i.e. his/her decision and his/her actions have to be in accordance with all the *legal requirements* that are in place for other public bodies and tribunals.[76]

However, the courts do not quash the ombudsmen's decisions on a daily basis. They only interfere with these decisions 'if it is clear that the Ombudsman in reaching a decision has misdirected himself as to a matter of law or has failed to have regard to a relevant consideration or has had regard to an irrelevant consideration.'[77] In order to illustrate the general attitude of the English courts to quashing the decisions of the ombudsmen one can

69 Ibid., para. 41.
70 Ibid., paras. 43 and 58.
71 *R v Parliamentary Commissioner for Administration (ex parte Balchin & Anor)* [1999] EWHC Admin 484 (24 May 1999), para. 49.
72 Ibid., para. 47.
73 Ibid.
74 *R v Parliamentary Commissioner for Administration ex p Balchin* (No 3) (2000) 79 P&CR 157 and The Law Commission, Consultation Paper No. 196, p. 15.
75 See, Opinion of Lord Macphail in Petition of Argyll and Bute Council against Judicial Review of a Decision of the Scottish Public Services Ombudsman, [2007] CSOH 168.
76 See, also Chapter 5.
77 *R (on the application of Turpin) v Commissioner for Administration* [2001] EWHC Admin 503, (28 June 2001), para. 36.

quote Justice Morison. In *R (on the application of Doy) v Local Administration*, where he dismissed the application for a judicial review of the decision of the LGO, he noted that:

> 'In essence, the Ombudsman and not the court is the arbiter of what constitutes maladministration. The court's supervisory role is there to ensure that he has acted properly and lawfully. However much the court may disagree with the ultimate conclusion, it must not usurp the Ombudsman's statutory function. It is likely to be very rare that the court will feel able to conclude that the Ombudsman's conclusions are perverse, if only because he must make a qualitative judgment based upon his [his department's] wide experience of having to put mistaken administration onto one side of the line or the other. I have to say that in this case I would not have made the same judgment as the Ombudsman; but I am not asked to make any personal judgment and the real question is whether any reasonable Ombudsman was entitled to hold the view expressed in this careful report.'[78]

3.1.2.1.2 Judicial review of actions of other institutions

Sometimes a judicial review of decisions of other public bodies can have a direct impact on ombudsmen as well. An explicit example of this practice can be observed in case of *R (on the application of Bradley & Ors) v Secretary of State for Work & Pensions & Ors* where the courts dealt with an application for a judicial review of the decision of the *government department* not to accept the recommendations included in a PO report.

> Lord Justice Chadwick here argued that the PO serves as an independent and authoritative investigator that the Members of Parliament can use as a better instrument to protect the citizen.[79] Lord Justice Wall expressed the position of the courts towards the ombudsman and de facto contributed to institutional coordination of these bodies. He stated that 'the role of the Ombudsman under the 1967 Act is not only to report to Parliament, but, where appropriate, vigorously to alert Parliament to an injustice which has occurred through maladministration. It is, therefore, for Parliament to provide the remedy, subject only to the role of the courts in ensuring that the acts of the Ombudsman herself and the role of the relevant Departments in responding to her reports are themselves lawful.'[80]

This judgment is used in the further text of the book.[81] It is not excluded that there are other judicial review cases that have an indirect impact on any of the ombudsmen.

3.1.2.2 The case work of the tribunals

Although since the TCE 2007Act the tribunals have officially been a part of the judiciary, the position of the tribunal system is notably different to the position of the courts. The

78 *R (on the application of Doy) v Local Administration* [2001] EWHC Admin 361 (27 April, 2001), para. 16.
79 *R (on the application of Bradley & Ors) v Secretary of State for Work & Pensions & Ors* [2008] EWCA Civ 36, para. 40.
80 Ibid., para. 142.
81 See, section 4.1.2.1.

tribunals do not have a *law-creating* function.[82] Their roles are closely connected with the acts establishing them. The authoritative interpretation of the primary or secondary legislation by the tribunals beyond their particular remit is at least questionable. Nonetheless, despite the endeavour to unify the tribunals under one roof or one umbrella of the FTT one can still observe different 'shades' of tribunals within the FTT. Tribunals existing outside the unification created by the TCE 2007 Act may sometimes deal with issues that do not directly connect with the state administration and might, for instance, deal with cases between individuals.[83]

The information received during the interviews with the judges of different tribunals showed the following main point. From the perspective of the tribunals, *the work of tribunals as such does not conflict with the work of the ombudsmen*. They adhere to the purpose that is given to them by their establishing statute. This was best described by Judge Herwald, Mental Health (FTT), who referred to the tribunals as *creatures of statute*. This means that the tribunals are closely connected with the statutes that have developed them and provided them with competences. Hence, they have to fulfil their functions with close adherence to the establishing statute. Similarly, just as the ombudsmen's decisions, also the tribunals' decisions are amenable to judicial review. Still, they are different institutions. All the judges interviewed confirmed this opinion. His Honour Judge Martin, President of the FTT (Chamber on Social Entitlements) in this connection said:

> 'We [the tribunals and the ombudsmen] see ourselves as having basically different responsibilities. But there may be an overlap in terms of the citizen who has a problem which is in two halves and for each half there is a different body that he could contact.'

Also Judge Laverick, FTT (Local Government Standards in England), confirmed that:

> 'Ombudsmen and tribunals are two different parallel ways of achieving a remedy, but we don't do the same thing.'

The considerable differences in competences including the close connection to the law and the lack of powers to create generally binding rules are one of the reasons why it was not possible to find any formal institutional coordination mechanism between the tribunals and the ombudsmen in the casework of the five chosen tribunals.[84]

3.1.3 The 'ombudsprudence' of the Parliamentary Ombudsman and the Local Government Ombudsman

In connection with the two researched ombudsmen one has to ask oneself whether the reports or other decisions of these ombudsmen have the power to establish a formal coordination mechanism between them and the judiciary. One must take into account that the reports of the PO are legally non-binding recommendations or advice on better

82 Compare, Slapper & Kelly 2011 or Elliot & Quinn 2008.
83 See, the Employment Tribunals, <www.justice.gov.uk/tribunals/employment> (accessed on 31 July 2013).
84 See, section 3.1.1.

administration. Although the previous section notes that the local bodies should follow the recommendations of the LGO unless challenged in judicial review, this does not make them *generally* legally binding.[85] This confirms that the reports of the two researched ombudsmen cannot formally coordinate relations with the judiciary. Still, the reports often *include* or *express the* ombudsman's opinions on certain issues concerning the relations between them and the judiciary. Such examples can be found in the annual reports of the PO and the LGO. Examples included in the annual reports confirm that ombudsmen accept the existing mechanisms of formal coordination (e.g. the possibility of a judicial review of their decisions).[86]

Although the ombudsmen in England do not have the power to formally coordinate their relations with the judiciary one can occasionally see that especially the PO can *add* to the existing institutional coordination. An outstanding example can be found in a special report of the PO: *'A Debt of Honour' The ex gratia scheme for British groups interned by the Japanese during the Second World War of 12 July 2005.*[87]

> The case dealt with a governmental scheme of ex gratia payments for British citizens interned by the Japanese during the Second World War. The case was filed before the courts as well as before the PO. First of all, a judicial review procedure had been started by the ABCIFER (the Association of British Civilian Internees Far Eastern Region). Justice Scott Baker noted during this procedure that the scheme by Parliament 'was not clear and unambiguous and was devoid of relevant qualifications.'[88] He stated that 'moral detriment could in some circumstances be sufficient but bitter disappointment in the present case was not enough.'[89] He concluded that 'he had to decide whether the Secretary of State had acted unlawfully and broken any principle of law in defining the boundary of the scheme as he did. This was not the case and the scheme was not considered to be irrational.'[90] The Court of Appeal accepted that the announcement of the scheme *was less clear* than it should have been but there was nothing there to suggest that the Government was intending to introduce a qualification which would exclude a significant number of persons who would otherwise be eligible to receive payment.[91] The Court concluded that 'we do not think that the introduction of this scheme was well handled by the Government. But for the reasons that we have given, the appellant has failed to satisfy us that the scheme was *unlawful*.'[92] Both the original claim and the appeal were thus dismissed.
>
> The attention of the PO was triggered by an *individual complainant* who had been detained by the Japanese during WWII but according to the specified scheme was not able to receive the ex gratia payment and was not a member of the ABCIFER. The PO

85 See, section 3.1.2.1.1.

86 See, Annual Report of the PO 2009/10 (*Making an impact*), p. 35; Annual Report of the PO 2007/08 (*Bringing wider public benefit from individual complaints*), p. 4 or Annual Report of the LGO 2009/10 (*Delivering public value*), p. 23.

87 For more on the special reports of the PO see, section 1.1.1.3.2.

88 *R (on the application of Association of British Civilian Internees Far East Region) v Secretary of State for Defence,* [2002] EWHC 2119 (Admin), para. 31.

89 Ibid., para. 36.

90 Ibid., para. 55.

91 *R (on the application of Association of British Civilian Internees Far Eastern Region) v Secretary of State for Defence,* [2003] EWCA Civ. 473, para. 59.

92 Ibid., para. 87.

> postponed the investigation until the courts had decided on the claim of the ABCIFER. After the position of the courts was ascertained the PO decided to recommence the investigation. She emphasized that the complaint was not directed at whether the scheme was *lawful* but that it concerned the injustice suffered in consequence of *maladministration*. In her view, 'the complaint was not one wholly amenable to an application for judicial review, as maladministration is not synonymous with acting unlawfully.'[93] The PO dealt with the previous judgments concerning the ABCIFER as the complainant could (should) have *theoretically* used the same *alternative legal remedy*.[94] She argued that it was proper that she should have had regard to the ABCIFER challenge to the lawfulness of some of the actions about which the complainant complained but it was *also proper that she should not question the decisions of the courts about the scheme*.[95] Thus, the PO decided to investigate only *maladministration falling short of unlawfulness*.

This case leads to interesting conclusions. First of all, the PO clearly distinguished between her own jurisdiction and that of the courts. The PO did not give a ruling on the issue of the legality of the decision by the Government. She stuck to the institutional coordination designed in the 1967 Act and emphasised her connection with maladministration. Secondly, the case underlines the fact that the same issue *can* be approached by the courts from the point of view of illegality in the judicial review procedure and by ombudsmen from the position of maladministration, even at the same time, and even after the courts have exercised the judicial review procedure, that in their opinion should be the last and final remedy.[96] This is confirmation that the same case can *theoretically* and *practically* lead to two different results: one concerning *lawfulness* and one concerning *maladministration*. A questionable though hypothetical matter is whether the PO would have investigated the case if the *ABCIFER had filed a complaint of maladministration* after the unsuccessful judicial review proceedings or whether the courts would have quashed this decision of the PO if there would have been a claim for judicial review against her report. This case leads to the conclusion that the institutional coordination of ombudsman–judiciary relations included in *the case law* is not always strictly applied by the PO.

3.1.4 Short summary

The most important formal institutional coordination mechanisms that deal with ombudsman-judiciary relations in England are included in written law and the case law of the courts. The law creates the framework where ombudsmen, the courts and tribunals exercise their functions. An institutional coordination of ombudsman-judiciary relations does exist, although it is general. The law, on the one hand, greatly limits ombudsmen so that they do not venture too far into the world of the judiciary, while, on the other, it allows the ombudsmen to protect individuals against infringements of a different set of norms than the legal norms. Judgments of the courts interpreting the law and explaining the

93 Special report *Debt of Honour*, para. 25.

94 See, section 3.1.1 and the explanation of 'the *has* option'.

95 Special report *Debt of Honour*, para. 32.

96 See, section, 3.1.2.1.

powers and the position of the ombudsmen add to the formal institutional coordination of their relations. This is amplified by the fact that the English courts have the power to assess the legality of the decisions of ombudsmen. The decisions of tribunals do not determine special institutional rules for ombudsman–tribunal relations. The ombudsmen in their reports confirm the existing limits laid down in the law and the case law. Only rarely do they give a new dimension to the existing institutional coordination.

3.2 Informal institutional coordination in England

Although England is a common law country and unwritten procedures are presumably present in the practice of its institutions, *informal institutional coordination* is not something that is extensively present in ombudsman-judiciary relations. However, one cannot say that their relations are coordinated only formally, since as previously mentioned the formal institutional coordination of these relations is rather general. One can presume that there is some *institutional practice.*

The informal institutional coordination of ombudsman-judiciary relations does not lie at the heart of academic interest. Not even in the UK itself. Because of that, it is not possible to obtain much information on such coordination from written sources. Thus, this section builds on interviews with ombudsmen, their investigators, judges and members of the AJTC. The interviews are illustrations of the practice of these bodies and they are usually the sole source of data. Still, these data are only *individual opinions of the specialists.* They are by no means official statements by these institutions.

3.2.1 Informal interaction?

The ombudsmen, courts and tribunals are state institutions. Although England does not have one document that can be called a constitution, they are *constitutional* bodies. The formal interaction between these institutions is set in primary legislation and the case law. However, I investigated if there is some kind of informal interaction, as there usually is a difference between the letter of law and reality. Because of that can one detect an *informal interaction* between ombudsmen and the judiciary. In this connection Ms Abraham, the Parliamentary Ombudsman (2002-2012), noted that:

> 'I would like to think that in the last few decades or so the judiciary in the wider sense has acquired a broader understanding of the work of ombudsmen and respect for it. Let me just show you some illustrations after we adopted the principles [of good administration]. These are letters that I keep. This is Lord Justice Sedley writing to me about the principles for remedy and commending what we have done. And this is Lord Woolf writing to me about the principles generally. And I think that they are both illustrations that at some pretty senior level in the judicial population there is understanding and respect for the work of ombudsmen, and particularly in relation to the codification of principles.'[97]

97 This codification of the principles is not codification by Parliament as a statute but only on the internet site of the PO. See, also section 5.1.1 and Annex 3 b) and c).

Dr O'Brien (the former Interim Director of Policy and Public Affairs at the PO Office) argued that real interaction between these institutions is limited because:

> 'The courts and tribunals do not play a direct or specific role in the investigation of complaints. It is sometimes said that the ombudsman investigates 'in the shadow of the law', and this expression perhaps captures the extent to which court judgments indirectly influence the standards applied by the ombudsman and the processes adopted. The ombudsman is subject to judicial review by the courts and to that extent 'has a judge over her shoulder'.'

The Deputy Master of the Administrative Court, Ms Knapman, does not see a possibility for broad interaction between the Administrative Court and the ombudsmen although she does not deny it. To the question whether there is interaction between these institutions she answered:

> 'Not really, there is no special interaction between us. We have had exchange visits. But not in terms of how the ombudsman deals with cases. But there is an issue which affects most of the ombudsmen. And that is that if you apply to the court you cannot then go to the ombudsman. So if you exercise your judicial review remedy then you cannot go to the ombudsman.'

Judge Holbrook, the Employment Tribunal and the FTT (Charity Tribunal), noted that the ombudsmen and the tribunals do not necessarily cover the same area and thus their interaction is almost non-existent. Still it depends on the character of the tribunal:

> 'I sit in a range of jurisdictions dealing with disputes concerning residential leasehold property. The employment and property cases which I hear are invariably 'party v party' disputes (that is, they are *not* challenges to administrative decisions taken by public bodies) and so they are not the province of the various UK ombudsmen bodies. The charity jurisdiction is slightly different, because it does concern appeals made in respect of certain decisions and actions of the Charity Commission, which is the regulator for the charity sector. However, appeals to the tribunal concern substantive decisions made by the Commission rather than *service level complaints*. Consequently, there is no cross-over between the Tribunal's jurisdiction and matters which may be investigated by the PHSO.'

Similarly Judge O'Brien, FTT (Mental Health), explained that the majority of tribunals usually do not have a particular connection with the ombudsman system:

> 'I doubt whether the tribunals generally give a second thought to ombudsmen. In most cases, a tribunal's remit is tightly drawn by statute. There may be rare occasions when a decision of an ombudsman is taken into account, but most tribunals operate so narrowly within their own conventions of practice and procedure that it's unlikely they will find much space for the ombudsmen. I am not aware of any specific MHT perception of ombudsmen or their discretionary powers.'

Last but not least, His Honour Judge Martin, President of the FTT (Chamber on Social Entitlements), confirmed that there is no special interaction between his chamber of the FTT and the ombudsmen:

> 'We have no institutional links, no formal links. I do not have regular meetings with the ombudsman. We see ourselves as having basically different responsibilities. But there may be an overlap in terms of the citizen who has a problem which is in two halves and for each half there is a different body that he could contact.'

3.2.2 *Informal cooperation and an exchange of information?*

Although formal institutional cooperation as included in written law and in the case law is relatively limited, a specific part of the interaction between the judiciary and the ombudsmen that might require attention is their *informal cooperation*. The interviews show that cooperation between these institutions, even an informal one, is almost a non-issue. Even though there are some actual exceptions, any cooperation, including the informal one between the LGO or the PO and the judiciary, is very rare. The ombudsmen and the judiciary perceive themselves as being almost completely distinct with regard to their roles and spheres of interest. A distinction while being *mutually aware of the other institutions* was noted by Ms Seex (the Local Government Ombudsman):

> 'I do not think there is any explicit cooperation between us [the judiciary and the ombudsmen], but I think the people who work in both systems are aware of the work of the others. And particularly at the Local Government Ombudsmen level, our staff is fully aware of what the tribunals do in housing benefits, claims or special educational needs.'

She confirmed that the judicial review procedure, at least in cases dealing directly with ombudsmen, attracts the attention of the other ombudsmen:

> 'Although we do not have an active cooperation and dialogue with the courts, obviously our investigators and the ombudsmen are very aware of the cases that are decided in the High Court, the Court of Appeal and the European Court and will be informed by those judgments and decisions.'

Similar answers were given by other representatives of the ombudsman offices.

On the other hand, tribunal judges do not see much space for cooperation with the ombudsmen. Judge O'Brien, FTT (Mental Health), noted that since ombudsmen and some of the tribunals may cover completely different issues, their cooperation is reduced:

> 'I am not aware of any special co-operation between the Mental Health Review Tribunal and the various ombudsmen, including the PHSO. The tribunal jurisdiction is narrowly drawn by the Mental Health Act 1983 and is in effect exclusively concerned with the lawfulness of the detention of mental patients. This is not something with which any UK ombudsman is likely to be actively engaged, except very indirectly.

That indirect involvement might arise from complaints about the administration of the detention system or the quality of care afforded by a psychiatric unit but will fall short of adjudication on the actual issue of detention. I suspect that the 'culture' of the tribunals and of the ombudsmen is so different that neither party really sees the other as a significant actor in its sphere of activity.'

His Honour Judge Martin, President of the FTT (Chamber on Social Entitlements), however admitted that coordination might sometimes be adequate:

'I think it might be useful if we had a power to make a reference to the ombudsman because we are well placed, given the volume of cases we see, to recognize patterns of poor administration. Individual citizens are usually interested only in "my case" and nothing else, so we may lose that overview of "this is the tenth case with the similar problem so something is going wrong." We do not feel very comfortable saying we are like a manager or auditor for a government department who is working closely with them. It would be better for us to be able to say: here are a number of problems and we see a pattern. Who can we refer them to? The ombudsman would be the best place because they are the experts on the administration. They could accept a referral from us almost as they are accepting it from MPs.'

A somewhat broader possibility for cooperation was noted by Mr Laverick, a former senior officer of the LGO and a judge at the FTT (Local Government Standards in England):

'In the context of that question [cooperation between ombudsmen and the judiciary] I think that there was a problem in that the courts reserve for themselves this right of judicial review over everything. They tend to approach it from the position that "the way that the court operates is the best way of dealing with things". Because ombudsmen are not working with resolving legal arguments, the courts have been fairly good with ombudsmen. But to some extent I think that with the ombudsmen and also with the tribunals, the courts think that if you are not following their methods of procedure, there must be a much greater risk that you are doing it wrong. They need to be better educated about the way tribunals and ombudsmen in general operate. I think that it would be much better if they were much more flexible.'

He admitted that cooperation may have its benefits:

'I say yes, there certainly ought to be more cooperation. For instance, there are bodies which adjudicate upon decisions to refuse admissions to schools of first choice. They are called Admissions Tribunals. Now they may well benefit from having had the ombudsman look at the way that decision has been taken, because the ombudsman may discover relevant facts which the parents who have been to the appeal probably wouldn't discover. For example, if you want your child to go to school around the corner and you're told that the school is full, you as a parent are unlikely to get information that shows that the school is only full because there have been 3 children who have been allowed in who according to the rules shouldn't have been. Now the ombudsman might be able to find that out, so it would be useful to have some broader cooperation.'

An absence of actual cooperation between the High Court and the ombudsmen was noted by the Deputy Master of the Administrative Court, Ms Knapman. She noted that:

> 'We don't have any particular cooperation. We are two parallel systems.'

She explained that cooperation by way of referring the case to ombudsmen is not possible at the moment as the statutory provisions do not enable ombudsmen to investigate whether the case has been covered by a court of law. She argued that:

> 'I don't think that there is a position that the Court would normally stay the proceedings and refer the case to the ombudsman. This change would have to come by way of legislation. There are not many cases where the court would say: "Stop! Let's go to the ombudsman". They might say you shouldn't be here, you should be at the ombudsman and we are not going to carry on. But they don't have to transfer the case to the ombudsman. It is probably connected with the idea that judicial review is the remedy of last resort and you should exhaust the alternative remedies first.'

One can also point to the consultation reports of the Law Commission. This body commenced consultation on more substantive cooperation between the judiciary and ombudsmen.[98] It discussed the possibility for the courts to stay proceedings and to refer the case to ombudsmen. The Law Commission looked at the discretion of ombudsmen to refer points of law to the courts for determination. This consultation noted that it would be necessary to change the statutory bars and thus amend the law if such authority was established for the courts.[99] In most cases the bodies consulted were positive about power of the Administrative Court to stay proceedings in connection with an investigation by the ombudsman. The Law Commission in recommendation 4 of the law reform report presented to Parliament in 2011 recommended 'that the Administrative Court should have an express power to stay an action before it, in order to allow a public services ombudsman to investigate or otherwise dispose of the matter.'[100] In recommendation 7 of the same report it also recommended that 'the public services ombudsmen be given a specific power to make a reference to the Administrative Court asking a question on a point of law.'[101] Despite the endeavour of the Law Commission, this recommendation was not followed.

The previous pages confirm that there is some awareness of the mutual functions of the ombudsmen and the judiciary. They confirm that for now there is no special informal cooperation or any special issue that could be covered by their cooperation. Although they are not *a priori* against cooperation and in some cases cooperation might be an asset, the presently designed system does not enable these institutions to cooperate.

98 The Law Commission Consultation Paper No. 187, paras. 5.27-5.53, the Law Commission Consultation Paper No. 196, paras. 4.47-4.75 and the Law Commission (LAW COM No 329), paras. 3.50-3.88.

99 See, section 3.1.1.

100 The Law Commission (LAW COM No. 329), para. 3.88.

101 Ibid., para. 4.95.

Interaction can be seen in light of the *exchange of information* between these bodies. Although the judgments and the reports are discussed in the following chapter, already at this juncture one can point to the fact that the results of the work of the ombudsmen and judiciary might be of interest to the other institutions. The exchange of information as such is not covered by formal mechanisms. However, I presumed that the exchange of information (including their decisions) may occur in an informal way. The interviewees confirmed that a formal and informal exchange of information is rare and it is not an everyday practice of either of these institutions. As confirmed by Dr O'Brien, the former Interim Director of Policy and Public Affairs at the PO Office:

> 'There is no direct exchange of information between the Parliamentary Ombudsman office and the courts in connection with an exchange of court decisions and our reports.'

Also Ms Seex (the Local Government Ombudsman) confirmed that:

> 'There is no formal exchange of information between tribunals or courts and the Local Ombudsmen. No, except through the AJTC.'

The position of the judges is rather similar. They do not recognise any direct exchange of information. For instance, His Honour Judge Martin, President of the FTT (Chamber on Social Entitlements), stated in this connection:

> 'No, there is no formal way of exchanging information. However, there is nothing to stop me contacting Ann Abraham, who I know anyway, but there is the question whether we can identify common ground that would be useful. So at the moment it's only an informal way, because I know her and if I meet her and we talk I can say this is what's happening in my field, what's happening in your field? So there are informal, but very ad hoc exchanges although she would be aware of the Annual Report on the standards of decision-making that the tribunals publish and she may pick up some issues there.'

Mr Laverick, a former senior officer of the LGO service and a judge at the FTT (Local Government Standards in England), argued that:

> 'There is no formal way of exchanging information but there are a variety of informal examples, for example, at different conferences. There are some conferences that are specifically about some common issues. But it is three or four times a year that I came across the ombudsman. So there are occasions that I'm at the same places as they are. When I was the Pensions Ombudsman I would have come across the High Court judges. There are also other mostly social occasions and garden parties. And to be honest sometimes we had time to talk about interesting cases. These social occasions offer possibilities for some 'shop gossip'.'

Ms Knapman, the Deputy Master of the Administrative Court, noted that the ombudsmen must be individually proactive concerning the Court's judgments as:

> 'We [the Administrative Court] do not notify individual decisions to ombudsmen. Every substantive decision, every judgment is on the internet site of BAILII (British and Irish Legal Information Institute). They are in the public domain. If ombudsmen wanted this court to be aware of their decisions then they could clearly send them to me or to the court manager. But there is no point in sending us a decision that is not related to a case of ours.'

The absence of general norms that would formally establish an exchange of information between the researched subjects and the almost non-existent informal exchange of information can bring us to a similar conclusion as in the Netherlands. Ombudsmen and the judiciary in England try to adhere to their own spheres as closely as possible. There is no practice of exchanging judgments and reports between these bodies with the exception of their annual reports. An informal exchange of information is not completely excluded and can be found on the level of mutual, collegial and interpersonal relations rather than on the level of the ombudsmen and the judiciary as state institutions.

3.2.3 A short summary

As shown above, the *informal interaction* between the judiciary and the ombudsmen in England to a large extent is bound by and connected with their formal institutional coordination. From the previous pages it becomes clear that even though an informal interplay between the judiciary and ombudsmen does exist, it is usually connected with the highest representatives of the offices, i.e. ombudsmen themselves and the senior judges and at the level of informally *talking shop* or it is connected with general mutual awareness. However, this informal interplay tries to take into account, as far as possible, the formal framework set by the law and interpreted by the courts. Despite the impression that the interplay between ombudsmen and the judiciary exists in the framework of the statement *'this is my sphere and I stick to it'*, one can discover *mutual respect* and *awareness* between ombudsmen and the judiciary and also some informal, though very limited interconnection.

3.3 Summary

This chapter tried to find an answer to the question of *how the relations between ombudsmen and the judiciary in England are coordinated on the institutional level and what the content of this coordination is.* One can conclude that in England the *institutional coordination* has almost exclusively a *formal character*. Primary legislation sets the general framework for relations between the researched bodies. Formal mechanisms of coordination included in the written law are supported by the case law of the English courts that interpret the provisions of the law and sometimes stretch them. The tribunals and the ombudsmen do not add much to the development of the *formal institutional coordination* as they are either not connected with the power to make generally binding rules or this power cannot be deduced from the character of their offices. Written English law and the jurisprudence determine two different normative concepts for the ombudsmen and the courts – *maladministration* and *illegality.* As regards the tribunals, one can note that they generally assess *compliance with particular statutory requirements.*

In connection with the institutional coordination of ombudsman-judiciary relations in England one can discover the following mechanisms:

- *Formal barring mechanisms*, which limit the powers of the ombudsman in connection with the judgments or proceedings of the judiciary. These mechanisms include the statutory bars and limitations on ombudsmen regarding the subjects under their control and
- *Mechanisms covering formal issues*, as evidenced by the collecting powers of the ombudsman, contempt and obstruction.

The case law of the English senior courts often confirms and specifies the character of these relations. Based on the development of the case law of the English courts and the development of the judicial review procedure, the ombudsmen in England are *amenable to judicial review*. The legality of the actions and decisions of ombudsmen can be assessed by the courts. This fact puts the relations between the ombudsmen and the courts into a different position. Ombudsmen and the tribunals have, from the point of view of institutional coordination, probably fewer common grounds than the ombudsmen and the courts. The tribunals are closely connected with establishing statutes that do not allow an assessment of the administration in a way comparable with the ombudsmen.

Informal institutional interplay between the researched bodies exists only rarely. One can find it during high-level official meetings (e.g. annual conference of the AJTC) or based on mutual and friendly connections between judges and ombudsmen ('talking shop'). There is no specific cooperation or exchange of information that would go beyond formally established mechanisms.

A special *semi-formal forum* where ombudsmen, tribunals and even the courts can come together was (until July 2013) the AJTC. It was the only forum where these bodies could mutually discuss general issues such as the development of the administrative justice system and exchanging information.

Despite a relatively clear institutional delimitation of the powers of the ombudsmen and the judiciary there are still some areas that are not coordinated in the most *user-friendly* manner. This is for instance the ambiguity of the use of the judicial review procedure as a remedy of last resort and the statutory discretion given to ombudsmen to investigate cases even in the case of judicial or tribunal procedures (*Debt of Honour* case). As Dr Thompson (a member of the AJTC) put it:

> 'You have got a couple of what I would call 'Catch-22' situations, where in judicial review the rule says judicial review should be the last resort. The statutory bar on the ombudsman seems to be saying the same thing. So you could have a situation where the poor citizen is being told by both of these possibilities: "The other one is the one where you should be going to first!"'

Chapter 4

CASE COORDINATION OF OMBUDSMEN-JUDICIARY RELATIONS IN ENGLAND?

The second research question is connected with the *formal results* of the procedures of the ombudsmen and the judiciary in England, i.e. their 'decisions', the judgments of the courts and tribunals and the reports and other decisions of the ombudsmen. This chapter explains the *mutual significance of the reports of the ombudsmen and the judgments of the judiciary and their content in England and their possible interconnections.*

First of all, this chapter addresses the possible *formal case coordination* between the judgments and reports (4.1) and, secondly, it devotes attention to the *practical interplay* between these institutions in connection with their findings (4.2). The summary concludes the chapter (4.3).

4.1 Formal case coordination of ombudsman-judiciary relations?

Primary legislation, delegated legislation, the jurisprudence of the courts and tribunals and the ombudsprudence of the researched ombudsmen can include some mechanisms of *formal case coordination* between ombudsmen and the judiciary.

4.1.1 Formal case coordination of ombudsman-judiciary relations in codified law?

Primary legislation, delegated legislation and the *case law* of the courts formally coordinate ombudsmen and the judiciary at the *institutional level.*[1] In connection with the judgments and reports of ombudsmen the law does not provide any *real coordination mechanisms.*

A close inspection of the ombudsman statutes (the 1967 Act and the 1974 Act) and the statutes on the courts (especially the 1981 Act) and tribunals (statutes establishing the 5 chosen tribunals, the TCE 2007 Act and other regulations) does not *directly* show the applicability of the report by the ombudsman in court (tribunal) proceedings or *vice versa* the applicability of the court or tribunal judgment in the investigation of the ombudsmen.

The procedural rules of the courts and the tribunals are in this connection somewhat *clearer*. If one looks at the CPR, especially Rules 32 and 54, it is possible that these rules

1 See, section 3.1.1.

design general provisions concerning the use of *evidence in court proceedings*. If we concentrate on the judicial review procedure, then it shows that the *claim form* (for judicial review) must be accompanied by the *bundle of documents*.[2] Although the CPR do not refer in particular to the *reports of the ombudsman*, this bundle should include *copies of any document on which the claimant proposes to rely*. These copies of the documents may undoubtedly also include reports or other decisions of the ombudsman. Furthermore, during the proceedings the parties may, according to Rule 54.16 (2), rely on written evidence (including written ombudsman reports). Supperstone and Knapman argue that the only general rule which can be stated in connection with the judicial review procedure and evidence is that *all relevant evidence is admissible*, subject to exceptions.[3] Thus, the report of an English ombudsman is *a priori* not rejected. Still, an individual must submit it as evidence when asked at the permission stage as in the judicial review procedure fresh evidence is usually not taken into account.[4]

Similarly, the procedural rules of the tribunals do not forbid the use of ombudsmen's reports as evidence in their proceedings. For instance, the Tribunal Procedure Rules for the General Regulatory Chamber enable the tribunals to *permit or require party or another person to provide documents, information or submissions*.[5] In this connection the tribunals have a rather broad discretion as they may admit any evidence whether or not it is admissible in a civil trial in the UK or whether it was available to a previous decision maker.[6] Thus, it is not excluded that a report or another decision of an ombudsman can be relied upon before the tribunals.

In connection with ombudsmen, the application of judgments as evidence in their investigations is rather unclear. Neither the 1967 Act nor the 1974 Act describe the possibility for individuals or an ombudsman himself to rely on the judgment of a court or tribunal. However, due to the broad investigative powers of the PO and the LGO and their practice, individuals can support their statements with court or tribunal judgments in the ombudsman investigation.[7]

A close inspection of the ombudsman statutes (the 1967 Act and the 1974 Act) and the statutes on the courts (especially the 1981 Act) and tribunals (specialised statutes establishing the 5 chosen tribunals, the TCE 2007 Act and other regulations) did not reveal any other special formal mechanism that would *expresis verbis* coordinate relations between the findings of ombudsmen and the judiciary.

Although there is no specific regulation of these matters it is necessary to keep in mind the already mentioned *institutional coordination* by the statutory bars established for ombudsmen.[8] Because of these legal provisions ombudsmen have to acknowledge the

2 Rule 54.6 (2), the CPR and sec. 5.6, Practice Direction 54A.
3 Supperstone & Knappman 2008, p. 87.
4 See, *R v West Sussex Quarter Sessions, ex. p Albert and Maud Johnson Trust Ltd* [1974] QB 24.
5 Article 5 (3) d., the Tribunal Procedure (FTT) (General Regulatory Chamber) Rules 2009, Sec. I. 2009 No. 1976 (L. 20). A similar general power is also included in the tribunal procedure rules of other chambers of the FTT.
6 Ibid., Art. 15 (2) a.
7 See, section 4.2.1.1.
8 See, section 3.1.1.

existence of legal proceedings and/or the results thereof (based on the facts of the case) as they can bar their investigations. Thus, the law presumes that court/tribunal judgments have an indirect impact on an ombudsman's investigation.

4.1.2 Formal case coordination in the case law of the judiciary?

As shown in the previous chapter,[9] the courts can influence *institutional coordination* between them and ombudsmen. Apart from that they can influence *case coordination*. One can thus mention several judgments that have had an impact on the character of the ombudsmen reports in England.

4.1.2.1 Judiciary and the reports of the PO

The 1967 Act does not state that the reports of the PO are legally binding administrative (or other) decisions. The reports are only *recommendations* which, traditionally, are not legally binding.[10] This legally non-binding character of the PO's reports has been confirmed by the courts. Confirmation of this development can be found in *R (on the application of Bradley & Ors) v Secretary of State for Work & Pensions & Ors.*

> The court here dealt with an application for a judicial review of the decision of the Secretary of State for Work and Pensions who had rejected the recommendations included in the report of the PO. The Court of Appeal confirmed that 'the Secretary of State is entitled to reject a finding of maladministration and prefer his own view.'[11] 'There was nothing which suggested that in introducing legislation for the appointment of a Parliamentary Commissioner, the Government intended that Ministers (or the complainant) should be bound by findings in any report which the Commissioner might think it appropriate to make.'[12] The Court also underlined that it is not enough that the public body rejected the report on rational grounds as 'it is necessary that its decision to reject the Ombudsman's findings in favour of its own view is, itself, not irrational having regard to the legislative intention which underlies the 1967 Act.'[13]

Thus, the judgment on the one hand confirms the legally non-binding character of the reports of the PO. On the other hand, however, it notes that it is not enough for a public body to simply reject the PO's finding of maladministration as it *must have a rational reason for rejecting a finding which the Ombudsman has made after an investigation under the powers conferred by the 1967 Act.* The decision of a public body rejecting the PO's report should be *reasoned* and it *should not be irrational.* It should have *cogent reasons* for not accepting the PO's findings.[14] Here the *Bradley* judgment in my opinion modifies the character of the reports of the PO. Although it confirms its legally non-binding character, it also notes that the report is more than *an ordinary recommendation* that can be simply

9 See, section 3. 1.2.1.
10 See, Slapper & Kelly 2011, pp. 83-153.
11 *R (on the application of Bradley & Ors) v Secretary of State for Work & Pensions & Ors*, para. 51.
12 Ibid., para. 40.
13 Ibid.
14 See, Coe & Gay 2010, p. 3 or Elliott et al. 2011, p. 252.

overlooked. The court here *de facto* creates a legal *obligation* for the administration *to give reasons for rejecting the application of the recommendations included in the PO's report.* This possibly implies that the PO's report is more than just a piece of paper.

4.1.2.2 The judiciary and the reports of the LGO

In connection with the LGO there are two judgments that interpret the character of LGO findings. First of all, one has to mention the landmark case of *R v Local Commissioner for Administration, ex p Eastleigh Borough Council.*

> Lord Donaldson MR stated that in connection with the LGO, the Parliamentary intention was that 'reports by ombudsmen should be loyally accepted by the local authorities concerned.'[15] He supported his argument with the provisions of the 1974 Act which 'require the local authority to make the report available for inspection by the public and to advertise this fact, to notify the ombudsman of the action which it has taken and proposes to take in the light of his report' and which 'entitle the ombudsman to make a further report if the local authority's response is not satisfactory.'[16] Judicial review by the courts is the only possible remedy against the report of the ombudsman. Lord Donaldson reiterated that 'in the absence of a successful application for judicial review and the giving of relief by the court, local authorities should not dispute an ombudsman's report and should carry out their statutory duties in relation to it.'[17]

Thus, it seems that *local authorities should follow the recommendations of the LGO unless they are successfully challenged in the judicial review procedure.* The character of the LGO's reports differs from the character of the PO's reports as described above. The reports of the LGO are *factually binding on the administration unless they are challenged in the judicial review procedure.*

The latest development in the case law may indicate a different direction. In *R (on the application of Gallagher & Anor) v Basildon District Council,* similar to the *Bradley* case, a public body had rejected the recommendations included in the LGO report.

> Justice Parker here stated that 'as for the case law, the Eastleigh judgment cannot be authority for the proposition that recommendations are binding or that the rejection of recommendations must be based on "cogent reasons".'[18] He noted that at the time of *Eastleigh* the LGO had no statutory power to make recommendations. He reiterated that Parliament intended that local authorities should be entitled to consider the impact on the fair and efficient allocation of scarce local resources in deciding whether to accept a recommendation of the LGO and, in an appropriate case, to reject such a recommendation because of a disproportionate effect on such resources.[19]

15 *R v Local Commissioner for Administration, ex p Eastleigh Borough Council,* [1988] QB 866. See, also section 3.1.2.1.
16 Ibid.
17 Ibid.
18 *R (on the application of Gallagher & Anor) v Basildon District Council* [2010] EWHC 2824 (Admin), para. 28.
19 Ibid., para. 27.

Thus, based on this development a council can reject the recommendations of the LGO but this rejection must not be unreasonable or unlawful. It is questionable whether this judgment is in line with Eastleigh or whether it somehow changes the legal status of the reports of the LGO.

4.1.2.3 Tribunals and the reports of the researched ombudsmen

A close inspection of the casework of the chosen tribunals does not show that these tribunals develop any particular rule that directly or indirectly adds to the case coordination of the reports of the ombudsmen and their decisions.

4.1.3 Formal case coordination in the 'ombudsprudence'?

The reports and other decisions of the LGO and the PO are not binding on the English judiciary. Ombudsmen cannot *establish* or *create* a mechanism that can institutionally coordinate their relations with the judiciary. The same holds true in connection with *case coordination*. Ombudsmen can only *confirm* the existence of a mechanism that was created by written law or the case law of the courts. The practice of the PO and the LGO and their actual views concerning judgments is described in the following section.

4.2 Interplay between ombudsmen and the judiciary regarding their reports and judgments

As described above, there is only limited formal case coordination between the ombudsmen and the judiciary. This coordination is rather general and offers a possibility for a broad interpretation. Due to this fact and in order to be able to answer the second research question in a comprehensive manner, it is useful to look at the practice of the researched ombudsmen, the courts and the tribunals.

4.2.1 Practice of the researched ombudsmen

The interviewed ombudsmen agreed that court and occasionally tribunal judgments have some importance for their investigation. Although ombudsmen deal with maladministration, the judgments of the judiciary are not overlooked. Sometimes they are taken into consideration. The interviews and the investigation of the ombudsprudence confirm that ombudsmen *occasionally* make cross-references in their findings to judgments, courts and tribunals. These cross-references are only made on an *ad hoc* basis. Ms Abraham, Parliamentary Ombudsman (2002-2012), noted:

> 'Occasionally, [we do refer to courts in our reports]. But it would be quite unusual. I suppose there are certain areas in which that can be done. For example, there was a case called Bournewood, which is about the liberty of people with incapacity and that is featured as something that we have referred to. Sometimes, if we are looking at cases of complaints about maladministration by the UK Boarder Agency, there may have been decisions in the courts and we get records from there. So it does happen. But what I am

> saying is we don't feel that it's off limits but I would think that the majority of the cases that we report on are unlikely to have a reference to court judgments in them.'

Dr O'Brien (the former Interim Director of Policy and Public Affairs at the PO Office) added that:

> 'If there is directly relevant case law, this will be taken into account, even though the ombudsman does not apply a precedent in any formal way.'

The *ad hoc* character of references by the ombudsmen to court judgments was also highlighted by Ms Seex (the Local Government Ombudsman) who stated that there is a possibility to refer to case law through the written rules:

> 'I would say that we do refer to and rely on case law when it's necessary and appropriate in particular circumstances of that complaint. But a lot of what we do is looking at regulations or just standards of good administrative practice where you would not really need the case law. For example, when we look at a complaint about the allocation of places in schools to children, there is lots of case law on the standards of what should be in a decision letter about any important administrative action. And we could refer to all of those cases if we wanted to. But we don't need to because there is a statutory code that actually sets it out very clearly and therefore we rather rely on the code rather than the case law because it is simpler and easier and you know where to find it.'

A former senior officer of the LGO service, Mr Laverick, stated that there is a difference in the importance that is given to judgments by an ombudsman and vice versa:

> 'The PO and the LGO would take account of the law as it has been found by the High Court. The declarations of the law that are made by the High Court are binding on them but it is not the other way around. The ombudsmen should look at what the courts do but it does not count the other way around.'

Although the two researched ombudsmen are different institutions, they have a relatively similar practice of dealing with judgments of the judiciary. First of all, both ombudsmen are rather careful when referring to the courts. When referring to the courts they try to evade the creation of an illusion of some formal connection with the judiciary that can lead to a perception that they are an inferior court. Ombudsmen make cross-references to the judiciary only if there is a need to do so. The cross-references are *not premeditated*, they are *ad hoc* and, with the exception of the annual reports, they are *connected with a particular case*. The research shows that the PO and the LGO refer to the courts and tribunals only on rare occasions with a rather limited scope. When discussing the PO one can only presume this practice, as his/her investigative reports are not accessible. Only in a handful of their published reports can one find any reference to the judiciary. The following scheme points to the amount of cross-references to the judiciary made by the ombudsmen between 1/1/2005 – 31/7/2013.[20]

20 As noted in Part 1 this limitation is not applicable in connection with the PO.

Scheme 2 – **Amount of ombudsmen's cross-references to the judiciary**

Cross-references	To a court	To a tribunal	Accessible ombudsprudence 1/1/2005 –31/7/2013
The LGO*	in 33 reports in 57 decision statements	in 12 reports in 47 decision statements	542 reports 107 decision statements
The PO	in 37 accessible reports	in 17 accessible reports	42 reports (including special reports). Five of these reports are digests of cases which include another 60 cases.

* See, the internet site of the LGO < http://www.lgo.org.uk/decisions/ > (accessed on 31 July 2013).

Despite the small amount of cross-references to the judiciary made by the ombudsmen it is possible to find the following typology of the cross-references. Because of the relatively limited number of cases the typology of both researched ombudsmen is described together.

4.2.1.1 A typology of ombudsman cross-references to the judiciary

1. Competence cross-references

In the practice of both ombudsmen one can find cases in which they explain why in a particular case they can act or conversely why the investigations are not possible. By these cross-references to the judiciary, the ombudsmen do not refer to rules adopted by the judiciary; they only explain their ability or inability to deal with the cases in connection with the judiciary. In the *Report on an investigation into a complaint against the London Borough of Newham* the LGO noted that:

> 'The Act says that I cannot conduct any investigation into "the commencement or conduct of civil or criminal proceedings in any court of law". However, I retain jurisdiction to investigate administrative actions prior to the issue of court proceedings and, where the Council instructs agents for enforcement of court orders, the actions of those agents (unless they are agents of the Court).'[21]

In the *Report on an investigation into a complaint against Wiltshire County Council* the LGO made a cross-reference to a tribunal in the following sense:

> 'Where a complaint is made to me for which the complainant has a remedy available by way of appeal to an independent tribunal, I may investigate the complaint if I consider it unreasonable to expect the complainant to appeal.(Local Government Act 1974, s26(6)(a)) But where the complainant has already appealed, I lose all discretion in the matter. (R v Commissioner for Local Administration, ex p PH [1999]).'[22]

Even the PO sometimes explains why he/she can deal with the case. This was done it, for example, in the special report *A Debt of Honour.*

21 Report on an investigation into complaint no. 08 019 113 against the London Borough of Newham, para. 6.
22 Report on an investigation into complaint no. 06/B/06454 against Wiltshire County Council, para. 18.

> The PO had to deal with a possible alternative remedy for the complainant. She stated that 'my predecessor received the referral of Professor Hayward's complaint ... While my predecessor was considering whether to investigate Professor Hayward's complaint, he was informed that the Association of British Civilian Internees Far Eastern Region (ABCIFER) had initiated an application for judicial review impugning the *legality* of the scheme ... . Professor Hayward was not party to the judicial review proceedings concerned with the position of civilian internees and he had never been a member of the organisation which initiated them. It was my conclusion that he had not exercised an alternative remedy through ABCIFER's actions.'[23]

Hence, the two researched ombudsmen usually refer in their reports to the judiciary or its proceedings when assessing their own competence to deal with the case at hand. They only do so in 'borderline' cases that can have some connection with the judiciary.[24]

2. Factual (descriptive) cross-references

The PO and the LGO also make cross-references to the judiciary when they describe the facts of the case. Although the competence of both ombudsmen is limited in cases where the complainant has or had an alternative legal remedy[25] sometimes the previous judiciary proceedings can be connected with the case or the complainant. By these cross-references to the judiciary, the ombudsmen only describe the actual facts of a particular case. For example, in the *Report on an investigation into a complaint against Wirral Metropolitan Borough Council* the LGO stated:

> 'Mr H appealed to a Special Education Needs and Disability Tribunal about the content of S's statement and the school that was named. In November 2006 the Tribunal's decisions included a ruling that the Statement should name the school preferred by Mr H ... .'[26]

In the practice of the PO it is possible to find such references, for instance, in the report *Investigation into delays in making payments under the Arable Area Payments Scheme* where the PO stated as a matter of fact that:

> 'The High Court judgment of 10 February 1998 established that there was a legal entitlement for farmers to recover payments under the scheme provided that the qualifying conditions were fulfilled, and "the respondent [Ministry of Agriculture, Fisheries and Food] accepts that if I conclude, as I have, that the section [of the Supreme

23 Special report *A Debt of Honour*, paras. 18 and 23.

24 See, also the Report on an investigation into complaint no. 07B05001 against Oxfordshire County Council, para. 64; Report on an investigation into complaint no. 05/C/00898 against Trafford Metropolitan Borough Council, para. 25 or the Report *A Further Investigation of the Prudential Regulation of Equitable Life?* of 19 July 2004, p. 13.

25 See, section 3.1.1.

26 Report on an investigation into complaint no. 07/C/03447 against Wirral Metropolitan Borough Council, para. 4.

> Court Act] is in principle applicable to these claims so that action by writ might have been brought in respect of them, interest should be payable … .'[27]

By these factual cross-references the ombudsmen refer to the judiciary only when they describe the facts of the case that are important for the investigated complaint.[28]

3. Explanatory cross-references

Sometimes the ombudsmen can explain the power of the courts or tribunals to the parties which are subject to their investigation and/or the obligations that the parties have towards the judiciary. An explanatory reference can be found, for example, in the *Report on an investigation into a complaint against the London Borough of Newham.* The LGO here noted that:

> 'Before making a person bankrupt a statutory demand must be served on them, which details the debts owed. If no suitable arrangement is made and the debt is still owed then the creditor may issue a bankruptcy petition. A County or High Court judge will decide if the debtor is to be made bankrupt. If a bankruptcy order is made then the case will be passed to the Official Receiver, who may appoint a Trustee in Bankruptcy to realise the debtor's assets for the benefit of the creditors.'[29]

A short, but very expressive explanatory reference was included in the *Report on an investigation into a complaint against Bradford Metropolitan District Council* where the LGO very clearly expressed that *only the courts can determine whether a council has acted lawfully.*[30]Another explanatory reference can be found in the report *Environmentally unfriendly,* a report of a joint investigation by the PO and the LGO. The PO here referred to the general powers of the courts in the following way:

> 'Although the Agency had issued section 71 notices (paragraph 29) to Mr R and Mr M to try and get the evidence about ownership, Mr M's solicitors had told them that they had lost the relevant file relating to the purchase of the land. The officer said that section 71 notices were generally used to establish specific information which could then be used as the basis for an interview. However, if a person incriminated themselves in their response to such a notice, it could be ruled inadmissible by the court.'[31]

27 Report on an *Investigation into delays in making payments under the Arable Area Payments Scheme* of 10 July 2000, para. 17.

28 See, also Report on an investigation into complaint no. 05/C/03466 against Gateshead Metropolitan Borough Council, para. 12; Report on an investigation into complaint no. 06/B/06454 against Wiltshire County Council, para. 23; the Report *The Ostrich Farming Corporation Limited* of 27 April 1999, para. 41 or the Report *'Small mistakes, big consequences'* of 19 November 2009, p. 37.

29 Report on an investigation into complaint no. 08 019 113 against the London Borough of Newham, para. 13.

30 Report on an investigation into complaint no. 06/C/02472 against Bradford Metropolitan District Council, para. 46.

31 The Report *Environmentally unfriendly: a report of a joint investigation by the PO and the Local Government Ombudsman* of 20 January 2010, para. 90.

In the report *The Prudential Regulation of Equitable Life* the PO explained that *questions and disputes about the interpretation of legislation are matters for the courts to determine.*[32] By these cross-references, the ombudsmen explain the powers of the judiciary.[33]

4. Supportive cross-references

In some reports it is possible to observe more substantial cross-references to the judiciary. Some cross-references are connected with the application of certain norms previously explained or interpreted by the judiciary. They confirm that the LGO and the PO are well aware of the case law of the English courts and, when necessary, they make use thereof. The ombudsmen can support their findings with the judgments or they can refer to the rule that was previously developed by the judiciary. An example can be found in the *Report on an investigation into a complaint against St Helens Metropolitan Borough Council* where the LGO referred to a particular court judgment in order to refer to a particular rule interpreted by the courts:

> 'The public inspection and personal notification duties must be carried out by a Council as soon as practicable after the TPO [Tree preservation order] has been made. This term is not defined in The Town and Country Planning (Trees) Regulations 1999, but is one which is commonly used in a number of areas of law, and it has been considered by the Courts on a number of occasions. It means that action must be taken as soon as is reasonably feasible (see Mary Devoy v World Duty Free (Europe) Ltd LTL 8/1/2001).'[34]

In the *Report on an investigation of a complaint against Herefordshire Council* the LGO found support in a court judgment explaining the law:

> '7. The Courts have affirmed that officers may deal with working amendments to a planning permission where the variations are not considered material and that it is appropriate for officers to decide whether a proposed amendment is minor or material. But it has been held that interested parties should be informed of requested changes that may directly affect them.
> 8. In Breckland District Council v Secretary of State 1992, the Court ruled that third parties had a right to be informed of and consulted on any amendment that materially affected them. In British Telecommunications v Gloucester City Council 2001, the High Court ruled that it was appropriate for local planning authorities to take a pragmatic approach when considering amendments to a planning application. The question was whether the change was so substantial that, in the interests of fairness, a fresh application should be lodged.'[35]

32 The Report *The Prudential Regulation of Equitable Life, Part II: Full Text of Representative Investigation* of 30 June 2003, para. 5.

33 See, Report on an investigation into complaint no. 06/B/01231 against Manchester City Council, para. 3; Report on an investigation into complaint nos. 05/C/14043 and 05/C/14757 against Birmingham City Council, para. 5; or Report on an investigation into complaint no. 06/B/06454 against Wiltshire County Council, para. 6.

34 Report on an investigation into complaint no. 05/C/01218 against St Helens Metropolitan Borough Council, para. 10.

35 Ibid., para. 7.

In the *Report on an investigation into a complaint against York City Council* the LGO found support in a judgment in connection with a recommendation for a remedy:

> 'To remedy this injustice I recommend that the Council should: 1. Calculate the financial loss caused to Mrs Sharpe and give that sum, plus interest at the County Court rate, as reimbursement; ...'[36]

Similarly, the PO, when recommending financial compensation, advised the administrative institution to use an interest rate specified in the rules for relevant courts. This was done in the report *'Cold Comfort'*:

> 'Payments for financial loss should be calculated by looking at how much the complainant has demonstrably lost or what extra costs they incurred. In addition, and as described in the Principles for Remedy, an appropriate interest rate should be applied to payments for financial loss, aimed at restoring complainants to the position they would have been in had the maladministration not occurred. As a general principle, and if there is not a good reason to use another rate, I recommend using the rate specified in the rules for the relevant courts.'[37]

Thus by these cross-references the ombudsmen directly grasp a certain rule adopted by the judiciary and apply it in their own procedure.[38]

5. Cross-references connected with a finding of maladministration and recommendations
The last type of references that can be found is in cases where the ombudsman finds an instance of maladministration in the conduct of an administrative body that is directly connected with the application of a particular decision of the judiciary. By these cross-references ombudsmen de facto require the administration to follow the court judgments and hence they add to legal certainty. For instance, in the *Report on an investigation into a complaint against Northampton Borough Council* the LGO found that:

> 'All of the above failings also took place against the backdrop of Ms Adams facing the threat of eviction as a result of the Council's decision to pursue recovery action through the Courts from August 2005 onwards. The knowledge that this action was proceeding should have lent both extra care and urgency to the Council's processing of Ms Adams' benefit claims. But the evidence is that even in the light of these proceedings, no extra priority was given to resolving Ms Adams' benefit claims, with the Council even failing to comply with the order of the County Court to resolve the benefit position as a matter of urgency. This was maladministration.'[39]

36 Report on an investigation into complaint no. 04/B/01280 against York City Council, para. 54.

37 The Report *Cold Comfort: the Administration of the 2005 Single Payment Scheme by the Rural Payments Agency*, para. 38.

38 See, for example, Report on an investigation into complaint nos. 04/C/07580, 04/C/07906, 04/C/07909, 04/C/08472 and 04/C/09824 against Rossendale Borough Council para. 11, Report on an investigation into complaint no. 07/A/12661 against the London Borough of Camden.

39 Report on an investigation into complaint no. 05/B/16773 against Northampton Borough Council, para. 81.

A similar cross-reference was also included in the *Report on an investigation into a complaint against Birmingham City Council* where the LGO found that:

> 'Natasha was two years old when she first came to the notice of the Council, having swallowed her mother's methadone. By the time she was four, in May 2000, the Council's initial assessment suggested that she was living in a violent home with at least one drug-using parent. She was made the subject of a Care Order which placed her in the care of the Council. … Yet the Council failed to have any contact with Natasha, to supervise the placement or to comply in any way with the Contact Order made by the Courts for the next eighteen months. That was very clearly maladministration.'[40]

Based on these examples, ignoring the decisions of the judiciary can lead to the assessment that there was maladministration. Due to the limited number of published reports of the PO I was not able to find this type of reference in the practice of this ombudsman. However, the LGO refers to the judiciary in this particular way also in other cases.[41]

Sometimes the ombudsmen recommend the public body to commence court or tribunal proceedings. This happened in *Report on an investigation into a complaint against the London Borough of Camden* where the LGO noted this point:

> 'I must now seek to put Mrs Gordon in the position that she would have been, had no maladministration occurred. My draft report recommended that the Council should apply to the court for the annulment of Mrs Gordon's bankruptcy, on the grounds she was not capable of managing her own affairs at the time and pay the costs of this action. I am pleased to say that the Council has applied for an annulment.'[42]

A similar reference is made in *Report on an investigation into a complaint against Cornwall County Council* where the LGO recommended that the Council should properly implement a tribunal decision.

> The commissioner 'recommended that the Council should: ensure that the provision ordered by the Special [Educational] Needs and Disability Tribunal in December 2006 is implemented, including the timely preparation of Individual Education Plans.'[43]

Similar cases can be found in the practice of the PO. In the report *Tax Credits: Putting Things Right* the PO makes a recommendation to file an appeal with an independent tribunal.

> In this connection the PO states that '[a] statutory test for the recovery of overpayments has been applied for many years. This test seems to strike the right balance between the obligations on the part of the administrators and those on the part of the recipients.

40 Report on an investigation into complaint nos. 05/C/14043 and 05/C/14757 against Birmingham City Council, para. 57.

41 Report on an investigation into complaint no. 07/C/03447 against Wirral Metropolitan Borough Council, para. 17.

42 Report on an investigation into complaint no. 07/A/12661 against the London Borough of Camden, para. 43

43 Report on an investigation into complaint no. 06/B/04337 against Cornwall County Council, para. 43

It is therefore difficult to understand why this model of a statutory test should not be applied in tax credits cases, with a right of appeal to an independent tribunal. I therefore recommend that consideration is given to the adoption of a statutory test for recovery of excess payments and overpayments of tax credits, consistent with the test that is currently applied to social security benefits, with a right of appeal to an independent tribunal.'[44]

4.2.1.2 A short summary

As can be seen from the previous examples, the LGO and the PO are aware of the courts and the tribunals, their powers and their decisions and sometimes they make cross-references to these decisions or powers. These references are not very common or premeditated. They are made on an *ad hoc basis* and are connected with individual cases. The references are limited to mentioning the courts or tribunals that are in some way connected with the individual case at hand. In the actual practice of the ombudsmen it is possible to identify cross-references where the ombudsmen *explain* their ability to deal with cases, *explain* the powers of the judiciary, *describe* the facts of the case or *make use of* the rule adopted by the judiciary. These references do not change the character or authority of the report but they allow us to understand the attitude and knowledge of the ombudsman about the judiciary.

In general, the courts and their judgments receive wider attention than tribunals and their judgments. Still, the types of references to the tribunals and to the courts in the reports of the PO and the LGO are similar. As the majority of the PO's ombudsprudence is not accessible one can only guess at how these issues are dealt with in the PO's investigation reports.

4.2.2 Practice of the courts

The judiciary is not obliged to consider the reports or other decisions of the PO or the LGO. This is connected with the ombudsmen's inability to create the law and the applicability of the judicial review procedure to their actions and decisions. Ms Knapman, the Deputy Master of the Administrative Court, noted that:

> 'The Administrative Court takes into account also the reports of the ombudsmen but only if they are a part of a challenge to ombudsmen. But it is very rare, unless the parties were seeking to rely on the facts within the ombudsman report and there was no dispute as to what are the facts, because for the court it would be very unlikely to distinguish them and to have a different view.'

Nonetheless, there are situations in which the English courts make cross-references to ombudsmen and/or their reports. Scheme 3 shows a limited amount of accessible cases where the courts made cross-references to ombudsmen.

44 The Report *Tax Credits: Putting Things Right* of 21 June 2005, paras. 5.64-5.66.

Scheme 3 – **Cross-references by the courts to the researched ombudsmen**[45]

Cross-references in accessible judgments 1/1/2005 – 31/7/2013 to	**PO**	**PCA**	**PHSO**	**LGO**
Courts	23	29	8	54

The research into these judgments proved that the typology of the references differs from the typology as included in the previous national case (the Netherlands). This is connected with the possibility of the courts to review the legality of the ombudsmen's decisions. Because of that, one can distinguish the following typology of references to the ombudsmen and their decisions.

The majority of *accessible* cross-references by the English courts to ombudsmen and/or their decisions was made *in the judicial review procedure.* The courts can make these cross-references when they review ombudsmen's actions or when they review the actions of other bodies.[46] During the *review of ombudsmen's actions* the courts deal with these actions and/or decisions because of the possibility that the decision or action of the ombudsman was not lawful. As the courts in these proceedings assess the legality of the decisions/actions taken by ombudsmen, it is not strange that they refer to ombudsmen reports or quote from them.[47] During a *review of the decisions or actions of bodies other than ombudsmen* the courts only make cross-references to the ombudsman if there is a connection between the reviewed action of the other public body and the ombudsman. For example, the rejection of recommendations included in the report of the ombudsman by a public body can lead to a judicial review of the action of this body.[48]

The courts can also make cross-references to the ombudsmen *outside the judicial review procedure,* for example, in appellate proceedings, in proceedings dealing with human rights or in statutory review proceedings. However, at least according to www.bailii.org, these cases are not as common (or as commonly published) as the cases connected with a judicial review.

As there are only a handful of cases where the courts have made cross-references to the ombudsmen both of these categories are approached together. One can find the following types of cross-references by the courts to ombudsmen and/or their decisions.[49]

1. Factual (descriptive) cross-references

Usually, when dealing with claims for a judicial review of an ombudsman's decision, the courts describe the facts of the case in great detail. Sometimes they even quote the important parts of the contested report or decision. These references are made because of the need for a precise description of the facts of the case. For example, in *R (on the*

45 These examples were found on the site <www.bailii.org>.

46 See, section 3.1.2.

47 See, *R (on the application of Adams) v The Commission for Local Administration In England & Ors* [2011] EWHC 2972 (Admin), para. 5.

48 See, sections 3.1.2.2 and 4.1.2.1.

49 This typology will not be very broad as important 'landmark' cases involving a judicial review of ombudsman decisions were discussed in section 3.1.2.1.1.

application of Abernethy) v Local Government Ombudsman Sir Swinton Thomas noted as a matter of fact that:

> 'On 10th October 1996 Mr Abernethy complained about the council's decision to the LGO. The ombudsman – in two letters dated 8 January 1998 and 12 March 1998 – refused to investigate the complaint principally because he considered that Mr Abernethy had suffered no significant injustice as a result of the council's decision.'[50]

In this cross-reference the court only depicted the investigation of the LGO as one of the facts of the dispute. The majority of the judgments in the judicial review proceedings include these cross-references.[51]

2. Explanatory (interpretative) cross-references

The English courts tend to explain or reiterate the powers of the ombudsmen. This tendency is often connected with the need to explain the powers and obligations of the ombudsmen and to explain why an ombudsman can decide the dispute in one way or another. These cross-references may also include an explanation of the status of the courts in connection with the ombudsmen and their proceedings. Sometimes these explanations are connected with an authoritative interpretation of the law. An example of this cross-reference can be found in *R (on the application of Abernethy) v Local Government Ombudsman:*

> 'I well understand the strength of feeling that Mr Abernethy has about all these matters, but as I am sure he appreciates, the court could only interfere with a decision by an Ombudsman if an error of law has been identified….'[52]

In the case *R (on the application of Evison) v the Commissioner for Local Administration in England* Mr Justice Cranston explained that:

> 'Generally speaking, however, the situation is that once an individual who complains about maladministration by a local government authority has taken legal action, that effectively bars him from having the matter dealt with by the Ombudsman. The underlying policy is clear. The claimant has a choice: either to proceed before the Ombudsman and have the matter dealt with by his informal investigative techniques; or to take legal action. Once legal action is taken, the right to pursue a complaint before the *Local Government Ombudsman* is effectively barred.'[53]

50 *R (on the application of Abernethy) v Local Government Ombudsman* [2002] EWCA Civ 552, para. 3.

51 See, for example, *R (on the application of Balchin & Ors) v Parliamentary Commissioner for Administration*, [1999] EWHC Admin 484 or *R v Parliamentary Commissioner for Administration ex p. Dyer* [1993] EWHC (Admin 3) or *R (on the application of Klimas) v Prosecutors General Office of Lithuania* [2010] EWHC 2076 (Admin). Outside the judicial review procedure see, for example, *Neil Martin Ltd v Revenue and Customs* [2006] EWHC 2425 (Ch), paras. 51-53 or *Poole & Ors v Her Majesty's Treasury* [2006] EWHC 2731 (Comm), para. 148.

52 *R (on the application of Abernethy) v Local Government Ombudsman* [2002] EWCA Civ 1520, para. 13.

53 *R (on the application of Evison) v The Commissioner for Local Administration & Anor* [2008] EWHC 3568 (Admin), para. 12.

In these cross-references the courts interpret the competences of ombudsmen.[54]

3. Assessing cross-references

As the judicial review procedure can lead to a judgment as to whether or not an action or a decision of the ombudsman is in accordance with the law, the courts must assess the ombudsman's action or decision against certain rules. They then make a cross-reference to the ombudsman in these judgments. For example, in the case of *R (on the application of Mahajan) v Local Government Ombudsman* Justice Munby assessed that:

> '21. The Local Government Ombudsman's summary grounds for contesting this part of the claim are as follows: "The decision of the Ombudsman to discontinue the investigation was a lawful exercise of the Ombudsman's discretion and there is no basis whatsoever for impugning that decision."
> 22. I entirely agree with that. The summary grounds continue: "It is submitted that the court is not entitled to substitute its decision for that of the Ombudsman (which is what the claimant in effect invites the court to do) and there are no arguable grounds for concluding that the Ombudsman has gone wrong in law. Again, I entirely agree with that.'[55]

Another assessment cross-reference can be found in, for instance, *R (on the application of Murray) v Parliamentary Commissioner for Administration)* where Lord Justice Potter stated:

> 'Finally, I would observe that I have seen no hint or suspicion of bias on the part of the Ombudsman in the exercise of his discretion under sec. 5(2) (b) which seems to me to have been one of reason and good sense in that, whatever the applicant's motivation for seeking an investigation of the Legal Aid Board's maladministration, it can do nothing to secure for him an effective remedy for the original and continuing source of his grievance.'[56]

Although only a handful of actions or decisions by ombudsmen are substantially reviewed in the judicial review procedure, one can find other examples where the courts have assessed the compliance of the ombudsman's action or decision with the law.[57]

54 See also, *R (on the application of Adams) v The Commission for Local Administration In England & Ors* [2011] EWHC 2972 (Admin), para. 30; *R(on the Application of Scholarstica Umo) v Commissioner for Local Administration In England* [2003] EWHC 3202 (Admin), para. 17; or *R (on the Application of Atapattu) v The Secretary of State for the Home Department* [2011] EWHC 1388 (Admin). Outside the judicial review procedure see, for example, *Home Office v Mohammed & Ors* [2011] EWCA Civ 351, paras. 25-26 or *Equitable Life Assurance Society*, Re [2002] EWHC 140 (Ch), para. 22.

55 *R (on the application of Mahajan) v Local Government Ombudsman* [2007] EWHC 1135 (Admin).

56 *R (on the application of Murray) v Parliamentary Commissioner for Administration* [2002] EWCA Civ 1472, para. 37.

57 See, for example, *R (on the application of Balchin & Ors) v Parliamentary Commissioner for Administration,* [1999] EWHC Admin 484, para. 49 or *R (on the application of Senior-Milne) v the Parliamentary and Health Service Ombudsman* [2009] EWHC 2240 (Admin), para. 33.

4. Inspirational cross-references

There are also so-called inspirational cross-references. One can find them outside the judicial review procedure. In some cases, the courts are not interested in an assessment of the legality of the ombudsman reports but they take into account the ombudsprudence or practice of ombudsmen. Hence, the report of the ombudsman can *possibly* become a *source of inspiration* and a *source of information for the court*. One of the examples of this practice is a claim for damages under the HRA 1998 included in the judgment *R (on the application of Bernard) v London Borough of Enfield.*

> In this case the court dealt with damages in accordance with the HRA 1998. Justice Sullivan in this connection looked into the recommendations of the LGO for inspiration as to the amount of awards for breaches of this act. He stated that 'many complaints to the LGO are made by or on behalf of disabled persons who contend that they have been deprived of benefits or assistance as a result of maladministration. This is in broad terms what has occurred in the present case.'
>
> He added that 'I have found the awards recommended by the LGO of great assistance. In effect, they are seeking to give just satisfaction for the adverse consequences of administrative failings of the kind which occurred in the present case. But it is important to bear in mind that in every case the Ombudsman's report will try to explain how the maladministration occurred. Part of the remedy is invariably a recommendation that the Council apologise to the claimant, if it has not already done so. In very many cases assurances are given that procedures have been improved so as to reduce the risk of similar mistakes in the future.
>
> The LGO's recommended awards are the best available United Kingdom comparables. Although I am awarding damages under sec. 8 as just satisfaction for a breach of the claimants' Article 8 rights, this case is, in essence, an extreme example of maladministration which has deprived the second claimant of much needed social services care.'[58]

Hence, the recommendations of the LGO proved to be interesting for the judiciary. Apart from that Justice Sullivan appreciated the work of the LGO. A similar approach was adopted by Justice Tugendhat in *W v Westminister City Council.*[59] One can point to the judgment of the Court of Appeal in *Anufrijeva v London Borough of Southwark* where the court stated that:

> 'The levels of awards made by the Criminal Injuries Compensation Board and by the Parliamentary Ombudsman and the Local Government Ombudsman may all provide some rough guidance where the consequences of the infringement of human rights are similar to that being considered in the comparator selected. In cases of maladministration where the consequences are not of a type which gives rise to any right to compensation under our civil law, the awards of the Ombudsman may be the *only* comparator.'[60]

58 *R (on the application of Bernard) v London Borough of Enfield* [2002] EWHC 2282 (Admin), paras. 45-60.
59 *W v Westminister City Council* [2005] EWHC 102 (QB), para. 248.
60 *Anufrijeva v London Borough of Southwark* [2003] EWCA Civ 1406, para. 74.

Although these cases are connected with the HRA 1998 and at the time of these proceedings the courts did not have enough experience in how to approach the remedying of breaches of this act, one cannot *a priori* exclude that the courts may possibly find inspiration in ombudsman reports in other cases.[61] However, even if the court finds inspiration or an interesting point in the report of the ombudsman it does not mean that this will always be noted in the written judgment.

4.2.3 Practice of the chosen tribunals

As noted in Chapter 3, only the practice of five chosen tribunals and their accessible jurisprudence was included and considered in this research. Although the tribunals are part of the judiciary and although *the TCE 2007 Act* introduced the possibility for the Upper Tribunal to exercise the judicial review procedure, this power of the Upper Tribunal does not extend to the PO or the LGO.

In general, the reports of the ombudsmen are not that important for the practice of the tribunals. This however depends on the particular powers of the tribunal. For example, Judge Laverick, FTT (Local Government Standards for England), noted that the reports of the LGO have some importance for the work of this tribunal:

> 'If an ombudsman has already investigated a Councillor's participation in a planning application and has said that the Councillor was present at the meeting and did speak, then we would accept that as evidence of those facts subject to any challenges that the party wishes to make. We start on the assumption that what the ombudsman has found was right, factually right, but we wouldn't be bound if it was proved to us that she has got it wrong. But we certainly wouldn't say that there is no way that you can come up with what the ombudsman said. But we would say, looking at that planning example, that the judgment has to be made on whether the Councillor had the kind of interest which should have prevented him from participating. We certainly wouldn't be bound by the ombudsman on how that judgment should be. We will decide on that and that's the question of the judgment and not the fact.'

Judges Birrell, O'Brien and Herwald, all FTT (Mental Health), conversely noted that the reports of the ombudsmen do not play any special role in connection with this particular tribunal. This is because it is rare for applicants to this tribunal to use the reports of ombudsmen in order to support their own arguments. In connection with his practice as a FTT (Special Educational Needs) judge, Judge Herwald noted that:

> 'In many years I have had only one or two cases where parties have produced the report of the ombudsman which has carried some weight, but to be honest it has been on a completely different point. So even if it was produced, it dealt with different things. Of course, I have taken that into account but usually it was never mentioned in my decision. But that is because it has not been necessarily relevant. All it was saying was that the council had acted in a way that shows that there was maladministration but that would not necessarily impact my decision at all, because today I am making a

61 See, for example, *Secretary of State for Defence v Elias* [2006] EWCA Civ 1293.

> decision as to whether or not the law applies in a particular way to a particular child in education. If I am forcing the issue, it might carry some weight in the sense that if the council was 'maladministrating' the issue years ago then maybe I am not happy with its decision today. But also then I would have to decide on the evidence before me.'

Judge Holbrook, Employment Tribunal and FTT (Charity), confirmed that the reports of ombudsmen could be used as evidence although it is difficult to imagine the circumstances in which this would be done. After researching the casework of the chosen tribunals it was possible to find the following facts as regards *case coordination*.

1. The research proved that the decisions of the *FTT* (*Mental Health*) are published only to a limited extent. The official internet site of the English judiciary[62] includes only a minimum amount of judgments by this particular tribunal and none of the published decisions referred in any way to any of the researched ombudsmen and/or their reports. Neither www.bailii.org nor www.osscsc.gov.uk/Aspx includes any decision by this particular tribunal or the Upper Tribunal dealing with an appeal against the decision of this tribunal that refers to the PO or the LGO or their decisions.

2. Decisions of the *FTT* (*Local Government Standards for England*) are accessible online.[63] An investigation of this search engine showed that between 1/1/2005 – 31/7/2013 this tribunal made cross-references to ombudsmen, particularly to the LGO, in 26 cases. Despite this limited number of cross-references it was possible to find the following types of cross-references to the ombudsman. Apart from the *factual references* that only describe the facts of the case[64] and the *explanatory references* where the tribunal explains the legal possibilities for the applicant, such as filing a complaint with the ombudsman,[65] it was possible to find a *reference where the tribunal assessed the participation of a councillor in the investigation of the LGO in connection with a breach of conduct by this councillor*. In these cases the Tribunal assessed whether the complaint by the councillor with the LGO (often as a private person) could have led to a breach of the *Code of Conduct of the local council*. For example, in *Case APE 0377: Reference in relation to a possible failure to follow the Code of Conduct* (Hudson, Great Yarmouth Borough Council).

> The tribunal in this case dealt with allegations by an ethical standards officer who stated, among other things, that a councillor, by complaining to the LGO that a planning officer of the Council was professionally incompetent, had failed to comply with Great Yarmouth Borough Council's Code of Conduct. Next to factual references where the tribunal described the involvement of the LGO in the said case, it assessed whether complaining to the LGO in this case resulted in a breach of the Council's Code

62 <www.judiciary.gov.uk/media/tribunal-decisions/mh-trib-decisions.htm> (accessed on 31 July 2013).

63 <www.adjudicationpanel.tribunals.gov.uk/Public/Decisions.aspx> (accessed on 31 July 2013).

64 For example, APE 0376: *Reference in relation to a possible failure to follow the Code of Conduct* (Sandy, Rushmoor Borough Council) or APE 0323: *Reference in relation to a possible failure to follow the Code of Conduct* (Watts, West Oxfordshire District Council).

65 For example, APE 0276: *Reference in relation to a possible failure to follow the Code of Conduct* (Cobbledick, Bude Stratton Town Council) or LGS/2009/0477: *Reference about possible failure to follow the Code of Conduct* (Shropshire Council Standards Committee Andrews).

> of Conduct. The tribunal stated that it 'fully accepted that a councillor had a right to complain if he felt that an officer of the Council was not fulfilling his role competently. However, that did not give a councillor the right to make wild allegations to besmirch the name of officers. The Case Tribunal felt that the Respondent had misused a legitimate route for complaint, i.e. to the local government ombudsman, to continue making allegations which had been demonstrated to have no substance.'[66]

Here the tribunal did not assess the quality of the LGO's report, nor was it interested in the rules or principles used by the LGO. It used the report as evidence in order to assess the alleged breaches of the Code of Conduct. A similar example can be found in Case No: LGS/2011/0559: *Appeal by a former member of a local authority against a Standards Committee decision* (Bence, Darlington Borough Council Standards Committee).

> The tribunal here took into account the report of the LGO where the ombudsman had found an instance of maladministration. The procedure before the LGO started with a complaint by a councillor. Also by pointing to this complaint the tribunal discovered a *personal interest of the appellant* (the councillor) that was likely to prejudice her judgement of the public interest when acting as a councillor in the case which in the end led to a failure to comply with the Code of Conduct.[67]

These references have an *ad hoc* character. One can find similar examples in other decisions by this tribunal.[68]

3. In connection with the *FTT* (*Charity*) only a handful of cases were published online on the official site of the tribunal[69] and on the internet site <www.bailii.org>. Unfortunately, none of the published decisions included a reference to the two researched ombudsmen. Internet sites that include the decisions of the Upper Tribunal <www.osscsc.gov.uk/Aspx> do not include decisions that refer to the researched ombudsmen connected with the Charity Tribunal.

4. As the *FTT* (*Social Security and Child Support*) does not publish appeal hearing decisions or disclose them to any parties other than the appellants, their representatives (if they have one), and the first-tier agency that made the original decision,[70] it was not possible to assess whether this tribunal makes any cross-references to the two researched ombudsmen in its decisions. The internet site that publishes the decisions of the Upper Tribunal in connection with social security or child support <www.osscsc.gov.uk/Aspx> does not include decisions that refer to ombudsmen.

66 Para. 4.4.3.1, APE 0377: *Reference in relation to a possible failure to follow the Code of Conduct* (Hudson, Great Yarmouth Borough Council).

67 Paras. 9-13 and 20-23, Case No: LGS/2011/0559: *Appeal by a former member of a local authority against a Standards Committee decision* (Bence, Darlington Borough Council Standards Committee).

68 See, APE 0311: *Reference in relation to a possible failure to follow the Code of Conduct* (Small, Lamerton Parish Council).

69 <www.charity.tribunals.gov.uk/decisions.htm> (accessed on 31 July 2013).

70 See, House of Lords, Summer Recess 2012, Written Answers and Statements, First-tier Social Security and Child Support Tribunals, Question asked by the Countess of Mar, point 2.

5. The official internet site of the *Employment Appeal Tribunal* includes a list of judgments <www.employmentappeals.gov.uk/Public/Search.aspx>. However, on the mentioned site I was not able to find any decisions that made a cross-reference to an ombudsman.

4.2.4 A short summary

Based on the previous sections it is possible to summarise the main conclusions of the cross-referencing practice of the English judiciary. First of all, one must repeat the fact that the English judiciary occasionally refers to ombudsmen. Secondly, this practice is relatively limited and ad hoc. The judiciary only does this if the inclusion of such a cross-reference is necessary. One can see that the courts' cross-references to the ombudsmen are often connected with *the judicial review procedure*. But sometimes they can also be found outside *the judicial review procedure* (e.g. proceedings according to the HRA 1998). In general, one can talk about four main roles of the courts' references to the ombudsmen and their reports. They:
- *inform the readers* of the judgments about the facts of the case, which may include previous investigations or reports of ombudsmen; or they
- *explain the powers of the ombudsmen* or their reports, in connection with their own procedure; or they
- *assess the actions of the ombudsmen* if it is a case of judicial review; or they occasionally
- *point to the possible inspiration* that can be drawn from the ombudsman reports.

The cross-referencing practice of the tribunals is almost non-existent. This can be explained by the statutory limitations on the tribunals and thus the often marginal overlap of their functions with those of the ombudsmen.

4.3 Summary

This chapter provides an answer to the question *about the mutual significance of the reports of the ombudsmen and the judgments of the judiciary in England and their content for the other researched institutions and concerning their interrelations.*

Formal case coordination as included in the English written law is limited. The primary legislation does not include particular rules dealing with the case coordination of the ombudsmen and the judiciary. Delegated legislation, especially the procedural rules of the judiciary, include general provisions that can be linked with this subject. A considerable part of the answer to this research question can be deduced from the *institutional coordination* between the ombudsmen and the judiciary as state institutions that was discussed in Chapter 3 especially the statutory bars on the ombudsmen that *de facto* require them to acknowledge previous judgments and to take them into account. The jurisprudence of the *courts* includes several rules that can influence the character of the reports of the PO or the LGO. The actions of the courts can only be initiated by an individual but the results of court proceedings can also be applicable as a precedent to other similar situations. The *tribunals* have not created any special mechanism for case coordination in connection with the reports of the ombudsmen. The practice of the ombudsmen does not do that either. Their reports do not legally bind the judiciary. Formally, they only confirm and apply the existing formal mechanisms, they do not and cannot create new ones.

The *practice of the ombudsmen and the judiciary* explains the *mutual attitude* of the ombudsmen towards the decisions of the judiciary and *vice versa*. From the *practice of the ombudsmen* one can see that the PO and the LGO are well aware of the case law of the courts. Their cross-references to judgments and the judiciary are not premeditated and are not used on a large-scale basis. One can however find cases where ombudsmen make cross-references to the judiciary because they need to *explain their own competences*, to *explain the competences of the judiciary* or to *support their own findings*.

The *courts* and the *tribunals* are usually aware of the ombudsmen and their reports or other decisions. A priori it is not excluded or forbidden to take into account the reports of ombudsmen in court and tribunal proceedings and vice versa. This practice is however connected with the needs of the judiciary. As the decisions of the ombudsmen are amendable to judicial review, the courts are aware of such decisions; however, only in connection with this procedure. On limited occasions one can find examples where the reports or practice of the ombudsmen raises the interest of the judiciary outside the judicial review procedure. In connection with the English tribunals one can observe a very limited or non-existent interest on the part of the tribunals in the reports of the ombudsmen as such. This is explained by the very narrowly defined fields of competence of several tribunals and hence the marginal overlap of their powers with those of the two ombudsmen. As the English tribunal system is broad one can note different approaches by different tribunals. Still, the ombudsprudence does not play a significant role in the work of tribunals.

Hence, one can observe that within the English judiciary, as it is currently organised, there are differences of opinion concerning the position of reports by ombudsmen. On the one hand, there are courts (at least senior courts) that are aware of the existence of ombudsmen's reports and if there is a need they can review these 'decisions' or even look at them for inspiration. On the other hand, the tribunals have only a very limited or marginal interest in ombudsmen's reports.

Chapter 5

NORMATIVE COORDINATION OF OMBUDSMAN-JUDICIARY RELATIONS IN ENGLAND

For centuries the English courts have had an important impact on the development of English law as its character is closely interconnected with the tradition of judicially developed and followed legal rules (the common law).[1] Their normative function is obvious. The tribunals, on the other hand, are in general only connected with statutory review and not with the development of norms. The normative function of the PO or the LGO does not receive as broad academic attention as the normative function of the judiciary. Until recently, the ombudsmen have not been promoting their normative concepts in a coordinated campaign. This chapter tries to answer the question of *what is the mutual significance of the normative standards of the ombudsmen and of the judiciary in England and what are the interrelations of these normative standards.*

First of all, the chapter discusses the normative standards developed by the PO and the LGO and the judiciary (5.1). This is followed by describing the *formal normative coordination* of these institutions and the possible similarity between their normative standards (5.2). The following section provides a research-based description of the practical application of these normative standards (5.3). The chapter ends with a summary (5.4).

5.1 The development of normative standards by ombudsmen and the judiciary in England

Before describing the *normative coordination* between the two researched ombudsmen and the judiciary, it is useful to generally discuss the relationship between maladministration and unlawfulness. The judiciary is clearly connected with assessing compliance with the law. Maladministration is the province of the ombudsmen and apart from them there are no other English state authorities that deal with this concept. Although the courts sometimes dabble with this issue, they do not expressly or purposely decide on maladministration.[2] In general, maladministration also covers conduct that is not in accordance with the law, i.e. conduct that is unlawful. But a decision may be taken within the legal parameters of the decision-maker, in terms of both substance and procedure, but it may nevertheless

1 Cf. Slapper & Kelly 2011 or Elliot & Quinn 2008.
2 See, section 1.3.

be tainted by maladministration.[3] Nonetheless, ombudsmen do not act as a surrogate of the court in determining whether there has been unlawful conduct[4] as *overseeing legality is within the jurisdiction of the courts in the specialised judicial review procedure.* But the substantive overlaps between maladministration and unlawfulness include, for example, bias, fettering discretion, taking into account irrelevant considerations or a failure to follow a code of practice.[5] As it can often be difficult to draw the line between maladministration and unlawful administrative action, or between maladministration and negligent administrative action, there is 'a strong potential for an overlap between the jurisdictions of the courts and ombudsmen.'[6]

Some authors claim that unlawful behaviour is also maladministration although there are also views to the contrary. For example, in connection with the LGO, Arden et al. state that 'simply because a local authority's policy or decision is clearly ultra vires, this of itself does not necessarily amount to maladministration.'[7] They argue that the LGO, hearing a complaint made against an authority arising out of the (common) practice of determining mandatory renovation grants under a queuing system which took longer than the applicable statutory time-limit for determinations, had accepted that it was very difficult for local authorities to *comply with the statutory requirements.*[8] They continue that the LGO alleged that the queuing system – although it led to non-compliance with the statutory obligation – was *administratively unavoidable and proper* and *a fair and reasonable procedure* for managing demand and matching it with available resources.[9] The LGO do not always follow this pattern. Their practice shows that unlawfulness often leads to maladministration.[10] This position of maladministration and unlawfulness was confirmed by the incumbent Local Government Ombudsman, Ms Seex, and by the former senior officer of the LGO, Mr Laverick, who during the interviews noted that:

> 'I used to talk about unlawfulness as a sort of circle and maladministration as a wider concept of it. I used to say that if you are unlawful you are also acting with maladministration.'

Conversely, Ms Abraham (the Parliamentary Ombudsman 2002-2012) expressed, during the interview, the opinion that 'unlawful behaviour should not be automatically considered maladministration as the ombudsman has to have the discretion to decide whether there was an instance of maladministration or not.' Some reports of the PO include *maladministration falling short of unlawfulness,* i.e. behaviour that is lawful but still maladministration.[11] Thus the PO makes a clear difference between unlawfulness and

3 Stott & Felix 1997, p. 243.
4 *R v Local Commissioner for Administration in North and North East England, ex parte Liverpool City Council* [2001] 1 All ER 462, para. 48.
5 Woolf et al. 2007, p. 49.
6 The Law Commission Consultation Paper No. 187, p. 99.
7 Arden et al. 1999, p. 770.
8 Ibid.
9 Unfortunately, Arden et al. refer only to the '*decision dated May 31, 1995*' without any other identification of the report. Without that one cannot find the decision among the reports published by the LGO.
10 See, also section 5.3.1.
11 See, for example, the already mentioned special report *A Debt of Honour.* See, section 3.1.3.

maladministration. Despite several possible overlaps unlawfulness must not necessarily lead to maladministration.

5.1.1 *The Parliamentary Ombudsman, the Local Government Ombudsmen and normative standards*

Although the normative concept of both researched ombudsmen is maladministration, they nowadays approach it from an opposite position and assess compliance with principles of good administration. As noted by Mr Medlock, Training Team Manager at the PO Office:

> 'We [the PO] did not define what maladministration looks like. We focus on benchmarks of good administration, which we use as our comparing tool to say whether something has fallen away from it or not. To define maladministration, it would limit out discretion and that might be wrong.'

5.1.1.1 Principles of Good Administration of the Parliamentary Ombudsman

In the last ten years one can see a proactive approach by the PO to the development of his/her normative standards. Between 2006 and 2008 the PO developed three different sets of principles applicable to the work of the administration: the *Principles of Good Administration*, the *Principles for Remedy* and the *Principles of Good Complaint Handling.*[12] These principles have been primarily developed for public bodies because they outline the *approach that public bodies should adopt when delivering good administration* and customer services, and how they should respond when things go wrong.[13] Before the adoption of the principles the PO had a 12-week consultation with government departments, the NHS, the Public Administration Select Committee of the House of Commons, and other key groups and individuals in which he gave them an opportunity to express their opinions on the draft principles.[14] These three sets share the *same* six principles that include several sub-principles, an explanation of the meaning of the principles and the supporting text for each of the principles. The general principles of good administration are:

1. the principle *getting it right* includes several sub-principles, e.g. acting in accordance with the law and with regard for the rights of those concerned or acting in accordance with the public body's policy and guidance (published or internal);
2. the principle *being customer focused* includes several sub-principles, e.g. ensuring people can access services easily or informing customers what they can expect and what the public body expects of them;
3. the principle *being open and accountable* includes several sub-principles, e.g. stating its criteria for decision making and giving reasons for decisions or handling information properly and appropriately etc.

12 They were revised and published as a complete set in 2009 or 2010.

13 Principles of Good Administration of the PO, p. 1.

14 Press release 04/06 of 19 October 2006, *Ombudsman consults on principles of good administration.*

4. The principle *acting fairly and proportionately* includes several sub-principles, e.g. treating people impartially, with respect and courtesy or treating people without unlawful discrimination or prejudice, and ensuring no conflict of interests.
5. The principle *putting things right* includes several sub-principles, e.g. acknowledging mistakes and apologising where appropriate or putting mistakes right quickly and effectively.
6. The principle *seeking continuous improvement* includes several sub-principles, e.g. reviewing policies and procedures regularly to ensure they are effective or asking for feedback and using it to improve services and performance.

All sub-principles included in the PO's six main principles of good administration are enumerated in Annex 3 b).

Based on the interviews with the PO and her investigators these principles are used when assessing individual complaints. Ms Abraham confirmed during her interview that the principles should be applied by the public bodies and by the PO in his/her practice. As she noted during the interview 'we should live them and not laminate them'. Mr Medlock, Training Team Manager at the PO Office, noted during the interview that the principles are general and flexible rules:

> 'Now with the principles of good administration we have established benchmarks. But the way in which they are phrased shows that they aren't solid rules. They are not to be a trapdoor but they provide a very nice framework in which case-workers can work.'

The *Principles of Good Administration* are intended to promote a shared understanding of what is meant by good administration in order to help public bodies provide a first-class service to their customers.[15] The *Principles for Remedy* are intended to promote a shared understanding of how to put things right when they have gone wrong and to help public bodies provide fair remedies.[16] Last but not least, the *Principles of Good Complaint Handling* are intended to promote a shared understanding of what is meant by good complaint handling and to help public bodies deliver first-class complaint handling to all their customers.[17] The Principles for Remedy and the Principles of Good Complaint Handling are considered to be an integral part of good administration.[18] The *Principles of Good Complaint Handling* and the *Principles for Remedy* are thus specialised principles of good administration that deal with a specific component of administrative actions – *remedying* and *internal complaint resolution*. In general, they can be perceived as part of the broader *Principles of Good Administration*. The following pages, however, include only an analysis of the broadest *Principles of Good Administration*.[19]

15 Principles of Good Administration, p. 1.
16 Principles for Remedy, p. 1.
17 Principles of Good Complaint Handling, p. 1.
18 Publication on Principles for Remedy, p. 1.
19 From a comparative perspective it is necessary to state that also the other researched ombudsmen have special lists of normative standards that are connected with a special part of administrative behaviour. However, as these lists of specialised normative standards do not cover the same issues, this research covers only those normative standards that cover *administrative conduct as a whole*.

5.1.1.2 The LGO and normative standards

The LGO and the *Commission for Local Government in England* are also active in the development of normative standards. The LGO approach the content of maladministration from the opposite side – as good administration. In July 2013 their guidance did not include normative standards preventing *bad* administration or maladministration but it did include guidelines for attaining *good* administration. A document adopted by the Commission, *Good Administrative Practice,* includes 42 rules called axioms of *good* administrative practice. The axioms have a slightly different character than the principles of the PO. They are not created as broad statements but rather as legally non-binding *instruction norms for local authorities* on how to deal with an individual and his case in a good administrative manner. They are rather precise. The axioms are connected with specific activities of the local administration when dealing with a case. They are coordinated around 8 specific domains within the practice of local authorities where good administrative practices are required.

The first domain, *law,* includes axioms such as understand what the law requires the council to do and fulfil those requirements or ensure that all staff working in any particular area of activity understand and fulfil the legal requirements relevant to that area of activity.

The domain *policy* includes axioms such as communicate relevant policies and rules to customers or ensure that all staff understand council policies relevant to their area of work.

The domain *decisions* includes axioms such as ensure that decisions are not made or action taken prematurely or ensure that irrelevant considerations are not taken into account in making a decision.

The domain *action prior taking decision* includes axioms such as carry out a sufficient investigation so as to establish all the relevant and material facts or seek appropriate specialist advice as necessary.

The domain *administrative processes* includes axioms as compile and maintain adequate records or monitor progress and carry out regular appraisals of how an issue or problem is being dealt with.

The domain *customer relations* includes axioms such as avoid making misleading or inaccurate statements to customers or keep customers regularly informed about the progress of matters which are of concern to them.

The domain *impartiality and fairness* includes axioms such as avoid unfair discrimination against particular individuals, groups or sections of society or maintain a proper balance between any adverse effects which a decision may have on the rights or interests of individuals and the purpose which the council is pursuing.

The last domain, *complaints,* includes axioms such as have a simple, well-publicised complaints system and operate it effectively or take remedial action when faults are identified, both to provide redress for the individuals concerned and to prevent a recurrence of the problem in the future. All 42 axioms of the LGO/Commission are enumerated in Annex 3 c).

The document *Good Administrative Practice* was published for the first time in 1993, which predates the PO's Principles of Good Administration by almost 15 years. The axioms are created to assist councils in the promotion of good administrative practice for all services and functions and the achievement of high standards for their customers. They should assist the councils in their understanding of what the LGO expect by way of good practice. And they should contribute to the prevention of maladministration and secure a reduction in the volume of complaints to the LGO.[20] Thus, this guidance has a reparatory but also a preventive character. Although this document determines some important conclusions which can be drawn from the LGO's investigations and observations[21] it is questionable how and whether these standards are actually used at all in the practice of the LGO. The LGO in their reports do not expressly refer to a breach of the principle of good administration as included in the Axioms.[22]

5.1.2 The English judiciary and normative standards

5.1.2.1 The courts and their normative function

The normative function of the English courts cannot be questioned. The development of law by the courts and the unwritten character and durability of the common law are some of the major differences between the English legal system and those of continental Europe. In the modern English judicial review procedure, but also previously, the courts have been discovering and developing legal principles which they have applied to actions while assessing the legality of governmental actions. These legal principles are nowadays used as *grounds for judicial review* and they represent a collection of non-statutory (uncodified) judicial principles that are used while assessing the legality of administrative decisions.

There is no statutory codified list of grounds for judicial review. However, in legal theory one can find different typologies of the grounds for judicial review. This book uses the typology devised by Lord Diplock as developed in Feldman 2009.[23] Based on that, one can enumerate several general legal principles that are used as assessment standards for administrative conduct. Generally, there are *three main* groups of grounds applied by the courts when assessing the lawfulness of actions by public bodies in the judicial review procedure – *illegality in the strict sense*, *procedural fairness* and *substantive control over discretion*.[24]

1. *Illegality in the strict sense* includes the following legal principles:
   a) *Legal authority to act* means that the public body must have a legal authority to act and to perform its functions. It may act only in accordance with an explicit or implied legal authority.[25]
   b) As a legal principle, the *exercise of conferred discretionary powers* means that if decision-making power is conferred upon a person or a body it is for this body or person and nobody else to exercise that power.[26] This principle also includes the

20 Good Administrative Practice, Guidance on good practice 2, p. 1.
21 Ibid., p. 26.
22 See, <www.lgo.org.uk/decisions/search/> (accessed on 31 July 2013).
23 See, section 2.1.2.
24 This typology does not question the existence of these grounds for judicial review. It takes them for granted.
25 Sunkin 2009, p. 623.
26 Ibid., p. 625.

inability of the body in question to delegate decision-making responsibility, unless it is expressly or implicitly authorised to do so.[27]

c) The *proper purpose principle* means that powers can be used only for the purposes for which they have been expressly or implicitly conferred.[28] This power should not be used for extraneous or improper purposes or on the basis of irrelevant considerations.
d) According to the *relevancy principle* public bodies have to take account of factors that the empowering provisions expressly or implicitly require them to consider.[29]
e) Last but not least, illegality also includes cases where the public body acts in a way that is incompatible with the *human rights* included in the ECHR and incorporated into domestic law by the HRA 1998.[30]

2. *Procedural Fairness* is another broad legal principle that has been traditionally developed by the courts and which is used in order to assess the legality of the actions of public bodies. It contains several legal principles, which directly relate to the *decision-making procedure*. Traditionally, this ground includes two principles of natural justice: *audi alteram partem* (hear both sides) and *nemu iudex causa sua* (no man should be a judge in his own case).[31] Apart from a *general right to a fair hearing* procedural fairness includes the *right to procedural fairness* and *the rule against interest and bias*. It also encompasses, for example:
   - the right to be given prior notice of what is proposed and an effective opportunity to make representations before the decision is made or implemented,
   - the right to make oral or written representations,
   - the right to receive an adequate disclosure of points that are adverse to the person's interests so that there is an opportunity to comment on them or
   - the right to legal representation, but this also includes duties for the decision maker to make inquiries, to conduct an oral hearing or to cross-examine witnesses. Last but not least, procedural fairness entails an *obligation to give reasons* although in English law there is no general requirement to give reasons for administrative decision making. This principle is strongly influenced by primary legislation.[32]
3. *Substantive control over discretion* is the third broad ground for judicial review. It includes several different and general principles.
   a) *Irrationality* as a ground for judicial review includes the traditional and modern perception of Wednesbury unreasonableness (a *decision is so unreasonable that no reasonable authority could ever have come to it*).[33]
   b) Although Lord Diplock described *proportionality* as one of the *possible future principles*,[34] today it is discussed whether proportionality is an independent ground

27 Ibid., p. 632.
28 Ibid., p. 641.
29 Ibid., p. 648.
30 Ibid., p. 662ff.
31 Bailey 2009, p. 669.
32 Cf. Ibid., pp. 667-719.
33 Lord Greene in *Associated Provincial Picture Houses Ltd v Wednesbury Corporation* [1948] 1 KB 223, HL. See, also Craig 2009, p. 720.
34 See, section 2.1.2.

for judicial review.[35] Despite this discussion there are cases where the English judiciary has explicitly applied the proportionality test or has reasoned in an analogous manner.[36] Due to the impact of European Union law, proportionality is creeping into English law as one of the general principles of Union law. Last but not least, the application of the proportionality test can be found in human rights cases in accordance with the HRA 1998.[37]

c) *Legitimate expectations* is another ground that can be used as a ground for judicial review. On the one hand, it requires the existence of a procedural right that the applicant possesses as a result of behaviour by a public body which generated the expectation. On the other hand, this principle refers to seeking a particular benefit founded upon the governmental action that should justify the expectation.[38]
d) Craig includes in this general ground for judicial review also the concept of *equality*. This concept generally entails a number of different issues including the perception that everybody should be subject to the same law and that officials should not be given any special privileges or that similar groups should be treated similarly and different groups treated differently.

All these grounds for judicial review are included in the case law of the courts and are used as assessment standards in the judicial review procedure. The grounds for judicial review are thus broad, are built up on a case-by-case basis and are internally complex *clusters* of principles that, from a theoretical point of view, are connected together in general categories. They are still being developed and their content can potentially change. Occasionally, a specific part of these legal principles can be codified.

5.1.2.2 The tribunals and their normative function

Although the tribunals are formally a part of the judiciary, it is questionable whether they have an impact on the development of normative standards or whether they have a normative function similar to that of the courts. Certainly, the tribunals are amenable to judicial review. In their procedures they must be consistent with the principles that are used as grounds for judicial review by the courts. However, applying principles is not the same thing as actively developing them.

Tribunals were originally created in an uncoordinated way on an *ad hoc* basis. Although nowadays most tribunals are under the umbrella of the FTT one cannot say that all parts of the FTT are identical concerning their functions. It is possible to see a differentiation between the individual parts of this tribunal. Hence, it is not excluded that a certain part of the FTT would develop certain standards in their decision-making processes. Nonetheless, the tribunals are closely connected with their establishing statutes. They are *creatures of the statute* and their functions and roles are closely connected with

35 See, *R v Secretary of State for Defence ex parte Association of British Civilian Internees: Far East Region* (2003) QB 1397.
36 Craig 2009, p. 724.
37 See, *R v Secretary of State for the Home Department (on application of Daly)* [2001] UKHL 26.
38 Craig 2009, p. 730.

the establishing statute and thus sometimes they only assess compliance with a particular statute. Another point that moves tribunals away from norm development is their *traditional dispute resolution character*. Tribunals were never created in order to substitute the roles of the courts at least not in their norm-creating function.[39] Their work was traditionally linked with the speedy and low-cost solution of problems and not always with norm development.[40] Nonetheless, some of the tribunals have been connected with the 'norm-creating' function.[41] As mentioned by His Honour Judge Martin, President of the FTT (Social Entitlement Chamber), tribunals are not closely connected with the development of normative standards:

> 'We [tribunals] see ourselves as a part of the judicial system because we are linked into the judicial system. The measure that we are applying all the time is the *law on entitlement*. We are not applying what might be administrative standards of efficient and effective organization, and we aren't applying what you might call customer service principles.'

The difference between the individual parts of the FTT was noted by Judge Laverick, FTT (Local Standards for the Administration in England), who pointed to the fact that the *law* is the main normative standard, although this tribunal assesses compliance with other standards, especially the *Code of conduct for the local bodies*.[42]

> 'We take into account legal norms and also the Code of Conduct. The Code of Conduct sets a minimum standard of behaviour. The Code of Conduct can be in some ways regarded as setting down the principles that you must treat people with respect; you mustn't participate when you have a prejudicial interest; you must not bully the people. That is not altogether dissimilar from the kinds of publications that the various ombudsmen made.'

Codes of conduct or codes of practice that can be taken into account by the tribunals include, for instance, the *Code of Practice* of the Mental Health Act 1983 or the *Model Code of Conduct for the Local Authorities*. But these documents are statutory instruments (*secondary legislation*) and they are not adopted by the tribunals but by the bodies that are entitled to adopt them. The tribunals only *apply* them when assessing compliance with the statute. However, the competence of the Upper Tribunal to judicially review the actions and decisions of inferior bodies enable this tribunal to be active in norm development. Judicial review, even if exercised by the Upper Tribunal, is connected with the possibility to develop principles which are applicable in the judicial review procedure.

39 Cf. Cane 2009, p. 182ff.

40 Cf. Slapper & Kelly 2011, pp. 574-577.

41 According to Harlow and Rawlings this is the case with the Civil Aviation Authority that has both adjudicative and rule-making powers. See, Harlow & Rawlings 2006, p. 461.

42 See, the Local Authorities (Model Code of Conduct) Order 2007, 2007 No. 1159.

5.2 Coordination between normative standards and norm development?

The following section searches for the existence of *formal coordination* between the normative standards developed and used by the English judiciary and ombudsmen. This section also discusses the *similarity* between these normative standards.

5.2.1 Formal coordination between the normative standards of ombudsmen and the judiciary in England?

It is questionable whether in England there is any *formal normative coordination* between the ombudsmen and the judiciary at all. A search of the primary and secondary legislation dealing with these institutions did not show any reference that would *explicitly* or *implicitly* deal with normative coordination between ombudsmen and the judiciary. The only exceptions are connected with *institutional coordination* and *possibly* with *case coordination*.[43] The jurisprudence is silent on this coordination. One can thus conclude that there is no formal normative coordination between ombudsmen and the judiciary.

This does not mean that in England there is no *interconnection* between the normative standards of the judiciary and those of ombudsmen. The actual normative interconnection between the judiciary and ombudsmen is perceived in a careful manner. While stressing the differences between the two systems, Dr Thompson (a member of the AJTC) argued that there is a difference between the normative standards of the two researched ombudsmen and the judiciary, although this difference is not that great because

> 'The ombudsmen themselves probably feel that they should be careful what they do and therefore as they are carrying out the investigation they have to be able to stand over it at the end. Therefore they feel that there needs to be a minimum due process in their processes.'

Prof. Seneviratne (a member of the AJTC) argued that:

> 'The ombudsmen are more likely to contribute to the development of good administrative practice. This is what they are striving to do. They want the public bodies to act legally as well, but they are not pushing the development of the law. They are pushing the development of good administrative practice.'

As the difference between unlawfulness and maladministration is to a certain extent blurred, one can speculate about the relationship between the contents of these normative concepts. If one looks at the normative standards of these institutions and their application one can observe several similarities. While taking into account the closeness of unlawfulness and maladministration, these similarities give rise to questions about the existence of normative interplay between these normative standards. Here one can perceive the existence of a *formal similarity between the normative standards* and their *substantive similarity*.

43 See, sections 3.1.1 and 4.1.1.

5.2.2 Similarity between normative standards

The *formal similarity between the normative standards* is similarity in the denomination of the normative standards used by the ombudsmen and the judiciary. In England it virtually does not exist. The grounds for judicial review, although they are legal principles, are broad and general. So is their terminology.[44]

The normative standards of the PO are codified as *broad statements* but they do not resemble legal principles in any way. They are developed to cover a broader concept such as good administration. The denomination of principles as *Get it right* or *Be customer focused* extensively departs from the legal world. Their simplicity and general accessibility to their addressees are the goals of the PO.[45] Although the axioms of the LGO do not resemble legal principles, they are drafted in a more 'lawyer-friendly' way. They are drafted as *concrete instruction norms* for the local administration and not only as vague, though flexible principles. They do not have specific names, but they are included in similar groups, so it is difficult to assess the formal similarity between the axioms and the legal principles used by the judiciary. The missing formal similarity between the normative standards may evoke the conclusion that there is no similarity between these standards whatsoever. While formal similarity can be a certain indicator of the development and interplay between the normative standards it is by no means decisive. It is more important to look at the substance of the normative standards.

The *substantive similarity between normative standards* relates to the substantive content (substance) of the normative standards that prohibits or requires certain administrative conduct. Thus, this comparison of the normative standards does not look at the denomination of the standards but at their content. The normative standards protect a certain value. A similarity between these values points to the similarity between the contents of the normative standards. Then it can occur that the ombudsmen and the judiciary protect the same value by using different methods and standards of a different character. The following two schemes show that one can discover a substantive overlap between protected values by the normative standards of the ombudsmen and the courts. They also show that not all of the existing normative standards are overlapping. The following two schemes identify this substantial overlap.

44 See, section 5.1.2.1.

45 The Principles of Good Administration of the PO are a winning document of the Plain Language Commission and was accredited with the Clear English Standard.

Scheme 4 – **Principles of Good Administration of the PO – Grounds for judicial review – substantial overlap of written standards**

	Principles of Good Administration of the PO	Court ground for judicial review / primary and secondary legislation	Value protected
	Example*	Example**	Overlap identified
1.	Get it right (a)	- Legal authority to act - Exercise conferred the discretionary powers - Proper purpose (implied) - Legislation	Compliance with the law (including human rights), legal certainty
	- Mr D's complaint about the Child Support Agency (in Report – Putting things right: complaints and learning from DWP)	*Entick v Carrington (1765)* 19 St TR 1030, *R v Somerset CC, ex p Fewings* [1995] 1 All E 513	Disregarding the law and legal obligations can lead to unlawfulness and to maladministration.
2.	Get it right (b)	- Exercise of conferred discretionary powers - Fettering discretion	Compliance with the law (including human rights), legal certainty
	- Mr D's complaint about the Child Support Agency (in Report – Putting things right: complaints and learning from DWP)	*R v North West Lancashire Health Authority, ex p A* [2000] 1 WLR 977, 991 or *R (on application of Holding & Barnes plc) v Secretary of State for Environment* [2001] UHL 23; [2001] 2 WLR 1389at 143	Ignoring the policy can lead to unlawfulness and to maladministration.
3.	Get it right (e)	- Irrationality - Relevancy principle	Reasonableness of administration
	- Mr Q's complaint about Jobcentre Plus and the Child Benefit Office (in Report – Putting things right: complaints and learning from DWP)	*Associated Provincial Picture Houses v Wednesbury Corp* [1948] 1 KB 223, 233-234 and 228.	Taking irrelevant considerations into account can lead to illegality and to maladministration.
4.	Being customer focused (c)	- Substantive legitimate expectations	Trust in administrative promises
	- Complaint about the Healthcare Commission (in Report – Improving public service: a matter of principle)***	*R v North and East Devon Health Authority, ex p Coughlan* [2001] QB 213, CA; *R* (on the application of *Munjaz*) *v Mersey Care NHS Trust* [2005] UKHL 58.	Not keeping to legitimate promises can lead to unlawfulness and to maladministration.
5.	Being open and accountable (b)	- Right to Procedural Fairness	Knowledge of the content of the administrative decisions and their conclusions
	- Mr W's application for asylum (in Report – 'Fast and fair?')	Implied duty to give reasons is included for example in *R v Civil Service Appeal Board, ex p Cunningham [1992] ICR 817* or in *R v Higher Education Funding Council, ex p Institute of Dental Surgery [1994] 1 WLR 241, 263*	Not giving reasons for an administrative decision can lead to maladministration and potentially to unlawfulness.

6.	**Acting fairly and proportionately (a)**	**- Procedural fairness (Prohibition of bias)**	Impartiality of administration
	- Complaint about the Healthcare Commission (in Report – Improving public service: a matter of principle)***	*R v Secretary of State for the Environment, ex p. Kirkstall Valley Campaign* [1996] 3 All ER 304; *R v Advertising Standards Authority, ex p International Fund for Animal Welfare* (QBD,11/11/1997)	Partiality of the administration can lead to maladministration and potentially to unlawfulness.
7.	**Acting fairly and proportionately (b)**	**- Procedural fairness (Prohibition of bias)** **- Non-discrimination (HR)**	Non-discriminatory administration
	- Mr H's complaint about the Disability and Carers Service and Jobcentre Plus (in Report – Putting things right: complaints and learning from DWP)	- *R v Secretary of State for the Environment, ex p. Kirkstall Valley Campaign* [1996] 3 All ER 304; *Secretary of State for Defence v Elias* [2006] EWCA Civ 1293	Unjustified discrimination can lead both to maladministration and to unlawfulness.
8.	**Acting fairly and proportionately (c)**	**- Irrationality and Relevancy principle (objectivity)** **- Legitimate expectations (consistency issues)** **- Equity (consistency people)** **- Procedural fairness (Prohibition of bias)**	Objectiveness and consistency of the administration
	- Complaint about HM Courts Service (in Report – Putting things right: complaints and learning from DWP)	*Associated Provincial Picture Houses v Wednesbury Corp* [1948] 1 KB 223, 233-234 and 228; *R* (on the application of *Munjaz) v Mersey Care NHS Trust* [2005] UKHL 58; *Edwards v SOGAT* [1971] Ch 354	A non-objective administration can lead to maladministration and to illegality. An inconsistent administration can lead to a breach of the equality principle and discrimination and to maladministration.
9.	**Acting fairly and proportionately (d)**	**- Proportionality** **- Irrationality (a contratio)** **- Procedural Fairness.**	Balance between the aims and means of administrative actions.
	- Complaint about Jobcentre Plus of the Department for Work and Pensions (in Report – Improving public service: a matter of principle)	*R v Secretary of State for Environment, Transport and Regions (ex p Holding & Barnes plc)* [2001] UKHL 23, 2 WLR 1389; *Associated Provincial Picture Houses v Wednesbury Corp* [1948] 1 KB 223, 233-234.	Disproportionate administrative actions can amount to maladministration and potentially also be unlawful.

* These examples can include cases where the finding of maladministration is based on a combination of several acts of malpractice and not only on a breach of one particular principle.

** Examples included here refer to cases where the said principle was applied or developed by the courts.

*** This complaint was dealt with by the health branch of the PO office.

The scheme shows that the normative standards developed by the PO and those developed by the courts sometimes substantially overlap. This overlap is connected with several matters such as the objectiveness of the administration, the proportionality of the administration, compliance with the law or non-discrimination on the part of the administration. Although this overlap is not an absolute one, it is possible to see that these standards tend to protect the same *general value*. When looking at the scheme it can also be observed that most of the principles overlap only *partially*. The principles of the PO have a very broad character and even if a part of a principle protects the same value as the legal principle of the courts, its other parts can protect the values protected by some other legal principle or values that are not protected by the courts.

Sometimes one can see that the substantive overlap is *explicit* but in other cases it is only *implied*. This is connected with the fact that both versions of the normative standards are rather broad and they can cover various, though similar situations. In this connection one can see that the overlap is connected with two main areas: *compliance of the public bodies with the rules including the law* and *fair administrative procedure*. The scheme shows that the principles of the PO and the grounds for judicial review used by the courts are not completely separated. This brings concepts of lawfulness and good administration closer together. It also shows that it is possible to identify an area of interrelatedness between the PO and the courts.

The normative standards that are *not included* in this scheme *do not substantially overlap*. They protect different values. These values are not covered by the standards of the other institution and their protection is the responsibility of either the PO or the courts. Exclusively ombudsman standards include, for instance, the principle *Seek continuous improvement* but also principles that are connected with remedial actions and are included in the broad principle *Put it right*. Some of the traditionally perceived ombudsman principles such as *courtesy* or *sensitivity* must obviously be included in the group of non-overlapping normative standards.

Apart from that, one can point to the matter of lawfulness and of compliance with human rights. While compliance with the law is required by the first general principle of good administration of the PO there is no explicit inclusion of human rights in the principles of the PO, with the exception of the requirement of non-discrimination. However, in my opinion compliance with human rights can be implied from the PO's standards (see, Scheme 4, point 1) especially after the inclusion of the HRA 1998 into the English legal system.

Although there is no real formal similarity between the normative standards of the LGO and those of the courts one can discover several *substantial similarities*.

Scheme 5 – **Axioms of the LGO/Commission – Grounds for judicial review – substantial overlap of written standards**

	Axioms of the LGO/ Commission[5]	Grounds for judicial review / primary and secondary legislation	Value protected
	Example*	Example**	Overlap identified
1.	- **Axiom 1**	- **Legal authority to act,** - **Exercise conferred the discretionary powers** - **Proper purpose (implied)**	Compliance with the law (including human rights), legal certainty.
	- Report on an investigation into complaint nos. 07/C/14706 and 07/C/14724 against Calderdale Metropolitan Borough Council (2009)	*Entick v Carrington (1765)* 19 St TR 1030, *R v Somerset CC, ex p Fewings* [1995] 1 All E 513; *Blackpool Corp v Locker* [1948] 1 KB 349	Disregarding the law and legal obligations can lead to unlawfulness and to maladministration.
2.	- **Axiom 2**	- **Legal authority to act (implied)**	Compliance with the law and legal certainty.
	- Report on an investigation into complaint nos. 06/A/16418, 06/A/17287 & 07/A/02844 against Woking Borough Council (2007)	*Entick v Carrington (1765)* 19 St TR 1030, *R v Somerset CC, ex p Fewings* [1995] 1 All E 513; *Blackpool Corp v Locker* [1948] 1 KB 349	Lack of legal authority to act can lead to maladministration as well as to unlawfulness.
3.	- **Axioms 8, 11–13, 22 and 23**	- **Relevancy principle**	Objectiveness of administrative actions
	- Report on an investigation into complaint nos. 05/B/00448 and 05/B/00897 against Staffordshire County Council (2006) or Report on an investigation into complaint no. 04/C/07540 against Kirklees Metropolitan Borough Council (2006)	*Associated Provincial Picture Houses v Wednesbury Corp* [1948] 1 KB 223 and 228.	Not taking relevant considerations into account and taking irrelevant ones into consideration can lead to illegality and maladministration.
4.	- **Axiom 14**	- **Proper purpose principle**	Legal certainty and trust in the administration
	- Report on an investigation into complaint no. 08 004 707 against the Governing Body of Herschel Grammar School (2008)	*R (on application of Spath Holme Ltd) v Secretary of State for Environment* [2001] 2 AC 349	Using powers for a different purpose than the one included in the law can be unlawful and can amount to maladministration.

	Axioms of the LGO/ Commission[5]	Grounds for judicial review / primary and secondary legislation	Value protected
	Example*	Example**	Overlap identified
5.	**- Axioms 15-17, 19-21, 35, 39**	**- Procedural fairness (general)**	Fairness of administrative procedures
	- Report on an investigation into complaint no. 07B13868 against Bromsgrove District Council (2009)	Implied duty to give reasons is included for example in *R v Civil Service Appeal Board, ex p Cunningham* [1992] ICR 817 or in *R v Higher Education Funding Council, ex p Institute of Dental Surgery* [1994] 1 WLR 241, 263	Lack of procedural fairness can lead to maladministration and to unlawfulness. For example, unreasoned administrative decisions can potentially lead to maladministration and to unlawfulness
6.	**- Axiom 18**	**- Exercise conferred the discretionary powers**	Legal certainty and trust in the administration
	Report on an investigation into complaint nos. 05/B/14123 and 05/B/14124 against West Devon Borough Council (2006)	*Blackpool Corp v Locker* [1948] 1 KB 349	A delegation of powers made without sufficient authorisation can lead to maladministration and to unlawfulness.
7.	**- Axiom 36**	**- Prohibition of bias**	Unbiased administration
	- Report on an investigation into complaint nos. 06/A/15080 & 07/A/00517 against Forest Heath District Council (2008)	*R v Secretary of State for the Environment, ex p. Kirkstall Valley Campaign* [1996] 3 All ER 304 or *R v Advertising Standards Authority, ex p International Fund for Animal Welfare* (QBD,11/11/1997)	In general, a biased administration can lead to maladministration and to unlawfulness.
8.	**- Axiom 37**	**- Illegality (discrimination)**	Non-discriminatory administration
	- Report on an investigation into complaint no. 05/C/00426 against Manchester City Council (2006)	*Secretary of State for Defence v Elias* [2006] EWCA Civ 1293	A discriminatory administrative action rule and biased decisions can lead to maladministration and to unlawfulness.

* These examples can include cases where the finding of maladministration is based on a combination of several acts of malpractice and not only on a breach of one particular principle.

** Examples included here refer to cases where the said principle was applied or developed by the courts.

As can be seen from this scheme it is possible to find several substantive overlaps between the grounds for judicial review and the axioms of the LGO. As in the previous case also here the similarity is almost completely connected with *compliance with legal requirements* and with *compliance with the requirements of procedural justice.*

The Axioms of the LGO are not as broad as the principles of the PO but *de facto* create a step-by-step guide for good administrative actions by the local authorities. They are rather *precise instructions for local authorities.* Because of that an overlap of one axiom with more grounds for judicial review is rare. Grounds for judicial review are in this case more general. The substantive overlap between these normative standards points to the closeness between the concepts of lawfulness and good administration. It also confirms a possible interrelatedness between the LGO and the courts. The substantively overlapping normative standards confirm the protection of a similar general value. The same values are protected by the courts and by the LGO while using different techniques and ways of protecting the values. It often occurs in a different context.

One can note that some of the normative standards do not overlap. They can be found on the side of the LGO as well as on the side of the courts. Some of the standards of the LGO are connected with clearly *extra-legal requirements*. These are issues that are not covered by the standards of the courts. These include, for example, Axiom 33 – *Reply to letters and other enquiries and do so courteously and within a reasonable period; and have a system for ensuring that appropriate action is taken on every occasion* or Axiom 34 – *Keep customers regularly informed about the progress of matters which are of concern to them.*

In the list of Axioms of the LGO one cannot find a reference to compliance with human rights (with the exception of the prevention of discrimination) although compliance with human rights can be implied from Axiom 1 that requires local bodies to act in compliance with the law. Apart from human rights one cannot find in this list any axioms expressly dealing with equality or proportionality.

Both lists of principles shown above *de facto* confirm that the courts and the ombudsmen can apply normative standards that protect similar *general values*. And in connection with these values one can see substantive room for possible cooperation.

5.3 Normative standards and practice

Although the previous pages have shown that there is substantive similarity between the normative standards of the English courts it is questionable whether these principles are the same when applied by the institutions in their practice. In general, the interviewed ombudsmen have admitted that in practice, on certain occasions, the normative standards of the courts are taken into account. As for the possible interconnection between the Principles of Good Administration and the law Ms Abraham pointed to the first principle 'Get it right' that technically includes the principle *'Get it lawful/legal'* but:

> "Getting it right', it's not just about the law. It's getting it right in terms of what's good practice. Sometimes it is about good professional practice. Sometimes it is about your own guidance. So there's a lot to getting it right. The *law is just a starting point*.'

Dr O'Brien (the former Interim Director of Policy and Public Affairs at the PO Office) noted that:

> 'Even where there is specific legislation (e.g. on anti-discrimination) the ombudsman will 'take account of' the law rather than attempt to 'apply' it. It is the ombudsman's Principles of Good Administration that will be the more explicit standard to be applied, although they in turn will *have been shaped by accepted common law principles* of administrative behaviour.'

Ms Seex (the Local Government Ombudsman) confirmed that the LGO take the legal norms into account, although they are not the only norms that can aid them:

> 'I would say that we do decide the case also on other than legal norms. There are other norms and I think they are the norms on efficient management of public services and efficient administration which are more detailed. They are more microcosmic than legal norms. I think that there is a sort of ombudsman's view on how public authorities should treat citizens which is rooted in legal norms very definitely but probably goes further down the line into a sort of microcosm of the interrelationship between the citizens and the public service dealing with them.'

The LGO and the PO are aware of the law and when necessary they take into account the normative standards developed and applied by the courts. The law can be perceived as a starting point when looking for maladministration. Undoubtedly, this is connected with the fact that their work is amendable to judicial review and with the fact that maladministration and illegality are partially overlapping concepts.[46] The attitude of the courts is somewhat different. As argued by Ms Knapman, the Deputy Master of the Administrative Court:

> 'The judges know that there are principles of the ombudsmen. But they would refer to them only if the claimant, respondent or even the interested party raised the issue that the decision maker had acted or did not act in accordance with these principles. Then I think the court might take notice of them. But the court would not find itself bound by them on the basis that they were challenged. They are just guidance by the PO or LGO for the local authorities or other administrative bodies but not for the court. They don't have a statutory format. They are only recommendations.'

In the application of normative standards other than those that are directly connected with their work, the tribunals are even more careful than the courts or ombudsmen. They are often closely linked with the establishing statute and they often do not have the discretion to apply different standards than those that are prescribed by the law. However, some of the tribunals can assess compliance with secondary legislation such as, for instance, codes of practice. Judge O'Brien, FTT (Mental Health), noted that:

> 'The Mental Health Review Tribunal operates within a tight statutory framework. The Mental Health Act 1983 and the various regulations arising from it in effect prescribe the standards to be applied to decisions about the lawfulness of detention. There is also an extensive statutory Code of Practice. However, I would be surprised if the PO's principles have featured at all.'[47]

46 See, section 5.1.

47 See also, section 4.2.3.

5.3.1 *Primary and secondary legislation including human rights as a normative standard*

The English legal system does not recognise a code of administrative procedure that would codify unwritten general principles of administrative law. However, it cannot be said that the English courts are lost in the plethora of unwritten and uncodified norms or that the statutes of Parliament do not play any role in assessing the legality or good administration of administrative actions. Primary and secondary legislation are a starting point for assessing the legality of these actions in the judicial review procedure. Their breach inevitably leads to unlawfulness. A breach of a particular written legal norm gives grounds for the application of a general, unwritten legal assessment standard. Also for the majority of the tribunals, the written law is the most important normative standard that is applied in their practice, as their review is mostly a *statutory review*. Last but not least, a breach of written law or written legal obligations can lead to maladministration.

Ms Abraham has emphasised on several occasions that her role is not to adjudicate legal issues.[48] Nonetheless, when looking at the first principle of the Principles of Good Administration – *Get it right,* one can observe that this broad principle inter alia requires a public body to act in accordance with the law, i.e. to *get it lawful.*[49] I therefore presume that a breach of the law by a public body can lead to a breach of this principle. However, as noted in the practice of the PO a failure to meet one or more of the Principles of Good Administration does not necessarily indicate maladministration.[50] Hence, a breach of the *get it right/ get it lawful* principle must not necessarily lead to maladministration. Ms Abraham noted in this connection that:

> 'Not every example of maladministrative behaviour is also unlawful behaviour. That is very clear. But the interesting thing is if the ombudsman is to find a breach of the law, there is a separate question: how would the ombudsman find that because she can't determine it? But if the ombudsman finds a breach must she then conclude that there is maladministration? I say no to that.'

Unfortunately, the published ombudsprudence of the PO does not include a case where the PO would explicitly use a breach of primary or secondary legislation as a foundation for a finding of maladministration while applying the Principles of Good Administration. It is not excluded that there is such a case among the non-published cases although 'the PO does not do statements on breaches of law as that is not the Ombudsman's role.'[51] However, it is not possible to exclude a situation where the PO would regard a breach of written law as one of the reasons for finding maladministration. This can be supported by some partially published reports included in the digests of cases where the PO has found

48 Cf. Abraham & O'Brien 2006.
49 See, Annex 3 b).
50 Report of the PO, *Putting things right: complaints and learning from DWP*, 2009, p. 91.
51 Interview with Ms Abraham.

maladministration connected with a breach of the 'get it right' principle and potentially also of its 'get it lawful' part.[52]

The LGO occasionally uses written law as a normative standard. Axiom 1 of the LGO/Commission requires local authorities to *understand what the law requires the council to do and fulfil those requirements*. Thus, it is probable that a breach of the law by a public body within the competence of the LGO can lead to maladministration although the LGO 'cannot formally find that the administrative action was unlawful.'[53] But they cannot overlook breaches of the law. This practice was confirmed by the LGO also in the *Report on an investigation into complaint no. 04/A/05724 against St Albans City and District Council.*

> In this case the complainant argued that the local authorities had taken a decision for which they did not have legal authority. The LGO argued that although 'he cannot come to findings of law, his own legal advice is that the decision maker acted unlawfully but it is still effective and remains extant unless and until it is quashed by the courts.'[54] In this case, however, the LGO decided that this did not lead to a finding of maladministration by the LGO although maladministration was in fact found for other reasons.

However, in the *Report on an investigation into complaint no. 09 017 510 about Kent County Council and complaint no. 09 017 512 about Dover District Council* the LGO expressly connected the finding of maladministration with a breach of the statutory duties of the Council.

> The LGO here stated that 'when J went to Dover's housing office in January 2009 the housing officer should have accepted he was homeless and provided suitable temporary accommodation. The failure to do so was contrary to the law and so maladministration.'[55]

Thus even though the LGO cannot say, with legal consequences, that there was a breach of the law such breaches are not overlooked.[56] A breach of the law here apparently means: maladministration.

Although this is not the place for a general description of the system or the development of human rights in England it is necessary to note that in the English legal system human rights stem from different sources, either from the common law tradition, historical

52 Report of the PO, *Putting things right: complaints and learning from DWP*, 2009, p. 90, or Report of the PO, *Small mistakes, big consequences*, 2009, p. 20 or p. 44. None of the cases included in these reports uses a breach of the written law as the only reason for finding of maladministration. In both cases a breach of several principles, whether 'codified' or not, were needed for that statement.

53 Report on an investigation into complaint no. 04/A/05724 against St Albans City and District Council.

54 Ibid., para. 46.

55 Report on an investigation into complaint no. 09 017 510 about Kent County Council and complaint no. 09 017 512 about Dover District Council, para. 79.

56 Similar cases where a breach of the law led to maladministration can be found in Report on an investigation into complaint nos. 07/C/14706 and 07/C/14724 against Calderdale Metropolitan Borough Council or Report on an investigation into complaint no. 08 001 152 against the London Borough of Lewisham.

documents (e.g. the Magna Carta 1215, the Bill of Rights 1689), norms of international law (e.g. ECHR) or from statutory legislation often influenced by external sources (e.g. HRA 1998).[57] The HRA 1998 gave effect to most of the rights guaranteed by the ECHR that by then had only a limited impact in English law.[58] The HRA 1998 requires all public bodies, including the courts, to act in a way that is compatible with the ECHR.[59]

It is questionable whether the PO or the LGO use human rights as assessment standards. Their remit does not *explicitly* extend to the investigation of violations of human rights. They do not directly engage in questioning whether a public body has breached human rights requirements. They are not primarily *human rights ombudsmen*.[60] Similarly, neither the PO's Principles nor the LGO's axioms explicitly require public bodies to comply with human rights with the exception of the prohibition of discrimination.

However, as noted by the PO, the principles, in particular *Getting it right*, *Being customer focused*, *Being open and accountable* and *Acting fairly and proportionately*, provide a *practical application of human rights principles based on the concept of fairness*.[61] When looking into the casework of the PO it is possible to find a handful of cases where the issue of human rights is noted. These were found, for instance, in the reports *Six Lives* (2009) and *Care and support provided to a person with Down's syndrome* (2011) both investigated jointly with the LGO. Still, these reports were adopted by the health branch of the PHSO. In connection with the parliamentary branch of the PO, due to the limited accessibility of the ombudsman's reports I did not find any report that directly used human rights as a normative standard. However, because of the character of human rights, the broad character of ombudsman principles (especially the principle *get it right*) and the endeavour of the PO to *seek higher ethical authority than the domestic law*[62] one cannot exclude the use of human rights as a potential assessment standard for the PO. However, the PO, while taking breaches of human rights into account, might not be so eager (just as in connection with breaches of the law) to adjudicate on these breaches. Still, a failure to take human rights into account by the administration could possibly lead to maladministration.[63]

Although the axioms of the LGO are not as broad as the Principles, there is also an axiom requiring local bodies to 'get it lawful' (Axiom 1). As there is now (since 1998) the Human Rights Act, local bodies must act in compliance with this act as well. It is not for the LGO to say whether there has been a breach of the HRA 1998. However, human rights were taken into account by the LGO in several reports. Apart from the previously noted joint reports with the PHSO one can point to the *Report on an investigation into a complaint against the London Borough of Lewisham* where the LGO noted that *the Human Rights Act 1998 makes it unlawful for a public authority to act in a way that is incompatible*

57 Cf. Feldman 2002 or Hoffman & Rowe 2009.
58 Ibid.
59 Sec. 6, HRA 1998.
60 Cf. Remac 2013.
61 Response to the Government Equalities Office consultation paper: '*Building a fairer Britain: Reform of the Equality and Human Rights Commission*'.
62 Cf. Abraham & O'Brien 2006.
63 See, joint reports with the LGO *Six Lives* (2009) or *Care and support provided to a person with Down's syndrome* (2011).

with a citizen's rights under the ECHR.[64] The LGO here connected maladministration with a breach of the human rights protected by the HRA 1998.[65] Similar cases of the application of human rights, at least via the prism of the HRA 1998, can also be observed in some other reports of the LGO. For example, in the *Report on an investigation into a complaint against Blaby District Council* the LGO reached the conclusion that the Council, in the complainant's case, had failed to take into account the application of human rights which in the end (at least indirectly) led to maladministration.[66] Similar examples can be found in other cases.[67] Although the LGO is not an ombudsman who explicitly assesses the compliance of local bodies with human rights, one cannot *a priori* exclude that this ombudsman will approach this issue in his/her practice from the position of maladministration.

5.3.2 General principles of law as normative standard

Uncodified general principles of administrative law exist as grounds for judicial review.[68] They are developed and applied by the English courts. Although grounds for judicial review are included in the law books, academic articles and judicial decisions, they are not codified in a statute. These normative standards exist without a codification in law and their legal persuasiveness is connected with the character of the English common law system and the long practice of the English courts in shaping the law.[69] They are *the law* and they are legally binding. They must be complied with by public bodies and by tribunals. The actual application of these legal principles as assessment standards is documented in the case law of the courts.

In connection with the tribunal system in England one can say that the use of uncodified legal principles beyond the statutory English law by the tribunals as a normative standard is not *a priori* excluded. Apart from the practice of the Upper Tribunal in the judicial review procedure, where the tribunal has to apply the grounds for judicial review developed by the courts, the application of unwritten principles can be connected with the so-called *overriding objective* of the tribunals.

The *overriding objective* of the tribunals is *an obligation for the tribunals to deal with cases fairly and justly*. This objective is included in the procedural rules of the tribunals.[70] Since the procedural rules of the tribunals do not explain what the phrase '*dealing with cases fairly and justly*' entails, the tribunals could possibly apply, while dealing with cases

64 Report on an investigation into complaint no. 08 001 152 against the London Borough of Lewisham, 25 August 2009, paras. 2 and 41.

65 Ibid. paras. 41 and 46.

66 Report on an investigation into complaint no. 09 006 783 against Blaby District Council, paras. 7 and 44 and Report Summary.

67 See, Report on an investigation into complaint no. 05/A/15987 against Tandridge District Council, Report on an investigation into complaint nos. 06/A/16993, 06/A/16997 and 06/A/17360 against Basildon District Council or Report on an investigation into complaint no. 06/A/10428 against the London Borough of Havering.

68 Compare, Slapper & Kelly 2011 or Woolf et al. 2009.

69 Slapper & Kelly 2011, p. 179ff.

70 See, for example, The Tribunal Procedure (First-tier Tribunal) (General Regulatory Chamber) Rules 2009 S.I. 2009 No. 1976 (L. 20), sec. 2.

fairly and justly, unwritten legal principles such as procedural fairness. Because of that it is thus questionable whether the tribunals are really *applying* non-written principles as normative assessment standards. Of course, when exercising their functions, the tribunals must adhere to the legal standards developed by the courts, as their actions are amendable to judicial review. However, the application of uncodified principles as assessment standards for the tribunals is not entirely excluded as the tribunals, even those that are covered by the umbrella of the FTT, are varied.

In the following examples I would like to point to two *different* but *substantively overlapping assessment standards* that can be found in the practice of the courts as well as in the practice of the PO and the LGO. Firstly, it is a partially overlapping *duty for the administration to take relevant considerations into account* and not to consider ones which are irrelevant. The judicial standard that encompasses this rule is the *relevancy principle.* In the practice of the two researched ombudsmen one can find a reflection of this duty in Axioms 11 (*Ensure that irrelevant considerations are not taken into account in making a decision*) and 13 (*Ensure that adequate consideration is given to all relevant and material factors in making a decision*) of the LGO and in the principle *Get it right: Taking reasonable decisions, based on relevant considerations* of the PO.

The core of *the relevancy principle used by the courts* is that public bodies must take account of factors that the empowering provisions expressly or implicitly require them to consider, and they must exclude from their deliberations factors that the legislation requires to be excluded.[71] In a case of lacking legal provisions that prescribe the factors to be considered, public bodies have discretion. The use of discretion has to be in accordance with the policies determined by the public body. According to Sunkin, 'the relevancy arises in a variety of aspects including fairness, rationality or human rights obligations.'[72] However, the decision might be allowed to stand where it can be justified or when the irrelevant factor was minor, peripheral or insubstantial.[73]

The PO and the LGO require the administration to take relevant considerations into account. This was the case in the *Report on an investigation into complaint no. 04/C/07540 against Kirklees Metropolitan Borough Council.*

> In this case the LGO assessed whether a planning decision of the Council was flawed by maladministration. The investigation discovered that the Council, when deciding on the application for planning permission for the construction of a house, did not take into account its own responsibility to *enhance and preserve the special nature of the conservation area* that stemmed from the Planning Policy Guidance which includes several matters relevant to an application to be taken into account.[74] The LGO did not express an opinion on the possibility to build the house but directed the Council's

71 Sunkin 2009, p. 649 and *R (on application of J (child) v North Warwickshire BC* [2001] EWCA Civ 315.

72 Ibid., pp. 648-649.

73 Ibid., p. 650.

74 Report on an investigation into complaint no. 04/C/07540 against Kirklees Metropolitan Borough Council, para. 75ff.

> attention to its obligation to take all necessary considerations into account.[75] Not taking these particular issues into account was one of the reasons why the LGO found maladministration.

Similarly, in the *Report on an investigation into complaint no. 07C13163 about Birmingham City Council* the LGO noted that ignoring the relevant factors set out in the Council's adult protection procedure was one of the reasons leading to maladministration.[76]

A case where not taking relevant considerations into account had led to maladministration was described in *Mr Q's complaint about Jobcentre Plus and the Child Benefit Office* included in the PO report *Putting things right: complaints and learning from DWP.*

> In this partially published report, the PO dealt with Mr Q's complaint about an ex gratia payment. The complainant was a widower who for 6 years had not received bereavement benefits. The request for an ex gratia payment was refused. The state agency Jobcentre Plus alleged that Mr Q could have contacted it sooner as this issue was widely advertised and it had no obligation to invite widowers to apply for this benefit. The PO found this response by the public body to be inadequate. The PO argued that the complainant was in a vulnerable group whose human rights had been violated and that he would have no reason to make a claim unless he was informed about the changes to the law. According to the PO, the onus was on Jobcentre Plus to try to inform him of his new eligibility.[77] She argued in this connection that Jobcentre Plus had not given due weight to all relevant considerations such as the fact that bereaved fathers make up a group which would be particularly difficult to reach through a publicity campaign or the fact that there might be a failure in their databases and scanning processes. As it failed to do this, its decision to refuse Mr Q's request had been taken with maladministration.[78]

In both cases, the ombudsmen pointed to considerations that were connected with a particular issue of the cases and which were important for the decision, whether this was a planning decision or a decision on a request for an ex gratia payment. In the first case the issues needed to be taken into account stemmed from the obligations of the Council included in the *policy* and/or the *statute.* Here one can see an overlap with the legal principle of relevancy even though the LGO assessed the issue from the perspective of maladministration. In the second case these issues stemmed from the general ability of the public body to evaluate all possible external matters that could have influenced its decision and which were in no way connected with its legal obligation or policy.

In these examples the application of the ombudsmen principles do not differ that much from the legal principle. In the first case (LGO) one can accept that if the court would have dealt with this case it could have reached a similar conclusion. In the second case (PO), it is not so obvious that the court would deal with this case in a similar fashion as the PO. The PO here pointed to the specific circumstances of the complainant. The

75 Ibid., para. 76.

76 Report on an investigation into complaint no. 07C13163 about Birmingham City Council, para. 70.

77 *Mr Q's complaint about Jobcentre Plus and the Child Benefit Office* (report – *Putting things right: complaints and learning from DWP),* p. 28.

78 Ibid., pp. 26-29.

court, while assessing the position of the complainant from the position of unlawfulness, could take into account the same specific circumstances. However, one cannot confirm this. It is rather speculation as to whether the court would decide the case in one way or the other.

In connection with this particular principle it is necessary to underline that, apart from the legal issues that could have been taken into account, it mostly depends on the *factual issues* that could have influenced the decision of the public body and the *discretion* of this body. Although these examples are only a tiny fraction of all the possible judgments and reports, from a methodological point of view they illustrate a possible practical overlap between certain assessment standards of the LGO and the PO and those of the courts.

The second example is connected with a *duty to give reasons for administrative decisions.* Today, despite certain developments, the English common law still does not recognise a general duty to give reasons for an administrative decision.[79] Although it may be questioned whether a breach of this duty can lead to the illegality of the decision and its subsequent quashing, in certain cases, while taking into account the particular issues of the case, the courts require reasons for an administrative decision.[80] As Elliott puts it, 'there is a presumption that reasons need not to be given and the onus is on the claimant to establish that some feature of the case displaces that presumption.'[81] Despite the developing character of this principle it is not clear whether a breach of this principle will lead to the illegality and subsequent quashing of the administrative decision. However, if this obligation was included in legal statutes the court could look at it as a breach of statutory obligations.

In the practice of the ombudsmen it is possible to find this standard in the LGO's Axiom 16 (*Give reasons for an adverse decision and record them in writing for the customer concerned*) and in the PO's principle *Being open and accountable: Stating its criteria for decision making and giving reasons for decisions.* The duty to give reasons was addressed in the *Report of the LGO on an investigation into complaint no. 06/B/09241 against Oswestry Borough Council.*

> The LGO found maladministration leading to injustice because the Council had failed to give reasons for granting permission, against an officer's advice, for an application which was not in compliance with the General Development Procedure Order 1995 (a statutory instrument). The LGO accepted that 'the Planning Committee was entitled to depart from the officer's advice but only where there was good reason to do so, based on clear and legitimate planning grounds.'[82] He based this statement on the fact that the obligation to give reasons was expressly included in this order. Thus the LGO did not push this obligation beyond the actual wording of secondary legislation.

79 Lord Mustill in *R v Secretary of State for the Home Department, ex p. Doody* [1994] 1 AC 531 at 564 or Justice Beatson in *R v Birmingham Crown Court (on the application of Birmingham City Council)* [2009] EWHC 3329 (Admin) para. 46.

80 See, *R v Higher Education Funding Council, ex p Institute of Dental Surgery* [1994] 1WLR 242.

81 Elliott 2011, p. 59.

82 Report of the LGO on an investigation into complaint no. 06/B/09241 against Oswestry Borough Council, para. 71.

Similarly in the *Report on an investigation into complaint no. 09 017 510 about Kent County Council and complaint no. 09 017 512 about Dover District Council* the LGO found maladministration because the Council did not give the complainant a written and reasoned decision which was in accordance with *its statutory duty*. Because of that the complainant could not ask for its review or appeal. This constituted maladministration.[83]

Sometimes, however, one can discover some uncertainty in the use of this particular standard by the LGO. For example, in the *Report on an investigation into complaint nos. 10 008 980 & 10 012 328 against Walsall Metropolitan Borough Council* the LGO found an instance of maladministration because there was no record of the reasons for the Council's decision to remove a planning condition.[84] However, maladministration was in fact found because of a failure to keep such a record and not because of omitting the reasons for this decision. Nevertheless, a breach of the duty to give reasons for an administrative decision can be implied from some other reports of the LGO.[85]

In the *Complaint about Jobcentre Plus of the Department for Work and Pensions* included in the report *Improving public service: a matter of principle* the PO also mentioned a breach of this particular principle, although it was not possible to assess the actual reason as to why this principle had been breached as this particular report was included in a digest of several cases that were described only in a general fashion.

In connection with the standard used by the courts one can argue that the ombudsmen, while dealing with the reasons for administrative decisions, do not go further than the courts. One can see that the ombudsmen can find maladministration if there has been a breach of this duty if it stems from statutory rules or the internal rules of the public body. In this case it is possible to presume that a breach of these rules would be similarly considered by the courts.

For now, there is no general duty for the administration to give reasons for decisions. This principle is in a stage of development. Although there are some attempts to broaden the legal principle to administrative institutions, there is no clear legal obligation in form of a general legal principle for the administration to do so.[86] A duty for public bodies to give reasons for administrative decisions can however stem from primary or secondary legislation.[87] However, a duty to give reasons exists as the ombudsmen's principle of good administration. In this case the standards of the ombudsmen can act as a possible inspiration for the further development of the case law and the legal principles.

83 Report on an investigation into complaint no. 09 017 510 about Kent County Council and complaint no. 09 017 512 about Dover District Council, paras. 10 and 81.

84 Report on an investigation into complaint nos. 10 008 980 & 10 012 328 against Walsall Metropolitan Borough Council, para. 88.

85 See, Report on an investigation into complaint nos. 07/B/04448, 07/B/04816 and 07/B/05311 against the Governing Body of All Saints Benhilton Church of England Primary School, Report on an investigation into complaints nos. 06/B/05262, 06/B/07971, 06/B/08615, 06/B/09497 and 06/B/10920 against the London Borough of Greenwich.

86 Elliott 2011, p. 60. See, also *R v Secretary of State for the Home Department, Ex parte Doody* [1994] 1 AC 531, Mountview Court Properties Ltd v Devlin 91970) 21 P & CR 689 or *R (on the application of Hasan) v Secretary of State for Trade and Industry* [2008] EWCA Civ 131.

87 SH Bailey 2009, p. 711ff.

5.3.3 Exclusively ombudsman principles as normative standard

As shown by the two previous comparative schemes, the normative standards of the LGO and the PO and the normative standards of the courts sometimes substantively overlap. However, some of the ombudsman principles remain within the *extra-legal sphere,* i.e. they are normative standards that do not reflect the normative standards of the courts. These include, in connection with the PO, for instance, principle 6 *Seeking continuous improvement* or principle 4 *Acting fairly and proportionately: Treating people impartially, with respect and courtesy* where especially the issue of courtesy in administrative relations is not covered by the legal standards of the judiciary. In connection with the normative standards of the LGO it is, for example, Axiom 29 *Monitor progress and carry out regular appraisals of how an issue or problem is being dealt with* or Axiom 33 *Reply to letters and other enquiries and do so courteously and within a reasonable period; and have a system for ensuring that appropriate action is taken on every occasion.*

Although the principles used by the courts in the judicial review procedure are very broad and the judicial review procedure is still developing it is not possible to compare the application of the exclusively ombudsmen principles with those of the judiciary, as the courts do not apply them in their practice. However, because of this almost unlimited development of the judicial review procedure one cannot exclude the fact that the courts possibly look into the normative standards of the ombudsmen for inspiration as to the development of their principles. As doing so may be necessary for the development of the law, the courts cannot ignore the standards of the ombudsmen mereby because they are 'only' extra-legal standards. Still, it is highly unlikely that this practice, even if it does occur, will be very broad.

5.4 Summary

This chapter tries to answer the question of *the mutual significance of the normative standards of the ombudsmen and the judiciary in England* and *their interrelations.*

First of all, one must note that there is *no formal normative coordination* between the normative standards of the judiciary and those of the ombudsmen. But the courts, (possibly) the tribunals and the ombudsmen do develop normative standards for their own domain: legal norms and good administration norms. They are generally aware of the existence of the normative standards used by the other bodies. The PO and the LGO are aware of the normative standards of the judiciary. These standards (as grounds for judicial review) apply to them as a standard for their behaviour. There might be some knowledge about the ombudsmen's standards among the judges but it cannot be proven that they take these standards into consideration when dealing with individual cases.

The normative standards of the ombudsmen and the judiciary exist alongside each other. Despite this, there is almost no *formal similarity* (similarity concerning the denomination of the normative standards used by the ombudsman and the judiciary) between legal standards and ombudsnorms. However, there is some *substantive similarity* (similarity between the values protected by legal norms and by ombudsnorms) between some normative standards of the courts and those of the ombudsmen. Thus, normative standards of a different character can have some interrelation. This substantive similarity between the normative standards leads to a certain similarity between unlawfulness and maladministration. Generally, maladministration is broader than unlawfulness although the judicial review procedure also covers, apart from illegality in the *strict sense,* matters such as *procedural fairness* and *irrationality.* At the same time matters such as procedural fairness as a legal principle are connected with the character of the English common law. Conversely, when looking at the normative standards of the PO and the LGO one can see that these normative standards are *not only extra-legal* i.e. they only cover maladministration in a strict sense, but they also connect maladministration with a breach of the law. Such a breach *can lead*, as a consequence, to maladministration.

Although, formally, ombudsmen do not have the competence to adjudge breaches of legality and human rights, their normative standards can be applicable to behaviour that is not in accordance with the law or human rights. This leads to the conclusion that even if they state that it is not for them to issue statements on breaches of legality, in the case of breaches of the law or legal norms (including human rights) they approach this breach from the perspective of maladministration. From this perspective, they can give *an opinion on compliance with the law.* Hence, as long as it is necessary for a finding of maladministration, they de facto *interpret the law.*

Hence, in connection with the development of the law and normative principles that are applicable to the administration (public bodies) one can imagine that there is normative coordination between the ombudsmen and the English judiciary.

PART IV

RELATIONS BETWEEN THE EUROPEAN OMBUDSMAN AND THE COURT OF JUSTICE OF THE EUROPEAN UNION

Part IV of the book discusses the relations between the *European Ombudsman* (*EUO*) and the *Court of Justice of the European Union* (*Court*).[1] Since its establishment as one of the European Union's institutions,[2] the EUO has been the subject of numerous publications, academic articles and research.[3] The EUO represents a combination of a traditional public administration ombudsman and an institution that deals with the activities of internal administrative bodies belonging to a *supranational institution*[4] and he exercises control which is similar to the control of public authorities by national ombudsmen.[5]

This part starts with a short description of the most important characteristics of the EUO and his functions (Chapter 1). The Court is briefly described in Chapter 2. Chapter 3 discusses the *institutional coordination* between the EUO and the Court. Chapter 4 deals with *case coordination* between these institutions and Chapter 5 looks at the *normative coordination* of the standards applied by the EUO and the Court.

1 The term '*the Court*' in this case includes the three judicial institutions of the EU – the Court of Justice, the General Court and the Civil Service Tribunal. See, Chapter 2.

2 The following pages will use the terms 'the European Union', 'Union law', 'the Union legal system' etc. Terms such as 'the European Communities' or 'the Community legal system' etc. are used only in connection with a quotation from historical documents including judgments of the Court and decisions of the EUO.

3 See, Magnette 2003, Heede 2000, De Leeuw 2009 and may others.

4 Here I will simply state that the European Union is a supranational institution. The character of the European Union itself has raised and probably still raises many questions. See, for example, Klabbers 2002. Furthermore, it is worth noting that although the Union does not have precisely the same internal organisation as national states one can see that there are institutions that, in their own way, reflect the division of power.

5 Popescu-Slaniceanu et al. 2010, p. 193.

Chapter 1

THE EUROPEAN OMBUDSMAN

The EUO is not an original Union or Community institution. The treaties from the 1950s are completely silent on this. In the 1950s hardly anyone could foresee how far European unification would expand. Also by that time an ombudsman institution was still only a *Nordic experiment*. The development of ombudsman institutions worldwide and changes in the perception of the political and societal accountability of the administration in the former Communities resulted in calls for the creation of a body that could deal with complaints against the malpractice of the European institutions. The historical roots of the ombudsman principle and its modern development in the European countries led to the idea of an ombudsman for the European Union.[1] Until July 2013 only Mr Söderman (Finland) and Prof. Diamandouros (Greece) had held the post of the European Ombudsman, both leaving their personal imprint on the institution.[2]

Although the history of the EUO has already been covered in various sources,[3] one must note that the EUO was established by mutual cooperation between the Union institutions and the Member States. Support for the idea of an ombudsman was by no means universal in either the Commission or the EUP.[4] This was one of the many reasons why the creation of the EUO was not such an easy matter. The difficulties and hesitations encountered in setting up the office of the EUO were also explained by differences in national civic cultures.[5] Also in the early 1990s only 7 of (the then) 12 Member States had a national body which fulfilled functions of the ombudsman and by that time only 5 of these ombudsmen had more than 10 years' experience in dealing with complaints against the

1 Annual Report of the EUO 1996, p. 4.

2 On 1 October 2013, Prof. Diamandouros decided to leave the post of the EUO. The new EUO is Ms E. O'Reilly (Ireland), the former Ombudsman of Ireland, who took up the position on the same day. She was elected on 3 July 2013 by the EUP.

3 See, for example, Kourtikis 2010, p. 37.

4 Bellamy & Warleigh 2001, p. 76.

5 Magnette 2003, p. 680.

administration.[6] Despite this, the EUO was established. This underlined the commitment of the Union to democratic, transparent and accountable administration.[7]

The EUO was established in 1992[8] by the Treaty of Maastricht and its provisions are currently, in July 2013, integrated in the TFEU. He is also mentioned in the Charter of Fundamental Rights of the European Union (*Charter*)[9] and several sources of secondary Union law.[10] The TEU is however silent on this Union institution.[11]

1.1 Functions of the European Ombudsman

Although the roles and functions of the EUO are described differently by several other authors and by the EUO himself[12] this chapter points to five ombudsman functions that were discussed in Part 1 and applied to the previous three ombudsman institutions.

1.1.1 Control function and protection and dispute resolution function

The *control function* of the EUO is directly connected with his role as an investigator of administrative conduct. His control function is based on Art. 228 (1) TFEU which empowers the EUO to *conduct inquiries for which he finds grounds.* He is a key part of the EU's complaint-handling procedures and a force for change within the institutions of the EU.[13] The EUO is one of several EU mechanisms that individuals can use in order to protect their interests and in order to settle their disputes with the Union. But he is the only Union institution that provides protection against *instances of maladministration.*

The *protection and dispute resolution function* of the EUO can be commenced in three ways: by a complaint submitted to the EUO directly by a complainant, by a complaint submitted to him by a Member of the EUP (an MEP) and by the EUO's inquiries of his own initiative.[14] Based on the *Decision of the EUP on the Regulations and General Conditions Governing the Performance of Ombudsman's duties* (the EUO statute)[15] the EUO has to *seek a solution with the institution or body concerned to eliminate the instance*

6 In 1992, the year when the Maastricht Treaty was signed, only Denmark (1955), the UK (1967), France (1973), Portugal (1975), Spain (1978), the Netherlands (1982) and Ireland (1984) had a national ombudsman.

7 Special Report from the EUO to the EUP following the own-initiative inquiry into the existence and the public accessibility, in the different Community institutions and bodies, of a Code of Good Administrative Behaviour (OI/1/98/OV).

8 The first EUO was elected by the EUP in 1995. Nonetheless, the institution has existed (on paper) since the signing of the Treaty of Maastricht (1992). The Treaty came into force in November 1993.

9 The Charter of Fundamental Rights of the European Union, OJ: 2010/C 83/02.

10 This includes the Decision of the EUP on the Regulations and General Conditions Governing the Performance of Ombudsman's duties, Decision of the EUO adopting implementing provisions, Regulation No. 1049/2001, Regulation No. 1922/2006 or the Rules of procedure of the EUP (Rules 204-206) etc.

11 OJ C 115/13.

12 Cf., Hertogh 1996, Reif 2004, p. 367ff or Strategy for mandate 2010, p. 6.

13 Giddins et al. 2000, p. 140.

14 Also the French *Défenseur des Droits* can start his investigation in any of these ways.

15 Decision adopted by the EUP on 9 March 1994 (OJ L 113, 4.5.1994) and later amended by its decisions of 14 March 2002 (OJ L 92, 9.4.2002) and 18 June 2008 (OJ L 189, 17.7.2008).

of maladministration and satisfy the complainant.[16] Art. 6 of the *Decision of the European Ombudsman adopting implementing provisions* (the Implementing decision)[17] goes even further. It obliges the EUO *to co-operate as far as possible with the institution concerned in seeking a friendly solution to eliminate maladministration and to satisfy the complainant.*

1.1.1.1 Subjects and matters within the competence of the European Ombudsman

The TFEU and the Statute of the EUO extend the EUO's control powers only to *Union institutions, bodies, offices or agencies (Union institutions).*[18] Neither the TFEU nor other sources of EU law include a list of Union institutions that can be controlled by the EUO. The EUO refers to the Union institutions listed on the official Union internet site *http://europa.eu/.*[19] Apart from the Union institutions enumerated in Art. 13 TEU the EUO includes within this term also *bodies set up by legislation*, such as the European Centre for Disease Prevention and Control.[20] However, he expressly excludes from his competences the Committees of the EUP.[21] As his control powers only extend to *Union institutions* the EUO is not empowered to deal with complaints filed against *institutions of the Member States* or the *Member States* themselves, not even if they deal with matters that fall within the scope of the EU. Although this limitation was introduced in order to avoid any overlap with national ombudsmen,[22] the EUO often expresses his dissatisfaction with a large number of received complaints that concern the institutions of the Member States.[23] *The Court of Justice of the European Union* is however excluded from the EUO's competence. The TFEU states that the EUO can receive complaints against the activities of all Union institutions except for *the activities of the Court of Justice of the European Union acting in its judicial role.*[24]

According to the TFEU the EUO investigates *instances of maladministration in the activities of the Union institutions.*[25] The term *activities of the Union institutions* is rather broadly explained by the EUO. Apart from the 'actions' of Union institutions, the term also includes the *inactivity of the institution,* e.g. delays.[26] In this connection Heede argues that the EUO is of the opinion that all activities by the Union institutions are included in

16 Art. 3 (5) Statute.

17 The Implementing decision was adopted on 8 July 2002 and subsequently amended by the decisions of the EUO of 5 April 2004 and 3 December 2008.

18 Art. 228 (1) TFEU, Art. 2 (2) of the Statute.

19 <www.ombudsman.europa.eu/atyourservice/interactiveguide.faces> (accessed on 31 July 2013).

20 Annual Report of the EUO 2011, p. 12.

21 Ibid., 13.

22 Peters 2005, p. 703.

23 According to Annex A of the Annual Report of the EUO 1996, 598 complaints (65% of all received complaints) were outside the remit of the EUO. From this number 542 complaints were outside the EUO's mandate because they were not filed in connection with an activity of a Community institution or body (Annual Report of the EUO 1996, p. 102). In 2012, this number was lower as only 30% (1,710) of all received complaints fell within the mandate of national ombudsmen (Annual Report of the EUO 2012, p. 5 and 19).

24 In relation to the Court, the EUO's limitations are discussed in detail in section 3.1.1.

25 Art. 228 (1) TFEU, Art. 2 (2) Statute.

26 See, for example, Special Report from the EUO to the EUP following the DR to the Commission in complaint 289/2005/(WP)GG etc.

his mandate irrespective of the fact that they are conducted under another framework. Thus, they can include a *factual activity*, an *administrative decision* as well as a *legislative act*.[27] Although the Treaty of Lisbon widened the EUO's mandate to include possible maladministration within the framework of the Common Foreign and Security Policy, including the Common Security and Defence Policy,[28] the control function of the EUO does not encompass all of the activities of the Union institutions. The EUO cannot conduct inquiries in cases where the alleged facts are or have *been subject to legal proceedings* (Art. 228 (1) TFEU) and he cannot question the *soundness of a court's ruling* (Art. 1 (3) Statute).[29]

1.1.1.2 Complaints and own initiative inquiries

Although a complaint to the EUO does not involve any fees, there are some criteria that have to be met when complaining to the EUO. Based thereon, the EUO determines whether a complaint is within his mandate and, if so, whether it is admissible.[30]

The general criteria are included in the TFEU and are specified in the Statute of the EUO. First of all, the *direct connection of the complainant with the Union* is required. Only a citizen of the Union or a natural person residing in a Member State of the Union or a legal person having its registered office in a Member State of the Union can complain to the EUO.[31] The person lodging the complaint must be *identifiable*. Anonymous complaints are not admissible.[32] Nonetheless, an individual complaining with the EUO does *not need to have a personal interest* in the case or he or she does not need to be affected by the alleged maladministration.[33] As complainants do not need to show any individual or direct interest the complaint to the EUO is often described as an *actio popularis* complaint.[34]

The complaint has to be directly connected with the activities of *Union institutions, bodies, offices or agencies (Union institutions)*.[35] It has to concern instances of *maladministration* and it has to be filed within a *time-limit of two years* since the date when the facts on which the complaint is based came to the attention of the person lodging the complaint.[36] However, the complaints submitted to the EUO do not affect the time-limits for appeals in administrative or judicial proceedings.

27 Heede 2000, p. 120.
28 Annual Report of the EUO 2011, p. 12.
29 In relation with the Court, the EUO's limitations are discussed in detail in section 3.1.1.
30 Art. 3.1 Implementing decision.
31 Art. 228 (1) TFEU, Art. 2 (2) Statute.
32 Art. 2 (3) Statute, Annual Report of the EUO 2011, p. 16.
33 See, *What can the European Ombudsman do for you?: An overview of the Ombudsman's work and how he could help yo*u, European Communities, 2008, p. 10.
34 Ebbesson 2002, p. 91. For an *actio popularis* complaint to the EUO see, for example, Decision of the EUO on complaint 2216/2003/(BB)MHZ against the European Personnel Selection Office; Decision on complaint 1042/25.11.96/SKTOL/FIN/BB against the Commission or Decision of the EUO on complaint 2130/2007/ELB against the Commission.
35 Art. 228 (1) TFEU, Art. 2 (2) Statute.
36 Art. 2 (4) Statute.

Last but not least, the Union institution in question must have the possibility do deal with the complaint internally before the EUO is approached.[37] If there has been no such procedure the EUO informs the complainant and recommends that he should complain with the institution concerned and the case is then closed.[38] This procedure is not required when the institution is aware of the issue concerned and has already had an opportunity to define its position.[39]

The EUO is empowered to conduct inquiries for which *he finds grounds on his own initiative*. This power of the EUO stems from Art. 228 (1) TFEU. He uses this power in two types of cases. The first one is connected with cases of maladministration brought to his attention by a subject who is not entitled to make a complaint such as, for example, a Union institution.[40] Secondly, an own-initiative inquiry will occur when the EUO reacts to suspected systemic problems and wants to deal with them.[41] Own-initiative inquiries are used only exceptionally, although it is an increasing practice.[42] One of the first own-initiative inquiries led to drafting the text of the *European Code of Good Administrative Behaviour* (the Code).[43]

1.1.1.3 Inquiry procedure

The inquiry of the EUO has to be able to support his vital role which lies in maintaining citizens' trust in the EU.[44] The EUO has to be impartial and independent when exercising this role. Only then can he build trust through dialogue between citizens and the EU and foster the highest standards of behaviour in the Union's institutions.[45] The inquiry involves two stages.

In the *preliminary control stage,* the EUO has to examine whether the complaint is within his mandate and whether it meets the criteria of admissibility. If the complaint falls outside his mandate or does not meet the admissibility criteria the EUO will close the file and inform the complainant. If he is not competent to deal with an inquiry he will try to transfer the complaint to a competent body or the complainant will be given appropriate advice about a competent body to which he can turn.[46] If the complaint is within his mandate and meets the necessary criteria, the EUO determines whether there are sufficient grounds for the inquiry.

37 Art. 2 (3) Statute.
38 See, Decision of the EUO closing his inquiry into complaint against the Commission 1574/2010 or Decision of the EUO on complaint 1054/2007/MHZ against the Commission.
39 See, Decision of the EUO on complaint 2130/2007/ELB against the Commission.
40 Annual Report of the EUO 2010, p. 17.
41 See, Strategy for mandate 2010, p. 5, Press release no. 7/2006, 31 January 2006.
42 In 2012 the EUO used this procedure in 15 cases, in 2011 in 14 cases and in 2010 in 12 cases. See, Annual Report of the EUO 2012, p. 18.
43 See, Case: OI/1/98/OV. The Code is discussed in sections 1.1.3.2 and 5.1.1
44 Press release no. 20101125IPR00555.
45 Strategy for mandate (no. 32), p. 6.
46 Annual Report of the EUO 2010, p. 17 or Arts. 2.4, 2.5, 3.2 Implementing decision.

The *substantive inquiry* starts if there are grounds for an inquiry. The Union institution complained against has three months to submit its opinion on the complaint.[47] The complainant can submit his observations within one month.[48] The EUO can make *further inquiries*. Then the complainant and the Union institution have another month to react.[49] During the inquiry the EUO has the traditional investigative powers including the right to require the Union bodies to supply him with documents and information for the purpose of an inquiry; the right to inspect the file; the right to require officials and servants of Union institutions to give evidence; the right to make inquiries on the spot; or the right to commission necessary studies and expert reports.[50]

Apart from a *formal written inquiry* the EUO can also make use of *informal procedures*. Based on the Statute of the EUO and the Implementing decision the EUO should try to *achieve a friendly solution* whenever possible if an inquiry leads to a finding of maladministration.[51] A friendly solution may involve a suitable remedy, such as amending a decision, offering an apology or providing compensation.[52] This procedure has proved to be rather successful in the practice of the EUO. In 2009, 179 cases were solved by the EUO's friendly solution or settled by the institution.[53] In 2012, however, this number fell to 80 cases.[54] A friendly settlement is not appropriate when the EUO deals with a complaint filed by a person who does not have a direct interest in the case *(actio popularis complaint)*.[55] If a friendly solution is not possible, the EUO closes his case with a decision with a *critical remark* or he can make a *draft recommendation*.[56] If the friendly solution is successful the case is closed with a reasoned decision that can include *further* or *critical remarks*.[57]

In the practice of the EUO it is also possible to find *settling the case to the complainant's satisfaction by an institution* which is not the same thing as a friendly settlement by the EUO.[58] In this situation the EUO, after receiving a complaint or starting an inquiry on his own initiative, informs the Union institution about the complaint or the inquiry and he asks it to submit useful comments. If the Union institution at this stage realises its mistake and changes or adapts its actions and these actions lead to the satisfaction of

47 Art. 4.3 Implementing decision.
48 Art. 4.5 Implementing decision.
49 Art. 4.7 Implementing decision.
50 See, Arts. 5.1-5.5 Implementing decision and Art. 3 Statute.
51 Annual Report of the EUO 2007, p. 20 and Art. 3 (5) Statute.
52 Strategy for Mandate 2010, p. 4. An example of a friendly settlement is Decision of the EUO closing his inquiry into complaint 784/2009/(GP)IP against the European Police College, where the EUO proposed to pay the complainant, in accordance with the principles of good administration, € 600 in order to cover her expenses. The parties agreed to this proposal and the EUO could close the case.
53 Annual Report of the EUO 2010, p. 29.
54 Annual Report of the EUO 2012, p. 31.
55 Decision of the EUO on complaint 2216/2003/(BB)MHZ against the European Personnel Selection Office.
56 For critical remarks or DRs see, section 1.1.3.1.
57 See, Decision of the EUO closing his inquiry into complaint 1581/2010/(FS) GG against the Commission or Decision of the EUO closing his inquiry into complaint 1633/2008/DK against the Commission etc.
58 See, Decision of the EUO closing his inquiry into complaint 1581/2010/(FS) GG against the Commission.

the complainant the EUO closes the investigation.[59] The inquiry of the EUO ends with a decision by which he closes the file.

1.1.2 *Redress function*

The EUO is generally perceived as a remedy which is an alternative to the protection of individuals provided by the Court.[60] However, he is not empowered to order a Union institution to change a decision or to provide redress, even if a complaint is found to be justified.[61] He can only recommend a remedy and/or criticise. Potentially, he can request political support from the EUP. This does not change the fact that it is the Union institution that has the discretion to accept the EUO's recommendations or not. There are no actual legal sanctions if the Union institution rejects or even ignores the EUO's recommendations. The only real risk in not accepting them lies in possible damage to its public image through the EUO's naming and shaming powers. The EUO's recommendations are not enforceable and their acceptance depends on the will of the Union institution concerned. When recommending remedies the EUO is not strictly bound by Union law and he can also recommend remedies that are not expressly available to the Court. He can *inter alia* recommend that the institution in question acknowledges its mistake and apologises;[62] offers compensation to the complainant;[63] corrects inaccuracies and misleading statements;[64] changes its practice;[65] or reconsiders its position and bears the appropriate consequences.[66] This list is not final. As Magnette puts it, the EUO's coercive means are more uncertain than those of a Court which can condemn and impose sanctions accompanied by financial penalties and damages, but his capacity to choose his priorities and make inquiries is larger than that of the Court.[67]

1.1.3 *Normative function and educative function*

The *normative function* of the EUO is connected with his normative concept – maladministration (or its opposite good administration). As *maladministration* is a

59 For example, in Decision of the EUO closing his inquiry into complaint 2497/2010/FOR against the European Banking Authority, the EUO had sent the EBA a letter to announce the opening of his inquiry into the allegation made by the complainant that the EBA had not provided him with access to information. After sending this letter to the EBA, the institution met the complainant's request and provided him with the requested information. Because of this *settlement by an institution* the EUO closed the case.

60 See, Diamandouros 2011 or Davis 2000.

61 Annual Report of the EUO 1995, p. 6.

62 See, DR of the EUO in his inquiry into complaint 882/2009/VL against the Commission or DR of the EUO in his inquiry into complaint 2403/2008/OV against the Commission.

63 See, DR of the EUO in his inquiry into complaint 1146/2007/BU against the Commission or DR of the EUO in his inquiry into complaint 3800/2006/JF against the Commission.

64 See, DR to the Commission in complaint 1476/2005/(BB)GG or DR to the Commission in complaint 1475/2005/(IP)GG.

65 See, DR of the EUO in his inquiry into complaint 2755/2009/JF against the Commission or DR of the EUO in his inquiry into complaint 856/2008/BEH against the European Anti-Fraud Office (OLAF).

66 See, DR of the EUO in his inquiry into complaint 882/2009/VL against the Commission.

67 Magnette 2003, p. 682.

unique and legally undefined concept, it needs to be given substance so that the Union institutions can learn what rules or standards should be followed if they *want* to actually act without maladministration.[68] The EUO is not obliged to refer in his decisions to a particular norm or principle of good administration that has been breached by the Union institution and thus the creation and application of the norms do not seem to be a top priority. Despite this, the EUO drafted a document that in the end became the *European Code of Good Administrative Behaviour* and which represents the EUO/EUP codification of principles of good administration in the Union.[69] Apart from that he has also adopted several guidance documents. The application of the Code can be seen in the practice of the EUO and in his decisions.

The *potential educational function* is reflected in the effect of the normative function of the EUO and his impact on the practice of the Union institutions. A possible learning impact can be seen on several levels. The EUO's decisions are published on his official internet site[70] and this enables individuals, and also the Union's civil servants, to access them. Also his guidance has a potential learning effect. Last but not least, the EUO asks the Union institutions, on an annual basis, to explain how they have dealt with his recommendations and critical or further remarks.

1.1.3.1 Decisions of the European Ombudsman

If a friendly settlement of an alleged dispute by the EUO fails, he can adopt a *decision* that is addressed to the Union institution, to the individual and sometimes to the EUP.[71] The decisions are posted on the EUO's official internet site. Announcements concerning the adoption of annual and special reports are also published in the Official Journal of the EU.[72]

A *draft recommendation* (DR) is adopted if a friendly solution is not possible or is unsuccessful and it is *possible* for the institution concerned to eliminate the instance of maladministration. A DR is also adopted if the instance of maladministration has a *general implication*.[73] The Union institution should send the EUO a detailed opinion on his draft recommendation. An unsatisfactory response can lead to a special report to the EUP.

A *reasoned decision with a critical remark* is prepared if a friendly solution is not possible or is unsuccessful and it is *no longer possible* to eliminate the instance of maladministration. It can be used also in cases where the Union institution fails to accept a draft recommendation but a special report to the EUP is not necessary.[74] A critical remark provides confirmation for the complainant that his or her complaint was justified and

68 Good administration, on the other hand, has the character of a fundamental right in EU law. See, section 5.1.
69 Another document that codifies the perception of good administration in the EU is the Charter. Its Art. 41 codifies the *right* to good administration. See, Chapter 5.
70 <www.ombudsman.europa.eu/en/cases/home.faces> (accessed on 31 July 2013).
71 Decisions of the EUO are not administrative decisions. They are neither legally binding nor enforceable.
72 Art. 16.1 Implementing decision.
73 Art. 8.1 Implementing decision.
74 Ibid.

indicates to the institution or body concerned what it has done wrong.[75] It concerns only *individual cases* of maladministration and not *general malpractice* by Union institutions. Although *decisions with further remarks* are not expressly mentioned in Union law, they do exist in practice of the EUO.[76] Further remarks are only general recommendations by the EUO to improve the future performance of Union institutions.[77] They do not imply criticism[78] and they are *not premised on a finding of maladministration.*[79]

Art. 8.4 of the Implementing decision states that if a Union institution fails to respond satisfactorily to a draft recommendation, the EUO *may* send a *special report* to the EUP. Up until July 2013 only 18 such reports had been drawn up with the latest being in 2012.[80] Special reports are technically the ultimate weapon of the EUO as he can bring the issue to the attention of the EUP that can theoretically back him up and exercise its political influence.[81] Thus, drawing up this report only makes sense in situations where the EUO expects to receive support from the EUP.[82] As the Parliament is not excluded from the EUO's powers, it is possible that the EUO will direct a special report to the EUP because he was not satisfied with its detailed opinion on a draft recommendation.[83] Although the special report is the final step in the EUO's inquiry,[84] he still closes the file with the decision. This decision can include critical remarks, further remarks or recommendations.[85] According to Art. 11.2 of the Implementing decision the EUO may also send such *other special reports* to the EUP as he thinks appropriate to fulfil his responsibilities under the Treaties and the Statute of the EUO. Interestingly enough, neither the Statute nor the TFEU recognise *other special reports.* Last but not least, in accordance with Art. 228 (1) TFEU the EUO is obliged to submit an *annual report* to the EUP on the outcome of his inquiries.

1.1.3.2 Guidance of the European Ombudsman

Apart from the decisions connected directly with the inquiry into maladministration, the EUO also adopts various guidance documents on good administrative conduct. In this guidance the EUO expresses his opinion as to how the Union institutions *should conduct themselves* so that their actions do not contain instances of maladministration.

The most comprehensive guidance instrument by the EUO is the *European Code of Good Administrative Behaviour* (the Code). It is intended to explain in more detail

75 Annual Report of the EUO 2008, p. 17.

76 See, Decision of the EUO closing his inquiry into complaint 920/2010/VIK or in in Decision of the EUO closing his inquiry into complaint 783/2010/(ANA)DK against the Research Executive Agency.

77 Annual Report of the EUO 2010, p. 28.

78 Annual Report of the EUO 2009, p. 44.

79 *Follow-up to Critical and Further Remarks: How the EU Institutions responded to the Ombudsman's Recommendations in 2010*, p. 5.

80 Special Report of the EUO concerning his inquiry into complaint 2591/2010/GG against the Commission.

81 Cf., Jones 1997, p. 51.

82 Peters 2005, p. 706.

83 Such a situation has occurred. See, Special Report from the EUO to the EUP following the DR to the EUP in complaint 341/2001/(BB)IJH.

84 See, Decision of the EUO on complaint 1391/2002/JMA against the Commission.

85 See, Decision of the EUO closing his inquiry into complaint 676/2008/RT against the Commission or Decision of the EUO on own-initiative inquiry OI/2/2003/GG against the Commission.

what the Charter's right to good administration should mean in practice.[86] It includes the principles that shall be respected by the Union institutions and their officials in their relations with the public.[87] Although the Code was approved by a resolution of the EUP in September 2001, it is not legally binding.[88]

The second guidance instrument by the EUO is relatively fresh as it was published in 2012: *Public service principles for the EU civil service.* This document introduces five general public service principles that constitute a *high-level distillation of the ethical standards for EU civil servants.*[89] The third guidance material for the Union institutions is *The European Ombudsman's guide to complaints* (2012) that generally recommends to the Union institutions how to deal with complaints. Apart from these guidance instruments the EUO also adopts guidelines for potential complainants. These include documents such as *An information sheet for businesses and organisations* (2007), *What can the European Ombudsman do for you?* (2008) or *Problems with the EU? Who can help you?* (2011). They do not specify the Code or other guidance instruments. These documents merely instruct complainants as to *how, when* and *where* to complain.

In connection with the EUO and his educative function it is also necessary to mention a study on the compliance of Union institutions with critical and further remarks and recommendations – *Follow-up to Critical and Further Remarks: How the EU Institutions responded to the Ombudsman's Recommendations in 2010.*[90] The study contains examples where, as a result of the follow-up on the EUO's remarks, real improvements have been made in areas ranging from transparency to recruitment.[91]

One can connect the EUO with five general functions of the ombudsman. The EUO, by controlling the Union administration, adds to the protection of individuals. He broadens their possibilities of dispute resolution and remedying. Last but not least, he can use his normative powers to develop standards that can potentially impact the administrative conduct of the Union institutions.

Before going any further, however, it is necessary to note a term that is connected with all the functions of the EUO, a term that lies at the heart of the EUO's interest – *maladministration* in the Union sense. Art. 228 (1) of the TFEU empowers the EUO to receive complaints concerning instances of *maladministration* in the activities of the Union institutions. Although maladministration is legislatively acknowledged, neither primary nor secondary Union law defines this concept. It is the EUO who should give content to the term.

In the Annual Report 1995 the EUO stated that there is maladministration *if a Community institution or body fails to act in accordance with the Treaties and with the Community acts that are binding upon it, or if it fails to observe the rules and principles*

86 *The European Code of Good Administrative Behaviour*, Introduction, Publication Office, 2005, p. 7.

87 Art. 1, Code.

88 For a better description of the normative standards included in the Code see, section 5.1.1.

89 *Public Service Principles for the EU Civil Service*, Introduction, p. 2. These principles include: Commitment to the European Union and its citizens; Integrity; Objectivity; Respect for others and Transparency.

90 <www.ombudsman.europa.eu/en/cases/followups.faces> (accessed on 31 July 2013).

91 *Follow-up 2010*, p. 3. In 2010, an overall follow-up on the critical and further remarks occurred in 78% of cases, while critical remarks were followed up in 68% of cases and further remarks in 95% of cases (p. 9).

of law established by the Court of Justice and the Court of First Instance.[92] In the same report the EUO gave a non-exhaustive list of examples of maladministration which included administrative irregularities, administrative omissions, abuse of power, negligence, unlawful procedures, unfairness, malfunction or discrimination etc.[93] For some reason this definition was not considered to be satisfactory, and in its resolution dealing with the Ombudsman's Annual Report for 1996 the Parliament expressed *the need to define the term maladministration.*[94] The Annual Report 1997 already contains such a definition. The EUO stated that *maladministration occurs when a public body fails to act in accordance with a rule or principle which is binding upon it.*[95] In accordance with this definition good administration requires respect for the rule of law, for the principles of good administration, and for fundamental rights.[96] In a publication from 2008, '*What can the European Ombudsman do for you?*', the EUO offers another definition of maladministration. Maladministration is here described as *poor or failed administration which occurs if an institution fails to act in accordance with the law, fails to respect the principles of good administration, or violates human rights.*[97]

Thus, good administration includes more than acting in accordance with the law.[98] In fact it is a broader review criterion than the criterion used by the Court.[99] If one looks closely at the previous definitions, it is possible to see that the concept of good administration encompasses compliance with three issues: *law, fundamental rights* and *principles of good administration.*[100] The relation between legality and maladministration in a Union sense is described in Chapter 5.

92 Annual Report of the EUO 1995, p. 9.

93 Ibid.

94 Report of the EUP on the Annual Report on the activities of the EUO in 1996 (C4-0293/97), para. 4 states that the EUP *points out that the role of the Ombudsman should support the institutional balance laid down by the Treaties and, in particular, the correct exercise of the discretionary powers of the Commission, the Parliament and the Court of Justice; therefore, it is necessary to have a clear definition of the term maladministration.*

95 Annual Report of the EUO 1997, p. 23.

96 Annual Report of the EUO 2010, p. 15.

97 *What can the European Ombudsman do for you?: An overview of the Ombudsman's work and how he could help you*, European Communities, 2008, p. 7.

98 Diamandouros 2007, p. 3.

99 Diamandouros 2011a.

100 Strategy for the mandate 2010, p. 4.

Chapter 2

THE COURT OF JUSTICE OF THE EUROPEAN UNION

The Court of Justice of the European Union (the Court) is probably one of the most influential Union institutions for the development of the law. As it receives a great deal of academic attention, and as it is not the goal of this book to describe the Union court system in its entirety, the following pages approach it only as the *administrative court of the Union.*[1]

2.1 Administrative court of the Union?

The Court was established in 1952 as one of the original institutions of the *Coal and Steel Community.* Although the communities and the Treaties have changed, the Court has always represented the judicial power of the Communities and the Union. Today it is the judicial body of two organisations – the EU and EURATOM.

The Court consists of three separate judicial bodies: the Court of Justice, the General Court and the European Union Civil Service Tribunal. *The Court of Justice* (COJ) acts as a court of first instance and as an appellate court. As the court of first instance it deals with preliminary proceedings[2] and with infringement proceedings.[3] As an appellate court the COJ deals with appeals against the judgments of the General Court. Its judgments are final and cannot be appealed against or otherwise contested. The *General Court* (EUGC) was created in 1988 as the *Court of First Instance* (CFI) and was rebranded in December 2009.[4] Its original role was to relieve the COJ of some of its heavy workload.[5] At first instance it deals with actions for the annulment of an act, failures to act and liability cases. As an appellate court, it deals with appeals against the decisions of the *Civil Service Tribunal*

1 Cf. Arnull 2006, Tridimas 2012 or Craig & de Búrca 2011 etc.

2 Which are an important tool in the development of Union law and the Ius Commune.

3 According to Art. 256 (1) TFEU the EUGC has jurisdiction to hear and determine at first instance actions or proceedings referred to in Arts. 263, 265, 268, 270 and 272, with the exception of those assigned to a specialised court set up under Art. 257 and those reserved in the Statute for the Court of Justice. Thus, the COJ has first-instance jurisdiction over disputes involving Member States or only the Union institutions. The EUGC acts at first instance in cases involving individuals including reviewing legality and a failure to act by the Union institutions.

4 The term 'Court of First Instance' in this text is only used in connection with historical documents.

5 See, Harris 2007, p. 222 or Craig & de Búrca 2011, p. 68.

(EUCST). The EUCST is so far the only specialized court of the Union.[6] It adjudicates in disputes between the EU and its civil servants. It was created in 2004. It may try to facilitate an amicable settlement of disputes between the Union and its civil service.[7] The legal framework of the Court is in general included in the texts of the Treaties, the Statute of the Court and the Rules of Procedure of individual courts.[8]

Because of the character of the EU and the division of power within its institutions, the Court differs from national administrative courts. Traditional parties to the Court proceedings are the Union institutions and the Member States. Individuals (natural or legal persons) are still considered to be non-privileged applicants. Ginter notes that 'private parties are in essence only granted standing when the challenged acts are decisions that by nature relate to the special situation of this applicant.'[9] Individuals can be parties to proceedings before the EUGC or EUCST and in appellate proceedings also before the COJ. In other cases they cannot directly address the Court.

The Court acts as an *administrative court* in cases where an individual is in a dispute with a Union institution. These cases include actions that can be *directly* commenced by an individual e.g. *actions for annulment*, *actions because of a failure to act* or *actions for damages*. Because of that, the consideration of the Court in this book is limited:

1. for purposes of *general institutional issues* to the field where the Court acts as an administrative court and deals with cases of disputes between a Union institution and individuals; and
2. for purposes of *issues of the development of normative standards* this field is broader as the Court discovers and develops legal principles also in proceedings where it does not act as an administrative court (i.e. preliminary or infringement proceedings).

2.2 The Court's proceedings (general)

This section describes the proceedings before the EUGC as the EUGC is the court that at first instance deals with individuals as an administrative court.[10] The Statute of the EUGC talks about two obligatory stages of the procedure: written and oral.[11]

The *written stage* deals with communication with the parties and all the necessary documents. A *written application* to the Registry of the Court is obligatory to commence the proceedings.[12] The parties to the proceedings must be legally represented. After the

6 The TFEU leaves open the possibility to create other specialized tribunals (Art. 257 (2) TFEU).

7 Art. 7 (4) Annex I to the Statute of the Court of Justice of the European Union.

8 These include the TEU (Arts. 13, 19 or 24), the TFEU (Section 5, its protocol No. 3), the Euratom Treaty, the Statute of the Court of Justice of the European Union, the Rules of Procedure of the Court and other sources of secondary Union law (e.g. Regulation (EC) No. 1049/2001 of the EUP and of the Council of 30 May 2001 regarding public access to EUP, Council and Commission documents or other sources of secondary Union law) etc.

9 Ginter 2002, p. 383.

10 Although the proceedings before all three courts are undoubtedly comparable, the appellate proceedings before the COJ or proceedings before the EUCST have their specific characteristics. See, Rules of procedure of the COJ and Rules of procedure of the EUCST.

11 Chapters 1 and 2, Rules of procedure of the EUGC.

12 Art. 44 Rules of procedure of the EUGC.

application is served on the defendant, he usually has two months to lodge *a defence*.[13] The application can be supplemented by *a reply* by the applicant and *a rejoinder* by the defendant. The Judge-Rapporteur prepares a preliminary report that contains recommendations for the EUGC as to whether organisation of procedure measures or measures of inquiry should be undertaken and whether the case should be referred to a different sitting of the court. As there are no permanent Advocates General (AG) at the EUGC, the court can authorise one of the judges to act as an AG in a particular case.[14]

The *oral stage* includes the hearing by the EUGC. Questions can be posed to the representatives of the parties. The EUGC can summon witnesses on application by a party or of its own motion.[15] It can also require an expert report. The judgment is delivered in open court and the parties are given notice to attend in order to hear it.[16] Judgments are binding from the date of their delivery and they have to state the reasons for reaching such a decision. They are always unanimous as there are no dissenting, concurring or separate opinions as in some national courts or at the European Court of Human Rights.[17]

The unsuccessful party is usually ordered to pay the costs of the proceedings. Generally, there is no court fee but the parties must be legally represented, so there are expenses for legal representation. Still, a party may apply for legal aid.

An *appeal* may be brought before the COJ against the judgment of the EUGC.[18] It has to be limited to points of law. In appellate proceedings the COJ does not deal with factual questions but only with questions of law. An appeal must be based on a lack of competence, a breach of procedure as well as an infringement of Union law by the EUGC.[19] If the COJ finds the appeal to be well founded it quashes the decision of the EUGC and either gives a final judgment on the matter or refers the case back to the EUGC for a new judgment.[20] In the latter case the EUGC is bound by the decision of the COJ on points of law.[21] An appeal does not have suspensory effect. Nearly identical provisions also apply to appeals against final decisions of the EUCST before the EUGC.[22]

2.3 Normative standards of the Court

In accordance with Art. 263 (2) TFEU the Court has to review the legality of Union acts on the grounds of (i) a lack of competence (the *ultra vires* doctrine),[23] (ii) an infringement

13 Arts. 45, 46 Rules of procedure of the EUGC.
14 Art. 2 Rules of procedure of the EUGC.
15 Art. 68 (1) Rules of procedure of the EUGC.
16 Art. 84) Rules of procedure of the EUGC.
17 Cf. ECHR in *Kopp v. Switzerland*, Judgment of 25 March 1998, 27 EHRR91 etc.
18 Art. 256 (1) TFEU.
19 Art. 58 Statute of the Court.
20 If there is a serious risk of the unity or consistency of Union law being affected it is also possible that the COJ will *review* the decision of the EUGC. This review can only be proposed by the AG. An individual does not have this remedy. See Art. 256 (2) and (3) TFEU.
21 Art. 61 Statute of the Court.
22 Cf. Arts. 9-13 of Annex I to the Statute and Art. 256 (2) TFEU.
23 Cf. Case C-110/02 *Commission v Council* [2004] ECR I-6333, para. 51 or Case C-376/98 *Germany v EUP and Council (Tobacco Advertising)* [2000] ECR I-8419 etc.

of an essential procedural requirement,[24] (iii) an infringement of the Treaties or any rule of law relating to their application,[25] and (iv) a misuse of powers.[26] Apart from these Treaty-established grounds, especially in cases where the Court has to consider the legality of acts by the Union institutions, the Court has been discovering and developing principles against which it assesses the legality of actions by the Union institutions or their inactivity. These principles are developed in connection with point (iii): an infringement of the Treaties or any rule of law relating to their application, which gives the Court rather broad normative powers.

These principles have the status of *general principles of Union law*. They are a set of rules that overarch or underpin the Union's legal order.[27] They act as guidelines for legislative enactments and as measures against which Union law is judged.[28] General principles of law discovered by the Court confirm the strong position of the Court in the area of the development of the law and they are an important tool for the judicial development of Union law.[29]

The Court has been developing these principles since its creation in the 1950s. A breakthrough in this development occurred in 1957 in the *Algera* judgment where it *inter alia* held that 'unless the court is to deny justice it is therefore obliged to solve the problem by reference to the rules acknowledged by the legislation, the learned writing and the case law of the member countries.'[30] This case made it clear that the Court acknowledges that unwritten principles play an important role in the European legal order. Existing gaps within written Union law have almost exclusively been bridged by Member States having recourse to the general principles of Union law, be they statutory or constitutional.[31] Even though there are also other explanations for the development of principles,[32] the gap-filling function of the principles is probably the most outstanding one.[33] While developing these principles the Court usually looks at legal principles which already exist in the Member States or at principles that exist in international law.[34] It is common practice that before the introduction of a new principle into the legal order of the EU, the Court conducts an extensive research of legal principles which already exist in the national legal orders of

24 Cf. Case C-76/01 P *Eurocoton and others v Council* [2003] ECR I-10091 in connection with the obligation to provide reasons for a legal act (Art. 296 TFEU) or Case 138/79 *SA Roquette Frères v Council* [1980] ECR 3333.

25 An infringement of the Treaty constitutes a general ground within which other grounds are subsumed. Chalmers et al. 2006, p. 436.

26 Cf. Case 105/75 *Giuffrida v Commission* [1976] ECR 1395, where the Court annulled a decision of the Commission on this particular ground or Case C-84/94 *UK v Council* [1995] ECR I-5755.

27 Horspool & Humphreys 2006, p. 128.

28 Ibid.

29 Iglesias 1999, pp. 1-16.

30 Joined cases 7/56 and 3/57 to 7/57, *Algera v Common Assembly of the ECSC* [1957] ECR 39.

31 Schwarze 2001, p. 62.

32 Raitio 2000, pp. 47-48.

33 Groussot 2006, pp. 10-11.

34 There is a tendency for the Court to borrow principles also from other legal branches, i.e. from criminal law. In the judgment Case C-45/08 *Spector Photo Group and Van Raemdonck* [2009] ECR I-12073, the Court discussed *inter alia* the applicability of the principle of the presumption of innocence (paras. 43-44).

the Member States.[35] Some of the principles discovered by the Court have already been codified in provisions of the Treaties[36] while others have the character of unwritten legal norms. Still, they are law.

So far there is no finalised set of all the general principles of Union law as they are still developing.[37] This book divides the Court's principles into two groups. Firstly, there are principles *primarily* dealing with relations between the Member States and the Union (or national law and European Union law), i.e. *principles with a strategic political character*. And secondly, there are principles that *a priori* serve as a guarantee for individuals in their relations with the European or national administrations within the scope of Union law, i.e. *procedural guarantee principles*. Principles with a strategic political character include, for example, the principle of the direct effect of Union law or the principle of the supremacy of Union law over domestic law. However, as they primarily deal with relations between national law and Union law and between the EU and its Member States rather than with the EU and individuals, they are not discussed here.[38] In this book attention is devoted to principles with a guarantee character as they potentially function as a standard to *balance the unequal status of individuals in their relations with the EU and its institutions*. These are discussed in detail in Chapter 5.

2.4 Remedies of the Court

An individual can only institute *annulment proceedings* against an act addressed to that individual,[39] an act which is of direct and individual concern to the individual, and against a regulatory act[40] which is of direct concern to that individual and does not entail implementing measures. He has to do this within a time limit of two months from the publication of such an act. His rights may be limited by special conditions and arrangements laid down in acts setting up Union institutions.[41] If the action is well founded, the Court declares the act concerned to be void, although (some of) the effects of the void act may be retained by the Court.[42] As Skouris noted 'the Court claims a monopoly in the annulment of acts of the Community institutions so as to ensure that those acts apply, or do not apply,

35 *Algera* Judgment part – The revocability of administrative measures giving rise to individual rights, p. 55.

36 The principle of equality and non-discrimination is codified in Art. 18 TFEU, the principle of proportionality in Art. 5 (4) TEU and the principle of the prohibition of discrimination because of sex in Art. 157 TFEU.

37 A typology of the Court's principles can be found in, for example, Craig & de Búrca, 2011, Chalmers at al. 2006.

38 For a further study of political principles see, Craig & de Búrca, 2011, Chalmers at al. 2006 etc.

39 This occurs, for instance, when an individual brings a case against the Commission's decision to impose a fine on this particular individual.

40 With respect to 'regulatory acts' the individual does not have to establish an *individual* concern; however, he/she must establish a *direct* concern. The meaning of *'regulatory act'* is not defined by the TFEU but in the Order of the General Court in Case T18/10 *Inuit Tapiriit Kanatami and Others* v *Parliament and Council* [2011] ECR II-5599 and in a judgment of the General Court in Case T-262/10 *Microban v Commission* [2011] ECR II-7697 the EUGC states that regulatory acts are *all acts of general application apart from legislative acts*.

41 Art. 263 (5) TFEU.

42 Art. 264 (2) TFEU.

uniformly throughout the whole of the European Union.'[43] An action for annulment does not have suspensory effect.[44] Thus the commencement of proceedings does not *ex lege* result in a suspension of the application of the contested act. However, if requested, the Court can suspend its application or prescribe any necessary interim measure.[45]

If the Union institution *fails to act,* an individual can start a procedure before the Court to put an end to this inactivity. The procedure (similar to the annulment procedure) takes place before the General Court. First of all, the Union institution has to be called upon to act within a time limit of *two months.* If the Union institution does not act within this time limit an action can be brought before the Court within a further period of two months. This *de facto* creates a preliminary procedure that has to be followed before the Court will deal with the case. Secondly, an individual has to have an *interest* in taking this action. Art. 265 (3) TFEU specifies that an individual can complain to the Court when the Union institution has failed to address to him/her an act that is not an opinion or a recommendation.[46] In practice, the Court also accepts actions for a failure to act in relation to an act which has not formally been addressed to individuals but concerns them *directly and individually.* In its decision the Court declares that the Union institution has failed to act *but it does not order it to act.* This obligation remains with that institution as the Court decision has only a declaratory character.[47]

If an individual believes that a Union institution has caused him to suffer damage, he can bring an *action for damages* before the Court.[48] Jurisdiction lies with the EUGC.[49] He has to do this within five years of the occurrence of the event giving rise to damage.[50] Non-contractual liability is primarily relevant in situations in which individuals are directly confronted with unlawful acts by a Union institution or servant.[51] An individual must establish the existence of a *wrongful act, damage* and *causation.* In the case of a wrongful act he has to show that there has been a sufficiently serious breach of a superior rule intended to confer rights on individuals.[52] Damage must be actual and certain and not only hypothetical or speculative.[53] It must also be a sufficiently direct consequence of the unlawful conduct of the Union institution concerned.[54] The conditions for the

43 Skouris 2009, p. 4. In connection with the claim of the Court's exclusive jurisdiction to control the legality and/or validity of Union law see, for example, Case C-314/85 Foto-Frost v Hauptzollamt Lübeck-Ost [1987] ECR 4199.

44 Art. 278 TFEU.

45 For criteria which are relevant for the determination of an application for interim measure see Jans et al. 2006, p. 248.

46 See, for example, Case T442/07 *Ryanair v Commission* [2011] ECR II-0333.

47 For example, in the judgment of 16 February 1993 in Case C-107/91*ENU v Commission* where the Court only declared that *the Commission failed to take a decision on the request submitted to it by the applicant.*

48 The EU has an obligation in accordance with *the general principles common to the laws of the Member States* to make good any damage caused by its institutions or by its servants in the performance of their duties. Art. 340 TFEU.

49 Art. 268 TFEU in connection with Art. 256 TFEU.

50 Art. 46 TFEU.

51 Jans et al. 2007, p. 256.

52 Case C-352/98 P *Bergaderm and Goupil v Commission* [2000] ECR I-5291.

53 Case 51/81 *De Franceschi v Council and Commission* [1982] ECR 117.

54 Joined cases 64 and 113/76, 167 and 239/78, 27, 28 and 45/79, 64/76 *Dumortier v Council* [1979] ECR 3091, judgment, para. 21.

liability of Union institutions depend on the extent of the Union institutions' *discretion*. In *Bergaderm*, the Court held that the degree of discretion is a decisive test for considering the liability of an Union institution.[55] Thus, the higher the degree of discretion the Union institution has, the lesser possibility there is that it will be held liable.[56]

In order to complete the picture concerning the remedies available to individuals it should be noted that according to Art. 266 TFEU the institution whose act has been declared void or whose failure to act has been declared contrary to the Treaties shall be required to take the necessary measures to comply with the judgment of the Court. However this obligation does not affect obligations which may result from an application for damages under Art. 340 TFEU.

As noted before, an individual can appeal against a decision of the General Court and against a decision of the EUCST.

55 Case C-352/98 P *Bergaderm and Goupil v Commission* [2000] ECR I-5291.

56 For a more thorough description of the currently valid conditions for non-contractual liability see the Union law textbooks. For example, Kaczorovska 2010, p. 473ff.

Chapter 3

INSTITUTIONAL COORDINATION OF OMBUDSMAN-JUDICIARY RELATIONS IN THE EU

This chapter tries to draw a comprehensive picture of the institutional coordination of the EUO and the Court. It addresses the formal institutional coordination of this relationship (3.1). It is followed by a description of the practice of possible informal coordination between these Union institutions (3.2). The chapter ends with a summary that attempts to the answer the first research question: how the relations between the EUO and the Court are coordinated on the institutional level and what is the content of this coordination (3.3).

3.1 Formal institutional coordination in the EU

When looking for an answer to the first research question, it is necessary to look for the existence of formal coordination mechanisms. The following subsections show that these mechanisms can be found in various sources. The first source that must be taken into account is *written Union law*, both, primary or secondary. The second source is *the case law of the Court* as the Court is the Union institution that has a considerable impact on the development and character of Union law. Although the EUO is one of two investigated subjects, he cannot create law or take decisions that can bind the Court. Because of that, it is questionable whether he can add something *new* to the *formal institutional coordination* of his relation with the Court.

3.1.1 Written Union law

EU law does not have a sole legislator that creates legal rules as can be seen in national states. Based on the character of legal norms and their creator, we can traditionally talk about *primary Union law*[1] that includes the *Founding Treaties* and their amendments and changes, but also the *Charter of Fundamental Rights*. Primary Union law is adopted by the *Union's Member States*. One can also talk about *secondary Union law* which includes a plethora of legal instruments (directives, regulations, decisions etc.) adopted by the

1 *Primary Union law* is a generally used term (cf. Griller 2000, p. 36). Some authors go a step further, for example, Fairhust states that *the treaties (including their amendments) form a 'constitution' of the European Communities and the Union*. See, Fairhust 2010, p. 56.

Union institutions that have themselves been established by the provisions of primary or even secondary Union law. Union law has to be complied with by the Member States and their institutions (when acting within the scope of Union law) and, naturally, the Union institutions. In general, the relationship between primary and secondary Union law can be compared, by analogy, with the relationship between national constitutional law and national statutory law. However, a strict classification of Union law into primary law and secondary law is not complete as there are definitely sources of law that do not belong to any of the two groups. These are the *general principles of Union law.* They must be in compliance with primary Union law but rules of secondary Union law that breach these principles can be quashed by the Court. They are discussed in section 2.3 and Chapter 5. This subchapter was researched with the help of the official internet site of the European legislation, *EUR-lex.*

3.1.1.1 Primary Union law

The Founding Treaties, their amendments and the *Accession Treaties* are the primary source of Union law.[2] So is the *Charter.* Although in the pre-Lisbon era the Charter had a rather unclear status, today it has the same legal value as the Treaties, thanks to the amended Art. 6 (1) of the TEU, and is thus considered to be a source of law with the status of primary Union law.[3] The only *formal institutional coordination* of the EUO and the Court in primary Union law is included in the TFEU (Art. 228) and in the Charter (Art. 43). The institutional coordination in these sources deals with the *implied legal bar on the EUO*, the *mandatory bar on the EUO* and the *indirect formal institutional coordination of the EUO and the Court.*

1. Implied legal bar on the EUO

Art. 228 (1) TFEU includes an important limitation to the competences of the EOU in connection with the Court. This provision highlights that the EUO is empowered to receive complaints concerning instances of maladministration in the activities of the Union institutions, bodies, offices or agencies, with *the exception of the Court of Justice of the European Union acting in its judicial role*. Thus, the conduct of the Court when acting in its judicial role can never be reviewed by the EUO. The same limitation on the EUO is also included in Art. 43 of the Charter. These two provisions give rise to the question whether the EUO is empowered to receive complaints when the Court is *not* acting in its judicial role.[4]

2 The Founding Treaties include e.g. the Paris Treaty, the Rome Treaties, the Treaty on the EU. The Amending Treaties include e.g. the Single European Act, the Amsterdam Treaty, the Lisbon Treaty etc. The Accession Treaties are the treaties with individual Member States when joining the Union.

3 Art. 6 (1) TEU states that the Charter *shall have the same legal value as the Treaties.*

4 This is not excluded. See, for example, Special Report by the EUO to the EUP following the own-initiative inquiry into public access to documents (616/PUBAC/F/IJH) of Annual Report of the EUO 1995.

2. Mandatory legal bar on the EUO

Art. 228 (1) TFEU also underlines another limitation on the EUO's powers. Its second part states that the EUO conducts inquiries for which he finds grounds, either on his own initiative or on the basis of complaints submitted to him directly or through an MEP, *except where the alleged facts are or have been the subject of legal proceedings*. Thus, although the TFEU grants the EUO exclusive powers to investigate complaints about instances of *maladministration,* it also limits these powers when the facts *have been* or *are assessed* in legal proceedings. This provision is a mandatory cessation for the EUO and his investigation.[5] This mandatory legal bar is connected with legal proceedings in general. It includes legal proceedings of the Court but also other courts, for instance national courts. Nonetheless, Union law does not bar the EUO from investigating cases where the facts *could* be or *could have been* theoretically a subject of legal proceedings. Only *actual* or *past* legal proceedings can hinder the EUO's power to investigate a complaint.[6] This limits the competences of the EUO, but it also limits the chances of individuals to have their interests protected. The same facts can lead to different conclusions by the Court and the EUO because the normative concepts of the Court and the EUO are not identical.[7] If the Court has dealt with the facts of a case from the perspective of lawfulness, it does not mean that it has assessed the facts in the same way as the EUO from the perspective of maladministration. Hence, this bar does not take into account the possibility that the EUO can make a different assessment when compared to the Court.

3. Indirect formal institutional coordination of the EUO and the Court

Indirectly, the *formal institutional coordination of the EUO and the Court* stems from several provisions of the TFEU and is exercised in the practice of the Court. In various decisions the Court explains its inability to *review the legality of the EUO's decisions* according to Art. 263 (1) TFEU, its inability to deal with the EUO's failure to act according to Art. 265 TFEU and its ability to assess the EUO's liability for non-contractual damage according to Art. 340 TFEU (in connection with Art. 268 TFEU).[8]

From the previous examples it is obvious that primary Union law provides only a limited picture of the *institutional coordination* of the EUO and the Court.

3.1.1.2 Secondary Union law

Secondary Union law sometimes only reiterates and repeats the provisions of primary Union law. Nonetheless, it sometimes introduces some novelties. The Statute of the EUO

5 See, for example, Decision of the EUO on complaint 1357/2010/(PL)MHZ against the Commission of 7 September 2010.

6 Other provisions of the TFEU that deal with the institutional coordination of the EUO and the Court contain organisational issues. For example, Art. 228 (2) TFEU discusses the role of the Court towards the EUO in connection with the EUO's dismissal. Based on the proposal of the EUP, the Court can dismiss the EUO if he no longer fulfils the conditions required for the performance of his duties or if he is guilty of serious misconduct. So far the Court has not used this power.

7 See, section 5.1.

8 See, section 3.1.2.

and the Implementing decision discuss the institutional coordination of the EUO and the Court with regard to:

1. Limitations of the EUO

Art. 1 (3) of the *Statute of the EUO* states that the EUO *may not intervene in cases before the courts* or *question the soundness of a court's ruling*. His role is to uncover maladministration in the activities of the Community institutions and bodies, *with the exception of the Court of Justice* and *the Court of First Instance acting in their judicial role*.[9] This confirms primary Union law by stating that the Court cannot be investigated by the EUO. An addition is the provision that the EUO *cannot intervene in cases before the Court*. It is not clear whether this intervention is the same as the intervention described in Art. 40 of the Statute of the Court. Also the rulings of the Court and their soundness cannot be questioned by the EUO. The EUO notes that *he cannot, directly or indirectly, question the practice of the EU judicature, nor can he assess in abstracto the correctness of the applicable rules of EU law and their compliance with general principles of law*.[10] Thus, the EUO may have a different opinion concerning a certain (factual or legal) question than the Court but he cannot directly criticise or asses it. This limitation on the EUO's competences is also included in the *Implementing decision*. Its Art. 10.3 states that if legal proceedings are instituted in relation to matters under investigation by the EUO, he closes the case and the outcome of any inquiries he has carried out up to that point is filed without further action.

2. Advice to address another authority

According to Art. 2 (5) of the Statute of the EUO, the EUO may *advise the person lodging the complaint to address it to another authority*. Although the Statute does not stipulate that the EUO can *transfer a complaint* or *a case* to the Court, the provision of such advice to a complainant may eventually lead to the commencement of Court proceedings and the subsequent closure of the case and the winding up of an investigation by the EOU. However, the EUO is by no means obliged to inform a complainant about this possibility. He only has the *choice* to *routinely inform* the citizen concerned about which measures should be taken in order to best serve his interests, including an indication of the judicial remedies.[11]

3. The possibility to inform the Court

According to Art. 10.4 of the *Implementing decision*, the EUO can inform the relevant national authorities and, if appropriate, also a *Union institution* or body of such criminal law matters as may come to his notice in the course of an inquiry. The EUO can also inform a Union institution of facts which, in his view, could justify disciplinary proceedings. Theoretically, it is not excluded that the EUO can provide the Court with certain information concerning criminal or disciplinary proceedings. Whether the Court would

9 Art. 2 (1) Statute of the EUO.

10 Decision of the EUO closing his inquiry into complaint 1859/2011/(BEH)JN against the Commission, para. 28.

11 Case T-209/00 *Lamberts v Mediator* [2002] ECR II-2203, judgment, para. 68.

admit such information and how it would deal with this information depends entirely on the circumstances of the case and on the discretion of the Court.

4. Organisational matters
Secondary Union law also deals with organisational matters such as the *dismissal* of the EUO by the Court (Art. 8 of the Statute of the EUO), the *solemn undertaking* by the EUO (the oath) before the COJ (Art. 9 (2) of the Statute of the EUO) or the remuneration, allowances and pension to be paid to the EUO who, in this connection, occupies the position of a judge of the COJ (Art. 10 (2) Statute of the EUO).

Regulations and *directives*, as important sources of secondary Union law, only rarely refer to the EUO or his relations with the Court or create a certain formal mechanism for the coordination of these relations. However, in some situations, regulations give individuals certain rights to *address the Court or the EUO when asking for access to documents.*

In accordance with *Regulation (EU) No. 1095/2010 of the EUP and of the Council* decisions taken by the European Supervisory Authority may be the subject of a complaint to the EUO *or* of proceedings before the COJ.[12] This regulation (and some others) basically follows primary Union law in giving an individual the possibility to choose between following 'the path' of the EUO or that of the Court. However, the main regulation dealing with access to European Parliament, Council and Commission documents, *Regulation (EC) No. 1049/2001 of the EUP and of the Council,* states that:

> '... in the event of a total or partial refusal [to provide access to information], the institution shall inform the applicant of the remedies open to him or her, namely instituting court proceedings against the institution *and/or* making a complaint to the Ombudsman, under the conditions laid down in Articles 230 and 195 of the EC Treaty, respectively.'[13]

This regulation suggests that theoretically an individual can use both remedies simultaneously. However, this possibility is explicitly excluded by primary Union law and by the Court's jurisprudence.

A rare reference to the status of the EUO in connection with the Court can also be found in some *resolutions of the European Union Parliament* (although these do not have the character of Union law). First of all, resolutions can play a role in the case of a special report by the EUO as the EUO may advise that his special reports are adopted as resolutions.[14] Secondly, although the resolutions of the EUP are not legally binding and they have a political character, they can shed more light on EUO-Court relations. For instance, in the *Resolution on the annual report on the activities of the European*

12 Regulation (EU) No. 1095/2010 of the EUP and of the Council of 24 November 2010 establishing a European Supervisory Authority (European Securities and Markets Authority), amending Decision No. 716/2009/EC and repealing Commission Decision 2009/77/EC, Art. 72 (3).

13 Regulation (EC) No. 1049/2001 of the EUP and of the Council of 30 May 2001 regarding public access to EUP, Council and Commission documents, OJ L 145, Art. 8.

14 Craig & de Búrca 2008, p. 63. See also Special Report from the EUO to the EUP following his DR to the Commission in Complaint 185/2005/ELB.

Ombudsman in 1996, the EUP *inter alia* pointed out that the role of the EUO should be to support the institutional balance laid down by the Treaties and, in particular, the correct exercise of the discretionary powers of the Commission, the EUP and the Court of Justice.

Unfortunately, no other similar examples have been found in other resolutions of the EUP.

From the research into secondary Union law one can see that its provisions usually only reiterate and repeat the provisions of primary Union law. Only on rare occasions does it introduce a new point that is applicable to the institutional coordination of the EUO and the Court.

3.1.2 The case law of the Court

The case law of the Court plays an important role also in connection with the institutional coordination of the EUO and the Court. Not only because the Court gives a binding interpretation and an explanation of Union law and ensures that in the interpretation and application of the Treaties the law is observed[15] but also because the Court can influence the validity of acts by Union institutions and deal with the non-contractual liability or inactivity of the Union institutions.

The possibility to judicially *review the legality of the EUO's decisions* in accordance with Art. 263 (1) TFEU is discussed in Case T-196/08 *Srinivasan v Mediator* (not published) and Case *C-580/08 P Srinivasan v Mediator* [2009] ECR I-110:

> In this case, the applicant complained to the Commission about infringement of Community law by the Irish authorities. After the Commission decided to take no further action on this complaint, he complained to the EUO. The EUO has not found any maladministration in the action of the Commission and closed the case. The discontent complainant brought the case against the EUO before the CFI. He *inter alia* asked the CFI to annul the EUO's decision. The CFI here stated that 'a reasoned decision by the Ombudsman concluding the substantive examination of a complaint by deciding to take no further action on it does not constitute a measure capable of being challenged by an action for annulment, since such a decision does not produce legal effects on third parties, within the meaning of Art. 263 TFEU.'[16] This decision was confirmed in the appellate proceedings by the COJ which decided to dismiss the appeal.[17]

The Court confirmed that the EUO is not an institution that can make decisions that have legal effect vis-à-vis third parties and that the annulment of his decisions is excluded from its competence. This case law has also been followed in the later practice of the Court.[18]

15 Art. 19 (1) TEU.

16 Case T-196/08 *Srinivasan v Mediator* (not published), order, paras. 11-12.

17 Case C580/08 P *Srinivasan v Mediator* [2009] ECR I-110, order, paras. 44-48.

18 Cf. Case T-290/08 AJ *Apostolov v Mediator* (not published) or Case T-477/11 AJ *BW v Commission and Mediator* (not published).

In connection with *actions for failure to act* in accordance with Art. 265 TFEU, the Court has decided in a similar fashion. In Case T-103/99 *Associazione delle Cantine Sociali Venete v Mediator*[19] *and the European Parliament,* the Court specified the possibility to deal with *actions for failure to act by the EUO,* particularly a failure to make a finding of maladministration on the part of the Commission.

> An applicant lodged a complaint with the EUO following the Commission's refusal to allow him to have access to its documents. As the EUO had not made a finding of maladministration in the conduct of the Commission the applicant started proceedings before the CFI. He claimed that the Court should declare that the EUO had unlawfully failed to make a finding of maladministration. The Court here decided on the admissibility of the action. In para. 46 it stated that 'the Ombudsman is not a Community institution within the meaning of (the third paragraph of) Article 175 of the Treaty (now Article 265 TFEU), so that the application, to the extent that it refers to a failure to act on the Ombudsman's part, must be declared inadmissible.'[20] It underlined that 'an action for failure to act made by a natural or legal person is nevertheless admissible only when the institution in question has failed to address to that person an act other than a recommendation or an opinion or to adopt a measure which would have concerned him directly and individually.'[21] This decision was confirmed in subsequent case law.[22]

The Court here expressly stated that it is not possible to admit an action for failure to act by the EUO. Although the application did not address the matter of the annulment of the EUO's decision, the Court here also concluded that the EUO's report does not constitute a challengeable act of direct and individual concern to it within the meaning of Art. 265 TFEU.[23] This statement was also confirmed in the previously discussed *Srinivasan* decision.

The *non-contractual liability of the EUO* was dealt with by the Court in Cases *T-209/00 Lamberts v Mediator* and *C-234/02 Mediator v Lamberts.* In these two cases the Court had to answer the question of whether conduct by the EUO can give rise, in accordance with Art. 340 TFEU, to the non-contractual liability of the Union.[24]

> The case was started by an unsuccessful candidate of internal competition at the Commission. Although the EUO did find maladministration in the conduct of the Commission, the complainant was not happy with his decision as he was not able to re-sit the competition at the Commission. Following the EUO's closure of the case the

19 For some reason, the titles of the judgments of the Court in which the EUO is a party to the proceedings describe the EUO as a 'Mediator'. However, the text of the judgments uses the term 'European Ombudsman'.

20 Case T-103/99 *Associazione delle Cantine Sociali Venete v Mediator and Parliament* [2000] ECR II-4165, order, para. 46.

21 Ibid., para. 47.

22 Cf. in Case T-144/06 *O'Loughlin v Mediator and Ireland* (not published) the Court stated that *in so far as the action seeks a declaration that the Ombudsman unlawfully failed to act, it is clear from the case law that the Ombudsman is not a Community institution within the meaning of Article 232 EC* (today Art. 263 TFEU), para. 15 of the Order of the CFI of 5 September 2006.

23 *Associazione delle Cantine Sociali Venete,* order, para. 50.

24 Art. 340 TFEU includes a general obligation for the Union to make good any damage caused by its institutions or by its servants in the performance of their duties.

> complainant claimed compensation in the form of material and non-material damages before the Court. The Court stated in its findings that it has jurisdiction in disputes relating to compensation for damage caused by Community *institutions*. In this connection, it interpreted the term 'institution' in a broad sense, not only in connection with the former Art. 7 TEC,[25] but emphasised that the term also covers, with regard to the system of non-contractual liability established by the Treaty, 'all other Community bodies established by the Treaty and intended to contribute to the achievement of the Community's objectives and the Ombudsman is clearly a body established by the Treaty, which conferred on him the powers set out in (now Article 228 (1) TFEU).'[26]

The CFI concluded that it has jurisdiction to entertain an action for compensation also against the EUO.

> In dealing with appeals against this judgment the COJ stated that 'a finding of liability owing to damage occasioned by the EUO's activity does not concern the personal liability of the Ombudsman but that of the Community and that it does not appear that the possibility that, under certain circumstances, the Community may incur liability owing to conduct on the part of the EUO in the performance of his duties which is contrary to Community law is of such a nature as to call into question the EUO's independence.'[27]

The COJ underlined that a breach of Union law is attributable to a Union institution if the conditions set in the case law are met. But a judicial review by the Court *must be carried out with due regard for the specific nature of the Ombudsman's function*.[28]

> It stated that the CFI was entitled to find that 'not only does the Ombudsman enjoy very wide discretion as regards the merits of the complaints [...] but also even if review by the Community judicature must consequently be limited, it is possible that in very exceptional circumstances a citizen may be able to demonstrate that the Ombudsman has committed a sufficiently serious breach of Community law in the performance of his duties likely to cause damage to the citizen concerned.'[29]

The Court concluded that in connection with an action for damages it is possible to appropriately assess *the lawfulness of the EUO's conduct*.

> It highlighted that 'in the context of an action founded on the noncontractual liability of the Community and seeking reparation for loss allegedly caused by the manner in which the EUO dealt with a complaint, it is appropriate to assess the *lawfulness of the Ombudsman's conduct in the performance of his duties*.'[30]

25 Art. 7 TEC at the time of the Court's judgment enumerated the Union institutions. However, it did not include the EUO. This article has been partially replaced by Art. 13 TEU as amended by the Treaty of Lisbon. The inclusion of the EUO as a Union institution is still lacking, however.

26 Case T-209/00 *Lamberts v Mediator* [2002] ECR II-2203, judgment, paras. 48-52.

27 Case C-234/02 *Mediator v Lamberts* [2004] ECR I-2803, judgment, para. 48.

28 Ibid., para. 51.

29 Ibid., para. 52.

30 Ibid., para. 62.

The precedent set in this decision was followed in the subsequent case law of the Court and the EUO (as an EU institution) was obliged to pay damages to an individual.[31] The Court thus confirmed that the EUO can be liable for non-contractual damage. This liability will only arise in *very exceptional circumstances* and under the conditions set by the case law of the Court there must be a *sufficiently serious breach of Union law* that causes the damage. Another conclusion is that the Court can, in limited circumstances of non-contractual liability, assess the *lawfulness of the EUO's conduct.*

In *Lamberts v Mediator* the Court confirmed the *alternative character of the EUO's protection,* as the EUO is *an alternative remedy to that of an action before the Community Court in order to protect their interests.*[32] It explains that these two remedies cannot be pursued at the same time and that that complaint with the EUO does not affect the time-limits for appeals to the Court. It is for the citizen to decide which of the two available remedies is likely to serve his interests best.[33] This case law was confirmed later.[34]

Last but not least, in Case T-369/11 *Diadikasia Symvouloi Epicheiriseon v Commission*, the EUGC confirmed that the EUO *constitutes a non-contentious means of obtaining redress.*[35]

3.1.3 The 'ombudsprudence' of the European Ombudsman

As noted above, the decisions of the EUO are not legally binding. Because of this the 'ombudsprudence' of the EUO cannot formally coordinate EUO-Court relations. The EUO does not have this power. He can only *confirm* and *apply* the mechanisms which exist in Union law. This approach can be seen in his decisions, for instance, in *Decision of the EUO closing his inquiry into complaint 793/2007/(WP) BEH against the EUP.*

> The EUO here argued that 'he is mindful of the fact that, pursuant to Article 19 of the TEU, the Court of Justice shall ensure that the law is observed in the interpretation and application of the Treaties. There can thus be no doubt that it is the Court, and the Court alone, which can authoritatively interpret EU law. The Ombudsman bears this in mind when he has to take a view on the legality of an institution's behaviour. He will, therefore, not normally find maladministration in this regard if the interpretation of the relevant legal rules put forward by an institution does not appear to be without merit.'[36]

The EUO here confirmed the status of the Court as the supreme institution providing a legally binding interpretation of Union law.[37] He argued that he *can only open inquiries*

31 Cf. Case T-412/05 *M v Mediator* [2008] ECR II-197. The Court here expressly stated that *Le Médiateur européen est condamné à payer à M. M une indemnité de 10 000 euros.* (See the following Chapter).

32 *Lamberts v Mediator,* para. 65.

33 Ibid., para. 66.

34 See, for example, Case T176/08 *infeurope v Commission* [2009] ECR II-00119 or Case T-294/04 *Internationaler Hilfsfonds v Commission* [2005] ECR II-2719.

35 Case T-369/11 *Diadikasia Symvouloi Epicheiriseon v Commission* (not yet published), para. 64.

36 Decision of the EUO closing his inquiry into complaint *793/2007/(WP)BEH* against the EUP, paras. 78-81.

37 See also, Annual Report of the EUO 1995, p. 5.

into the Court's non-judicial work and that *the Court is the highest authority in interpreting EU law.*[38]

3.1.4 *A short summary*

Union law delimits the roles, goals and competences of the EUO and the Court. The *formal institutional coordination* of the relations between these institutions is included in the written law and in the case law of the Court. Primary and secondary Union law in connection with this particular research lay down a *general framework* for the actions of these institutions. This framework sets several limitations for the EUO in the case of legal proceedings. Conversely, it does not create many limitations for the Court. The most important limitation is the Court's inability to annul the EUO's 'decisions'.

Nonetheless, when acting in its judicial role, the Court is protected against investigations by the EUO. Although some provisions of written Union law deal directly with EUO-Court relations, they are rather general and leave space for the Court's interpretation and for the practice of these institutions.

The case law of the Court is more precise than written Union law. It explains the main relations between the Court and the EUO including a possibility for the Court to review the legality of the EUO's conduct and decisions. The EUO can only follow and apply the mechanisms for institutional coordination laid down in Union law and the case law of the Court.

3.2 Informal institutional coordination in the EU

When describing the possible existence of *informal institutional coordination* between the EUO and the Court one must take into account the character of the work of both institutions, the law-developing function of the Court, the partially overlapping functions of the Court and the EUO and the character of EU law.

As there is no published information that deals with *informal* institutional coordination between the EUO and the Court this section almost exclusively builds on individual interviews with the ombudsman, his investigators and judges. These interviews were *de facto* the only source of information. The opinions given during the interviews are only *personal opinions provided during those interviews* and they do not in any way represent the official opinion of the Union institution in question.

3.2.1 *Informal interaction between the EUO and the Court?*

All of the interviewees confirmed that the relations between the EUO and the Court are not very broad. They all also confirmed that beyond what is laid down in Union law, there is not much interplay either. At the same time they did not completely exclude the existence of such an interaction. Prof Diamandouros (European Ombudsman 2005 -2013), noted

38 Annual Report of the EUO 2011, pp. 26 and 44.

that on the informal level there are some interpersonal and informal inter-institutional relations that do not influence the final decision-making of the institutions. He stated that:

> 'There are clearly no formal relations between the Courts and the Ombudsman. The Ombudsman is a separate institution that is independent of, and distinct from, the Courts. But this does not mean that there are no relations between the two. There are, in fact, strong and fruitful relations between my office and the Courts. I systematically meet the Presidents of all three courts in Luxembourg and I also meet members of the Courts. We are invited to attend official ceremonies of the Courts. So, we have very good informal relations that allow us to exchange views and compare practices but we do not have any kind of formal relations because we need to keep our institutions apart.'

Mr Sant'Anna, the Director of Directorate A, Office of the EUO, added that if there are any relations with the Court then they are at the highest level between the Ombudsman and the judges, rather than the between the employees of the EUO office and judges:

> 'There are absolutely no relations with the Court about concrete complaint handling of the case. I have to be clear about that. As for unofficial relations, there are many. For instance, the Ombudsman regularly meets the Presidents of the Courts in Luxembourg, even the President of the Strasbourg Court, and they exchange viewpoints on the evolution and developments in matters relating to the functioning of the institutions, transparency issues etc. Concrete particular cases are never part of these unofficial meetings.'

Also Mr Grill, the Director of Directorate B and Acting Head of the Complaints and Inquiries Unit, Office of the EUO, confirmed that the interaction with the Courts is not extensive or investigation-oriented. He reiterated that:

> 'There is no special relationship between the Court and us. But of course, we quite clearly respect each other. We had a couple of lectures from judges here in Strasbourg which were very interesting. Next to that in connection with the Court there is nothing out of the usual.'

The position of the interviewed judges of the Court was very similar. They all confirmed that relations with the EUO do not go beyond the provisions of Union law. If there are any informal or unofficial relations, they are on a high level and they are often linked with official occasions rather than with the fulfilment of the judicial functions of the Court. Mr Barents (a judge at the EUCST) noted that:

> 'The Ombudsman sometimes visits us. He also visited us about four weeks ago. And he was here also a couple of years ago. But these visits are rather informative ones. They usually confirm our own roles and importance, as different institutions. They have the character of protocol visits rather than going to the substance of the case. And actually, the Ombudsman postponed his last visit here as there were some cases against the Ombudsman by his former employees before the EUCST. Then the Ombudsman did not approach us, because of his independence. Even though this official meeting was about something other than the case concerned.'

A similar answer was also given by Mr Van der Woude (a judge at the EUGC), who stressed the possibility of interrelations with the EUO in connection with the administration of the Court:

> 'There are no institutional relations as such. Still, there may be official visits, of course, but that will be more for the President of the Court than for individual judges. I do not believe that there are some actual institutional relations. I get a copy of his Annual Report and basically that is it. I know that it is not very satisfactory as an answer but it is true.'

Nonetheless he noted that in connection with access to information there might be a theoretical interconnection between the powers of the EUO and the Court:

> 'One place where we would have a legal interaction with the Ombudsman albeit indirectly is the Regulation on access to documents. Regulation 1049/2001, Art. 8 (3) states that once the institution has reached its final decision whether or not it will grant access to documents an individual can go either to the Court or to the Ombudsman or even to both. And in fact this alternative shows that these institutions are two different things. Another place where you may have some relation is the issue of access to the files in competition cases.'

Also Prof. Prechal (a judge at the COJ) and Prof. Meij (a former judge at the CFI) noted that there is no special interconnection between the Court and the EUO. As confirmed by Prof. Prechal, if there are any relations these are rather *informal* and are connected with *official meetings* between the President of the Court and the EUO or *interpersonal meetings* between individual judges and the EUO; however, these meetings do not deal with cases being investigated.

As can be seen from the previous explanations there is no extensive interrelation between the EUO and the Court. There is no interplay whatsoever in connection with the investigated cases and, as confirmed by the interviewees, if there is a case that can potentially endanger their impartiality or independence or it can give rise to questions thereon, the interrelations can be even more limited.

3.2.2 *Informal cooperation and exchange of information?*

As the EUO and the Court both deal with disputes between the Union institutions and individuals, it was presumed that sometimes there might be cooperation between them. As confirmed by the previous subchapter there is no special interplay between them. The situation is similar also as regards their possible cooperation. Prof. Diamandouros (the European Ombudsman 2005-2013) noted that cooperation can exist but only within existing boundaries:

> 'It depends what you mean by broader cooperation … clearly the strengthening within these boundaries is important. Cooperation as such includes next to these meetings and invitations of judges also for example working lunches with judges. Of course, my Secretary General and my directors also have their own contacts. So we have informal

contacts. Thus strengthening in the way of doing more of the same is fine. But there has to be a clear line of demarcation. Hence strengthening and deepening yes, but I think that the informal way is better than formalising the relationship as it could lead to questioning our independence.'

Mr Grill, the Director of Directorate B and Acting Head of the Complaints and Inquiries Unit, Office of the EUO, did not see any possibility as to how the employees of the EUO Office could cooperate with the Court:

> 'The Ombudsman is an alternative to the Court and when it comes to us (legal officers), he relies on our help and on our assistance and, of course, it would not be appropriate to call the judges in Luxembourg and to ask them what they would do in such a situation. And of course, the Court will never do the same in connection with us. The relations we have are on the level of relations among the EU institutions. There is nothing mysterious about it and there is clearly nothing behind the scenes except trying to find out where the Court is going in the development of the law so we can use these directions for our decisions. We study the judgments of the Court and we apply them as we are bound to apply them. But apart from that there is nothing special.'

While talking about possible cooperation between the EUO and the Court the interviewed judges pointed to different standards of control by the Court and the EUO. Mr Barents (a judge at the EUCST) pointed to the fact that although these concepts might overlap, their character does not enable them to cooperate. He underlined the different character of the control exercised by the Court and by the EUO. He argued that:

> 'There is neither formal nor informal cooperation between these two institutions. In fact, we have totally different roles. The Ombudsman examines cases of maladministration and we occupy ourselves with controlling the legality of the decisions of the institutions. So we are exercising legality control. These two types of control are fundamentally different. The control exercised by the Ombudsman is what you may call full control or control of opportunity – control d'opportunité. Was the decision taken? Was it efficient? Was there certain action? Was it done in a correct manner? What we do is to look whether there has been a substantial legal error. Is there a manifest or serious error of judgement? But the case of maladministration is not necessarily a serious error of judgment. The error might be accidental and it must not necessarily be an illegality.'

In his opinion, based on the law that is nowadays applicable in the Union, there is not much room for cooperation between the EUO and the Court. He stated that:

> 'Frankly I can't see how we could cooperate given the fact that we are operating on different rules. So the question is even if it was legally possible to cooperate, what would be the added value of such cooperation? And I don't think that there would be any.'

Similarly, limited cooperation between the EUO and the Court was also noted by Mr Van der Woude (a judge at the EUGC) who also pointed to their different roles.

> 'I believe that illegality that is approached by the Court and maladministration that is approached by the Ombudsman are relatively different things. Our roles are also different.'

From a theoretical point of view he could imagine cooperation between the Court and the EUO. Although he noted that such cooperation would require legislative changes and it would necessarily change the position of the EUO in the system of protection within the Union:

> 'Theoretically, there can be certain cooperation. But not in the way of the Ombudsman calling the Court and the Court calling the Ombudsman. But I think about streamlining the procedures. You can think about the Ombudsman procedure as a certain preliminary stage before starting legal action. Legal action should be something of a last resort. And, for example, in access to documents cases it would be an idea to have the Ombudsman procedure as a preliminary step. Of course, his decisions cannot be challenged, but you could say that if the individual does not get access to the documents he should first go to the Ombudsman, and only after the Ombudsman has decided that the institution must take the decision will that decision be challenged. But at least there will be some kind of mediating filter before leading to the Court.'

Prof. Prechal (a judge at the COJ) underlined the complementary role of the EUO towards the Court. She also pointed to their different roles and different normative standards of control. Especially these two main points rather limit them to their own sphere and technically exclude cooperation. Also Prof. Meij (a former judge at the CFI) underlined that there was no cooperation with the EUO as the context of the case before both institutions must not be the same and both institutions need to retain their independence.

The interviewees were rather sceptical about any potential cooperation between the EUO and the Court. As they explained, Union law nowadays does not really allow cooperation. Still, the strengthening of cooperation as a conservation of the existing situation is sometimes perceived to be possible. A different type of active cooperation would require changes in the positions of the EUO and the Court, and also changes to the law.

When one looks at the definition of maladministration in the Union sense,[39] one can observe that it is rather broad and that it does not exclude the EUO's competence to assess the compliance of EU institutions with legal principles. In this connection one may ask the question how the EUO becomes acquainted with the law. And also one can ask how (and if at all) the Court becomes acquainted with the decisions of the EUO. These points can theoretically give rise to the question of whether there is any exchange of information, including especially concerning the results of their work – judgments and decisions. In this connection one may wonder how (and if at all) these institutions become acquainted with the cases of the other institution. Prof. Diamandouros (the European Ombudsman 2005 -2013) noted that the case law of the Court plays an important role. However, he did

39 See, section 1.1.3.2.

not mention any specific way of exchanging information between these two institutions beyond electronic or written means:

> 'The existing system of informal exchanges and of informal contacts allows us to monitor very carefully and systematically the case law of the Court, which we use via the eur.lex instrument. Via that system we can follow all the jurisprudence of the Court which we use among other things as a guidance and as a source of inspiration when taking decisions. ... I think we have sufficiently intense informal exchanges of information with the Courts but we need to bear in mind the need to avoid possible damage to our independence. I don't see the need for formalising these connections with the Court. Because that could be a danger for the Ombudsman as we could be seen as a lower, inferior court.'

Mr Grill, the Director of Directorate B and Acting Head of the Complaints and Inquiries Unit, Office of the EUO, also confirmed that a direct exchange of information between the EUO office and the Court does not exist:

> 'We have been told by the Court that they read our decisions, that they follow our case work but we do not send our decisions to the Court saying "here they are, please read them." If they want they can find them on the website similar to individuals who can find information about our work.'

He also confirmed that the case law of the Courts is important for the EUO:

> 'As regards our own actions, cases and investigations are handled by lawyers and these lawyers are trained in European law and therefore they take a natural interest in the case law of the Courts. All of them follow the case law, some more vigorously than others of course. For example, I study each and every judgment that comes out of the Court, obviously with a different degree of attention depending on the subject concerned. For example, trademark issues that are not directly relevant to our work are not the main centre of our attention. But of course, we follow the Courts' case law.'

Mr Sant'Anna, the Director of Directorate A, Office of the EUO, stated that:

> 'An exchange of information takes place on an unofficial basis. We have no privileged channel of communication, we have only traditional tools, eur.lex or the internet page of the Court that allow us to access the case work of the three Luxembourg Courts including the opinions of the Advocates General. They [the lawyers] have to follow them every day or at least they should keep up with the developments in the case law as everybody can organise their time in any way they wish. But this is the thing, the case law of the Court is important.'

The way in which the Courts and the judges approach the EUO case work is somewhat different. All the judges interviewed confirmed that becoming acquainted with the EUO case work occurs on an *ad hoc* rather than on a general basis. They all also confirmed that it happens only in connection with a particular case and it should be raised by one of the parties to the proceedings. Mr Barents (a judge at the EUCST) stated that:

> 'There is no practice of getting acquainted with Ombudsman cases, not in a general way. That would only happen in a specific case if the plaintiff refers to a decision that is taken by the Ombudsman. Then we would ask, according to the rules of procedure, for a copy of that decision. It is thus only on an ad hoc basis or in an annual report. We receive the annual report of the Ombudsman with a letter by its author. And sometimes you look in that report and read a portion thereof and then it is filed somewhere and often forgotten. That is the reality. It is not the case that the Ombudsman sends all individual reports to the judges and we can look at each decision. We can read them if we want to. We can find them on the internet.'

Also Mr Van der Woude (a judge at the EUGC) denied any special way of exchanging information with the EUO:

> 'To my knowledge there isn't any special way of exchanging information. The Ombudsman sends his annual report. I read it, though I do not read it in extenso but I do have a look at it. It can also happen that the Ombudsman's decision is part of the file. Then I would be aware of it because then the party would submit it to me. They will submit it to the Court and then I would read it as part of the file. So it is connected with a particular case and it is a passive way of becoming familiar. It is passive and ad hoc, thus somebody should refer to it or submit it as evidence. Of course, if there is a judge who is interested in the work of the Ombudsman he can study his decisions. But there is no institutional necessity to do so.'

This practice was confirmed by Prof. Meij (a former judge at CFI). Prof. Prechal (a judge at the COJ) confirmed that COJ judges only come into contact with the EUO's ombudsprudence on limited occasions because the COJ deals mostly with the legal assessment of appeals.

The statements by representatives of these two different Union institutions confirm two interesting points. Firstly, they all confirm that there is no special way of exchanging information between these two institutions including their case work. Nowadays, these institutions have very transparent practices and they post their case work on their official internet sites. This makes it possible for anybody (including other institutions) to access it. Secondly, they have a different practice in becoming acquainted with the case law of the other institution. While the 'EUO people' do this on a premeditated, deliberate and general basis, judges of the Court only do so in connection with the annual report or when the EUO's report has a connection with a particular case. There is *no practice* and *no need* for the judges of the Court to become acquainted with the case work of the EUO on a general basis.

3.2.3 A short summary

There is no special *informal institutional coordination* between the EUO and the Court beyond what is included in written Union law. If there are any 'informal' relations these are usually connected with protocol issues or official Union actions, seminars, meetings etc. There is no special interplay between the EUO and the Court. Both institutions deal with their own issues and do not intermingle in the affairs of the other institution. The rules that divide the setting for these two institutions are closely followed and there is no real room for cooperation. Mutual cooperation as well as the exchange of information are also limited. As both institutions try to apply different, though overlapping legislative standards and try to retain their independence they do not look for possibilities of mutual cooperation. The exchange of information does not overstep the level of free access to the information of the Union institutions. It is usually ad hoc and depends on an individual case. Both institutions know where to look.

3.3 Summary

How are the relations between the European Ombudsman and the Courts coordinated on the institutional level and what are the contents of this coordination? This question was observed from the position of formal and informal institutional coordination between the EUO and the Court.

The *formal institutional coordination* between the EUO and the Court is included in primary and secondary Union law that establish a general framework for their institutional relations. This delimitation is not absolute and is supplemented by the jurisprudence of the Court. The Treaties lay down a general framework for the workings of the Union institutions and they go deeper into the substance, but only in a limited way. Secondary Union law provides only a little more concrete coordination of the researched relations. Still, that coordination is only marginal. Very often it only reaffirms the provisions of primary Union law. Union law does not presume a broad interplay between the EUO and the Court. There is a clear delimitation of powers between these institutions. The case law of the Court is in this connection more enlightening. The Court explains that in limited circumstances it is possible to assess the legality of the EUO's conduct. The judicial review by the Court is however limited to the conduct of the EUO and must be connected with procedures under Art. 340 TFEU, i.e. the non-contractual liability of Union institutions while taking into account the specific character of the EUO's roles. The main mechanisms for institutional coordination between the EUO and the Court include:

- *Mechanisms that limit the competence of the EUO towards the Court.* Based on them the EOU cannot act if there were legal proceedings which covered the same facts as the investigation of the EUO. The EUO is also limited in connection with the Court as it cannot assess its conduct and search for maladministration. There are also
- *Mechanisms that provide formal issues concerned with the EUO* (dismissal, the oath, remuneration) and based on the case law there are also
- *Mechanisms that limit the competence of the Court towards the EUO.* Based on its case law the Court has decided that the EUO's decisions cannot be quashed in a judicial review or that actions for a failure to act are (for now) excluded.

Beyond the relations that are included in Union law, there are no really specific ways of *informal institutional coordination* between the EUO and the Court. Their informal institutional correlation is connected with official occasions where the representatives of both institutions meet and can converse. And although these meetings offer room to 'talk shop' they usually deal with more general institutional issues such as transparency or accessibility but, as confirmed by both sides, they never go into the contents of individually assessed cases. Also their informal cooperation is almost non-existent. And so is the exchange of information. Still it is possible to point to a different perception of their case work. While the EUO closely observes the development of the case law by the Court (despite his direct connection with good administration), the Court occasionally takes ombudsprudence into account. Both institutions consider the EUO's investigation to be an alternative to the Court's proceedings.

Chapter 4

CASE COORDINATION OF OMBUDSMAN-JUDICIARY RELATIONS IN THE EU?

This chapter ascertains the issue of *the significance of the decisions of the EUO and the judgments of the Court and their contents for the other researched institutions and their interrelations*. Thus, the second research question is connected with the formal results of the pondering processes of the EUO and the Court, the judgments of the Court and the decisions of the EUO.[1] This question is approached in a twofold way. Firstly, this chapter addresses it from the position of a possible *formal case coordination* between the EUO and the Court (4.1). And secondly, it discusses the *practical interplay* of these institutions in connection with their findings (4.2). The chapter concludes with a summary (4.3).

4.1 Formal case coordination of ombudsman-judiciary relations?

When looking for a formal case coordination of the researched relations this section follows the pattern adopted by the previous chapter. It looks at the possible sources of the formal coordination: written Union law, the case law of the Court and also the ombudsprudence of the EUO.

4.1.1 Formal case coordination in written Union law?

The research into written Union law, both primary and secondary, shows that case coordination between the EUO and the Court is not extensively dealt with. Legal provisions dealing with this issue are infrequent.

Primary Union law does not go further than what was already described in the previous chapter. It provides only a general description of EUO-Court relations. Nevertheless, the mechanisms that can be at least *indirectly* applicable to case coordination are included in *Art. 228 (1) TFEU* which requires the EUO to stop or not to initiate his proceedings if he finds out that the alleged facts are or have been the subject of legal proceedings.[2] And although this article does not compare the decisions of the researched institutions, it *de facto* requires the EUO to be aware of the case law of the Court. This

1 Decisions of the EUO are here perceived in a broad sense. They include 'decisions to closing the inquiry', 'draft recommendations' or 'special reports', etc.

2 See, section 3.1.1.

requirement of awareness is connected with inquiries started by a complaint as well as own-initiative inquiries. This provision, however, does not require the EUO to study or follow the Court's judgments, it merely requires him to be aware of the factual issues of the previous or present Court cases. Other provisions of primary Union law are silent on case coordination.

Secondary Union law does not go much further than primary law. The only provision that tackles the said issue is included in Art. 1 (3) of the Statute of the EUO that requires the EUO *not to question the soundness of a court's ruling.* Here, the Statute directly connects the EUO with a particular ruling of the Court. From the text of the Statute it is not clear when this limitation is applicable, whether it is in the EUO's own findings or generally and whether it also includes public speeches or interviews by the EUO. Nonetheless, the provision de facto assumes that the EUO will, in some way and for some reason, be acquainted with the findings of the Court and that he will be theoretically able to give his opinion about this document. The other provisions of secondary law do not deal with this issue and they follow the institutional framework predetermined by primary law.[3]

4.1.2 Formal case coordination in the case law of the Court?

The Court, in its jurisprudence, interprets several legal provisions applicable to the EUO. Sometimes it explains the character and importance of his decisions for other Union institutions and also for its own practice.

The character of the EUO decision was described in previously mentioned orders of the Court in Case T-103/99 *Associazione delle Cantine Sociali Venete v Mediator and EUP* and Case T-196/08 *Srinivasan v Mediator.*[4] In these two decisions, the CFI confirmed that the report where the EUO finds a case of maladministration *does not, by definition, produce legal effects vis-à-vis third parties within the meaning of Article 263 of the Treaty.*[5] Both decisions also confirm that the findings of the EUO are not legally binding.[6]

In Case T-209/00 *Lamberts v Mediator* the CFI specifically pointed to the *character of a critical remark* by the EUO[7] and the report which may contain a recommendation. The court here also explained that these instruments are not *designed to protect the individual interests of the citizen concerned against damage which may arise as a result of maladministration on the part of a Community institution or body.*[8] Thus, the CFI confirmed the limited ability of these instruments to actually protect the legal interests of individuals and de facto their legally non-binding character.

Another interesting judgment that explains the position of an EUO decision is included in Case T-371/03 *Le Voci v Council,* where the CFI stated that *in accepting the recommendation of the EUO in an individual case the Union institution does not take on itself an obligation to follow the recommendation on a systematic basis if the scope of the decision*

3 See, sections 3.1.1 and 3.1.2.
4 See, section 3.1.2.
5 *Associazione delle Cantine Sociali Venete*, order, para. 37, *Srinivasan v Mediator*, order, para. 11.
6 *Associazione delle Cantine Sociali Venete*, order, para. 50, *Srinivasan v Mediator*, order, para. 11.
7 See, section 1.1.3.1.
8 *Lamberts* v *Mediator,* para. 87.

of the EUO was connected only with a particular case.[9] This judgment clearly notes that the recommendations of the EUO in individual cases do not have the character of the generally applicable rules that must be followed by the Union institution. A recommendation that was accepted by the administration in the individual case does not have to be applied to other similar cases, even if the administrative institution has accepted that it must apply the recommendation in an individual case.

The order of the President of the CFI in Case T-193/04 R *Tillack v Commission* as supported by the order of the President of the CFI in Case T-294/04 *Internationaler Hilfsfonds eV v Commission* solved the possibility of using the report of the EUO in the Court's proceedings, at least in connection with damages. Both orders underlined that *the EUO's decisions are subject to their own conditions, which are not the same as those that must be met in order to found a right to compensation that is awarded by the Court.* They highlight that *a finding of abuse by the EUO cannot simply be treated as a sufficiently serious breach of a rule of law.* But cases generally conclude that the *EUO's decisions are not binding on the Court and do not relieve it of its obligation to consider whether the conditions in question have been met.*[10] These orders distinguish between the character of the judgments and the decisions of the EUO. The decision of the EUO is not simply adopted as it stands; the Court applies its own processes and its own considerations.

In the judgment in Case T-193/04 *Tillack v Commission* this case law was de facto confirmed. The CFI explicitly argued that *the classification as an 'act of maladministration' by the EUO does not mean, in itself, that the conduct of a Union institution constitutes a sufficiently serious breach of a rule of law within the meaning of the case law.*[11] The CFI thus confirmed that the finding of maladministration by the EUO does not overlap with the finding of a *sufficiently serious breach of a rule of law by the Court.* The findings of the Court and the EUO therefore must have different consequences.

Also in Case T-377/07 *Evropaïki Dynamiki v Commission* the CFI also stated that a *complaint lodged with the EUO cannot constitute evidence for the purposes of establishing a misuse of powers.*[12] Although it is not completely clear whether the CFI was referring to the 'result of the EUO investigation (decision)' or to the sole fact of 'lodging the complaint with the EUO' this statement is *de facto* in line with its previous case law and it confirms that the EUO decisions, his findings or possibly lodging a complaint with the EUO do not have the necessary authority to persuade the CFI to build its judgment on the findings of the EUO. Thus in the judicial proceedings individuals cannot only rely on a finding of maladministration by the EUO.

As shown above, the case law of the Court is much more expressive and more concrete than written Union law. However, it does not answer all the issues concerning case coordination between the EUO and the Court. Nonetheless, it gives an indication of the opinion of the Court. The decisions of the EUO are accepted as fact rather than

9 Case T-371/03 Le Voci v Council [2005] FP-I-A-00209, judgment, para. 126.

10 Case T-193/04 R *Tillack v Commission*, order, para. 60, Case T-294/04 *Internationaler Hilfsfonds eV v Commission*, order, para. 39.

11 Case T-193/04 *Tillack v Commission*, judgment, para. 128.

12 Case T-377/07 *Evropaïki Dynamiki v Commission* [2011] ECR II-0442, judgment, para. 114.

as persuasive authority. In general, it is not enough for an individual to support his case before the Court with a finding of maladministration by the EUO.

4.1.3 Formal case coordination in the ombudsprudence?

As noted in the previous section, the EUO does not adopt decisions that can in any way bind the Court. Because of that the EUO *cannot create* any new rules that would be applicable to case coordination. One can find some cases where the EUO has de facto *confirmed* either the rules laid down in written Union law or in the case law. Such an example is included in the Draft recommendation to the Commission concerning complaint 2283/2004/GG where the EUO confirmed that he is not able to assess the soundness of the Court's ruling as *it is abundantly clear that he has no mandate to deal with a request for correction of a judgement pronounced by a Community court.*[13] A similar confirmation of this practice can be found in other documents of the EUO.[14]

4.2 Interplay between the European Ombudsman and the Court in connection with their findings

In order to be able to answer the second research in a comprehensive manner one has to look at the practice of the researched institutions. The Union law does not give a satisfactory or complete answer to this question. In the practice of the EUO and the Court one can discover how these institutions mutually perceive its findings.

4.2.1 Practice of the European Ombudsman

The interviews with the EUO and the senior members of his office confirm that the judgments of the Court play an important and inspirational (but also necessarily limiting) role for his inquiries and work. They confirmed this despite the fact that the EUO deals with instances of maladministration and not with illegality. The EUO is not ignorant of the Court's case law and, when necessary, the Court judgments are taken into the account. The interviews and the research into the ombudsprudence confirm that the EUO very often makes cross-references to the judgments of the Court. Prof. Diamandouros (the European Ombudsman, 2003-2013) argues that the use of the Court's case law is strictly connected with the development of the ombudsman ideas:

> 'My lawyers systematically follow the Court's case law. If you consult our decisions, you can find references to cases of the Court that are not yet published. We do that with the eur.lex instrument which has a complete list of the Court's decisions. My officers are expected to read the judgments so that they can identify ways in which the case law can give us opportunities for developing our own ideas.'

13 Para. 4.11.

14 See, for example, Decision of the EUO closing his inquiry into complaint 1935/2008/FOR against the Commission or Decision of the EUO on complaint 3255/2005/IP against the Commission or Annual Report of the EUO 2011.

Union law, including the case law, has importance for the EUO. Here he noted that:

> 'You start with the law and you go beyond it. I will use the usual formulation: it is an absolutely necessary, but not a sufficient condition. You cannot do without the law but if you stay only within the law you are giving up the very reason for being an ombudsman. But if you forget the law and say that I will deal only with the other issues, then obviously you are undermining yourself. So you have to take the law as the minimum condition and build upon it, by integrating principles of good administration and fundamental rights into your work. This way, you can serve citizens best.'

The use of the case law of the Court in the EUO's practice was also highlighted by Mr Sant'Anna, the Director of Directorate A, Office of the EUO:

> 'The case law of the Court is the first thing we look into. However, the Ombudsman's role is to discover and solve instances of maladministration. And maladministration is more than just a breach of the law, but surely it includes breaches of the law. So the first 'commandment' is not to break the law, and the law at the European level is developed by the Court. The law is determinant for our work. So the first thing we would look for is what the Court has said because the case law of the Court sets the boundaries that should not be crossed. The Ombudsman cannot dispute if the Court had said that a rule is the law. Thus the Ombudsman will always apply the law as interpreted or developed by the Court.'

Also Mr Grill, the Director of Directorate B and the Acting Head of the Complaints and Inquiries Unit, Office of the EUO, noted the importance of the case law:

> 'Clearly we have to respect the Court's case law and we cannot develop a solution that would be contrary to what the Court has said. That is clearly our approach to case law. We have to take it into consideration. Also many complainants and many institutions refer in their submissions to the case law. We are thus obliged to look at it and find out whether these references are correct, whether these judgments mean what the party indicates.'

He however underlined that applying only a legality approach is not what the EUO is doing in his procedures:

> 'The Ombudsman cares about legality but obviously he believes that good administration is more than obeying the law. For example, we have many cases where the complainant argues that what the administration has said is unlawful. Then we have to find out whether this is true or not. In many cases it is possible and necessary to achieve more than that. The complainant may be unhappy about other aspects as well. The Court may check the legality and nothing else, but the Ombudsman can go further and say that the administration has complied with the law but it did not do so in a very citizen-friendly manner. The obligation to be polite, for instance, is not explicitly laid down in European law. So the decision could be that the administrative decision was properly taken but the way in which it was communicated was clearly not in conformity with good administration. We have to distinguish between the legality aspect and the good administration aspect.'

The interviews confirm that the EUO and his staff are well aware of the existence of the Court's case law. The case law of the Court is taken seriously into account when dealing with individual complaints.

The actual approach of the EUO towards the jurisprudence of the Court can be found in his cross-referencing practice. The EUO's cross-references to the Court are connected with all three individual courts. Sometimes one can find a cross-reference to a national or an international court. As the latter two courts are not part of this research, the research criteria when going through the databases of the EUO decisions were in particular the terms '*Court of Justice*', '*General Court*', '*Court of First Instance*', '*Civil Service Tribunal*' and the terms '*Community Courts*' or '*Union Courts*'. Researching the references was done via the EUO's official internet site www.ombudsman.europa.eu/en/cases/home.faces.

The EUO makes cross-references to the Court only in connection with the case at hand and this practice is only different in the general annual reports, where he expresses his general opinions and the Court is often mentioned. The research proves that the EUO refers in his decisions to the Court and its case law quite often. Between the years 2005-2013 the EUO referred to the Court in numerous cases. The following scheme shows the numbers of references by the EUO to the Court. The numbers included in the following scheme are not absolute as one decision of the EUO can include general references to several courts.

Scheme 1 – **Cross-references by the EUO to the Court and its decisions**

References found in the EUO decisions	**Decisions closing inquiry** (1/1/2005 -31/7/2013)	**Draft resolutions** (1/1/2005-15/7/2013)	**Special reports** (1/1/2005-15/7/2013)
Court of Justice	512	59	8
Court of First Instance	294	37	3
General Court	89	16	1
Civil Service Tribunal	73	13	0
Community courts	320	29	3
Union courts	68	8	0

Based on these cross-references it was possible to create the following typology.

4.2.1.1 A typology of the cross-references to the Court

1. Competence cross-references

Before the EUO starts dealing with the substance of the dispute, he must deal with all potential objections concerning his competence to deal with the complaint. At the same time he can also discover that he does not have the competence to deal with the complaint. Thus, he must often explain why in this particular case he can or conversely cannot deal with the complaint. This cross-referencing can be found in, for instance, the *Draft recommendation to the Commission in complaint 1844/2005/GG.*

> The EUO here dealt with a claim by an individual to access documents connected with infringement proceedings which had been rejected by the Commission. During the EUO's inquiry the Commission argued that there was a case pending before the CFI in which its decision to refuse access to documents was being challenged. The EUO had to consider his own competence to deal with the complaint. Before examining the issue he addressed 'the Commission's reference to Case T-380/04(6). Article 195 of the EC Treaty provides that the EUO shall conduct inquiries for which he finds grounds "except where the alleged facts are or have been the subject of legal proceedings". However, it emerges from the summary of the case published in the Official Journal that this application concerns the Commission's refusal to grant access to "the main contract, the sub-contracts, the costs of the construction items, the invoices and the final report relating to the construction of the Spata airport". It is thus clear that this application does not concern the facts that have been submitted to the Ombudsman in the present complaint. The case pending before the Court of First Instance consequently does not affect the Ombudsman's power to deal with this complaint.'[15]

Hence, the EUO discovered that despite legal proceedings before the Court he had competence to deal with the complaint as the facts of the case were not identical.

The opposite was found, for instance, in *Decision of the EUO concerning complaint 966/2009/JMA against the Commission.*

> Here during the course of the inquiry the Commission informed the EUO that the subject matter of the complaint was also the subject of a legal action which the complainant had brought before the EUGC. The EUO then stated that 'it appears that the subject matter of this aspect of the complaint before the Ombudsman has been the object of an action brought by the complainant before the General Court and registered under reference number T-377/09. Accordingly, in view of the applicable legal provision, the Ombudsman cannot deal any further with this aspect of the complaint and, therefore, closes it.'[16]

The EUO here showed that he is not willing to go against primary Union law. These references to the Court do not deal with matters of substance in the judgment but only with the possibility of the EUO to investigate a complaint. One can find other similar examples.[17]

2. Factual (descriptive) cross-references

Although it is excluded for the EUO to investigate the same facts as those that were or are investigated in legal proceedings, in his decision the EUO may make cross-references to legal proceedings that were directly or indirectly connected with the complaint or the complainant. The EUO here does not deal with the contents of the judgment or legal principles but only with the *fact* that there were Court proceedings. For example, in

15 DR to the Commission in complaint 1844/2005/GG, para. 1.8.

16 Decision of the EUO concerning complaint *966/2009/JMA* against the Commission, para. 30.

17 See, for example, Special Report from the EUO to the EUP following the DR to the Council of the European Union in complaint *2395/2003/GG* or DR to the Council of the European Union in complaint *1487/2005/GG*, part Inquiry.

Decision of the EUO closing his inquiry into complaint 2904/2005/(TN)FOR against the Commission the EUO states as a matter of fact that:

> 'On 9 August 2000, the complainant lodged an action against the Ombudsman and the EUP before the Court of First Instance (now the General Court), claiming compensation for material and non-material damage allegedly suffered as a result of the manner in which the Ombudsman dealt with complaint 687/98/BB. The Court of First Instance (now the General Court) dismissed the action as unfounded, since the complainant did not demonstrate that the Ombudsman had breached any of his administrative duties in dealing with complaint.'[18]

The EUO here, as a matter of fact, noted the existence of the previous proceedings before the Court that had a certain relation to the complainant. Another factual cross-reference can be found in *Draft recommendation of the EUO in his inquiry into complaint 1161/2010/BEH against the European Commission.*

> In this draft recommendation the EUO noted, as a matter of fact, that 'the complainant turned to the Commission and requested access to certain documents relating to a number of infringement cases, which were then pending before the Court of Justice.'[19]

Although cross-references to the Court included in this provision were also raised in the further part of the draft recommendation, here they represent only a description of the facts of the case and the dispute at hand. In factual cross-references the EUO does not deal with the contents of judgments. These cross-references only describe the previous proceedings that have a factual or legal connection with the case at hand. They can also be found in other decisions.[20]

3. Explanatory cross-references

Although it may appear that the ombudsman's investigations or inquiries are not much connected with the law and legal proceedings, the reality in the case of the EUO is somewhat different. Individuals and Union institutions almost always use Court judgments in order to support their own arguments and claims, even in the EUO inquiry. This case law of the Court is then mostly cross-referenced in the decision of the EUO as he has to deal with these arguments by the parties. The EUO cannot overlook previous actions of the Court as they are directly connected with his possibility to deal with complaints and, at the same time, the Court's judgments can resume their task of developing the law.[21] After the parties to the EUO's inquiry submit their arguments he has to deal with this knowledge in order to solve the problem at hand. He has to assess the information provided by the parties, interpret their arguments and possibly apply them to the investigated dispute. The

18 Decision of the EUO closing his inquiry into complaint *2904/2005/(TN)FOR* against the Commission, paras. 2-3.

19 DR of the EUO in his inquiry into complaint *1161/2010/BEH* against the Commission, para. 2.

20 See, for example, DR of the EUO in his inquiry into complaint *1953/2008/MF* against the EUP; Special Report from the EUO to the EUP following his DR to the Commission in Complaint *185/2005/ELB*.

21 Cf. Broberg & Fenger 2010, p. 33.

EUO is here in a position of a *de facto* interpreter of Court decisions but not an appraiser of these decisions as he does not have this competence.[22] Thus, the EUO makes cross-references to the judgments because he needs to assess their applicability to the case and to explain whether in this particular case this argument supports the position of the parties or not. This practice can be found in *Decision of the EUO closing his inquiry into complaint 793/2007/(WP)BEH against the EUP*.

> The complainant here originally requested the EUP to provide access to certain documents. As his request was rejected, he complained to the EUO that the EUP had *inter alia* failed to deal properly with his application to access certain documents. In this connection the complainant argued that 'according to the EUP, the directives for the award of public contracts did not apply to the financing of EUP's D4-D5 buildings, given that, pursuant to a contract between the EUP and the developer, the latter was in charge of ensuring the external financing of the building project.' He furthermore alleged that 'this statement appeared to contradict the *jurisprudence of the Court of Justice* which followed from the Court's case law that "a contract cannot cease to be a public works contract when the rights and obligations of the contracting authority are transferred to an undertaking which is not a contracting authority.'[23]
>
> The EUP took the view that this jurisprudence was irrelevant and did not apply to contracts awarded by the EUP because unlike in the case covered by this judgment, the EUP was not a contracting authority. Thus, the EUO assessed the applicability of this case law to the case at hand. He assessed the arguments and stated that the *EUP's interpretation of the law was plausible*.[24] He concluded that 'the EUP can no longer be considered as having failed to address the implications of the said judgment of the Court of Justice.'[25]

As the EUO was satisfied with this explanation by the EUP and its interpretation of the law and the Court's jurisprudence he closed the case in this part of the complaint. Another similar example is included in *Draft recommendation of the EUO in his inquiry into complaint 2493/2008/(BB)TS against the European Medicines Agency (EMA)*.

> The complainant asked the EMA to provide access to documents containing details of all suspected serious adverse reactions relating to a certain medicine. He complained about the rejection of his application to obtain access to these documents. During the EUO's inquiry, the EMA *inter alia* presented an argument by which it sought to justify its refusal to provide access to the requested documents. The EMA pointed to a judgment of the CFI (T-2/03, Verein für Konsumenteninformation v Commission) according to which 'an institution must retain the right, in particular cases where concrete, individual examination of the documents would entail an unreasonable amount of administrative work, to balance the interest in public access to the documents against the burden of work so caused, in order to safeguard, in those particular cases, the interests of good administration.'[26]

22 See, section 3.1.1.
23 Decision of the EUO closing his inquiry into complaint *793/2007/(WP)BEH* against the EUP, para. 28.
24 Ibid., paras. 84-85.
25 Ibid., para. 87.
26 DR of the EUO in his inquiry into complaint *2493/2008/(BB)TS* against the European Medicines Agency, para. 19.

The EUO had to consider the applicability of this judgment to the case. He stated that 'the issue which the Court dealt with in this judgment was not whether the principle of proportionality constituted, as such, a justification for not providing access to the requested documents, but whether it was permissible, on the basis of the principle of proportionality, for the Commission to refrain from carrying out a concrete, individual examination of each of the documents in response to a request for access'.[27]

The case covered by the judgment arose because the Commission had refused to carry out a concrete and individual examination of each of the documents while the file in question contained over 47,000 pages. The EUO highlighted that the EMA did not invoke the volume of work required to deal with the request for access 'as a reason for refraining from carrying out a concrete, individual examination of each of the documents' but it relied, instead, on an administrative burden, as such, as an additional exception to the right of access to documents.'[28] According to the EUO, this was not in accordance with the Court's case law. The EUO argued that 'the principle of proportionality cannot, on its own, stand as a reason to refuse a request for access to documents. It is not a valid and adequate ground for refusing access to documents.'[29]

The EUO thus assessed whether the argument by a party (a judgment of the Court) was applicable to this particular situation. Because of that the EUO was placed in a position where he was required to judge the applicability of the rule laid down by the court. As in the previous case, he *de facto* interpreted and explained the applicability of this rule and the jurisprudence to the dispute at hand. Similar cross-references can be found in other EUO decisions.[30]

4. Supportive cross-references

The EUO cannot overlook rules in which the Court interprets Union law. Sometimes a cross-reference to the Court's jurisprudence can assist the EUO in dealing with an issue. Whether an application of the Court's rule is appropriate or necessary depends on the EUO's assessment. The applicability of this rule can be raised by a party to the proceedings as in the previous type of reference, although sometimes during the inquiry it is the EUO who comes up with an applicable Court rule. As the judgments of the Court are legally binding, they can boost the persuasive authority of the decisions of the EUO. As the legal binding authority of the Court cannot be overlooked by the Union's institutions, the EUO may approach these rules in order to give his legally non-binding findings a *quasi-binding* character. The application of the rules found by the Court may improve the chances of his findings or recommendation being accepted by the Union's institutions. The only drawback to this approach is that interpretations of Court judgments by the EUO are only non-binding. Thus, even though the EUO interprets the judgment in a certain way, the Union institution may have a different legal opinion. Then they can reach

27 Ibid., para. 89.

28 Ibid., para. 90.

29 Ibid., para. 105.

30 See, Decision of the EUO closing his inquiry into complaint *3106/2007/(TS)FOR* against the European Medicines Agency; Decision of the EUO closing his inquiry into complaint *224/2005/ELB* against the Commission; Decision of the EUO closing his inquiry into complaint *1953/2008/MF* against the EUP; DR of the EUO concerning his inquiry into complaint *2273/2008/MF* against the Commission.

a position where there are two antagonistic statements concerning the applicability of the jurisprudence and neither of the institutions wants to surrender its position. A supportive cross-reference can be found in *Draft recommendations of the EUO in his inquiry into complaint 715/2009/(VIK)ANA against the European Commission.*

> The complainant here *inter alia* alleged that the Commission had failed to provide him with access to the minutes of his meeting with the Commission and delayed the handling of his confirmatory application for access. The Commission supported its rejection to provide access to the minutes by Regulation No. 1049/2001 regarding public access to EUP, Council and Commission documents. The EUO here made use of a rule already adopted by the Court. He noted 'that the COJ has stated on multiple occasions that the right of access to Commission documents exists as a matter of principle, and a decision to refuse access is valid only if it is based on one of the exceptions laid down in Article 4 of Regulation 1049 /2001.'[31]
>
> The EUO here made a cross-reference to Case T-2/03 *Verein für Konsumenten-information v Commission* according to which the application of the exception may only be justified by the institution if access to the document specifically and actually undermines the protected interest and there is no overriding public interest in disclosure. However, the risk of a protected interest being undermined must be reasonably foreseeable and not purely hypothetical.[32] Based on that, the EUO did not accept the arguments of the Commission. He stated that 'it is clear from the case law that the risk for the Commission's decision-making process must be clearly foreseeable and not merely hypothetical. The Commission did not demonstrate the existence of a concrete risk which could undermine its decision-making process.'[33]

The EUO thus found that as the Commission did not take this case law into account, it wrongly refused access to the minutes of the meeting and that resulted in an instance of maladministration. Here he *de facto* supported his own decision by the rule which already existed in the Court's jurisprudence. Another example can be found in *Draft recommendation to the European Personnel Selection Office (EPSO) concerning complaint 2826/2004/PB.*

> Here the EUO supported his decision and his proposition for a friendly settlement by a Court judgment. In this case a participant in an open competition had been excluded from the competition on the ground that she did not comply with specific educational requirements for Ireland. During the investigation, the EUO found that the Notice of Competition did not sufficiently meet the legal requirements which in this case were included in the case law of the Court. He noted that in connection with his proposed friendly settlement he 'reminded EPSO of the established case law of the Community Courts, according to which the essential function of the Notice of Competition is to give those interested in applying for a competition the most accurate information possible about the conditions of eligibility for the post to enable them to judge whether they should apply for it: "the Selection Board is not empowered to exclude a candidate from

31 DRs of the EUO in his inquiry into complaint *715/2009/(VIK)ANA* against the Commission, para. 69.
32 Ibid., para. 71.
33 Ibid., para. 75.

> the tests on the ground that he does not meet a requirement which was not mentioned in the notice of competition".'[34]
>
> During the investigation he found that the complainant had been excluded because of a requirement that was not included in the Notice of Competition and because of that 'the Selection Board's decision to exclude the complainant was in breach of the legal framework.'[35] He found support for this decision in Case F-25/05 *Mc Sweeney and Armstrong v Commission* which concerned the same open competition as the one at issue in the present complaint. In that case, the Tribunal accepted actions for annulment filed by candidates 'who had been excluded for the same reason as the complainant had been in the present case.'[36] Although the EPSO originally did not want to accept the fact that it should apply the decision of the EUCST also to applicants who were not direct participants to the court proceedings, in the end it accepted the recommendation of the EUO 'to reconsider its position and take measures to provide an effective remedy to the complainant for the unlawful decision adopted by the Selection Board in this case.'[37]

Thus, the EUO here not only backed up his own decision by a decision of the Court but also explicitly stated that the unlawful situation resulted in (potential) maladministration in the action of the Union institution. When necessary, the EUO can thus make use of the Court's case law in order to support his own findings. Similar references can be found in other EUO decisions.[38]

4.2.1.2 A short summary

The research confirms that cross-references by the EUO to the Court and its judgments are, although partially *ad hoc*, premeditated. Union law, including the jurisprudence of the Court, is the first issue that is looked at when the EUO is assessing the complaint. Despite the fact that the EUO makes cross-references to the Court and its judgments, he provides his own view of the rule included in the judgments. These rules are not overtaken without checking on their applicability for the case at hand. Although his practice is closely connected with the case law of the Court, his ability to assess the application of the judgment to the particular investigated case does not put him in the position of an inferior court. The EUO is not the *fourth Union court*. Still, his practice confirms that jurisprudence plays an important role in finding instances of maladministration. The actual cross-references to the courts are used to *state* the facts, to *explain* the competences and the applicability of the judgment to the inquiry and to *support* his own findings. One can conclude that the law, including the case law of the Court, plays an important role in the practice of the EUO. The connection between the EUO and the Court's case law through

34 DR to the European Personnel Selection Office (EPSO) concerning complaint *2826/2004/PB*, para. 1.7.

35 Ibid., para. 1.10.

36 Ibid., para. 1.11.

37 Ibid.

38 See, DR of the EUO concerning his inquiry into complaint *640/2011/AN* against the Commission; DR of the EUO in his inquiry into complaint *1260/2010/RT* against the Commission; DR of the EUO in his inquiry into complaint 301/2008/IP against the Commission; Special Report from the EUO to the EUP following his DR to the Commission in Complaint *185/2005/ELB*; DR of the EUO in his inquiry into complaint *1146/2007/BU* against the Commission or DR to the European Anti-Fraud Office in complaint 2350/2005/GG.

the standards applied by the EUO and the subsequent overlap between maladministration and unlawfulness is discussed in the following chapter.

4.2.2 Practice of the Court

The research into the jurisprudence of the Court shows that the Court sometimes makes cross-references to the EUO in cases where the EUO *is a party to the proceedings* before the Court and in cases where the EUO is *not a party to the proceedings*. However, the Court's practice of cross-referencing the EUO is rather scarce and minimal. This subchapter examines the decisions of all three European courts and evaluates the results jointly. Apart from the decisions of the Court it also discusses the cross-referencing practice in the opinions of the AG. And although these do not have binding authority, they can be a very persuasive factor that might foresee the development of Union law.

The judges of the Court argue that they cross-reference the EUO and his decisions only if this is necessary in the case at hand. Mr Barents (a judge at the EUCST) stated that theoretically it is possible to use the report of the EUO in the proceedings before the Court:

> 'If the action of the plaintiff would be to establish the illegality of the action in question and either to annul it or to obtain damages, the Court would exercise legality control and examine whether the act or the behaviour in question had led to a serious error in judgement or a manifest error in judgement.

The report [of the EUO] will be approached as evidence. It would be information in the file on the basis of which the decision is taken. But I do not think that the decision of the Ombudsman has any special particular value in this respect, in the sense that the Ombudsman will find maladministration and we will immediately say that this is illegal. No, that is not the way. There is no automatic relationship meaning that if the Ombudsman has adopted a decision or found an instance of maladministration the court would change the procedure and the findings just because of that.'

Mr Van der Woude (a judge at the EUGC) confirmed that although the report of the EUO will not be overlooked, he did underline the ad hoc element in using the report of the EUO:

> 'If an individual has already dealt with this issue before the ombudsman, who has given him a favourable report and the body does not act as it should, I believe that this will be taken into account. It will not lead to the annulment of the administrative decision as such but it is part as an annex. This may show that, for example, the decision is not well reasoned or it has not been properly prepared or the person was not heard and, on top of that, the ombudsman has said that the individual was right. I would attach, at least personally, a certain authority to the report. Of course, it depends on the context. It certainly carries some weight. It is an objective element by a third party who does not have any personal interest in the case. If it was a case of maladministration I would take that into consideration. But the fact that there is maladministration does not mean that the legal principle has been violated.'

Also Prof. Prechal (a judge at the COJ) and Prof. Meij (a former judge at the CFI) confirmed that the report of the EUO, if submitted, is taken into account, although this only occurs in a few cases and in the case of the COJ almost never.

The database of the Court's case law <http://curia.europa.eu> was the main source of the information for this part of the research. The actual amount of cross-references to the EUO in the decisions of the Court and in the opinions of the AGs is arranged in the following scheme.[39] The scheme confirms that the Court acknowledges and makes cross-references to the EUO and his decisions. However, the amount of the Court's references to the EUO is minimal and compared to the number of decisions adopted yearly by the Court they can easily be overlooked.[40]

Scheme 2 – **Cross-references by the Court to the EUO between 1/1/1995 – 31/7/2013**[41]

	COJ	EUGC (CFI)	EUCST	AG
Judgment	23	61	9	-
Order	11	28	3	-
Opinion	-	-	-	26
	COJ	EUGC (CFI)	EUCST	AG
EUO (party to the Court proceedings)	4	15	1	1
EUO (not a party to the Court proceedings)	30	77	11	25

The scheme confirms that there are cross-references to the EUO in all three courts. The highest number is connected with the EUGC as in most administrative law cases it is this court that acts at first instance and in these cases individuals often rely on the report of the EUO. This number could have been higher; however, since 2006 civil service cases have been transferred from EUGC to the EUCST. The COJ deals with administrative law cases mostly as a cassation court. The lowest number of references is connected with the EUCST. It is influenced by the specialised character of this Tribunal and by the relatively short time of its existence. In the practice of the court one can find the Court's cross-references in two types of cases; in cases where the *EUO is a party to the Court proceedings* and in cases where the *EUO is not a party to the Court proceedings*.

39 The official internet site of the Court also includes other documents, for example, applications or summaries of judgments. None of these documents has been included in this research.

40 According to *Annual Report 2012 of the Court* in 2012 the COJ completed 595 cases (p. 89), the EUGC completed 688 cases (p. 181) and the EUCST completed 121 cases (p. 229).

41 Only the decisions of the Court referring to the EUO are included in this scheme. Decisions with references to *other* ombudsmen, whether national or specialised (for instance, the Postal service ombudsman as mentioned in Case C-148/10 *DHL International* [2011] ECR I-9543) are not included here. Also it must be highlighted that these numbers reflect only the decisions of the EUO in the English language. The number of published decisions in other official Union languages, especially French, can be different. Similarly, sometimes decisions dealing with the EUO are published online only in other languages, e.g. Spanish (cf. Joined cases T-219/02 and T-337/02 *Lutz Herrera* v *Commission* [2004] FP-I-A-0319). Occasionally, a case is published on the webpage of the Court without any further information about its contents. This is, for example, Case T-3/06 AJ *Wenzel v Commission and Mediator* that does not provide any information about the case whatsoever.

4.2.2.1 Cross-referencing practice of the Court in cases where the EUO is a party to the proceedings

The cases included in this group are cases where the Court *technically* embarks on a judicial review of the conduct of the EUO and his decisions or expresses its opinion on this issue. The Court here deals with disputes between the EUO and individuals. This includes cases where the Court has to deal with actions for the annulment of the EUO's decision, actions based on the EUO's failure to act, actions for damages caused or appeals against decisions of the lower court dealing with a case where the EUO was a party to the proceedings. Scheme 2 shows that these cases are not very numerous. The most important cases that can be included in this first group, which delimit the borders of the judicial review of the EUO's actions, were discussed before.[42] They include:

1. Case T-103/99 *Associazione delle Cantine Sociali Venete v Mediator and European Parliament*, order, sets a precedent in connection with actions for a failure to act by the EUO and partially with the annulment of the EUO decision.
2. Case T-196/08 *Srinivasan v Mediator*, order and a decision on an appeal, C-580/08 P *Srinivasan v Mediator*, developing the previous case law on the annulment of the EUO's decision.
3. Cases T-209/00 *Lamberts v Mediator* and C-234/02 *Mediator v Lamberts* set a precedent in connection with the non-contractual liability of the EUO.
4. Other specific decisions in which the Court deals directly with the EUO confirm the case law in the previous three cases.[43] Although in July 2013 there are some cases pending against the EUO that still need to be decided it is very probable that the existing case law will not be changed and that the Court will follow its previous case law.[44]

In these decisions one can find the following types of cross-references to the EUO.

1. Factual (descriptive) cross-references

In its decisions the Court describes the facts of the case in great detail. These descriptions can include the actions of the EUO. The factual cross-references are included in the decisions of the Court as there is often a need for a clear and precise description of a dispute and its developments. This reference can be found, for instance, in Case T-196/08 *Srinivasan v Mediator*, where the CFI *inter alia* stated, as a matter of fact, that:

> 'By letter of 7 April 2008, the Ombudsman informed the applicant that, on the basis of his investigation following the complaint, he had found no maladministration on the part of the Commission and therefore decided to close his file.'[45]

42 See, section 3.1.2.

43 Cf. Case T-412/05 *M v Mediator* [2008] ECR II-197; Case T-144/06 – *O'Loughlin v Mediator and Ireland* (not published) or Case T-168/08 AJ *Meister v Commission and Mediator* (not published).

44 See, Case C-535/12 P *Faet Oltra v Mediator* (not published); Case T-406/12 P-AJ *BG v Mediator* (not published) or Case T-217/11 *Staelen v Mediator* (information not available).

45 Case T-196/08 *Srinivasan v Mediator* (not published), order, para.4.

This cross-reference to the EUO only includes the facts which, according to the judges, were necessary for the readers of the judgment. In further parts of this decision the Court refers to the EUO also in other ways. One can find such references also in other judgments.[46]

Among the descriptive references one can also include *formal* cross-references where the Court refers to its previous case law that dealt with the EUO (e.g. referring to case *Lamberts v Mediator*) or where it makes cross-references to legal provisions that also refer to the EUO.[47]

2. Explanatory cross-references

The Court is the institution that authoritatively interprets Union law. The Court does this also in connection with the EUO. These cross-references clarify, at least to the parties to the proceedings, the powers, roles or functions of the EUO. They can also explain the EUO's limitations. Thus, the Court here does not refer to the EOU because of the principle used by the EUO or because of the issue discussed in his decision but because of the need to explain the provisions of primary or secondary Union law. Still, the principles stemming therefrom are often used as a precedent. An explanatory cross-reference can be found in Case T-209/00 *Lamberts v Mediator.*

> The Court here inter alia explained that 'neither a critical remark nor a report of the EUO is designed to protect the individual interests of the citizens against damage which may arise as a result of maladministration on the part of a Community institution or body.'[48] In this judgment the Court also noted and explained the character of its relations with the EUO. It described the EUO as *an alternative non-judicial remedy to that of an action before the Community Court.*[49]

Another explanatory reference can be found in Case T-103/99 *Associazione delle Cantine Sociali Venete v Mediator and Parliament.* Here the Court explained the character of the EUO's decision.

> The CFI here *inter alia* stated that 'the report of the EUO that is sent to the EUP does not, by definition, produce legal effects vis-à-vis third parties within the meaning of Article 173 of the Treaty (today 263 TFEU).'[50]

By the explanatory references the Court authoritatively clarified and interpreted the legal provisions connected with the EUO that, based on the existing disputes, required a necessary and a clear explanation. Similar references can be found in other judgments.[51]

46 See, *Lamberts v Mediator*, para. 23 or *Associazione delle Cantine Sociali Venete*, order, para. 9.
47 Case T-209/00 *Lamberts v Mediator*, judgment, paras. 1-15.
48 *Lamberts* v *Mediator,* para. 87.
49 Ibid., para. 65.
50 *Associazione delle Cantine Sociali Venete*, order, para. 37.
51 *Mediator v Lamberts,* paras. 62-63 or Case T-196/08 *Srinivasan v Mediator* (not published).

3. Assessment cross-references

Although the Court found out that the decision of the EUO is not a decision that can be annulled and there is no point in assessing its legality,[52] it adopted the rule that the *legality of the EUO's conduct* can be overseen in connection with the non-contractual liability of the EUO.[53] It is important to underline that it is the *legality of conduct* by the EUO and *not the legality of his decisions* that the Court assesses. The best example of the assessment reference can be found in Case T-412/05 *M v Mediator* where the Court had to decide on a claim for damages connected with the non-contractual liability of the EUO.

> The case was commenced by an official of the Commission who argued that due to the negligence of the EUO he had been named in one of his decisions. The CFI found that one of the earlier published versions of the EUO decision had indeed named the officer. Then, the CFI had to determine whether this conduct was in compliance with the legal requirements. The Court found two exceptions to the principle of confidentiality that would allow the EUO to name the official. They argued that '*la première exception concerne le cas dans lequel la désignation nominative est nécessaire eu égard à la gravité des faits et en tenant compte de l'objectif poursuivi par l'institution ou l'organe communautaire. La deuxième exception concerne le cas dans lequel la confidentialité risque de prêter à confusion ou encore de jeter le doute sur l'identité des personnes impliquées, ce qui est susceptible de nuire aux intérêts de personnes concernées mais non visées par les irrégularités dénoncées.*'[54]
>
> In connection with the naming of the officer the Court *inter alia* found that '*force est de constater en l'espèce, premièrement, que la désignation du requérant n'était pas indispensable pour atteindre l'objectif que poursuit la dénonciation d'un cas de mauvaise administration. La désignation nominative du requérant n'était pas non plus nécessaire afin d'éviter un risque de confusion.*'[55] And, last but not least, it stated that '*il est constant que le Médiateur n'a pas entendu le requérant avant d'adopter sa [Implementing decision], qui était d'application au moment de ladite décision, disposait explicitement que, « [s]i un fonctionnaire ou autre agent est nommément critiqué dans une plainte, il est normalement invité à présenter des observations.*'[56]
>
> Based on the facts of the case the Court concluded that '*il résulte de tout ce qui précède que le Médiateur, en identifiant nommément le requérant … a violé le droit au*

52 *Associazione delle Cantine Sociali Venete*, order, para. 50.

53 *Mediator v Lamberts*, para. 62.

54 See, Case T-412/05 *M v Mediator* [2008] ECR II-197, paras. 130-131 (published only in French). The first exception concerns cases in which naming is necessary due to the seriousness of the facts while it takes into account the objective pursued by the Union institution. The second exception concerns cases in which confidentiality can lead to confusion or it can raise doubts about the identity of the individuals involved which is likely to damage the interests of the affected persons which is not presumed by these irregularities (translated by the author).

55 In the present case it must note that, firstly, the naming of the complainant was not indispensable for reaching the objective followed by the exposure of the case of maladministration. At the same time, the naming of the complainant was not necessary in order to prevent the risk of confusion (translated by the author).

56 Ibid., paras. 134-136. It is undisputed that the EUO did not hear the complainant before adopting his [Implementing decision], which was not applicable at the moment of the said decision and which explicitly stated that '[i]f an official or other servant is specifically complained against in a complaint, he/she is normally invited to submit his/her comments' (translated by the author).

> *respect de la vie privée de celui-ci, le principe de proportionnalité ainsi que le principe du contradictoire.*'[57]

These breaches led to the decision of the CFI that the EUO was obliged to pay damages to the complainant. Thus, the Court here expressly *assessed the legality of the conduct of the EUO*. Next to the fact that it confirmed the previous case law, it also clearly underlined that a breach of legal principles by the EUO's conduct can lead to the non-contractual liability of the Union. These cross-references to the EUO were made in order to assess the EUO's conduct.

In cross-references to the EUO in proceedings where the *EUO is one of the parties*, the Court mostly describes the formal status of the EUO, the status of the EUO's decisions and its own connection with these decisions. I assume that these cross-references show how the Court perceives the EUO as a Union Institution.

4.2.2.2 Cross-referencing practice of the Court in cases where the EUO is not a party to the proceedings

The second group of cases where the Court has made cross-references to the EUO are cases where the EUO is *not a party* to the proceedings. Here one can find the following cross-references.

1. Factual (descriptive) cross-references
Before dealing with the substance of the case the Court describes the facts and legal provisions that are important for the reader of the decision. Generally, the decisions of the Court include *summaries of the facts* which do not need to contain all the facts relied upon by the parties to the proceedings but only the facts that the Court considers important.[58] These facts can include a cross-reference to the EUO. They can be found, for example, in the judgment in Case T-19/07 *Systran and Systran Luxembourg v Commission.*

> In this case the applicant asked for compensation for damage owing to illegalities following an invitation to tender by the Commission. The CFI stated, as a matter of fact, that 'the complaint against the Commission was submitted to the European Ombudsman on 28 July 2005, who presented the results of his investigation on 28 September 2006.'[59] The judgment is silent as to what these results were or how they were used by this court.

By these cross-references the Court, as a matter of fact, indicates that there was a previous EUO inquiry leading to a finding. These references *do not mean* that the Court accepts the facts discovered by the EUO or that it rejects them. The Court does not refer to facts

57 Ibid., para. 140. From all the above-mentioned facts is clear that the EUO by identifying the complainant by his name … has breached the complainant's right to respect for private life, the principle of proportionality and the principle of adversarial proceedings (translated by the author).

58 Case C-580/08 P, *Srinivasan v Mediator,* order, para. 21.

59 Case T-19/07 *Systran and Systran Luxembourg v Commission* [2010] ECR II-6083, judgment, para. 289.

found by the EUO but it considers the *previous Ombudsman inquiry or his decisions to be a fact* which is necessary to mention in the decision. Similar examples can be found in its other judgments.[60]

As in the previous case, one can include among the descriptive references also *formal* cross-references where the Court refers to its previous case law that dealt with the EUO (e.g. referring to case *Lamberts v Mediator*) or where it makes cross-references to a legal provision that also refers to the EUO.[61]

2. Explanatory cross-references

Sometimes the Court in its cross-references to the EUO *explains* some issues or legal provisions directly connected with the EUO. Such a situation can be found in the order of the CFI in Case T-294/04 – *Internationaler Hilfsfonds v Commission*.

> In this case the applicant *inter alia* asked the Court to decide that the Commission should reimburse the costs it had incurred in the proceedings before the EUO, namely the 'lawyers' fees incurred by the applicant. The CFI here stated that 'in the institution of the Ombudsman, the Treaty has given citizens of the Union an alternative remedy to that of an action before the Community Court in order to protect their interests'.[62] '[...] and since these two remedies cannot be pursued at the same time. It is therefore for the citizen to decide which of the two available remedies is likely to serve his interests best.'[63]
>
> The CFI furthermore continued that 'unlike proceedings before the Community courts, proceedings before the Ombudsman are designed in such a way as to make recourse to legal advice unnecessary. It suffices to set out the facts in the complaint and there is no need to set out any legal arguments. Accordingly, it is implicit in the individual's freedom to choose to be legally represented in the proceedings before the Ombudsman that he must bear such costs personally. It is precisely on account of the lack of such freedom of choice in proceedings before the Community courts, in which representation by a lawyer is obligatory, that judicial proceedings entail a decision on costs which includes lawyers' fees.'[64]

The CFI thus explained that *lawyers' fees incurred in proceedings before the EUO are not recoverable by way of an action for damages*.[65] This decision by the CFI was confirmed in appellate proceedings before the COJ.[66]

Another example of an explanatory reference can be found in the judgment of 4 October 2006 in Case T193/04 R *Tillack* v *Commission*.

60 Cf. Case F-120/06 *Dálnoky v Commission* [2007] FP-I-A-1-0269, order, para. 14; Case C-28/08 P *Commission v Bavarian Lager* [2010] ECR I-6055, judgment, paras. 27-28; or Case T-298/09 *Evropaïki Dynamiki v Commission* [2011] ECR II-0300, judgment, para. 61.

61 See, for example, Case T-250/08 *Batchelor v Commission* [2011] ECR II-2551, judgment, para. 6 or Case T-407/07 *CMB and Christof v Commission* [2011] ECR II-0286, judgment, para. 5.

62 Case T-294/04 *Internationaler Hilfsfonds v Commission* [2005] ECR II-2719, order, para. 42.

63 Ibid., para. 48.

64 Ibid., para. 52.

65 Ibid., para. 55.

66 Case C-331/05 P *Internationaler Hilfsfonds v Commission* [2007] ECR I-5475, judgment, paras. 25-27.

> The applicant in this case relied on the EUO's finding which found maladministration in actions of the European Anti-Fraud Office (OLAF). In this connection the CFI explained that 'classification as an "act of maladministration" by the Ombudsman does not mean, in itself, that OLAF's conduct constitutes a sufficiently serious breach of a rule of law within the meaning of the case law.'[67]

Thus, the CFI explained that the EUO's findings of maladministration do not automatically make the action of the Union institution unlawful. Conduct in which the EUO found an instance of maladministration does not need to be, at the same time, conduct in which the Court will find unlawfulness. The CFI did not expressly exclude the possibility that an instance of maladministration can lead to unlawfulness. This judgment also confirms the argument that if an applicant wants the Court to annul a decision of a Union institution because of its unlawfulness, the EUO's finding of maladministration as the only evidence to support his arguments is not in principle sufficient.

An explanatory reference can also be found in the judgment in Case T-371/03 *Le Voci v Council.*

> Here an unsuccessful applicant in an open competition brought an action before the Court to declare the competition invalid. After the applicant had disputed the result before the selection board and the original result was confirmed, he requested a copy of his written test with corrections. In the request he referred to the decision of the EUO (2097/2002/GG). The selection board did not provide him with this written test, although it did state that it was progressing in providing access to these kinds of documents in accordance with the EUO's recommendation. Subsequently, he lodged an appeal before the CFI and pointed out that the EUO had addressed a written recommendation to the Council, where he expressed the view that the Council's refusal to grant the complainant access to a marked test paper was an instance of maladministration. He also emphasised that the Council had accepted that recommendation by the EUO in its entirety.[68]
>
> In connection with this argument the CFI stated that 'it must be borne in mind that in accepting the recommendation of the European Ombudsman the Council did not in any way undertake to disclose marked tests in future on a systematic basis, as the scope of that decision of the Council was limited to that particular case.'[69] The CFI also noted that the Council relied on its case law that *allowed* it to provide the candidate with a marked copy, which does not in any way mean that the Council recognised that 'it was under an obligation to do so in similar cases.'[70] Subsequently it dismissed this part of applicant's action.

Although it is not mentioned expressly the CFI here *inter alia* directly regulated the application of the EUO's recommendations by the Union institution. It confirmed the character of the EUO's recommendations and the discretion of the Union institutions to *ignore* EUO recommendations. The Union institution is under no legal obligation to make

67 Case T-193/04 *Tillack v Commission* [2006] ECR II-3995, judgment, para. 128.
68 Case T-371/03 *Le Voci v Council* [2005] FP-I-A-209, judgment, para. 112.
69 Ibid., para. 126.
70 Ibid.

systematic changes even if it accepts the EUO's recommendations in individual cases. Similar cases can be found in the Court's case law.[71]

The interpretation of the law by the Court can sometimes be questionable. This can be found, for example, in Case T-294/03 *Gibault v Commission.*

> The applicant was an unsuccessful applicant in an open competition. After his plea to reconsider his result was rejected by the chairman of the selection board, he lodged a complaint against the decision. This complaint was rejected by the appointing authority. He then started proceedings before the CFI. He asked the Court to annul the decision of the selection board or to annul the said competition. One of the arguments relied upon by the applicant was that the selection board's evaluation is final and a candidate who has failed has in reality no opportunity of contesting it.[72] In this context he referred to the Draft recommendation of the EUO dealing with the secrecy which forms part of the Commission's recruitment procedures.[73]
>
> The Commission stated that the opinions of the EUO cannot be taken into account in proceedings concerning the legality of competitions based on tests. Also the CFI adopted a negative position and stated that 'the argument that the applicant bases on the inquiry undertaken by the European Ombudsman is irrelevant. Under [Article 228 TFEU], the Ombudsman is empowered only to investigate and give his views in cases of maladministration, which cannot include infringement of a legal provision or of a general principle amenable to review by the Community judicature.'[74]

This statement gives rise to several questions about its actual meaning. On the one hand, it can mean that the EUO is not able to investigate or give his views in cases of maladministration which include infringements of a legal provision or of a general principle *if* the CFI is reviewing the case. Such a statement by the CFI would confirm written Union law.

On the other hand, if one takes this statement literally it can lead to a different conclusion. If the EUO had to apply this statement literally, he would only be able to investigate instances of maladministration which do not deal with a breach of the law or a breach of general principles of law, i.e. *maladministration falling short of unlawfulness.* Thus, the EUO would have to consider the complaint firstly from the position of the law and if the law had not been breached only then would he be able to investigate the breach of those principles or rules that exist 'outside the law'. However, if there was a possible breach of the law he would have to drop the case. This would also considerably limit his discretion to deal with cases and it would de facto define maladministration in a very narrow sense. If this decision was really applied to the practice of the EUO then it would be going much further than barring the EUO from investigating those cases where there are or were legal proceedings.[75] It would prevent him from investigating cases with a

71 Cf. Case T-424/08 *Nexus Europe (Ireland) v Commission* [2010] ECR II-96, para. 66 or Case T-377/07 *Evropaïki Dynamiki v Commission* [2011] ECR II-0442, para. 114.

72 Case T-294/03 *Gibault v Commission* [2005] FP-I-A-141, judgment, para. 33.

73 DR of the EUO to the Commission in the own-initiative inquiry 1004/97/PD of 8 March 1999.

74 *Gibault v Commission*, judgement, para. 45.

75 See, section 3.1.1.

possibility of legal proceedings whether a complainant wants them or not. Because of that one can assume that the CFI had the first explanation in mind.

3. Distinguishing cross-references

Although it is rather rare the Court can express a positive or negative opinion as to the EUO´s findings. These cross-references to the EUO are closely connected with the content and the substance of his decisions. Such a reference can be found in Case T-424/08 *Nexus Europe (Ireland) v Commission* where the applicant applied for compensation for the loss allegedly suffered as a consequence of the Commission making certain amendments to the contract concluded with the applicant.

> The Court dealt with this contract because of an *arbitration clause* which enabled it to hear any disputes between the Community and its co-contractors as to the application or interpretation of the contract.[76] Amendments to the contract were concluded by both parties and dealt with the reimbursement model of the applicant. Thanks to the amendments, the eligible costs of the applicant were lowered in more than half of its original amount. However, as these amendments were added to the contract 3 years after signing the original contract the applicant was not reimbursed for all the work. Before resorting to the Court, the applicant had filed a complaint with the EUO where he had claimed for compensation for material and non-material damage suffered.
>
> The judgment stated that the EUO found that there had been an instance of maladministration in the conduct of the Commission as 'it failed to provide the applicant with a coherent and reasonable account of the legal basis for its actions.'[77] The EUO also proposed that the Commission should make a fair and appropriate payment and withdraw, in explicit terms, any suggestion of fraud or serious financial irregularity. This proposition was accepted by the Commission which was willing to pay to the applicant the sum proposed by the EUO. The applicant, however, did not agree with the proposed sum and started the action for compensation in the form of damages before the Court.
>
> In the Court proceedings the applicant inter alia referred to the findings of the EUO and to the breach of the principle of sound administration. In connection with the validity of the contract the Court stated that 'the question whether the conduct of the Commission infringes the principle of sound administration is irrelevant. Even if, by failing to provide a coherent explanation as to the reasons justifying the request for the amendment of the 2001 contract and by threatening at the same time to exercise powers such as the suspension of future payments, the Commission had breached its duty of sound administration, that fact alone cannot invalidate the 2004 contract, which from the moment it was concluded has governed with retroactive effect the rights and obligations of the parties.'[78] The Court dismissed the action and did not award damages to the applicant despite the fact that the EUO had found maladministration in the same case.

The Court in this case did not follow the EUO's line of reasoning and it assessed only the legal side of the dispute. It *de facto* confirmed that the finding of maladministration by the

76 Case T-424/08 *Nexus Europe (Ireland) v Commission* [2010] ECR II-96, para. 7.
77 Ibid., para. 25.
78 Ibid., para. 66.

EUO did not have to cover the same issues as those that were important for the decision of the Court. It showed that it is in no way bound by an EUO decision. Obviously the Court takes into consideration only those sources that are connected in one way or another with the law. The recommendations and decisions of the EUO are not such a source. Similar cross-references can also be found in other Court decisions.[79]

The typology of cross-references included in cases where the EUO *is not a party to the proceedings* before the Court does not considerably differ from cases where the EUO is a party to the proceedings. This is connected with the fact that there are only limited cases where the Court has made cross-references to the EUO. Still, these cross-references can be various in character. They can describe the *facts of the case* or only *formally refer to the EUO*. But they can also express the *Court's attitude towards the EUO* and *answer more substantive issues*.

4.2.2.3 Practice in the opinions of the Advocates General

Opinions of the AG are not decisions of the Court. At the same time they are not legally binding on the Court or any other Union institution. Nonetheless, they represent a potential and an influential source of information for the Court. Sometimes they even include a summary of the applicable law and even national principles.[80] Parties to the Court's proceedings sometimes refer to the opinions of the AG[81] and this is also true for the parties to EUO inquiries.[82]

As to the typology it is possible to find almost the same categories of references as in the case of the Court. First of all, one can find *factual references* to the EUO where the AG only refers to the EUO because he is describing the facts of the case. As the AGs provide the Court with an independent legal opinion on the appeal against the decision of the EUGC they can point to a fact that might have been overlooked by the EUGC or a fact which has not been taken into account. For example, in the opinion in Case C-470/00 – *EUP v Carlo Ripa di Meana and Others* AG Mischo pointed to facts of the case that included an investigation by the EUO.

> As a matter of fact he stated that 'these two Members (of the EUP) … made a complaint of maladministration against the EUP to the Ombudsman. Subsequently, the complaint was rejected by the Ombudsman on the ground that these two opportunities to acquire knowledge of the time-limit for the submission of the application sufficiently protected both the Members and the requirements of good administration.'[83]

79 See, Case T-160/03 *Afcon v Commission* [2005] ECR II-981, judgment, para. 13.

80 See, Opinion of AG Lagrange in Joined cases 7/56, 3/57 to 7/57 *Dineke Algera, Giacomo Cicconardi, Simone Couturaud, Ignazio Genuardi, Félicie Steichen v Common Assembly of the European Coal and Steel Community*.

81 Cf. Case T-433/10 P *Allen and Others v Commission* (not yet published).

82 DR of the EUO concerning his inquiry into complaint 640/2011/AN against the Commission, para. 36.

83 Opinion of AG Mischo in Case C-470/00 *Parliament v Carlo Ripa di Meana and Others* [2004] ECR I-4167, para. 68.

The opinion does not deal with the issue of the EUO in any more detail but includes it only as a matter of fact. Similar references can be found in other opinions.[84] There are also *formal references* where the AGs refer to previous Court decisions that include the term 'Ombudsman' in their name.[85]

In the opinion to Case C-234/02 P *Mediator v Lamberts*, AG Geelhoed *inter alia* tried to explain the main characteristics of the EUO. *Explanatory references* can be found here as well.

> He explained that 'the EUO does not offer any legal protection in the proper sense and that he is to be regarded as an administrative body whose task – primarily via complaints – is to identify in the public interest instances of maladministration by the Community institutions and to help to put an end to that maladministration.'[86]

Similarly AG Kokott in her opinion to Case C427/07 *Commission v Ireland* explained that *the Ombudsman may offer an unbureaucratic alternative to court proceedings.*[87] Sometimes the opinion of the AG can be different from the opinion of the EUGC (CFI). This was the case concerning the opinion of AG Mengozzi in Case C-362/08 P *Internationaler Hilfsfonds v Commission* in which the AG tried explain of the character of the EUO decision differently from the CFI.

> In the opinion the AG underlined that part of the appeal should be upheld on the ground that 'the CFI wrongly classified the Ombudsman's decision finding an instance of maladministration in relation to the processing of the application for access to documents in this case as not constituting a (substantial) new factor (or fact) within the meaning of the case law on acts merely confirming a previous act not challenged within the time-limits for bringing court proceedings.'[88]
>
> According to him 'the classification of a decision of the Ombudsman ... as a 'substantial new fact' is not ... precluded by either Article 2(6) of Decision 94/262 or Article 195 EC, contrary to the finding of the Court of First Instance.'[89] He furthermore alleged that 'the approach of treating a decision by the Ombudsman ... as a substantial new fact justifying reconsideration by the administration of a previous decision which has become definitive ensures the effectiveness of a finding of an instance of maladministration by the Ombudsman and at the same time preserves the discretion of the requested institution.'[90]

The COJ subsequently set aside the judgment of the General Court and returned the case.[91] However, it did not address the issue whether the EUO decision creates as a *new*

84 See, for example, Opinion of AG Tizzano in Case C-193/01 P *Pitsiorlas v Council and ECB* [2003] ECR I-4837, para. 5.8. or also Opinion of AG Jacobs in Case C-227/04 P *Lindorfer v Council* [2007] ECR I-6767.

85 See, for example, Opinion of AG Léger in C-40/03 P *Rica Foods v Commission* [2005] ECR I-6811.

86 Opinion of AG Geelhoed in Case C-234/02 P *Mediator v Lamberts* [2004] ECR I-2803, para. 63.

87 Opinion of AG Kokott in Case C427/07 *Commission v Ireland* [2009] ECR I-6277.

88 Opinion of AG Mengozzi in Case C-362/08 P *Internationaler Hilfsfonds v Commission* [2010] ECR I-669, para. 145.

89 Ibid., para. 170.

90 Ibid., para. 174.

91 Case C-362/08 P *Internationaler Hilfsfonds v Commission* [2010] ECR I-669, judgment paras. 53-60.

factor that should/has to be taken into account. Similar types of references can be found in other opinions by AGs.[92] Other types of references were not found.

An important issue that should be noted is that AG opinions represent only the *personal view of a legal expert* on the issues raised by the dispute and on a solution which could be adopted.[93] The Court is in no way bound by them. Thus, they do not represent a view of the Union or of the Court but only individual opinions of the AGs. Still they can sometimes facilitate the decision-making of the Court as they are considered to be a fruitful source of the development of the jurisprudence.[94]

4.2.2.4 A short summary

When we want to analyse the practice of the Court, the first issue that is obvious to observe is the fact that in connection with the bulk of decisions adopted by the Court since 1995 when the EUO was established, only a very small amount of decisions of the Court actually make cross-references to the EUO. Between 1/1/1995 and 31/7/2013 there has been an average of only 8 decisions per year where the Court has made cross-references to the EUO. This is a negligible amount of cases. Still, even this small amount of cases confirms that the Court *de facto* acknowledges the existence of the EUO as an independent Union institution.

The experiences of the judges and the decisions of the Court confirm that the EUO and his decisions *are not that important for the work of the Court*. Next to the fact that the EUO's decisions do not play an important role in the practice of the Court it is confirmed that if the decision of the EUO is to be used by the Court two facts have to apply. Firstly, the decision of the EUO should be connected with the case at hand. This means that the EUO's ombudsprudence is consulted only in *ad hoc cases*. Secondly, the case law confirms that only the decision of the EUO on its own is not going to persuade the Court about its unlimited application. All applicants must also support their statements with some other argument, as the findings of the EUO that there was maladministration are not enough for the Court to conclude that there was illegality.

4.3 Summary

This chapter discusses the question of *what is the significance of the decisions of the EUO and the judgments of the Court and their content for the other researched institution in the EU and what are their interrelations?*

One can say that written *Union law* does not give a comprehensive answer to this question. Directly, it deals with the question only marginally. Indirectly, the answer can be partially deduced from the institutional coordination of the EUO and the Court. Written Union law creates a framework for the EUO and the Court that bars the EUO from

92 See, Opinion of AG Mengozzi in C-362/08 P *Internationaler Hilfsfonds v Commission* [2010] ECR I-669 or Opinion of AG Trstenjak in C-331/05 P *Internationaler Hilfsfonds v Commission* [2007] ECR I-5475.

93 Darmon 1988, p. 431.

94 Ibid.

dealing with facts that were already covered by the Court. The Court's jurisprudence in general underlines the differences between these two findings and between their practical application and impact. While the decisions of the Court are legally binding and must be complied with by the Union's institutions, including the EUO, the decisions of the EUO do not play any particular role in the practice of the Court and their application in Court practice is limited.

The *practice* of both institutions is different. While the EUO uses Union law and the jurisprudence of the Court as a starting point when looking for instances of maladministration, the Court very often overlooks the existence of previous EUO decisions in the same or in a similar case. Only exceptionally does the Court deal with *cases against the EUO* and *with issues that have already been dealt with* by the EUO. The EUO, when dealing with complaints, does not adopt any individually binding decision that would give any enforceable right to an individual. Based on the case law the EUO's decisions do not create rights vis-à-vis third parties. They are not the law. From the perception of the Court, the EUO's inquiry is an alternative remedy to the Court proceedings. But it is excluded that these two remedies are pursued at the same time if the same facts are discussed.

Although the EUO deals with complaints covering problems 'beyond legality' the impact of the law and case law of the Court is indeed visible. The EUO can refer to the Court when *describing the facts* of the case, when *explaining its competences* and possibly also when *supporting his own decisions*. Also, the EUO very often has to deal with arguments by the parties that are supported by the judgments of the Court. In these cases he is often in a position of being a *factual interpreter of a particular judgment* and of the Court's rules. The EUO does not need to wait for the arguments of the parties as he actively looks for case law that could be applicable to a dispute and that can theoretically assist him in finding an instance of maladministration in the action of the Union institution in question.

In general, the decisions of the EUO can be submitted before the Court as a part of the file. The Court will not however look for these decisions of the EUO of its own volition. Even if it is accepted as evidence, the decision of the EUO does not have any special status in the Court's proceedings. If the EUO has found maladministration in a certain action by a Union institution, it does not mean that the Court will automatically follow his opinion in finding a breach of the law, a failure to act or damage as a result thereof. Simultaneously, if the Court deals with a decision of the EUO as a piece of evidence it does not base its own decision on facts found *only* by the EUO. The EUO is not in the position of an *authoritative fact-finder* for the Court. Nonetheless, the Court must not, but potentially can accept facts found by the EUO as relevant for its judgement.

Chapter 5

NORMATIVE COORDINATION OF OMBUDSMAN-JUDICIARY RELATIONS IN THE EU

Both the Court and the EUO are active in the development of normative standards. The EUO develops and applies normative standards while investigating instances of maladministration, the Court develops and applies them while ensuring that in the interpretation and application of the Treaties the law is observed.[1] The Court's normative standards attract a great deal of interest among researchers as they have a direct impact on the reputation and the actual functioning of the Union's legal order and, eventually, also on the legal systems of the Member States.[2] Despite the general acceptance of the EUO's normative function, his normative standards are only occasionally the subject of academic research.[3] This chapter tries to add to this research by answering the question of *what is the mutual significance of the normative standards of the ombudsman and the judiciary in the European Union and what are the interrelations of these normative standards.*

Firstly, it characterises the relation between legality and maladministration in the Union sense and it looks at the normative standards of these normative concepts (5.1). This is followed by looking for a formal normative coordination of the EUO and the Court and the similarity between these normative standards (5.2). The next section provides a research-based description of the character of the normative standards as applied in the practice of the EUO and the Court (5.3). The chapter ends with a summary (5.4).

5.1 Maladministration in the Union sense, legality and development of normative standards

The normative concept of maladministration in the Union sense is not identical to unlawfulness. Maladministration does not equal unlawfulness; these concepts have close but not entirely identical meanings. Generally, the EUO is entitled to address complaints to uncover failures in acting lawfully.[4] The EUO has on several occasions clearly explained that 'illegality in matters within the Ombudsman's mandate necessarily

1 Art. 228 TFEU and Art. 19 TEU.
2 Cf. Tridimas 2007.
3 See, for example, De Leeuw 2009.
4 Hsieh 2005, p. 6.

implies maladministration, however maladministration does not automatically entail illegality.'[5] However, the definition of maladministration created in the Annual Report 1997[6] does not limit maladministration to cases where the rule or principle that is being violated is legally binding.[7] Because whilst an unlawful act always constitutes an act of maladministration, vice versa this is not always true and 'there may be maladministration even if the institution has not acted unlawfully.'[8] The EUO's perception of the relation between legality and maladministration can thus be depicted in the following diagram:

This diagram can be supported by a number of EUO decisions. For example, in Draft recommendation of the EUO in his inquiry into complaint 2904/2005/TN against the Commission the EUO stated that 'it is true that while "illegality" implies maladministration, a finding of maladministration does not automatically mean that there was also "illegality"'.[9] This is sometimes questioned by authors. For instance, Dimitrakopoulos argues that there can also be so-called 'illegality beyond (the concept of) maladministration.'[10]

Although the EUO, according to the Treaties, is the only institution that deals with maladministration, the concept has occasionally been brought to the attention of the Court. The term *maladministration* was used by the Court and the AGs also in the pre-Ombudsman era, i.e. before 1995.

In Joined cases 176/86 and 177/86 *Houyoux and Guery* v *Commission* (an application for the annulment of a Commission decision) the Court stated that the applicant *had been misled* as a result of *negligence* on the part of the Commission and that he had suffered damage as a result of the Commission's *maladministration*.[11] Maladministration here includes *misleading the applicant* and *not rectifying the error in good time*. However, maladministration did not lead to the annulment of the decision or an order to pay damages to the applicant. Nonetheless, having regard to all the circumstances of the case, the Court assessed the damage *ex aequo et bono* and ordered the Commission to pay the damages.[12]

Similarly in Joined Cases 173/82, 157/83 and 186/84 *Castille* v *Commission*, the Court stated that a *delay in the work* of the Commission was not compatible with the *principle*

5 Annual Report 2010, p. 15.
6 See, section 1.1.3.
7 Annual Report 2010, p. 15.
8 Diamandouros 2011a.
9 DR of the EUO in his inquiry into complaint 2904/2005/TN against the Commission, para. 51.
10 Dimitrakopoulos 2010, p. 55.
11 Joined Cases 176/86 and 177/86 *Houyoux and Guery v Commission* [1987] ECR 4333, para. 14.
12 Ibid., para. 18 (a).

of sound administration and that the Commission had to bear the financial consequences arising from such maladministration.[13]

In Case T-68/91 *Barbi v Commission* the CFI noted that the Commission's delay constituted maladministration. The Court found that 'the Commission was guilty of maladministration by failing to draw up the applicant's staff report within the time limit prescribed by the Staff Regulations and substituting for it in the contested promotion procedure a promotion proposal less favourable than the staff report later drawn up.'[14]

In Case C-294/95 P *Ojha v Commission*, the Court stated that any non-performance of the duty to provide assistance could only lead to the annulment of the decision refusing the assistance requested and, in some cases, may constitute maladministration for which the Community may be liable.[15]

An interesting statement about the relation between legality and maladministration was made in Case T-53/91 *Mergen v Commission*. Here the CFI stated that 'since the Commission has not acted unlawfully, there can be no question of maladministration.'[16] The CFI here directly connected the unlawfulness of the conduct of Union institutions with maladministration. If we use the argument *a contrario* then a lawful action is always action with good administration. This, however, is not an opinion which is identical to the present development of the relationship between maladministration and unlawfulness. Nowadays the Court usually deals with the term maladministration only in connection with the EUO.[17]

Based on these examples, the EUO is not the only European institution that can give content to term maladministration. The Court sometimes connects legal implications with maladministration (especially in connection with damages). Nowadays, the Court mentions maladministration in its judgments almost exclusively as a term connected with the competence of the EUO. In the pre-Ombudsman era, the practice of the Court in dealing with maladministration did exist but it never specialized in this concept.[18]

5.1.1 The European Code of Good Administrative Behaviour

Since the establishment of the EUO as a Union institution, the EUO has tried to connect maladministration or rather good administration with standards of administrative conduct.[19] These attempts by the EUO led to a speedy development of the draft of the

13 Joined cases 173/82, 157/83 and 186/84 *Castille* v *Commission* [1986] ECR 497, judgment, para. 34.

14 Case T-68/91 *Barbi v Commission* [1992] ECR II-2127, judgment, para. 45.

15 Case C-294/95 P *Ojha v Commission* [1996] ECR I-5863, judgment, para. 53.

16 Case T-53/91 *Mergen v Commission* [1992] ECR II-2041, judgment, para. 66.

17 See, for example, Case *Lamberts v Mediator*.

18 Another explanation for the use of the term *maladministration* in the pre-Ombudsman era judgments is an inappropriate translation. In French versions of judgments the Court, when talking about maladministration, used the term *une faute de service*. The EUO, on the other hand, in French versions of his own documents translates maladministration as *un cas de mauvaise administration*. Thus, it is questionable whether terms that are used by the Court and by the EUO and are translated into English as *maladministration* actually mean the same thing. At the same time one can note that the Court translates the term maladministration (when connected with the EUO) as *un cas de mauvaise administration*. (C-234/02 P, *Lamberts v Mediator*, para. 9 ff.).

19 Annual Report of the EUO 1995, p. 5.

European Code of Good Administrative Behaviour and its adoption by a resolution of the EUP (*the Code*).

The Code is a concentrated list of principles that *should be used by the EUO* when assessing whether the actions of Union institutions lead to an instance of maladministration and by the Union administration when dealing with individuals. The Code is based on an idea presented by the MEP Perry in 1998. On this basis and on the basis of 'numerous complaints which brought to the EUO's attention instances of maladministration and in order to enhance relations between the European citizens and the Community'[20] the EUO started own-initiative inquiries. In this inquiry he asked 19 Community institutions whether they had already adopted, or would agree to adopt, a code of a good administrative conduct applicable to their officials in their relations with the public.[21] In 1999, the EUO recommended these institutions to adopt a draft Code.[22] The draft Code was supposed to be a kind of *blueprint* for other codes of conduct of the Union institutions that should have been adopted in the form of a decision and published in the Official Journal.[23] Although these institutions were not very keen to adopting it,[24] the Code was approved with some changes in a resolution of the EUP.[25] The resolution urged the Commission to submit a legislative proposal containing this Code under Art. 308 of the *Treaty establishing the European Community*.[26] The Commission however indicated that it had no intention whatsoever of setting forth a proposal to transform the Code into a binding regulation.[27] The said resolution also asked the EUO to 'apply the Code in examining whether there is maladministration, so as to give effect to the citizens' right to good administration in Article 41 of the Charter of Fundamental Rights of the European Union.'[28] Subsequently, the EUO *de facto* promised 'to take into account the rules and principles contained in the Code in his inquiries into possible instances of maladministration in the activities of the Community institutions and bodies.'[29] Thus, the Code should have become an official list of the assessment standards of the EUO.

Nowadays, the Union does not have a *single legal document* that contains one code of good administrative conduct. Although several Union institutions adopted the EUO/EUP

20 Special Report from the EUO to the EUP following the own-initiative inquiry into the existence and the public accessibility, in the different Community institutions and bodies, of a Code of Good Administrative Behaviour (OI/1/98/OV), p. 2.
21 Annual Report of the EUO 2002, p. 19.
22 DR to the European institutions, bodies and agencies in the own-initiative inquiry OI/1/98/OV of 13 September 1999.
23 DR (OI/1/98/OV), recommendation 3.
24 At the time only the European Agency for the Evaluation of Medicinal Products and the Translation Centre for the Bodies of the European Union adopted a code of conduct based on the EUO's draft.
25 EUP Resolution on the EUO 's Special Report to the EUP following the own-initiative inquiry into the existence and the public accessibility, in the different Community institutions and bodies, of a Code of Good Administrative Behaviour (C5-0438/2000 – 2000/2212 (COS)).
26 Ibid., point 1.
27 Mendes 2009, p. 3.
28 EUP Resolution C5-0302/2001 – 2001/2043(COS), point 7.
29 Letter from the EUO (Söderman) to the President of the EUP (Cox) regarding the European Code of Good Administrative Behaviour of 11 March 2002 and Annual Report of the EUO 2002, p. 19.

Code[30] there are institutions that have adopted their own code of administrative conduct including the Commission[31] and the Council.[32]

The Code is constructed as a combination of the experiences of other Union institutions and the EUO's own experience while taking into account the principles of European administrative law contained in the case law of the Court and drawing inspiration from national laws.[33] It includes judicially *non-enforceable* rules and principles. When looking at the list of principles included in the Code one can here find a number of original ombudsman principles such as fairness, courtesy or the keeping of adequate records. It also includes a *non-binding* codification of principles that overlap with provisions of primary or secondary Union law and the case law. It includes principles that are designated by the EUO as principles connected with the law, human rights or good administration in a narrow sense. The diversity of the principles included in the Code has been confirmed by the EUO. He argues that in the Code one can find legal rights and principles, such as proportionality, the right to be heard and legitimate expectations. But also fairness, reasonableness, helpfulness and courtesy as they *form an essential part of a culture of service.*[34]

The Code includes the as principles Lawfulness (Art. 4), Absence of discrimination (Art. 5), Proportionality (Art. 6), Absence of abuse of power (Art. 7), Impartiality and independence (Art. 8), Objectivity (Art. 9), Legitimate expectations, consistency and advice (Art. 10), Fairness (Art. 11), Courtesy (Art. 12), Reply to letters in the language of the citizen (Art. 13), Acknowledgment of receipt and indication of the competent official (Art. 14), Obligation to transfer to the competent service of the Institution (Art. 15), Right to be heard and to make statements (Art. 16), Reasonable time-limit for taking decisions (Art. 17), Duty to state grounds of decisions (Art. 18), Indication of the possibilities of appeal (Art. 19), Notification of decision (Art. 20), Data protection (Art. 21), Requests for information (Art. 22), Request for public access to documents (Art. 23) and Keeping adequate records (Art. 24).[35]

During the interview with Prof. Diamandouros (the European Ombudsman 2005-2013) he noted:

30 The Code has also been adopted by the European Centre for the Development of Vocational Training (2011) and the European Training Foundation (2002). The Code of good administrative behaviour adopted by the European Investment Bank (2001) resembles that of the EUO. So do the codes of Community Plant Variety Office (2001), the European Foundation for the Improvement of Living and Working Conditions Decision (2000) and the European Environmental Agency (2000).

31 Code of Good Administrative Behaviour of the Commission, Official Journal of the European Communities: OJ L 267/63, 20 October 2000.

32 Code of Good administrative Behaviour for the General Secretariat of the Council of the European Union and its staff in their professional relations with the public, Official Journal of the European Communities: OJ C 189/1, 25 June 2001.

33 The Code, Introduction, 2005, p. 6.

34 Diamandouros 2011 a.

35 For individual articles of the Code see, Annex 3 d).

> 'The European Code of Good Administrative Behaviour is our major instrument. It is a standard for judging administrative behaviour. On the basis of the Code we issue critical remarks and elaborate other kinds of recommendations. But it is not the only instrument we use.'

Due to the existence of different codes of good conduct, the applicability of the Code as a *general* assessment standard by the EUO is questionable. Its potential educative function is diminished. Its applicability on a broader scale becomes rather ambiguous as, in practice, the EUO has to consider also the codes of good conduct of other institutions. Mr Grill, the Director of Directorate B and the Acting Head of Complaints and Inquiries Unit, Office of the EUO, noted:

> 'We [the EUO office] respect other institutions' codes and on occasions we use them. Normally, we check their codes as to whether they are consistent with ours. Then we might use their code as a standard and we can say that, for example, the Commission's code was not applied in this case. So in those cases where there is no difference you might find the references to the institution's code and to our own.'

Despite that, the actual application of the Code raises questions. It seems that an interest of the EUO in the Code, at least in connection with the decision making, dwindles with the passing of time. It is true that all posted draft recommendations and special reports of the EUO include a general description of the case *types of maladministration alleged* and these indeed include a reference to the Code.[36] This reference, however, is often the only reference to the Code. The text of the decision or the conclusions of the EUO only exceptionally refer back to the Code. Most of the EUO decisions lack a clear and explicit connection between a finding of maladministration and the Code as a list of assessment standards which the EUO agreed to apply. When the EUO discovers maladministration he only rarely refers to the Code concerning the *standard* that was *breached* by the action of the Union institution. Between 1 January 2005 and 31 July 2013 the EUO directly referred to the Code in only 36 of the 209 draft recommendations and in 1 out of 8 of the special reports. A clear statement of the *type of maladministration found and the principle breached* might enhance the clarity of the breached normative standard. A 'lack of interest' in the Code is also visible in the EUO's annual reports although today's practice of the EUO is more consistent with the Code than the one from before 2009.[37] Despite the questionable use of the Code by the EUO and by the Union institutions, some authors believe that all is not yet lost. According to Mendes the Code remains a valuable source to understand the meaning of good administration in EU law and to perceive possible future developments in this matter.[38]

36 Cf. DR of the EUO in his inquiry into complaint 1260/2010/RT against the Commission. It states *Types of maladministration alleged – (i) breach of, or (ii) breach of duties relating to: Duty to state the grounds of decisions and the possibilities of appeal [Arts. 18 and 19 ECGAB].*

37 Compare the schemes included in the Annual Reports 2008-2011. (Annual Report 2008, p. 44; Annual Report 2009, p. 42; Annual Report 2010, p. 27 and Annual Report 2011, p. 29).

38 Mendes 2009, p. 3.

5.1.2 General principles of Union law and the Court

General principles of Union law as discovered and further developed by the Court receive much more attention and respect than principles of good administrative conduct developed by the EOU. The Court has a unique opportunity of resorting in its judgments to general principles of law which are not contained in the Treaties. General principles of law express constitutional standards underlying the Union's legal order and recourse to them is an integral part of the Court's methodology.[39] The Court, as an administrative court, *reviews the legality* of the acts of Union institutions. The general principles of law are then, apart from written Union law, used as standards for this particular goal.

Although the Court has not developed a comprehensive list of these principles, they are a popular theme for academics and scholars who try to fill this missing gap. As noted in Chapter 2, only those principles with the character of a procedural guarantee are described in this part. These principles *de facto* bring a balance between two unequal subjects – a Union institution and an individual (a natural or legal person).

The general principles of law with a guarantee character include *inter alia*:

1. *The principle of legal certainty*[40] that requires the administration to respect acquired rights. It includes the *principle of non-retroactivity*[41] which imposes limits on the retroactive effect of regulations and the withdrawal of decisions.
2. *The principle of legitimate expectations*[42] requires that the Union institutions fulfil the legitimate or justified expectations which they have created.[43]
3. *The principle of proportionality*[44] means that the adverse consequences of a certain measure for one or more interested individuals may not be disproportionate in relation to the purposes and objectives served by that measure.[45]
4. *The principle of equality*[46] (or the *principle non-discrimination*)[47] requires that equal cases must be treated equally and unequal cases unequally.[48]
5. *The rights of defence*[49] are a broad umbrella principle that includes several mostly procedural sub-principles.[50] In accordance with Art. 41 Charter this principle includes the right to be heard,[51] the right to be informed about the facts of which the individual

39 Tridimas 2007, p. 33.

40 See, Joined cases 42 and 49/59 *SNUPAT v High Authority* [1961] ECR 109.

41 See, Case C-60/02 *Rolex* [2004] ECR I-651.

42 See, Case 81/72 Commission v Council [1973], ECR 575, Case 112/77 *Topfer* [1978] ECR 1019, Joined cases 2005 to 2015/82 *Deutsche Milchkontor* [1983] ECR 2623 etc.

43 Tridimas 2007, p. 252.

44 See, Case 11/70 *Internationale Handellsgezelschaft* [1970] ECR 1125.

45 Cf. Jans et al. 2011.

46 See, Case 71/85 *Netherlands v Federatie Nederlandse Vakbeweging* (FNV) [1986] ECR 3855or Joined cases 75/82 and 117/82 *Razzouk and Beydoun* [1984] ECR 1509.

47 See, Case C-13/94 *P v. S* [1996] ECR I-2143 (sex discrimination), Case 147/79 *Hochstrass* [1980] ECR 3005 (nationality discrimination), Case C-280/93 *Germany v. Council* [1994] ECR I-4973 (discrimination in the area of agriculture) etc.

48 Compare Tridimas 20076 or Jans et al. 2011.

49 See, Case 17/74 *Transocean Marine Paint Association* [1974], ECR 1063, Case 85/76 *Hoffmann-La Roche* [1979] ECR 461.

50 Compare, Tridimas, 2007.

51 See, Case C-349/07 *Sopropé* [2009] ECR I-10369.

is accused, the right to have access to the file, protection against self-incrimination,[52] the right to legal assistance and the right to legal privilege.[53]

6. *The reasonableness of the time for a decision*[54] is included in Arts. 41 and 47 Charter. The reasonableness of the time for the administrative decision depends on the individual circumstances of each particular case, its context and complexity.[55]
7. *The principle of transparency*[56] as a relatively new principle requires openness by the administration and is concerned with the availability, accessibility and clarity of information offered by the administrative authority.[57]
8. *The fundamental principles* guaranteed by the ECHR and those that stem from the constitutional traditions common to the Member States have nowadays the character of general principles of law.[58] The fundamental rights are also included in the Charter.
9. *Impartial and fair handling of individual affairs* by the Union institutions is included in Arts. 41 and 47 Charter. The Union administration should act in an unbiased manner and it should avoid conflicts of interests. This should include subjective as well as objective impartiality.[59]

General principles of Union law, such as the reasonableness of the time for a decision, the impartial and fair handling of individual affairs, the principle of proportionality or the rights of defence are sometimes included in a general *principle of good administration* that has been developed in the case law of the Court.[60] It is questionable whether this legal principle can be characterised as a 'general principle of Union law'.[61] Nonetheless, both the *principle of good administration* as found in the case law of the Court and the *right to good administration* as codified in Art. 41 of the Charter are devised in a broad way and one can presume that their development will continue.[62]

As one can write a whole book about each of the above-mentioned principles, the following description only points to their general characteristics. The description is by no means exhaustive. The general principles of law are developed in individual cases and they are subsequently applied in a general way to future similar cases. They are characterised by their open-endedness.[63] This quality enables their repeated use in comparable situations. The general principles of law often set a minimum standard of administrative

52 See, Case 374/87 *Orkem* [1989] ECR 3283.
53 See, Case C-550/07 P *Akzo & Akcros* [2010] ECR I-8301.
54 Tridimas includes this principle under the guise of the rights of defence as a part of the right to good administration. According to him this duty of the Union administration derives from the principle of legal certainty. Tridimas 2007, pp. 410-415.
55 See, Case T-190/00 *Regione Siciliana* [2003] ECR II-5015 and Tridimas 2007, p. 412.
56 See, Case C-231/03 *Coname* [2005] ECR I-7287. See, also Buijze 2013.
57 Cf, Jans at al. 2011.
58 Art. 6 (3) TEU.
59 Case C-439/11 P *Ziegler SA v European Commission* (not yet published) judgment, para. 131.
60 See, Kristjánsdóttir 2013, Nehl 2009 or Statskantoret, 2005, p. 12 – 13. See, also, for instance, C-282/95 P *Guérin automobiles v Commission* [1997] ECR I-1503 (reasonable time), C-501/00 *Spain v Commission* [2004] ECR I-6717 (duty to state reasons) or C-428/05 *Laub* [2007] ECR I-5069 (the possibility of completing the documents relating to the payment of the refund after the expiry of the relevant periods).
61 See, Groussot 2006 or Tridimas 2007.
62 See, for example, Nehl 2009, pp. 322-336.
63 Jans et al. 2007, p. 115.

behaviour and are used as standards against which the Court reviews the actions of the administration.[64] An action that is contrary to general principles of law is always unlawful and is contrary to Union law. They are partially codified in several documents including the TFEU, TEU, Charter and a number of provisions of secondary law.[65] In spite of their codification, general principles of law still retain the character of binding law.[66] They exist as unwritten principles in the case law and can be further developed. Some of the principles (for instance, the principle of legitimate expectations) have not (yet) been codified and exist only in the case law.

The general principles of law are often based on constitutional traditions common to the Member States but also on some principles of international law. Some of them can be linked with the case law of the European Court of Human Rights. As it can be difficult to find a legal principle that exists for *all* the Member States the Court looks for a common legal notion. For this goal it often investigates the existing principles of all or only some of the Member States.[67] This means that some general principles of law may not be recognised as *legal principles in the national law* of all Member States.

The Court is the only Union institution which develops these principles. This enables it to embark on a constant and uniform revision and development of these principles. If it is necessary to broaden the application of a certain principle, the Court can do this. This possibility of the Court to influence the applicability of the principles is a stable element in their continuous development. When discovered by the Court the principles gain the status of unwritten law. This allows a transformation of an extra-legal standard into a legal one.[68] The general principles of law do not only apply to the Union institutions but also to the Member States, at least when they act within the scope of Union law.[69]

5.1.3 The European Charter of Fundamental Rights

Apart from a legally non-binding Code and legally binding general principles of law it is necessary to point to *the Charter*. The catalogue of human or fundamental rights was included in primary Union law in 2009. Art. 6 TFEU nowadays notes that the Union recognises the rights, freedoms and principles set out in the Charter which shall have the same legal value as the Treaties. Until its inclusion among the sources of primary Union law the Charter had a dubious legal status. It existed as a *solemn proclamation* by the Commission, the EUP and the Council.[70] Also the Court occasionally questioned its

64 Ibid.

65 For example, the principle of proportionality is partially codified in Art. 5 (4) TEU or the principle of non-discrimination can be found also in Council Directive 2000/43/EC of 29 June 2000 implementing the principle of equal treatment between persons irrespective of racial or ethnic origin.

66 Cf. Jans et al. 2011 or Tridimas 2007.

67 *Algera* Judgment part – The revocability of administrative measures giving rise to individual rights, p. 55.

68 For a discussion on the 'judicial discovery' of the general principles of law, see, Widdershoven & Remac 2012.

69 This happens, for example, when the Member States implement the provisions of Union law or invoke a permitted derogation therefrom (for example, free movement rights).

70 See the text of the Charter as published on 18 December 2000 in the Official Journal of the European Communities, (C 364/01).

binding character.[71] Nowadays, it functions as a 'road map' and identifier of EU rights.[72] Partially, it contains rights that correspond with the rights guaranteed by the ECHR and it is mainly addressed to the institutions and bodies of the Union.[73]

In connection with the EUO, the Charter is interesting at least from two perspectives. Firstly, it includes Art. 41 that codifies *the right to good administration,* and, secondly, Art. 43 that reaffirms *the right to complain with the European Ombudsman.*

Art. 41 of the Charter is the first ever codified expression of individuals' *'right' to good administration.*[74] The *right to good administration* was included in the Charter also because of the explicit and open insistence of the EUO.[75] After the Lisbon Treaty, this article moved good administration from *a non-binding normative concept* to *an expressly recognised fundamental right.* Its status as an independent right with the aim of providing guarantees for individuals during administrative procedures suggests that it was meant to have a substantive meaning.[76] Its purpose is to provide guarantees for individuals during administrative procedures.[77] The right to good administration included in the Charter is only a *partial* codification of what the Court had already discovered in its case law. The right to good administration as included in the Charter is an umbrella right that includes various, mainly *procedural rights* including the *right to have affairs handled impartially, fairly* and *within a reasonable time* by the institutions, bodies, offices and agencies of the Union or *the right to be heard.* It is a non-exhaustive enumeration of basic principles of good administration.[78] As a partial codification of the Court's case law, Art. 41 includes also the rights that were not explicitly included in the Court's jurisprudence.[79] This includes, for example, the *right to have affairs handled fairly by the Union institutions.* This right, included in the nowadays legally binding Charter, broadens the possibilities of individuals to have their interests protected. It also broadens the duties of the Court. Today, the Court has to assess the compliance of the actions of the Union institutions with a new legal standard that requires a further legally binding interpretation.[80] The *fairness of administrative actions* is an open-ended principle and covers procedural as well as substantive matters. It will be interesting to see how the Court will deal with this issue if it will be expressly raised by the applicant during proceedings. Potentially, the practice of the EUO in assessing the fairness of the administrative conduct might help.[81] That, however, depends on the decision of the Court.

71 See, for example, Joined cases T-377/00, T-379/00, T-380/00, T-260/01 and T-272/01 *Philip Morris International v Commission* [2003] ECR II-0001, judgment, para. 122.

72 Douglas-Scott 2011, p. 649.

73 It is also addressed to Member States *when they are implementing Union law* (Art. 51(1)). See also, Morano-Foadi & Andreadakis 2011, p. 596.

74 Söderman 2004, p. 114.

75 Söderman 2000. See, also Mendes 2009.

76 Kristjánsdóttir 2013, p. 252.

77 Ibid., p. 247.

78 Cf. Addink 2005, p. 25, Mendes 2009, p. 3 or Söderman, p. 114.

79 See, Kańska 2004 or Mendes 2009.

80 In Joined Cases T458/09 and T171/10 *Slovak Telekom a.s. v European Commission* (not yet published), the EUGC connected the right to have affairs handled impartially, fairly and within a reasonable time with *the duty of the competent institution to examine carefully and impartially all the relevant aspects of the individual case* (para. 68).

81 See, for example, Draft recommendation of the EUO to the Commission in complaint 1617/2005/(BB)JF, Draft recommendation of the EUO to the Commission in complaint 2437/2004/GG or Draft

Although both the Code and the Charter were created during a similar period of time and although the EUO actively promoted the inclusion of Art. 41 in the Charter, both documents clearly have a different legal character.[82] The Charter has the status of primary Union law, while the Code remains on the level of a non-binding document. The EUO sees breaches of the rights contained in Art. 41 of the Charter as *prima facie* evidence of maladministration.[83] This is also underlined by the argument that the Code states what the Charter's right to good administration should mean in practice.[84] Prof. Diamandouros (the European Ombudsman 2005-2013) during the interview confirmed that the application of the Charter supports the Code:

> 'There is a strengthening of the Code as we proceed with the Charter, because the Charter essentially invokes rights that are legally binding. It also includes some rights included in the Code, so I believe that the development is a reinforcement rather than a diminution of the Code.'

5.2 Formal normative coordination and the similarity between normative standards?

The following subchapter discusses two different issues. After pointing to the limited existence of a *formal coordination* between the normative standards developed and used by the Court and those of the EUO it points to a *formal* and *substantive similarity* between these normative standards.

5.2.1 Formal coordination between the normative standards of the Court and of the European Ombudsman

Is there any *formal* normative coordination between the Court and of the EUO? *Primary Union law* is fairly limited in this connection. As previously discussed, the TFEU establishes a general framework for these two institutions without going into the details of this particular relation. The TUE only confirms the existence of general principles of law. In accordance with Art. 6 (3) TEU these principles include *fundamental rights*, as guaranteed by the ECHR and as they result from the constitutional traditions common to the Member States. The Court's power to ad hoc 'discover' legal principles is confirmed by years of undisputed practice by the Court and the application of these normative standards by the Union institutions and by the Member States. According to Art. 19 TEU, the Court ensures that the law is observed in the application and interpretation of the Treaties. The term *'law'* in this case also includes general principles of law.[85] The normative standards of the EUO are not expressly noted in primary Union law. It only acknowledges maladministration as its normative concept. However, the general character of this

recommendation of the EUO to the Commission in own-initiative inquiry OI/3/2007/GG.

82 Söderman 2004, p. 144.

83 Chalmers et al. 2006, p. 440.

84 The European Code of Good Administrative Behaviour, Foreword, 2013, p. 2.

85 See, Joined cases C-46/93 and C-48/93 *Brasserie du pêcheur v Bundesrepublik Deutschland and The Queen/ Secretary of State for Transport, ex parte Factortame and Others* [1996] ECR I-1029, judgment, para. 27.

concept implies a discovery of the normative standards by the EUO. Nowadays, there is an undisputed practice of the EUO developing the principles of the good administrative conduct of the Union institutions. The research shows that primary Union law does not include any specific provision that would coordinate these normative standards in any way. It does not say anything about the mutual application of these normative standards by the EUO and the Court.

Secondary Union law does not say much either. Although the provisions of the Statute and the Implementing decision are broader than the provisions of primary law, they are silent about the normative function of the EUO or the character of his normative standards. Secondary Union law does not deal with the relation between the different normative standards of the EUO and the Court or their mutual applicability or importance.

In the *Court's jurisprudence* one can discover a handful of decisions that at least partially set some rules for this specific relationship. An example can be found in the already mentioned Order of the President of the CFI in the Case *Tillack v Commission*.

> The President of the CFI in this case *inter alia* noted that 'it is sufficient to state that the mere fact that in 2003 the European Ombudsman found an 'instance of maladministration' does not for all that mean that the principle of good administration as interpreted by the Community judicature has been infringed here.'[86]

This remark clearly shows a distinction between a breach of the *principle of good of administration* as developed by the Court and the *finding of an instance of maladministration* by the EUO. The EUO's finding of maladministration does not directly lead to a breach of the legal principle of good administration as *these principles are not identical*. In the Order in the Case *Gorostiaga Atxalandabaso v EUP* the CFI explained the character of a breach of *the Code*.

> It noted that 'the [Code] is only a resolution of the EUP amending a draft which had been submitted to it by the European Ombudsman and calling on the Commission to submit a legislative proposal in that respect on the basis of Article 308 EC. Therefore, regardless of whether a provision such as that [in Article 20 of the Code] also refers to decisions other than those having adverse effect, it must be made clear that it is not a legal provision.'[87]

Although the Charter now has a different legal authority and although the Code, in the EUO's words, *tells citizens what the right to good administration, contained in Article 41 of the Charter, means in practice*,[88] the Court did not amend its opinion about the binding or persuasive authority of the Code. The latest case law of the Court follows the same line of thinking as noted in the previous case. In Case *PC-Ware Information Technologies v Commission* the EUGC rejected the argument of the applicant that the Commission had breached its legal obligations due to a breach of the Code.

86 Case T193/04 R *Tillack v Commission*, order, para. 60.

87 Case T-132/06 *Gorostiaga Atxalandabaso v Parliament* [2007] ECR II-0035, order, para. 73.

88 *The European Code of Good Administrative Behaviour*, Introduction, Publication Office, 2013, p. 2.

> Since 'the code of good behaviour is not a legal provision but a resolution of the EUP amending a draft which had been submitted to it by the European Ombudsman and calling on the Commission to submit a legislative proposal in that respect. Therefore, that code is not a measure binding on the Commission and the applicant cannot claim any rights on the basis of it.'[89]

Apart from these decisions, the Court has not expressed its opinion on this particular issue. Based on the previous paragraphs one can conclude that written law Union law and the Court's jurisprudence provide only a limited formal normative coordination between the Court and the EUO.

5.2.2 Similarity between the normative standards

Although there is almost no formal normative coordination of the EUO and the Court, one can find several similarities between their normative standards. One can here discover *formal similarity between the normative standards* as well as *substantive similarity.*

A *formal similarity* between these principles is obvious. First of all, the Code is clearly reminiscent of a statutory act. It has been drafted in a way which can evoke that officials have a certain binding obligation to do something or to act in a certain way. According to the Code officials *shall* act in certain way. The obligation in the Code is not softened by terms such as *should* or *could*. The provision that officials *shall* act is reminiscent of a legal obligation. Some of the principles included in the Code are also laid down as *rights* or *duties* such as the right to be heard or the duty to state the grounds for a decision which can add to the ambiguity of their character.

When looking at the denomination of the principles included in the Code one can also see that some of them have the same name as in the general principles of law. These principles include the principle of proportionality, the absence of discrimination or the duty to state the grounds for a decision. Still, most of the principles do not share this formal similarity. But because of the way in which they were adopted, they might be mistaken for the law. A formal similarity between these normative standards is an indicator of a possible interconnection between these normative standards.

A *substantial similarity* is connected with the content and substance of the researched normative standards. Looking into the content of the principles included in the Code one can see that some of them, at their core, protect the same value as general principles of law. However, the character of these standards is different. So is the way in which this value is protected. Because of that, some values are protected in a 'double way' – by the EUO and by the Court. The normative standards protecting the same value are substantially similar. One can here develop a scheme that points to a substantial overlap between some of the principles included in the Code and in the general principles of law.

89 Case T-121/08 *PC-Ware Information Technologies v Commission* [2010] ECR II-1541, para. 90

Scheme 3 – **Principles of the Code, the general principles of Union law and standards included in written Union law – a substantial overlap**

	Principles included in the Code	**General principles of Union law / Written Union law**	**Value protected**
	Example*	Example**	Overlap identified
1.	**- Lawfulness (Art. 4) - Absence of abuse of power (Art. 7)**	**- Lawfulness as a general principle of law - Art. 19 (1) TEU - Art. 263 (1) TFEU**	Compliance with the law (including human rights), legal certainty
	Draft recommendation concerning complaint 2826/2004/PB, Decision concerning complaint 696/2008/(WP)OV	C-1/94 *Cavarzere Produzioni Industriali and Others v Ministero dell'Agricoltura e delle Foreste and Others* [1995] ECR I-2363.	A disregard of the law and legal obligations can lead to unlawfulness as well as maladministration. So can an abuse of powers.
2.	**- Absence of discrimination (Art. 5)**	**- Non-discrimination - Art. 3(3) TEU - Art. 18, 45 (2), 49, 157 TFEU - Art. 20, 21 Charter - Norms of secondary law**	Non-discrimination in administrative actions
	Draft recommendation concerning complaints 2986/2008/MF and 2987/2008/MF	Case C-29/95 *Eckehard Pastoors and Trans-Cap GmbH v Belgian State* [1997] ECR I-285.	Unjustified discrimination can lead both to maladministration and to unlawfulness.
3.	**- Proportionality (Art. 6)**	**- Principle of proportionality - Art. 5 (4) TEU - Art. 49, 52 Charter**	Balance between the aims and means of administrative actions.
	Draft recommendation concerning complaint 640/2011/AN	Case C-210/10 *Urbán* (not yet published).	Disproportionate administrative actions can to lead to maladministration and to unlawfulness.
4.	**- Legitimate expectations, consistency and advice (Art. 10)**	**- Legitimate expectations**	Trust in legitimate administrative promises
	Draft recommendation concerning complaint 3031/2007/(BEH) VL	Case 112/77 *Töpfer v Commission*, ECR [1978] 1019.	Not keeping to legitimate promises can lead to unlawfulness and maladministration.
5.	**- Right to be heard and to make statements (Art. 16)**	**- Right to be heard - Art. 41 Charter**	Fair procedural opportunities for the parties
	Draft recommendation concerning complaint 3800/2006/JF	Case C-349/07 *Sopropé* [2009] ECR I-10369; Case F-51/07 *Phillippe Bui Van v Commission* [2008] FP-I-A-1-0289.	Not giving an opportunity for an individual to submit comments before a decision is taken can lead to unlawfulness and to maladministration.

6.	**- Impartiality and independence (Art. 8)** **- Fairness (Art. 11)**	**- Rule against bias** **- Art. 41(1),(2) Charter**	Impartiality of the administration
	Draft recommendation concerning complaint 642/2008/TS	Joined cases C-341/06 P and C-342/06 P *Chronopost SA and La Poste v Union française de l'express (UFEX) and Others*, [2008] ECR 1-4777or T-195/05 *Deloitte Business Advisory NV v Commission* [2007] ECR II-187.	Partiality on the part of the administration can lead to maladministration and to unlawfulness.
7.	**- Reasonable time-limit for taking decisions (Art. 17)**	**- Art. 41Charter** **- Reasonableness of time for decision**	Reasonable speed of administrative actions
	Draft recommendations concerning complaint 862/2011/AN	T-59/05 *Evropaïki Dynamiki v Commission* [2008] ECR II-157 or Case T-394/03 *Angeletti v Commission* FP-I-A-2-00095.	Unreasonable speed by the administration can lead to maladministration and to unlawfulness.
8.	**- Duty to state grounds of decisions (Art. 18)**	**- Duty to state reasons** **- Art. 41(1), (2) Charter** **- Art. 296 TFEU** **- Norms of secondary law**	Knowledge of the content of the administrative decisions and their conclusions
	Draft recommendation concerning complaint 1450/2007/(WP)BEH	Case 24/62 *Germany v Commission (BrennWein)*, [1963] ECR, 63, Joined cases T-439/10 and T-440/10 *Fulmen v Council* (not yet published).	Lack of reasons for an administrative decision can lead to maladministration and unlawfulness.
9.	**- Request for information (Art. 22)** **- Request for public access to documents (Art. 23)** **- Keeping of adequate records (Art. 24)**	**- Transparency** **- Art. 41 (2) Charter**	Clarity of administrative actions
	Draft recommendations concerning complaint 1947/2010/PB	Case C-231/03 *Coname* [2005] ECR I-7287.	Unclear administrative actions can lead to maladministration and to unlawfulness.
10.	**- Reply to letters in the language of the citizen (Art.13)**	**- Art. 41(4) Charter**	Comprehensibility of administrative decisions
	Draft recommendation concerning complaint 2293/2007/(ID)PB	Case T-148/89 *Trefilunion SA v Commission* [1995] ECR II-1063 or Case T-120/99 *Kik v OHIM* [2001] ECR II-2235.	Not replying in the language of the applicant can lead to maladministration and to unlawfulness.

* These examples can include cases where the finding of maladministration is based on a combination of several acts of malpractice and not only on a breach of one particular principle.
** Examples included here refer to cases where the said principle was applied or developed by the Court.

Based on the scheme and on a comparison of the content of the principles included in the Code and the general principles of law one can find two main groups of normative standards developed and used by these institutions, the *normative standards of the EUO and the Court that overlap* and *standards that do not*.

The existence of *substantively overlapping standards* practically confirms that the EUO and the Court protect the same general values. They do this in their own way of offering protection and by assessing the actions of the Union institutions against the standards with a different character. The scheme shows that if we take the Code as the most important assessment tool of the EUO we can identify at least 10 standards of good administrative practice that directly, fully or partially overlap with the general principles of law. These principles included in the Code reflect or are reflected in the general principles of law. *Hence, the EUO de facto becomes a reviewer of the lawfulness of administrative actions, but only to the extent of an overlap between these normative standards and only within the limits of his competence to reveal instances of maladministration in the actions of Union institutions.* That, however, does not make his principles legally binding, it merely underlines the fact that a value can be protected by the Court and by the EUO. This does not mean, however, that they can be protected at the same time.[90]

The principles included in the Code are sufficiently clear. Because of that an overlap can be identified. They usually overlap only with one particular general principle of law. The only exception is the requirements that can be connected with *transparency.* Transparency as a legal principle is rather broad and 'recent'. From scheme 3 it seems that under this principle there are overlaps with four different principles of good administration or the EUO which are in this case more concrete.[91] The principles included in the Code sometimes *overlap* with the normative standards that are included in written Union law. As it is the Court that primarily assesses compliance with written Union law (whether general principles of law or not) the overlap shows that the EUO and the Court once again protect the same general values though in a different way and manner. This overlap does not lead to a change in the character of the EUO's principles.

The *non-overlapping normative standards* include only the ombudsman principles of the EUO. From the previous scheme one can note that not all of the normative standards of the EUO that are included in the Code reflect the general principles of law. There are cases of standards of administrative conduct that can be characterised as *exclusively ombudsman principles.* These standards protect values that are not in any way protected by written or unwritten law and thus they are not protected by the Court. They include principles of administrative conduct such as courtesy, keeping adequate records or the helpfulness of the administration. In these cases, the value behind the normative standards is only protected by the EUO.

90 See, section 3.1.1.

91 Buijze claims that transparency is already a general principle of Union law. See, Buijze 2013.

5.3 Normative standards in practice

The EUO and the Court in their practice apply various normative standards. When they evaluate administrative conduct these standards have the character of *assessment standards* against which they evaluate the conduct.

The EUO has on several occasions underlined that his work is connected with situations that require a *legal assessment* of a situation but also an assessment of a situation *beyond legality*.[92] According to the EUO, an exclusive focus on legality is not sufficient in order to establish and sustain a culture of service so that the Union administration *inter alia* acts openly, fairly, reasonably, carefully and consistently or acknowledges mistakes and offers apologies where appropriate and aims for a continuous improvement in performance. In that respect there needs to be room for *life beyond legality*.[93] Hence apart from a consideration and assessment of the legal aspects of the case, non-legal aspects should be assessed as well. This division was also mentioned during the interview with Prof. Diamandouros (the European Ombudsman 2005-2013) who noted that:

> 'In the contemporary world, a full and a well-functioning ombudsman institution, and certainly in the European legal order, needs to operate at 3 different levels which provide for assessment criteria. Clearly, the first one is the law. The second one is good administration and the third is fundamental rights. So we provide for three distinctive bodies of rules because the Ombudsman has, as you can see, a privileged area that is maladministration. Maladministration is today very strongly complemented by fundamental rights, because as you know the Charter is now legally binding.'

The Court is primarily connected with an assessment of compliance with legal requirements, whether procedural or substantive, including fundamental rights. This point was also confirmed by the interviews with the judges of the Court. For example, Mr Barents (a judge at the EUCST) pointed to the fact that the legality control is the only standard used by the Court when acting as an administrative court. He noted that:

> '[The Court's] standard is legality control which means that either there is a specific legal rule that has been violated or if it concerns an action that is based on the discretionary power then we apply what is called marginal control, i.e. is there a serious error of judgment. We can put it in football terminology. During the game you have the linesmen who look whether the ball is either in or out of play. If it is in then it is ok. If it is out then it is no good. We also look at whether the action is inside the law.'

It is questionable whether the Court actually uses principles that are not directly connected with the law.

The following pages look at the application of written Union law (including fundamental rights), general principles of law and normative standards of the EUO as the potential assessment standards of the EUO and the Court. The following sections try to

92 Diamandouros 2006.
93 Diamandouros 2007b.

explain whether the EUO and the Court use the same normative standards in a similar fashion or whether there is a different applicability of the normative standards.

5.3.1 Statutory law including human rights as the normative standard

The Union institutions must follow the provisions of primary or secondary Union law. A breach of substantive or procedural requirements included in written Union law if found by the Court leads to unlawfulness and if found by the EUO leads to maladministration. As it is the Court that assesses compliance with the law and the EUO who assesses compliance with the requirements of good administration (that also includes compliance with the law), one must see that written Union law plays a considerable role in their practice.

In accordance with the Treaties the Court assesses whether in the implementation and application of the Treaties the law has been observed. It is responsible for the assessment of compliance with the law during the implementation and application of primary Union law. At the same time it has an immense power to say what the law is. The term 'law' is interpreted by the Court extensively and it includes also uncodified legal principles. The Court is obliged to use legal provisions as normative standards. As the Court is the only Union institution that can authoritatively assess the compliance of the actions of Union institutions with Union law and declare them unlawful, it is not necessary to discuss the application of written Union law as a normative standard of the Court in any special way. In connection with the EUO this can however be different.

Already in his Annual Report 1997 the EUO stated that 'the ombudsman's first and most essential task must be to establish whether it has acted lawfully.'[94] Similarly Prof. Diamandouros (the European Ombudsman 2005-2013) confirmed during the interview that the legal principles play an important role in the practice of the EUO. He noted that:

> 'You start with the law and you go beyond it. It is an absolutely necessary but not a sufficient condition. You cannot do without the law but if you stay only within the law you are giving up the very reason for being an ombudsman. But if you forget the law and say that I will deal only with the other issues, then obviously you are undermining yourself. So you have to take the law as the minimum condition and build upon it, by integrating principles of good administration and fundamental rights into your work.'

Although the Code tries to describe what is traditionally perceived as principles of good administration, it does not overlook the issue of legality. It is an example of how the Ombudsman can foster high standards of behaviour in the EU civil service through a non-legally binding text.[95] Acting according to the law and the application of rules and procedures laid down in Union legislation are expressly included in the Code (Art. 4). Acting in a way which contradicts Union law and its legal principles thus *constitutes an instance of maladministration*. The EUO does not deny the application of Union law and legal principles.[96] This confirms an interest of the EUO in the assessment of the compliance

94 Annual Report of the EUO 1997, p. 24.
95 Diamandouros 2011b.
96 Ibid.

of administrative conduct with the legal requirements but from the perspective of compliance with good administration principles. One can find several decisions where the EUO has found an instance of maladministration because the actions of the Union institution were not in compliance with the law. These actions led to a breach of the Code. A case where a breach of Union law led to a breach of normative standards (and to maladministration) can be found in *Draft recommendations of the EUO in his inquiry into complaint 2482/2009/ (BU)KM against the Commission.*

> The EUO had to deal with a complaint against the wrongly refused reimbursement of a Commission employee's expenses. During the investigation the EUO found that the Commission had not acted in compliance with the *General implementing provisions adopting the Guide to missions for officials and other servants of the European Commission*, C(2004) 1313. Although the EUO did not expressly state that this led to maladministration in his draft recommendation, he did state that 'the Commission should pay interest on the mission expenses which it *unlawfully* recovered from the complainant.'[97]

An almost identical decision by the EUO can also be found in *Draft recommendation of the EUO in his inquiry into complaint 2749/2009/KM against the Commission.* Another example can be found in *Draft recommendation of the EUO in his inquiry into complaint 856/2008/BEH against the European Anti-Fraud Office (OLAF)* where the EUO expressly pointed to unlawful conduct by OLAF that led to maladministration.

> The complainant *inter alia* argued that by delegating powers to open and closed investigations to the Director in charge of investigations and operations, who is not the "Director of the Office" within the meaning of the Regulation, OLAF failed to comply with Regulation 1073/1999. During the inquiry the EUO found that this practice by OLAF did not comply with the said regulation. Because of that the EUO concluded that 'OLAF did not establish that its practice of delegating the power to open and closed decisions from the Director-General to the Director in charge of investigations and operations is *in accordance with the law*.'[98] This constituted an instance of maladministration. Still, during the inquiry the EUO confirmed that the Court alone can authoritatively interpret EU law.[99]

Cases where the EUO points to a breach of Union law can also be found in other decisions.[100] From these examples, one can conclude that the law as a normative standard has its place in the practice of the EUO. A breach of the law in this practice leads to maladministration. The EUO in this connection does not try to surpass the work of the Court. This is connected with the fact that he cannot authoritatively say that there has

97 DRs of the EUO in his inquiry into complaint 2482/2009/(BU)KM against the Commission.

98 DR of the EUO in his inquiry into complaint 856/2008/BEH against the European Anti-Fraud Office (OLAF), para. 104.

99 Ibid., 49.

100 See, Decision closing the inquiry into complaint 920/2010/VIK against the Commission, DR of the EUO in his inquiry into complaint 3307/2006/(PB)JMA against the Commission or DR of the EUO in his inquiry into complaint 882/2009/VL against the Commission.

been a *breach of the law leading to illegality*. Still, he can say that there has been a *breach of the law leading to an instance of maladministration*.

Apart from the law, *human rights* are also approached as normative standards. As the European Communities were originally created only as an organisation to liberate the market there was not much space for human rights. This changed after the Court started with the development of fundamental rights in the Communities.[101] In several judgments it confirmed that fundamental rights form an integral part of the general principles of law whose observance it ensures.[102] It also acknowledged a whole series of fundamental rights as fundamental Union rights.[103] In the pre-Lisbon era the Court discovered as general principles of law, for example, the principle of human dignity (and integrity),[104] the freedom of expression,[105] the right to religious freedom[106] or the principle of the non-retroactivity of penal provisions.[107] Still, the human rights protection in the EU was not very clear as the fundamental rights of individuals were mainly based on the Court's jurisprudence. However, the changes included in the Lisbon Treaty considerably influenced the perception of fundamental rights in the EU.[108] Nowadays fundamental rights in the EU have the character of *written law* or *general principles of Union law*.[109] As they are part of the law any breach leads to unlawfulness. The Court has noted this in various decisions.[110]

Human rights play a role in connection with the practice of the EUO. The EUO's perception of 'life beyond legality' goes very much hand in hand with a firm commitment to the centrality of human rights as the source of political value.[111] Although the EUO does not put himself in the shoes of the ombudsmen who deal *predominantly* with human rights issues, he accepts that most of the ombudsmen in Europe could identify themselves also with an issue of human rights.[112] The character of maladministration in an Union sense and his discretion open the EUO doors to the use of human rights as an assessment normative standard. The EUO considers the Charter to be an important standard that he takes into account when looking for instances of maladministration. A breach of the Charter constitutes in the practice of the EUO an instance of maladministration as it is

101 See, Case C-29/69 *Stauder v Stadt Ulm* [1969] ECR 419.

102 See, Case C-299/95 *Friedrich Kriemzow v. Austrian State* [1997] ECR I-2629, para. 14.

103 Jans et al.2007, p. 120.

104 See, Case C-36/02 *Omega* [2004] ECR I-9609, Case C-377/98 *Netherlands v. Parliament and Council*, [2001] ECR I-7079 etc.

105 See, Case C-288/89 *Collectieve Antennevoorziening Gouda* [1991] ECR I4007, para. 23; Case C-148/91 *Veronica Omroep Organisatie* [1993] ECR I487, para. 10; and *TV10*, para. 19 etc.

106 See, Case C-130/75 *Prais v Council* [1976] ECR-1589.

107 See, Case 63/83 *Kirk* [1984] ECR 2689, paras. 21 and 22; Case C-331/88 *Fedesa and Others* [1990] ECR I4023, para. 44; and Joined Cases C387/02, C391/02 and C403/02 *Berlusconi and Others* [2005] ECR I3565, paras. 74-78.

108 See, Craig 2010, pp. 199-200.

109 Art.6 (3) TEU.

110 See, for example, Case T-590/10 *Thesing and Bloomberg Finance v ECB* (not yet published) or Case T-496/10 *Bank Mellat v Council and Commission* (not yet published).

111 Abraham 2008b, p. 687.

112 Diamandouros 2007b.

necessarily *a failure of a pubic body to act in accordance with a rule or principle which is binding upon it.*[113] Thus, human rights can be one of the normative standards of the EUO.

The application of human rights as normative standards of the EUO can be found in several of his decisions. For example, the principle of non-discrimination was raised in *Draft recommendation of the EUO in his inquiries into complaints 2986/2008/MF and 2987/2008/MF against the EUP.*

> The EUO here dealt with a complaint where the complainants argued that due to the change of the practice by the EUP they were discriminated against. During the inquiry the EUO discovered that this practice was *inter alia* not in compliance with the principle of non-discrimination. He highlighted that the EUP's Practice gives its officials a clear financial advantage over officials of every other institution.[114] The EUO summarised that EUP's Practice inter alia is 'leading to the unfair financial treatment of its officials, depending on the dates of their respective promotions.'[115] This led to the conclusion that the practice of the EUP was in breach of Art. 5 of the Code (the absence of discrimination) and to maladministration.

Another example of this practice can be found in *Draft recommendation of the EUO in his own-initiative inquiry OI/4/2009/PB concerning the Commission.*

> This particular inquiry concerned the protection of the rights of defence. The EUO during the inquiry reiterated the character of the rights of defence as included in the Charter (Art. 41 (2)) and in the case law of the Court (Case F-51/07 *Phillippe Bui Van v Commission*). After the inquiry and without an express confirmation of the instance of maladministration he recommended 'the Commission to ensure that its services *fully respect the fundamental right to be heard*' in relation to recovery measures that they adopt against present or former staff. The Commission should lay down a general rule to the effect that, unless exceptional circumstances require otherwise, the relevant service must grant the individual concerned the opportunity to state his or her views on the substance before it decides to adopt the recovery measure.[116]

The research thus confirms that the EUO uses human rights as normative assessment standards during his inquiries. He uses them while assessing breaches of human rights stemming from the Charter, the Court's jurisprudence and on some occasions also directly from the Code (Arts. 4 or 5). As shown in the second example the EUO occasionally supports his finding of a breach of fundamental rights by referring to the Charter or the Court's case law. One can find other EUO decisions using fundamental rights as an assessment standard.[117]

113 Annual Report of the EUO 1997 (p. 23).

114 Ibid., para. 52.

115 Ibid., para. 53.

116 DR of the EUO in his own-initiative inquiry OI/4/2009/PB concerning the Commission.

117 See, DR of the EUO in his inquiry into complaint 2575/2009/ (TS)(TN)RA against the European Medicines Agency or DR of the EUO in his own-initiative inquiry into case OI/3/2008/FOR against the Commission.

5.3.2 General principles of Union law as the normative standard

Scheme 3 shows that several of the normative standards of the EUO substantively overlap with the general principles of law as it is possible to identify a general value that is protected by these standards. This raises the question of to what extent are these substantively overlapping normative standards identical. During interview, Mr Grill, the Director of Directorate B and the Acting Head of the Complaints and Inquiries Unit, Office of the EUO added that:

> 'The standards applied by the Ombudsman are by necessity the same as those applied by the Court in so far as assessing the *legality of a given act of an EU institution is concerned*. However, the Ombudsman considers that maladministration can also occur where an EU institution has complied with the law. To that extent, his standards can be more than those of the Court. The extent of the duties to inform candidates of the results of their applications in recruitment procedures is a good example. According to established case law, it is sufficient to inform candidates about the mere result (for example, 30 out of 40 points). The Ombudsman is much more demanding in this respect.... Given that the right to good administration is now legally binding, it cannot be excluded that the Court's future case law on this right could limit the Ombudsman's scope of action. If the Court were to hold, in the above-mentioned example, that limiting the information to be given to candidates to points is not only legal but *also compatible with the right to good administration* it would clearly be difficult for the Ombudsman to hold otherwise.'

Despite a close connection and overlap between the EUO's normative standards and the practice of the Court in the following two examples (the *principle of proportionality* and the *principle of legitimate expectations*), it is possible to point to the flexibility of the overlapping assessment standards of the EUO and the Court and to the fact that the same general value can be protected by different subjects by using different methods.

The principle of proportionality is a traditional legal principle that has existed in Union law since the 1950s when the Court referred to a generally accepted rule of law that the reactions to an illegal action must be proportionate to the scale of that action.[118] Nowadays it also has Treaty status.[119] The application of the principle of proportionality can be found in several judgments of the Court. In many cases the Court uses a 'three-step proportionality test' to assess the actions of the Union institutions or of the Member States, although sometimes the Court dispenses with this test.[120] In a very simplistic way this test requires the administrative measure to be *suitable* and *necessary* as regards the interest or aim it protects. The interest must be *legitimate* and last but not least the measure must be proportionate *in stricto sensu*.[121] Despite the fact that the principle is partially codified

118 Case 8/55 *Fédéchar v High Authority*, [1954-56] ECR 245, 256, see also Tridimas 2006, p. 141.

119 Art. 5 (4) TEU requires that *under the principle of proportionality, the content and form of Union action shall not exceed what is necessary to achieve the objectives of the Treaties.*

120 For example, Case T-85/09 *Kadi v Commission* [2010] ECR II-05177.

121 See, Opinions of AG Van Gerven in Case C-312/89 *Sidef Conforama* [1991] ECR I-997.

in the TEU and in secondary Union law, the unwritten Court-developed principle is still used by the Court. This principle is applicable in several situations.[122]

Proportionality has been used in several EUO decisions such as in *Draft recommendation of the EUO concerning his inquiry into complaint 640/2011/AN against the Commission.*

> Here the EUO dealt inter alia with an allegation that the Commission had failed to ensure the publication of the consultation paper on taxation, published only in English, in all the official languages of the Union. The Commission's argument was based on urgency, the technicality of the document and the available resources. The EUO argued, in connection with urgency, that not translating anything into any language at any stage of the consultation process was *clearly disproportionate.*[123] The EUO concluded that the Commission by its action (not publishing all its consultation documents in all of the official languages of the Union, or providing citizens with a translation upon request) had acted with maladministration by *unjustifiably* and *disproportionately* restricting the right of non-English-speaking citizens to be consulted by not making the Consultation Paper available to them in languages other than English.[124]

Although in *Draft recommendation of the EUO in his inquiry into complaint 2365/2009/ (MAM)KM against the Commission* the EUO did not deal with a complaint about the disproportionate actions of an Union institution, the EUO pointed to the necessity of the Union institutions acting in compliance with the proportionality principle.

> The complaint dealt inter alia with a discontented official whose articles were not published on Intracomm (the Commission's intranet). The EUO here agreed that the Commission has an editorial policy in this matter and that freedom of speech does not mean an obligation for others to publish. In this connection he pointed to possible limitations to the freedom of expression. In his opinion 'subject to the principle of proportionality, limitations may be made only if they are necessary and genuinely meet objectives of general interest recognised by the Union or the need to protect the rights and freedoms of others.'[125]

Proportionality was raised in *Draft recommendation of the EUO in his inquiry into complaint 861/2012/RA against the EUP.*

> The complaint concerned the use of the Irish language on the website of the EUP. According to the complainant, the EUO had failed to make its internet site and other relevant pages on its website available in Irish. The complainant argued that the EUP had violated a wide range of legal rules and principles. The EUP disagreed. It pointed to a serious shortage of Irish translators and because of that it decided to apply a temporary derogation from its Rules of Procedure which stated that 'all its documents should be

122 Jans et al. distinguish three situations where this principle is applied: in connection with a review of Union legislation, in connection with a restriction of national free movement rights and in the assessment of law enforcement decisions, especially sanctions. See, Jans et al. 2007, pp. 146-163.

123 DR of the EUO concerning his inquiry into complaint 640/2011/ AN against the Commission, para. 39.

124 Ibid., para. 43.

125 DR of the EUO in his inquiry into complaint 2365/2009/ (MAM)KM against the Commission, para. 32.

> drawn up in the official languages.' During the inquiry the EUO noted that 'the invoked reasons of staff shortages cannot suffice to entitle Parliament to disregard completely the status of Irish as an official EU language, unless the difficulties it would face by giving some effect to this reality are insurmountable.'[126] He noted that 'Parliament's reason for not translating *anything* into Irish in *any section* of its website is *clearly disproportionate*.'[127] The EUO concluded that 'Parliament's reasons are insufficient to justify not making at least some of the most relevant pages on its website available in Irish.' This, in his view, unjustifiably and disproportionately limited the use of Irish on its website. This constituted an instance of maladministration.[128]

From these three cases one can see that the *application* of the proportionality principle by the EUO is not that different from the application by the Court even though the EUO does not expressly refer to the proportionality test. Both institutions weigh administrative action against the consequences for individuals. If the administration cannot *justify* its actions as to the consequences of these actions such actions can lead to disproportionality not only in the eyes of the Court but also in the eyes of the EUO. The EUO also often uses similar wording as the Court as he often talks about a *clear disproportionality*.[129] Still, one can only speculate whether these cases would succeed before the Court based on the breach of proportionality principle. However, as the EUO does not need to follow the Court's principle of proportionality in extra-legal matters it is possible that he might apply this principle in a different, more lenient fashion than the Court. Hence, the requirements of the Court might be satisfied, but the EUO's requirements might not.

Also the *principle of legitimate expectations* is a traditional legal principle that has found its way into the practice of the EUO.[130] Legitimate expectations in the perception of the Court can arise from the actions of the Union institutions[131] as well as from Union legislation.[132] In the view of the Court legitimate expectations can also arise concerning policy rules or guidelines. Only *competent authorities* can raise these expectations. An individual can rely on expectations if he is acting *in good faith*. An individual, however, cannot invoke legitimate expectations if the change of law was *foreseeable*, as in this case the expectations are not worthy of protection. Also an individual will not be successful if he could have *reasonably discovered the inaccuracy* of the information. Last but not least, legitimate expectations will not be allowed *contra legem*.[133]

126 DR of the EUO in his inquiry into complaint 861/2012/RA against the EUP, para. 32.

127 Ibid.

128 Ibid., para. 41.

129 For instance, in Case C-212/11 *Jyske Bank Gibraltar Ltd v Administración del Estado* (not yet published) or in Case C-234/03 *Contse SA and Others* [2005] ECR I-9315 the Court talks about administrative action that was *clearly disproportionate*.

130 Case 112/77 *Töpfer* [1978] ECR 575.

131 Case 289/81 *Mavridis v Parliament* [1983] ECR 1731.

132 Case C-152/88 *Sofrimport v Commission* [1992] ECR I-2477.

133 See, Jans et al. 2007 or Tridimas 2006.

As shown in the previous scheme the legal principle of legitimate expectations substantially overlaps with the EUO's principle of legitimate expectations. It was used in *Decision of the EUO closing his inquiry into complaint 2656/2010/AN against the Commission*.

> The complainant *inter alia* argued that the Commission had wrongly refused to pay travel expenses for members of the experts' families travelling to Jamaica. The Commission noted that these persons do not fall within the category of eligible staff. The EUO found that the reimbursement provisions included in the contract between the Commission and the complainant were not sufficiently clear. At the same time he noted that the Commission for a longer period of time had interpreted the contract so that these persons were eligible for reimbursement. In his view such an interpretation of a contract could give rise to legitimate expectations. He noted that the complainant could rely on such expectations as to the expenses connected with moving from their residence to Jamaica and back.[134] This, however, does not mean that it raises legitimate expectations if these persons are travelling for a holiday.[135] The case did not lead to a finding of maladministration as the Commission accepted the EUO's proposal for a friendly solution.

Another case where the EUO dealt with legitimate expectations is included in *Decision of the EUO closing his inquiry into complaint 633/2010/OV against the Commission*.

> The complainant argued that, on the basis of the information communicated to new staff when he joined the Commission, he had the 'legitimate expectation' to receive 9 merit points for his probationary period, which would then have been converted, under the new rules, into 5 points. The Commission disapproved of that. The rules for awarding promotion points are included in the staff regulations that had subsequently changed. The EUO found that the Commission had stated that new staff were also told that the rules were going to change. The complainant did not comment on this argument nor dispute it. Thus, the EUO concluded that no precise assurances were given to new staff as regards their right to obtain 9 points.[136] In order to support his argument he referred to the judgment in Case C-443/07 P *Centeno Mediavilla* according to which new staff cannot rely on the principle of the protection of legitimate expectations in order to oppose the adoption of new rules, especially in a sphere in which the institution enjoys a considerable degree of discretion.[137] The EUO did not find maladministration in the actions of the Commission.

The third example of the application of this principle is in *Decision of the EUO closing his inquiry into complaint 2855/2008/ELB against the EUP*.

> In this case the complainant *inter alia* claimed that the EUP had breached his legitimate expectations by revising the number of years transferred to the EU pension scheme. He noted that there was a difference between the draft and the final decision of the EUP.

134 Decision of the EUO closing his inquiry into complaint 2656/2010/AN against the Commission, paras. 58 and 60.

135 Ibid., para. 61.

136 Decision of the EUO closing his inquiry into complaint 633/2010/OV against the Commission, para. 59.

137 Ibid., para. 60.

In the opinion of the EUP the draft decision included an obvious error in calculation and thus no legitimate expectations could have been raised. The EUO concluded that the complainant's dealings with the EUP did not entitle him to a legitimate expectation. In order to support this conclusion he noted that based on the case law of the Court in cases where there are doubts about the soundness of a payment made to him or her, the interested party must approach the administration in order to allow it to make all the necessary verifications (Case T-156/96 Jensen v Commission). This was not the case. The EUO also relied on the judgment in Case T-324/04 F v Commission [2007] where the CFI found that the fact that the administration did not notice an irregular payment when checking or rechecking an official's file does not, in itself, give rise to any legitimate expectations on the part of the person concerned. Thus, this conduct by the EUP did not lead to a breach of the principle.

The previous three examples of the application of the principle of legitimate expectations do not differ from the application of this principle by the Court. Especially in the last two cases one can observe that the EUO supported his finding on legitimate expectations by the rules adopted by the Court. The closeness between the application of the legal principle of legitimate expectations and the good administration principle of legitimate expectations is obvious.

From the previous two examples one *cannot conclude* that the normative standards of the EUO are applied in a *more flexible fashion* than the substantively overlapping normative standards of the Court. This is connected with the fact that in the practice of the EUO these principles have been used in a limited number of cases. Nonetheless, in both examples it is possible to see a connection between the perception of the EUO and that of the Court. The Ombudsman often applies the principles in a very similar fashion as the Court. This is underlined by the fact that the EUO often refers to the contents of these principles as applied by the Court in its jurisprudence. Nonetheless, the EUO does not expressly use the same tests as the Court. Based on the previous examples and the relatively close-to-Court application of these principles by the EUO one can only hypothesize whether the EUO applies his principles that substantively overlap with the general principles of law more loosely or more strictly than the Court.

5.3.3 *Exclusively ombudsman principles as normative standards?*

The principles of good administration included in the Code requirements that do not substantively overlap with the general principles of law include, for example, the requirement of courtesy (Art. 12), the requirement to acknowledge receipt and an indication of the competent official (Art. 14), the requirement to transfer to the competent service of the institution (Art. 15) or the requirement to keep adequate records (Art. 24). The existence of these extra-legal principles of the EUO can be explained by the fact that compliance with good administration requires more than just respect for legality.[138] As these requirements do not have legally binding authority they do not have to be taken into

138 Annual Report of the EUO 2010, p. 35.

account by the Court. As Mr Barens (a judge at the EUCST) stated, the Court only rarely makes use of some other norms or normative standards:

> 'In principle the EUCST does not need to take into account other norms than the legal norms. Though if the court is confronted with a number of possible interpretations then for reasons of equity we say that this is the best interpretation for the poor applicant. This is possible. But in principle we are not applying different sets of norms. We carry out a legal review and in fact we cannot do anything else. We have to review legality and nothing but legality. From time to time there are considerations of equity or the economy of procedure. We can qualify them as semi-legal norms, although it is difficult to say. The Ombudsman can cover those other issues.'

As the extra-legal requirements of the EUO do not in any way overlap with the general principles of law one cannot compare their application.

5.4 Summary

This chapter discussed the question of *what is the mutual significance of the normative standards of the EUO and the Court and what are the interrelations of these normative standards?*

As can be seen from the previous pages, the EUO and the Court actively approach their normative standards. The development of normative standards by the EUO and the Court is a manifestation of their normative functions. The Court is active in the development of legally binding general principles of law and the EUO is active in the development of legally non-binding principles of good administrative conduct.

There is almost no *formal normative coordination*. Primary as well as secondary law are rather silent about this issue. The jurisprudence of the Court is more informative although it is connected with ad hoc situations. Based on its case law, a breach of the EUO's normative standard (even if it is substantively overlapping) does not lead to a breach of the general principles of law or to a breach of Union law as such.

In connection with some principles it is possible to identify a *formal similarity* that is connected with the denomination of the principles. At the same time it is possible to observe a *substantial similarity* as to the content of several normative standards. From the previous schemes it is possible to see that some of the normative standards of the EUO and the Court can protect the same values. For instance, non-discrimination in administrative actions is protected by the EUO as well as by the Court. Thus, theoretically, if all the conditions are met, the protection of this value can be exercised by the EUO as well as by the Court, although not at the same time. It can be presumed that this similarity between the protected values can bring these institutions closer at least in connection with their normative standards.

The EUO has never explicitly or implicitly rejected the application of the law and legal principles as assessment standards in his investigation. Also, the provisions of Union law do not prohibit him from using law and legal principles in his investigations as assessment standards. If we look at the Code and at the practice of the EUO we can see that the EUO actually considers lawfulness as a very important principle. At the same time, the EUO clearly sees himself as an institution that can go further than the Court, at least in connection with maladministration that is a broader concept than unlawfulness. The broad character of this concept connects the EUO also with the assessment of the lawfulness of the actions of the Union institution, but only to the extent to which lawfulness overlaps with the requirements of good administrative conduct. Nonetheless, a strong accent on the legality review by the EUO can lead to a questioning of his role as an independent institution with competence to assess compliance with the concept that only partially overlaps with lawfulness.

At the same time human rights are normative standards of the both institutions. As the general principles of law are the law, they play the same role in the EUO's practice as written Union law. Nonetheless, in some cases one can observe that the EUO can give the value which is also protected by the general principles of law a different dimension, a dimension of good administrative conduct. Last but not least, one can see that the EUO can possibly provide the Court with principles that do not, *for now,* exist as legal principles but only as part of the EUO's requirements of good administration.

PART V

FINDINGS, AMENDMENTS, COMPARISON AND CONCLUSIONS

Part V, as the final part of this book, builds on the data and information accumulated and presented in the substantive parts. This part reiterates the theories that are applicable to an analysis of the matter researched. It also provides readers with the main substantive findings of the research and with explanations for these findings. By doing this, Part V answers the research questions.

As this evaluation is an opportunity to express my own opinion about the findings, in several places I make some recommendations on amendments to the existing designs of the relations between ombudsmen and the judiciary. While pointing to the findings this part provides a comparison between the three existing designs of the relations between ombudsmen and the judiciary. However, it does not make a conclusive judgment about the 'best' out of the three researched systems.

Chapter 1

THEORIES AND OMBUDSMAN-JUDICIARY RELATIONS

In order to analyse the data received throughout the research, one has to place the analysis within the theoretical framework. In this connection one can discover a *possible institutional coordination*, a *possible case coordination* and a *possible normative coordination* of ombudsman-judiciary relations. While institutional coordination and case coordination are linked with the *doctrine of the division of powers* and especially with the *doctrine of checks and balances* and are intended to help realise the *accountability of the administration*, normative coordination can be analysed from the *perspective of relations between the law and morality* or *law and another normative system*. The term 'coordination' is perceived through the eyes of *organizational theory* and *coordination theory*. Based on these theories one can see ombudsmen and the judiciary as two subjects of the same 'organisation' – the state, that should be coordinated in order to reach their goals.

Ombudsmen and the judiciary *are two separate state institutions*. Despite that, one can discover several issues that connect them and that can bring them closer together. The most important issue is that the judiciary and the ombudsmen both function as *dispute resolution mechanisms*. However, while the judiciary is perceived as a *traditional* dispute resolution mechanism, ombudsmen have the character of an *alternative* resolution mechanism. This character of dispute resolution is linked with their different powers and competences, different methods of dispute resolution or the protection of different values. Nonetheless, dispute resolution as a connecting factor *cannot* be overlooked. Because of this, their actions should *somehow* be coordinated so that ombudsmen *and* the judiciary can fully exercise their own special functions.

The division of competences between state institutions is crucial for the functioning of modern democratic states. The judiciary, legislation and the executive have their specific and unique state powers and functions. Although an ombudsman is not included among any of the traditional bearers of state power as described by Montesquieu or Locke, one cannot overlook the fact that nowadays the ombudsman institution is a common component of the state apparatus. The practice of the ombudsman in dispute resolution brings him close to the judiciary. This closeness is also connected with the overlapping spheres of action and the similarity between their competences. Because of these similarities, an *institutional coordination* of the ombudsmen and the judiciary seems to be necessary. A deficiency in this coordination can lead to uncertainty about the bodies providing the dispute resolution in general or about the institution that should deal with a particular case. In this connection one needs to speak of the *coordination of mutual interaction between ombudsmen and the judiciary*.

Regarding the *original relations between the individual and the administration* the position of the ombudsmen as well as the judiciary is only *subsidiary* or *secondary*. Generally, they are only involved in relations between the individual and the state administration *in the case of a dispute* and as dispute resolution mechanisms. They both stand between the state administration and the individual and they *check and balance the powers of the (state) administration* – the executive. The ombudsmen stand alongside the judiciary as independent controllers of administrative conduct. The position of the judiciary and the administration is delimited by their particular place in the *trias politica*. They have their own competences and roles. The judiciary takes binding decisions, but by these decisions it does not entirely replace the role of the administration. Only occasionally does the judiciary replace the decision of the administration by its own decision. Conversely, ombudsmen cannot 'bite' by means of their reports. They cannot legally bind the administration or replace its decisions. Therefore, they do not need to guard the exercise of their competences against transgressing into the domain of the competence of the administration as much as the courts do. Still, they cannot do something that does not belong to their competences.

Both institutions add to the protection of individuals. They not only add to the system of checks of balances between the bearers of state power but also to the checks and balances between the bearers of state power and those virtually without this power (individuals). From the perspective of individuals, the *institutional coordination* and the *case coordination* of the judiciary and the ombudsmen are a considerable addition to the protection of their rights and an addition to the solution of the problems that have led to a dispute. The combination of the powers of the judiciary and those of the ombudsmen may enable a full exercise of their powers and this can potentially improve the possibilities and chances of individuals against the administration. This does not mean that the ombudsmen or the judiciary are *a priori* on the side of the individual. They vigorously guard their impartiality.

Ombudsmen are often empowered to bring new aspects to dispute resolution. They can generally exercise their powers following an individual complaint or on their own initiative. The latter possibility is something that the judiciary cannot do. The addition of ombudsmen to the checks and the protection of individuals against state power consists of the informal way in which they use investigative and dispute resolution methods that are not primarily applied by the judiciary. These aspects also include a normative quality check on the actions of the administration and the possibility to provide the administration with recommendations. The recommendations do not legally bind the administration, but they seek to change administrative processes by way of persuasion. Also the ombudsmen's sanctions are limited to *naming* and indirectly to *shaming* the perpetrators breaching behavioural standards. When exercising these functions, the ombudsman institutions stand *alongside* the judiciary. With these aspects the ombudsmen *add something extra* to the protection of individuals, dispute resolution and the checks and balances provided by the judiciary.

The discussion on the normative standards of the courts and the normative standards of the ombudsmen can be linked to the *discussion between law and morality* (or law and another normative system) and it can perceive the ombudsmen as a *moral or* at least *a normative alternative to the judiciary*. The starting point in this perception is that the ombudsmen and the judiciary apply two sets of different normative standards – the ombudsmen apply *ombudsnorms* (moral norms) and the judiciary applies *legal norms*.

The legal norms applied by the judiciary can include moral norms although they are not identical. Moral norms are generally broader than legal norms. Still, moral norms included in judgments or codified in the law become a part of the legal norms of the country. The law and the legal principles, whether codified or not (including human rights), are the most important normative standard that is applied by the judiciary. While the normative standards that are applied by the judiciary are clearly *legal norms*, the normative standards applied by the ombudsmen do not have such a clear-cut character. They are *something else*. As such, they are not legally binding or legally enforceable. An individual will not succeed if he asks the judiciary to enforce an ombudsnorm. The research however shows that ombudsmen's normative standards have two different levels. Firstly, the ombudsmen can apply the *normative standards that substantially overlap with the legal principles* and, secondly, they apply *normative standards that do not overlap with the law* (extra-legal ombudsnorms) and are applicable to conduct uncovered by the law. This division is connected with the general character of the normative concept that is assessed by the ombudsmen (good administration, maladministration etc.) and with the incumbent ombudsman's perception of this concept. The overlapping standards can lead to the conclusion that the ombudsmen partially apply legal norms. However, the application of normative standards which substantively overlap with legal norms *does not* a priori *mean* that these standards have the character of legal norms or law or that they are applied in the same way. Conversely, the courts assess legal issues. Their role is to assess compliance with the law. They do this even if the law potentially codifies moral norms. Because of that one can draw the following scheme.[1]

Scheme 1 – **Ombudsnorms and legal norms**

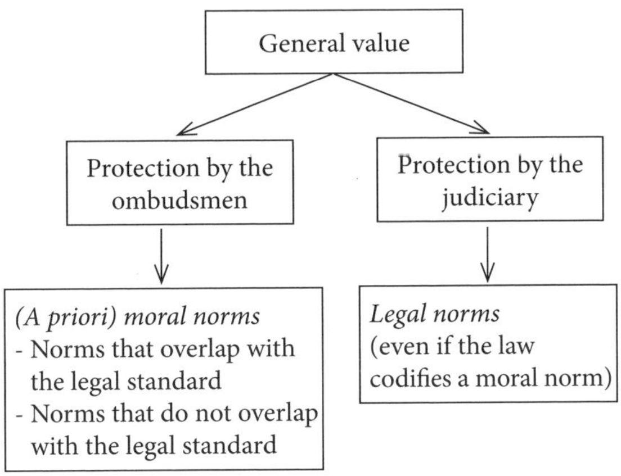

1 Compare, scheme 3, section 2.2, Part I.

The main difference between the normative standards of the judiciary and those of ombudsmen clearly lies in the binding power of these standards. A first look at the standards could lead to the somewhat rash statement that the normative standards of the courts are binding while those of the ombudsmen are not. This statement is only correct, however, if one refers to the power of these standards to *legally bind* their addresses. However, in connection with the researched ombudsmen one cannot overlook a high level of the administration's compliance with their reports and recommendations. Although one can ask why the administration follows the recommendations of the ombudsmen, this level of compliance confirms that the reports of the ombudsmen are taken seriously. This shows that the normative standards of the ombudsmen and the findings based thereon have a *factual binding effect*. Although the ombudsmen's recommendations can appeal to a higher moral norm (such as the norm that *civil servants should behave politely when in contact with citizens*), their factual binding power is not always connected with morality in a strict sense. When one looks at the character of the ombudsnorms one can see that they do not always include some *moral rule* in the sense of some higher value norms. Sometimes these norms simply allow the problem of the administration to be approached from a different perspective than the law, especially from the perspective of *good administration*. This does not make them norms in the sense of general moral rules but that also does not mean that they necessarily fit within the category of legal norms. Thus, as noted before one can discover *moral norms in a strict sense* (e.g. the norm of courtesy or impartiality) and *moral norms in a broader sense* (e.g. the norm organising the administrative procedure).

The term coordination, as used throughout this book, has been borrowed from organisational theory and coordination theory. It is a broad term that covers the *processes of managing formal and informal cooperative, collaborating or competitive dependencies between ombudsmen and the judiciary in order to reach their common goals.*[2] The main *common goals* of the judiciary and the ombudsmen can be described as dispute resolution and potentially also the correct functioning of the administration and the protection of individuals. Of course, one can also note different goals of the judiciary and ombudsmen, such as, for example, *law enforcement* by the judiciary, a power that is not present in the competences of ombudsmen. In ombudsman-judiciary relations one can find several bases for their *collaboration* but also various *competitive dependencies*. Thus, the term *coordination* must be perceived as a term including both *cooperation* (when ombudsmen and the judiciary exercise their control function over the administration) and *competition* (when ombudsmen and the judiciary stand against each other). A broad perception of coordination enables the researched relations to be approached from all possible angles. Thus, coordination is not perceived in this book as a strict, formal and legally pre-set way of organising the work and competences of the ombudsmen and the judiciary but as a mélange of mutual interrelations between these institutions and the need to organise them.

2 See, Mintzberg 1979, p. 2 and Malone & Crowston 1994, p. 90.

Chapter 2

FINDINGS, EVALUATIONS AND AMENDMENTS

The section on the theoretical framework included in Part 1 delimits the research questions. The parts describing the situation in the Netherlands, England and the EU provide the data leading to the answers to these questions. The research questions are rather broad, hence one cannot answer them in a simple one-sentence way. Because of that, the answer to each of these research questions consists of *main findings* that are linked with their substance and *the analysis of these findings.*

2.1 Question 1 (institutional coordination)

The first research question is:

How are the relations between ombudsmen and the judiciary as state institutions coordinated in the researched systems, and what is the content of this coordination?

2.1.1 Findings

The research into all three systems confirms the existence of some *institutional coordination* between the ombudsmen and the judiciary. The three different legal systems (common law, continental law and European law) coordinate ombudsman-judiciary relations in a surprisingly similar way, although they retain their own specifics and develop and coordinate these relations relatively autonomously. Nonetheless, based on the previous parts, the chapters on institutional coordination (Chapters 3), one can underline the following general findings that constitute an answer to the first research question.

> **Finding 1**
> *Despite their similarities, the ombudsmen and the judiciary are different bodies. Ombudsmen are not only dispute resolution mechanisms.*

Although this finding may seem rather obvious or even well known, in practice it is not always so. The majority of legal academics and law practitioners are well aware of the powers of the judiciary. They solve disputes between parties, while using formal procedures that lead to a legally binding judgment. They assess compliance with the law by using codified or uncodified legal norms. The general knowledge concerning ombudsmen is not equally widespread. Although they have been around in large numbers for at least fifty years, one can see that there is a continuous tendency for ombudsmen to reiterate their powers and to underline their independence. Ombudsmen are traditionally perceived as an *extra-legal alternative* to the courts. The term *alternative* means that dispute resolution can (sometimes) be exercised by ombudsmen *or* by the judiciary. It also means that ombudsmen have some additional '*extras*' that are not linked with dispute resolution or law enforcement.

These additional powers include especially the *own-initiative investigations* (EU, NL and partially also LGO);[1] the possibility to *make non-binding recommendations* (all the researched ombudsmen);[2] the ability to identify *structural problems in the functioning of the administration* and to point them out (all the researched ombudsmen);[3] the potential to *develop norms of conduct* and guidance to administrative conduct (all the researched ombudsmen);[4] and last but not least, the *discretion of the ombudsmen* to approach the problem between the individual and the (state) administration in any possible way that in his/her view may *contribute to a solution of the core of this problem* (all the researched ombudsmen).[5] The existence of these *special competences* in connection with relations between the individual and the administration and their application shows that the ombudsmen are not identical to the judiciary. The ombudsmen are not a kind of inferior court. These competences also show that the ombudsmen are *more than a dispute resolution mechanism*. Of course, one should *not see* ombudsmen as a miraculous cure for all administrative problems but at the same time one cannot ignore their '*extras*' and their potential, compared to the judiciary.

Finding 2
The legislator formally establishes a general institutional framework with powers and competences for the ombudsmen and the judiciary.

The legislators in all three legal systems are the main and primary *formal* coordinators of ombudsman-judiciary relations. In England, this formal coordination is included predominantly in the statutes establishing the two researched ombudsmen (the 1967 Act and the 1974 Act). The situation is similar in the Netherlands (WNo and GALA). In the EU formal coordination is included in the TFEU and some other provisions of secondary Union law. The statutes establishing the courts or tribunals do not deal with the researched relationship.[6] This coordination is often general and needs interpretation either in the case law of the judiciary or in the reports or decisions of the ombudsmen. The general

1 See, Part II, section 1.1.1.2; Part III, section 1.2.1.1.2 and Part IV, section 1.1.1.2.
2 See, Part II, sections 1.1.2 and 1.1.3; Part III, sections 1.1.1.2, 1.1.1.3, 1.2.1.2 and 1.2.1.3 and Part IV, sections 1.1.2 and 1.1.3.
3 See, Part II, section 1.1.2; Part III, sections 1.1.1.2 and 1.2.1.2 and Part IV, section 1.1.2.
4 See, Part II, section 1.1.3; Part III, sections 1.1.1.3 and 1.2.1.3 and Part IV, section 1.1.3.
5 See, Part II, section 1.1.2; Part III, sections 1.1.1.2 and 1.2.1.2 and Part IV, section 1.1.2.
6 See, Part II, section 3.1.1; Part III, section 3.1.1 and Part IV, section 3.1.1.

framework, as designed by the legislator, often limits ombudsmen.[7] Formally, only the law and with some limitations also the case law of the courts coordinate the institutional relations between the ombudsmen and the judiciary.[8]

The formal relations between the ombudsmen and the judiciary are *not generally* seen as being problematic. Generally, there is a belief that the legal borders between the ombudsmen and the judiciary are clearly set and that there is no special need to explain these relations any further.

Finding 3

The protection and dispute resolution of the judiciary often limit the protection and dispute resolution of the ombudsmen. The protection and dispute resolution of the ombudsmen do not limit the protection and dispute resolution of the judiciary.

The framework set by the legislator, occasionally confirmed by the case law of the courts and the practice of the researched institutions, *limits* the protection and dispute resolution provided by ombudsmen. In England, the ombudsman institutions cannot generally act when the individual *has* or *had* a right of appeal to a tribunal or has or had a remedy by way of proceedings in any court of law.[9] In the EU, the EUO cannot investigate in cases where the alleged facts are or have been the *subject of legal proceedings*.[10] In the EU and in England the legislators do not distinguish between the impact of different types of courts or tribunals on the ombudsman investigation. *Any* court or tribunal proceedings where an individual has or had a remedy (ENG) or *any* legal proceedings dealing with alleged facts (EU) bar the investigation/inquiry of the ombudsmen. In the Netherlands, the legislator distinguishes between the impact of a judgment of the administrative courts (an absolute bar for the NO) and the impact of a judgment of a civil or criminal court (a discretion-based bar for the NO). If the complaint is *closely linked with a case pending* before *any* Dutch court the NO has to halt the investigation.[11] In all three cases the limitation on ombudsmen is connected with the closeness of the contents of a complaint filed with the ombudsman and an application filed with the courts. In general, the ombudsmen *cannot exercise* their protection when the judiciary *is exercising* or has already *exercised* its protection. Conversely, however, the judiciary is not limited by investigations/inquiries by the ombudsmen. In all three cases the judiciary can act even if the ombudsmen are investigating the complaints or have already investigated them.[12] This finding confirms that the ombudsman's protection is *additional* and *supplementary* to the protection by the judiciary and it *does not replace* the protection by the judiciary.

Although the ombudsmen when exercising their competences are in principle limited by the competences of the judiciary, some of them are provided with discretion to disregard this fact. In England the ombudsmen can investigate a complaint despite

7 See, Finding 3 (institutional coordination).
8 See, Part II, section 3.1; Part III, section 3.1 and Part IV, section 3.1.
9 See, Part III, sections 1.1.1.1.1, 1.2.1.1 and 3.1.1.
10 See, Part IV, sections 1.1.1.1 and 3.1.1.
11 See, Part II, section 3.1.1.
12 See, Part II, section 3.1; Part III, section 3.1 and Part IV, section 3.1.

previous court or tribunal proceedings if *under the particular circumstances it is not reasonable to expect the complainant to use this right or remedy.*[13] In the Netherlands, the NO has discretion in connection with a judgment of a civil or criminal court.[14] In the EU, the EUO does not have a similar discretion. Neither the TFEU nor another provision of primary or secondary Union law allows the EUO to exercise his/her discretion and to investigate facts that have already been covered by legal proceedings.[15] This discretion of the ombudsmen confirms that even in the case of protection provided by the Court the individual's problem is not necessarily solved. When ombudsmen are provided with this discretion and they apply it, the application of this competence is a *real alternative* to protection by the judiciary from the perspective of citizens.

Finding 4

The interaction between the ombudsmen and the judiciary almost strictly follows the framework designed by the legislator and the interpretation of the courts. Beyond this framework, any (formal or informal) interaction between these institutions is only marginal and occurs on an ad hoc basis.

The ombudsmen and the judiciary try to exercise their functions strictly within the framework designed by the law and/or interpreted in the case law. None of the three researched legal systems foresees a broad interaction between the ombudsmen and the judiciary. A formal interaction, apart from the limitation on the ombudsmen, is also rare. The interaction that exists *beyond* the formal framework occurs during official or unofficial mutual meetings or consultations between these institutions. Still, it occurs only in isolated instances. In the EU, this interaction does not usually go beyond the level of formal gatherings where these institutions reiterate and explain their mutual roles. They do not delve deeply into the substance of their working problems, although sometimes general issues are discussed. These institutions protect their autonomy by officially reiterating their status and the strict delimitation of their spheres of interest.[16] In the Netherlands, this interaction goes beyond explaining their mutual roles. Occasionally, one can see that there are situations where the NO and the administrative courts discuss general substantive issues that can affect the whole system of administrative justice or a specific issue (e.g. the enforcement of decisions, the remedying of damages).[17] In England there is only occasional interaction. However, until August 2013 the English system recognised the AJTC – a specialised institution that kept the whole administrative justice system under review. This forum, with the PO as an ex officio member, ensured that the relationships between the courts, tribunals, ombudsmen and alternative dispute resolution providers satisfactorily reflected the needs of users.[18]

13 See, Part III, section 3.1.1.
14 See, Part II, section 3.1.1.
15 See, Part IV, section 3.1.1.
16 See, Part IV, section 3.2.1.
17 See, Part II, sections 3.2.1 and 3.2.2
18 See, Part III, section 3.1.1 also the AJTC internet site.

The limited interaction between the ombudsmen and the judiciary shows that occasionally there are mutually interesting themes. This limitation proves, however, that the ombudsmen and the judiciary try to approach these matters on their own and only rarely in cooperation. The research also suggests that communication between the ombudsmen and the judges is often easier if the incumbent ombudsman is a former judge or lawyer. The ombudsman is then often seen as *one of us,* as the *one who understands.*[19]

Finding 5

The courts sometimes explain their ability to review the legality of the reports or actions of ombudsmen. Even if they deduce that they have these powers, they generally respect the competences of the ombudsmen.

In all three systems, this particular issue is resolved differently. Formally, neither GALA nor other Dutch statutes allow the administrative courts to review the legality of the reports or actions of the NO. A report of the NO does not have the character of an administrative legal act (*besluit*). Theoretically, there can be civil proceedings against the NO in relation to damages because of his/her investigation or report; however, the research did not show that such proceedings have actually occurred.[20] In the EU, the Court has expressly stated that the decision of the EUO does not produce legal effects for third parties, within the meaning of the TFEU. Thus, the action for the annulment of an EUO decision is excluded. However, the Court has declared that it has the power to assess the *lawfulness of the EUO's conduct* in the performance of his/her duties connected with the non-contractual liability of the EUO as a Union institution.[21] In England, the courts, but not the tribunals, have deduced that they have the authority to judicially review the reports and actions of the PO and the LGO. These ombudsmen are not outside the purview of a judicial review.[22]

This particular finding can be explained by the fact that the main role of the administrative courts (apart from solving disputes between individuals and the administration) is also to assess compliance of actions of state institutions with the law. Theoretically, they are the *guardians of the lawfulness* of administrative institutions' actions. This is linked with their position in the system of checks and balances in democratic states. Furthermore, even if the courts have the power to judicially review the actions of ombudsmen, they argue that they are not prepared to do this on daily basis.[23] At the same time, they do not assess whether the substance of the ombudsman's report is correct, i.e. whether there was a breach of the normative standards of the ombudsman. They assess whether the ombudsman's actions when investigating the complaints or writing the report have had an impact on its legality. The limited inclination of the courts to assess the legality of the substance of the ombudsmen's actions can be explained by their different standards of control and by the respect of the courts for the work of the ombudsmen, their meticulous investigations and the thoroughness of their actions.

19 See, Part II, section 3.2.1.
20 See, Part II, sections 4.2.2 and 3.1.2.
21 See, Part IV, section 3.1.2.
22 See, Part III, section 3.1.2.1.1.
23 Ibid.

2.1.2 Evaluation of findings and possible amendments to the existing designs

When one looks at the assessed relations from the perspective of institutional coordination, one can see that the situation in all three cases is without considerable problems. The ombudsmen and the judiciary in the Netherlands, England and the EU have their own competences, their own roles and their own functions. The application of the doctrine of checks and balances between the ombudsmen and the judiciary works in practice. The judiciary assesses the compliance of the administrative actions and decisions with the law. It uses the formal procedures in which it is rather passive because of the mainly adversarial character of its proceedings. Its judgements are legally binding and enforceable. The ombudsmen, conversely, assess the compliance of administrative actions and conduct with *'something else'* than law. They often act actively, in an inquisitorial manner. Their reports and decisions are neither legally binding nor enforceable. Sometimes they can start to control the administration on their own.

Both institutions try to remain within their own spheres. They try to be as independent and as impartial as possible, sometimes even at the expenses of *potential cooperative actions*. To remain within their spheres and to exercise their functions independently, ombudsmen are often limited in their investigations when there is or was a judicial procedure covering the same facts as a complaint to the ombudsmen. Occasionally, the courts have the ability to review the actions (and decisions) of the ombudsmen. Nevertheless, institutionally, the actions of these institutions are formally coordinated in a way that allows the ombudsmen and the judiciary to work autonomously without obstructing the other institution.

An evaluation of the findings falling under the first research question may lead to questions about the *suitability of the statutory bars limiting the ombudsmen's investigations/inquiries* or at least about their suitability as they are currently devised. Is the removal of these statutory bars or their limitation a positive and adequate thing to do?

Theoretically, the removal of these bars can lead to a situation where two different state institutions, ombudsmen and the judiciary, separately deal with similar or even the same facts. They can assess these facts from two different perspectives, while using different methods and possibly also different normative standards. The legal problem underlying the dispute is dealt with by the judiciary and the 'good administration' problem underlying the dispute is dealt with by the ombudsman. Then the procedures of the ombudsmen and the judiciary and their outcomes can impact an administrative body simultaneously. Hence the legality of the administrative decision (or another legally relevant action) and the quality of administrative conduct can be assessed by the judiciary and the ombudsmen at the same time. Can the work of ombudsmen and the judiciary and a system for the protection of individuals exist without these limitations for the ombudsmen? In my opinion this is possible and can lead to several positives. Especially if one takes into account that the positions of the judiciary and the ombudsmen are, as they often put it themselves: *we do something different than they do*. Furthermore, one can see a tendency in some countries to deformalize their court procedures and to give the judiciary certain powers directed at speeding up procedures or using more problem-solving methods. This is the case in the Netherlands and its NZB policy that tries to combine the work of the judiciary (legality review) with techniques that potentially take over some elements from the ADR (e.g. mediation).

Due to seemingly different scopes of control by the ombudsmen and the judiciary, they should be allowed to approach the same administrative actions from two different perspectives – lawfulness and good (proper) administration. They should be allowed to do this at the same time. Then they can cover all possible angles of the administrative actions. I admit that the removal or redesigning of the statutory bars on ombudsmen could have a considerable impact on the existing designs of ombudsman-judiciary relations, but it can possibly lead to a more comprehensive and clearer protection of individuals and it might lead to the final solution of the problem that is the subject of the dispute. Any change to the statutory bars would require changes to the law in all three systems, whether it is statutory law in England and the Netherlands or the TFEU in the EU. The removal of the statutory bars barring the ombudsmen from exercising their powers can enable the assessment of lawfulness by the judiciary *and* good/proper administration by the ombudsmen at the same time. Of course, the impact of the removal of these bars should be properly researched and, if this step is taken, it should also solve matters relating to relations between the results of the ombudsman investigations and the court proceedings. A partial investigation into the possibility to remove these bars has already been undertaken, for example, in the UK by the Law Commission. For now, however, it has not received the necessary support of the legislator. In my opinion these limitations on ombudsmen should be changed as the ombudsmen a priori deal with a different normative concept than the judiciary and their decisions, reports and recommendations do not have legally binding effect. Hence, this section leads to the following recommendation.

The statutory bars barring ombudsmen from investigating complaints if they cover the same facts as applications to the judiciary should be removed.

Apart from the removal of the statutory bars one can think of the movement of cases between the judiciary and the ombudsmen. It is always possible that an application with the court entirely or partially includes issues that do not fall under the assessment of legality but they might nonetheless be assessed by the ombudsman. Generally, the judiciary does not have an obligation to refer the case to the ombudsman or at least to inform him about the case. Furthermore, if the judiciary has already dealt with the case, ombudsmen usually cannot assess the same facts.

If, during its proceedings, the judiciary encounters recurring malpractice that is not connected with legality but falls within the scope of matters to be considered by ombudsmen, it does not have any obligation regarding this malpractice. In these situations the judiciary should *be allowed* to inform an ombudsman about the malpractice. The information provided by the judiciary can then theoretically lead to the ombudsmen's own-initiative investigations. At the moment, in none of the researched systems can the judiciary act in such a way. It would be more *individual-friendly* and *problem solving* if the judiciary were to be allowed to inform ombudsmen about a *clear-cut case of maladministration* or *improper administration*. At the same time, information by the court to the ombudsmen about recurring malpractice could lead to an ombudsman's own-initiative investigation and also to the possible resolution of the malpractice (e.g. several applications against the same tax office alleging, in addition to unlawful tax deductions, also impolite or offensive behaviour by its employees). These powers of the judiciary may influence the prevention of similar future applications as the problem can be solved by the administration after interference by the ombudsman. One can also think of cases where ombudsmen would receive a complaint that could be better dealt with by the courts and referring the case to the courts would be an adequate solution (for example, if the ombudsman would deal with a complaint including an administrative decision that can be appealed against). Still, it is more difficult to imagine this situation as ombudsmen often see in a breach of the law also a breach of their normative concept.

Based on the above-mentioned considerations one can recommend the following *amendment* to the existing design of the ombudsmen and the judiciary.

> **The judiciary should have the competence to refer a case to the ombudsman if it clearly maladministration (improper administration) falling short of unlawfulness. At the same time the judiciary should have the competence to inform the ombudsman about possible structural administrative problems. In both cases the ombudsman should have the discretion to investigate these cases.**

The existing designs of the ombudsmen and the judiciary show that there is not much communication between them, either formally or otherwise. Nobody can compel these institutions to engage in mutual communication. A general forum for communication between ombudsmen and the judiciary is lacking in the Netherlands and in the EU. Only in England can one see such a forum that allowed ombudsmen and the judiciary to communicate if and when necessary (AJTC). One can argue that the AJTC was created because of the ambiguous and overcomplicated system of English administrative justice, but one cannot deny that the AJTC, apart from its investigative and other functions, is the forum that facilitated mutual communication between individual subjects of the administrative justice system, including ombudsmen and judges. In the Netherlands and in the EU any communication between ombudsmen and the judiciary is only ad hoc and informal. One can observe that occasionally there are meetings between the NO and the judges of the ABRvS or the EUO and the judges of the Court.

Still, it is nothing but speculation to say that such a communication forum would work in the EU or in the Netherlands. However, one cannot exclude the fact that communication between ombudsmen and the judiciary as state institutions may have some advantages and can be used in order to discuss matters or challenges common to both institutions, to strengthen the development of certain norms, to explain '*how we do it*' or only just to reiterate the functions and goals of these bodies. In my opinion, although ombudsmen and the judiciary are different institutions with different roles, they still have common themes. Because of that I can recommend an *amendment* that can be added to the existing designs.

There should be a communication forum where ombudsmen and the judiciary could discuss certain issues connected with improving the protection offered to individuals, their own roles, their different points of view or other matters connected with their functions.

2.2 Question 2 (case coordination)

The second research question is:

What is the significance of the ombudsman reports and the court judgments and their contents for the other researched institutions and what are their interrelations?

2.2.1 Findings

Despite the limited interaction between the ombudsmen and the judiciary as state institutions, the results of their work, their judgments and their reports sometimes attract their mutual attention. In the practice of the ombudsmen and the judiciary one can discover cases where they make cross-references to each other's judgments or reports and/or use parts of these documents in their own findings. The findings that lead to an answer to this question are mainly based on the research described in the chapters dealing with case coordination (Chapters 4).

Finding 1
Relations between ombudsmen and the judgments of the judiciary as well as the judiciary and the ombudsmen's decisions are regulated only marginally.

Although the legislator formally regulates the general relations between the ombudsmen and the judiciary as *state institutions*, the interrelations between the *judgments* and the *reports* are not comprehensively regulated.[24] Formally, in all three systems it is confirmed that judgments of the judiciary are legally binding and can be enforced. Conversely, the reports of the ombudsmen have only the character of legally non-binding recommendations. All three systems require ombudsmen to take judgments into account. As a court (or tribunal) judgment can mean the halting of an ombudsman's investigation, in their investigation ombudsmen must check whether there are/have been court or tribunal proceedings (ENG), whether there are/have been legal proceedings dealing with the facts covered by the complaint (EU) or whether there has been a judgment by an administrative or ordinary (civil or criminal) court or whether there are court proceedings which are still pending (NL).[25] In the EU, there is also an express and mandatory obligation for the EUO not to question the soundness of the court's ruling.[26] Thus *ex lege*, ombudsmen must discover whether there is a court (or a tribunal) judgment or proceedings leading to such a judgment that potentially cover the same substance as the complaint, because

24 See, Part II, section 4.1; Part III, section 4.1 and Part IV, section 4.1.
25 See, Finding 3 (Institutional coordination).
26 See, Part IV, section 3.1.1.2.

they can have a negative impact on the ombudsman's ability to deal with the case. If there are such proceedings and judgments, the ombudsmen must assess whether the court judgment covered the same issues as the complaint (depending on the precise wording of their obligations). Hence, ombudsmen are obliged to consider and even to consult existing court judgments. The judiciary, however, is not under any obligation to consult or consider the reports of ombudsmen. This includes individual investigation reports, annual reports or any other reports or decisions of the ombudsmen.

Finding 2

When necessary, ombudsmen, while drafting their reports, make cross-references to the case law of the courts (and the law in general). While drafting their judgments, the judiciary only rarely makes cross-references to the reports of the ombudsmen. The reasons for this practice vary.

The application of judgments in ombudsmen's investigations and ombudsmen's reports in court/tribunal proceedings is confirmed by the practice of these institutions. In all three systems one can find examples where ombudsmen make cross-references to judgments in their reports.[27] Similarly, while reading the judgments of the judiciary one can discover some cross-references to the ombudsmen and/or their reports.[28] These mutual cross-references do *not* occur in every judgment or in every report, but only if there is a factual or normative connection between these institutions and their 'decisions' and if the institutions consider explicit cross-references to be necessary. The cross-references confirm that the judiciary and the ombudsmen formally acknowledge the existence and practice of the other institution that is active in the resolution of disputes between the state and individuals. Hence, these institutions are occasionally aware of the 'case work' of the other institution and they are potentially familiar with some aspects of the work of the other institution that, as they argue, *does something different than we do.*

As the ombudsmen in all three researched systems provide a form of protection that differs from that of the judiciary, it comes as no real surprise that the cross-references to the court's case law are relatively similar. A more surprising fact is that cases where the judiciary makes cross-references to the ombudsmen's reports are also rather similar.[29] There are various cases in which judgments are used in ombudsmen's inquiries or investigations and vice versa. These include, for example, *factual cross-references* describing, in detail, the facts of the case while referring to the procedure of the other institution; *competence cross-references* explaining the possibility or impossibility for ombudsmen to deal with a case because of the actions of the judiciary; *supportive cross-references* where judgments finding a breach of the law are used by ombudsmen in order to support their own decisions and reports; or *distinguishing cross-references* where the ombudsmen and the judiciary reach different findings in similar situations.[30] A special type of cross-referencing, *assessment*

27 See, Part II, section 4.2.1; Part III, section 4.2.1.1 and Part IV, section 4.2.1.

28 See, Part II, section 4.2.2; Part III, sections 4.2.2 and 4.2.3 and Part IV, section 4.2.2.

29 See, Part II, section 4.2.2; Part III, section 4.2.2 and Part IV, section 4.2.2.

30 See, Part II, sections 4.2.1 and 4.2.2; Part III, sections 4.2.1, 4.2.2 and 4.2.3 and Part IV, sections 4.2.1 and 4.2.2.

cross-references, exists in cases where the judiciary reviews the legality of the actions and/or the reports of the ombudsmen (ENG, EU). One cannot therefore say that the reports of the ombudsmen and the judgments of the courts have no significance for the other institutions whatsoever. However, one must take into account the *ad hoc* character of such practice and the fact that this practice is not very common.

> **Finding 3**
> *The ombudsmen acknowledge the applicability of judgments for their investigations/inquiries. Sometimes they consider them to be decisive in an investigated case. The judiciary does not ignore the existence of ombudsmen's reports in their proceedings. However, it does not consider them to be decisive for its judgments.*

In all three cases, ombudsmen are *ex lege* obliged to consider the existence of judgments (Finding 1). Firstly, the *ex lege* consideration is connected with the *facts covered by the judgments*. If a judgment covers the same facts as those covered by a complaint the statutory bars can be applicable. Secondly, the judgment can be considered by the ombudsman if he/she applies a rule which has been previously interpreted by the court. The normative definitions that are provided by the courts (administrative or other courts) can be applied by ombudsmen in their investigations to prove a particular point. This practice exists in the Netherlands, in the EU and in England (LGO).[31] Thirdly, the consideration of judgments can be connected with the rules applied by the courts as a *yardstick* (as an assessment standard).

The judgments might also prove important for ombudsmen when developing their normative standards. Compliance with the law is often perceived as an internal part of a broader concept of good or proper administration.[32] This can theoretically lead ombudsmen to believe that the judgments of the courts are decisive in an individual case. A breach of the law found in the judgment *can* lead to a breach of the requirements of good or proper administration.[33]

Conversely, the judiciary is not in any way required to study or consult ombudsmen's reports and it is certainly not bound by them.[34] Investigations by the ombudsmen do not bar the judiciary from assessing issues that have already been evaluated by ombudsmen (for example, damages). The recommendations of the ombudsmen are addressed *to the administration* and *not to the judiciary*. Last but not least, good or proper conduct by the administration *is not* necessarily the same as lawful conduct by the administration. This is the reason why one can observe a certain judicial reluctance to take into account the facts found and conclusions reached by the ombudsmen. In doing that the court can theoretically come to a decision that does not reflect the applicable law. The courts assess compliance with the law and not with a general normative concept such as good or proper administration.[35] Although the courts are not obliged to take the reports of the ombudsmen

31 See, Part II, section 4.2.1; Part III, section 4.2.1.1 and Part IV, section 4.2.1.
32 See, Part II, section 5.1; Part III, section 5.1 and Part IV, section 5.1.
33 See, the findings connected with normative coordination included in the following section.
34 See, Part II, section 4.2.2; Part III, section 4.2.2 and Part IV, sections 4.2.2.
35 See Findings 2 and 4 (normative coordination).

into account, if a report is submitted to them (by a party), they do not ignore it.[36] If an individual supports his statements with an ombudsman's report the courts generally consider it. But in most cases, the reports of ombudsmen that find maladministration or improper administration are not enough for the court to find a breach of the law. One can find examples where the courts state that the finding of maladministration or improper administration by an ombudsman is not enough to support the individual's claim of unlawfulness.[37] Although the ombudsman is an institution with constitutionally recognised investigative and dispute resolution powers, these powers are not enough for a court to uphold an individual claim that is based solely on the report of an ombudsman. This is connected with a different yardstick which is applied by ombudsmen. One can thus distinguish between two issues – *facts included in the report* and the *normative standard used in the report*. There are cases where the courts have expressly argued that even though the facts were ascertained by the ombudsman, they cannot rely on them.[38] Still, sometimes depending on the circumstances of the case, they can take them into account.[39] The normative standards are discussed in the following subsection.

Finding 4

An individual can rely on ombudsmen's reports in court proceedings and on judgments during an ombudsman's investigation/inquiry. Nonetheless, it is the ombudsmen and the judiciary who decide what authority judgments or reports have in connection with particular cases.

When protecting their interests, individuals can rely in court proceedings on the reports of the ombudsmen and vice versa they can rely on judgments in ombudsmen's investigations.[40] In none of the described systems is this possibility expressly excluded. If an individual supports his contentions with a court judgment that does not mean that the ombudsman will automatically accept the judgment as decisive in the case at hand. In the practice of the ombudsmen one can see that they do decide whether certain judgments are applicable to a particular case.[41]

The same happens if an individual supports his statements with an ombudsman's report in court proceedings. The courts decide whether the report should apply to the case at hand. *A priori* they do not take the report as being applicable or non-applicable to the case.[42] The reports of the ombudsmen *do not* however *have* any *special status* or *specific persuasive authority*. Their application and their value are evaluated by the judiciary just as any other argument that supports or disproves the contentions of the parties to the proceedings.

The practice of the researched institutions shows that they decide whether the judgments or the reports have some importance for their case. If that is not so, they

36 See, Part II, section 4.2.2; Part III, section 4.2.2 and Part IV, sections 5.1.1 and 5.2.1.

37 See, Part II, sections 3.1.2 and 5.2.1 and Part IV, sections 3.1.2, 4.1.2 and 5.2.1.

38 See, Part II, section 4.2.2; Part III and Part IV, section 4.2.2.

39 See, Part II, sections 4.2.1 and 4.2.2 and Part III, section 4.2.2.

40 See, Part II, sections 4.2.1 and 4.2.2; Part III, sections 4.2.1 and 4.2.2 and Part IV, sections 4.2.1 and 4.2.2.

41 See, Part II, section 4.2.1; Part III, section 4.2.1 and Part IV, section 4.2.1.

42 See, Part II, section 4.2.2 and Part IV, section 4.2.2.

point to this fact. Due to the inquisitorial character of the ombudsman investigation, the ombudsmen sometimes make use of a judgment of their own initiative. For example, if an individual relies on the case law of the courts, ombudsmen sometimes point to more recent court judgments (EUO). The judiciary mostly deals with ombudsmen's findings only when steered in that direction by the parties and not of its own initiative.[43] During these procedures ombudsmen become the *interpreters of the judgments* and the judiciary the *interpreter of the reports*. One can here see a difference in the binding authority and consequences of these interpretations.

2.2.2 Evaluation of findings and possible amendments to the existing designs

Case coordination among ombudsmen and the judiciary is directly connected with their institutional coordination, with the substance of disputes between individuals and the administration and with the normative concepts of the ombudsmen and the judiciary. In all three systems the *reports* of the ombudsmen and the *judgments* of the courts can be accessed by the other institution. The only exception is the ombudsprudence of the PO whose investigative reports are published only exceptionally. Furthermore, the accessibility of the jurisprudence of the English tribunals is fairly limited and the jurisprudence of all researched courts (with the exception of the Court of the EU) is not published online in its entirety.

In the practice of the ombudsmen one can see an occasional cross-reference to judgments or an application of the rules included in judgments. This practice is mostly *ad hoc*, although it is sometimes premeditated and in the case of the EUO it is the starting point for the ombudsman's inquiry. The cross-referencing practice of the judiciary exists as well, but it is almost completely coincidental. Within the judiciary one can also see various approaches towards the ombudsprudence, from no interest at all (some of the English tribunals) to an assessment as to whether the ombudsmen's reports and actions are in compliance with the law (the English Administrative Court). In general, there is *no common approach* towards the ombudsprudence and its importance for the judiciary. The ombudsprudence is very often ignored.

The individuals or administration in dispute often support their arguments by referring to the judgments of the judiciary or the reports of the ombudsmen. Because of the character of their work ombudsmen sometimes look for and make use of certain judgments of their own initiative. The judiciary, mainly because of the adversarial character of their work, do not do this. Formally, the law requires ombudsmen to be aware of judgments as these can theoretically have an influence on their ability to investigate a complaint. This is not applicable to the judiciary. The judiciary is not required to know the contents of ombudsmen's reports. It does not need to be aware of their existence. Hence, when the judiciary makes cross-references to the ombudsmen, it does so for a certain reason.

Similar to the case of institutional coordination, one cannot see major problems in case coordination between ombudsmen and the judiciary that would lead to their inability

43 See, Part II, section 4.2.2 and Part IV, section 4.2.2.

to exercise their functions properly. The absence of visible problems does not mean that the design of ombudsmen-judiciary relations cannot be any different or that it cannot be somehow amended. One can think about this matter as regards the checks and balances of the ombudsmen and the judiciary in relation to the administration. Case coordination between the ombudsmen and the judiciary may improve the way in which they exercise their functions. This coordination can also bring an additional balance into relations between individuals and the administration and it can potentially enhance the procedural possibilities of individuals.

The different binding character of the reports and the judgments is clear. Legally binding judgments by the judiciary stand next to the legally non-binding reports (and other decisions) of the ombudsmen. The legally non-binding character of the reports does not mean that they have no binding effect at all as the majority of the ombudsmen's recommendations are in fact followed. This makes it interesting, as ombudsmen can use only the authority of their office to persuade the administration that their recommendations are worth following. Only sometimes do ombudsmen turn to national parliaments for the political support. On the other hand, the administration does not have any option but to follow the judgments of the judiciary.

Ombudsmen are constitutionally acknowledged institutions. They are provided with specific investigative powers which are to a certain extent similar to those of the judiciary. They can hear witnesses, they can ask for expert reports and they can even carry out on-site investigations. They can be asked to order any of these actions by any party to the investigation but they can also act in an *inquisitorial manner*. Some of them can start an investigation of their own motion. The judiciary does not have this authority. The judiciary acts only if it is required to act and its procedures are in principle of an *adversarial character*. The extensive investigative powers of the ombudsmen, their own-motion investigations and their need to persuade the administration about their correctness without the possibility to force it to follow their recommendations place ombudsmen in the position of *meticulous fact-finders*. Their investigations must be precise so that the administration can accept their findings without protest. The ombudsmen's particular specialisation and their flexible investigating powers give rise to the question of why the judiciary does not more often take the factual findings of ombudsmen as a starting point. Cooperation in this area can considerably strengthen the checks and balances that these institutions provide in relation to the administration and it can potentially speed up problem solving. Because of this one can make the following recommendation.

> **The judiciary should not a priori reject the facts found by ombudsmen during their investigations. If they are relevant for the legal question, the judiciary could take them as a starting point in its assessment unless proved otherwise during the proceedings.**

Apart from the facts, the judgments and the reports can be interesting for the ombudsmen and the judiciary also because of the *normative standards* used in the particular decision. Case coordination between them can enhance the clarity of the normative standards used. The practice of the ombudsmen or the judiciary is not always as clear as it could be. Normative coordination is however evaluated in the following section.

In connection with case coordination one can also ask whether the parties to the proceedings or to the investigation can support their arguments by judgments and reports and the value of this support. The absence of any explanation as to whether one can use the report of the ombudsman in court proceedings (and vice versa) may impact the chances of individuals and a speedy solution to the case. Individuals and the administration often rely on reports by ombudsmen or judgments by the courts in the proceedings or in the investigation of the other institution. An average complainant or applicant may not see any difference between a court judgment and a report of the ombudsman. As the law is usually silent on this and the case law is often ad hoc and unclear, individuals possibly assume that these documents have a similar character and thus that they can be relied upon during the procedures of the other institutions. Naturally, these 'decisions' can prove the individual's contentions in the proceedings of the other institution, but this is not obligatory. The absence of a clear explanation as to why an ombudsman's report was not accepted in judicial proceedings or why a court judgment was not applied by an ombudsman in his/her investigation can lead to uncertainty for individuals and even potentially negatively affect their trust in the system of protection against the administration and thus in the entire system of checks and balances in relation to the administration. For this reason one can recommend the following amendment to the existing design.

The judiciary and ombudsmen should pay more attention to the explanation for the importance of the findings of the other institutions for their own proceedings or investigation, if these findings have been raised by one of the parties to their procedures.

2.3 Question 3 (normative coordination)

The third research question is:

What is the mutual significance of the normative standards of ombudsmen and the judiciary in the researched systems and what are the interrelations between these normative standards?

2.3.1 Findings

In their procedures both the judiciary and the ombudsmen apply certain normative standards as assessment criteria. Against these normative standards they assess the actions of the administration. The chapters of this book dealing with normative coordination (Chapters 5) describe and discuss the existing *significance, coordination* and *interrelation* between the normative standards of the researched institutions. Based on the data provided in these chapters one can answer the research question with the following findings.

Finding 1

The legislator acknowledges the existence of different normative concepts of the ombudsmen and the judiciary. The coordination of this matter is left to their practice.

In connection with the normative concepts and normative standards of the ombudsmen and the judiciary one can observe that the legislators almost never address this particular matter. In England, the legislator connects both researched ombudsmen with the concept of maladministration (in the English sense).[44] In the infancy of the English ombudsman institutions, the legislator also provided them with a 'manual' to explain the meaning of the term.[45] In the EU, the legislator connects the EUO with the concept of maladministration (in the Union sense) without providing him with any narrower identification of its contents.[46] In the Netherlands, ombudsmen are linked with a normative concept of proper administration. They are also expressly required to use this as an assessment standard and to refer to it in their reports.[47] Sometimes the judiciary tries to provide ombudsmen with 'guidance' as to the content of their normative concepts. This is the case, for example, in England where the courts have tried to explain the contents of maladministration,[48] but also in the EU where the Court often describes a delay as an instance of maladministration.[49] But these are only isolated cases. In all three cases the administrative courts are linked with the assessment of compliance with the law. The law is often their only normative standard.[50]

In all of the researched systems, the normative concepts of the ombudsmen exist without a legal definition or a delimitation of their content. These concepts therefore have considerable flexibility without a legal limitation. At the same time, ombudsmen are given broad discretion as regards their investigations but also in connection with the powers to 'clarify' the content and substance of this normative concept. In order to do that, they develop and redevelop numerous normative standards. This development is generally accepted and it is relatively unlimited as long as these normative standards do not require the administration to act in direct contradiction with their procedural or substantive obligations.

Finding 2

Ombudsmen and the judiciary develop their normative standards separately. Nonetheless, during the development of these standards inspiration can be drawn from other, already existing standards.

The ombudsmen included in this research develop normative standards that are applied when assessing compliance with good or proper administration. Their normative function is accepted in all three legal systems. This development took some time and it led to the

44 See, Part III, section 1.3.
45 Ibid.
46 See, Part IV, sections 1.1.1 and 5.1.
47 See, Part II, sections 1.1.1 and 5.1.
48 See, Part III, section 1.3.
49 See, Part IV, section 5.1.
50 See, Part II, sections 5.1.2 and 5.3; Part III, sections 5.1.2 and 2.1.2 and Part IV, sections 5.1.2 and 5.3.

creation of '*codified*' lists of normative standards. These normative standards then function as *assessment standards* (when applied by ombudsmen) and as *standards of conduct* (when applied by the administration). The EUO has developed (in cooperation with the European Parliament) the Code of Administrative Conduct.[51] The PO has developed three sets of Principles of Good Administration.[52] The LGO have developed the Axioms of Good Administration.[53] The NO has developed, and recently redeveloped, Guidelines on Proper Conduct and several lists of normative standards of administrative conduct which are applicable in particular parts of administrative conduct.[54]

The normative standards of the ombudsmen have been developed in a relatively short period of time, usually within a few years after the establishment of the ombudsman institution. The exception is the PO as his/her lists of normative standards were developed and published after almost 40 years of the institution's existence. The normative standards of the ombudsmen give substance to the general normative concept assessed by the ombudsmen, whether it is maladministration or proper administration etc. Because of the flexible character of these normative concepts, the ombudsnorms can also protect (in their own way) the conduct that is protected by the judiciary. Good administrative conduct and proper administrative conduct often require the administration to comply with *the law* including *human rights* and with the *requirements of good or proper administration in a narrow sense.* Thus compliance with the law and human rights has found its way also into the normative standards of the ombudsmen primarily connected with evaluating compliance with a general normative concept such as good administration.

The judiciary assesses compliance with the law. While doing so it applies normative standards – *statutory law* and both *codified* and *uncodified* legal principles. In all three legal systems one can find cases of the judicial discovery and development of legal principles.[55] The courts have considerably longer experience in the development of normative standards than the ombudsmen. They have been developing their standards for decades or even longer. The legal principles developed by the courts are sometimes codified in statutory law. This is partially the case with the Dutch and Union practice.[56]

The normative standards of the ombudsmen and the judiciary have not been developed in a vacuum. They do not develop out of nothing, they rather react to developments in society and in the law. Hence it can happen that the normative standards of different institutions *reflect* this development and each other. The normative standards of the ombudsmen have their basis in the investigative practice of the ombudsmen, in the practice of the administration and, theoretically, also in the practice of other institutions i.e. in external influences. Also the courts, when developing legal principles, are not entirely free of external influences. They may be influenced from the outside. This is the case, for example, with the *principle of transparency* and the *principle or reasonable time* which since the mid-1990s have been a part of the agenda of the EUO and are nowadays also

51 See, Part IV, sections 1.1.3.1 and 5.1.1.
52 See, Part III, sections 5.1.1.1 and 1.1.1.3.1.
53 See, Part III, sections 5.1.1.2 and 1.2.1.3.1.
54 See, Part II, sections 1.1.3.1 and 5.1.1
55 See, Part II, section 5.1.2; Part III, section 5.1.2 and Part IV, section 5.1.2.
56 See, Part II, section 5.1.2 and Part IV, section 5.1.2.

used by the Court and, according to some authors, amount to two of the general principles of Union law.[57] Still it is rare that the normative standards of the courts expressly reflect those of the ombudsmen. It depends on the willingness and the need of the judiciary to look for normative standards outside the traditional legal sphere.

Finding 3

One can distinguish a formal and substantive overlap between some normative standards of the ombudsmen and the judiciary. Some of the normative standards of these institutions, however, do not overlap at all.

The research confirms that between the normative standards of the ombudsman and the judiciary there are occasional formal and/or substantive overlaps.[58] A *formal overlap* is an overlap in the *denomination* of the normative standards. It is possibly linked with the ombudsman's perception of his/her role towards the law and with the assessment of compliance with the law. If the perception of the ombudsman's role is close to the assessment of compliance with the law, then also the formal overlap may be greater. When one looks at the list of the normative standards of the EUO, one can see that these standards are quite often called the same in general principles of Union law. Moreover, the Code itself resembles a statute.[59] In the Netherlands, this overlap is very small, at least in connection with the latest version of the Guidance on proper conduct of the Dutch NO.[60] In England such an overlap does not exist (the PO) or is limited (LGO).[61]

A *substantive overlap* between the normative standards is the overlap of the *contents* of the normative standards. The existence of this overlap confirms the proximity of the normative standards of the ombudsmen and the judiciary. As shown previously, a substantive overlap exists in the majority of normative standards developed and used by the investigated institutions.[62] One can also see that there is some substantive overlap between the normative standards of the ombudsmen and the statutory law, if the law codifies the standards developed by the judiciary.[63] This indicates that ombudsmen and the judiciary, while developing and applying their standards, potentially protect the same general values that are connected with certain types of (positive or negative) administrative behaviour. The substantive overlap between the normative standards links this value with *double* protection – '*soft*' protection by the ombudsman and '*hard*' protection by the judiciary. The *substantive* overlap between the normative standards of the ombudsmen and the judiciary shows that values that are primarily protected by the judiciary (compliance with the law including human rights) can in a specific way be protected by the ombudsmen as well.

Some general values are only protected by the ombudsmen. These are the values that do not have any specific legal protection by the judiciary. Surprisingly enough, in all

57 See, and Part IV, section 5.1.2.and Buijze 2013.
58 See, Part II, section 5.2.2; Part III, section 5.2.2 and Part IV, section 5.2.2.
59 See, Part IV, section 5.2.2.
60 See, Part II, section 5.2.2.
61 See, Part III, section 5.2.2.
62 See, Part II, section 5.2.2; Part III, section 5.2.2 and Part IV, section 5.2.2.
63 Ibid.

of the researched systems one can see that the majority of the legal principles developed by the courts (if not all of them) are in some way reflected in the normative standards of the ombudsmen.[64] However, this premise is not applicable vice versa as some normative standards of the ombudsmen are not reflected in legal principles at all. This can be explained by the greater flexibility of the normative concepts that are connected with the ombudsmen and by the fact that lawfulness and compliance with a concept such as good administration are not identical but only partially overlap. This allows ombudsmen to protect the values that are *not protected* by the judiciary. They include values protected by, for example, the principle of good administration such as *seek continuous improvement* (PO) or requirements of *courtesy* of the NO, the LGO or the EUO.

One can presume that the values that are *only* protected by the ombudsmen's normative standards can, but must not, also receive protection from the courts. One cannot exclude a *future development of the law* including general principles of law. As standards having a potential to influence the development of legal principles, one can mention, for example, the principle of *fairness*, the *principle of transparency* or the *principle of a reasonable time for a decision* of the EUO. They can possibly become principles of national law as well. Also proportionality as perceived by the PO can creep into the judgments of the English courts where, with the exception of the application of European law, proportionality does not have a stable place among the grounds for a judicial review. Conversely, one can hardly imagine that the judiciary will create a legal principle requiring the administration to *act politely* or *courteously*. This means that not all of the values protected by the ombudsmen have a tendency to be also protected by the law and the judiciary. They might not be protected by legal norms but only by ombudsnorms.

Finding 4

A breach of the normative standards of the court can be evaluated by ombudsmen as a breach of their normative standards. Despite a substantive overlap between the normative standards, a breach of the ombudsmen's normative standards is only rarely identified by the courts as a breach of their normative standards.

The vast majority of the normative standards developed by the judiciary are reflected in the normative standards of the ombudsmen. A breach of a legal principle or a breach of written law can directly lead to a breach of the ombudsmen's standards. This is connected with the perception that the concept of good or proper administration often overlaps with the concept of lawfulness but it also provides protection for values existing 'beyond the law.'

The researched ombudsmen have different perspectives on the relationship between lawfulness and good/proper administration. According to the NO, unlawful conduct is not always also improper conduct and improper conduct does not always lead to unlawfulness.[65] According to the PO unlawfulness is not necessarily maladministration (in the English sense) and maladministration does not have to lead to unlawful conduct.[66]

64 See, schemes in Part II, section 5.2.2; Part III, section 5.2.2 and Part IV, section 5.2.2.
65 See, Part II, section 5.1.
66 See, Part III, section 5.1.1.1.

The LGO often connects unlawful conduct with maladministration (in the English sense) but maladministration does not have to lead to unlawful conduct.[67] According to the EUO unlawful conduct always leads to maladministration (in the Union sense) but maladministration does not always lead to unlawful conduct.[68] Thus, all four ombudsmen included in the research *distinguish between the concept of good/proper administration* and *the concept of lawfulness*. From this perspective one can note that while in the case of the EUO and the LGO unlawfulness can be seen as an internal part of maladministration, in the case of the PO and the NO these concepts are separate. If we use the ombudsmanquadrant develop by the NO[69] we can have four different situations where the administrative conduct in question can be either:

Administrative conduct	**Good or proper**	**Maladministrative or improper**
Lawful	Lawful and proper (good)	Lawful but improper (maladministrative)
Unlawful	Unlawful but proper (good)	Unlawful and improper (maladministrative)

This scheme shows that there is a difference between compliance with the law and compliance with ombudsnorms. They are parallel concepts. The conduct of the administration should comply with legal principles *as well as* with ombudsnorms. Because of this it can be *theoretically* possible that unlawful conduct can be good or proper, i.e. unlawfulness does not directly lead to maladministration or improper conduct. This is applicable at least in connection with the NO and the PO. The situation is different in the practice of the EUO (and possibly also that of the LGO) as here a breach of a legal principle *presupposes* a breach of the normative standard of the ombudsmen and thus also maladministration. Unlawfulness in these cases always leads to maladministration.

The perception of the ombudsmen is not identical with the perception of the judiciary. Generally, the judiciary does not identify a breach of the ombudsmen's normative standard as a breach of its standards.[70] Although one can find cases where the judiciary underlines an *overlap* between normative concepts such as good or proper administration and lawfulness, the judiciary does not give the same significance to a breach of the normative standards of the ombudsmen compared to a breach of legal principles. A priori, it clearly distinguishes between its normative standards and those of the ombudsmen and between their legal consequences. Not even in the EU, where the EUO rather closely applies and follows the normative standards of the judiciary, is the Court *a priori* prepared to follow the report of the ombudsman as regards its normative standards.[71] For the courts, a finding of maladministration or improper administration does not automatically lead to a finding of unlawful conduct. These are only the findings of an extrajudicial institution. The judiciary strictly distinguishes between these normative standards.

67 See, Part III, section 5.1.1.2.
68 See, Part IV, sections 5.1 and 5.3.1.
69 See, Part II, section 5.1, Annual Report of the NO 2005 and Annual Report of the NO 2006.
70 See, Part II, sections 3.1.2, 4.1.2 and 5.3 and Part IV, sections 4.1.2 and 5.3.
71 See, Part IV, sections 4.1.2 and 5.1.2.

One can explain this reluctance on the part of the judiciary to apply the ombudsmen's normative standards by the fact that these standards do not have the status of law or of legally binding standards. The courts are not obliged to use them or take them into account. The normative standards of the ombudsmen, even if they protect the same general value, are *not the law*. The courts can completely ignore them and they often do so.

This finding confirms that ombudsmen are aware of the normative standards of the courts while the courts have only limited knowledge about the specific contents of the normative standards of the ombudsmen. Nonetheless, there are examples where the high echelons of the judiciary or even the judges of the lower courts are well aware of the normative standards of the ombudsmen although they do not use them in practice.[72]

Finding 5
In the case of a substantive overlap, the normative standards of the ombudsmen can potentially have a different application than the normative standards of the judiciary.

Although the substantive parts do not discuss and closely compare all the normative standards of the ombudsmen and the judiciary, from the perspective of the normative standards that were compared (i.e. as a qualitative statement) this finding proves to be applicable. The previous text closely compares several substantively overlapping standards of the ombudsmen and the judiciary.[73] Based on these comparisons, one can see that the ombudsmen's normative standards can sometimes cover aspects that are not included in the overlapping legal principles of the courts.[74] This practice can be seen, for example, in connection with the NO's requirement of proportionality that can be applied more *leniently* than the principle of proportionality as applied by the courts.[75] This practice has not really been confirmed in the EU or England.

This practice does not broaden or change the legal principles as such. It may however possibly lead to a further development of the legal principles by the courts, but only if the courts know about this practice. This finding is connected with the different character of the concept of good or proper administration and lawfulness. The former is more flexible and so are its normative standards. Because of this flexibility, the protection of the substantively overlapping normative standards of the ombudsmen and the courts can be different. The standards of the ombudsmen can provide protection against administrative conduct that is lawful but is morally or administratively unacceptable.

2.3.2 Evaluation of findings and possible amendments to the existing designs

The starting point for an evaluation of findings linked with *normative coordination* between the normative standards of the ombudsmen (*ombudsnorms*) and those of the judiciary (*legal norms*) is that these normative standards are *different* or rather that they are *not identical* even though one can occasionally discover a substantive overlap between

72 See, Part II, section 5.3 and Part III, sections 5.1.1 and 5.3.
73 See, Part II, section 5.2.2; Part III, section 5.2.2 and Part IV, section 5.2.2.
74 See, Part II, sections 5.2.2 and 5.3.1 and Part IV, sections 5.2.2 and 5.3.1.
75 See, Part II, section 5.3.2.

them. This necessary difference is linked with a different kind of protection provided by ombudsmen and the judiciary. The normative standards of the judiciary are the law and legal principles. They are legally binding and enforceable. The normative standards of ombudsmen have the character of non-binding moral principles. These are either *moral principles in a strict sense* (e.g. polite conduct by the administration) or *broader moral principles* (e.g. the principle of good administrative organisation). Normative standards are closely connected with the normative concept that is covered by these institutions. They reflect the content of this normative concept.

When one looks at the normative coordination between the ombudsmen and the judiciary in the three researched legal systems one can see that there is almost no normative coordination. In the law one can find the *acknowledgements of the existence* of different normative standards applied by the ombudsmen and the judiciary but there is almost *no formal coordination*. From the present design of the systems, one can see that normative standards are developed by the ombudsmen and the judiciary *autonomously*. Although this development sometimes goes in different directions, one can see that the normative standards often protect similar or overlapping values. Ombudsmen as well as the judiciary try to conserve their competences and to keep their distance not only as state institutions but also as regards their normative standards. It is possible to question this status quo. Although ombudsmen and the judiciary apply *a priori* different standards, there are substantive overlaps among these standards. Then one can see that ombudsmen can apply the overlapping standards in a more lenient way and thus they can give legal principles a new dimension. Precisely this possibility of the ombudsmen can enable the judiciary to see whether there is some room for the development or redevelopment of their own principles. Thus, at least in connection with some normative standards, such coordination might prove useful.

Although ombudsnorms are different from legal norms one can see that these standards cover two types of conduct, conduct that can also be covered by legal principles (*'legal' ombudsnorms*) and conduct which is not covered by legal principles (*extra-legal ombudsnorms*). This division depends on the ombudsman's perception of good or proper administration. Despite this duality of the ombudsnorms, *the ombudsnorms are not the law or legal principles*. This is connected with the fact that the 'legal' ombudsnorms are not always completely identical to the legal norms as the overlap can be only partial and they can also partially cover extra-legal issues. Still, the ombudsmen by developing 'legal' ombudsnorms can stretch or broaden traditional legal principles. By doing that, they can add to the protection of individuals provided by the judiciary. The extra-legal ombudsnorms covering conduct *beyond the law* such as courtesy, de-escalation or cooperation with individuals, should be constantly developed by ombudsmen because the judiciary is not interested in the development of these standards in the first place and because this is something that the 'good administration' ombudsmen should do. Although ombudsmen often reiterate the importance of the development of ombudsnorms, one can sometimes see a certain satisfaction on the part of ombudsmen after ombudsnorms have been '*codified*' (as in the case of the EUO). Still, normative concepts of proper/good administration are general and flexible and they need continuous development. Because of that, ombudsmen should *constantly develop and interpret* their standards for the benefit of the administration. They should clarify their meanings as this can help them in their practice but also it can help the administration in striving for '*good*' administration. Here one can recommend the following change.

> **Ombudsmen should constantly (re)develop and apply their normative standards in practice. They should do this for the benefit of the administration, for the sake of clarity and to uphold their standards and for the sake of protecting individuals and society as a whole.**

The development of normative standards by the ombudsmen should be consistent but flexible. The finding of maladministration or improper administration should be clearly presented and explained in the reports of the ombudsmen or their conclusions. The findings should also include a clear notification of the norm that was breached. The connection between the facts of the case, maladministration or improper administration and the normative standards should be implicitly included in the reports of the ombudsmen. This can enhance the clarity of these normative standards and the potential educational function of ombudsmen. Conversely, the absence of any identification of a breached normative standard can diminish these roles. As noted before in the text, ombudsnorms can be an inspiration for the judiciary and possibly also for the development of the law. Because of that one can make the following recommendation.

> **Ombudsmen should always refer to and explain the *applied* and *breached* normative standards in the findings and/or conclusions of their reports.**

An interpretation and assessment of compliance with *the* law is the *domain of the courts*. Due to the general character of the normative concepts that should be protected by the ombudsmen, these ombudsmen can also develop the norms covering conduct that can be perceived as unlawful. A substantive overlap between these standards and the practice of the institutions confirm this. At this point one can imagine that there might be some *normative coordination between these institutions*. As shown by all three case studies, the development and application of normative standards by the ombudsmen and the judiciary is *relatively independent*. One can imagine that ombudsmen develop and apply their normative standards in a more lenient fashion than the judiciary, i.e. differently. On the one hand, it is necessary that ombudsmen apply and develop their principles in a more lenient and more flexible way because they evaluate compliance with a general normative concept that is *not identical with lawfulness*. On the other hand, this normative concept often requires the administration to act *in compliance with the law and legal principles*. Especially this second point can be used in order to question the ombudsman's leniency. An over-lenient approach by the ombudsman to a normative standard overlapping with *written law* can lead to uncertainty about the contents of this standard. Ombudsmen as a state institution are naturally bound by the law. Of course, one can argue that ombudsmen only develop their '*own*' normative standards in order to give content to the concept that is different from lawfulness. But a very lenient approach by ombudsmen can in this case (an overlap with written law) possibly undermine ombudsmen's authority and it can potentially question the need for more than one normative system in the state. But if the ombudsmen's normative standards overlap with *unwritten legal standards*, the ombudsmen should conversely have the freedom to adopt a more lenient and flexible approach. Still, the development of this principle should not ignore the value that was protected by this unwritten legal standard.

One can ask where is the line between a positive development of the ombudsnorms covering the same issues as written or unwritten law and a negative development? Although the answer to this question depends on each and every particular case, one can make the following recommendations.

When developing normative standards which overlap with written law, ombudsmen should follow the meaning of written law, unless it is necessary to cover an extra-legal dimension of the conduct.

When developing normative standards which overlap with unwritten legal principles, ombudsmen should do this freely; however, their development should take into account the general value that is protected by unwritten legal principles.

One can look at the normative coordination also from the point of view of the possible impact of ombudsmen on the standards of the judiciary. Although some values are now only protected by extra-legal ombudsnorms it is not excluded that in the future these values will require protection by the law. Thus these standards might become legal principles or legally codified rules. The same can be said about the ombudsnorms which overlap with legal norms as these can also cover, thanks to a more lenient approach by ombudsmen, matters that are not explicitly included in a legal principle. The development of the law cannot be completely foreseen or isolated. It is connected with the needs and the development of society. As ombudsnorms are built on the practice or malpractice of the administration, they can inspire the judiciary to develop a particular principle if it is necessary for the protection of individuals to deal with this malpractice also in a legally binding manner. The protection provided by the ombudsnorms may cover situations previously not imagined by the judiciary. Ombudsmen can guide the development of legal principles into new territories, for example, the involvement of the EUO in the development of transparency in the EU. Ombudsmen can therefore add something new to the development of the law and legal principles. Also because of this, the courts should not completely ignore ombudsnorms. One can here suggest the following amendment to the existing design.

The judiciary should not overlook the normative standards of ombudsmen, as they may potentially have a positive impact on the development of the law. It is thus necessary for the judiciary to be aware of the normative standards of ombudsmen.

2.4 General conclusions

Although this book describes ombudsman-judiciary relations in three different legal systems one cannot overlook the fact that these relations have a considerable *number of similarities* and that they are regulated in a very similar way.

Ombudsmen and the judiciary are *two different state institutions*. They have their own competences, their own sphere of work, their own methods and their own normative concepts and standards. Despite their differences, one must accept that their goals and roles are rather similar, at least from the perspective of dispute resolution. They provide an independent and impartial *dispute resolution* system between individuals and the state administration. By doing so, they add to the checks and balances and to the protection of individuals in their relations with the administration. They also enable the solution of problems (legal or otherwise) and inevitably they can also enhance the trust of individuals in the administrative justice system. By definition, ombudsmen *should complement* the judiciary.

Ombudsmen and the judiciary are positioned between individuals and the administration. While exercising their functions one can discover some coordination of their actions. This coordination is not only formal, although their informal interplay tends to be marginal. Nowadays, however, coordination between ombudsmen and the judiciary is relatively limited. The *institutional coordination* of ombudsmen and the judiciary determines the competences and roles between them as state institutions. In this regard one cannot overlook the role of the *legislator* which actively sets the general framework for the work of ombudsmen and their general relations with the judiciary. The design of the institutional coordination predestines any other type of coordination between these institutions. Because of that, *the case coordination* linked with the findings of the ombudsmen and the judiciary and the *normative coordination* regarding their normative standards are limited and connected with the practice of these institutions.

One can imagine a further coordination of the actions of the ombudsmen and the judiciary in the sense of *mutual cooperation*. Such coordination may allow the judiciary and the ombudsmen to use their powers more comprehensively. It can also bring more clarity to their normative standards and enable mutual coordination during their development. Last but not least, it can lead to a better understanding of the different types of protection afforded to individuals and can provide them with a complete assessment of their disputes with the administration. Thus, cooperation between ombudsmen and the judiciary can influence the fulfilment of their roles, the protection of individuals, the development of normative concepts and standards and dispute resolution as such.

Ombudsmen and the judiciary as state institutions have their strengths and weaknesses. First of all, the protection of individuals and the dispute resolution provided by the judiciary are often not enough. If this was so, there would not be a need for the ombudsman institution in the first place. However, individuals often need more than just a formal confirmation that they were right and that the administration was wrong. They need their problem to be solved. Ombudsmen can provide *additional* dispute resolution. They can react to the particular problem and if the administration is willing to cooperate, they can work on its swift and informal removal. Their informal methods of dispute resolution and their non-legally binding problem-prevention recommendations can add to the formal legally binding assessments of the judiciary. Ombudsmen also have specific powers that can push them beyond the mechanism for solving disputes. For instance, their own-interest investigations and their non-binding recommendations provide a considerable addition to the protection of individuals. *They are not only dispute resolution mechanisms.* At the same time one must understand that ombudsmen are not a panacea for the administration. They cannot heal or prevent all its problems. Undoubtedly, they can bring a more 'moral' sense into the administration but they can only do this within the limits and competences given to them.

Generally, ombudsmen and the judiciary understand that their *different roles* and *different powers* allow them to approach disputes from different perspectives. They should however try to understand that only one way of solving disputes is often not enough to solve *the problem* between an individual and the administration in a comprehensive manner. The first step in this understanding can be reached through broader communication. Such communication can perhaps show that they are not mutual competitors but that they can work together towards general goals within the competences that are given to them. It is not enough to say *we do something else and that is why we do not need to cooperate.* It is more challenging to say *we do something else, but we also keep in mind that our general goals can bring us closer and help us to work better and in the interest of individuals, the administration and society as a whole.*

SAMENVATTING

Coördinatie van ombudsmannen en rechtspraak
Een vergelijking van de verhoudingen tussen ombudsmannen en rechtspraak in Nederland, Engeland en de Europese Unie.

De ombudsman is een instelling die in moderne democratische staten een snelle ontwikkeling doormaakt. Er is nog maar een handjevol landen dat geen ombudsman heeft op nationaal of tenminste op lokaal niveau. Meestal vertegenwoordigen ombudsmannen de *'verlengde arm van het nationaal parlement'* binnen de staatsoverheid. Zij doen onafhankelijk en onpartijdig onderzoek naar gedragingen van de overheid. Bij hun onderzoek van dit gedrag toetsen zij dit aan beoordelingsnormen. In het algemeen kunnen zij overheidsgedragingen toetsen aan verschillende normatieve concepten zoals wetgeving, aan een algemeen concept zoals goed of behoorlijk bestuur, of aan mensenrechten. Ombudsmannen functioneren ook als mechanisme voor conflictoplossing tussen de overheid en particulieren. Zij zijn echter niet de enige overheidsinstelling die voor verbolgen particulieren conflicten beslecht. De meeste landen hebben andere, meer *traditionele* mechanismen die met de beslechting van deze conflicten zijn belast. Deze traditionele mechanismen zijn algemene rechterlijke instanties of gespecialiseerde bestuursrechtelijke colleges. In vergelijking met deze traditionele mechanismen hebben ombudsmannen meestal een aantal specifieke aanvullende bevoegdheden ('ombudsman extra's'): ze kunnen onderzoek doen op eigen initiatief, kunnen aanbevelingen doen, die juridisch overigens niet bindend zijn, en kunnen structurele problemen binnen de overheid vaststellen en beoordelen.

Er is nog relatief weinig onderzoek gedaan naar de verhoudingen tussen ombudsmannen en rechtspraak. Binnen een aantal landen is een poging hiertoe gedaan, maar er bestaat geen onderzoek dat echt een internationale vergelijking trekt. Tot nu toe dan. In dit onderzoek benadert de auteur de verhoudingen tussen ombudsman en rechtspraak vanuit een vergelijkend perspectief. Het biedt een antwoord op de volgende drie vragen betreffende de coördinatie tussen ombudsmannen en de rechtspraak:

- *Hoe vindt in de onderzochte rechtssystemen coördinatie plaats van de verhoudingen tussen ombudsmannen en rechtspraak als overheidsinstellingen, en wat houdt deze coördinatie in?*;

- *Welke betekenis hebben rapporten en vonnissen (en hun inhoud) voor deze instellingen onderling, en welke verbanden bestaan er?*; en
- *Welke betekenis hebben de beoordelingsnormen van ombudsmannen en van de rechtsprekende instanties voor elkaar, en welk verband bestaat er tussen deze verschillende soorten beoordelingsnormen?*

Het onderzoek is uitgevoerd in drie volkomen verschillende systemen: het rechtssysteem van Engeland (*common law*), het rechtssysteem van Nederland (continentaal recht) en het rechtssysteem van de Europese Unie. Methodologisch gezien vormt het onderzoek een combinatie van traditioneel juridische desk-top research en kwalitatief empirisch onderzoek, omdat een deel van de gegevens gebaseerd is op mondelinge en schriftelijke interviews. Het onderzoek beschouwt deze drie verschillende systemen als drie verschillende casestudies naar de verhoudingen tussen ombudsmannen en rechtspraak.

In het algemeen functioneren ombudsmannen en rechterlijke instanties naast elkaar. De rechterlijke macht en de ombudsmannen zijn allebei overheidsinstellingen. Zij oefenen overheidsbevoegdheden uit die door de wetgever in de wet zijn vastgelegd. Deze bevoegdheden oefenen zij uit op een vergelijkbaar gebied: dat van *de bescherming van burgers tegen de overheid*. Als men op een algemene manier kijkt naar de rol die zij spelen, wordt het duidelijk dat rechtspraak en ombudsman functioneren als *mechanisme voor conflictoplossing tussen particulieren en de (staats)overheid*. In vergelijking met de oorspronkelijke verhouding tussen particulieren en de overheid hebben zowel de ombudsmannen als rechterlijke instanties *een secundaire positie*. Rechterlijke instanties vormen hier een *traditioneel mechanisme voor conflictoplossing*, terwijl de ombudsmannen een *alternatief mechanisme voor conflictoplossing* zijn. Op basis van deze veronderstelling vormen ombudsmannen een alternatief ten opzichte van de conflictoplossingsfunctie van rechterlijke instanties. Het is echter niet *slechts* een alternatief, aangezien ombudsmannen andere aspecten van overheidsgedragingen kunnen beoordelen dan de rechterlijke macht of juist dezelfde overheidsgedragingen kunnen beoordelen met andere methoden en technieken dan die van de rechterlijke macht, zoals het informeel benaderen van de overheid, als mediator proberen op te treden in het conflict, of een minnelijke schikking proberen te bereiken tussen de strijdende partijen. Ondanks de verschillen tussen deze twee instellingen kan men niet voorbijgaan aan hun *mogelijke* overeenkomsten en overlapgebieden, wat vervolgens vragen oproept over de wenselijkheid van coördinatie tussen deze instellingen.

Als men de uitgangspunten van *Mintzbergs organisatietheorie* toepast op de verhouding tussen ombudsmannen en rechterlijke instanties, gelden er twee fundamentele en tegengestelde vereisten: *de verdeling van arbeid over verschillende taken* en *de coördinatie van deze taken om het gestelde doel te bereiken*. Als we de overheid zien als een grote 'organisatie', zijn deze twee criteria ook zichtbaar. Coördinatie is volgens Mintzberg gebaseerd op verschillende mechanismen die moeten worden beschouwd als de meest elementaire componenten van de structuur, de lijm die organisaties bijeen houdt. Deze mechanismen zijn: onderlinge aanpassing, direct toezicht, standaardisatie van werkprocessen, standaardisatie van output, standaardisatie van vaardigheden en standaardisatie van normen. Coördinatie in deze betekenis wordt dus niet beschouwd als coördinatie die alleen aanwezig is in formele en juridisch bindende normen. Overeenkomstig met deze theorie wordt in dit onderzoek de coördinatie tussen ombudsmannen en rechtspraak beschouwd als het *managen van samenwerkende of concurrerende afhankelijkheden tussen ombudsmannen en rechtspraak om gedeelde doelstellingen te bereiken*. Dit onderzoek onderscheidt drie verschillende niveaus in de coördinatie van de verhoudingen tussen ombudsman en rechterlijke macht: institutionele coördinatie, zaakscoördinatie en normatieve coördinatie. Het eerste niveau (*institutionele coördinatie*) is het breedst, omdat het gaat om de coördinatie tussen ombudsmannen en rechterlijke instanties als *overheidsinstellingen*. Dit niveau houdt verband met de *doctrine van de machtsverdeling* en de *doctrine van checks-en-balances tussen ombudsmannen en rechtspraak*. Het tweede niveau (*zaakscoördinatie*) gaat om coördinatie tussen ombudsmannen en rechtspraak als mechanismen voor conflictoplossing tussen particulieren en de overheid. Dit houdt verband met de opvatting van *de ombudsmannen en rechterlijke instanties als checks-en-balances tegenover de uitvoerende macht*. Het derde niveau (*normatieve coördinatie*) is het smalst. Dit houdt verband met de beoordelingsnormen die door deze instellingen worden toegepast en ontwikkeld, zowel binnen als buiten hun eigen procedures. Dit beoordelingskader kan worden beschouwd vanuit de gezichtspunten *wetgeving en moraal* en *wetgeving en goed bestuur*.

Op het niveau van ***institutionele coördinatie*** heeft het onderzoek resultaten opgeleverd ten aanzien van de institutionele organisatie van ombudsmannen en rechterlijke instanties. Net als voor de andere twee coördinatieniveaus zijn deze resultaten gebaseerd op een analyse van de verhoudingen tussen ombudsmannen en rechterlijke instanties in Nederland, Engeland en de Europese Unie.

De eerste conclusie op dit niveau is nogal voor de hand liggend. Deze luidt dat *ondanks hun overeenkomsten, ombudsmannen en de rechterlijke instanties verschillende organen zijn* en dat *ombudsmannen meer zijn dan alleen een mechanisme voor conflictoplossing*. De bevoegdheden van de rechterlijke macht zijn in principe algemeen bekend. In de rechtspraak worden conflicten opgelost tussen partijen in formele procedures die uitmonden in juridisch bindende uitspraken. Rechterlijke instanties toetsen naleving van de wet op basis van gecodificeerde of niet-gecodificeerde *rechts*normen. Ombudsmannen zijn niet zo algemeen bekend als rechtspraak. Hoewel ombudsmannen in West Europa al sinds de jaren zestig bestaan, hebben ze duidelijk nog de neiging om hun bevoegdheden te bevestigen en hun onafhankelijkheid te benadrukken. Ombudsmannen worden traditioneel gezien als een *alternatief mechanisme voor conflictoplossing*, naast de rechter. Uit dit onderzoek blijkt dat de term 'alternatief' niet alleen inhoudt dat een conflict kan worden opgelost door ombudsmannen *of* door rechterlijke instanties, maar ook dat ombudsmannen een aantal extra, aanvullende competenties hebben die hen en hun wijze van conflictoplossing onderscheiden van die van de rechtspraak. Deze pluspunten omvatten *onderzoek op eigen initiatief*; de mogelijkheid om *niet-bindende aanbevelingen te doen*; de mogelijkheid om *structurele problemen bij de overheid* te onderzoeken en onder de aandacht te brengen; de mogelijkheid om *gedragsnormen te ontwikkelen* en richtlijnen te ontwikkelen voor overheidsgedragingen; en bovendien nog de *keuzevrijheid van ombudsmannen* om het probleem tussen de particulier en de (staats)overheid zodanig te benaderen dat dit *zou kunnen leiden tot de oplossing van de kern van het probleem.* Het feit dat deze bevoegdheden bestaan en door ombudsmannen ook worden toegepast toont aan dat er verschillen bestaan tussen ombudsmannen en rechterlijke instanties. Uit deze bevoegdheden blijkt ook dat een ombudsman meer is dan een soort eerstelijnsrechter voor 'small claims'. Uiteraard moeten ombudsmannen ook weer niet worden beschouwd als panacee voor alle overheidsproblemen.

De tweede conclusie is ook vrij voor de hand liggend en luidt dat *de wetgever alleen in formele zin een algemeen institutioneel kader vaststelt met bevoegdheden en competenties voor ombudsmannen en rechterlijke instanties.* In de onderzochte systemen zijn ombudsmannen opgezet als onderdeel van een systeem waarbinnen de rechtspraak al functioneerde. De rechterlijke macht, als een van de traditionele dragers van overheidsbevoegdheid, heeft de bevoegdheid om conflicten op te lossen tussen particulieren en de (staats) overheid. Deze conflicten worden opgelost aan de hand van het geldende recht. De ombudsmannen, daarentegen, lossen conflicten op die te maken hebben met de normatieve concepten van goed of behoorlijk bestuur. De wetgever heeft aldus verschillende normatieve concepten vastgesteld voor de ombudsmannen en de rechterlijke macht als algemene kaders waarbinnen deze overheidsinstellingen hun competenties en bevoegdheden uitoefenen. Uit deze conclusie blijkt dat de wetgever een belangrijke rol speelt in het bestaan van deze instellingen en in de bepaling van hun bevoegdheden en de door hen te hanteren normatieve maatstaven.

De derde conclusie op het niveau van de institutionele coördinatie luidt dat *de bescherming en de conflictoplossing door rechtsprekende instanties vaak een beperking vormen voor de bescherming en conflictoplossing door de ombudsmannen, terwijl de bescherming en de conflictoplossing door de ombudsmannen in principe geen beperking vormen voor de bescherming en conflictoplossing door rechtsprekende instanties.* De drie systemen in dit onderzoek laten zien dat in formele zin de bescherming die wordt geboden door ombudsmannen in enigerlei mate beperkt is als een rechtsprekende instantie haar functie al uitoefent of heeft uitgeoefend. Ombudsmannen zijn vaak verplicht hun onderzoeken te staken (of überhaupt niet te beginnen) als de inhoud van de klacht al eerder behandeld is, of op dat moment wordt behandeld, door de rechter. Dit betekent dat ondanks de *verschillende* normatieve kaders van ombudsmannen en rechterlijke instanties, zij zich niet op hetzelfde moment met *dezelfde* zaakinhoud kunnen bezighouden. Andersom, dat wil zeggen als ombudsmannen de inhoud van de zaak al hebben behandeld, kan de rechtspraak zich over het algemeen wèl bezighouden met de zaak vanuit het gezichtspunt van rechtmatigheid. Het blijkt dat ombudsmannen af en toe wel de vrijheid hebben om klachten te onderzoeken, zelfs als deze inhoudelijk al zijn behandeld door de rechter, maar dit komt niet vaak voor (en de behandeling door ombudsmannen richt zich dan vaak op een ander aspect van de zaak dan de rechter heeft behandeld).

De vierde conclusie luidt dat *de interactie tussen ombudsmannen en rechterlijke instanties bijna exact het door de wetgever vastgestelde kader en de interpretatie door de rechter volgt. Buiten dit kader is de (formele of informele) interactie tussen deze instellingen slechts marginaal en vindt uitsluitend plaats op ad-hoc basis.* Hoewel ombudsmannen en rechters onafhankelijk en onpartijdig zijn in hun conflictoplossing en daarmee tussen particulieren en de overheid in staan, is hun onderlinge interactie uiterst beperkt, en zelfs bijna niet-bestaand. Formeel gezien houden deze instellingen zich strikt aan hun belangensferen en algemene kaders. Slechts heel af en toe staan wettelijke bepalingen expliciet een vorm van samenwerking toe tussen ombudsmannen en rechtspraak. Hierdoor is formele interactie en samenwerking tussen hen nogal ongebruikelijk. Dit geldt ook voor informele interactie. De bestaande communicatie of samenwerking vindt uitsluitend plaats op adhoc basis, en is geenszins van te voren bepaald. De informele interactie kan variëren van onofficiële gesprekken tussen rechters en ombudsmannen tijdens conferenties, tot officieel overleg tussen rechtbankpresidenten en ombudsmannen. Deze beperkte interactie wordt meestal verklaard door de verschillende competenties, de verschillende normatieve concepten en de verschillende werkwijzen. Ook bestaat de neiging om de noodzaak van absolute institutionele onafhankelijkheid te benadrukken.

De vijfde en laatste conclusie op het niveau van institutionele coördinatie luidt dat *rechters soms toelichting geven wat betreft hun eigen bevoegdheid om de rechtmatigheid van de rapporten of handelingen van ombudsmannen te toetsen* en dat *zelfs als zij concluderen dat zij in het betreffende geval deze bevoegdheden hebben, zij over het algemeen de competenties van de ombudsmannen respecteren.* In sommige systemen toetst de rechter de rechtsgeldigheid van handelingen en besluiten van ombudsmannen. Deze bevoegdheid bestaat meestal niet op basis van wetgeving, maar rechters leiden deze af uit de algemene bevoegdheid van hun gerecht. Uit dit onderzoek blijkt dat rechters voorzichtig zijn in het gebruik van deze competentie. Het feit dat een rechter de handelingen van een ombudsman aan het recht kan toetsen, verandert echter het karakter van de verhouding tussen deze twee. Bij het uitoefenen van hun functies moeten ombudsmannen rekening houden met een '*rechter die over hun schouder meekijkt*.' Een interessant punt is dat deze bevoegdheid van de rechters niet kan worden opgevat als een vorm van beroep tegen rapporten of andere besluiten van ombudsmannen. Gerechtelijke toetsing houdt meestal alleen verband met de vraag of de ombudsman, bij het onderzoek van een klacht, rechtmatig te werk is gegaan. Dat impliceert de mogelijkheid om de rechtsgeldigheid van de handelingen van een ombudsman te toetsen aan de normen voor buitencontractuele aansprakelijkheid.

Het niveau van de ***zaakscoördinatie*** staat in direct verband met de institutionele coördinatie en met het feit dat beide typen instellingen functioneren als mechanismen voor conflictoplossing. Dit niveau betreft de eventuele coördinatie tussen de *formele resultaten* van de overwegingen en besluitvormingsprocessen van ombudsmannen en rechters: hun rapporten en hun uitspraken. Dit heeft de volgende conclusies opgeleverd.

De eerste conclusie op dit niveau is dat *verhoudingen tussen ombudsmannen en gerechtelijke instanties, en tussen rechtspraak en ombudsmanrapporten slechts in zeer beperkte mate geregeld zijn.* De wetgever bepaalt alleen het 'speelveld' voor ombudsmannen en rechterlijke instanties, en de algemene regels. Er wordt niets gezegd over verbanden tussen rapporten en uitspraken, hoewel de wetgever wel vaak een beperking oplegt wat betreft de bevoegdheid van een ombudsman om gerechtelijke uitspraken te controleren. De wetgever legt vaak regels vast over de bewijsvormen die de rechter in beschouwing mag nemen bij de behandeling van een zaak. De rapporten van ombudsmannen worden hiervan niet uitgesloten. Andersom wordt deze keus voor ombudsmannen meestal aan henzelf overgelaten.

De tweede conclusie luidt dat *indien noodzakelijk, ombudsmannen in hun rapporten verwijzingen opnemen naar jurisprudentie (en naar wetgeving in het algemeen).* Andersom *neemt de rechterlijke macht in zijn uitspraken slechts zeer zelden verwijzingen op naar rapporten van ombudsmannen.* Ombudsmannen en de rechterlijke macht bestaan geen van beide in een normatief of maatschappelijk vacuüm. In alle drie de onderzochte systemen kwamen zaken naar voren waarin ombudsmannen verwijzen naar rechterlijke uitspraken. De redenen hiervoor kunnen worden gezocht in de noodzaak om de lezer van de rapporten *informatie te verschaffen* over de feiten van de zaak, om *toelichting te geven* over de toepasselijkheid van de uitspraak in het onderzoek van de ombudsman, of om *gebruik te maken* van een eerder door de rechter vastgestelde regel en zo de eigen bevindingen te *schragen.* Ombudsmannen voeren geen beoordeling uit van de kwaliteit van de uitspraken of bevindingen van de rechter. De rechtspraak verwijst soms ook naar ombudsmannen of hun rapporten, om vergelijkbare redenen. Rechters proberen de lezer van de uitspraken *informatie te verschaffen* over de feiten van de zaak, *uitleg te geven* over de toepasselijkheid van het rapport of de bevoegdheden van de ombudsman in het algemeen. Bij uitzondering *maken ze gebruik* van de eerder door een ombudsman toegepaste regel of gebruiken ze zijn rapport om hun eigen bevindingen te *schragen.* In zaken waarin rechters de rechtmatigheid van handelingen van ombudsmannen kunnen toetsen, lichten ze deze toetsing toe. Over het algemeen gebeurt dit op ad-hoc basis en wordt het niet vooraf gepland. In dat geval valt er een verschil te zien in de inquisitoire benadering van ombudsmannen en de overwegend contradictoire benadering van de rechterlijke macht.

De derde conclusie luidt dat *ombudsmannen de toepasselijkheid van gerechtelijke uitspraken op hun onderzoeken erkennen. Soms beschouwen ze deze als doorslaggevend in een onderzochte zaak. In de rechtspraak wordt het bestaan van de rapporten van ombudsmannen zeker niet genegeerd, maar worden ze in uitspraken niet als doorslaggevend beschouwd.* Hieruit blijkt dat ombudsmannen zich bewust zijn van gerechtelijke uitspraken, en wel op dezelfde manier als waarop ze zich bewust zijn van wetgeving. Indien noodzakelijk wordt rekening gehouden met jurisprudentie (en met wetgeving). Indien de rechter in zijn beoordeling van de rechtsgeldigheid van een overheidshandeling concludeert dat deze niet rechtsgeldig is, kan het zijn dat de ombudsman in een vergelijkbare zaak concludeert dat er sprake is een van een schending van standaarden van goed bestuur. Dit hangt echter af van het verband tussen rechtsgeldigheid en goed of behoorlijk bestuur. Aan de andere kant kan niet worden gesteld dat de rechtspraak niet bekend is met de rapporten van ombudsmannen, hoewel deze daar slechts zelden worden gebruikt. Ombudsmanrapporten hebben geen bijzondere status binnen het bewijs dat aan rechters wordt voorgelegd. Een ombudsmanrapport is voor een rechter in principe niet voldoende om te concluderen dat er een overtreding van een rechtsnorm heeft plaatsgevonden of om een schadevergoeding toe te kennen.

De vierde en laatste conclusie op het niveau van de zaakscoördinatie laat zien dat *een particulier in gerechtelijke procedures een beroep kan doen op ombudsmanrapporten, en in een ombudsmanonderzoek op gerechtelijke uitspraken. Het zijn echter de ombudsmannen en de rechterlijke instanties zelf die beslissen welke betekenis deze uitspraken of rapporten hebben in een bepaalde zaak.* Dit onderzoek laat zien dat particulieren in gerechtelijke procedures zich regelmatig beroepen op ombudsmanrapporten, en in ombudsmanonderzoeken op gerechtelijke uitspraken. *A priori* houden wetgeving en secundaire wetgeving en ook de praktijk van deze instellingen de mogelijkheid open voor particulieren om zich op deze documenten te beroepen. Indien dergelijke documenten aan hen worden voorgelegd, nemen ze deze in beschouwing. Indien ze belangrijk zijn voor het onderzoek van een ombudsman of voor de gerechtelijke procedure, zullen deze instellingen ernaar verwijzen. Indien een rapport of uitspraak waar naar is verwezen niet van toepassing is, zullen rechters of ombudsmannen dit toelichten. Er bestaat een algemene regel dat als in een uitspraak wordt geoordeeld dat er sprake is van schending van een rechtsnorm, dit niet direct leidt tot een ombudsmanrapport waarin wordt geoordeeld dat er sprake is geweest van wanbestuur of onbehoorlijk bestuur en, andersom, dat als in een ombudsmanrapport wordt geconcludeerd dat er sprake is geweest van wanbestuur of onbehoorlijk bestuur, dit niet direct leidt tot een uitspraak waarin wordt geoordeeld dat er een rechtsnorm is geschonden. Een uitspraak of een rapport vormt slechts deel van al het bewijs dat door ombudsmannen en rechtspraak moet worden meegewogen.

Het derde coördinatieniveau, dat van de ***normatieve coördinatie*** tussen ombudsmannen en rechterlijke macht, houdt verband met de beoordelingsnormen die zij toepassen bij het toetsen van de overheidshandeling in kwestie.

De eerste conclusie is dat *de wetgever erkent dat er verschillende normatieve concepten bestaan voor ombudsmannen en voor rechtspraak. De coördinatie hiervan wordt overgelaten aan de praktijk.* De wetgever is nogal zwijgzaam als het gaat om normatieve coördinatie. Toch speelt deze een zekere rol, omdat het de wetgever is die de competenties verdeelt tussen ombudsmannen en rechtspraak, en expliciet bepaalt dat het de rechterlijke instanties zijn die de naleving van rechtsnormen toetsen en dat het de ombudsmannen zijn die de naleving van een algemeen normatief concept beoordelen, zoals goed of behoorlijk bestuur. Hoewel de wetgever aangeeft wat de wet is (in het wetgevingsproces), legt deze zelden uit wat goed/behoorlijk bestuur of wanbestuur inhoudt. De inhoud van deze termen wordt overgelaten aan de ombudsmannen. Slechts zelden biedt de wetgever of de jurisprudentie de ombudsmannen 'hulp' als het gaat om de betekenis van deze termen. Op dezelfde manier zwijgt de wetgever over de verhouding tussen normatieve concepten zoals goed/behoorlijk bestuur en rechtmatigheid. De wetgever laat dit onderwerp over aan de onderlinge praktijk van ombudsmannen en de rechtspraak en, uiteraard, aan wetenschappers.

De tweede conclusie op dit niveau luidt dat *ombudsmannen en de rechtspraak hun verschillende beoordelingsnormen onafhankelijk van elkaar ontwikkelen. Bij de ontwikkeling van deze beoordelingsnormen kan echter inspiratie worden geput uit andere al bestaande beoordelingsnormen.* Zowel ombudsmannen als rechterlijke instanties hebben normatieve functies. In het algemeen kan de rechtspraak nieuwe juridische principes ontdekken. Deze nieuwe juridische principes kunnen blijven bestaan in de vorm van ongeschreven recht of kunnen worden gecodificeerd in wetgeving of zelfs constitutioneel recht. De algemene rechtsprincipes worden dan gebruikt als beoordelingsnormen van de rechtspraak. De normatieve functie van ombudsmannen houdt verband met de noodzaak om de inhoud van algemeen normatieve concepten zoals goed/behoorlijk bestuur toe te lichten. Deze toelichting houdt ofwel verband met de ontwikkeling van de vereisten van goed/behoorlijk bestuur, dat wil zeggen afzonderlijke principes van dit concept, ofwel met de ontwikkeling van algemene richtlijnen en aanbevelingen aangaande goed/behoorlijk bestuur.

Er is vastgesteld dat ombudsmannen hun normatieve functies actief benaderen door het ontwikkelen van vereisten voor goed/behoorlijk bestuur en het publiceren van algemene richtlijnen aangaande goed/behoorlijk bestuurlijk handelen.

De derde conclusie luidt dat *er een formele en inhoudelijke overlap bestaat tussen bepaalde beoordelingsnormen van ombudsmannen en van rechtspraak. Een aantal van de beoordelingsnormen van deze instellingen vertonen echter geen enkele overlap.* Hoewel de beoordelingsnormen van ombudsmannen en rechtspraak onafhankelijk van elkaar zijn ontwikkeld, zijn er overeenkomsten te zien tussen deze beoordelingsnormen. Deze overeenkomsten omvatten twee lagen. Er zijn *formele overeenkomsten* op het vlak van bewoordingen en aanduiding van de afzonderlijke standaarden. En er zijn *inhoudelijke overeenkomsten* op het vlak van de inhoud van de afzonderlijke standaarden. Het lijkt erop dat de meerderheid van de beoordelingsnormen die worden ontwikkeld door de rechtspraak op de een of andere wijze *terugkomen* in de beoordelingsnormen van ombudsmannen. Daarbij kan niet worden gesteld dat de beoordelingsnormen van ombudsmannen slechts reproducties vormen van rechterlijke principes of rechtsprincipes. De overlap komt niet voort uit de bindende kracht van juridische beoordelingsnormen, maar uit de waarde die daardoor beschermd wordt. Uit dit onderzoek blijkt dat deze inhoudelijk overlappende beoordelingsnormen dezelfde (of tenminste zeer vergelijkbare) algemene waarden beschermen. De waarde in kwestie is deel van het algemene maatschappelijke ethos. Afhankelijk van het belang van bepaalde waarden worden sommige 'op harde wijze' beschermd door de rechtspraak en ook 'op zachte wijze' door ombudsmannen. Toch vertonen sommige van de beoordelingsnormen van rechterlijke instanties en ombudsmannen geen enkele overlap; met andere woorden, de waarde in kwestie wordt óf alleen door ombudsmannen óf alleen door rechterlijke instanties beschermd. Hieruit blijkt dat de beoordelingsnormen van ombudsmannen niet geheel identiek zijn aan die van de rechtspraak: ze kunnen ook waarden beschermen die niet door de rechter worden beschermd.

De vierde conclusie luidt dat *schending van de beoordelingsnormen van de rechter door ombudsmannen kan worden opgevat als schending van hun eigen normatieve standaarden. Hoewel er inhoudelijke overlap bestaat tussen deze verschillende typen beoordelingsnormen, wordt een schending van de beoordelingsnormen van ombudsmannen slechts zelden door de rechter ook opgevat als schending van een rechtsnorm.* De beoordelingsnormen van ombudsmannen en van rechters verschillen van elkaar. Ondanks inhoudelijke overeenkomsten hebben schendingen van deze standaarden niet dezelfde consequenties. Een schending van beoordelingsnormen van rechters is automatisch ook een overtreding van het recht en bestraffing/handhaving hiervan kan worden afgedwongen. Een schending van de beoordelingsnormen van ombudsmannen brengt niet automatisch een dergelijke sanctie met zich mee. Het verschil tussen deze standaarden wordt benadrukt door het feit dat een schending van de beoordelingsnormen van de ene instelling niet altijd leidt tot een schending van de beoordelingsnormen van de andere instelling. Dit is echter ook niet geheel uitgesloten. In de ombudsprudentie komen zaken voor waarin een overtreding van een rechtsnorm ook leidt tot een schending van een ombudsnorm. Een schending van een ombudsnorm leidt echter slechts zelden direct tot een overtreding van een rechtsnorm. Dit houdt verband met het karakter van het normatieve concept dat door ombudsmannen beschermd wordt. Concepten als goed/behoorlijk bestuur zijn flexibeler en meeromvattend dan rechtmatigheid. Deze concepten omvatten meestal naleving van rechtsnormen (inclusief de mensenrechten) en naleving van vereisten van goed/behoorlijk bestuur in strikte zin. In alle onderzochte rechtssystemen kan *onderscheid worden gemaakt tussen het concept van goed/behoorlijk bestuur* en *het concept van rechtmatigheid.* Dit leidt tot vier verschillende categorieën van overheidsgedragingen:

overheidsgedraging	**goed of behoorlijk bestuur**	**wanbestuur of onbehoorlijk bestuur**
rechtmatig	rechtmatig en behoorlijk bestuur (goed bestuur)	rechtmatig maar onbehoorlijk bestuur (wanbestuur)
onrechtmatig	onrechtmatig maar behoorlijk bestuur (goed bestuur)	onrechtmatig en onbehoorlijk bestuur (wanbestuur)

Dit dit schema blijkt dat er een verschil kan zijn tussen naleving van de wet en naleving van ombudsnormen. Het gaat hier om parallelle concepten. Overheidsgedragingen dienen *zowel* te voldoen aan juridische principes *als* aan ombudsnormen.

De vijfde en laatste conclusie luidt dat *bij inhoudelijke overlap de beoordelingsnormen van ombudsmannen een andere toepassing kunnen hebben dan de beoordelingsnormen van rechters.* Als er inhoudelijke overlap bestaat tussen de verschillende beoordelingsnormen van ombudsmannen en van rechters betekent dit niet per se dat de toepassing van deze beoordelingsnormen hetzelfde is. In de praktijk van deze instellingen is te zien dat de beoordelingsnormen van ombudsmannen kunnen worden toegepast op een wijze die vergelijkbaar is met die van de rechter. In dat geval bepalen de beoordelingsnormen van de rechtspraak (rechtsnormen) over het algemeen een minimumstandaard voor overheidshandelen. Theoretisch is het zo dat als een instelling zich houdt aan deze minimumstandaard, dit gedrag (in het betreffende verband) zal gelden als rechtmatig en behoorlijk/goed. Het kan echter ook zo zijn dat de verschillende soorten beoordelingsnormen die inhoudelijke overlap vertonen door ombudsmannen op een andere, mildere wijze kunnen worden toegepast dan die van de rechtspraak. In dat geval stellen de ombudsnormen een minimumstandaard voor gedrag, althans voor ombudsmannen. Theoretisch is het dan zo dat als een instelling voldoet aan de rechtsnorm, haar handelingen toch niet voldoen aan de vereisten van behoorlijkheid/goed bestuur.

Analyse van de resultaten heeft verschillende algemene aanbevelingen opgeleverd, die mogelijk verbetering kunnen brengen in het werk van deze instellingen, maar ook verbeteringen in de kans die particulieren maken in conflicten met de overheid. In verband met *institutionele coördinatie* levert de analyse de volgende aanbevelingen op:

1. *Wettelijke beperkingen waardoor ombudsmannen een klacht niet kunnen onderzoeken als deze dezelfde feiten betreft als een verzoek bij de rechter dienen te worden geschrapt.*

2. *De rechter zou de bevoegdheid moeten hebben om een zaak te verwijzen naar de ombudsman indien deze duidelijk gaat om wanbestuur (onbehoorlijk bestuur) en er geen sprake is van onrechtmatig handelen. De rechtspraak zou bovendien bevoegd moeten zijn om de ombudsman op de hoogte te stellen van mogelijke structurele problemen bij de*

overheid. In beide gevallen zou de ombudsman de vrijheid moeten hebben om deze zaken te onderzoeken.

3. *Er zou een platform in het leven kunnen worden geroepen waar ombudsmannen en rechtspraak bepaalde onderwerpen kunnen bespreken die te maken hebben met het verbeteren van de bescherming van particulieren tegen de overheid, hun eigen rol, hun verschillende gezichtspunten of andere aan hun functies gerelateerde zaken.*

Deze aanbevelingen kunnen resulteren in een verbetering van de bescherming voor particulieren en in een volledig gebruik van het potentieel van de rechtspraak en ombudsmannen. Ten eerste bieden ombudsmannen in vergelijking met de rechter aanvullende bescherming. Ombudsmannen beoordelen naleving van een ander normatief concept dan rechters. Daarom zouden ombudsmannen de mogelijkheid moeten hebben om zich met het inhoudelijke probleem bezig te houden vanuit hun eigen perspectief van goed/behoorlijk bestuur, ook als de rechter zich al bezighoudt met het inhoudelijke probleem vanuit het perspectief van rechtmatigheid. Bovendien, als de rechtspraak en ombudsmannen de mogelijkheid zouden hebben om het deel van het probleem dat direct verband houdt met een ander normatief concept naar elkaar te verwijzen, zou het probleem in kwestie vanuit beide perspectieven kunnen worden opgelost (rechtmatigheid en goed bestuur). Duidelijke informatie over de positie van deze instellingen (met name de bevoegdheden van ombudsmannen) kan leiden tot beter begrip, maar ook tot effectievere uitoefening van hun bevoegdheden en tot een vollediger bescherming van particulieren tegen de overheid.

Op het gebied van de *zaakscoördinatie* levert de analyse de volgende aanbevelingen op:

1. *Rechterlijke instanties zouden de door ombudsmannen in hun onderzoeken gevonden feiten niet a priori moeten afwijzen. Als deze bevindingen relevant zijn voor de voorliggende rechtsvraag, zouden rechterlijke instanties deze als uitgangspunt kunnen nemen in hun beoordeling, tenzij in de gerechtelijke procedure het tegendeel wordt bewezen.*

2. *Rechterlijke instanties en ombudsmannen dienen meer aandacht te geven aan de toelichting die zij geven over het belang van de bevindingen van de andere instelling voor hun eigen procedure of onderzoek, indien deze bevindingen door een van de partijen in hun procedures worden aangevoerd.*

De resultaten van ombudsmanonderzoeken en gerechtelijke procedures (de rapporten en uitspraken) vormen de formele uiting van hun werk. De rapporten en de bevindingen daarin zijn gebaseerd op de feiten die in nauwgezet onderzoek door ombudsmannen zijn beoordeeld. De bevindingen van ombudsmannen vallen niet *a priori* gunstig uit voor particulieren, omdat ombudsmannen onpartijdig en onafhankelijk zijn. Om deze reden zouden door ombudsmannen aangetoonde feiten, als hiernaar in gerechtelijke procedures wordt verwezen, niet onmiddellijk door de rechtspraak mogen worden afgewezen uitsluitend en alleen omdat het 'slechts' een ombudsman was die deze heeft aangetoond. Particulieren voeren vaak ombudsmanrapporten aan in gerechtelijke procedures, en beroepen zich in ombudsmanonderzoeken vaak op gerechtelijke uitspraken. Voor particulieren is (zonder uitleg) het verschil tussen een rapport en een uitspraak vaak moeilijk te begrijpen. Als particulieren hun beweringen schragen met rapporten of uitspraken, zouden ombudsmannen en rechterlijke instanties moeten toelichten waarom deze worden gebruikt of het gebruik ervan juist wordt afgewezen.

Op het gebied van de *normatieve coördinatie* levert de analyse de volgende aanbevelingen op:

1. *Ombudsmannen moeten in de praktijk hun beoordelingsnormen continu blijven (her) ontwikkelen en toepassen. Dit moeten ze doen in het belang van de overheid, om duidelijkheid te scheppen en om hun standaarden te handhaven, en in het belang van de bescherming van particulieren en van de maatschappij in haar geheel.*

2. *Ombudsmannen moeten in de bevindingen en/of conclusies van hun rapporten altijd verwijzen naar en toelichting geven over de toegepaste en/of geschonden beoordelingsnormen.*

3. *Bij het ontwikkelen van beoordelingsnormen die overlap vertonen met geschreven rechtsnormen, zouden ombudsmannen de betekenis van de geschreven rechtsnormen moeten volgen.*

4. *Bij het ontwikkelen van beoordelingsnormen die overlap vertonen met ongeschreven rechtsbeginselen, moeten ombudsmannen de vrijheid nemen; zij moeten echter wel rekening houden met de algemene waarde die door deze ongeschreven rechtsbeginselen wordt beschermd.*

5. *Rechterlijke instanties moeten de beoordelingsnormen van ombudsmannen niet negeren, omdat deze een positief effect kunnen hebben op de ontwikkeling van het recht. Het is dus noodzakelijk dat de rechtspraak zich bewust is van de beoordelingsnormen van ombudsmannen.*

Voor ombudsmannen en de rechtspraak vormen hun beoordelingsnormen een uiting van hun normatieve functie. Op dit gebied zijn ombudsmannen actiever dan de rechterlijke macht. Dit houdt verband met de flexibiliteit, of meer de vaagheid, van hun normatieve concepten. Daarom dienen ze duidelijk toe te lichten wat een dergelijk normatief concept inhoudt. Uit alle drie de casestudies komt naar voren dat de ombudsmannen en rechterlijke instanties hun beoordelingsnormen *relatief onafhankelijk* van elkaar ontwikkelen en toepassen. Het is denkbaar dat ombudsmannen hun beoordelingsnormen op een minder strenge wijze invullen en toepassen dan de rechterlijke instanties. Aan de ene kant kan daartoe de noodzaak bestaan, omdat zij een beoordeling uitvoeren van de naleving van een algemeen normatief concept dat *niet gelijk is aan rechtmatigheid*. Aan de andere kant vereist dit normatieve concept vaak dat de overheid *zich houdt aan de wet en de algemene rechtsprincipes*. Met name vanwege dit tweede punt kunnen vraagtekens worden gesteld bij de een minder strenge invulling van een normatieve standaard door een ombudsman.

Als een ombudsman overdreven mild is wat betreft een normatieve standaard die overlapt met *geschreven recht* kan dit leiden tot onzekerheid aangaande de inhoud van deze standaard. Ombudsmannen zijn als overheidsinstellingen uiteraard aan de wet gebonden. Ombudsmannen hebben echter een grotere flexibiliteit bij het ontwikkelen van standaarden die overlap vertonen met *ongeschreven rechtsbeginselen*. Om duidelijkheid te scheppen aangaande hun normatieve concepten zouden zij in hun bevindingen moeten verwijzen naar de beoordelingsnormen die toegepast en/of geschonden zijn. Omdat de ontwikkeling van het recht en van vereisten van goed/behoorlijk bestuur verre van compleet is, zouden ombudsmannen en rechterlijke instanties ook aandacht moeten besteden aan de beoordelingsnormen van de andere instelling: deze kunnen een inspiratie vormen voor de verdere ontwikkeling van hun eigen normatief concept.

Dit onderzoek heeft laten zien dat ombudsmannen en rechtspraak twee verschillende overheidsinstellingen zijn, met ieder hun eigen bevoegdheden, hun eigen werk, hun eigen werkwijzen en hun eigen normatieve concepten en standaarden. Ondanks deze verschillen hebben zij ook wat gemeen: zij lossen conflicten op tussen particulieren en de overheid. Ze voegen beide wat toe aan de bescherming van particulieren. Ze pogen overheidsproblemen (juridisch of anderszins) op te lossen en vergroten zo het vertrouwen dat particulieren hebben in de overheid.

De handelingen van ombudsmannen en rechtspraak zouden verder gecoördineerd kunnen worden als het gaat om *onderlinge samenwerking*. Dergelijke coördinatie kan ervoor zorgen dat rechtspraak en ombudsmannen hun bevoegdheden vollediger benutten. Dit kan ook meer duidelijkheid brengen in hun beoordelingsnormen en zorgen voor onderlinge coördinatie tijdens de ontwikkeling daarvan. Bovendien kan het leiden tot een beter begrip van de verschillende soorten bescherming voor particulieren en zorgen voor een volledige beoordeling van hun conflict met de overheid. Samenwerking tussen ombudsmannen en rechtspraak kan derhalve een positieve invloed hebben op de uitvoering van hun rollen, op de bescherming van particulieren, op de ontwikkeling van normatieve concepten en standaarden, en op de conflictoplossing zelf.

Ombudsmannen en rechtspraak hebben als overheidsinstellingen ieder hun sterke en hun zwakke punten. Ten eerste zijn de conflictoplossing en de bescherming van particulieren door de rechtspraak vaak niet afdoende. Als dat wel het geval was, zou er überhaupt geen ombudsman nodig zijn. Particulieren hebben echter vaak behoefte aan meer dan alleen de formele bevestiging dat zij gelijk hadden en de overheid ongelijk: zij willen dat hun probleem ook wordt opgelost. Ombudsmannen kunnen zorgen voor *aanvullende conflictoplossing*. Zij kunnen reageren op het eigenlijke probleem en indien de overheid bereid is mee te werken kunnen zij bijdragen aan een snelle en informele oplossing. Hun informele conflictoplossing en juridisch niet-bindende aanbevelingen om problemen in de toekomst te voorkomen kunnen een mooie toevoeging vormen op de juridisch bindende toetsing door de rechtspraak. Ombudsmannen hebben ook specifieke aanvullende bevoegdheden, waardoor zij meer kunnen doen dan simpelweg functioneren als mechanisme voor conflictoplossing. Hun onderzoeken uit eigen beweging en hun niet-bindende aanbevelingen vormen een aanzienlijke aanvulling als het gaat om de bescherming van particulieren. *Zij zijn dus meer dan alleen een mechanisme voor conflictoplossing.* Men moet echter ook begrijpen dat ombudsmannen niet een panacee vormen voor alle problemen tussen overheid en burgers. Zij kunnen niet alle problemen oplossen of voorkomen. Ombudsmannen kunnen zonder twijfel de overheid een sterker 'moreel gevoel' bijbrengen, maar zij kunnen dat alleen binnen hun eigen bevoegdheden en beperkingen.

Over het algemeen zien ombudsmannen en rechtspraak in dat hun *verschillende rollen* en *verschillende bevoegdheden* hen ertoe in staat stellen conflicten vanuit verschillende perspectieven te benaderen. Ze zouden echter ook moeten proberen in te zien dat slechts één manier van conflictoplossing vaak niet voldoende is om *het eigenlijke probleem* tussen een particulier en de overheid volledig op te lossen. De eerste stap om dit te bereiken is een betere onderlinge communicatie. Dan zou kunnen blijken dat zij geen concurrenten zijn, maar gezamenlijk kunnen werken naar algemeen gedeelde doelen, ieder binnen de eigen competenties. Het is niet voldoende om simpelweg te stellen: *we doen verschillend werk en dus is samenwerking nergens voor nodig*. Er ligt een grotere uitdaging in: *ons werk verschilt, maar we zijn ons ervan bewust dat onze algemene doelstellingen ons nader tot elkaar kunnen brengen en ons kunnen helpen ons werk beter te doen in het belang van particulieren, de overheid en de maatschappij als geheel.*

Bibliography

Aalberts 2011

Aalberts C.T., De bestuurrechtlijke zitting nieuwe stijl, NTB 2011, 35.

Abraham 2008

Abraham A., *The Ombudsman as Part of the UK Constitution: A Contested Role?*, Parliamentary Affairs Vol. 61, No. 1, 2008.

Abraham 2008a

Abraham A., *The Ombudsman and the Executive: The Road to Accountability*, Parliamentary Affairs Vol. 61, No. 3, 2008.

Abraham 2008b

Abraham A., *The Future in International Perspective: The Ombudsman as Agent of Rights, Justice and Democracy*, Parliamentary Affairs Vol. 61, No. 4, 2008.

Abraham 2011

Abraham A., The Parliamentary Ombudsman and Administrative Justice: Shaping the next 50 years, JUSTICE Tom Sargant memorial annual lecture 2011.

Abraham & O'Brien 2006

Abraham A., O'Brien N., *The implementation of human rights and the role of Ombudspersons – 'from a negative position'*, Meeting and general assembly of the International Ombudsman Institute – European region, June 2006.

Addink 2005

Addink H., *Principles of Good Governance: Lessons from Administrative Law* in Curtin D. M., Wessel R. A. (eds.), *Good governance and the European Union : reflections on concepts, institutions and substance*, Intersentia, Antwerp, 2005.

Addink 2005b

Addink G.H., *The Ombudsman as the fourth power. On the foundations of Ombudsman law from a comparative perspective*, in: Van der Linden E.C.H.J. & Stroink F.A.M. (eds.) Judicial Lawmaking and Administrative Law, Intersentia, Antwerp, 2005.

Addink 2008

Addink G.H., *Goed bestuur: een norm voor het bestuur of een recht van de burger?* In Addink G.H., Jurgens G.T.J.M., Langbroek Ph. & Widdershoven R.J.G.M. (eds.), Grensverleggend bestuursrecht, Kluwer, Alphen aan den Rijn, 2008.

Addink 2010

Addink H., *Goed bestuur*, Kluwer, Deventer, 2010.

Addink 2011

Addink H., *Borgen van publieke waarden: behoorlijk of goed bestuur?*, Bestuurkunde 2011 – 2.

Addink et al. 2010

Addink H., Anthony G., Buyse B. & Flinterman C., *Human Rights & Good Governance*, SIM special 34, Utrecht, 2010.

Adriaansen 2004
Adriaansen M.P.L., *Beginselen van het bestuursrecht*, MKB - adviseur, Deventer 2004.

Akkermans et al. 2005
Akkermans P.W.C., Bax C.J., Verhey L.F.M., *Grondrechten: grondrechten en grondrechtsbescherming in Nederland*, Kluwer, Deventer, 2005.

Alder 2005
Alder J., *Constitutional and administrative law*, Palgrave Macmillan, 2005.

Andersen & Kragh 2010
Andersen P. H., Kragh H., *Sense and sensibility: Two approaches for using existing theory-building qualitative research,* Industrial Marketing Management 39 (2010).

Anthony 2002
Anthony G., *UK Public Law and European Law: The Dynamics of Legal Integration*, Hart Publishing, 2002.

Antoine 2008
Antoine R.-M. B., *Commonwealth Caribbean Law and Legal Systems*, Routledge-Cavendish, 2008.

Arden et al. 1999
Arden A., Manning J. & Collins S., *Local Government – Constitutional and Administrative Law,* Sweet and Maxwell, 1999.

Arnull 2006
Arnull A., *The European Union and its Court of Justice*, OUP Oxford, 2006.

Ayeni 2000
Ayeni V.O., *Ombudsman around the world: essential elements, evolution and contemporary issues*, in Ayeni V.O., Reif L., Hayden T., *Strengthening Ombudsman and Human Rights Institutions in Commonwealth Small and Island States: The Caribbean Experience*; Commonwealth Secretariat, 2000.

Bailey et al. 2002
Bailey S., Ching J., Gunn M. & Ormerod D., *Smith, Bailey and Gunn on the Modern English Legal System*, Sweet & Maxwell, 2002.

Bailey et al. 2005
Bailey S.H., Jones B. & Mowbray A.R., *Cases, Materials and Commentary on Administrative Law*, Sweet & Maxwell, 2005.

Bailey 2009
Bailey S.H., *Grounds for Judicial Review: Due Process, Natural Justice, and Fairness* in Feldman (ed.), English Public Law: Oxford Principles of English Law, OUP Oxford, 2009.

Barkhuysen & Claessens 2012
Barkhuysen T., Claessens M., *Naar een 'slagvaardiger' bestuursrecht met de Wet aanpassing bestuursprocesrecht?*, Ars Aequi, February 2012.

Barnett 2011
Barnett H., *Constitutional & Administrative Law*, Routledge-Cavendish, 2011.

Bellamy & Warleigh 2001
Bellamy R., Warleigh A., *Citizenship and Governance in the European Union*, Continuum, 2001.

Blokker et al. 2006
Blokker N., Lefeber R., Lijnzaad L., Van Bladel I. (eds.), *The Netherlands in Court: Essays in Honour of Johan G. Lammers,* Brill, 2006.

Bradley & Ewing 2006
Bradley A. & Ewing K., *Constitutional and Administrative Law*, Pearson Longman, 2006.

Brenninkmeijer 2006

Brenninkmeijer A., '*Eerlijk Bestuur,*' Van Slingelandtlezing, speech, 21 November 2006.

Brenninkmeijer 2007

Brenninkmeijer A., *Van Slingelandt-lezing Eerlijk bestuur: over rechtmatigheid en behoorlijkheid*, Bestuurskunde, 2007 – 1.

Brenninkmeijer 2012

Brenninkmeijer A., *Unitas politica*, 20 January 2012, <http://njblog.nl/2012/01/20/unitas-politica/>.

Brenninkmeijer & Van Hoogstraten 2008

Brenninkmeijer A.F.M., Van Hoogstraten W.J., *The Architecture of Good Administration*, Dutch Journal of Administrative Law, 2008.

Brenninkmeijer & Van Hoogstraten 2008a

Brenninkmeijer A.F.M., van Hoogstraten W.J., *De architectuur van behoorlijk bestuur. De bijdrage van de Nationale ombudsman aan behoorlijk bestuur in 25 jaar*, NTB 2008.

Brenninkmeijer & Van der Vlugt 2009

Brenninkmeijer A., van der Vlugt Y., *Mensenrechten behoorlijk gewaarborgd* in Barkhuysen T. et al. (eds.), *Geschakeld recht: verdere studies over Europese grondrechten ter gelegenheid van de 70ste verjaardag van prof. mr. E. A. Alkema.*, Kluwer, 2009.

Broberg & Fenger 2010

Broberg M. & Fenger N., Preliminary References to the European Court of Justice, OUP Oxford, 2010.

Buck et al. 2011

Buck T., Kirkham R., Thompson B., *The Ombudsman Enterprise and Administrative Justice*, Ashgate, London, 2011.

Burkens 1989

Burkens M.C., *Algemene leerstukken van grondrechten naar Nederlands constitutioneel recht*, Tjeenk Willink, 1989.

Burkens et al. 2006

Burkens M.C., Kummeling H.R.B.M., Vermeulen B.P., Widdershoven R.J.G.M., *Beginselen van de democratische rechtsstaat,* Kluwer, Alphen aan den Rijn, 2006.

Burkens et al. 2012

Burkens M.C., Kummeling H.R.B.M., Vermeulen B.P., Widdershoven R.J.G.M., *Beginselen van de democratische rechtsstaat,* Instituut voor staats- en bestuursrecht UU, Kluwer Bv, 2012.

Cadwell 1950

Caldwell L.G., *The Proposed Federal Administrative Court: The Arguments for its Adoption*, American Bar Association Journal, January 1950, Vol. 36.

Cane 1996

Cane P., *An Introduction to Administrative Law*, Clarendon Press, 1996.

Cane 2009

Cane P., *Administrative Tribunals and Adjudication*, Hart Publishing, 2009, p. 182ff.

Carrol 2006

Carroll A., *Constitutional and Administrative Law*, Longman, 2003.

Chalmers et al. 2006

Chalmers D., Hadjimmanuil C., Monti G. & Tomkins A., *European Union Law*, CUP Cambridge, 2006.

Coe & Gay 2010

Coe J., Gay O., *The Parliamentary Ombudsman and the MP filter*, Standard Note: SN/PC/05181, 2010.

Cordeiro & Filipe 2003
Cordeiro J.A.M., Filipe J. J., *Application of the Theory of Organized Activity to the Coordination of Social Information Systems, ECIS 2003 Proceedings.* Paper 41.
Cownie et al. 2007
Cownie F., Bradney A. & Burton M., *English Legal System in Context*, OUP Oxford, 2007.
Craig 2009
Craig P., *Grounds for Judicial Review: Substantive Control Over Discretion* in Feldman D. (ed.), *English Public Law: Oxford Principles of English Law*, OUP Oxford, 2009.
Craig 2010
Craig P., The Lisbon Treaty: law, politics and treaty reform, OUP Oxford, 2010.
Craig & de Búrca 2008
Craig P., de Búrca G., *EU Law: Text, Cases, and Materials*, OUP Oxford, 4th edition, 2008.
Craig & de Búrca 2011
Craig P., de Búrca G., *EU Law: Text, Cases, and Materials*, OUP Oxford, 2011.
Crawford 2002
Crawford C., *The Local Ombudsman: A Form of Alternative Dispute Resolution* in Samson C. & McBride J. (eds.), Solutions de rechange au règlement des conflits, Pu Laval Presse Univers, 2002.
Curtin & Wessel 2005
Curtin D. M., Wessel R. A. (eds.), *Good governance and the European Union : reflections on concepts, institutions and substance*, Intersentia, Antwerp, 2005.
Daadler et al. 1998
Daalder E.J., de Groot G.R.J., van Breugel J.M.E., *De parlementaire geschiedenis van de Algemene wet bestuursrecht*: Derde tranche, Alphen aan den Rijn: Samsom H.D. Tjeenk Willink 1998.
Damen 2008
Damen L.J.A., *Behoorlijk, en ook rechtmatig, of juist eerlijk?*, NTB 2008.
Damen et al. 2006
Damen L.J.A. et al., *Bestuursrecht 2: Rechtsbescherming tegen de overheid.* BJU, The Hague, 2006.
Damen et al. 2013
Damen L.J.A. et al., *Bestuursrecht 2, Rechtsbescherming tegen de overheid. Bestuursprocesrecht*, 4th ed., 2013, BJU, The Hague.
Darmon 1988
Darmon M., The role of the Advocate General in the Court of Justice of the European Communities, in S. Sheetreet (ed.), *The Role of courts in society*, Martinus Nijhoff Publishers, Dordrecht, 1988.
Davis 2000
Davis R. W., *Quasi-Judicial Review: The European Ombudsman as an Alternative to the European Courts*, [2000] 1 Web JCLI.
Davies 2003
Davies K., *Understanding European Union Law*, Routledge Cavendish; 2nd ed., 2003.
De Cruz 2007
De Cruz P., *Comparative Law in a Changing World*, Routledge-Cavendish, 3rd ed., 2007.
De Haan et al. 2001
De Haan P., Drupsteen Th. G., Fernhout R., *Bestuursrecht in de sociale rechtsstaat*, Kluwer, 2001.

De Leeuw 2009
De Leeuw M.E., *An Empirical Study into the norms of good administration as operated by the European Ombudsman in the field of tenders*, EUI Working papers, RSCAS 2009/20 Robert Schuman Centre for Advanced Studies.

De Meij & Van der Vlies 2000
De Meij J.M., Van der Vlies, I.C., *Inleiding tot het staatsrecht en het bestuursrecht*, Tjeenk Willink, Deventer, 2000.

De Vaus 2001
De Vaus D.A., *Research Design in Social Research*, Sage Publications Ltd, 2001.

De Waard 2009
De Waard B.W.N., in Barkhuysen T., Polak J.E.M., Schueler B.J., Widdershoven R.J.G.M., *AB Klassiek – Standaarduitspraken bestuursrecht, opnieuw en thematisch geannoteerd*, Kluwer, 2009.

Diamandouros 2005
Diamandouros N., Speech on the Occasion of the Formal Dinner with the EU Institutions, Bodies and Agencies to Mark the 10th Anniversary of the European Ombudsman Institution, Brussels, 17 November 2005.

Diamandouros 2006
Diamandouros N., Speech at the 4th International Conference of Information Commissioners, *'FOI: a European Perspective'*, Manchester, 2006 Open Government: a Journal on Freedom of Information. Volume 2, Issue 2., Published on 11 December 2006.

Diamandouros 2007
Diamandouros N., *'The principle of good administration in the recommendations of the European Ombudsman'*, speech, Sofia, 2007.

Diamandouros 2007a
Diamandouros N., *'Rethinking good administration in the European Union'*, speech, Strasbourg, 2007.

Diamandouros 2007b
Diamandouros N., *'Legality and good administration: is there a difference?'*, speech, Strasbourg, 2007.

Diamandouros 2011
Diamandouros N., *'Promoting ethical behaviour by EU civil servants: the role of the European Ombudsman'*, speech, Bristol, 2011.

Diamandouros 2011a
Diamandouros N., *'The work of the European Ombudsman and the European Network of Ombudsmen'*, speech, Strasbourg, 2011.

Diamandouros 2011b
Diamantouros N., *'Promoting ethical behaviour by EU civil servants: the role of the European Ombudsman'*, speech, Bristol 2011.

Dimitrakopoulos 2010
Dimitrakopoulos I., *Is an Illegal Community Act Necessarily an Instance of Maladministration, in the Sense of Article 195 EC?*, REALaw; vol. 2, No. I, 2010.

Douglas-Scott 2011
Douglas-Scott S., *The EU and Human Rights after the Treaty of Lisbon*, Human Rights Law Review (2011) 11(4).

Dragoş et al. 2010
Dragoş D., Neamtu B., Balica D., *The Romanian Ombudsman and its interaction with the courts – an exploratory research*, Transylvanian Review of Administrative Sciences, No. 31E/2010.

Dragos & Neamtu 2014
Dragos D. &; Neamtu B. (Eds.), Alternative Dispute Resolution in Administrative Proceedings, Springer, to be published in 2014.
Drewry 1997
Drewry G., *The Ombudsman: Parochial Stopgap or Global Panacea?*, in: Leyland P. & Woods T. (eds.) Administrative Law Facing the Future: Old Constraints & New Horizons, Blackstone Press Limited, 1997.
Drewry 2009
Drewry G., *The Judicialisation of 'Administrative' Tribunals in the UK: From Hewart to Leggatt*, Transylvanian Review of Administrative Sciences, No. 28 E SI/2009.
Ebbesson 2002
Ebbesson J. (ed.), *Access to Justice in Environmental Matters in the EU*, Kluwer Law International, 2002.
Elliott et al. 2011
Elliott M., Beatson J. and Matthews M., *Beatson, Matthews and Elliott's Administrative Law Text and Materials*, OUP Oxford, 4th edition, 2011.
Elliot & Quinn 2008
Elliot C., Quinn F., *English Legal System*, Pearson Education ltd., 2008.
Elliot 2011
Elliott M., *Has the Common Law Duty to Give Reasons Come of Age Yet?*, Public Law Iss. 1, 2011.
Endicott 2011
Endicott T., *Administrative Law*, OUP Oxford, 2011.
Fairhust 2010
Fairhust J. in *Law of the European Union*, Longman, 7th ed., 2010.
Feldman 2002
Feldman D., *Civil Liberties and Human Rights in England and Wales*, OUP Oxford; 2nd edition, 2002.
Feldman 2009
Feldman D. (ed.), *English Public Law: Oxford Principles of English Law*, OUP Oxford, 2009.
Gay 2008
Gay O., *The Ombudsman – the developing role in the UK*, Standard Note: SN/PC/04832, 2008.
Gerrits-Jansens 2000
Gerrits-Jansens M.P. in Addink G.H., Ten Berge J.B.J.M., Graat P.A.M.J., Langbroek P.M., *Kwaliteit van overheidsbestuur: enkele verkenningen van veranderingen in bestuursrechtelijke verhoudingen ten gevolge van de invoering van kwaliteitszorg bij de overheid*, Tjeenk Willink, Deventer, 2000.
Giddins et al. 2000
Giddins P., Gregory R., Harris A., The European Union Ombudsman in Warleigh A., *Understanding European Union Institutions*, Routledge, London, 2000.
Ginter 2002
Ginter C., *Access to Justice in the European Court of Justice in Luxembourg*, European Journal of Law Reform, Vol. 4, No. 3.
Goorden 1997
Goorden C.P.J., *Algemeen bestuursrecht compact*, The Hague, Tweede druk VUGA, 1997.
Gøtze 2009
Gøtze M., *The Danish Ombudsman – Citizens, Parliament and EU*, paper presented to the Annual Conference of EGPA – Study Group X (Law and Administration), September 2009.

Grainger et al. 2000
Grainger I., Fealy M., Spencer M., *Civil Procedure Rules in Action*, 2nd edition, Routledge Cavendish, 2000.
Griller et al. 2000
Griller S., Droutsas D.P., Falkner G. and Forgo K., *The Treaty of Amsterdam: Facts, Analysis, Prospects*, Springer Verlag GmbH, 2000.
Gregory 1999
Gregory R., *Building an Ombudsman Scheme: Statutory Provisions and Operating Practices*, in Reif L. (ed.), The International Ombudsman Anthology: Selected Writings from the International Ombudsman Institute, Kluwer law International, 1999.
Gregory 2001
Gregory R., *The Ombudsman: An Excellent Form of Dispute Resolution?*, in Reif L. (ed.), International Ombudsman Yearbook vol. 5, Kluwer Law International, 2001.
Gregory & Giddings 2000
Gregory R. & Giddings P., *The Ombudsman Institution: Growth and Development*, in Gregory R., Giddings P. (eds.), Righting Wrongs: The Ombudsman in Six Continents IOS Press, 2000.
Gregory & Giddings 2002
Gregory R. & Giddings P., *The Ombudsman and Parliament: A History of the Parliamentary and Health Service Ombudsman*, Politico's Publishing Ltd, 2002.
Groussot 2006
Groussot X., *General Principles of Community Law*, Europa Law Publishing, Groningen, 2006.
Gubrium & Holstein 2001
Gubrium J.F., Holstein J.A., *From the Individual Interview to the Interview Society*, in Gubrium J.F., Holstein J.A. (eds.), Handbook of Interview Research: Context & Method, Sage Publications 2001.
Gwyn 1973
Gwyn W. B., *The British PCA: "Ombudsman or Ombudsmouse?"*, The Journal of Politics, Vol. 35, No. 1, Feb., 1973
Habermas 1996
Habermas J., *Between Facts and Norms, Contributions to a Discourse Theory of Law and Democracy*, The MIT Press, Cambridge, Massachusetts, 1996.
Harlow 1978
Harlow C., *Ombudsmen in search of a role*, (1978) 41 MLR 446, pp. 450-453.
Harlow & Rawlings 2006
Harlow C., Rawlings R., *Law and Administration*, Cambridge UP, 2nd edition, 2006.
Harlow & Rawlings 2009
Harlow C., Rawlings R., *Law and Administration*, Cambridge UP, 3rd edition, 2009.
Harris 1999
Harris M., *Ombudsman or Tribunal? The Ombudsman as the Adjudicative Mechanism* in Partington M., Harris M. (eds.), *Administrative Justice in the 21st Century*, Hart publishing, 1999.
Harris 2007
Harris P., *An introduction to law*, CUP Cambridge, 7 ed., 2007.
Hawke & Parpworth 1998
Hawke N. & Parpworth N., *Introduction to Administrative Law*, Cavendish publishing ltd., 1998.

Heede 2000
Heede K., *European Ombudsman: redress and control at Union level*, Kluwer Law International, 2000.
Hertogh 1996
Hertogh, M., *The European Ombudsman: Different Roles in a Demanding Context*, in: Hesse J.J. & Toonen Th.A.J. (eds.), The European Yearbook of Comparative Government and Public Administration, Vol. III/1996, Baden-Baden: Nomos Verlagsgesellschaft, pp. 337-349.
Hofmann et al. 2011
Hofmann H.C.H., Rowe G.C. & Türk A.H., *Administrative Law and Policy of the European Union,* OUP Oxford, 2011.
Hoffman & Rowe 2009
Hoffman D., Rowe J.Q.C., *Human Rights in the UK: An Introduction to the Human Rights Act 1998*, Longman, 3rd edition, 2009.
Horspool & Humphreys 2006
Horspool M., Humphreys M., *European Union law*, OUP Oxford, 2006.
Hsieh 2005
Hsieh K., *The European Ombudsman's Role in EU Freedom of Information Protection*, presented at The Third European Union Studies Association – Asia Pacific Conference: Multilateralism and Regionalism in Asia-Pacific and Europe, Keio University, Tokyo, Japan, 8-10 December 2005.
Hubeau 2008
Hubeau B., *Klachtenbehandeling en ombudswerk in Nederland en België/Vlaanderen: zo dichtbij …en toch zo verschillend*, in Addink G.H., Jurgens G.T.J.M., Langbroek Ph.M., Widdershoven R.J.G.M., Grensverleggend bestuursrecht, Kluwer, 2008.
Iglesias 1999
Iglesias R., *Reflections on the General Principles of Community Law*, CJLS 1999.
Jacoby 1999
Jacoby D., *The Future of the Ombudsman* in L. Reif (ed.), The International Ombudsman Anthology: Selected Writings from the International Ombudsman Institute, Kluwer law International, 1999.
James 1997
James R., *Private Ombudsmen and Public Law,* Dartmouth Publishing, 1997.
Jans 2008
Jans J.H., *European Law and the Inapplicability of the 'Speciality Principle'*, Review of European Administrative Law, Vol. 1, No. 1, Europa Law publishing, 2008.
Jans et al. 2007
Jans J.H., de Lange R., Prechal S., Widdershoven R.J.G.M., *Europeanisation of Public Law*, Europa Law Publishing, 2007.
Jans et al. 2011
Jans J.H., Prechal S., Widdershoven R.J.G.M., *Inleiding tot het Europees bestuursrecht*, Nijmegen, Ars Aequi Libri, 2011.
Jansen 2006
Jansen P.G.M., *Beginselen van behoorlijk bestuur in het belastingrecht*, Sdu Fiscale & Financiele Uitgevers, Amersfoort, 2006.
Jones 1997
Jones A., *Britain and the European Union*, Edinburgh University Press, 1997.

Jones & Thompson 2007

Jones B. & Thompson K., *Administrative Law in the United Kingdom*, in Seerden R.J.G.H. (ed.), Administrative Law of the European Union, its Member States and the United States: A Comparative Analysis, Intersentia, 2007.

Kaczorowska 2010

Kaczorowska A., *European Union law*, Hoboken: Taylor & Francis, 2010.

Kańska 2004

Kańska K., *Towards Administrative Human Rights in the EU. Impact of the Charter of Fundamental Rights*, European Law Journal, Vol. 10, No. 3, May 2004, pp. 296–326.

Kirkham 2004

Kirkham R., *Prevention is Better than Litigation: the Importance of Good Administration*, Journal of Social Welfare and Family Law, 2004, Vol. 26, No. 3.

Kirkham 2007

Kirkham R., *The Parliamentary Ombudsman: withstanding the test of time*, p. 12, 4th Report, Session 2006-2007, presented to Parliament pursuant to Section 10(4) of the Parliamentary Commissioner Act 1967.

Kirkham et al. 2008

Kirkham R., Thompson B. and Buck T., *When putting things right goes wrong: enforcing the recommendations of the ombudsman*, 2008, Public Law 510.

Klabbers 2002

Klabbers J., *An introduction to international institutional law*, Cambridge University Press, 2002.

Kofler 2008

Kofler B., parts *European Union* and *United Kingdom of Great Britain and Northern Ireland* in Kucsko-Stadlmayer G. (ed.), European Ombudsman-Institutions: A comparative legal analysis regarding the multifaceted realisation of an idea, Springer, Vienna, 2008.

Kortmann & Bovend'Eert 2000

Kortmann C.A.J.M., Bovend'Eert P.P.T., *Dutch Constitutional Law*, Kluwer Law.

Kourtikis 2010

Kourtikis K., *Imitation and supranational politics: some lessons from the European Ombudsman and the European Court of Auditors*, European Political Science Review (2010), 2:1.

Kristjánsdóttir 2013

Kristjánsdóttir M. V., *Good Administration as a Fundamental Right*, Icelandic Review of Politics and Administration Vol. 9, Issue 1 (237-255), 2013.

Kucsko-Stadlmayer 2008

Kucsko-Stadlmayer G., *The Legal Structures of Ombudsman-Institutions in Europe – Legal Comparative Analysis*, Kucsko-Stadlmayer G. (ed.), European Ombudsman-Institutions: A comparative legal analysis regarding the multifaceted realisation of an idea, Springer, Vienna, 2008.

Langbroek 1997

Langbroek P., *General principles of Proper Administration in Dutch Administrative Law* in Hessel B., Hofmański P. (eds.), Government Policy and Rule of Law, Bauhaus, 1997.

Langbroek et al. 2013

Langbroek P., Buize. A. & Remac M., *Designing Administrative Pre-Trial Proceedings*, Eleven International publishing, 2013.

Langbroek & Remac 2011
Langbroek P., Remac M., *Ombudsman's Assessments of Public Administration Conduct: Between Legal and Good Administration Norms*, NISPAcee Journal of Public Administration and Policy, Vol. IV, No. 2, Winter 2011/2012, 2011.
Langbroek & Rijpkema 2004
Langbroek P.M., Rijpkema P., *Ombudsprudentie: Over de behoorlijkheidsnormen en zijn toepassing*, BJU, 2004.
Langbroek & Rijpkema 2006
Langbroek P., Rijpkema P., *Demands of proper administrative conduct: A research project into the ombudsprudence of the Dutch National Ombudsman*, Utrecht Law Review, Vol. 2, Is. 2, 2006.
Le Sueur et al. 1999
Le Sueur A.P., English R. & Herberg J.W., Principles of Public Law (Practice Notes), Routledge Cavendish, 2nd edition, London, 1999.
Lewis 2008
Lewis C., *Judicial Remedies in Public Law*, Sweet & Maxwell, 2008.
Leyland & Anthony 2008
Leyland P. & Anthony G., *Textbook on Administrative Law*, OUP Oxford, 2008.
Longley & James 1999
Longley D., James R., *Administrative justice: Central Issues in UK and European Administrative Law*, Cavendish Publishing Limited, 1999.
Magnette 2003
Magnette P., *Between parliamentary control and the rule of law: the political role of the Ombudsman in the European Union*, Journal of European Public Policy 10:5 October 2003: 677–694.
Maino 1999
Maino Ch., *Ethical Considerations: The Leadership Code of Papua New Guinea* in Reif L. (ed.), The International Ombudsman Anthology: Selected Writings from the International Ombudsman Institute, Kluwer law International, 1999.
Malone & Crowston 1994
Malone T. W., Crowston K., *The Interdisciplinary Study of Coordination*, ACM Computing Surveys, Vol. 26, No. 1, March 1994.
Maxwell 2005
Maxwell J.A., *Qualitative Research Design: An Interpretative Approach*, Applied Social Research Methods Series, Volume 41, Saga publications, 2005.
Mein et al. 2010
Mein A.G. et al., *Reflectie op de Nationale ombudsman*, Verwey-Jonker Instituut, 2010.
Mendes 2009
Mendes J., *Good administration in EU law and the European Code of Good Administrative Behaviour*, EUI Working Papers, Law 2009/09 European University Institute.
Meulenbroek 2008
Meulenbroek J.M.C., *Klachtrecht en ombudsman: een praktische handleiding*, Kluwer, 2008.
Michiels 2004
Michiels F.C.M.A. (ed.), *Staats- en Bestuursrecht, Kluwer*, Instituut voor Staats- en Bestuursrecht, Universiteit Utrecht, 2004.
Michiels 2006
Michiels F.C.M.A., *Hoofdzaken van het bestuutsrecht*, Kluwer, Deventer 2006.

Mintzberg 1979
Mintzberg H., *The structuring of organizations*, Prentice Hall, Engelwood Cliffs, 1979.
Mintzberg 1983
Mintzberg H., *Structure in Fives: Designing Effective Organizations*, Prentice-Hall, Engelwood Cliffs, 1983.
Montesh 2009
Montesh M., *The Functioning of Ombudsman (Public Protector) in South Africa: Redress and Checks and Balances?*, Transylvanian Review of Administrative Sciences, No. 28 E SI/2009.
Morano-Foadi & Andreadakis 2011
Morano-Foadi S., Andreadakis S., *Reflections on the Architecture of the EU after the Treaty of Lisbon: The European Judicial Approach to Fundamental Rights*, European Law Journal, Vol. 17, Issue 5, 2011.
Morgan 2009
Morgan D., '*The Ombudsman and the Judge: Redressing Grievance and Holding to Account*', Address to NI Ombudsman's 40th Anniversary Event, speech, 2009.
Mukoro 2008
Mukoro A., *The Ombudsman Phenomenon in African States Public Services*, CAFRAD No. 70/2008.
Nehl 2009
Nehl H. P., *Good administration as procedural right and/or general principle*, in Hofmann C.H. & Türk A.H. (eds.), Legal Challenges in EU Administrative Law: Towards an Integrated Administration, Edward Elgar Publishing Ltd, 2009.
Nicolai 1990
Nicolai P., *Beginselen van behoorlijk bestuur*, Kluwer, Deventer 1990.
O'Reilly 2007
O'Reilly E., *Human Rights and the Ombudsman*, Lecture of the Ombudsman of Ireland at the 2007 Biennial Conference of the British and Irish Ombudsman Association, University of Warwick, 27 April 2007.
Oosting 1995
Oosting M., *The National Ombudsman of the Netherlands and human rights*, in Smith F.J., Zwaak L.F. (eds.), International protection of human rights: selected topics, Utrecht, Studie- en Informatiecentrum Mensenrechten [SIM], 1995.
Pauliat 2008
Pauliat H., *The Treatment of Citizens' Complaints in the Justice Field: Is an Ombudsman Necessary?*, International Journal for Court Administration, Vol. 1 No. 2., 2008.
Paunio 2009
Paunio R.-L., '*The Ombudsman as Human Rights Defender*', speech at IOI's conference, Workshop 1: The Ombudsman as Human Rights Defender, 10 June 2009, Stockholm.
Pennarts 2008
Pennarts H., *Beginselen van behoorlijk bestuur*, Maklu-Uitgevers, Apeldoorn, 2008.
Peters 2005
Peters A., *The European Ombudsman and the European Constitution*, Common Market Law Review 42: 697-743, 2005.
Pearce 1999
Pearce D., *The Ombudsman: Review and Preview – Importance of Being Different* in L. Reif (ed.), The International Ombudsman Anthology: Selected Writings from the International Ombudsman Institute, Kluwer Law International, 1999.

Popescu-Slaniceanu 2010
Popescu-Slaniceanu I., Petrovszki D.M., Enescu C.I., *The Role of the European Ombudsman in the Implementation of the Right to Good Administration*, Acta Universitatis Danubius No. 2/2010: 193-208.

Purdue 2009
Purdue M., *Investigations by the Public Service Ombudsmen* in Feldman D. (ed.), English Public Law: Oxford Principles of English Law, OUP Oxford, 2009.

Raitio 2000
Raitio J., The Principle of Legality as a General Principle of EU Law, in Bernitz U., Nergelius J. (eds.), *General Principles of European Community Law: Reports from a Conference in Malmo, 27-28 August 1999*, Kluwer Law International, 2000.

Ramcharan 2002
Ramcharan B., *The United Nations High Commissioner for Human Rights: the Challenges of International Protection*, Martinus Nijhoff Publ., 2002.

Reif 2004
Reif L., *The Ombudsman Good Governance and the International Human Rights System*, Martinus Nijhoff Publishers, Leiden, 2004.

Remac 2013
Remac M., *Standards of Ombudsman Assessment: A New Normative Concept?*, Utrecht Law Review, Vol. 9, No. 3, pp. 62-78, July 2013.

Romano 2002
Romano C., *Advance tax rulings and principles of law: towards a European tax rulings system?*, IBFD Publications BV, Amsterdam, 2002.

Russell & O'Brien 2001
Russell P.H., O'Brien D.M. (eds.), Judicial Independence in the Age of Democracy: Critical Perspectives from Around the World, University of Virginia Press, 2001.

Sackers & Buruma 2008
Sackers H.J.B., Buruma Y. (eds.), *Kroniek van het strafrecht 2007*, Kluwer 2008.

Schlössels & Stroink 2006
Schlössels, R. J. N., Stroink F. A. M., *Kern van het bestuursrecht*, The Hague, BJU, 2006.

Schlössels 2013
Schlössels, R.J.N., *De harde kern van behoorlijkheid, Over rechtmatigheid, behoorlijkheid en de Nationale ombudsman*, in K. Groenendijk et al. (eds.), Issues that matter: mensenrechten, minderheden en migranten. Liber amicorum voor Prof. mr. R. Fernhout, Nijmegen, Wolf, 2013.

Schwarze 2001
Schwarze J., Judicial Review of Community Acts from a German point of view, in Wouters J., Stuyck J. (eds.), *Principles of Proper Conduct for Supranational, State and Private Actors in the European Union*, Intersentia, 2001.

Seerden & Wenders 2012
Seerden R., Wenders D., *Administrative Law in the Netherlands*, in Seerden R. (ed.), Administrative law of the European Union, its Member States and the United States: A Comparative Analysis, Intersentia Metro, 2012.

Senden 2004
Senden L., *Soft Law in European Community Law*, Hart Publishing, Oxford, 2004.

Seneviratne 2000
Seneviratne, M., *Ombudsmen 2000*, Nottingham L.J. 13 (2000).

Seneviratne 2002
Seneviratne M., *Ombudsmen: Public Services and Administrative Justice*, Butterworths, 2002.
Skouris 2009
Skouris V., '*The relationship of the European Court of Justice with the national constitutional courts*', speech, Budapest, 2009.
Slapper & Kelly 2011
Slapper G. & Kelly D., *The English Legal System: 2011-2012*, Routledge Cavendish, 2011.
Söderman 1997
Söderman J., '*Is there a classic parliamentary Ombudsman?*', speech, Vienna, 1997.
Söderman 2000
Söderman J., Speech of the European Ombudsman – *Public Hearing on the draft Charter of Fundamental Rights of the European Union*, Preliminary remarks, Brussels 2000.
Söderman 2004
Söderman J., Good Administration: a Fundamental Right, in Apap J.(ed.), *Justice and Home Affairs in the EU: Liberty and Security Issues After Enlargement*, Edward Elgar Publishing Ltd, 2004.
Spratt et al. 2004
Spratt Ch., Walker R., Robinson B., *Module A5: Mixed research methods*, Commonwealth of Learning, 2004.
Stern 2008
Stern J., parts *Netherlands, Sweden* in Kucsko-Stadlmayer G. (ed.), European Ombudsman-Institutions: A comparative legal analysis regarding the multifaceted realisation of an idea, Springer, Vienna, 2008.
Stott & Felix 1997
Stott D. & Felix A., *Principles of Administrative Law*, 1997.
Sunkin 2009
Sunkin M., *Grounds for Judicial Review: Illegality in the Strict Sense* in Feldman (ed.), English Public Law: Oxford Principles of English Law, OUP Oxford, 2009.
Supperstone & Knapman 2008
Supperstone M., Knapman L., (eds.), *Administrative Court Practice*, Oxford OUP, 2008.
Sweet & Keller 2008
Sweet A.S., Keller H., *Assessing the Impact of the ECHR on National Legal Systems* (2008). Faculty Scholarship Series. Paper 88.
Ten Berge 2007
Ten Berge G., De Nationale ombudsman en handhavingtoezicht in de Algemene wet bestuursrecht, in Blomberg A. et al. (eds.), *Van Utrecht via Brussel naar Maastricht*, Kluwer 2007.
Ten Berge et al. 1992
Ten Berge J.B.J.M, Gerrits-Janssens M.P., Stolk P.J., *Vereisten van behoorijkheid: Een analyse na tien jaar ombudsman*, Tjeenk Willink, Zwolle, 1992.
Ten Berge & Langbroek 2005
Ten Berge G., Langbroek P., *Surplus value of the Ombudsman* in Gammeltoft-Hansen H., Olsen J. (eds.), The Danish Ombudsman 2005: Part III, Folketingets Ombudsmand, Copenhagen, 2005.
Ten Berge & Widdershoven 2001
Ten Berge J.B.J.M, Widdershoven R.J.G.M., *Bescherming tegen de overheid: Nederlands algemeen Bestuursrecht 2*, Tjeenk Willink, 2001.

Tridimas 2007
Tridimas T., *The General Principles of EU Law*, OUP Oxford, 2 edition, 2007.
Tridimas 2012
Trinidas T., *The European Court of Justice and the EU Constitutional Order: Essays in Judicial Protection*, Hart Publishing Oxford, 2012.
Turpin & Tomkins 2007
Turpin C. & Tomkins A., *British Government and the Constitution: Text and Materials*, Cambridge University Press, 2007.
Van der Heijden 2005
Van der Heijden K., *Klachtenbehandeling door decentrale overheden*, Reed Business Information, The Hague, 2005.
Van der Vlugt 2011
Van der Vlugt Y.M., *De Nationale ombudsman en behoorlijk politieoptreden*, Boom Lemma Uit., The Hague, 2011.
Van Ettekoven & Verburg 2011
Van Ettekoven B.J. & Verburg D.A., *Nieuwe zaaksbehandeling bij de bestuursrechter*, Pionierskrant, zomer 2011.
Van Wijk et al. 2008
Van Wijk H.D., Konijnenbelt W. & Van Male R., *Hoofdstukken van bestuursrecht*, The Hague: Elsevier Juridisch, 2008.
Wade & Forsyth 2009
Wade W. & Forsyth C., *Administrative Law*, OUP Oxford, 2009.
Wakefield 2007
Wakefield J., *The Right to Good Administration*, Kluwer Law International, 2007.
Widdershoven & Remac 2012
Widdershoven R., Remac M., *General Principles of Law in Administrative Law under European Influence,* European Review of Private Law, 2012.
Woolf et al. 2013
Woolf H., Jowell J., Le Sueur A., Donnelly C. & Hare I., *De Smith's Judicial Review*, 7th ed., London, Sweet & Maxwell, Thomson Reuters, London, 2013.
Zweigert & Kötz 1998
Zweigert, K. & Kötz H., *Introduction to comparative law,* Clarendon Press, Oxford 1998.

The Law Commission Consultation Paper No. 187
The Law Commission Consultation Paper No. 187, *Administrative redress: public bodies and the citizen,* 2008.
The Law Commission Consultation Paper No. 196
The Law Commission Consultation Paper No. 196, *Public Service Ombudsmen,* 2010.
Law Commission (LAW COM No. 329)
Law Commission (LAW COM No. 329), *Public Service Ombudsmen,* June 2011.
Statskantoret 2005
Principles of Good Administration in the Member States of the European Union, Statskantoret, 2005:4.

Annual Reports of the Dutch National Ombudsman (2005-2012).
Annual Reports of the UK Parliamentary Ombudsman (2005-2012).
Annual Reports of English Local Government Ombudsmen (2008-2011).
Annual Reports of the European Ombudsman (1996-2012).

Table of cases

The Netherlands

HR 3-05-1977, NJ 1978, 692.
HR 12-04-1978 (*Doorbraakarresten*), NJ 1979/533.
HR 26-09-1979, AB 1980/210.
HR 14-04-1989, AB 1989, 207.
HR 16-06-1998, NJ1998, 800.
HR 16-12-1998, BB 2002, 634.
HR 23-04-2004, BNB 2004, 392.
HR 13-11-2007, JOL 2007, 754.
HR 11-07-2008, JOL 2008, 588.
HR 17-04-2009, BNB 2010, 114.
HR 28-09-2010, RvdW 2010, 1154.
HR 24-12-2010, BNB 2011, 82.
HR 25-01-2011, JOW 2011, 31.
HR 09-09-2011, NJ 2011, 553.
HR 30-09-2011, BNB 2012, 69.

ABRvS 03-02-1983, AB 1984, 283.
ABRvS 16-02-1987, NJ 1990, 464.
ABRvS 09-05-1996, JB 1996, 158 (Praxis en Maxis).
ABRvS 05-12-2007, AB 2008, 18.
ABRvS 15-02-2007, JV 2007, 168.
ABRvS 11-02-2009, AB 2009, 102.
ABRvS 30-03-2009, JB 2009, 128.

CRvB 31-10-1935, ARB 1936.
CRvB 18-02-1975, AB 1975/243.
CRvB 25-02-1999, TAR 1999, 70.
CRvB 28-05-1999, AB 2000, 262.
CRvB 24-02-1998, USZ 1998, 107.
CRvB 20-08-2004, LJN: AQ7407.
CRvB 04-05-2006, LJN: AX3238.
CRvB 09-10-2007, USZ 2007.
CBB 29-10-2010, LJN: BO2813.
CBB 10-11-2010, LJN: BP0447.
Hof Leeuwarden 16-01-2004, BB 2004, 451.
Hof Leeuwarden 02-12-2008, JA 2009, 34.

Hof Arnhem 13-07-2010, NTFR 2010, 2174.
Hof Arnhem 14-09-2010, NTFR 2010, 2334.
Hof Den Haag 14-12-2010, LJN: BO7396.
Hof Leeuwarden 16-08-2012, BB 2012, 531.

Rb. Den Haag 22-06-1994, V-N 1994/2526, 36.
Rb. Zutphen 12-10-1995, NJK 1996, 35.
Rb. Dordrecht 04-06-1999, AB 1999, 330.
Rb. Den Haag 10-04-2003, TAR 2003, 124.
Rb. Den Haag 23-06-2004, LJN: AP5823.
Rb. Alkmaar 18-04-2006, LJN: AW8127.
Rb. Assen 19-02-2007, LJN: AZ8836.
Rb. Den Haag 12-03-2007, NJF 2007.
Rb. Assen 19-02-2007, LJN: AZ8836.
Rb. Den Haag 12-11-2007, JV 2008, 61.
Rb. Den Haag 13-11-2007, LJN: BC1009.
Rb. Den Haag 17-12-2007, LJN: BC5117.
Rb. Den Haag 11-02-2009, LJN: BH9325.
Vzngr. Rb. Den Haag 02-03-2009, JA 2009, 69.
Vzngr. Rb. 's-Hertogenbosch 30-12-2009, JAR 2010.
Rb. Den Haag 14-08-2008, JV 2008.
Rb. Haarlem 31-03-2010, NTFR 2010, 1150.
Rb. Den Haag 19-05-2010, LJN: BM9244.
Rb. Den Haag 30-11-2010, BB 2011.
Rb. Maastricht 08-02-2011, JWR 2011, 40.
Rb. Den Haag 27-07-2011, LJN: BU1282.
Rb. Amsterdam 07-02-2012, LJN: BW8475.
Rb. Den Haag 11-07-2012, NJ 2012, 579.
Rb. Den Haag 20-08-2012, LJN: BX5425.
Rb. Rotterdam 20-03-2013, LJN: BZ5645.

UK/England

Anufrijeva v London Borough of Southwark [2003] EWCA Civ 1406.
Blackpool Corp v Locker [1948] 1 KB 349.
Edwards v SOGAT [1971] Ch 354.
Entick v Carrington (1765) 19 St TR 1029.
Mountview Court Properties Ltd v Devlin 91970) 21 P & CR 689.
R v Advertising Standards Authority, ex p International Fund for Animal Welfare (QBD,11/11/1997).
R v Civil Service Appeal Board, ex p Cunningham [1992] ICR 817.
R v Commissioner for Local Administration, ex p Croydon London Borough Council, [1989] 1 All ER.
R v Commissioner for Local Administration, ex p H [1999] COD 382, 314.
R v Cotswold District Council, ex p Barrington Parish Council (1997) 75 P & CR 515.
R v Local Commissioner for Administration for the North and East Area of England, ex parte Bradford Metropolitan City Council [1979] Q.B. 287.
R v Local Commissioner for Administration in North and North East England, ex p Liverpool City Council [2001] 1 All ER 462.
R v Local Commissioner for Administration for the South, the West, the West Midlands, Leicestershire, Lincolnshire and Cambridgeshire, ex p Eastleigh Borough Council, (1987) 86 LGR 145.

R v Local Commissioner for Administration for the South, the West Midlands, Leicestershire, Lincolnshire and Cambridgeshire, Ex parte Eastleigh Borough Council [1988] 3 W.L.R. 113.
R v Higher Education Funding Council, ex p Institute of Dental Surgery [1994] 1WLR 242.
R v HM the Queen in Council, ex p Vijayatunga [1988] QB 322.
R v Law Society, ex p Kingsley [1996] COD 59.
R v North and East Devon Health Authority, ex p Coughlan [2001] QB 213, CA.
R v North West Lancashire Health Authority, ex p A [2000] 1 WLR 977, 991.
R v Parliamentary Commissioner for Administration, ex p Balchin & Anor [1996] EWHC Admin 152.
R v Parliamentary Commissioner for Administration, ex p Balchin & Anor [1999] EWHC Admin 484.
R v Parliamentary Commissioner for Administration ex p Balchin (No 3) (2000) 79 P&CR 157.
R v Parliamentary Commissioner for Administration, ex p Dyer [1993] EWHC (Admin 3).
R v Sandwell Metropolitan Borough Council, ex p Wilkinson [1998] 31 HLR 22.
R v Secretary of State for Environment, Transport and Regions, ex p Holding and Barnes [2001] 2 All ER 929.
R v Secretary of State for the Environment, ex p Kirkstall Valley Campaign [1996] 3 All ER 304.
R v Secretary of State for the Home Department, ex parte Daly [2001] UKHL 21.
R v Secretary of State for the Home Department, Ex parte Doody [1994] 1 AC 531.
R v Somerset CC, ex p Fewings [1995] 1 All E 513.
R (on the application of Abernethy) v Local Government Ombudsman [2002] EWCA Civ 552.
R (on the application of Adams) v The Commission for Local Administration in England & Ors [2011] EWHC 2972 (Admin).
R (on the application of Association of British Civilian Internees Far East Region) v Secretary of State for Defence, [2002] EWHC 2119 (Admin).
R (on the application of Association of British Civilian Internees: Far East Region) v Secretary of State for Defence [2003] EWCA Civ. 473.
R (on the application of Atapattu) v The Secretary of State for the Home Department [2011] EWHC 1388 (Admin).
R (on the application of Bernard) v London Borough of Enfield [2002] EWHC 2282 (Admin).
R (on the application of Birmingham City Council) v Birmingham Crown Court [2009] EWHC 3329 (Admin).
R (on the application of Bradley & Ors) v Secretary of State for Work & Pensions & Ors [2008] EWCA Civ 36.
R (on the application of Doy) v Commissioner for Local Administration [2001] EWHC Admin 361.
R (on the application of Evison) v The Commissioner for Local Administration & Anor [2008] EWHC 3568 (Admin).
R (on the application of Gallagher & Anor) v Basildon District Council [2010] EWHC 2824 (Admin).
R (on the application of Hasan) v Secretary of State for Trade and Industry [2008] EWCA Civ 131.
R (on the application of Klimas) v Prosecutors General Office of Lithuania [2010] EWHC 2076 (Admin).
R (on the application of Mahajan) v Local Government Ombudsman [2007] EWHC 1135 (Admin).
R (on the application of Murray) v Parliamentary Commissioner for Administration [2002] EWCA Civ 1472.
R (on the application of Munjaz) v Mersey Care NHS Trust [2005] UKHL 58.
R (on the application of Scholarstica Umo) v Commissioner for Local Administration In England [2003] EWHC 3202 (Admin).
R (on the application of Senior-Milne) v the Parliamentary and Health Service Ombudsman [2009] EWHC 2240 (Admin).
R (on the application of Turpin) v Commissioner for Administration [2001] EWHC Admin 503.
W v Westminister City Council [2005] EWHC 102 (QB).

European Union

Case 8/55 *Fédéchar v. High Authority* [1954-56] ECR 245, 256.
Joined cases 7/56 and 3/57 to 7/57, *Algera v Common Assembly of the ECSC* [1957] ECR 39.
Joined cases 42 and 49/59 *SNUPAT v High Authority* [1961] ECR 109.
Case 24/62 *Germany v Commission (BrennWein)* [1963] ECR 63.
Case 29/69 *Stauder v Stadt Ulm* [1969] ECR 419.
Case 11/70 *Internationale Handellsgezelschaft* [1970] ECR 1125.
Case 81/72 *Commission v Council* [1973] ECR 575.
Case 17/74 *Transocean Marine Paint Association* [1974] ECR 1063.
Case 105/75 *Giuffrida v Commission* [1976] ECR 1395.
Joined cases 64 and 113/76, 167 and 239/78, 27, 28 and 45/79, 64/76 *Dumortier v Council* [1979] ECR 3091.
Case 85/76 *Hoffmann-La Roche* [1979] ECR 461.
Case 112/77 *Töpfer* [1978] ECR 1019.
Case 138/79 *SA Roquette Frères v Council* [1980] ECR 3333.
Case 147/79 *Hochstrass* [1980] ECR 3005.
Case 51/81 *De Franceschi v Council and Commission* [1982] ECR 117.
Case 289/81 *Mavridis v Parliament* [1983] ECR 1731.
Joined cases 2005 to 2015/82 *Deutsche Milchkontor* [1983] ECR 2623.
Joined cases 75/82 and 117/82 *Razzouk and Beydoun* [1984] ECR 1509.
Joined cases 173/82, 157/83 and 186/84 *Castille* v *Commission* [1986] ECR 497.
Case 71/85 *Netherlands v Federatie Nederlandse Vakbeweging (FNV)* [1986] ECR 3855.
Joined Cases 176/86 and 177/86 *Houyoux and Guery v Commission* [1987] ECR 4333.
C-314/85 *Foto-Frost v Hauptzollamt Lübeck-Ost* [1987] ECR 4199.
Case 374/87 *Orkem* [1989] ECR 3283.
Case C-152/88 *Sofrimport v Commission* [1992] ECR I-2477.
Case C-104/89 *Mulder and Others v Council and Commission* [2000] ECR I-00203.
Case C-107/91 *ENU v Commission* [1993] ECR I-599.
Joined cases C-46/93 and C-48/93 *Brasserie du pêcheur v Bundesrepublik Deutschland and The Queen / Secretary of State for Transport, ex parte Factortame and Others* [1996] ECR I-1029.
Case C-280/93 *Germany v. Council* [1994] ECR I-4973.
Case C-1/94 *Cavarzere Produzioni Industriali and Others v Ministero dell'Agricoltura e delle Foreste and Others* [1995] ECR I-2363.
Case C-13/94 *P v. S* [1996] ECR I-2143
Case C-84/94 *UK v Council* [1995] ECR I-5755.
Case C-29/95 *Eckehard Pastoors and Trans-Cap GmbH v Belgian State* [1997] ECR I-285.
Case C-282/95 P *Guérin automobiles v Commission* [1997] ECR I-1503
Case C-294/95 P *Ojha v Commission* [1996] ECR I-5863.
Case C-299/95 *Friedrich Kriemzow v. Austrian State* [1997] ECR I-2629.
Case C-352/98 P *Bergaderm and Goupil v Commission* [2000] ECR I-5291.
Case C-376/98 *Germany v EUP and Council (Tobacco Advertising)* [2000] ECR I-8419.
Case C-377/98 *Netherlands v. Parliament and Council* [2001] ECR I-7079.
Case C-501/00 *Spain v Commission* [2004] ECR I-6717
Case C-76/01 P *Eurocoton and others v Council* [2003] ECR I-10091.
Case C-36/02 *Omega* [2004] ECR I-9609.
Case C-60/02 *Rolex* [2004] ECR I-651.
Case C-110/02 *Commission v Council* [2004] ECR I-6333.
Case C-234/02 *Mediator v Lamberts* [2004] ECR I-2803.

Case C-231/03 *Coname* [2005] ECR I-7287.
Case C-234/03 *Contse SA and Others* [2005] ECR I-9315.
Case C-331/05 P *Internationaler Hilfsfonds v Commission* [2007] ECR I-5475.
Joined cases C-341/06 P and C-342/06 P *Chronopost SA and La Poste v Union française de l'express (UFEX) and Others*, [2008] ECR I-4777.
Case C-428/05 *Laub* [2007] ECR I-5069
Case C-342/06 P *Chronopost SA and La Poste v Union française de l'express (UFEX) and Others*, [2008] ECR I-4777.
Case C-349/07 *Sopropé* [2009] ECR I-10369.
Case C-550/07 P *Akzo & Akcros* [2010] ECR I-8301.
Case C-28/08 P *Commission v Bavarian Lager* [2010] ECR I-6055.
Case C-45/08 *Spector Photo Group and Van Raemdonck* [2009] ECR I-12073.
Case C-580/08 *P Srinivasan v Mediator* [2009] ECR I-110.
Case C-148/10 *DHL International* [2011] ECR I-9543.
Case C-210/10 *Urbán* (not yet published).
Case C-212/11 *Jyske Bank Gibraltar Ltd v Administración del Estado* (not yet published).
Case C-439/11 P *Ziegler SA v European Commission* (not yet published).
Case C-535/12 P *Faet Oltra v Mediator* (not yet published).

Case T-148/89 *Trefilunion SA v Commission* [1995] ECR II-1063.
Case T-53/91 *Mergen v Commission* [1992] ECR II-2041.
Case T-68/91 *Barbi v Commission* [1992] ECR II-2127.
Case T-103/99 *Associazione delle Cantine Sociali Venete v Mediator and the EUP* [2000] ECR II-4165.
Case T-120/99 *Kik v OHIM* [2001] ECR II-2235.
Case T-190/00 *Regione Siciliana* [2003] ECR II-5015.
Case T-209/00 *Lamberts v Mediator* [2002] ECR II-2203.
Joined cases T-377/00, T-379/00, T-380/00, T-260/01 and T-272/01 *Philip Morris International v Commission* [2003] ECR II-0001.
Joined cases T-219/02 and T-337/02 *Lutz Herrera* v *Commission* [2004] FP-I-A-0319.
Case T-212/03 *MyTravel Group plc v Commission* [2008] ECR II-1967.
Case T-371/03 *Le Voci v Council* [2005] FP-I-A-00209.
Case T-160/03 *Afcon v Commission* [2005] ECR II-981.
Case T-294/03 *Gibault v Commission* [2005] FP-I-A-141.
Case T-394/03 *Angeletti v Commission* [2006] FP-I-A-2-00095.
Case T-193/04 *Tillack v Commission* [2006] ECR II-3995.
Case T-294/04 *Internationaler Hilfsfonds v Commission* [2005] ECR II-2719.
Case T-59/05 *Evropaïki Dynamiki v Commission* [2008] ECR II-157.
Case T-195/05 *Deloitte Business Advisory NV v Commission* [2007] ECR II-187.
Case T-412/05 *M v Mediator* [2008] ECR II-197.
Case T-3/06 AJ *Wenzel v Commission and Mediator* (not published).
Case T-132/06 *Gorostiaga Atxalandabaso v Parliament* [2007] ECR II-0035.
Case T-144/06 *O'Loughlin v Mediator and Ireland* (not published).
Case T-19/07 *Systran and Systran Luxembourg v Commission* [2010] ECR II-6083.
Case T-377/07 *Evropaïki Dynamiki v Commission* [2011] ECR II-0442.
Case T-407/07 *CMB and Christof v Commission* [2011] ECR II-0286.
Case T442/07 *Ryanair v Commission* [2011] ECR II-0333.
Case T-121/08 *PC-Ware Information Technologies v Commission* [2010] ECR II-1541.
Case T-168/08 AJ *Meister v Commission and Mediator* (not published).
Case T176/08 *infeurope v Commission* [2009] ECR II-00119.

Case T-196/08 *Srinivasan v Mediator* (not published).
Case T-250/08 *Batchelor v Commission* [2011] ECR II-2551.
Case T-290/08 AJ *Apostolov v Mediator* (not published).
Case T-424/08 *Nexus Europe (Ireland) v Commission* [2010] ECR II-96.
Case T-85/09 *Kadi v Commission* [2010] ECR II-05177.
Case T-298/09 *Evropaïki Dynamiki v Commission* [2011] ECR II-0300.
Joined Cases T458/09 and T171/10 *Slovak Telekom a.s. v European Commission* (not yet published).
Case T18/10 *Inuit Tapiriit Kanatami and Others* v *Parliament and Council* [2011] ECR II-5599.
Case T-262/10 *Microban v Commission* [2011] ECR II-7697.
Case T-433/10 P *Allen and Others v Commission* (not yet published).
Joined cases T-439/10 and T-440/10 *Fulmen v Council* (not yet published).
Case T-496/10 *Bank Mellat v Council and Commission* (not yet published).
Case T-590/10 *Thesing and Bloomberg Finance v ECB* (not yet published).
Case T-369/11 *Diadikasia Symvouloi Epicheiriseon v Commission* (not yet published).
Case T-217/11 *Staelen v Mediator* (information not available).
Case T-477/11 AJ *BW v Commission and Mediator* (not published).
Case T-406/12 P-AJ *BG v Mediator* (not published).

Case F-120/06 *Dálnoky v Commission* [2007] FP-I-A-1-0269.
Case F-51/07 Phillippe Bui Van v Commission [2008] FP-I-A-1-0289.

Opinion of AG Lagrange in Joined cases 7/56, 3/57 to 7/57 *Dineke Algera, Giacomo Cicconardi, Simone Couturaud, Ignazio Genuardi, Félicie Steichen v Common Assembly of the European Coal and Steel Community*
Opinions of AG Van Gerven in Case C-312/89 *Sidef Conforama* [1991] ECR I-997.
Opinion of AG Mischo in Case C-470/00 *Parliament v Carlo Ripa di Meana and Others* [2004] ECR I-4167.
Opinion of AG Tizzano in Case C-193/01 P *Pitsiorlas v Council and ECB* [2003] ECR I-4837.
Opinion of AG Geelhoed in Case C-234/02 P *Mediator v Lamberts* [2004] ECR I-2803.
Opinion of AG Léger in C-40/03 P *Rica Foods v Commission* [2005] ECR I-681.
Opinion of AG Jacobs in Case C-227/04 P *Lindorfer v Council* [2007] ECR I-6767.
Opinion of AG Trstenjak in C-331/05 P *Internationaler Hilfsfonds v Commission* [2007] ECR I-5475.
Opinion of AG Kokott in Case C427/07 *Commission v Ireland* [2009] ECR I-6277.
Opinion of AG Mengozzi in Case C-362/08 P *Internationaler Hilfsfonds v Commission* [2010] ECR I-669.

Annex 1

INTERVIEW QUESTIONS

1. Questions - ombudsmen

a) *Institutional coordination between ombudsmen and the judiciary*

1. Are there any official or unofficial relations with the judiciary?
2. Does the judiciary play any role in the investigations of complaints? Does the judiciary play any role outside these investigations?
3. Is there any exchange of information between your office and the judiciary?
4. Do you refer complainants to the judiciary when you think that they could be better helped there?

b) *Case coordination between ombudsmen and the judiciary*

1. Do you make cross-references in your investigations to the court case law? Are such cross-references predetermined or it is done only on an ad hoc basis?
2. How are you informed about important court decisions that can influence you?
3. If you do operate with the court case law during the investigation, what is the main reason for such a practice?
4. Do you look for support in the court decisions? If yes, in what cases?
5. What is the actual role of the court case law in your investigation? Is there any coordination in this connection or do each of the investigators do this individually?

c) *Normative coordination between ombudsmen and the judiciary*

1. What kind of assessment standards do you use while investigating the complaints?
2. How do you, in practice, use these standards in your investigation?
3. If you were able support the conclusions of your decision with a) a court decision that includes a particular principle of law or b) with reference to your own assessment standards or c) with 'something else', what will you chose? Subject to what conditions would your decision depend?
4. In which cases do the use of principles of law seem to be a better solution and in which cases do your own assessment standards prevail?
5. What kind of assessment standards do you use when trying to solve the case with a friendly solution? How do you assess these situations?

2. Questions - the judiciary

a) Institutional cooperation between ombudsmen and the judiciary
1. Is there any co-operation between your office and the ombudsmen? If yes, in what way? If not, what do you think are the main reasons for non-cooperation?
2. Are there any official relations between your office and the ombudsmen (official meetings, presentations, official visits, official consultations)?
3. Can cooperation between the judiciary and the ombudsmen lead to a better protection of individuals or better administration?
4. Do you refer complainants to ombudsmen when you think that they could be better off there? Is this at all possible?
5. How do you perceive the ombudsmen's powers in connection with the role of the judiciary?

b) *Case coordination between ombudsmen and the judiciary*
1. Is there any formal or informal exchange of information between your office and ombudsmen? If yes, in what way is this done? Are you aware of the reports of ombudsmen?
2. Do you take into account in your decision-making process the reports of ombudsmen if they are submitted to you by a party to the proceedings? How?
3. Do you look into the reports of the ombudsmen for inspiration? If yes, in what connection?
4. How do you deal with the reports of ombudsmen if they deal with the same issues as you do, but from the point of view of good (proper) administration? Is it possible to use an ombudsman's report as evidence in court proceedings?

c) *Normative coordination between ombudsmen and the judiciary*
1. What kind of assessment standards do you use while deciding cases?
2. Do you, while deciding cases, take into consideration also other norms than the legal norms (e.g. moral norms, customer service principles, Codes of Conduct etc.)?
3. Do you think that there is a difference between applicability of principles used by ombudsmen and the principles used by you?
4. How do you perceive the ombudsmen's endeavour to create a normative system distinct from, though sometimes overlapping with the legal norms?
5. Can the normative standards of ombudsmen add something new to the development of legal principles?

3. Questions - Members of the AJCT (England)

1. Is it within the powers of the AJTC (whose main objective is to review the administrative justice system as whole) to influence the actions of subjects within the field of administrative justice so that these are in accordance with the principles of the AJTC?
2. Can the AJTC actually influence the interaction between these subjects so that they can attain similar general goals?

3. A substantial part of AJTC powers was transposed from the former Council on Tribunals and the PO is an ex lege member of the AJTC. Cannot these issues create an obstacle in the AJTC's ability to review the whole administrative justice system without prejudice?
4. How does the AJTC monitor the relationships between the first instance decision makers, ombudsmen, tribunals and the courts? What does the AJTC actually do with the results of monitoring?
5. Is there an official opinion of the AJTC on the relationships between these subjects (especially on the relationship between ombudsmen and the courts)?

4. Questions – academics (England)

1. Is the level of the cooperation between public sector ombudsmen and the courts/tribunals in your opinion sufficient? Is it necessary to improve cooperation between ombudsmen and the courts/tribunals subject to the English conditions?
2. What is your opinion on the applicability of the judicial review procedure to ombudsmen? Does this power of the judiciary endanger the discretionary powers of ombudsmen or their independence?
3. Can, in your opinion, the power to stay the (ombudsmen or court) proceedings and transfer the case to another authority strengthen the cooperation between these bodies?
4. Do ombudsmen in your opinion strive for legal certainty? Do they contribute in any way to the development of the law?
5. The concepts of maladministration and unlawfulness are not the same, although they do overlap. Their similarity and/or difference were mentioned on various occasions. Do you think that there is going to be a further mutual development of these concepts?
6. In connection with maladministration and unlawfulness do you think that there is any difference between the type of norms used by the courts and ombudsmen?

Annex 2

INTERVIEWED PERSONS

The Netherlands

- Dr *A. Brenninkmeijer,* the National Ombudsman,
- Mr *F. van Dooren,* the Substitute National Ombudsman,
- Ms *J. de Bruijn*, senior investigator at the NO Office,
- Mr *J. Prins*, senior investigator at the NO Office,
- Ms *Vegter*, senior investigator at the NO Office,
- Ms *Govers*, senior investigator at the NO Office,
- Ms *Bannier*, senior investigator at the NO Office,
- Mr *S. Sjouke*, Head of International Affairs of the NO Office,
- Ms *M.A.A Mondt-Schouten* (Afdeeling bestuursrechtspraak van de Raad van State),
- Mr *J.E. Jansen* (Centrale Raad van Beroep),
- Mr *R. van Zutphen*, President of the Trade and Industry Appeals Tribunal,
- Prof. *R. Widdershoven*, judge, the Trade and Industry Appeals Tribunal,
- Mr *J. Jansen*, judge, the Central Appeals Tribunal,
- Mr *J. van Schagen*, judge, Rechtbank Oost-Nederland and
- Mr *A. Verburg*, judge, Rechtbank Midden-Nederland.

England

- Ms *A. Abraham,* the Parliamentary Ombudsman 2002 – 2012,
- Ms *A. Seex,* the Local Government Ombudsman,
- Dr *N. O'Brien,* former Interim Director of Policy and Public Affairs at the PO Office,
- Ms *A. Harding*, Legal Adviser at the PO Office,
- Mr *A. Medlock*, Training Team Manager at the PO Office,
- Mr *D. Galligan*, Policy manager at the PO Office,
- Ms *J. Betteridge*, Casework manager at the PO Office
- Mr *P. Mende*, Public Affairs Analyst at the PO Office,
- Mr *D. Laverick,* former senior officer at the Local Government Ombudsman office (1975 1995) and judge, FTT (Local Government Standards in England),
- Ms *L. Knapman,* the Deputy Master of the High Court (High Court),
- His Honour *R. Martin,* FTT (President of Social Entitlement Chamber),
- Dr. *N. O'Brien,* judge, FTT (Mental Health),
- Mr *J. Holbrook*, judge, FTT (Charity) and Employment Tribunal,

- Mr *D. Birrell,* judge, FTT (Mental Health),
- Mr *B. Herwald,* FTT (Special Educational Needs, Immigration Tribunal, Mental Health),
- Prof. *M. Seneviratne* (Member of the AJTC) and
- Dr. *B. Thompson* (Member of the AJTC).

European Union
- Prof. *N. Diamandouros,* the European Ombudsman 2001 2013,
- Mr *J. Sant'Anna,* Director of Directorate A, Office of the EUO,
- Mr *G. Grill,* Director of Directorate B and Acting Head of the Complaints and Inquiries Unit, Office of the EUO,
- Prof. *S. Prechal* (judge, the Court of Justice),
- Mr *M. Van der Woude* (judge, the General Court),
- Mr *R. Barents* (judge, the Civil Service Tribunal),
- Prof *A. Meij* (former judge, the Court of First Instance) and
- Ms *C. Kristensen* (Registry of the Court).[1]

1 In December 2011 Ms Abraham was succeeded in the post of the Parliamentary Ombudsman by Dame J. Mellor. However, Dame Mellor was not interviewed. In October 2013 Prof. Diamantouros was succeeded in the post of the European Ombudsman by Ms E. O'Reilly. Ms O'Reilly was not interviewed.

Annex 3

LISTS OF NORMATIVE STANDARDS OF THE RESEARCHED OMBUDSMEN

(applicable on 31 July 2013.)

a) Guidelines of proper administration of the National Ombudsman (NL)

1. Transparent
Actions of public authorities should be open and foreseeable so that it is clear to citizens why government is taking a particular action.

2. Provide adequate information
Public authorities should ensure that citizens receive the information they need. The information should be clear, correct and complete. Public authorities should provide it proactively, not just when citizens ask for it.

3. Listen to citizens
Public authorities should listen actively to individual citizens, so that they feel that they are heard.

4. Adequate reasons
Public authorities should supply clear statements of the reasons for their actions and decisions. Such statements should explain the statutory basis for the action or decision, the facts taken into consideration and the way individual citizens' interests have been taken into account. Citizens should be able to understand the statements.

5. Respect for fundamental rights
Public authorities should respect the fundamental rights of citizens. Some of these fundamental rights guarantee protection against government action. For example: the right to physical integrity, the right to privacy, the right to respect for private and family life, the right to personal liberty, the right to freedom from discrimination. By contrast, other fundamental rights guarantee that public administration will take certain action. For example: the right to education or the right to health.

6. Promotion of active public participation
Public authorities should maximise public involvement in their operations.

7. Courtesy
Public authorities should be respectful, courteous and helpful towards citizens.

8. Fair play
Public authorities should give citizens the chance to exhaust all the procedural avenues open to them and should ensure fair play in this respect.

9. Proportionality
In pursuing its aims, public authorities should avoid measures that have an unnecessary impact on citizens' lives or that are disproportionate to the aims concerned.

10. Special care
When people are in government custody and therefore reliant on public authorities for their physical care, the authorities should provide that care.

11. Individualised approach
Public authorities should be prepared to waive general policies or rules in cases where their enforcement would have unintended or undesirable consequences.

12. Cooperation
Public authorities should cooperate spontaneously with other governmental and nongovernmental bodies in the interests of the citizen and should not send citizens from pillar to post.

13. Leniency
When mistakes have been made, public authorities should show leniency and flexibility in remedying them. They should not deny reasonable claims for compensation and should not burden citizens with unnecessary and complicated procedures and demands for proof.

14. Promptness
Actions by public authorities should be as prompt and effective as possible.

15. De-escalation
In all its contacts with individual citizens, public authorities should seek to prevent or halt escalation. Communication skills and a solution focused attitude are essential in this respect.

16. Integrity
Public authorities should act with integrity and use their powers only for the purposes for which they were conferred.

17. Trustworthiness
Public authorities should act within the framework of the law. They should be honest and fair-minded. They should do what they say and should comply with judgments of the courts.

18. Impartiality
Public authorities should be impartial in their attitude and unprejudiced in their actions.

19. Reasonableness
Before taking any decision, public authorities should weigh up the various interests involved. The outcome of this process must not be unreasonable.

20. Careful preparation
Public authorities should assemble all the information necessary to take a well-considered decision.

21. Effective organisation
Public authorities should ensure that their organisational and administrative systems promote the standard of their services to the public. They should work meticulously and avoid mistakes. Any errors that occur should be corrected as quickly as possible.

22. Professionalism
Public authorities should ensure that their employees work in accordance with relevant professional standards. Citizens are entitled to expect government employees to be expert in their particular field

b) Principles of Good Administration of the Parliamentary Ombudsman (EN)

1. Getting it right
a)[1] Acting in accordance with the law and with regard for the rights of those concerned.
b) Acting in accordance with the public body's policy and guidance (published or internal).
c) Taking proper account of established good practice.
d) Providing effective services, using appropriately trained and competent staff.
e) Taking reasonable decisions, based on all relevant considerations.

2. Being customer focused
a) Ensuring people can access services easily.
b) Informing customers what they can expect and what the public body expects of them.
c) Keeping to its commitments, including any published service standards.
d) Dealing with people helpfully, promptly and sensitively, bearing in mind their individual circumstances.
e) Responding to customers' needs flexibly, including, where appropriate, co-ordinating a response with other service providers.

3. Being open and accountable
a) Being open and clear about policies and procedures and ensuring that information, and any advice provided, is clear, accurate and complete.
b) Stating its criteria for decision making and giving reasons for decisions.
c) Handling information properly and appropriately.
d) Keeping proper and appropriate records.
e) Taking responsibility for its actions.

4. **Acting fairly and proportionately**
a) Treating people impartially, with respect and courtesy.
b) Treating people without unlawful discrimination or prejudice, and ensuring no conflict of interests.
c) Dealing with people and issues objectively and consistently.
d) Ensuring that decisions and actions are proportionate, appropriate and fair.

5. **Putting things right**
a) Acknowledging mistakes and apologising where appropriate.
b) Putting mistakes right quickly and effectively.
c) Providing clear and timely information on how and when to appeal or complain.
d) Operating an effective complaints procedure, which includes offering a fair and appropriate remedy when a complaint is upheld.

6. Seeking continuous improvement
a) Reviewing policies and procedures regularly to ensure they are effective.
b) Asking for feedback and using it to improve services and performance.
c) Ensuring that the public body learns lessons from complaints and uses these to improve services and performance.

1 Individual sub-principles are given here a letter only because of easier application in the further text. The sub-principles as included in the text of the Principles of Good Administration do not have these letters.

c) Axioms of Good Administration of the Local Government Ombudsmen (EN)

Law

1. Understand what the law requires the council to do and fulfil those requirements.
2. Ensure that all staff working in any particular area of activity understand and fulfil the legal requirements relevant to that area of activity.

Policy

3. Formulate policies which set out the general approach for each area of activity and the criteria which are used in decision making.
4. Ensure that criteria are clear and relevant and can be applied objectively so that decisions are not made on an inconsistent ad hoc or subjective basis.
5. Communicate relevant policies and rules to customers.
6. Ensure that all staff understand council policies relevant to their area of work.

Decisions

7. Ensure that the council does what its own policy or established practice requires.
8. Consider any special circumstances of each case as well as the council's policy so as to determine whether there are exceptional reasons which justify a decision more favourable to the individual customer than what the policy would normally provide.
9. Ensure that decisions are not taken which are inconsistent with established policies of the council or other relevant plans or guidelines unless there are adequate and relevant grounds for doing so.
10. Have regard to relevant codes of practice and government circulars; and follow the advice contained in them unless there are justifiable reasons not to do so.
11. Ensure that irrelevant considerations are not taken into account in making a decision.
12. Ensure that adequate consideration is given to all relevant and material factors in making a decision.
13. Give proper consideration to the views of relevant parties in making a decision.
14. Use the powers of the council only for their proper purpose and not in order to achieve some other purpose.
15. Ensure that decisions are not made or action taken prematurely.
16. Give reasons for an adverse decision and record them in writing for the customer concerned.
17. Ensure that any necessary decisions or actions are taken as circumstances require and within a reasonable time.
18. If a decision is being taken under delegated powers, ensure that there is proper and sufficient authority for this to be done and that use of delegated powers is appropriate in the circumstances.

Action prior taking decision

19. Carry out a sufficient investigation so as to establish all the relevant and material facts.
20. Seek appropriate specialist advice as necessary.
21. Consult any individuals or organisations who might reasonably consider that they would be adversely and significantly affected by a proposed action.
22. Detect major errors which materially affect an issue under consideration.
23. Give adequate consideration to the reasonable courses of action which are open to the council in any particular circumstances.
24. Ensure that a committee is provided with a report when circumstances require and that the report is materially accurate and covers all the relevant points.

Administrative processes

25. Ensure that the correct action is taken both to implement decisions when they are made and generally in the conduct of the council's business.
26. Have adequate systems and written procedures for staff to follow in dealing with particular areas of activity.

27. Have a system for ensuring proper liaison and co-operation between different departments, different sections of a department, or different areas in the authority.
28. Compile and maintain adequate records.
29. Monitor progress and carry out regular appraisals of how an issue or problem is being dealt with.
30. Seek to resolve difficulties or disagreements by negotiations in the first instance but take formal action when it is clear that informal attempts at resolution are not working.

Customer relations
31. Avoid making misleading or inaccurate statements to customers.
32. Formulate undertakings with care and discharge any responsibilities towards customers which arise from them.
33. Reply to letters and other enquiries and do so courteously and within a reasonable period; and have a system for ensuring that appropriate action is taken on every occasion.
34. Keep customers regularly informed about the progress of matters which are of concern to them.
35. Provide adequate and accurate information, explanation and advice to customers on issues of concern to them.

Impartiality and fairness
36. Ensure that the body taking a decision on a formal appeal from a dissatisfied customer does not include any person previously concerned with the case or who has a personal or otherwise significant interest in the outcome.
37. Avoid unfair discrimination against particular individuals, groups or sections of society.
38. Maintain a proper balance between any adverse effects which a decision may have on the rights or interests of individuals and the purpose which the council is pursuing.
39. Where an individual is adversely affected by a decision, or the decision is otherwise one which the individual potentially might wish to challenge, inform him or her of any rights of appeal or avenues for pursuing a complaint.
40. Ensure that members and officers are fully aware of the requirements for declaring an interest where appropriate and the reasons for doing so.

Complaints
41. Have a simple, well-publicised complaints system and operate it effectively.
42. Take remedial action when faults are identified, both to provide redress for the individuals concerned and to prevent recurrence of the problem in the future.

d) The European Code of Good Administrative Behaviour (EUO)

Article 1 - General provision
In their relations with the public, the institutions and their officials shall respect the principles which are laid down in this Code of Good Administrative Behaviour, hereafter referred to as "the Code".

Article 2 - Personal scope of application
1. The Code shall apply to all officials and other servants to whom the Staff Regulations and the Conditions of employment of other servants apply, in their relations with the public. Hereafter the term "official" refers to both the officials and the other servants.
2. The institutions and their administrations will take the necessary measures to ensure that the provisions set out in this Code also apply to other persons working for them, such as persons employed under private law contracts, experts on secondment from national civil services, and trainees.
3. The term "public" refers to natural and legal persons, whether they reside or have their registered office in a Member State or not.

4. For the purpose of this Code:
   a. the term "institution" shall mean an EU institution, body, office, or agency;
   b. "Official" shall mean an official or other servant of the European Union.

Article 3 - Material scope of application
1. This Code contains the general principles of good administrative behaviour which apply to all relations of the institutions and their administrations with the public, unless they are governed by specific provisions.
2. The principles set out in this Code do not apply to the relations between the institution and its officials. Those relations are governed by the Staff Regulations.

Article 4 - Lawfulness
The official shall act according to law and apply the rules and procedures laid down in EU legislation. The official shall in particular take care to ensure that decisions which affect the rights or interests of individuals have a basis in law and that their content complies with the law.

Article 5 - Absence of discrimination
1. In dealing with requests from the public and in taking decisions, the official shall ensure that the principle of equality of treatment is respected. Members of the public who are in the same situation shall be treated in a similar manner.
2. If any difference in treatment is made, the official shall ensure that it is justified by the objective relevant features of the particular case.
3. The official shall in particular avoid any unjustified discrimination between members of the public based on nationality, sex, race, colour, ethnic or social origin, genetic features, language, religion or belief, political or any other opinion, membership of a national minority, property, birth, disability, age, or sexual orientation.

Article 6 – Proportionality
1. When taking decisions, the official shall ensure that the measures taken are proportional to the aim pursued. The official shall in particular avoid restricting the rights of the citizens or imposing charges on them, when those restrictions or charges are not in a reasonable relation with the purpose of the action pursued.
2. When taking decisions, the official shall respect the fair balance between the interests of private persons and the general public interest.

Article 7 - Absence of abuse of power
Powers shall be exercised solely for the purposes for which they have been conferred by the relevant provisions. The official shall in particular avoid using those powers for purposes which have no basis in the law or which are not motivated by any public interest.

Article 8 - Impartiality and independence
1. The official shall be impartial and independent. The official shall abstain from any arbitrary action adversely affecting members of the public, as well as from any preferential treatment on any grounds whatsoever.
2. The conduct of the official shall never be guided by personal, family, or national interest or by political pressure. The official shall not take part in a decision in which he or she, or any close member of his or her family, has a financial interest.

Article 9 - Objectivity
When taking decisions, the official shall take into consideration the relevant factors and give each of them its proper weight in the decision, whilst excluding any irrelevant element from consideration.

Article 10 -Legitimate expectations, consistency, and advice

1. The official shall be consistent in his or her own administrative behaviour as well as with the administrative action of the institution. The official shall follow the institution's normal administrative practices, unless there are legitimate grounds for departing from those practices in an individual case. Where such grounds exist, they shall be recorded in writing.
2. The official shall respect the legitimate and reasonable expectations that members of the public have in light of how the institution has acted in the past.
3. The official shall, where necessary, advise the public on how a matter which comes within his or her remit is to be pursued and how to proceed in dealing with the matter.

Article 11 - Fairness

The official shall act impartially, fairly, and reasonably.

Article 12 – Courtesy

1. The official shall be service-minded, correct, courteous, and accessible in relations with the public. When answering correspondence, telephone calls, and e-mails, the official shall try to be as helpful as possible and shall reply as completely and accurately as possible to questions which are asked.
2. If the official is not responsible for the matter concerned, he or she shall direct the citizen to the appropriate official.
3. If an error occurs which negatively affects the rights or interests of a member of the public, the official shall apologise for it and endeavour to correct the negative effects resulting from his or her error in the most expedient way and inform the member of the public of any rights of appeal in accordance with Article 19 of the Code.

Article 13 - Reply to letters in the language of the citizen

The official shall ensure that every citizen of the Union or any member of the public who writes to the institution in one of the Treaty languages receives an answer in the same language. The same shall apply as far as possible to legal persons such as associations (NGOs) and companies.

Article 14 - Acknowledgement of receipt and indication of the competent official

1. Every letter or complaint to the institution shall receive an acknowledgement of receipt within a period of two weeks, except if a substantive reply can be sent within that period.
2. The reply or acknowledgement of receipt shall indicate the name and the telephone number of the official who is dealing with the matter, as well as the service to which he or she belongs.
3. No acknowledgement of receipt and no reply need be sent in cases where letters or complaints are abusive because of their excessive number or because of their repetitive or pointless character.

Article 15 - Obligation to transfer to the competent service of the institution

1. If a letter or a complaint to the institution is addressed or transmitted to a Directorate General, Directorate, or Unit which has no competence to deal with it, its services shall ensure that the file is transferred without delay to the competent service of the institution.
2. The service which originally received the letter or complaint shall inform the author of this transfer and shall indicate the name and the telephone number of the official to whom the file has been passed.
3. The official shall alert the member of the public or organisation to any errors or omissions in documents and provide an opportunity to rectify them.

Article 16 - Right to be heard and to make statements

1. In cases where the rights or interests of individuals are involved, the official shall ensure that, at every stage in the decision-making procedure, the rights of defence are respected.
2. Every member of the public shall have the right, in cases where a decision affecting his or her rights or interests has to be taken, to submit written comments and, when needed, to present oral observations before the decision is taken.

Article 17 - Reasonable time-limit for taking decisions

1. The official shall ensure that a decision on every request or complaint to the institution is taken within a reasonable time-limit, without delay, and in any case no later than two months from the date of receipt. The same rule shall apply for answering letters from members of the public and for answers to administrative notes which the official has sent to his or her superiors requesting instructions regarding the decisions to be taken.
2. If a request or a complaint to the institution cannot, because of the complexity of the matters which it raises, be decided upon within the above mentioned time-limit, the official shall inform the author as soon as possible. In such a case, a definitive decision should be communicated to the author in the shortest possible time.

Article 18 - Duty to state the grounds of decisions

1. Every decision of the institution which may adversely affect the rights or interests of a private person shall state the grounds on which it is based by indicating clearly the relevant facts and the legal basis of the decision.
2. The official shall avoid making decisions which are based on brief or vague grounds, or which do not contain an individual reasoning.
3. If it is not possible, because of the large number of persons concerned by similar decisions, to communicate in detail the grounds of the decision and where standard replies are therefore sent, the official shall subsequently provide the citizen who expressly requests it with an individual reasoning.

Article 19 - Indication of appeal possibilities

1. A decision of the institution which may adversely affect the rights or interests of a private person shall contain an indication of the appeal possibilities available for challenging the decision. It shall in particular indicate the nature of the remedies, the bodies before which they can be exercised, and the time-limits for exercising them.
2. Decisions shall in particular refer to the possibility of judicial proceedings and complaints to the Ombudsman under the conditions specified in, respectively, Articles 263 and 228 of the Treaty on the Functioning of the European Union.

Article 20 - Notification of the decision

1. The official shall ensure that persons whose rights or interests are affected by a decision are informed of that decision in writing, as soon as it is taken.
2. The official shall abstain from communicating the decision to other sources until the person or persons concerned have been informed.

Article 21 - Data protection

1. The official who deals with personal data concerning a citizen shall respect the privacy and the integrity of the individual in accordance with the provisions of Regulation (EC) 45/2001 of the European Parliament and of the Council of 18 December 2000 on the protection of individuals with regard to the processing of personal data by the Community institutions and bodies and on the free movement of such data.[2]
2. The official shall in particular avoid processing personal data for nonlegitimate purposes or the transmission of such data to non-authorised persons.

Article 22 - Requests for information

1. The official shall, when he or she has responsibility for the matter concerned, provide members of the public with the information that they request. When appropriate, the official shall give advice on how to initiate an administrative procedure within his or her field of competence. The official shall take care that the information communicated is clear and understandable.

2 OJ L 8/1, 12.1.2001.

2. If an oral request for information is too complicated or too extensive to be dealt with, the official shall advise the person concerned to formulate his or her demand in writing.
3. If an official may not disclose the information requested because of its confidential nature, he or she shall, in accordance with Article 18 of this Code, indicate to the person concerned the reasons why he or she cannot communicate the information.
4. Further to requests for information on matters for which he or she has no responsibility, the official shall direct the requester to the competent person and indicate his or her name and telephone number. Further to requests for information concerning another EU institution, the official shall direct the requester to that institution.
5. Where appropriate, the official shall, depending on the subject of the request, direct the person seeking information to the service of the institution responsible for providing information to the public.

Article 23 - Requests for public access to documents

1. The official shall deal with requests for access to documents in accordance with the rules adopted by the institution and in accordance with the general principles and limits laid down in Regulation (EC) 1049/2001.[3]
2. If the official cannot comply with an oral request for access to documents, the citizen shall be advised to formulate it in writing.

Article 24 - Keeping of adequate records

The institution's departments shall keep adequate records of their incoming and outgoing mail, of the documents they receive, and of the measures they take.

Article 25 - Publicity for the Code

1. The institution shall take effective measures to inform the public of the rights they enjoy under this Code. If possible, it shall make the text available in electronic form on its website.
2. The Commission shall, on behalf of all institutions, publish and distribute the Code to citizens in the form of a brochure.

Article 26 - Right to complain to the European Ombudsman

Any failure of an institution or official to comply with the principles set out in this Code may be the subject of a complaint to the European Ombudsman in accordance with Article 228 of the Treaty on the Functioning of the European Union and the Statute of the European Ombudsman.[4]

Article 27 - Review of operation

Each institution shall review its implementation of the Code after two years of operation and shall inform the European Ombudsman of the results of its review.

3 OJ L 145/43, 31.5.2001.

4 Decision of the European Parliament on the Regulations and General Conditions governing the performance of the Ombudsman's duties. OJ 1994 L 113, p. 15, as last amended by Decision of the European Parliament 2008/587/EC, Euratom of 18 June 2008, OJ 2008 L 189, p. 25.

CURRICULUM VITAE

Milan Remac was born in 1980 in Michalovce, Slovakia. He read law at P.J. Safarik University in Kosice, Slovakia from 1998 until 2003. Furthermore, he read International and European law at the University of Amsterdam, the Netherlands in 2006 – 2007. In connection with the latter study he was awarded the MTEC scholarship (MATRA Training for European Cooperation).

Between 2003 and 2006 he worked at the Ministry of Environment of the Slovak Republic and between 2007 and 2009 at the Ministry of Justice of the Slovak Republic (Office of the Agent of the Government before the European Court of Human Rights).

Between 2009 and 2013 he worked on his PhD thesis on mutual relations between ombudsmen and the judiciary at the Institute of Constitutional and Administrative Law, Montaigne Centre at Utrecht University, the Netherlands. During this period he authored and co-authored a number of articles which were published in various journals and anthologies. He also participated in several research projects including research on behalf of the World Bank. He also taught a course on European Administrative Law.

IUS COMMUNE EUROPAEUM

A peer-reviewed book series in which the common foundations of the legal systems of the Member States of the European Union are the central focus.

The *Ius Commune Europaeum* series includes horizontal comparative legal studies as well as studies on the effect of treaties within the national legal systems. All the classic fields of law are covered. The books are published in various European languages under the auspices of METRO, the Institute for Transnational Legal Research at the Maastricht University.

Recently published:
Volume 113: *Inside Policy Custody: An Empirical Account of Suspects' Rights in Four Jurisdictions*, J. BLACKSTOCK, E. CAPE, J. HODGSON, A. OGORODOVA and T. SPRONKEN
Volume 114: *Motive Matters! An Exploration of the Notion 'Deliberate Breach of Contract' and its Consequences for the Application of Remedies*, M. VAN KOGELENBERG
Volume 115: *Legal Education*, A.W. HERINGA
Volume 116: *Standing Up for your Right(s) in Europe. A Comparative Study on Legal Standing (Locus Standi) before the EU and Member States' Courts*, M. ELIANTONIO, C. BACKES, C.H. VAN RHEE, T. SPRONKEN and A. BERLEE
Volume 117: *European Union Property Law. From Fragments to a System*, E. RAMAEKERS
Volume 118: *Compensating Ecological Damage. Comparative and Economic Observations*, JING LIU
Volume 119: *Parliamentary Immunity. A Comprehensive Study of the Systems of Parliamentary Immunity of the United Kingdom, France, and the Netherlands in a European Context*, S. HARDT
Volume 120: *The Effects of Judicial Decisions in Time*, P. POPELIER, D. VANHEULE, B. VANLERBERGHE and S. VERSTRAELEN (eds.)
Volume 121: *The position of Small and Medium sized Enterprises in European Contract Law*, M. LOOS and I. SAMOY (eds.)
Volume 122: *Property Law Perspectives II*, B. AKKERMANS, E. MARAIS and E. RAMAEKERS (eds.)
Volume 123: *The Treaty on European Union 1993-2013: Reflections from Maastricht*, M. DE VISSER and A.P. VAN DER MEI (eds.)
Volume 124: *Inside Policy Custody: Training Framework on the Provisions of Suspects' Rights*, T. SPRONKEN *et al.*